Berlitz®

Spanish

phrase book

CEREZAS
590

Berlitz Publishing
New York   London   Singapore

Contacting the Editors
Every effort has been made to provide accurate information in this publication, but changes are inevitable. The publisher cannot be responsible for any resulting loss, inconvenience or injury. We would appreciate it if readers would call our attention to any errors or outdated information. We also welcome your suggestions; if you come across a relevant expression not in our phrase book, please contact us at: **comments@berlitzpublishing.com**

All Rights Reserved
© 2018 Apa Digital (CH) AG and Apa Publications (UK) Ltd.
Berlitz Trademark Reg. U.S. Patent Office and other countries. Marca Registrada. Used under license from Berlitz Investment Corporation.

Thirteenth Printing: March 2018
Printed in China

Editor: Helen Fanthorpe
Translation: updated by Wordbank
Cover Design: Rebeka Davies
Interior Design: Beverley Speight
Picture Researcher: Tom Smyth
Cover Photos: all images iStock and Shutterstock

Interior Photos: Neil Buchan-Grant/APA 111; Kevin Cummins/APA 38; Greg Gladman/APA 1, 12, 18, 57, 60, 100, 114, 169, iStockphoto 48, 117, 135, 149, 152; Britta Jaschinski/APA 16, 88, 92, 147, 157; Lucy Johnston/APA 15, 175; Sylvaine Poitau/APA 97; Gregory Wrona/APA 79, 101, 107, 132, 141.

Distribution

UK, Ireland and Europe
Apa Publications (UK) Ltd
sales@insightguides.com
United States and Canada
Ingram Publisher Services
ips@ingramcontent.com
Australia and New Zealand
Woodslane
info@woodslane.com.au
Southeast Asia
Apa Publications (SN) Pte
singaporeoffice@insightguides.com

Worldwide
Apa Publications (UK) Ltd
sales@insightguides.com

Special Sales, Content Licensing, and CoPublishing
Discounts available for bulk quantities. We can create special editions, personalized jackets, and corporate imprints. sales@insightguides.com; www.insightguides.biz

Contents

Food & Drink

People

Leisure Time

Special Requirements

In an Emergency

Dictionary

Pronunciation

This section is designed to make you familiar with the sounds of Spanish using our simplified phonetic transcription. You'll find the pronunciation of the Spanish letters and sounds explained below, together with their 'imitated' equivalents. This system is used throughout the phrase book; simply read the pronunciation as if it were English, noting any special rules below.

Underlined letters indicate that that syllable should be stressed. The acute accent ´ indicates stress, e.g. **río**, _ree_-oh. Some Spanish words have more than one meaning. In these instances, the accent mark is also used to distinguish between them, e.g.: **él** (he) and **el** (the); **sí** (yes) and **si** (if).

There are some differences in vocabulary and pronunciation between the Spanish spoken in Spain and that in the Americas, although each is easily understood by the other. This phrase book and dictionary is specifically geared to travelers in Spain.

Consonants

Letter	Approximate Pronunciation	Symbol	Example	Pronunciation
b	1. as in English	**b**	**bueno**	_bweh_-noh
	2. between vowels as in English, but softer	**b**	**bebida**	beh-_bee_-dah
c	1. before e and i like th in thin	**th**	**centro**	_thehn_-troh
	2. otherwise like k in kit	**k**	**como**	_koh_-moh
ch	as in English	**ch**	**mucho**	_moo_-choh

Letter	Approximate Pronunciation	Symbol	Example	Pronunciation
d	1. as in English	**d**	**donde**	_dohn_·deh
	2. between vowels and especially at the end of a word, like th in thin, but softer	**th**	**usted**	oos·_teth_
g	1. before e and i, like ch in Scottish loch	**kh**	**urgente**	oor·_khehn_·teh
	2. otherwise, like g in get	**g**	**ninguno**	neen·_goo_·noh
h	always silent		**hombre**	_ohm_·breh
j	like ch in Scottish loch	**kh**	**bajo**	_bah_·khoh
ll	like y in yellow	**y**	**lleno**	_yeh_·noh
ñ	like ni in onion	**ny**	**señor**	seh·_nyohr_
q	like k in kick	**k**	**quince**	_keen_·theh
r	trilled, especially at the beginning of a word	**r**	**río**	_ree_·oh
rr	strongly trilled	**rr**	**arriba**	ah·_rree_·bah
s	1. like s in same	**s**	**sus**	soos
	2. before b, d, g, l, m, n, like s in rose	**z**	**mismo**	_meez_·moh
v	like b in bad, but softer	**b**	**viejo**	_beeyeh_·khoh
z	like th in thin	**th**	**brazo**	_brah_·thoh

Letters f, k, l, m, n, p, t, w, x and y are pronounced as in English.

Vowels

Letter	Approximate Pronunciation	Symbol	Example	Pronunciation
a	like the a in father	**ah**	**gracias**	_grah•theeyahs_
e	like e in get	**eh**	**esta**	_ehs_•tah
i	like ee in meet	**ee**	**sí**	see
o	like o in rope	**oh**	**dos**	dohs
u	1. like oo in food	**oo**	**uno**	_oo_•noh
	2. silent after g and q		**que**	keh
	3. when marked ü, like we in well	**w**	**antigüedad**	ahn•tee•gweh•_dahd_
y	1. like y in yellow	**y**	**hoy**	oy
	2. when alone, like ee in meet	**ee**	**y**	ee
	3. when preceded by an a, sounds like y + ee, with ee faintly pronounced	**aye**	**hay**	aye

With over 400 million Spanish speakers worldwide, Spanish is the third most widely spoken language in the world and the official language of 21 different nations. Over 17 million people in the United States speak Spanish as their native language, and it is one of the official languages of the United Nations. Spanish is the fourth most popular language on the internet, behind English, Japanese and German. Below are estimated numbers of Spanish speakers around the globe.

Central America: 55 million
North America: 112 million
South America: 190 million
Spain: 40 million

How to use this Book

Sometimes you see two alternatives separated by a slash. Choose the one that's right for your situation.

ESSENTIAL

I'm on vacation

Estoy aquí de vacaciones/en viaje de [holiday]/business. *negocios. ehs·toy ah·kee deh bah·kah·theeyohn·ehs/ ehn beeyah·kheh deh neh·goh·theeyohs*

I'm going to...

Voy a... *boy ah...*

I'm staying at the... Hotel.

Me alojo en el Hotel... *meh ah·loh·khoh ehn ehl oh·tehl...*

Words you may see are shown in YOU MAY SEE boxes.

YOU MAY SEE...

ADUANAS	customs
ARTÍCULOS LIBRES DE IMPUESTOS	duty-free goods
ARTÍCULOS QUE DECLARAR	goods to declare

Any of the words or phrases listed can be plugged into the sentence below.

Bicycle & Motorcycle

I'd like to rent [hire]...
a bicycle
a moped
a motorcycle
How much per day/week?

Quiero alquilar... *keeyeh·roh ahl·kee·lahr...*
una bicicleta *oo·nah bee·thee·kleh·tah*
un ciclomotor *oon thee·kloh·moh·tohr*
una motocicleta *oo·nah moh·toh·thee·kleh·tah*
¿Cuánto cuesta por día/semana?
kwahn·toh kwehs·tah pohr dee·ah/seh·mah·nah

The Dating Game

Spanish phrases appear in purple.

Read the simplified pronunciation as if it were English. For more on pronunciation, see page 7.

Can I join you?

¿Puedo acompañarle m/acompañarla f?
pweh·doh ah·kohm·pah·nyahr·leh m/
ah·kohm·pah·nyahr·lah f

You're very attractive.

Eres muy guapo m/guapa f.
eh·rehs mooy gwah·poh m/gwah·pah f

For Grammar, see page 162.

Related phrases can be found by going to the page number indicated.

When different gender forms apply, the masculine form is followed by *m*; feminine by *f*

When addressing strangers, always use the more formal **usted** (singular) or **ustedes** (plural), as opposed to the more familiar **tú** (singular) or **vosotros** (plural), until told otherwise. If you know someone's title, it's polite to use it, e.g., **doctor** (male doctor), **doctora** (female doctor). You can also simply say **Señor** (Mr.), **Señora** (Mrs.) or **Señorita** (Miss).

Information boxes contain relevant country, culture and language tips.

YOU MAY HEAR...

Expressions you may hear are shown in You May Hear boxes.

Hablo muy poco inglés.
ah·bloh mooy poh·koh een·glehs

I only speak a little English.

Color-coded side bars identify each section of the book.

Survival

Arrival & Departure

ESSENTIAL

I'm on vacation/ business.

Estoy aquí de vacaciones/en viaje de negocios.
ehs·<u>toy</u> ah·<u>kee</u> deh bah·kah·<u>theeyohn</u>·ehs/
ehn <u>beeyuh</u>·kheh deh neh·<u>goh</u>·theeyohs

I'm going to...
Voy a... boy ah...

I'm staying at the... Hotel.
Me alojo en el Hotel... meh ah·<u>loh</u>·khoh
ehn ehl oh·<u>tehl</u>...

YOU MAY HEAR...

Su pasaporte, por favor.
soo pah·sah·<u>pohr</u>·teh pohr fah·<u>bohr</u>

Your passport, please.

¿Cuál es el propósito de su visita?
kwahl ehs ehl proh·<u>poh</u>·see·toh
deh soo hee·<u>see</u>·tah

What's the purpose of your visit?

¿Dónde se aloja?
<u>dohn</u>·deh seh ah·<u>loh</u>·khah

Where are you staying?

¿Cuánto tiempo piensa quedarse?
<u>kwahn</u>·toh <u>teeyehm</u>·poh <u>peeyehn</u>·sah
keh·<u>dar</u>·seh

How long are you staying?

¿Con quién viaja?
kohn keeyehn <u>beeyah</u>·khah

Who are you here with?

Border Control

I'm just passing through. **Estoy de paso.** *ehs·toy deh pah·soh*

I'd like to declare... **Quiero declarar...** *keeyeh·roh deh·klah·rahr...*

I have nothing to declare. **No tengo nada que declarar.** *noh tehn·goh nah·dah keh deh·klah·rahr*

YOU MAY HEAR...

¿Tiene algo que declarar?
teeyeh·neh ahl·goh keh deh·klah·rahr

Anything to declare?

Tiene que pagar impuestos por esto.
teeyeh·neh keh pah·gahr eem·pwehs·tohs pohr ehs·toh

You must pay duty on this.

Abra esta maleta.
ah·brah ehs·tah mah·leh·tah

Open this bag.

YOU MAY SEE...

ADUANAS	customs
ARTÍCULOS LIBRES DE IMPUESTOS	duty-free goods
ARTÍCULOS QUE DECLARAR	goods to declare
NADA QUE DECLARAR	nothing to declare
CONTROL DE PASAPORTES	passport control
POLICÍA	police

Money

ESSENTIAL

Where's…?	**¿Dónde esta…?** _dohn·deh ehs·tah…_
the ATM	**el cajero automático** _ehl kah·kheh·roh awtoh·mah·tee·koh_
the bank	**el banco** _ehl bahn·koh_
the currency exchange office	**la casa de cambio** _lah kah·sah deh kahm·beeyoh_
When does the bank open/close?	**¿A qué hora abre/cierra el banco?** _ah keh oh·rah ah·breh/theeyeh·rrah ehl bahn·koh_
I'd like to change dollars/pounds into euros.	**Quiero cambiar dólares/libras a euros.** _keeyeh·roh kahm·beeyahr doh·lah·rehs/lee·brahs ah ew·rohs_
I'd like to cash traveler's checks [cheques].	**Quiero cobrar cheques de viaje.** _keeyeh·roh koh·brahr cheh·kehs deh beeyah·kheh_

YOU MAY SEE...

INTRODUCIR TARJETA AQUÍ	insert card here
CANCELAR	cancel
BORRAR	clear
INTRODUCIR	enter
CLAVE	PIN
RETIRAR FONDOS	withdraw funds
DE CUENTA CORRIENTE	from checking [current] account
DE CUENTA DE AHORROS	from savings account
RECIBO	receipt

At the Bank

I'd like to change money/get a cash advance.	**Quiero cambiar dinero/un adelanto de efectivo.** _keeyeh•roh kahm•beeyahr dee•neh•roh/ oon ah•deh•lahn•toh deh eh•fehk•tee•boh_
What's the exchange rate?	**¿Cuál es el tipo de cambio?** _kwahl ehs ehl tee•poh deh kahm•beeyoh_
How much is the fee?	**¿Cuánto es la tasa?** _kwahn•toh ehs lah tah•sah_
I lost my traveler's checks.	**He perdido los cheques de viaje.** _eh pehr•dee•doh lohs cheh•kehs deh beeyah•kheh_

My card was lost.	**Se me ha perdido la tarjeta.**
	seh meh ah pehr·<u>dee</u>·doh lah tahr·<u>kheh</u>·tah
My card was stolen.	**Me han robado la tarjeta.**
	meh ahn roh·<u>bah</u>·doh lah tahr·<u>kheh</u>·tah
My card doesn't work.	**Mi tarjeta no funciona.** *mee tahr·<u>kheh</u>·tah*
	noh foon·<u>theeyoh</u>·nah
The ATM ate my card.	**El cajero automático se ha tragado mi tarjeta.**
	ehl kah·kheh·roh awtoh·mah·tee·koh seh ah
	trah·gah·doh mee tahr·kheh·tah

For Numbers, see page 167.

ATMs are located throughout Spain. Cash can be obtained from ATMs with Visa™, Eurocard™, American Express® and many other international cards. Instructions are often given in English. Debit cards are becoming a more accepted method of payment in Spain. Whether using a credit card or debit card, make sure you have your PIN (personal identification number) and that it is four digits. If you have an alphabetic PIN, be aware that Spanish ATMs do not have letters on the keypad. The best rates for exchanging money will be found at banks and ATMs. You can change money at travel agencies and hotels, but the rate will not be as good. Remember your passport when you want to change money.

YOU MAY SEE...

Spanish currency is the **euro**, **€**, divided into 100 **céntimos** (cents).
Coins: 1, 2, 5, 10, 20, 50 **cts.**; **€**1, 2
Notes: €5, 10, 20, 50, 100, 200, 500

Getting Around

ESSENTIAL

How do I get to town?	**¿Cómo se llega a la ciudad?** <u>koh</u>·moh seh <u>yeh</u>·gah ah lah theew·<u>dahd</u>
Where's...?	**¿Dónde está...?** <u>dohn</u>·deh ehs·<u>tah</u>...
the airport	**el aeropuerto** ehl ah·eh·roh·<u>pwehr</u>·toh
the train [railway] station	**la estación de tren** lah ehs·tah·<u>theeyohn</u> deh trehn
the bus station	**la estación de autobuses** lah ehs·tah·<u>theeyohn</u> deh awtoh·<u>booses</u>
the metro station	**la estación de metro** lah ehs·tah·<u>theeyohn</u> deh <u>meh</u>·troh
Is it far from here?	**¿A qué distancia está?** ah keh dees·<u>tahn</u>·theeyah ehs·<u>tah</u>
Where do I buy a ticket?	**¿Dónde se compra el billete?** <u>dohn</u>·deh seh <u>kohm</u>·prah ehl bee·<u>yeh</u>·teh
A one-way/return-trip ticket to...	**Un billete de ida/ida y vuelta a...** oon bee·<u>yeh</u>·teh deh <u>ee</u>·dah/<u>ee</u>·dah ee <u>bwehl</u>·tah ah...

How much?	**¿Cuánto es?** _kwahn_·toh ehs
Is there a discount?	**¿Hacen descuento?** _ah_·then dehs·_kwehn_·toh
Which…?	**¿De qué…?** deh keh…
gate	**puerta de embarque** _pwehr_·tah deh ehm·_bahr_·keh
line	**línea** _lee_·neh·ah
platform	**andén** ahn·_dehn_
Where can I get a taxi?	**¿Dónde puedo coger un taxi?** _dohn_·deh _pweh_·doh koh·_khehr_ oon _tah_·xee
Take me to this address.	**Lléveme a esta dirección.** _yeh_·beh·meh ah _ehs_·tah dee·rek·_theeyohn_
Where's the car hire?	**¿Dónde está el alquiler de coches?** _dohn_·deh ehs·_tah_ ehl ahl·kee·_lehr_ deh _koh_·chehs
Can I have a map?	**¿Podría darme un mapa?** poh·_dree_·ah _dahr_·meh oon _mah_·pah

Tickets

When's…to Madrid?	**¿Cuándo sale…a Madrid?** _kwahn_·doh _sah_·leh…ah mah·_dreeth_
the (first) bus	**el (primer) autobús** ehl (pree·_mehr_) awtoh·_boos_
the (next) flight	**el (próximo) vuelo** ehl (_proh_·xee·moh) bweh·loh
the (last) train	**el (último) tren** ehl (_ool_·tee·moh) trehn
Where do I buy a ticket?	**¿Dónde se compra el billete?** _dohn_·deh seh _kohm_·prah ehl bee·_yeh_·teh
One/Two ticket(s), please.	**Un/Dos billete(s), por favor.** oon/dohs bee·_yeh_·teh(s) pohr fah·_bohr_
For today/tomorrow.	**Para hoy/mañana.** _pah_·rah oy/mah·_nyah_·nah
A…ticket.	**Un billete…** oon bee·_yeh_·teh…
one-way	**de ida** deh _ee_·dah
return-trip	**de ida y vuelta** deh _ee_·dah ee _bwehl_·tah
first class	**de primera clase** deh pree·_meh_·rah _klah_·she

business class	**de clase preferente** deh _klah_·seh preh·feh·_rehn_·teh
economy class	**de clase económica** deh _klah_·seh eh·koh·_noh_·mee·kah
How much?	**¿Cuánto es?** _kwahn_·toh ehs
Is there a discount for…?	**¿Hacen descuento a…?** _ah_·thehn dehs·_kwehn_·toh ah…
children	**los niños** lohs _nee_·nyohs
students	**los estudiantes** lohs ehs·too·_deeyahn_·tehs
senior citizens	**los jubilados** lohs khoo·bee·_lah_·dohs
tourists	**los turistas** too·_rees_·tahs

The express bus/ express train, please. **El autobús exprés/tren exprés, por favor.** ehl awtoh·_boos_/trehn ex·presh, pohr fah·_bohr_

The local bus/ train, please. **El autobús/tren local, por favor.** ehl awtoh·_boos_/trehn loh·kahl, pohr fah·_bohr_

I have an e-ticket. **Tengo un billete electrónico.** _tehn_·goh oon bee·_yeh_·teh eh·lehk·_troh_·nee·koh

Can I buy a ticket on the bus/train? **¿Puedo comprar el billete a bordo del autobús/tren?** _pweh_·doh kohm·_prahr_ ehl bee·_yeh_·teh ah _bohr_·doh dehl awtoh·_boos_/trehn

Do I have to stamp the ticket before boarding? **¿Tengo que sellar el billete antes de embarcar?** _tehn_·goh keh seh·yahr ehl bee·yeh·teh ahn·tehs deh ehm·bahr·kahr

How long is this ticket valid? **¿Cuál es la validez de este billete?** kwahl ehs lah bah·lee·dehth deh ehs·teh bee·yeh·teh

Can I return on the same ticket? **¿Puedo volver con el mismo billete?** _pweh_·doh bohl·behr kohn ehl meesh·moh bee·yeh·teh

I'd like to…my reservation. **Quiero…mi reserva.** _keeyeh_·roh…mee reh·_sehr_·bah

cancel	**cancelar** kahn·theh·_lahr_
change	**cambiar** kahm·_beeyahr_
confirm	**confirmar** kohn·feer·_mahr_

For Time, see page 170.

Plane

Airport Transfer

How much is a taxi to the airport?	**¿Cuánto cuesta el trayecto en taxi al aeropuerto?** *kwahn·toh kwehs·tah ehl trah·yehk·toh ehn tah·xee ahl ah·eh·roh·pwehr·toh*
To...Airport, please.	**Al aeropuerto de..., por favor.** *ahl ah·eh·roh·pwehr·toh deh...pohr fah·bohr*
My airline is...	**Mi compañía aérea es...** *mee kohm·pah·nyee·ah ah·eh·reh·ah ehs...*
My flight leaves at...	**Mi vuelo sale a la/las...** *mee bweh·loh sah·leh ah lah/lahs...*
I'm in a rush.	**Tengo prisa.** *tehn·goh pree·sah*
Can you take an alternate route?	**¿Puede coger otro camino?** *pweh·deh koh·khehr oh·troh kah·mee·noh*
Can you drive faster/slower?	**¿Puede ir más deprisa/despacio?** *pweh·deh eer mahs deh·pree·sah/dehs·pah·theeyoh*

For Grammar, see page 162.

For Time, see page 170.

YOU MAY HEAR...

¿Con qué compañía aérea viaja? *kohn keh kohm·pah·nyee·ah ah·eh·reh·ah beeyah·khah*	What airline are you flying?
¿Nacional o internacional? *nah·theeyoh·nahl oh een·tehr·nah·theeyoh·nahl*	Domestic or international?
¿Qué terminal? *keh tehr·mee·nahl*	What terminal?

YOU MAY SEE...

LLEGADAS	arrivals
SALIDAS	departures
RECOGIDA DE EQUIPAJES	baggage claim
VUELOS NACIONALES	domestic flights
VUELOS INTERNACIONALES	international flights
MOSTRADOR DE FACTURACIÓN	check-in
FACTURACIÓN ELECTRÓNICA	e-ticket check-in
PUERTAS DE EMBARQUE	departure gates

Checking In

Where's check-in?	**¿Dónde está el mostrador de facturación?** _dohn·deh ehs·tah ehl mohs·trah·dohr_ _deh fahk·too·rah·theeyohn_
My name is...	**Me llamo...** _meh yah·moh..._
I'm going to...	**Voy a...** _boy ah..._
I have...	**Tengo...** _tehn·goh_
one suitcase	**una maleta** _oo·nah mah·leh·tah_
two suitcases	**dos maletas** _dohs mah·leh·tahs_
one piece of hand luggage	**una pieza de equipaje de mano** _oo·nah peeyeh·thah_ _deh eh·kee·pah·kheh deh mah·noh_
How much luggage is allowed?	**¿Cuánto equipaje está permitido?** _kwahn·toh eh·kee·pah·kheh ehs·tah pehr·mee·tee·doh_
Is that pounds or kilos?	**¿Son libras o kilos?** _sohn lee·brahs oh kee·lohs_
Which terminal/gate?	**¿De qué terminal/puerta de embarque?** _deh keh tehr·mee·nahl/pwehr·tah deh ehm·bahr·keh_
I'd like a window/an aisle seat.	**Quiero un asiento de ventana/pasillo.** _keeyeh·roh oon ah·seeyehn·toh deh_ _behn·tah·nah/pah·see·yoh_

When do we leave/arrive?	**¿A qué hora salimos/llegamos?** *ah keh oh·rah sah·lee·mohs/yeh·gah·mohs*
Is the flight delayed?	**¿Lleva retraso el vuelo?** *yeh·bah reh·trah·soh ehl bweh·loh*
How late?	**¿Cuánto retraso lleva?** *kwahn·toh reh·trah·soh yeh·bah*

YOU MAY HEAR...

¡Siguiente! *see·geeyehn·teh*
Next!

Su pasaporte/billete, por favor. *soo pah·sah·pohr·teh/bee·yeh·teh pohr fah·bohr*
Your passport/ ticket, please.

¿Va a facturar el equipaje? *bah ah fahk·too·rahr ehl eh·kee·pah·kheh*
Are you checking in any luggage?

Lleva exceso de equipaje. *yeh·bah ehx·theh·soh deh eh·kee·pah·kheh*
You have excess luggage.

Eso es demasiado grande para equipaje de mano. *eh·soh ehs deh·mah·seeyah·doh grahn·deh pah·rah eh·kee·puh·kheh deh mah·noh*
That's too large for a carry-on [to carry on board].

¿Hizo las maletas usted? *ee·thoh lahs mah·leh·tahs oos·teth*
Did you pack these bags yourself?

¿Le entregó alguien algún paquete? *leh ehn·treh·goh ahl·geeyehn ahl·goon pah·keh·teh*
Did anyone give you anything to carry?

Vacíese los bolsillos. *bah·thee·eh·seh lohs bohl·see·yohs*
Empty your pockets.

Quítese los zapatos. *kee·teh·seh lohs thah·pah·tohs*
Take off your shoes.

Se está efectuando el embarque del vuelo... *seh ehs·tah eh·fehk·too·ahn·doh ehl ehm·bahr·keh dehl bweh·loh...*
Now boarding flight...

Luggage

Where is/are...?	**¿Dónde está/están...?** _dohn·deh ehs·tah/_ _ehs·tahn_...
the luggage carts [trolleys]	**los carritos para el equipaje** _lohs kah·ree·tohs pah·rah ehl eh·kee·pah·kheh_
the luggage lockers	**las consignas automáticas** _lahs kohn·seeg·nahs awtoh·mah·tee·kahs_
the baggage claim	**la recogida de equipajes** _lah reh·koh·khee·dah deh eh·kee·pah·k hehs_
My luggage has been lost.	**Han perdido mi equipaje.** _ahn pehr·dee·doh mee eh·kee·pah·kheh_
My luggage has been stolen.	**Me han robado el equipaje.** _meh ahn roh·bah·doh ehl eh·kee·pah·kheh_
My suitcase is damaged.	**Mi maleta ha sufrido daños.** _mee mah·leh·tah ah soo·free·doh dah·nyohs_

Finding your Way

Where is/are...?	**¿Dónde está/están...?** _dohn·deh_ _ehs·tah/ehs·tahn_...
the currency exchange	**la casa de cambio** _lah kah·sah deh kahm·beeyoh_
the car hire	**el alquiler de coches** _ehl ahl·kee·lehr deh koh·chehs_
the exit	**la salida** _lah sah·lee·dah_
the taxis	**los taxis** _lohs tah·xees_
Is there...into town?	**¿Hay...que vaya a la ciudad?** _aye...keh bah·yah ah lah theew·dahd_
a bus	**un autobús** _on awtoh·boos_
a train	**un tren** _on trehn_
a metro	**un metro** _on meh·troh_

For Asking Directions, see page 34.

Train

Where's the train station?	**¿Dónde está la estación de tren?** *dohn·deh ehs·tah lah ehs·tah·theeyohn deh trehn*
How far is it?	**¿A qué distancia está?** *ah keh dees·tahn·theeyah ehs·tah*
Where is/are...?	**¿Dónde está/están...?** *dohn·deh ehs·tah/ehs·tahn...*
the ticket office	**el despacho de billetes** *ehl dehs·pah·choh deh bee·yeh·tehs*
the information desk	**el mostrador de información** *ehl mohs·trah·dohr deh een·fohr·mah·theeyohn*
the luggage lockers	**las consignas automáticas** *lahs kohn·seeg·nahs awtoh·mah·tee·kahs*
the platforms	**los andenes** *lohs ahn·deh·nehs*
Can I have a schedule [timetable]?	**¿Podría darme un horario?** *poh·dree·ah dahr·meh oon oh·rah·reeyoh*
How long is the trip?	**¿Cuánto dura el viaje?** *kwahn·toh doo·rah ehl veeyah·kheh*
Is it a direct train?	**¿Es un tren directo?** *ehs oon trehn dee·rehk·toh*
Do I have to change trains?	**¿Tengo que cambiar de trenes?** *tehn·goh keh kahm·beeyahr deh treh·nehs*
Is the train on time?	**¿El tren va puntual?** *ehl trehn bah poon·tooahl*

For Asking Directions, see page 34.

YOU MAY SEE...

ANDENES	platforms
INFORMACIÓN	information
RESERVAS	reservations
SALA DE ESPERA	waiting room
LLEGADAS	arrivals
SALIDAS	departures

Spain's major railway network is **RENFE, Red Nacional de Ferrocarriles Españoles**. **RENFE** offers a variety of train types, from express to local, national to international. You can purchase tickets or make reservations through the **RENFE** website or a travel agency, or at the station. It is sometimes necessary to purchase your tickets a day or two in advance for popular routes.

Departures

Which track [platform] for the train to…?	**¿De qué andén sale el tren a…?** *deh keh ahn·dehn sah·leh ehl trehn ah…*	
Is this the track [platform]/train to…?	**¿Es éste el andén/tren a…?** *ehs ehs·teh ehl ahn·dehn/trehn ah…*	
Where is track [platform]…?	**¿Dónde está el andén…?** *dohn·deh ehs·tah ehl ahn·dehn…*	
Where do I change for…?	**¿Dónde tengo que cambiar para…?** *dohn·deh tehn·goh keh kahm·beeyahr pah·rah…*	

YOU MAY HEAR…

¡Todos a bordo! *toh·dohs ah bohr·doh*	All aboard!	
Billetes, por favor. *bee·yeh·tehs pohr fah·bohr*	Tickets, please.	
Tiene que cambiar de tren en León. *teeyeh·neh keh kahm·beeyahr deh trehn ehn leh·ohn*	You have to change at Léon.	
Próxima parada: Madrid. *proh·xee·mah pah·rah·dah mah·dreeth*	Next stop, Madrid.	

On Board

Can I sit here?	**¿Le importa si me siento aquí?** *leh eem·pohr·tah see meh seeyehn·toh ah·kee*
Can I open the window?	**Puedo abrir la ventana?** *pweh·doh ah·breer lah behn·tah·nah*
That's my seat.	**Ése es mi asiento.** *eh·seh ehs mee ah·seeyehn·toh*
Here's my reservation	**Esta es mi reserva.** *ehs·tah ehs mee reh·sehr·bah*

Bus

Where's the bus station?	**¿Dónde está la estación de autobuses?** *dohn·deh ehs·tah lah ehs·tah·theeyohn deh awtoh·boo·sehs*
How far is it?	**¿A qué distancia está?** *ah keh dees·tahn·theeyah ehs·tah*
How do I get to…?	**¿Cómo se llega a…?** *koh·moh seh yeh·gah ah…*
Is this the bus to…?	**¿Es éste el autobús a…?** *ehs ehs·teh ehl awtoh·boos ah…*
How many stops to…?	**¿Cuántas paradas hay hasta…?** *kwahn·tahs pah·rah·dahs aye ahs·tah…*

Bus service in Spain is extensive. For local service within a town, you usually pay as you board the bus. The fare is generally a fixed price. In larger cities, bus tickets are interchangeable with subway tickets. **Un bono** (**metrobús** in Madrid), a ten-trip ticket, is the cheapest way to go. These tickets are available at newsstands, banks, lottery-ticket shops and subway stations. When using the **bono** on a bus, make sure to validate your ticket by stamping it in the machine next to the driver as you board. Signal that you wish to get off by pushing a button, located throughout the bus; a sign will light up that says **parada solicitada** (stop requested).

Can you tell me when to get off?	**¿Podría decirme cuándo me tengo que bajar?** *poh•dree•ah deh•theer•meh kwahn•doh meh tehn•goh keh bah•khahr*
Do I have to change buses?	**¿Tengo que hacer transbordo?** *tehn•goh keh ah•thehr trahns•bohr•doh*
Stop here, please!	**¡Pare aquí, por favor!** *pah•reh ah•kee pohr fah•bohr*

For Tickets, see page 19.

Metro

Where's the metro?	**¿Dónde está la estación de metro?** *dohn•deh ehs•tah lah ehs•tah•theeyohn deh meh•troh*
A map, please.	**Un plano, por favor.** *oon plah•noh pohr fah•bohr*

In Spain, there are **metro** (subway) systems in Madrid, Barcelona, Valencia and Bilbao. **Metro** systems are easy to use and reasonably priced. All three **metro** systems operate on a one-way, per-ride basis. You can save money by buying a 10-trip ticket or **un bono** (**metrobús** in Madrid), which can be purchased at **metro** stations, banks, newsstands and tobacco shops. In larger cities, **metro** and bus tickets are the same price and are interchangeable. To enter the subway system, slip your ticket through the slot in the turnstile; remember to grab your ticket, which now has the date printed on it, so that you can pass through the turnstile.

Which line for…?	**¿Qué línea tengo que coger para…?**
	keh lee-neh-ah tehn-goh keh koh-khehr pah-rah…
Which direction?	**¿Qué dirección?** *keh dee-rehk-theeyohn*
Do I have to transfer [change]?	**¿Tengo que hacer transbordo?** *tehn-goh keh ah-thehr trahns-bohr-doh*
Is this the metro [train] to…?	**¿Es éste el tren a…?** *ehs ehs-teh ehl trehn ah…*
How many stops to…?	**¿Cuántas paradas hay hasta…?** *kwahn-tahs pah-rah-dahs aye ahs-tah*
Where are we?	**¿Dónde estamos?** *dohn-deh ehs-tah-mohs*

For Tickets, see page 19.

Boat & Ferry

When is the ferry to…?	**¿Cuándo sale el ferry a…?** *kwahn-doh sah-leh ehl feh-rree ah…*
Can I take my car?	**¿Puedo llevar el coche?** *pweh-doh yeh-bahr ehl koh-cheh*
What time is the next sailing?	**¿A qué hora sale el siguiente barco?** *ah keh oh-rah sah-leh ehl see-geeyehn-teh bahr-koh*
Can I book a seat/cabin?	**¿Puedo reservar un asiento/camarote?** *pweh-doh reh-sehr-bahr oon ah-seeyehn-toh/kah-mah-roh-leh*
How long is the crossing?	**¿Cuánto dura la travesía?** *kwahn-toh doo-rah lah trah-beh-see-ah*

For Tickets, see page 19.

YOU MAY SEE…

| **BALSA SALVAVIDAS** | life boat |
| **CHALECO SALVAVIDAS** | life jacket |

In Spain, ferry and boat services run to and from the Balearic Islands (Mallorca, Menorca, Ibiza and Formentera), destinations in North Africa and the Canary Islands and ports in Genoa, Italy (from Barcelona) and southern England (from Bilbao and Santander).

Taxi

Where can I get a taxi?	**¿Dónde puedo coger un taxi?** _dohn·deh pweh·doh koh·khehr oon tah·xee_
Can you send a taxi?	**¿Puede enviar un taxi?** _pweh·deh ehn·beeyahr oon tah·xee_
Do you have the number for a taxi?	**¿Tiene el número de alguna empresa de taxi?** _teeyeh·neh ehl noo·meh·roh deh ahl·goo·nah ehm·preh·sah deh tah·xee_
I'd like a taxi now/ for tomorrow at...	**Quiero un taxi ahora/para mañana a la(s)...** _keeyeh·roh oon tah·xee ah·oh·rah/pah·rah mah·nyah·nah ah lah(s)..._
Pick me up at (place/time)...	**Recójame en/a la(s)...** _reh·koh·khah·meh ehn/ah lah(s)..._
I'm going to...	**Voy...** _boy..._
this address	**a esta dirección** _ah ehs·tah dee·rehk·theeyohn_
the airport	**al aeropuerto** _ahl ah·eh·roh·pwehr·toh_

In Spain, **coger** means to catch or get, as in: **¿Dónde puedo coger un taxi?** (Where can I catch a cab?). However, in Latin America, **coger** is a vulgarity for 'to have sex'. Use **tomar** (**¿Dónde puedo tomar un taxi?**) in Spanish-speaking Latin America.

YOU MAY HEAR...

¿Adónde se dirige? ah·*dohn*·deh seh   Where to?
dee·*ree*·kheh

¿Cuál es la dirección? kwahl ehs lah   What's the address?
dee·rehk·*theeyohn*

the train station	**a la estación de trenes** ah lah *ehs·tah·theeyohn* deh *treh*·nehs	
I'm late.	**Llego tarde.** *yeh*·goh *tahr*·deh	
Can you drive faster/slower?	**¿Puede ir más deprisa/despacio?** *pweh*·deh eer mahs deh·*pree*·sah/dehs·*pah*·theeyoh	
Stop/Wait here.	**Pare/Espere aquí.** *pah*·reh/ehs·*peh*·reh ah·*kee*	
How much?	**¿Cuanto es?** *kwahn*·toh ehs	
You said it would cost...	**Dijo que costaría...** *dee*·khoh keh kohs·tah·*ree*·ah...	
Keep the change.	**Quédese con el cambio.** keh·*deh*·seh kohn ehl *kahm*·beeyoh	
A receipt, please.	**Un recibo, por favor.** oon reh·*thee*·boh pohr fah·*bohr*	

For Grammar, see page 162.

In major Spanish cities, taxis are reasonably priced. Extra
fees are usually charged for trips to the airport, bus station
and train station and also for extra luggage. When entering the
taxi, make sure the meter is turned on; it should register a base fare
when the trip begins. The fare is then increased by a set amount per
kilometer traveled.

Bicycle & Motorbike

I'd like to hire…	**Quiero alquilar…** _keeyeh_·roh ahl·kee·_lahr_…
a bicycle	**una bicicleta** _oo_·nah bee·thee·_kleh_·tah
a moped	**un ciclomotor** oon thee·kloh·moh·_tohr_
a motorcycle	**una motocicleta** _oo_·nah moh·toh·thee·_kleh_·tah
How much per day/week?	**¿Cuánto cuesta por día/semana?** _kwahn_·toh _kwehs_·tah pohr _dee_·ah/seh·_mah_·nah
Can I have a helmet/lock?	**¿Puede darme un casco/candado?** _pweh_·deh _dahr_·meh oon _kahs_·koh/kahn·_dah_·doh

Car Hire

Where's the car hire?	**¿Dónde está el alquiler de coches?** _dohn_·deh ehs·_tah_ ehl ahl·kee·_lehr_ deh _koh_·chehs
I'd like…	**Quiero…** _keeyeh_·roh…
a cheap/small car	**un coche económico/pequeño** oon _koh_·cheh eh·koh·_noh_·mee·koh/peh·_keh_·nyoh
an automatic/ a manual	**un coche automático/con transmisión manual** oon _koh_·cheh awtoh·_mah_·tee·koh/ kohn trahns·mee·_seeyohn_ mah·noo·_ahl_
air conditioning	**un coche con aire acondicionado** oon _koh_·cheh kohn _ayee_·reh ah·kohn·dee·theeyoh·_nah_·doh
a car seat	**un asiento de niño** oon ah·_seeyehn_·toh deh _nee_·nyoh
How much…?	**¿Cuánto cobran…?** _kwahn_·toh _koh_·brahn…
per day/week	**por día/semana** pohr _dee_·ah/seh·_mah_·nah
for…days	**por…días** pohr…_dee_·ahs
per kilometer	**por kilómetro** pohr kee·_loh_·meh·troh
for unlimited mileage	**por kilometraje ilimitado** pohr kee·loh·meh·_trah_·kheh ee·lee·mee·_tah_·doh
with insurance	**con el seguro** kohn ehl seh·_goo_·roh
Are there any discounts?	**¿Ofrecen algún descuento?** oh·_freh_·thehn ahl·_goon_ dehs·_kwehn_·toh

YOU MAY HEAR...

¿Tiene permiso de conducir internacional? _teeyeh•neh pehr•mee•soh deh kohn•doo•theer een•tehr•nah•theeyoh•nahl_ — Do you have an international driver's license?

Su pasaporte, por favor. _soo pah•sah•pohr•teh pohr tah•bohr_ — Your passport, please.

¿Quiere seguro? _keeyeh•reh seh•goo•roh_ — Do you want insurance?

Tiene que dejar una fianza. _teeyeh•neh keh deh•khahr oo•nah fee•ahn•thah_ — I'll need a deposit.

Firme aquí. _feer•meh ah•kee_ — Sign here.

Fuel Station

Where's the fuel station?	**¿Dónde está la gasolinera?** _dohn•deh ehs•tah lah gah•soh•lee•neh•rah_
Fill it up.	**Lleno.** _yeh•noh_
. . . liters, please.	**. . . litros, por favor.** . . . _lee•trohs pohr fah•bohr_
. . . euros, please.	**Euros por favor** _ew•rohs pohr fah•bohr_
I'll pay in cash/by credit card.	**Voy a pagar en efectivo/con tarjeta de crédito.** _boy ah pah•gahr ehn eh•fehk•tee•boh/ kohn tahr•kheh•tah deh kreh•dee•toh_

YOU MAY SEE...

NORMAL	regular
SÚPER	super
DIESEL	diesel

Asking Directions

Is this the way to…?	**¿Es ésta la carretera a…?** *ehs ehs•tah lah kah•rreh•teh•rah ah…*
How far is it to…?	**¿A qué distancia está…?** *ah keh dees•tahn•theeyah ehs•tah…*
Where's…?	**¿Dónde está…?** *dohn•deh ehs•tah…*
…Street	**la calle…** *lah kah•yeh…*
this address	**ésta dirección** *ehs•tah dee•rek•theeyohn*
the highway [motorway]	**la autopista** *lah aw•toh•pees•tah*
Can you show me on the map?	**¿Me lo puede indicar en el mapa?** *meh loh pweh•deh een•dee•kahr ehn ehl mah•pah*
I'm lost.	**Me he perdido.** *meh eh pehr•dee•doh*

YOU MAY HEAR…

todo recto *toh•doh rehk•toh*	straight ahead
a la izquierda *ah lah eeth•keeyehr•dah*	left
a la derecha *ah lah deh•reh•chah*	right
en/doblando la esquina *ehn/doh•blahn•doh lah ehs•kee•nah*	on/around the corner
frente a *frehn•teh ah*	opposite
detrás de *deh•trahs deh*	behind
al lado de *ahl lah•doh deh*	next to
después de *dehs•pwehs deh*	after
al norte/sur *ahl nohr•teh/soor*	north/south
al este/oeste *ahl ehs•teh/oh•ehs•teh*	east/west
en el semáforo *en ehl seh•mah•foh•roh*	at the traffic light
en el cruce *en ehl kroo•theh*	at the intersection

YOU MAY SEE...

(symbol)	**ADELANTAMIENTO PROHIBIDO**	no passing zone
STOP	**STOP**	stop
(symbol)	**CALLE DE SENTIDO ÚNICO**	one-way street
(symbol)	**CEDA EL PASO**	yield [give way]
(symbol)	**ENTRADA PROHIBIDA**	no entry
(symbol)	**ESTACIONAMIENTO PROHIBIDO**	no parking
(symbol)	**FINAL DEL CARRIL LATERAL DERECHO**	right lane ends (merge left)
(50)	**PROHIBICIÓN VELOCIDAD MÁXIMA**	maximum speed limit

Parking

Can I park here?	**¿Puedo aparcar aquí?** _pweh_·doh ah·pahr·_kahr_ ah·_kee_
Where's...?	**¿Dónde está** _dohn_·deh ehs·_tah_
the parking garage/	**el garaje/aparcamiento?** ehl gah·_rah_·kheh/
parking lot?	ah·pahr·kah·_meeyehn_·toh
the parking meter?	**el parquímetro?** ehl pahr·_kee_·meh·troh
How much...?	**¿Cuánto cobran...?** _kwahn_·toh koh·_brahn_...
per hour	**por hora** pohr _oh_·rah
per day	**por día** pohr _dee_·ah
for overnight	**por la noche** pohr lah _noh_·cheh

Public parking is noted by a blue sign with a capital 'P'. Many towns have **zonas azules** (blue zones), where parking is allowed; buy a ticket at the nearby parking machine. Larger cities have an **ora zona** (hourly parking). Purchase a ticket for 30, 60 or 90 minutes and display it in your windshield. Tickets for the **ora zona** can be purchased at tobacconists, hotels and other retailers — look for the **ora zona** signs in the window. Note: Spain's **Guardia Civil de Tráfico** (highway patrol) may enforce payment of fines for illegal parking on the spot for non-residents of Spain.

Breakdown & Repair

My car broke down/ won't start.	**El coche se me ha averiado/no arranca.** *ehl koh·cheh seh meh ah ah·beh·reeyah·doh/ noh ah·rrahn·kah*
Can you fix it (today)?	**¿Puede arreglarlo (hoy mismo)?** *pweh·deh ah·rreh·glahr·loh (oy meez·moh)*
When will it be ready?	**¿Cuándo estará listo?** *kwahn·doh ehs·tah·rah lees·toh*
How much?	**¿Cuánto es?** *kwahn·toh ehs*
I have a puncture/ flat tyre (tire)	**Tengo un neumático pinchado/desinflado** *tehn·goh oon neoo·mah·tee·coh peen·chah·doh/ dehs·een·flah·doh*

Accidents

There was an accident.	**Ha habido un accidente.** *ah ah·bee·doh oon ahk·thee·dehn·teh*
Call an ambulance/ the police.	**Llame a una ambulancia/la policía.** *yah·meh ah oo·nah ahm·boo·lahn·theeyah/ lah poh·lee·thee·ah*

ESSENTIAL

Can you recommend a hotel?	**¿Puede recomendarme un hotel?** *pweh-deh reh-koh-mehn-dahr-meh oon oh-tehl*
I have a reservation.	**Tengo una reserva.** *tehn-goh oo-nah reh-sehr-bah*
My name is…	**Me llamo…** *meh yah-moh…*
Do you have a room…?	**¿Tienen habitaciones…?** *teeyeh-nehn ah-bee-tah-theeyoh-nehs…*
for one/two	**individuales/dobles** *een-dee-bee-doo-ah-lehs/doh-blehs*
with a bathroom	**con baño** *kohn bah-nyoh*
with air conditioning	**con aire acondicionado** *kohn ayee-reh ah-kohn-dee-theeyoh-nah-doh*
For…	**Para…** *pah-rah…*
tonight	**esta noche** *ehs-tah noh-cheh*
two nights	**dos noches** *dohs noh-chehs*
one week	**una semana** *oo-nah seh-mah-nah*
How much?	**¿Cuánto es?** *kwahn-toh ehs*
Is there anything cheaper?	**¿Hay alguna tarifa más barata?** *aye ahl-goo-nah tah-ree-fah mahs bah-rah-tah*
When's check-out?	**¿A qué hora hay que desocupar la habitación?** *ah keh oh-rah aye keh deh-soh-koo-pahr lah ah-bee-tah-theeyohn*
Can I leave this in the safe?	**¿Puedo dejar esto en la caja fuerte?** *pweh-doh deh-khahr ehs-toh ehn lah kah-khah fwehr-teh*
Can I leave my bags?	**¿Podría dejar mi equipaje?** *poh-dree-ah deh-khahr mee eh-kee-pah-kheh*
Can I have the bill/a receipt?	**¿Me da la factura/un recibo?** *meh dah lah fahk-too-rah/oon reh-thee-boh*

| I'll pay in cash/by credit card. | **Voy a pagar en efectivo/con tarjeta de crédito.** *boy ah pah•gahr ehn eh•fehk•tee•boh/ kohn tahr•kheh•tah deh kreh•dee•toh* |

If you didn't reserve accommodations before your trip, visit the local **Oficina de turismo** (Tourist Information Office) for recommendations on places to stay.

Somewhere to Stay

Can you recommend...?	**¿Puede recomendarme...** *pweh•deh reh•koh•mehn•dahr•meh*
a hotel?	**un hotel?** *oon oh•tehl*
a hostel?	**un albergue?** *oon ahl•behr•geh?*
a campsite	**un cámping?** *oon kahm•peeng?*
a bed and breakfast	**una pensión?** *oo•nah pehn•seeyohn*
What is it near?	**¿Qué hay cerca?** *keh aye thehr•kah*
How do I get there?	**¿Cómo se llega allí?** *koh•moh seh yeh•gah ah•yee*

At the Hotel

I have a reservation.	**Tengo una reserva.** _tehn_·goh _oo_·nah reh·_sehr_·bah
My name is...	**Me llamo...** meh _yah_·moh...
Do you have a room...?	**¿Tiene una habitación...?** _teeyeh_·neh _oo_·nah ah·bee·tah·_theeyohn_...
for one/two	**individual/doble** een·dee·bee·_dwahl_ /doh·bleh
with a toilet/shower	**con un baño/una ducha** kohn oon _bah_·nyoh/_oo_·nah _doo_·chah
with air conditioning	**con aire acondicionado** kohn _ayee_·reh ah·kohn·dee·theeyoh·_nah_·doh
with a single/ double bed	**con una cama/cama de matrimonio** kohn una _kah_·mah/_kah_·mah mah·tree·_moh_·neeyoh
that's smoking/ non smoking	**para fumadores/no fumadores** _pah_·rah foo·mah·_doh_·rehs/noh foo·mah·_doh_·rehs
For...	**Para...** _pah_·rah...
tonight	**esta noche** _ehs_·tah _noh_·cheh
two nights	**dos noches** dohs noh·chehs
a week	**una semana** _oo_·nah seh·_mah_·nah
Does the hotel have...?	**¿Tiene el hotel...?** _teeyeh_·neh ehl oh·_tehl_...

YOU MAY HEAR...

Su pasaporte/tarjeta de crédito, por favor. soo pah·sah·_pohr_·teh/tahr·_kheh_·tah deh _kreh_·dee·toh pohr fah·_bohr_	Your passport/credit card, please.
Rellene este formulario. reh·_yeh_·neh _ehs_·teh fohr·moo·_lah_·reeyoh	Fill out this form.
Firme aquí. _feer_·meh ah·_kee_	Sign here.

There's a variety of places to stay in Spain. Hotels are rated from one to five stars, with five stars being the most expensive and having the most amenities. **Paradores** are government-run inns located throughout the country. These inns are usually castles, monasteries, palaces and other landmark buildings that have been restored and converted into hotels. Reservations are recommended far in advance for **paradores**, as they are very popular, especially in the summer months. Other unique accommodations in Spain include spas, resorts, farm house rentals, apartment rentals, villas and camping.

a computer	**un ordenador**	oon ohr·deh·nah·<u>dohr</u>
an elevator [a lift]	**un ascensor**	oon ah·thehn·<u>sohr</u>
(wireless) internet service	**acceso (inalámbrico) a Internet**	ahk·<u>theh</u>·soh (een·ah·<u>lahm</u>·bree·koh) ah een·tehr·<u>neht</u>
room service	**servicio de habitaciones**	sehr·<u>bee</u>·theeyoh deh ah·bee·tah·<u>theeyoh</u>·nehs
a pool	**una piscina**	<u>oo</u>·nah pees·<u>thee</u>·nah
a gym	**un gimnasio**	oon kheem·<u>nah</u>·seeyoh
I need…	**Necesito…**	neh·theh·<u>see</u>·toh…
an extra bed	**otra cama**	<u>oh</u>·trah <u>kah</u>·mah
a cot	**un catre**	oon <u>kah</u>·treh
a crib	**una cuna**	<u>oo</u>·nah <u>koo</u>·nah

For Numbers, see page 167.

Price

How much per night/ week?	**¿Cuánto cuesta por noche/semana?** <u>kwahn</u>·toh <u>kwehs</u>·tah pohr <u>noh</u>·cheh/seh·<u>mah</u>·nah
Are there any discounts?	**¿Ofrecen algún descuento?** oh·freh·thehn ahl·goon dehs·kwehn·toh

| Does that include breakfast/sales tax [VAT]? | **¿Incluye el precio el desayuno/IVA?** _een·kloo·yeh ehl preh·theeyoh ehl deh·sah·yoo·noh/eh·beh·ah_ |

Preferences

Can I see the room?	**¿Puedo ver la habitación?** _pweh·doh behr luh uh·bee·tah·theeyohn_
I'd like a...room.	**Quiero una habitación...** _keeyeh·roh oo·nah ah·bee·tah·theeyohn_
better	**mejor** _meh·khohr_
bigger	**más grande** _mahs grahn·deh_
cheaper	**más barata** _mahs bah·rah·tah_
quieter	**más silenciosa** _mahs see·lehn·ceeyo·sah_
I'll take it.	**Me lo llevo** _meh loh yeh·boh_
No, I won't take it.	**No, no me lo llevo** _noh, noh meh loh yeh·boh_

Questions

Where's...?	**¿Dónde está...?** _dohn·deh ehs·tah..._
the bar	**el bar** _ehl bahr_
the bathrooms	**el baño** _ehl bah·nyoh_
the elevator [lift]	**el ascensor** _ehl ahs·thehn·sohr_
Can I have...?	**¿Puede darme...?** _pweh·deh dahr·meh..._
a blanket	**una manta** _oo·nah mahn·tah_
an iron	**una plancha** _oo·nah plahn·chah_
a pillow	**una almohada** _oo·nah ahl·moh·ah·dah_
soap	**jabón** _khah·bohn_
toilet paper	**papel higiénico** _pah·pehl ee·kheeyeh·nee·koh_
a towel	**una toalla** _oo·nah toh·ah·yah_
Do you have an adapter for this?	**¿Tiene un adaptador para esto?** _teeyeh·neh oon ah·dahp·tah·dohr pah·rah ehs·toh_
How do I turn on the lights?	**¿Cómo enciendo las luces?** _koh·moh ehn·theeyehn·doh lahs loo·thehs_

41

Can you wake me at…?	**¿Podría despertarme a la/las…?**
	poh·dree·ah dehs·pehr·tahr·meh ah lah/lahs…
Can I leave this in the safe?	**¿Puedo dejar esto en la caja fuerte?**
	pweh·doh deh·khahr ehs·toh ehn lah kah·khah fwehr·teh
Can I have my things from the safe?	**¿Podría darme mis cosas de la caja fuerte?**
	poh·dree·ah dahr·meh mees koh·sahs deh lah kah·khah fwehr·teh
Is there mail [post]/ a message for me?	**¿Hay correo/algún mensaje para mí?**
	aye koh·rreh·oh/ahl·goon mehn·sah·kheh pah·rah mee

When asking for a public restroom, it's more common and polite to use the term **servicio**. The term **baño** tends to be used when asking for a private bathroom such as in a home or a hotel room. Native speakers sometimes use both words interchangeably, but you will almost always see **servicio** on a sign.

YOU MAY SEE…

EMPUJAR/TIRAR	push/pull
BAÑO/SERVICIO	bathroom/restroom [toilet]
DUCHA	shower
ASCENSOR	elevator [lift]
ESCALERAS	stairs
LAVANDERÍA	laundry
NO MOLESTAR	do not disturb
PUERTA DE INCENDIOS	fire door
SALIDA (DE EMERGENCIA)	(emergency) exit
LLAMADA DESPERTADOR	wake-up call

| Do you have a laundry service? | **¿Tienen servicio de lavandería?** *teeyeh·nehn sehr·bee·theeyoh deh lah·bahn·deh·ree·ah* |

For Grammar, see page 162.

Problems

There's a problem.	**Hay un problema.** *aye oon proh·<u>bleh</u>·mah*
I lost my key/ key card.	**He perdido la llave/llave electrónica.** *eh pehr·<u>dee</u>·doh lah <u>yah</u>·beh/<u>yah</u>·beh eh·lehk·<u>troh</u>·nee·kah*
I've locked my key/ key card in the room.	**He dejado la llave dentro de la habitación.** *eh deh·<u>khah</u>·doh lah <u>yah</u>·beh <u>dehn</u>·troh deh lah ah·bee·tah·<u>theeyohn</u>*
There's no hot water/toilet paper.	**No hay agua caliente/papel higiénico.** *no aye <u>ah</u>·gwah kah·<u>leeyehn</u>·teh/pah·<u>pehl</u> ee·<u>kheeyeh</u>·nee·koh*
The room is dirty.	**La habitación está sucia.** *lah ah·bee·tah·<u>theeyohn</u> ehs·<u>tah</u> <u>soo</u>·theeyah*
There are bugs in the room.	**Hay insectos en la habitación.** *aye een·<u>sehk</u>·tohs ehn lah ah·bee·tah·<u>theeyohn</u>*
...doesn't work.	**...no funciona.** *... no foon·<u>theeyoh</u>·nah*
Can you fix...?	**¿Pueden arreglar...?** *<u>pweh</u>·dehn ah·rreh·<u>glahr</u>...*
the air conditioning	**el aire acondicionado** *ehl <u>ayee</u>·reh ah·kohn·dee·theeyoh·<u>nah</u>·doh*
the fan	**el ventilador** *ehl behn·tee·lah·<u>dohr</u>*
the heat [heating]	**la calefacción** *lah kah·leh·fahk·<u>theeyohn</u>*
the light	**la luz** *lah looth*
the TV	**la televisión** *lah teh·leh·bee·<u>seeyohn</u>*
the toilet	**el retrete** *ehl reh·<u>treh</u>·teh*
I'd like another room.	**Quiero otra habitación.** *<u>keeyeh</u>·roh <u>oh</u>·trah ah·bee·tah·<u>theeyohn</u>*

Spain's electricity is 220 volts. You may need a converter and/or an adapter for your appliances.

Checking Out

When's check-out?	**¿A qué hora hay que desocupar la habitación?** *ah keh <u>oh</u>•rah aye keh deh•soh•koo•<u>pahr</u>* *lah ah•bee•tah•<u>theeyohn</u>*
Can I leave my bags here until…?	**¿Puedo dejar mi equipaje aquí hasta…?** *<u>pweh</u>•doh deh•<u>khahr</u> mee eh•kee•<u>pah</u>•kheh* *ah•<u>kee</u> <u>ahs</u>•tah…*
Can I have an itemized bill/a receipt?	**¿Puede darme una factura detallada/un recibo?** *<u>pweh</u>•deh <u>dahr</u>•meh oo•nah fahk•<u>too</u>•rah* *deh•tah•<u>yah</u>•dah/oon reh•<u>thee</u>•boh*
I think there's a mistake.	**Creo que hay un error.** *<u>kreh</u>•oh keh aye* *oon eh•<u>rrohr</u>*
I made… phone calls.	**He hecho…llamadas.** *eh <u>eh</u>•choh…* *yah•<u>mah</u>•dahs*
I took…from the mini-bar.	**He tomado…del minibar.** *eh toh•<u>mah</u>•doh…* *dehl <u>mee</u>•nee•bar*
I'll pay in cash/ by credit card.	**Voy a pagar en efectivo/con tarjeta de crédito.** *boy ah pah•<u>gahr</u> ehn eh•fehk•<u>tee</u>•boh/* *kohn tahr•<u>kheh</u>•tah deh <u>kreh</u>•dee•toh*

Tipping in hotels, restaurants and bars isn't customary in Spain. However, if you wish to leave a tip for good service, it will be appreciated; just round up a bill to the nearest euro or two.

Renting

I reserved an apartment/a room.	**He reservado un apartamento/una habitación.** *eh reh·sehr·bah·doh oon ah·pahr·tah·mehn·toh/ oo·nah ah·bee·tah·theeyohn*
My name is...	**Me llamo...** *meh yah·moh...*
Can I have the key/key card?	**¿Puede darme la llave/llave electrónica?** *pweh·deh dahr·meh lah yah·beh/ yah·beh eh·lehk·troh·nee·kah*
Are there...?	**¿Hay...?** *aye...*
dishes	**platos** *plah·tohs*
pillows	**almohadas** *ahl·moh·ah·dahs*
sheets	**sábanas** *sah·bah·nahs*
towels	**toallas** *toh·ah·yahs*
kitchen utensils	**cubiertos** *koo·beeyehr·tohs*
When do I put out the bins/ recycling?	**¿Cuándo saco la basura/el reciclado?** *kwahn·doh sah·koh lah bah·soo·rah/ ehl reh·thee·klah·doh*
...is broken.	**...está estropeado m/estropeada f.** *...ehs·tah ehs·troh·peh·ah·doh/ehs·troh·peh·ah·dah*
How does... work?	**¿Cómo funciona...?** *koh·moh foon·theeyoh*
the air conditioner	**el aire acondicionado** *ehl ayee·reh ah·kohn·dee·theeyoh·nah·doh*
the dishwasher	**el lavavajillas** *ehl lah·bah·bah·khee·yahs*
the freezer	**el congelador** *ehl kohn·kheh·lah·dohr*
the heater	**la calefacción** *lah kah·leh·fahk·theeyohn*
the microwave	**el microondas** *ehl mee·kroh·ohn·dahs*
the refrigerator	**la nevera** *lah neh·beh·rah*
the stove	**el horno** *ehl ohr·noh*
the washing machine	**la lavadora** *lah lah·bah·doh·rah*

Domestic Items

I need...	**Necesito...** neh·theh·<u>see</u>·toh...
an adapter	**un adaptador** oon ah·dahp·tah·<u>dohr</u>
aluminum [kitchen] foil	**papel de aluminio** pah·<u>pehl</u> deh ah·loo·<u>mee</u>·neeyoh
a bottle opener	**un abrebotellas** oon ah·breh·boh·<u>teh</u>·yahs
a broom	**una escoba** <u>oo</u>·nah ehs·<u>koh</u>·bah
a can opener	**un abrelatas** oon ah·breh·<u>lah</u>·tahs
cleaning supplies	**productos de limpieza** proh·<u>dook</u>·tohs deh leem·<u>peeyeh</u>·thah
a corkscrew	**un sacacorchos** oon sah·kah·<u>kohr</u>·chohs
detergent	**detergente** deh·tehr·<u>khehn</u>·teh
dishwashing liquid	**líquido lavavajillas** <u>lee</u>·kee·doh lah·bah·bah·<u>khee</u>·yahs
bin bags	**bolsas de basura** <u>bohl</u>·sahs deh bah·<u>soo</u>·rah
a lightbulb	**una bombilla** <u>oo</u>·nah bohm·<u>bee</u>·yah
matches	**cerillas** theh·<u>ree</u>·yahs
a mop	**una fregona** <u>oo</u>·nah freh·<u>goh</u>·nah
napkins	**servilletas** sehr·bee·<u>yeh</u>·tahs
paper towels	**papel de cocina** pah·<u>pehl</u> deh koh·<u>thee</u>·nah
plastic wrap [cling film]	**film transparente** feelm trahns·pah·<u>rehn</u>·teh
a plunger	**un desatascador** oon deh·sah·tahs·kah·<u>dohr</u>
scissors	**tijeras** tee·<u>kheh</u>·rahs
a vacuum cleaner	**una aspiradora** <u>oo</u>·nah ahs·pee·rah·<u>doh</u>·rah

For In the Kitchen, see page 80.

At the Hostel

Is there a bed available?	**¿Hay camas disponibles?** aye <u>kah</u>·mahs dees·poh·<u>nee</u>·blehs
I'd like...	**¿Me puede dar...?** meh <u>pweh</u>·deh dahr...

With more than 100 hostels around Spain, finding an inexpensive place to stay should be easy. Hostels are inexpensive accommodations that have dormitory-style rooms and, sometimes, private or semi-private rooms. Some offer private bathrooms, though most have shared facilities. There is usually a self service kitchen on site. Reservations are recommended in advance in larger cities and popular destinations during the tourist season.

a single/ double room	**una habitación individual/doble** _oo_•nah _ah_•bee•tah•_theeyohn_ een•dee•bee•doo•_ahl/doh_•bleh
a blanket	**una manta** _oo_•nah _mahn_•tah
a pillow	**una almohada** _oo_•nah ahl•moh•_ah_•dah
sheets	**sábanas** _sah_•bah•nahs
a towel	**una toalla** _oo_•nah toh•_ah_•yah
Do you have lockers?	**¿Tienen consignas?** teeyeh•nehn kohn•seeg•nahs
When do you lock up?	**¿A qué hora cierran las puertas?** ah keh _oh_•rah _theeyeh_•rrahn lahs _pwehr_•tahs
Do I need a membership card?	**¿Necesito una tarjeta de socio?** neh•theh•_see_•toh _oo_•nah tahr•_kheh_•tah de _soh_•theeyoh
Here's my International Student Card.	**Aquí tiene mi carnet internacional de estudiante.** ah•_kee_ teeyeh•neh mee kahr•_neht_ een•tehr•nah•theeyoh•_nahl_ deh ehs•too•_deeyahn_•teh

Going Camping

Can I camp here?	**¿Puedo acampar aquí?** _pweh_•doh ah•kahm•_pahr_ ah•_kee_
Where's the campsite?	**¿Dónde está el cámping?** _dohn_•deh ehs•_tah_ ehl _kahm_•peeng

What is the charge per day/week?	**¿Cuánto cobran por día/semana?** *kwahn·toh koh·brahn pohr dee·ah/seh·mah·nah*
Are there…?	**¿Hay…?** *aye…*
cooking facilities	**instalaciones para cocinar** *eens·tah·lah·theeyoh·nehs pah·rah koh·thee·nahr*
electric outlets	**enchufes eléctricos** *ehn·choo·fehs eh·lehk·tree·kohs*
laundry facilities	**servicio de lavandería** *sehr·bee·theeyoh deh lah·bahn·deh·ree·ah*
showers	**duchas** *doo·chahs*
tents for hire	**tiendas de alquiler** *teeyehn·dahs deh ahl·kee·lehr*
Where can I empty the chemical toilet?	**¿Dónde puedo vaciar el váter químico?** *dohn·deh pweh·doh bah·thee·ahr ehl bah·tehr kee·mee·koh*

For Domestic Items, see page 46.

YOU MAY SEE…

AGUA POTABLE	drinking water
PROHIBIDO ACAMPAR	no camping
PROHIBIDO HACER HOGUERAS/BARBACOAS	no fires/barbecues

Communications

ESSENTIAL

Where's an internet cafe?	**¿Dónde hay un cibercafé?** _dohn_·deh aye oon thee·behr·kah·_feh_
Can I access the internet/check e-mail?	**¿Puedo acceder a Internet/revisar el correo electrónico?** _pweh_·doh ahk·theh·_dehr_ ah een·tehr·_neht_/reh·bee·_sahr_ ehl koh·_rreh_·oh eh·lehk·_troh_·nee·koh
How much per (half) hour?	**¿Cuánto cuesta por (media) hora?** _kwahn_·toh _kwehs_·tah pohr (_meh_·deeyah) _oh_·rah
How do I connect/ log on?	**¿Cómo entro al sistema/inicio la sesión?** koh·moh _ehn_·troh ahl sees·_teh_·mah/ ee·nee·_theeyoh_ lah seh·_seeyohn_
A phone card, please.	**Una tarjeta telefónica, por favor.** _oo_·nah tahr·_kheh_·tah teh·leh·_foh_·nee·kah pohr fah·_bohr_
Can I have your phone number?	**¿Me puede dar su número de teléfono?** meh _pweh_·deh dahr soo _noo_·meh·roh deh teh·_leh_·foh·noh
Here's my number/ e-mail address.	**Aquí tiene mi número/dirección de correo electrónico.** ah·_kee teeyeh_·neh mee _noo_·meh·roh/ dee·rehk·_theeyohn_ deh koh·_rreh_·oh eh·lehk·_troh_·nee·koh
Call me.	**Llámeme.** _yah_·meh·meh
E-mail me.	**Envíeme un correo.** ehn·_bee_·eh·meh oon koh·_rreh_·oh
Hello. This is…	**Hola. Soy…** _oh_·lah soy…
Can I speak to…?	**¿Puedo hablar con…?** _pweh_·doh ah·_blahr_ kohn…
Can you repeat that?	**¿Puede repetir eso?** _pweh_·deh reh·peh·_teer eh_·soh

I'll call back later.	**Llamaré más tarde.** *yah·mah·reh mahs tahr·deh*
Bye.	**Adiós.** *ah·deeyohs*
Where's the post office?	**¿Dónde está la oficina de correos?** *dohn·deh ehs·tah lah oh·fee·thee·nah deh koh·rreh·ohs*
I'd like to send this to...	**Quiero mandar esto a...** *keeyeh·roh mahn·dahr ehs·toh ah...*

Online

Where's an internet cafe?	**¿Dónde hay un cibercafé?** *dohn·deh aye oon thee·behr·kah·feh*
Does it have wireless internet?	**¿Tiene Internet inalámbrico?** *teeyeh·neh een·tehr·neht een·ah·lahm·bree·koh*
What is the WiFi password?	**¿Cuál es la contraseña de WiFi?** *kwahl ehs lah kohn·trah·seh·nyah deh weeh·feeh*
Is the WiFi free?	**¿Es gratuito el acceso WiFi?** *esh grah·too·ee·toh ehl ahk·theh·soh weeh·feeh*
Do you have bluetooth?	**¿Tiene Bluetooth?** *teeyeh·neh blue·tooth*
How do I turn the computer on/off?	**¿Cómo enciendo/apago el ordenador?** *koh·moh ehn·theeyen·doh/ah·pah·goh ehl ohr·deh·nah·dohr*
Can I...?	**¿Puedo...?** *pweh·doh...*
access the internet	**acceder a Internet** *ahk·theh·dehr ah een·tehr·neht*
check e-mail	**revisar el correo electrónico** *reh·bee·sahr ehl koh·rreh·oh eh·lehk·troh·nee·koh*
print	**imprimir** *eem·pree·meer*
plug in/charge my laptop/iPhone/iPad/BlackBerry?	**enchufar/cargar el portátil/iPhone/iPad/Blackberry?** *ehn·choo·fahr/kahr·gahr ehl pohr·tah·teel/i·fon/i·pad/Blackberry*

access Skype?	**acceder a Skype?** *ahk•theh•dehr ah skype*
How much per (half) hour?	**¿Cuánto cuesta por (media) hora?** *kwahn•toh kwehs•tah pohr (meh•deeyah) oh•rah*
How do I...?	**¿Cómo...?** *koh•moh...*
connect/ disconnect	**me conecto/me desconecto** *meh koh•nehk•toh/meh dehs•koh•nehk•toh*
log on/off	**Inicio/cierro la sesión** *ee•nee•theeyoh/ theeyeh•rroh lah seh•seeyohn*
type this symbol	**escribo este símbolo** *ehs•kree•boh ehs•teh seem•boh•loh*
What's your e-mail?	**¿Cuál es su dirección de correo electrónico?** *kwahl ehs soo dee•rehk•theeyohn deh koh•rreh•oh eh•lehk•troh•nee•koh*
My e-mail is...	**Mi dirección de correo electrónico es...** *mee dee•rehk•theeyohn deh koh•rreh•oh eh•lehk•troh•nee•koh ehs...*

Do you have a scanner? **¿Tienen un escáner?** *teeyeh•nehn oon ehs•kah•nehr*

Social Media

Are you on Facebook/ Twitter?	**¿Está en Facebook/Twitter?** *(polite form)* *ehs•tah ehn Facebook/Twitter*
	¿Estás en Facebook/Twitter? *(informal form)* *ehs•tahs ehn Facebook/Twitter*
What's your user name?	**¿Cuál es su nombre de usuario?** *(polite form)* *kwahl ehs soo nohm•breh deh oo•soo•ah•reeyoh*
	¿Cuál es tu nombre de usuario? *(informal form)* *kwahl ehs too nohm•breh deh oo•soo•ah•reeyoh*
I'll add you as a friend.	**Le añadiré como amigo.** *(polite form)* *leh ah•nyah•dee•reh koh•moh ah•mee•goh*
	Te añadiré como amigo. *(informal form)* *teh ah•nyah•dee•reh koh•moh ah•mee•goh*

YOU MAY SEE...

CERRAR	close
BORRAR	delete
CORREO ELECTRÓNICO	e-mail
SALIR	exit
AYUDA	help
MENSAJERO INSTANTÁNEO	instant messenger
INTERNET	internet
INICIO DE SESIÓN	login
NUEVO (MENSAJE)	new (message)
ENCENDER/APAGAR	on/off
ABRIR	open
IMPRIMIR	print
GUARDAR	save
ENVIAR	send
NOMBRE DE USUARIO/CONTRASEÑA	username/password
INTERNET INALÁMBRICO	wireless internet

I'll follow you on Twitter.	**Le seguiré en Twitter.** *(polite form)* *leh seh·gee·reh ehn Twitter*
	Te seguiré en Twitter. *(informal form)* *teh seh·gee·reh ehn Twitter*
Are you following...?	**¿Sigue a...?** *(polite form) see·geh ah*
	¿Sigues a...? *(informal form) see·gehs ah*
I'll put the pictures on Facebook/Twitter.	**Subiré las fotos a Facebook/Twitter.** *soo·bee·reh lahs foh·tohs ah Facebook/Twitter*
I'll tag you in the pictures.	**Le etiquetaré en las fotos.** *(polite form)* *leh eh·tee·keh·tah·reh ehn lahs foh·tohs*
	Te etiquetaré en las fotos. *(informal form)* *teh eh·tee·keh·tah·reh ehn lahs foh·tohs*

Phone

A phone card/ prepaid phone, please.	**Una tarjeta telefónica/Un teléfono prepago, por favor.** _oo•nah tahr•kheh•tah teh•leh•foh•nee•kah/ oon teh•leh•foh•noh preh•pah•goh pohr fah•bohr_
How much?	**¿Cuánto es?** _kwahn•toh ehs_
Where's the pay phone?	**¿Dónde está el teléfono público?** _dohn•deh ehs•tah ehl teh•leh•foh•noh poo•blee•koh_
What's the area code/ country code for…?	**¿Cuál es el prefijo/código de país para…?** _kwahl ehs ehl preh•fee•khoh/koh•dee•goh deh pah•ees pah•rah…_
What's the number for Information?	**¿Cuál es el número de información?** _kwahl ehs ehl noo•meh•roh deh een•fohr•mah•theeyohn_
I'd like the number for…	**Quiero que me dé el número de teléfono de…** _keeyeh•roh keh meh deh ehl noo•meh•roh deh teh•leh•foh•noh deh…_
I'd like to call collect [reverse the charges].	**Quiero llamar a cobro revertido** _keeyeh•roh yah•mahr ah koh•broh reh•behr•tee•doh_
My phone doesn't work here.	**Mi teléfono no funciona aquí.** _mee teh•leh•foh•noh no foon•theeyoh•nah ah•kee_
What network are you on?	**¿En qué red está?** _ehn keh rehd ehs•tah_
Is it 3G?	**¿Es 3G?** _ehs trehs kheh_
I have run out of credit/minutes.	**Me he quedado sin saldo/minutos.** _meh eh keh•dah•doh seen sahl•doh/meeh•noo•tohs_
Can I buy some credit?	**¿Puedo comprar una recarga de saldo?** _pweh•doh kohm•prahr oo•nah reh•kahr•gah deh sahl•doh_
Do you have a phone charger?	**¿Tiene un cargador de móvil?** _teeyeh•neh oon kahr•gah•dohr deh moh•beel_
Can I have your number?	**¿Me puede dar su número de teléfono?** _meh pweh•deh dahr soo noo•meh•roh deh teh•leh•foh•noh_
Here's my number.	**Aquí tiene mi número.** _ah•kee teeyeh•neh mee noo•meh•roh_

Please call me.	**Llámame, por favor.** _yah_·mah·meh pohr fah·_bohr_
Please text me.	**Envíame un mensaje de texto, por favor.**
	ehn·_beeyah_·meh oon mehn·_sah_·kheh deh _tehx_·toh
	pohr fah·_bohr_
I'll call you.	**Le _m_/La _f_ llamaré.** leh/lah yah·mah·_reh_
I'll text you.	**Te enviaré un mensaje de texto.**
	teh ehn·beeyah·_reh_ oon mehn·_sah_·kheh deh _tehx_·toh

Telephone Etiquette

Hello. This is...	**Hola. Soy...** _oh_·lah soy...
Can I speak to...?	**¿Puedo hablar con...?** _pweh_·doh ah·_blahr_ kohn...
Extension...	**Extensión...** ehks·tehn·_seeyohn_...
Speak louder/more	**Hable más alto/despacio, por favor.** _ah_·bleh
slowly, please.	mahs _ahl_·toh/dehs·_pah_·theeyoh pohr fah·_bohr_

Public phones are either coin- or card-operated, though
coin-operated phones are becoming less common. Phone cards
can be purchased in post offices, newsstands and tobacconists. For
international calls, calling cards are the most economical. You can
also make your long-distance calls at **locutorios** (call centers); these
additionally offer internet, fax and wireless phone-charging services
at reasonable prices. Calling internationally from your hotel may be
convenient, but the rates can be very expensive.

Important telephone numbers:

emergencies, 112

information, 010

operator assistance, 025

To call the U.S. or Canada from Spain, dial 00 + 1 + area
code + phone number. To call the U.K. from Spain, dial 00
+ 44 + area code (minus the first 0) + phone number.

YOU MAY HEAR...

¿Quién llama? *keeyehn yah·mah* — Who's calling?

Espere. *ehs·peh·reh* — Hold on.

Le paso. *leh pah·soh* — I'll put you through.

No está. *noh ehs·tah* — He/She is not here.

No puede atenderle en este momento. *noh pweh·deh ah·tehn·dehr·leh ehn ehs·teh moh·mehn·toh* — He/She can't come to the phone.

¿Quiere dejarle un mensaje? *keeyeh·reh deh·khahr·leh oon mehn·sah·kheh* — Would you like to leave a message?

Vuelva a llamar más tarde/en diez minutos. *bwehl·bah ah yah·mahr mahs tahr·deh/ehn deeyeth mee·noo·tohs* — Call back later/in 10 minutes.

¿Le puede llamar él *m*/ella *f* a usted? *leh pweh·deh yah·mahr ehl/eh·yah ah oos·tehth* — Can he/she call you back?

¿Me da su número? *meh dah soo noo·meh·roh* — What's your number?

Can you repeat that?	**¿Puede repetir eso?** *pweh·deh reh·peh·teer eh·soh*
I'll call back later.	**Llamaré más tarde.** *yah·mah·reh mahs tahr·deh*
Bye.	**Adiós.** *ah·deeyohs*

For Business Travel, see page 142.

Fax

Can I send/receive a fax here?	**¿Puedo enviar/recibir un fax aquí?** *pweh·doh ehn·bee·ahr/reh·thee·beer oon fahx ah·kee*
What's the fax number?	**¿Cuál es el número de fax?** *kwahl ehs ehl noo·meh·roh deh fahx*
Please fax this to...	**Por favor envíe este fax a...** *pohr fah·bohr ehn·bee·eh ehs·teh fahx ah...*

Post

Where's the post office/mailbox?	**¿Dónde está la oficina/el buzón de correos?** _dohn·deh ehs·tah lah oh·fee·thee·nah/ehl boo·thohn deh koh·rreh·ohs_
A stamp for this postcard/letter to...	**Un sello para esta postal/carta a...** _oon seh·yoh pah·rah ehs·tah pohs·tahl/kahr·tah ah..._
How much?	**¿Cuánto es?** _kwahn·toh ehs_
I want to send this package by airmail/express.	**Quiero mandar este paquete por correo aéreo/urgente.** _keeyeh·roh mahn·dahr ehs·teh pah·keh·teh pohr koh·rreh·oh ah·eh·reh·oh/oor·khen·teh_
A receipt, please.	**Un recibo, por favor.** _oon reh·thee·boh pohr fah·bohr_

Oficinas de Correos (post offices) in Spain offer more than just standard postal services. You may be able to fax, scan and e-mail documents and send money orders from the local post office. Services available vary by location.

Food & Drink

Eating Out

ESSENTIAL

Can you recommend a good restaurant/bar?	**¿Puede recomendarme un buen restaurante/bar?** *pweh·deh reh·koh·mehn·dahr·meh oon bwehn rehs·taw·rahn·teh/bahr*
Is there a traditional Spanish/an inexpensive restaurant nearby?	**¿Hay un restaurante típico español/barato cerca de aquí?** *aye oon rehs·taw·rahn·teh tee·pee·koh ehs·pah·nyohl/bah·rah·toh thehr·kah deh ah·kee*
A table for…, please.	**Una mesa para…, por favor.** *oo·nah meh·sah pah·rah…pohr fah·bohr*
Can we sit…?	**¿Podemos sentarnos…?** *poh·deh·mohs sehn·tahr·nohs…*
here/there	**aquí/allí** *ah·kee/ah·yee*
outside	**fuera** *fweh·rah*
in a non-smoking area	**en una zona de no fumadores** *ehn oo·nah thoh·nah deh noh foo·mah·doh·rehs*
I'm waiting for someone.	**Estoy esperando a alguien.** *ehs·toy ehs·peh·rahn·doh ah ahl·geeyehn*
Where are the toilets?	**¿Dónde están los servicios?** *dohn·deh ehs·tahn lohs sehr·bee·theeyohs*
A menu, please.	**Una carta, por favor.** *oo·nah kahr·tah pohr fah·bohr*
What do you recommend?	**¿Qué me recomienda?** *keh meh reh·koh·meeyehn·dah*
I'd like…	**Quiero…** *keeyeh·roh…*
Some more…, please.	**Quiero más…, por favor.** *keeyeh·roh mahs… pohr fah·bohr*

Enjoy your meal!	**¡Que aproveche!** *keh ah·proh·beh·cheh*
The check [bill], please.	**La cuenta, por favor.** *lah kwen·tah pohr fah·bohr*
Is service included?	**¿Está incluido el servicio?** *ehs·tah een·kloo·ee·doh ehl sehr·bee·theeyoh*
Can I pay by credit card?	**¿Puedo pagar con tarjeta de crédito?** *pweh·doh pah·gahr kohn tahr·kheh·tah deh kreh·dee·toh*
Can I have a receipt?	**¿Podría darme un recibo?** *poh·dree·ah dahr·meh oon reh·thee·boh*
Thank you!	**¡Gracias!** *grah·theeyahs*

Where to Eat

Can you recommend...?	**¿Puede recomendarme...?** *pweh·deh reh·koh·mehn·dahr·meh...*
a restaurant	**un restaurante** *oon rehs·taw·rahn·teh*
a bar	**un bar** *oon bahr*
a cafe	**un café** *oon kah·feh*
a fast-food place	**un restaurante de comida rápida** *oon rehs·taw·rahn·teh deh koh·mee·dah rah·pee·dah*
a tapas bar	**un bar de tapas** *oon bahr deh tah·pahs*
a cheap restaurant	**un restaurante barato** *oon rehs·taw·rahn·teh bah·rah·toh*
an expensive restaurant	**un restaurante caro** *oon rehs·taw·rahn·teh kah·roh*
a restaurant with a good view	**un restaurante con buenas vistas** *oon rehs·taw·rahn·teh kohn bweh·nash bees·tahs*
an authentic/ a non-touristy restaurant	**un restaurante auténtico/no turístico** *oon rehs·taw·rahn·teh awtehn·tee·koh/ noh too·reesh·tee·koh*

Reservations & Preferences

I'd like to reserve a table...	**Quiero reservar una mesa...** _keeyeh_•roh reh•sehr•_bahr_ _oo_•nah _meh_•sah...
for two	**para dos** _pah_•rah dohs
for this evening	**para esta noche** _pah_•rah _ehs_•tah _noh_•cheh
for tomorrow at...	**para mañana a la/las...** _pah_•rah mah•_nyah_•nah ah lah/lahs...
A table for two, please.	**Una mesa para dos, por favor.** _oo_•nah _meh_•sah _pah_•rah dohs pohr fah•_bohr_
We have a reservation.	**Tenemos una reserva.** teh•_neh_•mohs _oo_•nah reh•_sehr_•bah
My name is...	**Me llamo...** meh _yah_•moh...
Can we sit...?	**¿Podríamos sentarnos...?** poh•_dree_•ah•mohs sehn•_tahr_•nohs...
here/there	**aquí/allí** ah•_kee_/ah•_yee_
outside	**fuera** _fweh_•rah
in a non-smoking area	**en una zona de no fumadores** ehn _oo_•nah _thoh_•nah deh noh foo•mah•_doh_•rehs
by the window	**al lado de la ventana** ahl _lah_•doh de lah behn•_tah_•nah

YOU MAY HEAR...

¿Tiene reserva? *teeyeh·neh reh·sehr·bah*	Do you have a reservation?
¿Cuántos son? *kwahn·tohs sohn*	How many?
¿Fumador o no fumador? *foo·mah·dohr oh noh foo·mah·dohr*	Smoking or non-smoking?
¿Está listo m/lista f para pedir? *ehs·tah lees·toh/lees·tah pah·rah peh·deer*	Are you ready to order?
¿Qué va a tomar? *keh bah ah toh·mahr*	What would you like?
Le recomiendo... *leh reh·koh·meeyehn·doh...*	I recommend...
Que aproveche. *keh ah·proh·beh·cheh*	Enjoy your meal.

in the shade/sun	**¿Me puede dar una mesa a la sombra/al sol?** *meh pweh·deh dahr oo·nah meh·sah ah lah sohm·brah/ahl sohl*
Where are the toilets?	**¿Dónde están los servicios?** *dohn·deh ehs·tahn lohs sehr·bee·theeyohs*

For Grammar, see page 162.

How to Order

Waiter/Waitress!	**¡Camarero m/Camarera f!** *kah·mah·reh·roh/ kah·mah·reh·rah*
We're ready to order.	**Estamos listos para pedir.** *ehs·tah·mohs lees·tohs pah·rah peh·deer*
May I see the wine list?	**La carta de vinos, por favor.** *lah kahr·tah deh bee·nohs pohr fah·bohr*
I'd like...	**Quiero...** *keeyeh·roh...*
a bottle of...	**una botella de...** *oo·nah boh·teh·yah deh...*
a carafe of...	**una garrafa de...** *oo·nah gah·rrah·fah deh...*

a glass of…	**un vaso de…**	*oon bah·soh deh…*
Can I have a menu?	**La carta, por favor.**	*lah kahr·tah pohr fah·bohr*
Do you have…?	**¿Tiene…?**	*teeyeh·neh…*
a menu in English	**una carta en inglés**	*oo·nah kahr·tah ehn een·glehs*
a fixed-price menu	**el menú del día**	*ehl meh·noo dehl dee·ah*
a children's menu	**una carta para niños**	*oo·nah kahr·tah pah·rah nee·nyohs*
What do you recommend?	**¿Qué me recomienda?**	*keh meh reh·koh·meeyehn·dah*
What's this?	**¿Qué es esto?**	*keh ehs ehs·toh*
What's in it?	**¿Qué lleva?**	*keh yeh·bah*
Is it spicy?	**¿Es picante?**	*ehs pee·kahn·teh*
I'd like…	**Quiero…**	*keeyeh·roh…*
More…, please.	**Más…, por favor.**	*mahs…pohr fah·bohr*
With/Without…	**Con/Sin…**	*kohn/seen…*
I can't have…	**No puedo tomar…**	*noh pweh·doh toh·mahr…*
rare	**muy poco hecho *m*/hecha *f***	*mooy poh·koh eh·choh/eh·chah*
medium	**medio hecho *m*/hecha *f***	*meh·deeyoh eh·choh/eh·chah*
well-done	**bien hecho *m*/hecha *f***	*beeyehn eh·choh/eh·chah*
It's to go [take away].	**Es para llevar.**	*ehs pah·rah yeh·bahr*

For Drinks, see page 82.

YOU MAY SEE…

CARTA	menu
MENÚ DEL DÍA	menu of the day
SERVICIO (NO) INCLUIDO	service (not) included
ESPECIALIDADES DE LA CASA	specials

Cooking Methods

baked	**al horno** _ahl ohr·noh_
boiled	**hervido** _m_ /**hervida** _f ehr·bee·doh/ehr·bee·da_
braised	**a fuego lento** _ah fweh·goh lehn·toh_
breaded	**empanado** _m_ /**empanada** _f ehm·pah·nah·doh/ ehm·pah·nah·dah_
creamed	**con nata** _kohn nah·tah_
diced	**cortado en taquitos** _kohr·tah·doh ehn tah·kee·tohs_
fileted	**cortado en filetes** _kohr·tah·doh ehn fee·leh·tehs_
fried	**frito** _m_ /**frita** _f free·toh/free·tah_
grilled	**a la plancha** _ah lah plahn·chah_
poached	**escalfado** _m_ /**escalfada** _f ehs·kahl·fah·doh/ ehs·kahl·fah·dah_
roasted	**asado** _m_ /**asada** _f ah·sah·doh/ah·sah·dah_
sautéed	**salteado** _m_ /**salteada** _f sahl·teh·ah·doh/sahl·teh·ah·dah_
smoked	**ahumado** _m_ /**ahumada** _f ah·oo·mah·doh/ ah·oo·mah·dah_
steamed	**al vapor** _ahl bah·pohr_
stewed	**guisado** _m_ /**guisada** _f gee·sah·doh/gee·sah·dah_
stuffed	**relleno** _m_ /**rellena** _f reh·yeh·noh/reh·yeh·nah_

Dietary Requirements

I'm…	**Soy…** _soy…_
diabetic	**diabético** _m_ /**diabética** _f dee·ah·beh·tee·koh/ dee·ah·beh·tee·kah_
lactose intolerant	**alérgico** _m_ /**alérgica** _f_ **a la lactosa** _ah·lehr·khee·koh/ah·lehr·khee·kah ah lah lahk·toh·sah_
vegetarian	**vegetariano** _m_ /**vegetariana** _f_ _beh·kheh·tah·reeyah·noh/beh·kheh·tah·reeyah·nah_
I'm allergic to…	**Soy alérgico** _m_ /**alérgica** _f_ **a…** _soy ah·lehr·khee·koh/ah·lehr·khee·kah ah…_

I can't eat...	**No puedo comer...**	noh _pweh_•doh koh•_mehr_...
dairy products	**productos lácteos**	proh•_dook_•tohs _lahk_•teh•ohs
gluten	**gluten**	_gloo_•tehn
nuts	**frutos secos**	_froo_•tohs _seh_•kohs
pork	**carne de cerdo**	_kahr_•neh deh _thehr_•doh
shellfish	**marisco**	mah•_rees_•koh
spicy foods	**comidas picantes**	koh•_mee_•dahs pee•_kahn_•tehs
wheat	**trigo**	_tree_•goh
Is it halal/kosher?	**¿Es halal/kosher?**	ehs ah•_lahl_/koh•_sehr_
Do you have...?	**¿Tiene...?**	_teeyeh_•neh
skimmed milk	**leche desnatada**	leh•cheh dehs•nah•tah•dah
whole milk	**leche entera**	_leh_•cheh ehn•_teh_•rah
soya milk	**leche de soja**	_leh_•cheh deh _soh_•khah

Dining with Children

Do you have children's portions?	**¿Sirven raciones para niños?**	_seer_•behn rah•_theeyoh_•nehs pah•rah nee•nyohs
Can I have a highchair/child's seat?	**Una trona/silla para niños, por favor.**	_oo_•nah _troh_•nah/_see_•yah _pah_•rah _nee_•nyohs pohr fah•_bohr_
Where can I feed/ change the baby?	**¿Dónde puedo darle de comer/cambiar al niño?**	_dohn_•deh _pweh_•doh _dahr_•leh deh koh•_mehr_/ kahm•_beeyahr_ ahl _nee_•nyoh
Can you warm this?	**¿Puede calentar esto?**	_pweh_•deh kah•lehn•_tahr_ _ehs_•toh

For Traveling with Children, see page 144.

How to Complain

When will our food be ready?	**¿Cuánto más tardará la comida?**	_kwahn_•toh mahs tahr•dah•_rah_ lah koh•_mee_•dah
We can't wait any longer.	**No podemos esperar más.**	noh poh•_deh_•mohs ehs•peh•_rahr_ mahs
We're leaving.	**Nos vamos.**	nohs _bah_•mohs

I didn't order this.	**Esto no es lo que pedí.** *ehs·toh noh ehs loh keh peh·dee*
I ordered...	**Pedí...** *peh·dee...*
I can't eat this.	**No puedo comerme esto.** *noh pweh·doh koh·mehr·meh ehs·toh*
This is too...	**Esto está demasiado...** *ehs·toh ehs·tah deh·mah·seeyah·doh...*
cold/hot	**frío/caliente** *free·oh/kah·leeyehn·teh*
salty/spicy	**salado/picante** *sah·lah·doh/pee·kahn·teh*
tough/bland	**duro/soso** *doo·roh/soh·soh*
This isn't clean/fresh.	**Esto no está limpio/fresco.** *ehs·toh noh ehs·tah leem·peeyoh/frehs·koh*

Paying

The check [bill], please.	**La cuenta, por favor.** *lah kwehn·tah pohr fah·bohr*
Separate checks [bills], please.	**Cuentas separadas, por favor.** *kwehn·tahs seh·pah·rah·dahs pohr fah·bohr*
It's all together.	**Póngalo todo junto.** *pohn·gah·loh toh·doh khoon·toh*
Is service included?	**¿Está incluido el servicio?** *ehs·tah een·kloo·ee·doh ehl sehr·bee·theeyoh*
What's this amount for?	**¿De qué es esta cantidad?** *deh keh ehs ehs·tah kahn·tee·dahth*
I didn't have that.	**Yo no tomé eso. Tomé...** *yoh noh toh·meh eh·soh toh·meh...*
I had...	
Can I pay by credit card?	**¿Puedo pagar con tarjeta de crédito?** *pweh·doh pah·gahr kohn tahr·kheh·tah deh kreh·dee·toh*
Can I have a receipt/ an itemized bill?	**¿Podría darme un recibo/una cuenta detallada?** *poh·dree·ah dahr·meh oon reh·thee·boh/ oo·nah kwehn·tah deh·tah·yah·dah*
That was delicious!	**¡Estuvo delicioso!** *ehs·too·boh deh·lee·theeyoh·soh*
I've already paid.	**Ya he pagado** *yah eh pah·gah·doh*

Restaurants are generally required to include service charges as part of the bill, so tipping isn't customary. If you wish to leave a tip for good service, just round up the bill to the nearest euro or two.

Meals & Cooking

Breakfast

el agua *ehl ah·gwah*	water
el café/el té... *ehl kah·feh/ehl teh...*	coffee/tea...
con azúcar *kohn ah·thoo·kahr*	with sugar
con edulcorante artificial *kohn eh·dool·koh·rahn·teh ahr·tee·fee·theeyahl*	with artificial sweetener
con leche *kohn leh·cheh*	with milk
descafeinado *dehs·kah·feyee·nah·doh*	decaf
solo *soh·loh*	black
los cereales (calientes/fríos) *lohs theh·reh·ah·lehs (kah·leeyehn·tehs/free·ohs)*	(cold/hot) cereal
los fiambres *lohs fee·ahm·brehs*	cold cuts [charcuterie]

El desayuno (breakfast) is usually served from 8:00 a.m. to 10:00 a.m. **La comida** (lunch), generally the largest meal of the day, is served from 2:00-4:00 p.m. **La cena** (dinner) is typically smaller and lighter than in the U.S. or U.K., and is usually served after 9:00 p.m. For a snack between meals, you can get **tapas** in smaller restaurants and some bars.

la harina de avena *lah ah·ree·nah deh ah·beh·nah* — oatmeal

el huevo... *ehl weh·boh...* — egg...

  duro/pasado por agua *doo·roh/ pah·sah·doh pohr ah·gwah* — hard-/soft-boiled

  frito *free·toh* — fried

  revuelto *reh·bwehl·toh* — scrambled

los huevos a la flamenca *lohs weh·bohs ah lah flah·mehn·kah* — baked eggs with tomato, onion and ham

la leche *lah leh·cheh* — milk

la magdalena *lah mahg·dah·leh·nah* — muffin

la mantequilla *lah mahn·teh·kee·yah* — butter

la mermelada/la jalea *lah mehr·meh·luh·dah/khah·leh·ah* — jam/jelly

el muesli *ehl mwehs·lee* — granola [muesli]

el pan *ehl pahn* — bread

el panecillo *ehl pah·neh·thee·yoh* — roll

el queso *ehl keh·soh* — cheese

la salchicha *lah sahl·chee·chah* — sausage

el tocino *ehl toh·thee·noh* — bacon

la tortilla... *lah tohr·tee·yah...* — omelet

  de patatas *deh pah·tah·tahs* — with potato (and sometimes onion)

  de jamón *deh khah·mohn* — with ham

  paisana *payee·sah·nah* — with potatoes, peas and shrimp or ham

  de queso *deh keh·soh* — with cheese

  de setas *deh seh·tahs* — with mushrooms

la tostada *lah tohs·tah·dah* — toast

el yogur *ehl yoh·goor* — yogurt

el zumo de... *ehl thoo•moh deh...* ...juice
    manzana *mahn•thah•nah* apple
    pomelo *poh•meh•loh* grapefruit
    naranja *nah•rahn•khah* orange

Appetizers

las aceitunas (rellenas) *lahs* (stuffed) olives
ah•theyee•too•nahs (reh•yeh•nahs)
las albóndigas *lahs ahl•bohn•dee•gahs* meatballs
el bacalao *ehl bah•kah•laoh* dried salt cod
los boquerones en vinagre anchovies marinated
lohs boh•keh•roh•nehs ehn bee•nah•greh in garlic and olive oil
los callos *lohs kah•yohs* tripe in hot paprika sauce
los caracoles *lohs kah•rah•koh•lehs* snails
los champiñones al ajillo mushrooms fried in
lohs chahm•pee•nyoh•nehs ahl ah•khee•yoh olive oil with garlic
las croquetas *lahs kroh•keh•tahs* croquettes with various
    fillings
las gambas al ajillo *lahs gahm•bahs ahl* broiled shrimp in
ah•khee•yoh garlic
el pan con tomate *ehl pahn kohn* toasted bread with garlic,
toh•mah•teh tomato and olive oil
los pescados fritos *lohs pehs•kah•dohs* fried fish
free•tohs

Tapas are snacks, similar to appetizers, served in cafés and bars.
Many bars have their own specialties. When ordering, **una tapa**
is a mouthful, **una ración** is half a plateful and **una porción** is a
generous amount.

los pimientos lohs pee·*meeyehn*·tohs	peppers
los pinchos lohs *peen*·chohs	grilled, skewered meat
los quesos lohs *keh*·sohs	cheese platter
la tortilla española lah tohr·*tee*·yah ehs·pah·*nyoh*·lah	potato omelet

Soup

el caldo gallego ehl *kahl*·doh gah·*yeh*·goh	stew of cabbage, potatoes, beans and meat, from Galicia region
el cocido ehl koh·*thee*·doh	chickpea stew with potatoes, cabbage, turnips, beef, bacon, chorizo and black pudding
el consomé al jerez ehl kohn·soh·*meh* ahl kheh·*rehth*	chicken broth with sherry
la fabada asturiana lah fah·*bah*·dah ahs·too·*reeyah*·nah	white bean stew
el gazpacho ehl gahth·*pah*·choh	cold tomato soup
el marmitako ehl mahr·mee·*tah*·koh	tuna fish and potato stew, from the Basque region
la sopa… lah *soh*·pah…	…soup
castellana kahs·teh·*yah*·nah	with garlic, chunks of ham and a poached egg
de ajo blanco deh *ah*·khoh *blahn*·koh	with garlic and almond, served cold, popular in Andalucia
de habas deh *ah*·bahs	bean
de mariscos deh mah·*rees*·kohs	seafood
de pollo deh *poh*·yoh	chicken
de tomate deh toh·*mah*·teh	tomato
de verduras deh behr·*doo*·rahs	vegetable

Fish & Seafood

la almeja *lah ahl·meh·khah* — clam

el arenque *ehl ah·rehn·keh* — herring

el atún *ehl ah·toon* — tuna

el bacalao a la vizcaína *ehl bah·kah·laoh ah lah beeth·kayee·nah* — cod with dried peppers and onions

el bacalao *ehl bah·kah·laoh* — cod

el besugo *ehl beh·soo·goh* — sea bream

el boquerón *ehl boh·keh·rohn* — fresh baby anchovy

la caballa *lah kah·bah·yah* — mackerel

el calamar *ehl kah·lah·mahr* — squid

los calamares a la romana *lohs kah·lah·mahr·ehs ah lah roh·mah·nah* — deep-fried battered squid

el cangrejo *ehl kahn·greh·khoh* — crab

el chipirón *ehl chee·pee·rohn* — small whole squid

las cigalas *lahs thee·gah·lahs* — crayfish

las cigalas cocidas *lahs thee·gah·lahs koh·thee·dahs* — boiled crayfish

el fletán *ehl fleh·tahn* — halibut

la gamba *lah gahm·bah* — shrimp

las gambas en cerveza *lahs gahm·bahs ehn thehr·beh·thah* — shrimp in beer

la langosta *lah lahn·gohs·tah* — lobster

el lenguado *ehl lehn·gwah·doh* — sole

la lubina *lah loo·bee·nah* — sea bass

la mariscada *lah mah·rees·kah·dah* — cold mixed shellfish

los mejillones *lohs meh·khee·yoh·nehs* — mussels

los mejillones en escabeche *lohs meh·khee·yohn·ehs ehn ehs·kah·beh·cheh* — mussels in a marinade

la merluza *lah mehr·loo·thah* — hake

la merluza a la sidra *lah mehr·loo·thah ah lah see·drah*	hake in cider
el mero *ehl meh·roh*	grouper
la ostra *lah ohs·trah*	oyster
el pez espada *ehl pehth ehs·pah·dah*	swordfish
el pulpo *ehl pool·poh*	octopus
el pulpo a la gallega *ehl pool·poh ah lah gah·yeh·gah*	octopus with olive oil and paprika
el salmón *ehl sahl·mohn*	salmon
el tiburón *ehl tee·boo·rohn*	shark
la trucha *lah troo·chah*	trout
la trucha a la navarra *lah troo·chah ah lah nah·bah·rrah*	grilled trout stuffed with ham
la zarzuela de pescado *lah thahr·thweh·lah deh pehs·kah·doh*	mixed fish and seafood cooked in broth, served over bread

Meat & Poultry

la asadurilla de cordero *lah ah·sah·doo·rree·yah deh kohr·deh·roh*	lamb's liver
la butifarra *lah boo·tee·fah·rrah*	spiced pork sausage, popular in Cataluña and Valencia
los callos a la madrileña *lohs kah·yohs ah lah mah·dree·leh·nyah*	tripe stew, a Madrid specialty
la carne *lah kahr·neh*	meat
la carne de cerdo *lah kahr·neh deh thehr·doh*	pork
la carne picada *lah kahr·neh pee·kah·dah*	ground beef
la carne de vaca *lah kahr·neh deh bah·kah*	beef
el chorizo *ehl choh·ree·thoh*	highly-seasoned pork sausage
la chuleta *lah choo·leh·tah*	chop

el cochifrito navarro *ehl koh•chee•free•toh nah•bah•rroh* — deep-fried lamb pieces

el conejo *ehl koh•neh•khoh* — rabbit

el cordero *ehl kohr•deh•roh* — lamb

la cordorniz *lah kohr•dohr•neeth* — quail

las costillas de cerdo *lahs kohs•tee•yahs deh thehr•doh* — pork ribs

las empanadas *lahs ehm•pah•nah•dahs* — pastry filled with meat, chicken or tuna, a specialty of Galicia

los espárragos montañeses *lohs ehs•pah•rrah•gohs mohn•tah•nyeh•sehs* — calves's tails

la falda de buey *lah fahl•dah deh bwehy* — beef flank steak

el filete *ehl fee•leh•teh* — steak

las gallinejas *lahs gah•yee•neh•khahs* — fried lamb intestine

el guisado de riñones *ehl gee•sah•doh deh ree•nyoh•nehs* — kidney stew

el hígado *ehl ee•gah•doh* — liver

el jamón *ehl khah•mohn* — ham

el jamón ibérico *ehl khah•mohn ee•beh•ree•koh* — aged Iberian ham

el jamón serrano *ehl khah•mohn seh•rrah•noh* — dry-cured serrano ham

el lacón con grelos *ehl lah•kohn kohn greh•lohs* — salted ham with turnip greens, typical of Galicia

las magras con tomate *lahs mah•grahs kohn toh•mah•teh* — lightly fried ham dipped in tomato sauce

las manos de cerdo *lahs mah•nohs deh thehr•doh* — pig's feet [trotters]

las mollejas de ternera *lahs moh•yeh•khahs deh tehr•neh•rah* — veal sweetbread

la morcilla *lah mohr•thee•yah*	blood sausage
la paella... *lah pah•eh•yah...*	paella...
de carne *deh kahr•neh*	with chicken and sausage (may be made with beef)
de marisco *deh mah•rees•koh*	with seafood
de verduras *deh behr•doo•rahs*	with vegetables
valenciana *bah•lehn•theeyah•nah*	with chicken, shrimp, mussels, squid, peas, tomato, garlic, olive oil, paprika; from the Valencia region
zamorana *thah•moh•rah•nah*	with ham, pork loin, pig's feet; popular in the Zamora region
las patatas con chorizo *lahs pah•tah•tahs kohn choh•ree•thoh*	potatoes with chorizo sausage
el pato *ehl pah•toh*	duck
el pavo *ehl pah•boh*	turkey
el pollo *ehl poh•yoh*	chicken
el pollo frito *ehl poh•yoh free•toh*	fried chicken
el riñón *ehl ree•nyohn*	kidney
la salchicha *lah sahl•chee•chah*	sausage
el salchichón *ehl sahl•chee•chohn*	salami-type sausage
el solomillo *ehl soh•loh•mee•yoh*	filet mignon
la ternera *lah tehr•neh•rah*	veal
el tocino *ehl toh•thee•noh*	bacon
la trucha a la navarra *lah troo•chah ah lah nah•bah•rrah*	trout fried with a piece of ham
el venado *ehl beh•nah•doh*	venison

Paella is a specialty dish of Spain. Traditional paella, which originated in Valencia, includes rice, saffron, vegetables, rabbit and chicken. Paella de marisco (seafood paella) is a very popular version of this dish, especially along the coast. Other delicious versions are noted above.

Vegetables & Staples

la aceituna *lah ah•theyee•too•nah*	olive
la acelga *lah ah•thehl•gah*	chard
el aguacate *ehl ah•gwah•khah•teh*	avocado
el ajo *ehl ah•khoh*	garlic
la albahaca *lah ahl•bah•ah•kah*	basil
la alcachofa (salteada) *lah ahl•kah•choh•fah (sahl•teh•ah•dah)*	(sauteed) artichoke
la alcaparra *lah ahl•kah•pah•rrah*	caper
el anís *ehl ah•nees*	aniseed
el apio *ehl ah•peeyoh*	celery
el arroz… *ehl ah•rrohth…*	rice…
con habas y nabos *kohn ah•bahs ee nah•bohs*	with beans and turnips
a la cubana *ah lah koo•bah•nah*	with fried eggs and banana fritters
empedrado *ehm•peh•drah•doh*	with tomatoes and cod and a top layer of white beans
santanderino *sahn• tahn•deh•ree•noh*	with salmon and milk
el azafrán *ehl ah•thah•frahn*	saffron
los bajoques farcides *lohs bah•khoh•kehs fahr•thee•dehs*	red peppers stuffed with rice, pork and tomatoes; from Catalonia

la batata *lah bah-tah-tah*	yam
la berenjena *lah beh-rehn-kheh-nah*	eggplant [aubergine]
el brécol *ehl breh-kohl*	broccoli
los brotes de soja *lohs broh-tehs deh soh-khah*	bean sprouts
el calabacín *ehl kah-lah-bah-theen*	zucchini [courgette]
la cassolada *lah kahs-soh-lah-dah*	rice casserole with thrushes (a type of bird) and ribs, from Catalonia
la cebolla *lah theh-boh-yah*	onion
el champiñon (a la plancha/salteado) *ehl chahm-pee-nyohn (ah lah plahn-chah/sahl-teh-ah-doh)*	(grilled/sautéed) mushroom
la coliflor *lah koh-lee-flohr*	cauliflower
el espárrago *ehl ehs-pah-rrah-goh*	asparagus
la espinaca *lah ehs-pee-nah-kah*	spinach
la faba *lah fah-bah*	white bean
el guisante *ehl gee-sahn-teh*	pea
las habas a la catalana *lahs ah-bahs a lah kah-tah-lah-nah*	broad bean
la harina *lah ah-ree-nah*	flour
la judía *lah khoo-dee-ah*	bean
la judía verde *lah khoo-dee-ah behr-deh*	green bean
la lechuga *lah leh-choo-gah*	lettuce
la lenteja *lah lehn-teh-khah*	lentil
el maíz *ehl mah-eeth*	corn
la menestra *lah meh-nehs-trah*	vegetable stew
las migas de pastor *lahs mee-gahs deh pahs-tohr*	bread soaked in water then fried with pieces of bacon and dried peppers
el pan *ehl pahn*	bread

la pasta *lah pahs·tah*	pasta
la patata *lah pah·tah·tah*	potato
el pepino *ehl peh·pee·noh*	cucumber
el perejil *ehl peh·reh·kheel*	parsley
el pimiento relleno *ehl pee·meeyehn·toh reh·yeh·noh*	stuffed pepper
el pimiento rojo/verde *ehl pee·meeyehn·toh roh·khoh/behr·deh*	red/green pepper
el repollo *ehl reh·poh·yoh*	cabbage
la seta *lah seh·tah*	mushroom
el tomate *ehl toh·mah·teh*	tomato
la verdura *lah behr·doo·rah*	vegetable
la zanahoria *lah thah·nah·oh·reeyah*	carrot

Fruit

el albaricoque *ehl ahl·bah·ree·koh·keh*	apricot
el arándano *ehl ah·rahn·dah·noh*	blueberry
el arándano rojo *ehl ah·rahn·dah·noh roh·khoh*	cranberry
la cereza *lah theh·reh·thah*	cherry
la ciruela *lah thee·rweh·lah*	plum
el coco *ehl koh·koh*	coconut
la frambuesa *lah frahm·bweh·sah*	raspberry
la fresa *lah freh·sah*	strawberry
la fruta *lah froo·tah*	fruit
la guayaba *lah gwah·yah·bah*	guava
el kiwi *ehl kee·wee*	kiwi
la lima *lah lee·mah*	lime
el limón *ehl lee·mohn*	lemon
la mandarina *lah mahn·dah·ree·nah*	tangerine
el mango *ehl mahn·goh*	mango
la manzana *lah mahn·thah·nah*	apple

el melocotón *ehl meh•loh•koh•tohn*	peach
el melón *ehl meh•lohn*	melon
la naranja *lah nah•rahn•khah*	orange
la papaya *lah pah•pah•yah*	papaya
la pera *lah peh•rah*	pear
la piña *lah pee•nyah*	pineapple
el plátano *ehl plah•tah•noh*	banana
el pomelo *ehl poh•meh•loh*	grapefruit
la sandía *lah sahn•dee•ah*	watermelon
la uva *lah oo•bah*	grape

Cheese

el queso... *ehl keh•soh...*	...cheese
blando *blahn•doh*	soft, mild-flavored
de Burgos *deh boor•gohs*	soft, creamy regional variety
Cabrales *kah•brah•lehs*	tangy, blue-veined regional variety
cremoso *kreh•moh•soh*	cream
curado *koo•rah•doh*	ripe
de leche de cabra *deh leh•cheh deh kah•brah*	from goat's milk
duro *doo•roh*	hard
fuerte *fwehr•teh*	strong
Manchego *mahn•cheh•goh*	hard cheese from Manchego sheep's milk
Perilla *peh•ree•yah*	firm, bland regional variety
rallado *rah•yah•doh*	grated
requesón *reh•keh•sohn*	cottage
Roncal *rohn•kahl*	sharp goat cheese, salted and smoked, regional variety
suave *swah•beh*	mild
tipo roquefort *tee•poh roh•qeh•fohrt*	blue

Dessert

el arroz con leche *ehl ah‐<u>rroth</u> kohn <u>leh</u>‐cheh*	rice pudding
el brazo de gitano *ehl <u>brah</u>‐thoh deh khee‐<u>tah</u>‐noh*	sponge cake roll with cream filling
el buñuelo *ehl boo‐<u>nyweh</u>‐loh*	thin, deep-fried fritter, covered in sugar
el canutillo *ehl kah‐noo‐<u>tee</u>‐yoh*	custard pastry horn with cinnamon
el churro *ehl <u>choo</u>‐rroh*	deep-fried fritter sprinkled with sugar
la filloa *lah fee‐<u>yoh</u>‐ah*	crepe (used in sweet or savory dishes), typical of Galicia region
el flan *ehl flahn*	caramel custard
la galleta *lah gah‐<u>yeh</u>‐tah*	cookie [biscuit]
el helado *ehl eh‐<u>lah</u>‐doh*	ice cream
la leche frita *lah <u>leh</u>‐cheh <u>free</u>‐tah*	fried milk custard
la mantecada *lah mahn‐teh‐<u>kah</u>‐dah*	small sponge cake
la manzana asada *lah mahn‐<u>thah</u>‐nah ah‐<u>sah</u>‐dah*	baked apple
el pastel de queso *ehl pahs‐<u>tehl</u> deh <u>keh</u>‐soh*	cheesecake
el sorbete *ehl sohr‐<u>beh</u>‐teh*	sorbet
la tarta de Santiago *lah <u>tahr</u>‐tah deh sahn‐<u>teeyah</u>‐goh*	dense almond cake topped with powdered sugar
el tocino de cielo *ehl toh‐<u>thee</u>‐noh deh <u>theeyeh</u>‐loh*	egg yolk custard

Sauces & Condiments

salt	**la sal** *lah sahl*
black pepper	**la pimienta negra** *lah pee‐<u>meeyehn</u>‐tah <u>neh</u>‐grah*
mustard	**mostaza** *mohs‐tah‐thah*

| ketchup | **ketchup** *keht•choop* |
| sugar | **el azúcar** *ehl ah•thoo•kahr* |

At the Market

Where are the carts [trolleys]/baskets?	**¿Dónde están los carritos/las cestas?** *dohn•deh ehs•tahn lohs kah•rree•tohs/luhs thehs•tahs*
Where is …?	**¿Donde está…?** *dohn•deh ehs•tah…*
I'd like some of that/this.	**Quiero un poco de eso/esto.** *keeyeh•roh oon poh•koh deh eh•soh/ehs•toh*
Can I taste it?	**¿Puedo probarlo?** *pweh•doh proh•bahr•loh*
I'd like…	**Quiero…** *keeyeh•roh…*
a kilo/half-kilo of…	**un kilo/medio kilo de…** *oon kee•loh/meh•deeyoh kee•loh deh…*
a liter of…	**un litro de…** *oon lee•troh deh…*
a piece of…	**un trozo de…** *oon troh•thoh deh…*
a slice of…	**una rodaja de…** *oo•nah roh•dah•khah deh…*
More/Less.	**Más/Menos.** *mahs/meh•nohs*
How much?	**¿Cuánto es?** *kwahn•toh ehs*
Where do I pay?	**¿Dónde se paga?** *dohn•deh seh pah•gah*
A bag, please.	**Una bolsa, por favor.** *oo•nah bohl•sah pohr fah•bohr*
I'm being helped.	**Ya me atienden.** *yah meh ah•teeyehn•dehn*

YOU MAY HEAR...

¿Necesita ayuda?   Can I help you?
neh·theh·<u>see</u>·tah ah·<u>yoo</u>·dah

¿Qué desea? *keh deh·<u>seh</u>·ah*   What would you like?

¿Algo más? *<u>ahl</u>·goh mahs*   Anything else?

Son...euros. *sohn...<u>ew</u>·rohs*   That's...euros.

In Spain, food is often purchased at local family-run markets.
These are excellent places for regional and specialty foods, fresh
fruit and vegetables, meat and baked goods. **Hipermercados** (large
grocery store chains) are also common, but these are usually found
on the outskirts of town or in the suburbs. These stores have a larger
selection than regular supermarkets, and are often less expensive.
Alcampo, **Carrefour** and **Hipercor** are common chains. **El Corte
Inglés** is a popular department store chain that has a supermarket on
the ground floor in some locations, but it tends to have higher prices
than regular supermarkets.

In the Kitchen

bottle opener	**el abrebotellas** *ehl ah·breh·boh·teh·yahs*
bowl	**el cuenco** *ehl <u>kwehn</u>·koh*
can opener	**el abrelatas** *ehl ah·breh·<u>lah</u>·tahs*
corkscrew	**el sacacorchos** *ehl sah·kah·<u>kohr</u>·chohs*
cup	**la taza** *lah <u>tah</u>·thah*
fork	**el tenedor** *ehl teh·neh·<u>dohr</u>*
frying pan	**la sartén** *lah sahr·<u>tehn</u>*

ESSENTIAL

Can I see the wine list/ drink menu, please?	**La carta de vinos/bebidas, por favor.** *lah kahr·tah deh bee·nohs/beh·bee·dahs pohr fah·bohr*
What do you recommend?	**¿Qué me recomienda?** *keh meh reh·koh·meeyehn·dah*
I'd like a bottle/glass of red/white wine.	**Quiero una botella/un vaso de vino tinto/blanco.** *keeyeh·roh oo·nah boh·teh·yah/ oon bah·soh deh bee·noh teen·toh/blahn·koh*
The house wine, please.	**El vino de la casa, por favor.** *ehl bee·noh deh lah kah·sah pohr fah·bohr*
Another bottle/glass, please.	**Otra botella/Otro vaso, por favor.** *oh·trah boh·teh·yah/oh·troh bah·soh pohr fah·bohr*
I'd like a local beer.	**Quiero una cerveza española.** *keeyeh·roh oo·nah thehr·beh·thah ehs·pah·nyoh·lah*
Can I buy you a drink?	**¿Puedo invitarle m/invitarla f a una copa?** *pweh·doh een·bee·tahr·leh/ een·bee·tahr·lah ah oo·nah koh·pah*
Cheers!	**¡Salud!** *sah·looth*
A coffee/tea, please.	**Un café/té, por favor.** *oon kah·feh/teh pohr fah·bohr*
Black.	**Solo.** *soh·loh*
With…	**Con…** *kohn…*
milk	**leche** *leh·cheh*
sugar	**azúcar** *ah·thoo·kahr*
artificial sweetener	**edulcorante artificial** *eh·dool·koh·rahn·teh ahr·tee·fee·theeyahl*
A…, please.	**Un…, por favor.** *oon…pohr fah·bohr*
juice	**zumo** *thoo·moh*
soda	**refresco** *reh·frehs·koh*

Measurements in Europe are metric - and that applies to the weight of food too. If you tend to think in pounds and ounces, it's worth brushing up on what the metric equivalent is before you go shopping for fruit and veg in markets and supermarkets. Five hundred grams, or half a kilo, is a common quantity to order, and that converts to just over a pound (17.65 ounces, to be precise).

glass	**el vaso** *ehl bah·soh*
(steak) knife	**el cuchillo (de carne)** *ehl koo·chee·yoh (deh kahr·neh)*
measuring cup/spoon	**la taza/la cuchara medidora** *lah tah·thah/ lah koo·chah·rah meh·dee·doh·rah*
napkin	**la servilleta** *lah sehr·bee·yeh·tah*
plate	**el plato** *ehl plah·toh*
pot	**la olla** *lah oh·yah*
saucepan	**el cazo** *ehl kah·thoh*
spatula	**la espátula** *lah ehs·pah·too·lah*
spoon	**la cuchara** *lah koo·chah·rah*

YOU MAY SEE...

CONSUMIR PREFERENTEMENTE ANTES DE...	best if used by...
CALORÍAS	calories
SIN GRASA	fat free
CONSERVAR EN FRIGORÍFICO	keep refrigerated
PUEDE CONTENER TRAZAS DE...	may contain traces of...
FECHA LÍMITE DE VENTA...	sell by...
APTO PARA VEGETARIANOS	suitable for vegetarians

water	**agua** _ah_·gwah
sparkling/still	**con/sin gas** kohn/seen gahs
Is the tap water	**¿Se puede beber el agua del grifo?**
safe to drink?	_seh <u>pweh</u>·deh beh·<u>behr</u> ehl <u>ah</u>·gwah dehl <u>gree</u>·foh_

Non-alcoholic Drinks

el agua (con/sin gas) _ehl <u>ah</u>·gwah_ _(kohn/seen gahs)_	(sparkling/still) water
el café _ehl kah·<u>feh</u>_	coffee
el chocolate caliente _ehl choh·koh·<u>lah</u>·teh kah·<u>leeyehn</u>·teh_	hot chocolate
el granizado _ehl grah·nee·<u>thah</u>·doh_	iced drink
la horchata _lah ohr·<u>chah</u>·tah_	sweet drink made from tiger nuts and sugar
la leche _lah <u>leh</u>·cheh_	milk
la limonada _lah lee·moh·<u>nah</u>·dah_	lemonade
el refresco _ehl reh·<u>frehs</u>·koh_	soda
el té (con hielo) _ehl teh (kohn <u>eeyeh</u>·loh)_	(iced) tea
el zumo _ehl <u>thoo</u>·moh_	juice

Aperitifs, Cocktails & Liqueurs

el coñac _ehl koh·<u>nyahk</u>_	brandy
la ginebra _lah khee·<u>neh</u>·brah_	gin
el jerez fino _ehl kheh·<u>rehth</u> <u>fee</u>·noh_	pale, dry sherry
el jerez oloroso _ehl kheh·<u>rehth</u> oh·loh·<u>roh</u>·soh_	dark, heavy sherry
el licor _ehl lee·<u>kohr</u>_	liqueur
el oporto _ehl oh·<u>pohr</u>·toh_	port
el ron _ehl rohn_	rum
la sangría _lah sahn·<u>gree</u>·ah_	wine punch
el tequila _ehl teh·<u>kee</u>·lah_	tequila

YOU MAY HEAR...

¿Qué desea beber? keh deh·_seh_·ah beh·_behr_ — Can I get you a drink?

¿Con leche o azúcar? — With milk or sugar?
kohn _leh_·cheh oh ah·_thoo_·kahr

¿Agua con gas o sin gas? — Sparkling or still
_ah_·gwah kohn gahs oh seen gahs — water?

el vodka ehl _bohd_·kah — vodka
el whisky ehl _wees_·kee — whisky
el whisky escocés ehl _wees_·kee ehs·koh·_thehs_ — scotch

Beer

la cerveza... lah thehr·_beh_·thah... — ...beer
  en botella/de barril ehn boh·_teh_·yah/ — bottled/draft
  deh bah·_rreel_
  española/extranjera ehs·pah·_nyoh_·lah/ — local/imported
  ehx·trahn·_kheh_·rah
  negra/ligera _neh_·grah/lee·_kheh_·rah — dark/light
  rubia/pilsner _roo_·beeyah/peels·_nehr_ — lager/pilsner
  sin alcohol seen ahl·koh·_ohl_ — non-alcoholic

Many Spaniards love coffee and drink it throughout the day.
Bottled water is available, though tap water is used in the home
and is generally safe to drink. Restaurants will almost always serve
bottled water with meals, unless you specifically request **agua del
grifo** (tap water). Juice is usually served with breakfast, but it's not
common at lunch or dinner.

There are many popular brands of beer in Spain, including **San Miguel®**, **Cruzcampo®**, **Alhambra®**, **Mahou®**, **Estrella Damm®** and **Zaragozana®**. Each brand usually has several classes and types of beer available, though most will be a lager-type beer. The classes of beer include **clásica**, a light, pale, pilsner-type lager; **especial**, a heavier pilsner-type lager; **negra**, a dark, malty lager; and **extra**, a heavy, high-alcohol lager.

Wine

el cava *ehl kah·bah*	sparkling wine
el champán *ehl chahm·pahn*	champagne
el vino... *ehl bee·noh...*	...wine
de la casa/de mesa *deh lah kah·sah/ deh meh·sah*	house/table
espumoso *ehs·poo·moh·soh*	sparkling
tinto/blanco *teen·toh/blahn·koh*	red/white
seco/dulce *seh·koh/dool·theh*	dry/sweet

With 40 recognized wine regions, Spain has the largest land area under vine in the world and is the third largest producer and exporter of wine. The most well-known types of wine include red wine from Rioja and Ribera del Duero, sherries from Jerez, white wine from Rueda and red wine and white wine from Penedés. Another popular wine, especially in the summer time, is the sparkling white known as **cava**. Spanish wineries are known as **bodegas**; the winemaker is known as a **bodeguero**.

On the Menu

el aceite *ehl ah·theyee·teh*		oil
el aceite de oliva *ehl ah·theyee·teh deh oh·lee·bah*		olive oil
la aceituna *lah ah·theyee·too·nah*		olive
la acelga *lah ah·thehl·gah*		chard
la achicoria *lah ah·chee·koh·reeyah*		chicory
el agua *ehl ah·gwah*		water
el aguacate *ehl ah·gwah·kah·teh*		avocado
el ajo *ehl ah·khoh*		garlic
el ajo chalote *ehl ah·khoh chah·loh·teh*		shallot
la albahaca *lah ahl·bah·ah·kah*		basil
el albaricoque *ehl ahl·bah·ree·koh·keh*		apricot
la albóndiga *lah ahl·bohn·dee·gah*		meatball
la alcachofa *lah ahl·kah·choh·fah*		artichoke
la alcaparra *lah ahl·kah·pah·rrah*		caper
la alcaravea *lah ahl·kah·rah·beh·ah*		caraway
la almeja *lah ahl·meh·khah*		clam
la almendra *lah ahl·mehn·drah*		almond
el almíbar *ehl ahl·mee·bahr*		syrup
el anacardo *ehl ah·nah·kahr·doh*		cashew
las ancas de rana *lahs ahn·kahs deh rah·nah*		frog's legs
la anchoa *lah ahn·choh·ah*		anchovy
la anguila *lah ahn·gee·lah*		eel
la angula *lah ahn·goo·lah*		baby eel
el anís *ehl ah·nees*		aniseed
el aperitivo *ehl ah·peh·ree·tee·boh*		aperitif
el apio *ehl ah·peeyoh*		celery
el arándano *ehl ah·rahn·dah·noh*		blueberry
el arándano rojo *ehl ah·rahn·dah·noh roh·khoh*		cranberry

el arenque *ehl ah•rehn•keh*	herring
el arroz *ehl ah•rrohth*	rice
el arroz integral *ehl ah•rrohth een•teh•grahl*	whole grain rice
el arroz salvaje *ehl ah•rrohth sahl•bah•kheh*	wild rice
el asado *ehl ah•sah•doh*	roast
las asaduras *lahs ah•sah•doo•rahs*	organ meat [offal]
el atún *ehl ah•toon*	tuna
la avellana *lah ah•beh•yah•nah*	hazelnut
la avena *lah ah•beh•nah*	oat
las aves *lahs ah•behs*	poultry
el azafrán *ehl ah•thah•frahn*	saffron
el azúcar *ehl ah•thoo•kahr*	sugar
el bacalao *bah•kah•lao*	cod
los barquillos *lohs bahr•kee•yohs*	wafers/ice cream cones
la batata *lah bah•tah•tah*	sweet potato
el batido *ehl bah•tee•doh*	milk shake
la bebida *lah beh•bee•dah*	drink
la berenjena *lah beh•rehn•kheh•nah*	eggplant [aubergine]
la berraza *lah beh•rrah•thah*	parsnip
el berro *ehl beh•rroh*	watercress
la berza *lah behr•thah*	kale
el besugo *ehl beh•soo•goh*	sea bream
blando *blahn•doh*	soft
el bollo *ehl boh•yoh*	pastry
el brandy *ehl brahn•dee*	brandy
el brécol *ehl breh•kohl*	broccoli
los brotes de soja *lohs broh•tehs deh soh•khah*	bean sprouts
el buey *ehl bwehy*	ox
el buñuelo *ehl boo•nyweh•loh*	fritter
la caballa *lah kah•bah•yah*	mackerel
la cabra *lah kah•brah*	goat

el cabrito *ehl kah·bree·toh*	young goat
el cacahuete *ehl kah·kah·weh·teh*	peanut
el café *ehl kah·feh*	coffee
el café solo *ehl kah·feh soh·loh*	espresso
el calabacín *ehl kah·lah·bah·theen*	zucchini [courgette]
la calabaza *lah kah·lah·bah·thah*	pumpkin
el calamar *ehl kah·lah·mahr*	squid
el caldo *ehl kahl·doh*	broth
los callos *lohs kah·yohs*	tripe
la canela *lah kah·neh·lah*	cinnamon
el cangrejo *ehl kahn·greh·khoh*	crab
el capuchino *ehl kah·poo·chee·noh*	cappuccino
el caracol *ehl kah·rah·kohl*	snail
el caramelo *ehl kah·rah·meh·loh*	candy [sweet]
la carne *lah kahr·neh*	meat
la carne de cangrejo *lah kahr·neh deh kahn·greh·khoh*	crabmeat
la carne de cerdo *lah kahr·neh deh thehr·doh*	pork
la carne picada *lah kahr·neh pee·kah·dah*	ground beef
la carne de vaca *lah kahr·neh deh bah·kah*	beef
el carnero *ehl kahr·neh·roh*	mutton

las carrilladas *lahs kah•rree•yah•dahs*	cow's cheeks
casero *kah•seh•roh*	homemade
la castaña *lah kahs•tah•nyah*	chestnut
el cava *ehl kah•bah*	sparkling wine
la caza *lah kah•thah*	game
la cebolla *lah theh•boh•yah*	onion
la cebolleta *lah theh•boh•yeh•tah*	scallion [spring onion]
los cebollinos *lohs theh•boh•yee•nohs*	chives
la cecina de bovino *lah theh•thee•nah deh boh•bee•noh*	corned beef
el centeno *ehl thehn•teh•noh*	rye
el centollo *ehl thehn•toh•yoh*	spider crab
el cereal *ehl theh•reh•ahl*	cereal
la cereza *lah theh•reh•thah*	cherry
la cerveza *lah thehr•beh•thah*	beer
el champiñón *ehl chahm•pee•nyohn*	mushroom
el champán *ehl chahm•pahn*	champagne
la chirivía *lah chee•ree•bee•ah*	parsnip
el chipirón *ehl chee•pee•rohn*	small whole squid
el chocolate *ehl choh•koh•lah•teh*	chocolate
el chocolate caliente *ehl choh•koh•lah•teh kah•leeyehn•teh*	hot chocolate
el chorizo *ehl choh•ree•thoh*	highly-seasoned pork sausage
la chuleta *lah choo•leh•tah*	chop
el chuletón *ehl choo•leh•tohn*	T-bone steak
el ciervo *ehl theeyehr•boh*	deer
la cigala *lah thee•gah•lah*	crayfish
el cilantro *ehl thee•lahn•troh*	cilantro [coriander]
la ciruela *lah thee•rweh•lah*	plum
la ciruela pasa *lah thee•rweh•lah pah•sah*	prune

el clavo *ehl <u>klah</u>·boh*	clove
el cochinillo *ehl koh·chee·<u>nee</u>·yoh*	suckling pig
el coco *ehl <u>koh</u>·koh*	coconut
la codorniz *lah koh·dohr·<u>neeth</u>*	quail
la col *lah kohl*	cabbage
las coles de Bruselas *lahs <u>koh</u>·lehs deh broo·<u>seh</u>·lahs*	Brussels sprouts
la coliflor *lah koh·lee·<u>flohr</u>*	cauliflower
el comino *ehl koh·<u>mee</u>·noh*	cumin
la compota *lah kohm·<u>poh</u>·tah*	stewed fruit
con alcohol *kohn ahl·koh·<u>ohl</u>*	with alcohol
con nata *kohn <u>nah</u>·tah*	with cream
el condimento *ehl kohn·dee·<u>mehn</u>·toh*	relish
el conejo *ehl koh·<u>neh</u>·khoh*	rabbit
el congrio *ehl <u>kohn</u>·greeyoh*	conger eel
el consomé *ehl kohn·soh·<u>meh</u>*	consommé
el coñac *ehl koh·<u>nyahk</u>*	brandy
el corazón *ehl koh·rah·<u>thohn</u>*	heart
el cordero *ehl kohr·<u>deh</u>·roh*	lamb
la cordorniz *lah kohr·dohr·<u>neeth</u>*	quail
el coriandro *ehl koh·<u>reeyahn</u>·droh*	coriander
la croqueta *lah kroh·<u>keh</u>·tah*	croquette
el cruasán *ehl krwah·<u>sahn</u>*	croissant
crudo *<u>kroo</u>·doh*	raw
los dátiles *lohs <u>dah</u>·tee·lehs*	dates
descafeinado *dehs·kah·feyey·<u>nah</u>·doh*	decaffeinated
el edulcorante artificial *ehl eh·dool·koh·<u>rahn</u>·teh ahr·tee·fee·<u>theeyahl</u>*	artificial sweetener
la empanada *lah ehm·pah·<u>nah</u>·dah*	pastry filled with meat, chicken, tuna or vegetables

el encurtido *ehl ehn·koor·tee·doh*   pickled
la endibia *lah ehn·dee·beeyah*   endive
el eneldo *ehl eh·nehl·doh*   dill
la ensalada *lah ehn·sah·lah·dah*   salad
la escarola *lah ehs·kah·roh·lah*   escarole [chicory]
el espagueti *ehl ehs·pah·geh·tee*   spaghetti
la espaldilla *lah ehs·pahl·dee·yah*   shoulder
el espárrago *ehl ehs·pah·rrah·goh*   asparagus
las especias *lahs ehs·peh·theeyahs*   spices
la espinaca *lah ehs·pee·nah·kah*   spinach
el estragón *ehl ehs·trah·gohn*   tarragon
el falsán *ehl fayee·sahn*   pheasant
la falda de ternera *lah fahl·dah deh*   beef brisket
tehr·neh·rah
los fiambres *lohs feeyahm·brehs*   cold cuts [charcuterie]
el fideo *ehl fee·deh·oh*   noodle
el filete *ehl fee·leh·teh*   steak
el flan *ehl flahn*   caramel custard
el fletán *ehl fleh·tahn*   halibut
la frambuesa *lah frahm·bweh·sah*   raspberry
la fresa *lah freh·sah*   strawberry
la fruta *lah froo·tah*   fruit
los frutos secos *lohs froo·tohs seh·kohs*   nuts
la galleta *lah gah·yeh·tah*   cookie [biscuit]
la galleta salada *lah gah·yeh·tah sah·lah·dah*   cracker
la gamba *lah gahm·bah*   shrimp
el ganso *ehl gahn·soh*   wild goose
el garbanzo *ehl gahr·bahn·thoh*   chickpea
el gazpacho *ehl gahth·pah·choh*   cold tomato-based soup
la ginebra *lah khee·neh·brah*   gin
el gofre *ehl goh·freh*   waffle

la granada *lah grah-nah-dah*	pomegranate
el granizado *ehl grah-nee-thah-doh*	iced drink
la grosella espinosa *lah groh-seh-yah ehs-pee-noh-sah*	gooseberry
la grosella negra *lah groh-seh-yah neh-grah*	black currant
la grosella roja *lah groh-seh-yah roh-khah*	red currant
la guayaba *lah gwah-yah-bah*	guava
la guinda *lah geen-dah*	sour cherry
la guindilla en polvo *lah geen-dee-yah ehn pohl-boh*	chili pepper
el guirlache *ehl geer-lah-cheh*	nougat
el guisante *ehl gee-sahn-teh*	pea
la hamburguesa *lah ahm-boor-geh-sah*	hamburger
la harina *lah ah-ree-nah*	flour
la harina de avena *lah ah-ree-nah deh ah-beh-nah*	oatmeal
la harina de maíz *lah ah-ree-nah deh mah-eeth*	cornmeal
el helado *ehl eh-lah-doh*	ice cream
el (cubito de) hielo *ehl (koo-bee-toh deh) eeyeh-loh*	ice (cube)

el hígado *ehl ee·gah·doh*	liver
el higo *ehl ee·goh*	fig
el hinojo *ehl ee·noh·khoh*	fennel
la hoja de laurel *lah oh·khah deh lawoo·rehl*	bay leaf
el hueso *ehl weh·soh*	bone
el huevo *ehl weh·boh*	egg
el jabalí *ehl khah·bah·lee*	wild boar
la jalea *lah khah·leh·ah*	jelly
el jamón *ehl khah·mohn*	ham
el jengibre *ehl khehn·khee·breh*	ginger
el jerez *ehl kheh·rehth*	sherry
la judía *lah khoo·dee·uh*	bean
la judía verde *lah khoo·dee·ah behr·deh*	green bean
el ketchup *ehl keht·choop*	ketchup
el kiwi *ehl kee·wee*	kiwi
el lacón *ehl lah·kohn*	pork shoulder
la langosta *lah lahn·gohs·tah*	lobster
el lavanco *ehl lah·bahn·koh*	wild duck
la leche *lah leh·cheh*	milk
la leche de soja *lah leh·cheh deh soh·khah*	soymilk [soya milk]
la lechuga *lah leh·choo·gah*	lettuce
la lengua *lah lehn·gwah*	tongue
el lenguado *ehl lehn·gwah·doh*	sole
la lenteja *lah lehn·teh·khah*	lentil
el licor *ehl lee·kohr*	liqueur
el licor de naranja *ehl lee·kohr deh nah·rahn·khah*	orange liqueur
los licores *lohs lee·kohr·ehs*	spirits
la liebre *lah leyee·breh*	hare
la lima *lah lee·mah*	lime
el limón *ehl lee·mohn*	lemon

la limonada *lah leeh·moh·<u>nah</u>·dah* — lemonade

la lombarda *lah lohm·<u>bahr</u>·dah* — red cabbage

el lomo *ehl <u>loh</u>·moh* — loin

la lubina *lah loo·<u>bee</u>·nah* — (sea) bass

los macarrones *lohs mah·kah·<u>rrohn</u>·ehs* — macaroni

la magdalena *lah mahg·dah·<u>leh</u>·nah* — muffin

la maicena *lah mayee·<u>theh</u>·nah* — cornmeal

el maíz *ehl mah·<u>eeth</u>* — sweet corn

la mandarina *lah mahn·dah·<u>ree</u>·nah* — tangerine

el mango *ehl <u>mahn</u>·goh* — mango

las manos de cerdo *lahs <u>mah</u>·nohs deh <u>thehr</u>·doh* — pig's feet [trotters]

la mantequilla *lah mahn·teh·<u>kee</u>·yah* — butter

la manzana *lah mahn·<u>thah</u>·nah* — apple

la margarina *lah mahr·gah·<u>ree</u>·nah* — margarine

el marisco *ehl mah·<u>rees</u>·koh* — shellfish

la mayonesa *lah mah·yoh·<u>neh</u>·sah* — mayonnaise

el mazapán *ehl mah·thah·<u>pahn</u>* — marzipan

el mejillón *ehl meh·khee·<u>yohn</u>* — mussel

la mejorana *lah meh·khoh·<u>rah</u>·nah* — marjoram

la melaza *lah meh·<u>lah</u>·thah* — molasses

el melocotón *ehl meh·loh·koh·<u>tohn</u>* — peach

el melón *ehl meh·<u>lohn</u>* — melon

la menta *lah <u>mehn</u>·tah* — mint

el menudillo *ehl meh·noo·<u>dee</u>·yoh* — giblet

el merengue *ehl meh·<u>rehn</u>·geh* — meringue

la merluza *lah mehr·<u>loo</u>·thah* — hake

la mermelada *lah mehr·meh·<u>lah</u>·dah* — marmalade/jam

el mero *ehl <u>meh</u>·roh* — grouper

la miel *lah meeyehl* — honey

la molleja *lah moh·<u>yeh</u>·khah* — sweetbread

la morcilla *lah mohr-thee-yah*	black pudding
la mostaza *lah mohs-tah-thah*	mustard
el muesli *ehl mwehs-lee*	granola [muesli]
el nabo *ehl nah-boh*	turnip
la naranja *lah nah-rahn-khah*	orange
la nata *lah nah-tah*	cream
la nata agria *lah nah-tah ah-greeyah*	sour cream
la nata montada *lah nah-tah mohn-tah-dah*	whipped cream
las natillas *lahs nah-tee-yahs*	custard
la nuez *lah nwehth*	walnut
la nuez moscada *lah nwehth mohs-kah-dah*	nutmeg
el oporto *chl oh-pohr-toh*	port
el orégano *ehl oh-reh-gah-noh*	oregano
la ostra *lah ohs-trah*	oyster
la pacana *lah pah-kah-nah*	pecan
la paella *lah pah-eh-yah*	rice dish
la paletilla *lah puh-leh-tec-yah*	shank
el palmito *ehl pahl-mee-toh*	palm heart
el pan *ehl pahn*	bread
el panecillo *ehl pah-neh-thee-yoh*	roll
la papaya *lah pah-pah-yah*	papaya
la paprika *lah pah-pree-kah*	paprika
la pasa *lah pah-sah*	raisin
la pasta *lah pahs-tuh*	pasta
el pastel *ehl pahs-tehl*	pie
el pastel de queso *ehl pahs-tehl deh keh-soh*	cheesecake
la pata *lah pah-tah*	leg
la patata *lah pah-tah-tah*	potato
las patatas fritas *lahs pah-tah-tahs free-tahs*	French fries
las patatas fritas *lahs pah-tah-tahs free-tahs*	potato chips [crisps]
el paté *ehl pah-teh*	pâté

el pato *ehl pah·toh*	duck
el pavo *ehl pah·boh*	turkey
la pechuga (de pollo) *lah peh·choo·gah (deh poh·yoh)*	breast (of chicken)
el pepinillo *ehl peh·pee·nee·yoh*	pickle
el pepino *ehl peh·pee·noh*	cucumber
la pera *lah peh·rah*	pear
la perca *lah pehr·kah*	sea perch
la perdiz *lah pehr·deeth*	partridge
el perejil *ehl peh·reh·kheel*	parsley
el perrito caliente *ehl peh·rree·toh kah·leeyehn·teh*	hot dog
el pescadito *ehl pehs·kah·dee·toh*	small fish
el pescado *ehl pehs·kah·doh*	fish
el pescado frito *ehl pehs·kah·doh free·toh*	fried fish
pescado y marisco *pehs·kah·doh ee mah·rees·koh*	seafood
el pez espada *ehl peth ehs·pah·dah*	swordfish
el pichón *ehl pee·chohn*	young pigeon
pilsner *peels·nehr*	pilsner (beer)
el pimentón *ehl pee·mehn·tohn*	paprika
la pimienta *lah pee·meeyehn·tah*	pepper (seasoning)
la pimienta negra *lah pee·meeyehn·tah neh·grah*	black pepper
la pimienta inglesa *lah pee·meeyehn·tah een·gleh·sah*	allspice
el pimiento *ehl pee·meeyehn·toh*	pepper (vegetable)
la piña *lah pee·nyah*	pineapple
los piñones *lohs pee·nyohn·ehs*	pine nuts
la pintada *lah peen·tah·dah*	guinea fowl
la pizza *lah peeth·thah*	pizza

el plátano *ehl plah·tah·noh*	banana
el pollo *ehl poh·yoh*	chicken
el pollo frito *ehl poh·yoh free·toh*	fried chicken
el pomelo *ehl poh·meh·loh*	grapefruit
el puerro *ehl pweh·rroh*	leek
el pulpo *ehl pool·poh*	octopus
el queso *ehl keh·soh*	cheese
el queso de cabra *ehl keh·soh deh kah·brah*	goat cheese
el queso crema *ehl keh·soh kreh·mah*	cream cheese
el queso roquefort *ehl keh·soh roh·keh·fohrt*	blue cheese
el rábano *ehl rah·bah·noh*	radish
el rabo de buey *ehl rah·boh deh bwehy*	oxtail
el rape *ehl rah·peh*	monkfish
el ravioli *ehl rah·beeyoh·lee*	ravioli
la raya *lah rah·yah*	skate
el refresco *ehl reh·frehs·koh*	soda
relleno *reh·yeh·noh*	stuffed/stuffing
la remolacha *lah reh·moh·lah·chah*	beet
el repollo *ehl reh·poh·yoh*	cabbage
el requesón *ehl reh·keh·sohn*	cottage cheese
el requesón de soja *ehl reh·keh·sohn deh soh·khah*	tofu

los retoños de bambú *lohs reh·toh·nyohs deh bahm·boo* bamboo shoots

el riñón *ehl ree·nyohn* kidney

el róbalo *ehl roh·bah·loh* haddock

el romero *ehl roh·meh·roh* rosemary

el ron *ehl rohn* rum

el rosbif *ehl rohs·beef* roast beef

la rosquilla *lah rohs·kee·yah* doughnut

rubia *roo·beeyah* lager (beer)

el ruibarbo *ehl rwee·bahr·boh* rhubarb

la sal *lah sahl* salt

el salami *ehl sah·lah·mee* salami

la salchicha *lah sahl·chee·chah* sausage

el salmón *ehl sahl·mohn* salmon

el salmonete *ehl sahl·moh·neh·teh* red mullet

la salsa *lah sahl·sah* sauce

la salsa agridulce *lah sahl·sah ah·gree·dool·theh* sweet and sour sauce

la salsa alioli *lah sahl·sah ah·yee·oh·lee* garlic sauce

la salsa picante *lah sahl·sah pee·kahn·teh* hot pepper sauce

la salsa de soja *lah sahl·sah deh soh·khah* soy sauce

la salvia *lah sahl·beeyah* sage

la sandía *lah sahn·dee·ah* watermelon

el sándwich *ehl sahnd·weech* sandwich

la sangría *lah sahn·gree·ah* wine punch

la sardina *lah sahr·dee·nah* sardine

la semilla *lah seh·mee·yah* seed

la semilla de soja *lah seh·mee·yah deh soh·khah* soybean [soya bean]

el sésamo *ehl seh·sah·moh* sesame

los sesos *lohs seh·sohs* brains

la seta *lah seh·tah*	mushroom
la sidra *lah see·drah*	cider
el sifón *ehl see·fohn*	seltzer water
el sirope *ehl see·roh·peh*	syrup
la soja *lah soh·khah*	soy [soya]
el solomillo *ehl soh·loh·mee·yoh*	sirloin
la sopa *lah soh·pah*	soup
el sorbete *ehl sohr·beh·teh*	sorbet
el suero de leche *ehl sweh·roh deh leh·cheh*	buttermilk
la tarta *lah tahr·tah*	cake
el té *ehl teh*	tea
la ternera *lah tehr·neh·rah*	veal
el tequila *ehl teh·kee·lah*	tequila
el tiburón *ehl tee·boo·rohn*	shark
tinto *teen·toh*	red (wine)
el tocino *ehl toh·thee·noh*	bacon
el tofu *ehl toh·foo*	tofu
el tomate *ehl toh·mah·teh*	tomato
el tomillo *ehl toh·mee·yoh*	thyme
la tónica *lah toh·nee·kah*	tonic water
la tortilla *lah tohr·tee·yah*	omelet
la tortita *lah tohr·tee·tah*	large pancake served as an afternoon snack
la tostada *lah tohs·tah·dah*	toast
el trigo *ehl tree·goh*	wheat
la trucha *lah troo·chah*	trout
las trufas *lahs troo·fahs*	truffles
la uva *lah oo·bah*	grape
la vainilla *lah bayee·nee·yah*	vanilla
el venado *ehl beh·nah·doh*	venison
la verdura *lah behr·doo·rah*	vegetable

el vermut *ehl behr•moot*   vermouth
las vieiras *lahs bee•eyee•rahs*   scallop
el vinagre *ehl bee•nah•greh*   vinegar
el vino *ehl beeh•noh*   wine
el vino dulce *ehl bee•noh dool•theh*   dessert wine
el vodka *ehl bohd•kah*   vodka
el whisky *ehl wees•kee*   whisky
el whisky escocés *ehl wees•kee*   scotch
ehs•koh•thehs

la yema/clara de huevo   egg yolk/white
lah yeh•mah/klah•rah deh weh•boh
el yogur *ehl yoh•goor*   yogurt
la zanahoria *lah thah•nah•oh•reeyah*   carrot
la zarzamora *lah thahr•thah•moh•rah*   blackberry
el zumo *ehl thoo•moh*   juice

People

ESSENTIAL

Hello!	**¡Hola!** _oh_·lah
How are you?	**¿Cómo está?** _koh_·moh ehs·_tah_
Fine, thanks.	**Bien, gracias.** beeyehn _grah_·theeyahs
Excuse me! (to get attention)	**¡Perdón!** pehr·_dohn_
Do you speak English?	**¿Habla inglés?** _ah_·blah een·_glehs_
What's your name?	**¿Cómo se llama?** _koh_·moh seh _yah_·mah
My name is...	**Me llamo...** meh _yah_·moh...
Nice to meet you.	**Encantado _m_/Encantada _f._** ehn·kahn·_tah_·doh/ehn·kahn·_tah_·dah
Where are you from?	**¿De dónde es usted?** deh _dohn_·deh ehs oos·_teth_
I'm from the U.S./U.K.	**Soy de Estados Unidos/del Reino Unido.** soy deh ehs·_tah_·dohs oo·_nee_·dohs/ dehl _reyee_·noh oo·_nee_·doh
What do you do for a living?	**¿A qué se dedica?** ah keh seh deh·_dee_·kah
I work for...	**Trabajo para...** trah·_bah_·khoh _pah_·rah...
I'm a student.	**Soy estudiante.** soy ehs·too·_deeyahn_·teh
I'm retired.	**Estoy jubilado _m_/jubilada _f._** ehs·_toy_ khoo·bee·_lah_·doh/khoo·bee·_lah_·dah
Do you like...?	**¿Le gusta...?** leh _goos_·tah...
Goodbye.	**Adiós.** ah·_deeyohs_
See you later.	**Hasta luego.** _ah_·stah _lweh_·goh

For Grammar, see page 162.

When addressing strangers, always use the more formal **usted** (singular) or **ustedes** (plural), as opposed to the more familiar **tú** (singular) or **vosotros** (plural), until told otherwise. If you know someone's title, it's polite to use it, e.g., **doctor** (male doctor), **doctora** (female doctor). You can also simply say **Señor** (Mr.), **Señora** (Mrs.) or **Señorita** (Miss).

Language Difficulties

Do you speak English?	**¿Habla inglés?** _ah_•blah een•_glehs_
Does anyone here speak English?	**¿Hay alguien que hable inglés?** aye _ahl_•geeyehn keh _ah_•bleh een•_glehs_
I don't speak (much) Spanish.	**No hablo (mucho) español.** noh ah•bloh (_moo_•choh) ehs•pah•_nyol_
Can you speak more slowly?	**¿Puede hablar más despacio?** _pweh_•deh ah•_blahr_ mahs dehs•pah•_theeyoh_
Can you repeat that?	**¿Podría repetir eso?** poh•_dree_•ah reh•peh•_teer_ eh•_soh_
Excuse me?	**¿Cómo?** _koh_•moh
What was that?	**¿Qué ha dicho?** keh ah _dee_•choh
Can you spell it?	**¿Podría deletrearlo?** poh•_dree_•ah deh•leh•treh•_ahr_•loh
Please write it down.	**Escríbamelo, por favor.** ehs•_kree_•bah•meh•loh pohr fah•_bohr_

YOU MAY HEAR...

Hablo muy poco inglés. _ah_•bloh mooy _poh_•koh een•_glehs_

No hablo inglés. noh _ah_•bloh een•_glehs_

I only speak a little English.

I don't speak English.

Can you translate this into English for me?	¿Podría traducirme esto al inglés? *poh·dree·ah trah·doo·theer·meh ehs·toh ahl een·glehs*
What does this/ that mean?	¿Qué significa esto/eso? *keh seeg·nee·fee·kah ehs·toh/eh·soh*
I understand.	Entiendo. *ehn·teeyehn·doh*
I don't understand.	No entiendo. *noh ehn·teeyehn·doh*
Do you understand?	¿Entiende? *ehn·teeyehn·deh*

Making Friends

Hello!	¡Hola! *oh·lah*
Good morning.	Buenos días. *bweh·nohs dee·ahs*
Good afternoon.	Buenas tardes. *bweh·nahs tahr·dehs*
Good evening.	Buenas noches. *bweh·nahs noh·chehs*
My name is...	Me llamo... *meh yah·moh...*
What's your name?	¿Cómo se llama? *koh·moh seh yah·mah*
I'd like to introduce you to...	Quiero presentarle a... *keeyeh·roh preh·sehn·tahr·leh ah...*
Pleased to meet you.	Encantado *m* /Encantada *f*. *ehn·kahn·tah·doh/ehn·kahn·tah·dah*
How are you?	¿Cómo está? *koh·moh ehs·tah*
Fine, thanks. And you?	Bien gracias. ¿Y usted? *beeyehn grah·theeyahs ee oos·tehth*

When first meeting someone in Spain always greet him or her with **hola** (hello), **buenos días** (good morning) or **buenas tardes** (good afternoon). Spaniards even extend this general greeting to strangers when in elevators, waiting rooms and other small public spaces. A general acknowledgment or reply is expected from all. When leaving, say **adiós** (goodbye).

Travel Talk

I'm here...	**Estoy aquí...** *ehs-toy ah-kee...*
on business	**en viaje de negocios** *ehn beeyah-kheh deh neh-goh-theeyohs*
on vacation	**de vacaciones** *deh bah-kah-theeyoh-nehs*
studying	**estudiando** *ehs-too-deeyahn-doh*
I'm staying for...	**Voy a quedarme...** *boy ah keh-dahr-meh...*
I've been here...	**Llevo aquí...** *yeh-boh ah-kee...*
a day	**un día** *oon dee-ah*
a week	**una semana** *oo-nah seh-mah-nah*
a month	**un mes** *oon mehs*
Where are you from?	**¿De dónde es usted?** *deh dohn-deh ehs oos-tehth*
I'm from...	**Soy de...** *soy deh...*

For Numbers, see page 167.

Personal

Who are you with?	**¿Con quién ha venido?** *kohn keeyehn ah beh-nee-doh*
I'm here alone.	**He venido solo *m*/sola *f*.** *eh beh-nee-doh soh-loh/soh-lah*
I'm with my...	**He venido con mi...** *eh beh-nee-doh kohn mee...*
husband/wife	**marido/mujer** *mah-ree-doh/moo-khehr*
boyfriend/ girlfriend	**novio/novia** *noh-beeyoh/noh-beeyah*
friend	**amigo/amiga** *ah-mee-goh/ah-mee-gah*
friends	**amigos/amigas** *ah-mee-gohs/ah-mee-gahs*
colleague	**colega** *koh-leh-gah*
colleagues	**colegas** *koh-leh-gahs*
When's your birthday?	**¿Cuándo es su cumpleaños?** *kwahn-doh ehs soo koom-pleh-ah-nyohs*
How old are you?	**¿Qué edad tiene usted?** *keh eh-dahth teeyeh-neh oos-tehth*

I'm...	**Tengo...años.** _tehn_•goh...ah•nyohs
Are you married?	**¿Está casado m/casada f?** ehs•_tah_ kah•_sah_•doh/ kah•_sah_•dah
I'm...	**Estoy...** ehs•_toy_...
single	**soltero m/soltera f** sohl•_teh_•roh/sohl•_teh_•rah
in a relationship	**en una relación** ehn _oo_•nah reh•lah•_theeyohn_
engaged	**comprometido m/comprometida f** kohm•proh•meh•tee•doh/kohm•proh•meh•tee dah
married	**casado m/casada f** kah•_sah_•doh/kah•_sah_•dah
divorced	**divorciado m/divorciada f** dee•bohr•_theeyah_•doh/dee•bohr•_theeyah_•dah
separated	**separado m/separada f** seh•pah•_rah_•doh/ seh•pah•_rah_•dah
I'm widowed.	**Soy viudo m/viuda f** soy _beeyoo_•doh/_beeyoo_•dah
Do you have children/ grandchildren?	**¿Tiene hijos/nietos?** _teeyeh_•neh _ee_•khohs/_neeyeh_•tohs

For Numbers, see page 167.

Work & School

What do you do for a living?	**¿A qué se dedica?** ah keh seh deh•_dee_•kah
What are you studying?	**¿Qué estudia?** keh ehs•_too_•deeyah
I'm studying Spanish.	**Estudio español.** ehs•_too_•deeyoh ehs•pah•_nyohl_
I...	**Yo...** yoh...
work full-time/ part-time	**trabajo a tiempo completo/parcial** trah•_bah_•khoh ah _teeyehm_•poh kohm•_pleh_•toh/ pahr•_theeyahl_
am unemployed	**estoy en el paro** ehs•_toy_ ehn ehl _pah_•roh
work at home	**trabajo desde casa** trah•_bah_•khoh _dehs_•deh _kah_•sah

Who do you work for?	**¿Para quién trabaja?** _pah_·rah keeyehn _trah_·_bah_·khah
I work for…	**Trabajo para…** trah·_bah_·khoh _pah_·rah…
Here's my business card.	**Aquí tiene mi tarjeta.** ah·kee _teeyeh_·neh mee tahr·_kheh_·tah

For Business Travel, see page 142.

Weather

What's the forecast?	**¿Cuál es el pronóstico del tiempo?** kwahl ehs ehl proh·_nohs_·tee·koh dehl _teeyehm_·poh
What beautiful/ terrible weather!	**¡Qué tiempo más bonito/feo hace!** keh _teeyehm_·poh mahs boh·_nee_·toh/_feh_·oh ah·theh
It's cool/warm.	**Está fresco/cálido** esh·_tah_ frehs·koh/_kah_·lee·doh
It's cold/hot.	**Hace frío/calor.** _ah_·theh _free_·oh/kah·_lohr_
It's rainy/sunny.	**Está lluvioso/soleado.** ehs·_tah_ yoo·_beeyoh_·soh/ soh·lee·_ah_·doh
It's snowy/icy.	**Hay nieve/hielo.** aye _neeyeh_·beh/_eeyeh_·loh
Do I need a jacket/an umbrella?	**¿Necesito una chaqueta/un paraguas?** neh·theh·_see_·toh _oo_·nah chah·_keh_·tah/oon pah·_rah_·gwahs

For Temperature, see page 174.

ESSENTIAL

Would you like to go out for a drink/dinner?	**¿Le gustaría salir a tomar una copa/cenar?** *leh goos·tah·ree·ah sah·leer ah toh·mahr oo·nah koh·pah/theh·nahr*
What are your plans for tonight/tomorrow?	**¿Qué planes tiene para esta noche/mañana?** *keh plah·nehs teeyeh·nehs pah·rah ehs·tah noh·cheh/mah·nyah·nah*
Can I have your number?	**¿Puede darme su número?** *pweh·deh dahr·meh soo noo·meh·roh*
Can I join you?	**¿Puedo acompañarle m/acompañarla f?** *pweh·doh ah·kohm·pah·nyahr·leh/ah·kohm·pah·nyahr·lah*
Can I buy you a drink?	**¿Puedo invitarle m/invitarla f a una copa?** *pweh·doh een·bee·tahr·leh/een·bee·tahr·lah ah oo·nah koh·pah*
I like you.	**Me gustas.** *meh goos·tahs*
I love you.	**Te quiero.** *teh keeyeh·roh*

The Dating Game

Would you like to go out for…?	**¿Le gustaría ir…?** *leh goos·tah·ree·ah eer…*
coffee	**a tomar un café** *ah toh·mahr oon kah·feh*
a drink	**a tomar un copa** *ah toh·mahr oo·nah koh·pah*
dinner	**a cenar** *ah theh·nahr*
What are your plans for…?	**¿Qué planes tiene para…?** *keh plahn·ehs teeyeh·neh pah·rah…*

today	**hoy** _oy_
tonight	**esta noche** _ehs·tah noh·cheh_
tomorrow	**mañana** _mah·nyah·nah_
this weekend	**este fin de semana** _ehs·teh feen deh seh·mah·nah_
Where would you like to go?	**¿Adónde le gustaría ir?** _ah·dohn·deh leh goos·tah·ree·ah eer_
I'd like to go to…	**Me gustaría ir a…** _meh goos·tah·ree·ah eer ah…_
Do you like…?	**¿Le gusta…?** _leh goos·tah…_
Can I have your number/e-mail?	**¿Puede darme su número/dirección de correo electrónico?** _pweh·deh dahr·meh soo noo·meh·roh/dee·rehk·theeyohn deh koh·rreh·oh eh·lehk·troh·nee·koh_
Are you on Facebook/Twitter?	**¿Está en Facebook/Twitter?** _(polite form)_ _ehs·tah ehn Facebook/Twitter_
	¿Estás en Facebook/Twitter? _(informal form)_ _ehs·tahs ehn Facebook/Twitter_
Can I join you?	**¿Puedo acompañarle _m_/acompañarla _f_?** _pweh·doh ah·kohm·pah·nyahr·leh/ ah·kohm·pah·nyahr·lah_
You're very attractive.	**Eres muy guapo _m_/guapa _f_.** _eh·rehs mooy gwah·poh/gwah·pah_
Let's go somewhere quieter.	**Vayamos a un sitio más tranquilo.** _bah·yah·mohs ah oon see·teeyoh mahs trahn·kee·loh_

For Communications, see page 49.

Accepting & Rejecting

I'd love to.	**Me encantaría.** _meh ehn·kahn·tah·ree·yah_
Where should we meet?	**¿Dónde quedamos?** _dohn·deh keh·dah·mohs_
I'll meet you at the bar/your hotel.	**Quedamos en el bar/su hotel.** _keh·dah·mohs ehn ehl bahr/soo oh·tehl_

I'll come by at…	**Pasaré a recogerle *m*/recogerla *f* a las…** *pah·sah·reh ah reh·koh·khehr·leh/ reh·koh·khehr·lah ah lahs…*
What is your address?	**¿Cuál es su dirección?** *kwahl ehs soo dee·rehk·theeyohn*
I'm busy.	**Estoy ocupado *m*/ocupada *f*.** *ehs·toy oh·koo·pah·doh/oh·koo·pah·dah*
I'm not interested.	**No me interesa.** *noh meh een·teh·reh·sah*
Leave me alone.	**Déjeme en paz.** *deh·kheh·meh ehn pahth*
Stop bothering me!	**¡Deje de molestarme!** *deh·kheh deh moh·lehs·tahr·meh*

For Time, see page 170.

Getting Intimate

Can I hug/kiss you?	**¿Puedo abrazarte/besarte?** *pweh·doh ah·brah·thahr·teh/beh·sahr·teh*
Yes.	**Sí.** *see*
No.	**No.** *noh*
Stop!	**¡Para!** *pah·rah*
I love you.	**Te quiero.** *teh keeyeh·roh*

Sexual Preferences

Are you gay?	**¿Eres gay?** *eh·rehs gay*
I'm…	**Soy…** *soy…*
heterosexual	**heterosexual** *eh·teh·roh·sehks·wahl*
homosexual	**homosexual** *oh·moh·sehks·wahl*
bisexual	**bisexual** *bee·sehks·wahl*
Do you like men/women?	**¿Te gustan los hombres/las mujeres?** *teh goos·tahn lohs ohm·brehs/lahs moo·kheh·rehs*

Leisure Time

Sightseeing

ESSENTIAL

Where's the tourist information office?	**¿Dónde está la oficina de turismo?** _dohn•deh ehs•tah lah oh•fee•thee•nah deh too•rees•moh_
What are the main sights?	**¿Dónde están los principales sitios de interés?** _dohn•deh ehs•tahn lohs preen•thee•pah•lehs see•teeyohs deh een•teh•rehs_
Do you have tours in English?	**¿Hay visitas en inglés?** _aye bee•see•tahs ehn een•glehs_
Can I have a map/guide?	**¿Puede darme un mapa/una guía?** _pweh•deh dahr•meh oon mah•pah/oo•nah gee•ah_

Tourist Information

Do you have information on…?	**¿Tiene información sobre…?** _teeyeh•neh een•fohr•mah•theeyohn soh•breh…_
Can you recommend…?	**¿Puede recomendarme…?** _pweh•deh reh•koh•mehn•dahr•meh…_
a bus tour	**un recorrido en autobús** _oon reh•koh•rree•doh ehn awtoh•boos_
an excursion to…	**una excursión a…** _oo•nah ehx•koor•seeyohn ah…_
a sightseeing tour	**un recorrido turístico** _oon reh•koh•rree•doh too•rees•tee•koh_

Tourist offices are located in major Spanish cities and in many of the smaller towns that are popular tourist attractions. Ask at your hotel or check online to find the nearest office.

On Tour

I'd like to go on the tour to…	**Quiero ir a la visita de…** _keeyeh·roh eer ah lah bee·see·tah deh…_
When's the next tour?	**¿Cuándo es la próxima visita?** _kwahn·doh ehs lah proh·xee·mah bee·see·tah_
Are there tours in English?	**¿Hay visitas en inglés?** _aye bee·see·tahs ehn een·glehs_
Is there an English guide book/audio guide?	**¿Hay una guía/audioguía en inglés?** _aye oo·nah gee·ah/awoo·deeyoh·gee·ah ehn een·glehs_
What time do we leave/return?	**¿A qué hora salimos/volvemos?** _ah keh oh·rah sah·lee·mohs/bohl·beh·mohs_
We'd like to see…	**Queremos ver…** _keh·reh·mohs behr…_
Can we stop here…?	**¿Podemos parar aquí…?** _poh·deh·mohs pah·rahr ah·kee…_
to take photos	**para tomar fotos** _pah·rah toh·mahr foh·tohs_
for souvenirs	**para comprar recuerdos** _pah·rah kohm·prahr reh·kwehr·dohs_
for the toilet	**para ir al servicio** _pah·rah eer ahl sehr·bee·theeyoh_
Is it disabled-accessible?	**¿Tiene acceso para discapacitados?** _teeyeh·neh ahk·theh·soh pah·rah dees·kah·pah·thee·tah·dohs_

Seeing the Sights

Where is/are…?	**¿Dónde está/están…?** _dohn·deh ehs·tah/ehs·tahn…_
the battleground	**el campo de batalla** _ehl kahm·poh deh bah·tah·yah_
the botanical garden	**el jardín botánico** _ehl khahr·deen boh·tah·nee·koh_
the castle	**el castillo** _ehl kahs·tee·yoh_
the downtown area	**el centro** _ehl thehn·troh_
the fountain	**la fuente** _lah fwehn·teh_
the library	**la biblioteca** _lah bee·bleeyoh·teh·kah_
the market	**el mercado** _ehl mehr·kah·doh_
the museum	**el museo** _ehl moo·seh·oh_

the old town	**el casco antiguo** *ehl kahs·koh ahn·tee·gwoh*
the opera house	**teatro de la ópera** *ehl tehahtroh deh lah operh rah*
the palace	**el palacio** *ehl pah·lah·theeyoh*
the park	**el parque** *ehl pahr·keh*
the ruins	**las ruinas** *lahs rwee·nahs*
the shopping area	**la zona comercial** *lahs thoh·nah koh·mehr·theeyahl*
the town square	**la plaza** *lah plah·thah*
Can you show me on the map?	**¿Puede indicármelo en el mapa?** *pweh·deh een·dee·kahr·meh·loh ehn ehl mah·pah*
It's...	**Es...** *ehs...*
amazing	**increíble** *een·kreh·ee·bleh*
beautiful	**precioso** *preh·theeyoh·soh*
boring	**aburrido** *ah·boo·rree·don*
interesting	**interesante** *een·teh·reh·sahn·teh*
magnificent	**magnífico** *mahg·nee·fee·koh*
romantic	**romántico** *roh·mahn·tee·koh*
strange	**extraño** *ex·trah·nyon*
stunning	**impresionante** *eem·preh·seeyoh·nahn·teh*
terrible	**horrible** *oh·rree·bleh*
ugly	**feo** *feh·oh*
I (don't) like it.	**(No) Me gusta.** *(noh) meh goo·stah*

Religious Sites

Where is…?	¿Dónde está…? <u>dohn</u>·deh ehs·<u>tah</u>…
the cathedral	**la catedral** lah kah·teh·<u>drahl</u>
the Catholic/	**la iglesia católica/protestante**
Protestant church	lah ee·<u>gleh</u>·seeyah kah·<u>toh</u>·lee·kah/proh·tehs·<u>tahn</u>·teh
the mosque	**la mezquita** lah mehth·<u>kee</u>·tah
the shrine	**el santuario** ehl sahn·<u>twah</u>·reeyoh
the synagogue	**la sinagoga** lah see·nah·<u>goh</u>·gah
the temple	**el templo** ehl <u>tehm</u>·ploh
What time is mass/the service?	**¿A qué hora es la misa/el culto?** ah keh <u>oh</u>·rah ehs lah <u>mee</u>·sah/ehl <u>kool</u>·toh

Shopping

ESSENTIAL

Where's the market/ mall?	**¿Dónde está el mercado/centro comercial?** <u>dohn</u>·deh ehs·<u>tah</u> ehl mehr·<u>kah</u>·doh/ <u>then</u>·troh koh·mehr·<u>theeyahl</u>
I'm just looking.	**Sólo estoy mirando.** <u>soh</u>·loh ehs·<u>toy</u> mee·<u>rahn</u>·doh
Can you help me?	**¿Puede ayudarme?** <u>pweh</u>·deh ah·yoo·<u>dahr</u>·meh
I'm being helped.	**Ya me atienden.** yah meh ah·<u>teeyehn</u>·dehn
How much?	**¿Cuánto es?** <u>kwahn</u>·toh ehs
That one, please.	**Ése m /Ésa f, por favor.** <u>eh</u>·she/<u>eh</u>·sah pohr fah·<u>bohr</u>
That's all.	**Eso es todo.** <u>eh</u>·soh ehs <u>toh</u>·doh
Where can I pay?	**¿Dónde se paga?** <u>dohn</u>·deh seh <u>pah</u>·gah
I'll pay in cash/by credit card.	**Voy a pagar en efectivo/con tarjeta de crédito.** boy ah pah·<u>gahr</u> ehn eh·fehk·<u>tee</u>·boh/ kohn tahr·<u>kheh</u>·tah deh <u>kreh</u>·dee·toh
A receipt, please.	**Un recibo, por favor.** oon reh·<u>thee</u>·boh pohr fah·<u>bohr</u>

There are many types of markets in the towns of Spain. You can find a wide variety of goods at these markets, including fruit and vegetables, antiques, souvenirs, regional specialty items and so on. Your hotel or local tourist office will have information on the markets for your area. Most permanent markets are open daily from early morning till early afternoon; traveling market times vary by location. Inclement weather may cause a market to close early or not open at all.

At the Shops

Where is/are...?	**¿Dónde está/están...?** _dohn_·deh ehs·_tah_/ ehs·_tahn_...
the antiques store	**la tienda de antigüedades** lah _teeyehn_·dah deh ahn·tee·gweh·_dah_·dehs
the bakery	**la panadería** lah pah·nah·deh·_ree_·ah
the bank	**el banco** ehl _bahn_·koh
the bookstore	**la librería** lah lee·breh·_ree_·ah
the clothing store	**la tienda de ropa** lah _teeyehn_·dah deh _roh_·pah
the delicatessen	**la charcutería** lah chahr·koo·teh·_ree_·ah
the department stores	**los grandes almacenes** lohs _grahn_·dehs ahl·mah·_theh_·nehs
the gift shop	**la tienda de regalos** lah _teeyehn_·dah deh reh·_gah_·lohs
the health food store	**la tienda de alimentos naturales** lah _teeyehn_·dah deh ah·lee·_mehn_·tohs nah·too·_rahl_·ehs
the jeweler	**la joyería** lah khoh·yeh·_ree_·ah
the liquor store [off-licence]	**la tienda de bebidas alcohólicas** lah _teeyehn_·dah deh beh·_bee_·dahs ahl·koh·_oh_·lee·kahs
the market	**el mercado** ehl mehr·_kah_·doh
the music store	**la tienda de música** lah teeyehn·dah deh moosee·kah
the pastry shop	**la pastelería** lah pahs·teh·leh·_ree_·ah

the pharmacy [chemist]	**la farmacia** *lah fahr·mah·theeyah*
the produce [grocery] store	**la tienda de frutas y verduras** *lah teeyehn·dah deh froo·tahs ee behr·doo·rahs*
the shoe store	**la zapatería** *lah thah·pah·teh·ree·ah*
the shopping mall	**el centro comercial** *ehl then·troh koh·mehr·theeyahl*
the souvenir store	**la tienda de recuerdos** *lah teeyehn·dah deh rch·kwchr·dohs*
the supermarket	**el supermercado** *ehl soo·pehr·mehr·kah·doh*
the tobacconist	**el estanco** *ehl ehs·tahn·koh*
the toy store	**la juguetería** *lah khoo·geh·teh·ree·ah*

Ask an Assistant

When do you open/close?	**¿A qué hora abren/cierran?** *ah keh oh·rah ah·brehn/theeyeh·rrahn*
Where is/are...?	**¿Dónde está/están...?** *dohn·deh ehs·tah/ehs·tahn...*
the cashier	**la caja** *lah kah·khah*
the escalators	**las escaleras mecánicas** *lahs ehs·kah·leh·rahs meh·kah·nee·kahs*
the elevator [lift]	**el ascensor** *ehl ahs·thehn·sohr*
the fitting room	**el probador** *ehl proh·bah·dohr*
the store directory	**la guía de tiendas** *lah gee·ah deh teeyehn·dahs*

YOU MAY SEE...

ABIERTO/CERRADO	open/closed
CERRADO AL MEDIODIA	closed for lunch
PROBADOR	fitting room
CAJERO m **CAJERA** f	cashier
SOLO EFECTIVO	cash only
SE ACEPTAN TARJETAS DE CREDITO	credit cards accepted
HORARIO DE APERTURA	business hours
SALIDA	exit

Can you help me?	**¿Puede ayudarme?** _pweh_·deh ah·yoo·_dahr_·meh
I'm just looking.	**Sólo estoy mirando.** _soh_·loh ehs·_toy_ mee·_rahn_·doh
I'm being helped.	**Ya me atienden.** yah meh ah·_teeyehn_·dehn
Do you have...?	**¿Tienen...?** _teeyeh_·nehn...
Can you show me...?	**¿Podría enseñarme...?** poh·_dree_·ah ehn·seh·_nyahr_·meh...
Can you ship/wrap it?	**¿Pueden hacer un envío/envolverlo?** _pweh_·dehn ah·_thehr_ oon ehn·_bee_·oh/ehn·bohl·_behr_·loh
How much?	**¿Cuánto es?** _kwahn_·toh ehs
That's all.	**Eso es todo.** _eh_·soh ehs _toh_·doh

For Clothing, see page 124.

YOU MAY HEAR...

¿Necesita ayuda? neh·theh·_see_·tah ah·_yoo_·dah	Can I help you?
Un momento. oon moh·_mehn_·toh	One moment.
¿Qué desea? keh deh·_seh_·ah	What would you like?
¿Algo más? _ahl_·goh mahs	Anything else?

Personal Preferences

I'd like something…	**Quiero algo…** _keeyeh_•roh _ahl_•goh…	
cheap/expensive	**barato/caro** bah•_rah_•toh/_kah_•roh	
larger/smaller	**más grande/más pequeño** mahs _grahn_•deh/ mahs peh•_keh_•nyoh	
from this region	**de esta región** deh _ehs_•tah reh•_kheeyohn_	
Around…euros.	**Alrededor de los…euros.** ahl•reh•deh•_dohr_ deh lohs…_ew_•rohs	
Is it real?	**¿Es auténtico m/auténtica f?** ehs awoo•_tehn_•tee•koh/awoo•_tehn_•tee•kah	
Can you show me this/that?	**¿Puede enseñarme esto/eso?** _pweh_•deh ehn•seh•_nyahr_•meh _ehs_•toh/_eh_•soh	
That's not quite what I want.	**Eso no es realmente lo que busco.** _eh_•soh noh ehs reh•ahl•_mehn_•teh loh keh _boos_•koh	
No, I don't like it.	**No, no me gusta.** noh noh meh _goos_•tah	
It's too expensive.	**Es demasiado caro.** ehs deh•mah•_seeyah_•doh _kah_•roh	
I have to think about it.	**Quiero pensármelo.** _keeyeh_•roh pehn•_sahr_•meh•loh	
I'll take it.	**Me lo llevo.** meh loh _yeh_•boh	

119

Credit cards are widely accepted throughout Spain; you will need to show ID when using a credit card. Mastercard™ and Visa™ are the most commonly used; American Express® is accepted in most places. Debit cards are common in Spain and throughout Europe; these are usually accepted if backed by Visa™ or Mastercard™. Traveler's checks are not accepted everywhere; always have an alternate form of payment available. Cash is always accepted—some places, such as newsstands, tobacconists, flower shops and market or street stands, take cash only.

YOU MAY HEAR...

¿Cómo va a pagar? _koh•moh bah ah pah•gahr_ — How are you paying?

Su tarjeta ha sido rechazada. _soo tahr•kheh•tah ah see•doh reh•chah•thah•dah_ — Your credit card has been declined.

Su documento de identidad, por favor. _soo doh•koo•mehn•toh deh ee•dehn•tee•dahd pohr fah•bohr_ — ID, please.

No aceptamos tarjetas de crédito. _noh ah•thehp•tah•mohs tahr•kheh•tahs deh kreh•dee•toh_ — We don't accept credit cards.

Sólo en efectivo, por favor. _soh•loh ehn eh•fehk•tee•boh pohr fah•bohr_ — Cash only, please.

¿Tiene cambio/billetes más pequeños? _teeyeh•neh kahm•beeyoh/bee•yeh•tehs mahs peh•keh•nyohs_ — Do you have change/small bills [notes]?

Paying & Bargaining

How much?	**¿Cuánto es?** _kwahn•toh ehs_
I'll pay...	**Voy a pagar...** _boy ah pah•gahr..._
in cash	**en efectivo** _ehn eh•fehk•tee•boh_
by credit card	**con tarjeta de crédito** _kohn tahr•kheh•tah deh kreh•dee•toh_
by traveler's check [cheque]	**con cheque de viaje** _kohn cheh•keh deh beeyah•kheh_
A receipt, please.	**Un recibo, por favor.** _oon reh•thee•boh pohr fah•bohr_
That's too much.	**Eso es demasiado.** _eh•soh ehs deh•mah•seeyah•doh_
I'll give you...	**Le doy...** _leh doy..._
I have only... euros.	**Sólo tengo...euros.** _soh•loh tehn•goh... ew•rohs_

| Is that your best price? | **¿Es el mejor precio que me puede hacer?** *ehs ehl meh·khohr preh·theeyoh keh meh pweh·deh ah·thehr* |
| Can you give me a discount? | **¿Puede hacerme un descuento?** *pweh·deh ah·thehr·meh oon dehs·kwehn·toh* |

For Numbers, see page 167.

Making a Complaint

I'd like...	**Quiero...** *keeyeh·roh...*
to exchange this	**cambiar esto por otro** *kahm·beeyahr ehs·toh pohr oh·troh*
to return this	**devolver esto** *deh·bohl·behr ehs·toh*
a refund	**que me devuelvan el dinero** *keh meh deh·bwehl·bahn ehl dee·neh·roh*
to see the manager	**hablar con el encargado** *ah·blahr kohn ehl ehn·kahr·gah·doh*

Services

Can you recommend...?	**¿Puede recomendarme...?** *pweh·deh reh·koh·mehn·dahr·meh*
a barber	**una peluquería de caballeros** *oo·nah peh·loo·keh·ree·ah deh kah·bah·yeh·rohs*
a dry cleaner	**una tintorería** *oo·nah teen·toh·reh·ree·ah*
a hairstylist	**una peluquería de señoras** *oo·nah peh·loo·keh·ree·ah deh seh·nyoh·rahs*
a laundromat [launderette]	**una lavandería** *oo·nah lah·bahn·deh·ree·ah*
a nail salon	**un salón de manicura** *sah·lohn deh mah·nee·koo·rah*
a spa	**un centro de salud y belleza** *oon then·troh deh sah·lood ee beh·yeh·thah*
a travel agency	**una agencia de viajes** *oo·nah ah·khehn·theeyah deh beeyah·khehs*

Can you...this?	**¿Puede...esto?** _pweh_·deh..._ehs_·toh
alter	**hacerle un arreglo a** ah·_thehr_·leh oon
	ah·_rreh_·gloh ah
clean	**limpiar** leem·_peeyahr_
fix	**zurcir** thoor·_theer_
press	**planchar** plahn·_chahr_
When will it be ready?	**¿Cuándo estará listo?**
	kwahn·doh ehs·tah·_rah_ _lees_·toh

Hair & Beauty

I'd like...	**Quiero...** _keeyeh_·roh...
an appointment for	**pedir hora para hoy/mañana**
today/tomorrow	_peh·deer_ _oh_·rah _pah_·rah oy/mah·_nyah_·nah
some color	**teñirme el pelo** teh·_nyeer_·meh ehl _peh_·loh
some highlights	**hacerme mechas** ah·_thehr_·meh _meh_·chahs
my hair styled/	**hacerme un peinado** ah·_thehr_·meh
blow-dried	oon peyee·_nah_·doh
a haircut	**cortarme el pelo** kohr·_tahr_·meh ehl _peh_·loh

With its varied landscapes and more than 2,000 registered springs (mineral and other), Spain is a prime location for spas, wellness centers and health-based resorts. These facilities offer a variety of treatments, including relaxation therapies and herbal remedies. Day spas can be found throughout the country, especially in the larger cities, and resort and overnight spas often offer individual services to those not staying there. Many of these also offer a wide variety of other relaxing activities such as horseback riding, guided tours, golf and swimming. Some spas and resorts do not allow children, so check before booking if you are traveling with kids.

an eyebrow/ bikini wax	**depilarme las cejas/ingles** *deh·pee·lahr·meh lahs theh·khahs/een·glehs*
a facial	**hacerme una limpieza de cutis** *ah·thehr·meh oo·nah leem·peeyeh·thah deh koo·tees*
a manicure/ pedicure	**hacerme la manicura/pedicura** *ah·thehr·meh lah mah·nee·koo·rah/peh·dee·koo·rah*
a (sports) massage	**un masaje (deportivo)** *oon mah·sah·kheh (deh·pohr·tee·boh)*
a trim	**cortarme las puntas** *kohr·tahr·meh lahs poon·tahs*
Not too short.	**No me lo corte demasiado.** *noh meh loh kohr·teh deh·mah·seeyah·doh*
Shorter here.	**Quíteme más de aquí.** *kee·teh·meh mahs deh ah·kee*
Do you offer...?	**¿Hacen...?** *ah·thehn...*
acupuncture	**acupuntura** *ah·koo·poon·too·rah*
aromatherapy	**aromaterapia** *ah·roh·mah·teh·rah·peeyah*
oxygen treatment	**oxígenoterapia** *oh·xee·kheh·noh·teh·rah·peeyah*
Do you have a sauna?	**¿Tienen una sauna?** *teeyehn·ehn oo·nah sawoo·nah*

Antiques

How old is it?	**¿Qué antigüedad tiene?** *keh ahn·tee·gweh·dahd teeyeh·neh*
Do you have anything from the...period?	**¿Tiene algo de la epoca...?** *teeyeh·neh ahl·goh deh lah eh·poh·kah...*
Do I have to fill out any forms?	**¿Tengo que rellenar algún impreso?** *tehn·goh keh reh·yeh·nahr ahl·goon eem·preh·soh*
Is there a certificate of authenticity?	**¿Tiene el certificado de autenticidad?** *teeyeh·neh ehl thehr·tee·fee·kah·doh deh awoo·tehn·tee·thee·dahd*
Can you ship/wrap it?	**¿Puede llevármelo/envolvérmelo?** *pweh·deh yeh·bahr·meh·loh/ehn·bohl·behr·meh·loh*

YOU MAY HEAR...

Le queda genial *leh keh·dah kheh·neeyahl* That looks great on you.
¿Cómo le queda? *koh·moh meh khe·dah* How does it fit?
No tenemos su talla We don't have your size.
noh teh·neh·mohs soo tah·yah

Clothing

I'd like...	**Quiero...** *keeyeh·roh...*
Can I try this on?	**¿Puedo probarme esto?**
	pweh·doh proh·bahr·meh ehs·toh
It doesn't fit.	**No me queda bien.** *noh meh keh·dah beeyehn*
It's too...	**Me queda demasiado...**
	meh keh·dah deh·mah·seeyah·doh...
big/small	**grande/pequeño** *m* **/pequeña** *f*
	grahn·deh/peh·keh·nyoh/peh·keh·nyah
short/long	**corto** *m* **/corta** *f* **/largo** *m* **/larga** *f*
	kohr·toh/kohr·tah/lahr·goh/lahr·gah
tight/loose	**ajustado/ancho** *ah·khoos·tah·doh/ahn·choh*
Do you have this in size...?	**¿Tiene esto en la talla...?** *teeyeh·neh ehs·toh ehn lah tah·yah...*
Do you have this in a bigger/ smaller size?	**¿Tiene esto en una talla más grande/pequeña?** *teeyeh·neh ehs·toh ehn oo·nah tah·yah mahs grahn·deh/peh·keh·nyah*

YOU MAY SEE...

ROPA DE CABALLERO	men's clothing
ROPA DE SEÑORA	women's clothing
ROPA DE NIÑOS	children's clothing

Colors

I'd like something...	**Busco algo...** _boos_·koh _ahl_·goh...
beige	**beis** behyees
black	**negro** _neh_·groh
blue	**azul** ah·_thool_
brown	**marrón** mah·_rrohn_
green	**verde** _behr_·deh
gray	**gris** grees
orange	**naranja** nah·_rahn_·khah
pink	**rosa** _roh_·sah
purple	**morado** moh·_rah_·doh
red	**rojo** _roh_·khoh
white	**blanco** _blahn_·koh
yellow	**amarillo** ah·mah·_ree_·yoh

Clothes & Accessories

a backpack	**la mochila** lah moh·_chee_·lah
a belt	**el cinturón** ehl theen·too·_rohn_
a bikini	**el bikini** ehl bee·_kee_·nee
a blouse	**la blusa** lah _bloo_·sah
a bra	**el sujetador** ehl soo·kheh·tah·_dohr_
briefs/panties	**los calzoncillos/las bragas** lohs kahl·thohn·_thee_·yohs/lahs brah·gahs
a coat	**el abrigo** ehl ah·_bree_·goh
a dress	**el vestido** ehl behs·_tee_·doh
a hat	**el sombrero** ehl sohm·_breh_·roh
a jacket	**la chaqueta** lah chah·_keh_·tah
jeans	**los vaqueros** lohs bah·_keh_·rohs
pajamas	**el pijama** ehl pee·_khah_·mah
pants [trousers]	**los pantalones** lohs pahn·tah·_loh_·nehs
pantyhose [tights]	**las medias** lahs _meh_·deeyahs
a purse [handbag]	**el bolso** ehl _bohl_·soh

a raincoat	**el impermeable** *ehl eem·pehr·meh·ah·bleh*
a scarf	**la bufanda** *lah boo·fahn·dah*
a shirt	**la camisa** *lah kah·mee·sah*
shorts	**los pantalones cortos** *lohs pahn·tah·loh·nehs kohr·tohs*
a skirt	**la falda** *lah fahl·dah*
socks	**los calcetines** *lohs kahl·theh·tee·nehs*
a suit	**el traje de chaqueta** *ehl trah·kheh deh chah·keh·tah*
sunglasses	**las gafas de sol** *lahs gah·fahs deh sohl*
a sweater	**el jersey** *ehl khehr·seyee*
a sweatshirt	**la sudadera** *lah soo·dah·deh·rah*
a swimsuit	**el bañador** *ehl bah·nyah·dohr*
a T-shirt	**la camiseta** *lah kah·mee·seh·tah*
a tie	**la corbata** *lah kohr·bah·tah*
underwear	**la ropa interior** *lah roh·pah een·teh·reeyohr*

Fabric

I'd like…	**Quiero…** *keeyeh·roh…*
cotton	**algodón** *ahl·goh·dohn*
denim	**tela vaquera** *teh·lah bah·keh·rah*
lace	**encaje** *ehn·kah·kheh*
leather	**cuero** *kweh·roh*
linen	**lino** *lee·noh*
silk	**seda** *seh·dah*
wool	**lana** *lah·nah*
Is it machine washable?	**¿Se puede lavar a máquina?** *seh pweh·deh lah·bahr ah mah·kee·nah*

Shoes

I'd like…	**Quiero…** *keeyeh·roh…*
high-heels/flats	**zapatos de tacón/planos** *thah·pah·tohs deh tah·kohn/plah·nohs*
boots	**botas** *boh·tahs*

loafers	**mocasines** *moh·kah·see·nehs*
sandals	**sandalias** *sahn·dah·leeyahs*
shoes	**zapatos** *thah·pah·tohs*
slippers	**zapatillas** *thah·pah·tee·yahs*
sneakers	**zapatillas de deporte** *thah·pah·tee·yahs deh deh·pohr·teh*
In size…	**En la talla…** *ehn lah tah·yah…*

For Numbers, see page 167.

Sizes

small (S)	**pequeña (P)** *peh·keh·nyah (peh)*
medium (M)	**mediana (M)** *meh·deeyah·nah (ehm)*
large (L)	**grande (G)** *grahn·deh (kheh)*
extra large (XL)	**XL** *ehkees·ehleh*
petite	**tallas pequeñas** *tah·yahs peh·keh·nyahs*
plus size	**tallas grandes** *tah·yahs grahn·dehs*

Newsagent & Tobacconist

Do you sell English-language newspapers?	**¿Venden periódicos en inglés?** *behn·dehn peh·reeyoh·dee·kohs ehn een·glehs*
I'd like…	**Quiero…** *keeyeh·roh…*
candy [sweets]	**caramelos** *kah·rah·meh·lohs*
chewing gum	**chicle** *chee·kleh*
a chocolate bar	**una chocolatina** *oo·nah choh·koh·lah·tee·nah*
a cigar	**un puro** *oon poo·roh*
a pack/carton of cigarettes	**un paquete/cartón de tabaco** *oon pah·keh·teh/kahr·tohn deh tah·bah·koh*
a lighter	**un mechero** *oon meh·cheh·roh*
a magazine	**una revista** *oo·nah reh·bees·tah*
matches	**cerillas** *theh·ree·yahs*
a newspaper	**un periódico** *oon peh·reeyoh·dee·koh*
a pen	**un bolígrafo** *oon boh·lee·grah·foh*

a postcard	**una postal** _oo_•nah _pohs_•tahl
a road/town map of...	**un mapa de las carreteras/plano de...** oon _mah_•pah deh lahs kah•rreh•_teh_•rahs/_plah_•noh deh...
stamps	**sellos** _seh_•yohs

Photography

I'd like a/an... camera.	**Quiero una cámara...** _keeyeh_•roh _oo_•nah _kah_•mah•rah...
automatic	**automática** awoo•toh•_mah_•tee•kah
digital	**digital** dee•khee•_tahl_
disposable	**desechable** deh•seh•_chah_•bleh
I'd like...	**Quiero...** _keeyeh_•roh...
a battery	**una pila** _oo_•nah _pee_•lah
digital prints	**fotos digitales** _foh_•tohs dee•khee•_tah_•lehs
a memory card	**una tarjeta de memoria** _oo_•nah tahr•_kheh_•tah deh meh•_moh_•reeyah
Can I print digital photos here?	**¿Puedo imprimir aquí fotos digitales?** _pweh_•doh eem•pree•_meer_ ah•_kee_ _foh_•tohs dee•khee•_tah_•lehs

Souvenirs

bottle of wine	**la botella de vino** lah boh•_teh_•yah deh _bee_•noh
box of chocolates	**la caja de bombones** lah _kah_•khah deh bohm•_boh_•nehs
castanets	**las castañuelas** lahs kahs•tah•_nyweh_•lahs
doll	**la muñeca** lah moo•_nyeh_•kah
fan (wooden, flamenco)	**el abanico de madera** ehl ah•bah•_nee_•koh deh mah•_deh_•rah
key ring	**el llavero** ehl yah•_beh_•roh
postcard	**la postal** lah pohs•_tahl_
pottery	**la cerámica** lah theh•_rah_•mee•kah
serrano ham	**el jamón serrano** ehl khah•_mohn_ seh•_rrah_•noh
T-shirt	**la camiseta** lah kah•mee•_seh_•tah
terracotta bowl	**la cazuela de barro** lah kah•_thweh_•lah deh _bah_•rroh

Spain produces a wide range of souvenirs, from typical tourist T-shirts to high-quality regional crafts. Spanish wine is popular and quality examples, such as sherry from Jerez and red wine from Rioja, can be found all over. Olive oil is also a popular gift. Classic Spanish souvenirs include bullfighting mementos, such as figurines, posters or capes, castanets, hand-painted flamenco fans and guitars. Reproduction paintings by Spain's most famous artists, such as Picasso, Dalí, Miró, Goya, El Greco or Velázquez, are also popular. Specialty regional goods include copperware, earthenware, leather goods, jewelry, lace, porcelain and wood carvings. Spanish swords and other metal work from Toledo are unique gifts, and Lladro® porcelain figurines are very popular. To find a good representation of each region's specialty goods at reasonable prices, visit the markets in each town.

toy	**el juguete** ehl khoo•_geh_•teh	
wine	**el vino** ehl _bee_•noh	
Can I see this/that?	**¿Puedo ver esto/eso?** _pweh_•doh behr ehs•toh/eh•soh	
It's in the window/ display case.	**Está en el escaparate/la vitrina.** ehs•_tah_ ehn ehl ehs•kah•pah•_rah_•teh/lah bee•_tree_•nah	
I'd like…	**Quiero…** _keeyeh_•roh…	
a battery	**una pila** _oo_•nah _pee_•lah	
a bracelet	**una pulsera** _oo_•nah pool•_seh_•rah	
a brooch	**un broche** oon _broh_•cheh	
earrings	**unos pendientes** _oo_•nohs pehn•_deeyehn_•tehs	
a necklace	**un collar** oon _koh_•yahr	
a ring	**un anillo** oon ah•_nee_•yoh	
a watch	**un reloj de pulsera** oon reh•_lohkh_ deh pool•_seh_•rah	
I'd like…	**Quiero…** _keeyeh_•roh…	
copper	**cobre** _koh_•breh	

crystal	**cristal** krees·*tahl*
diamonds	**diamantes** deeyah·*mahn*·tehs
white/yellow gold	**oro blanco/amarillo** *oh*·roh *blahn*·koh/ah·mah·*ree*·yoh
pearls	**perlas** *pehr*·lahs
pewter	**peltre** *pehl*·treh
platinum	**platino** plah·*tee*·noh
sterling silver	**plata esterlina** *plah*·tah ehs·tehr·*lee*·nah
Is this real?	**¿Es auténtico?** ehs awoo·*tehn*·tee·koh
Can you engrave it?	**¿Puede grabármelo?** *pweh*·deh grah·*bahr*·meh·loh

Sport & Leisure

ESSENTIAL

When's the game?	**¿Cuándo empieza el partido?**
	kwahn·doh ehm·*peeyeh*·thah ehl pahr·*tee*·doh
Where's…?	**¿Dónde está…?** *dohn*·deh ehs·*tah*…
the beach	**la playa** lah *plah*·yah
the park	**el parque** ehl *pahr*·keh
the pool	**la piscina** lah pees·*thee*·nah
Is it safe to swim here?	**¿Es seguro nadar aquí?** ehs seh·*goo*·roh nah·*dahr* ah·*kee*
Can I rent [hire] golf clubs?	**¿Puedo alquilar palos de golf?** *pweh*·doh ahl·kee·*lahr* pah·lohs deh golf
How much per hour?	**¿Cuánto cuesta por hora?** *kwahn*·toh *kwehs*·tah pohr *oh*·rah
How far is it to…?	**¿A qué distancia está…?** ah keh dees·*tahn*·theeyah ehs·*tah*…
Can you show me on the map, please?	**¿Puede indicármelo en el mapa, por favor?** *pweh*·deh een·dee·*kahr*·meh·loh ehn ehl *mah*·pah pohr fah·*bohr*

Watching Sport

When's...?	¿Cuándo empieza...?
	kwahn·doh ehm·peeyeh·thah...
the baseball game	**el juego del béisbol** *ehl khooeh·goh dehl behees·bohl*
the basketball game	**el partido de baloncesto** *ehl pahr·tee·doh deh bah·lohn·thehs·toh*
the boxing match	**la pelea de boxeo** *lah peh·leh·ah deh bohks·eh·oh*
the cycling race	**la vuelta ciclista** *lah bwehl·tah thee·klees·tah*
the golf tournament	**el torneo de golf** *ehl tohr·neh·oh deh golf*
the soccer [football] game	**el partido de fútbol** *ehl pahr·tee·doh deh foot·bohl*
the tennis match	**el partido de tenis** *ehl pahr·tee·doh deh teh·nees*
the volleyball game	**el partido de voleibol** *ehl pahr·tee·doh deh boh·levee·bohl*
Who's playing?	**¿Quienes juegan?** *keeyeh·nehs khweh·gahn*
Where is...?	**¿Dónde está...?** *dohn·deh ehs·tah...*
the horsetrack	**el hipódromo** *ehl ee·poh·droh·moh*
the racetrack	**el circuito de carreras** *ehl theer·kwee·toh de kah·rreh·rahs*
the stadium	**el estadio** *ehl ehs·tah·deeyoh*
Where can I place a bet?	**¿Dónde puedo hacer una apuesta?** *dohn·deh pweh·doh ah·thehr oo·nah ah·pwehs·tah*

Playing Sport

Where is/are...?	**¿Dónde está/están...?** *dohn·deh ehs·tah/ ehs·tahn...*
the golf course	**el campo de golf** *ehl kahm·poh deh golf*
the gym	**el gimnasio** *ehl kheem·nah·seeyoh*
the park	**el parque** *ehl pahr·keh*
the tennis courts	**las canchas de tenis** *lahs kahn·chahs deh teh·nees*

How much per...?	**¿Cuánto cuesta por...?** _kwahn_•toh _kwehs_•tah pohr...
day	**día** _dee_•ah
hour	**hora** _oh_•rah
game	**partido** pahr•_tee_•doh
round	**juego** _khweh_•goh
Can I rent [hire]...?	**¿Puedo alquilar...?** _pweh_•doh ahl•kee•_lahr_...
golf clubs	**palos de golf** _pah_•lohs deh golf
equipment	**equipo** eh•_kee_•poh
a racket	**una raqueta** _oo_•nah rah•_keh_•tah

At the Beach/Pool

Where's the beach/pool?	**¿Dónde está la playa/piscina?** _dohn_•deh ehs•_tah_ lah _plah_•yah/pees•_thee_•nah
Is there...?	**¿Hay...?** aye...
a kiddie pool	**una piscina infantil** _oo_•nah pees•_thee_•nah een•fahn•_teel_
an indoor/ outdoor pool	**una piscina cubierta/exterior** _oo_•nah pees•_thee_•nah koo•_beeyehr_•tah/ehx•teh•_reeyohr_
a lifeguard	**un socorrista** oon soh•koh•_rrees_•tah
Is it safe...?	**¿Es seguro...?** ehs seh•_goo_•roh...
to swim	**nadar** nah•_dahr_
to dive	**tirarse de cabeza** tee•_rahr_•seh deh kah•_beh_•thah

Fútbol (soccer) is the most popular sport in Spain; most cities in Spain have their own professional teams with a large fan base. Note that fans are extremely dedicated, so be sure not to insult the team. Almost all activity in Spain stops when there is an important soccer game on.

Golf is also popular and the golf courses on the Costa del Sol are worth a round. Other popular sports include basketball, tennis, auto racing, horse racing, hiking and climbing. **Jai alai** is a popular fast-paced game involving balls and curved -wicker-basket gloves.

There are many casinos throughout Spain. Minimum entrance and gaming age is 18; ID is required and the dress code is business casual.

for children	**para los niños** *pah-rah lohs nee-nyohs*	
I'd like to hire...	**Quiero alquilar...** *keeyeh-roh ahl-kee-lahr...*	
a deck chair	**una tumbona** *oo-nah toom-boh-nah*	
diving equipment	**equipo de buceo** *eh-kee-poh deh boo-theh-oh*	
a jet ski	**una moto acuática** *oo-nah moh-toh ah-kwah-tee-kah*	
a motorboat	**una lancha motora** *oo-nah lahn-chah moh-toh-rah*	
a rowboat	**una barca de remos** *oo-nah bahr-kah deh reh-mohs*	
snorkeling equipment	**equipo de esnórquel** *eh-kee-poh deh ehs-nohr-kehl*	
a surfboard	**una tabla de surf** *oo-nah tah-blah deh soorf*	
a towel	**una toalla** *oo-nah toh-ah-yah*	
an umbrella	**una sombrilla** *oo-nah sohm-bree-yah*	
water skis	**unos esquís acuáticos** *oo-nohs ehs-kees ah-kwah-tee-kohs*	
a windsurfer	**una tabla de windsurf** *oo-nah tah-blah deh weend-soorf*	
For...hours.	**Por...horas.** *pohr... oh-rahs*	

Winter Sports

A lift pass for a day/five days, please.	**Un pase de un día/cinco días de acceso a los remontes.** *oon pah·seh deh oon dee·ah/theen·koh dee·ahs deh ahk·theh·soh ah lohs reh·mohn·tehs*
I'd like to hire [hire]...	**Quiero alquilar...** *keeyeh·roh ahl·kee·lahr...*
boots	**botas** *boh·tahs*
a helmet	**un casco** *oon kahs·koh*
poles	**bastones** *bahs·toh·nehs*
skis	**esquís** *ehs·kees*
a snowboard	**una tabla de snowboard** *oo·nah tah·blah deh snoh·bohrd*
snowshoes	**raquetas de nieve** *rah·keh·tahs deh neeyeh·beh*
Are there lessons?	**¿Dan clases?** *dahn klah·sehs*
These are too big/small.	**Me quedan demasiado grandes/pequeños.** *meh keh·dahn deh·mah·seeyah·doh grahn·dehs/ peh·keh·nyohs*
I'm a beginner.	**Soy principiante.** *soy preen·thee·peeyahn·teh*
I'm experienced.	**Tengo experiencia.** *tehn·goh ehx·peh·reeyehn·theeyah*
A trail [piste] map, please.	**Un mapa de las pistas, por favor.** *oon mah·pah deh lahs pees·tahs pohr fah·bohr*

Out in the Country

A map of..., please.	**Un mapa de..., por favor.** *oon mah·pah deh... pohr fah·bohr*
this region	**esta región** *ehs·tah reh·kheeyohn*
the walking routes	**las rutas de senderismo** *lahs roo·tahs deh sehn·deh·rees·moh*
the bike routes	**los senderos para bicicletas** *lohs sehn·deh·rohs pah·rah bee·thee·kleh·tahs*
the trails	**los senderos** *lohs sehn·deh·rohs*
Is it... easy/difficult?	**¿Es... fácil/difícil?** *ehs fah·theel/dee·fee·theel*

Spain has more than 2,400 miles (4,000 km) of coastline and more than 1,700 beaches, with 16 different **Costas** (coastal regions). Two of the more famous coastal regions are **Costa del Sol** and **Costa Blanca**. Spain's Balearic and Canary Islands boast some of the most beautiful beaches in the world. If you decide to go for a swim, check the safety flags at each beach. Green flags indicate the water is safe, yellow flags indicate that you should use caution and red flags indicate that the water is unsafe for swimming.

Is it far/steep?	**¿Está lejos/empinado?** chs·_tah_ l_ch_·khohs/ ehm·pee·_nah_·doh
I'm lost.	**Me he perdido.** meh eh pehr·_dee_·doh
How far is it to…?	**¿A qué distancia está…?** ah keh dees·_tahn_·theeyah ehs·_tah_…
Can you show me on the map, please?	**¿Puede indicármelo en el mapa, por favor?** _pweh_·deh een·dee·_kahr_·meh·loh ehn ehl _mah_·pah pohr fah·_bohr_
Where is…?	**¿Dónde está…?** _dohn_·deh ehs·_tah_…
the bridge	**el puente** ehl _pwehn_·teh

Spain has three mountain ranges, the Pyrenees, the Sierra Nevada and the Cantabrian, with an average altitude of 2,000 feet (600 m). There are more than 30 ski resorts throughout Spain with more than 620 miles (1,000 km) of ski runs combined. In addition to skiing, most resorts and ski areas offer other winter activities such as snowboarding, snowmobiling, sledding and dog-sledding.

the cave	**la cueva**	lah <u>kweh</u>•bah
the cliff	**el acantilado**	ehl ah•kahn•tee•<u>lah</u>•doh
the desert	**el desierto**	ehl deh•<u>seeyehr</u>•toh
the farm	**la granja**	lah <u>grahn</u>•khah
the field	**el campo**	ehl <u>kahm</u>•poh
the forest	**el bosque**	ehl <u>bohs</u>•keh
the hill	**la colina**	lah koh•<u>lee</u>•nah
the lake	**el lago**	ehl <u>lah</u>•goh
the mountain	**la montaña**	lah mohn•<u>tah</u>•nyah
the nature preserve	**la reserva natural**	lah reh•<u>sehr</u>•bah nah•too•<u>rahl</u>
the viewpoint	**el mirador**	ehl mee•rah•<u>dohr</u>
the park	**el parque**	ehl <u>pahr</u>•keh

YOU MAY SEE...

TELESQUÍ	drag lift
TELEFÉRICO	cable car
TELESILLA	chair lift
PRINCIPIANTE	novice
NIVEL INTERMEDIO	intermediate
EXPERTO	expert
PISTA CERRADA	trail [piste] closed

the path	**el camino** *ehl kah•mee•noh*
the peak	**el pico** *ehl pee•koh*
the picnic area	**la zona de picnic** *lah thoh•nah deh peek•neek*
the pond	**el estanque** *ehl ehs•tahn•keh*
the river	**el río** *ehl ree•oh*
the sea	**el mar** *ehl mahr*
the (thermal) spring	**el manantial (de aguas termales)** *ehl mah•nahn•teeyahl (deh ah•gwahs tehr•mah•lehs)*
the stream	**el arroyo** *ehl ah•rroh•yoh*
the valley	**el valle** *ehl bah•yeh*
the vineyard	**la viña** *lah bee•nyah*
the waterfall	**la cascada** *lah kahs•kah•dah*

Going Out

ESSENTIAL

What's there to do at night?	**¿Qué se puede hacer por las noches?** *keh seh pweh•deh ah•thehr pohr lahs noh•chehs*
Do you have a program of events?	**¿Tiene un programa de espectáculos?** *teeyeh•neh oon proh•grah•mah deh ehs•pehk•tah•koo•lohs*
What's playing tonight?	**¿Qué hay en cartelera esta noche?** *keh aye ehn kahr•teh•leh•rah ehs•tah noh•cheh*
Where's...?	**¿Dónde está...?** *dohn•deh ehs•tah...*
the downtown area	**el centro** *ehl thehn•troh*
the bar	**el bar** *ehl bahr*
the dance club	**la discoteca** *lah dees•koh•teh•kah*
Is there a cover charge?	**¿Hay que pagar entrada?** *aye keh pah•gahr ehn•trah•dah*

Spain is famous for its centuries-old tradition of bullfighting. Known as **tauromaquia** or **corrida de toros**, bullfighting is seen as an art and tradition by many, and as a cruel and violent act against animals by others. Whether you find it fascinating or appalling, the bullfight is a unique experience in Spain. The bullfighting season runs from March to October; many towns have a vibrant festival in March to open the season.

Entertainment

Can you recommend…?	**¿Puede recomendarme…?** _pweh_•deh _reh_•koh•mehn•_dahr_•meh…
a concert	**un concierto** oon kohn•_theeyehr_•toh
a movie	**una película** _oo_•nah peh•_lee_•koo•lah
an opera	**una ópera** _oo_•nah _oh_•peh•rah
a play	**una obra de teatro** _oo_•nah _oh_•brah deh teh•_ah_•troh
When does it start/end?	**¿A qué hora empieza/termina?** ah keh _oh_•rah ehm•_peeyeh_•thah/tehr•_mee_•nah
What's the dress code?	**¿Cómo hay que ir vestido _m_/vestida _f_?** _koh_•moh aye keh eer behs•_tee_•doh/behs•_tee_•dah
I like…	**Me gusta…** meh _goos_•tah…
classical music	**la música clásica** lah _moo_•see•kah _klah_•see•kah
folk music	**la música folk** lah _moo_•see•kah folk
jazz	**el jazz** ehl jazz
pop music	**la música pop** lah _moo_•see•kah pop
rap	**el rap** ehl rap

For Tickets, see page 19.

Nightlife

What's there to do at night?	**¿Qué se puede hacer por las noches?** *keh seh pweh•deh ah•thehr pohr lahs noh•chehs*
Can you recommend...?	**¿Puede recomendarme...?** *pweh•deh reh•koh•mehn•dahr•meh...*
a bar	**un bar** *oon bahr*
a cabaret	**un cabaré** *oon kah•bah•reh*
a casino	**un casino** *oon kah•see•noh*
a dance club	**una discoteca** *oo•nah dees•koh•teh•kah*
a flamenco performance	**un espectáculo de flamenco** *oon ehs•pehk•tah•koo•loh deh flah•mehn•koh*
a gay club	**una discoteca gay** *oo•nah dees•koh•teh•kah gay*

Tourist offices, travel agencies and guidebooks have extensive information regarding events throughout Spain. Dates of some annual events change each year, so check before you go. For listings of local events, check the daily newspapers or ask at your hotel or the local tourist office. Larger cities in Spain have many entertainment magazines and publications that are a good source for information. A few of the most popular annual events are listed below.

Carnaval is the festival that takes place the week before Lent. It's the Spanish equivalent of Mardi Gras.

Traditional Holy Week festivities are centered around Catholicism. Seville has some of the most spectacular and elaborate processional re-enactments of the religious events of Easter. Valencia is famous for building, then torching, giant papier-mâché figures.

The **Fiesta de San Fermín** is one of Spain's most famous events. The running of the bulls is an annual event that draws thousands of people to Pamplona and is televised worldwide.

YOU MAY HEAR...

Por favor apaguen sus teléfonos móviles.
*pohr fah·bohr ah·pah·gehn soos
teh·leh·foh·nohs moh·bee·lehs*

Turn off your cell
[mobile] phones,
please.

a jazz club	**un club de jazz** *oon kloob deh jazz*
a club with Spanish music	**un bar con música española** *oon bahr kohn moo·see·kah ehs·pah·nyoh·lah*
Is there live music?	**¿Hay música en vivo?** *aye moo·see·kah ehn bee·boh*
How do I get there?	**¿Cómo se llega allí?** *koh·moh seh yeh·gah ah·yee*
Is there a cover charge?	**¿Hay que pagar entrada?** *aye keh pah·gahr ehn·trah·dah*
Let's go dancing.	**Vamos a bailar.** *bah·mohs ah bayee·lahr*
Is this area safe at night?	**¿Esta zona es segura por la noche?** *ehs·tah tho·nah ehs seh·goo·rah pohr lah noh·cheh*

One of Spain's greatest cultural achievements is the **flamenco**.
A combination of music, song and dance, the **flamenco** is an
emotional performance that should not be missed when you are in
Spain. Major cities such as Madrid, Seville and other Andalucian towns
have **flamenco** performances year round. A **peña** is a small, intimate
membership club (some allow guests) where you can view **flamenco**
performed. **Tablaos** are typical public venues for **flamenco**. Seeing
flamenco at a **tablao** can be an expensive night out, but well worth
the money.

Special Requirements

Business Travel

ESSENTIAL

I'm here on business.	**Estoy aquí en viaje de negocios.** ehs·_toy_ ah·_kee_ ehn _beeyah_·kheh deh neh·_goh_·theeyohs
Here's my business card.	**Aquí tiene mi tarjeta.** ah·_kee_ teeyeh·neh mee tahr·_kheh_·tah
Can I have your card?	**¿Puede darme su tarjeta?** _pweh_·deh _dahr_·meh soo tahr·_kheh_·tah
I have a meeting with...	**Tengo una reunión con...** _tehn_·goh _oo_·nah rewoo·_neeyohn_ kohn...
Where's...?	**¿Dónde está...?** _dohn_·deh ehs·_tah_...
the business center	**el centro de negocios** ehl _thehn_·troh deh neh·_goh_·theeyohs
the convention hall	**el salón de congresos** ehl sah·_lohn_ deh kohn·_greh_·sohs
the meeting room	**la sala de reuniones** lah _sah_·lah deh rewoo·_neeyohn_·ehs

On Business

I'm here to attend...	**Estoy aquí para asistir...** ehs·_toy_ ah·_kee_ _pah_·rah ah·sees·_teer_...
a seminar	**a un seminario** ah oon seh·mee·_nah_·reeyoh
a conference	**a una conferencia** ah _oo_·nah kohn·feh·_rehn_·theeyah
a meeting	**a una reunión** ah _oo_·nah rewoo·_neeyohn_
My name is...	**Me llamo...** meh _yah_·moh...
May I introduce my colleague...	**Le presento a mi compañero** m/**compañera** f **de trabajo...** leh preh·_sehn_·toh ah mee kohm·pah·_nyeh_·roh/kohm·pah·_nyeh_·rah deh trah·_bah_·khoh...

I have a meeting/an appointment with...	**Tengo una reunión/cita con...** _tehn·goh oo·nah rewoo·neeyohn/thee·tah kohn..._
I'm sorry I'm late.	**Perdone que haya llegado tarde.** _pehr·doh·neh keh ah·yah yeh·gah·doh tahr·deh_
I need an interpreter.	**Necesito un intérprete.** _neh·theh·see·toh oon een·tehr·preh·teh_
You can contact me at the...Hotel.	**Puede contactarme en el Hotel...** _pweh·deh kohn·tahk·tahr·meh ehn ehl oh·tehl..._
I'm here until...	**Estaré aquí hasta...** _ehs·tah·reh ah·kee ahs·tah..._
I need to...	**Necesito...** _neh·theh·see·toh..._
make a call	**hacer una llamada** _ah·thehr oo·nah yah·mah·dah_
make a photocopy	**hacer una fotocopia** _ah·thehr oo·nah foh·toh·koh·peeyah_
send an e-mail	**enviar un correo electrónico** _ehn·beeyahr oon koh·rreh·oh ee·lehk·troh·nee·koh_
send a fax	**enviar un fax** _ehn·beeyahr oon fahx_
send a package (for next-day delivery)	**enviar un paquete (para entrega el día siguiente)** _ehn·beeyahr oon pah·keh·teh (pah·rah ehn·treh·gah ehl dee·ah see·geeyehn·teh)_
It was a pleasure to meet you.	**Ha sido un placer conocerle m/conocerla f.** _ah see·doh oon plah·thehr koh·noh·thehr·leh/koh·noh·thehr·lah_

For Communications, see page 49.

It is common to greet colleagues with **buenos días** (good day). Shake hands if it is the first time you are meeting someone in a professional setting, or if it is someone you haven't seen in a while. When leaving, simply say **adiós, gracias** (goodbye, thank you).

YOU MAY HEAR...

¿Tiene cita? _teeyeh_•neh _thee_•tah	Do you have an appointment?
¿Con quién? _kohn keeyehn_	With whom?
Está en una reunión. _ehs-_tah_ ehn _oo_•nah rewoo•_neeyohn_	He/She is in a meeting.
Un momento, por favor. _oon moh-_mehn_•toh pohr fah-_bohr_	One moment, please.
Siéntese. _theeyehn_•teh•seh	Have a seat.
¿Quiere algo de beber? _keeyeh_•reh _ahl_•goh deh beh-_behr_	Would you like something to drink?
Gracias por su visita. _grah_•theeyahs pohr soo bee-_see_•tah	Thank you for coming.

Traveling with Children

ESSENTIAL

Is there a discount for kids?	**¿Hacen descuento a niños?** _ah_•then dehs-_kwehn_•toh ah _nee_•nyohs
Can you recommend a babysitter?	**¿Puede recomendarme una canguro?** _pweh_•deh reh-koh-mehn-_dahr_•meh _oo_•nah kahn-_goo_•roh
Do you have a child's seat/highchair?	**¿Tienen una silla para niños/trona?** _teeyeh_•nehn _oo_•nah _see_•yah _pah_•rah _nee_•nyohs/_troh_•nah
Where can I change the baby?	**¿Dónde puedo cambiar al bebé?** _dohn_•deh _pweh_•doh kahm-_beeyahr_ ahl beh-_beh_

Out & About

Can you recommend something for kids?	**¿Puede recomendarme algo para los niños?** _pweh·deh reh·koh·mehn·<u>dahr</u>·meh <u>ahl</u>·goh pah·rah lohs <u>nee</u>·nyohs_
Where's...?	**¿Dónde está...?** _<u>dohn</u>·deh ehs·<u>tah</u>..._
the amusement park	**el parque de atracciones** _ehl <u>pahr</u>·keh deh ah·trahk·<u>theeyoh</u>·nehs_
the arcade	**el salón de juegos recreativos** _ehl sah·<u>lohn</u> deh <u>khweh</u>·gohs reh·kreh·ah·<u>tee</u>·bohs_
the kiddie [paddling] pool	**la piscina infantil** _lah pees·<u>thee</u>·nah een·fahn·<u>teel</u>_
the park	**el parque** _ehl <u>pahr</u>·keh_
the playground	**el parque infantil** _ehl <u>pahr</u>·keh een·fahn·<u>teel</u>_
the zoo	**el zoológico** _ehl thoh·oh·<u>loh</u>·khee·koh_
Are kids allowed?	**¿Se permite la entrada a niños?** _she pehr·<u>mee</u>·teh lah ehn·<u>trah</u>·dah ah <u>nee</u>·nyohs_
Is it safe for kids?	**¿Es seguro para niños?** _ehs seh·<u>goo</u>·roh pah·rah <u>nee</u>·nyohs_
Is it suitable for... year olds?	**¿Es apto para niños de...años?** _ehs <u>ahp</u>·toh <u>pah</u>·rah <u>nee</u>·nyohs deh... <u>ah</u>·nyohs_

For Numbers, see page 167.

YOU MAY HEAR...

¡Qué mono _m_/mona _f_! _keh <u>moh</u>·noh/<u>moh</u>·nah_	How cute!
¿Cómo se llama? _<u>koh</u>·moh seh <u>yah</u>·mah_	What's his/her name?
¿Qué edad tiene? _keh eh·<u>dahth</u> <u>teeyeh</u>·neh_	How old is he/she?

Baby Essentials

Do you have…?	**¿Tiene…?** _teeyeh·neh…_
a baby bottle	**un biberón** _oon bee·beh·rohn_
baby food	**la papilla** _lah papeeyah_
baby wipes	**toallitas** _toh·ah·yee·tahs_
a car seat	**un asiento para niños** _oon ah·seeyehn toh pah·rah nee·nyohs_
a children's menu/portion	**un menú/una ración para niños** _oon meh·noo/ oo·nah rah·theeyohn pah·rah nee·nyohs_
a child's seat/ highchair	**una silla para niños/trona** _oo·nah see·yah pah·rah nee·nyohs/troh·nah_
a crib/cot	**una cuna/un catre** _oo·nah koo·nah/oon kah·treh_
diapers [nappies]	**pañales** _pah·nyah·lehs_
formula	**fórmula infantil** _fohr·moo·lah een·fahn·teel_
a pacifier [dummy]	**un chupete** _oon choo·peh·teh_
a playpen	**un parque** _oon pahr·keh_
a stroller [pushchair]	**un cochecito** _oon koh·cheh·thee·toh_
Can I breastfeed the baby here?	**¿Puedo darle el pecho al bebé aquí?** _pweh·doh dahr·leh ehl peh·choh ahl beh·beh ah·kee_
Where can I change the baby?	**¿Dónde puedo cambiar al bebé?** _dohn·deh pweh·doh kahm·beeyahr ahl beh·beh_

Babysitting

Can you recommend a babysitter?	**¿Puede recomendarme una canguro?** _pweh·deh reh·koh·mehn·dahr·meh oo·nah kahn·goo·roh_
How much do they charge?	**¿Cuánto cuesta?** _kwahn·toh kwehs·tah_
I'll be back by…	**Vuelvo a la/las…** _bwehl·boh ah lah/lahs…_
If you need to contact me, call…	**Puede contactarme en el…** _pweh·deh kohn·tahk·tahr·meh ehn ehl…_

For Grammar, see page 162.

Health & Emergency

Can you recommend a pediatrician?	**¿Puede recomendarme un pediatra?** _pweh•deh reh•koh•mehn•dahr•meh oon peh•deeyah•trah_
My child is allergic to...	**Mi hijo m /hija f es alérgico m /alérgica f a...** _mee ee•khoh/ee•khah ehs ah•lehr•khee•koh/ ah•lehr•khee•kah ah..._
My child is missing.	**Mi hijo m /hija f ha desaparecido.** _mee ee•khoh/ ee•khah ah deh•sah•pah•reh•thee•doh_
Have you seen a boy/girl?	**¿Ha visto a un niño m /una niña f ?** _ah bees•toh ah oon nee•nyoh/oo•nah nee•nyah_

Disabled Travelers

ESSENTIAL

Is there...?	**¿Hay...?** _aye..._
access for the disabled	**acceso para los discapacitados** _ahk•theh•soh pah•rah lohs dees•kah•pah•thee•tah•dohs_
a wheelchair ramp	**una rampa para sillas de ruedas** _oo•nah rahm•pah pah•rah see•yahs deh rweh•dahs_

a disabled-accessible toilet	**un baño con acceso para discapacitados** *oon bah·nyoh kohn ahk·theh·soh pah·rah dees·kah·pah·th/ee·tah·dohs*
I need…	**Necesito…** *neh·theh·see·toh…*
assistance	**ayuda** *ah·yoo·dah*
an elevator [a lift]	**un ascensor** *oon ahs·thehn·sohr*
a ground-floor room	**una habitación en la planta baja** *oo·nah ah·bee·tah·theeyohn ehn lah plahn·tah bah·khah*

Asking for Assistance

I'm disabled.	**Soy discapacitado** *m*/**discapacitada** *f soy dees·kah·pah·thee·tah·doh/ dees·kah·pah·thee·tah·dah*
I'm deaf.	**Soy sordo** *m*/**sorda** *f.* *soy sohr·doh/sohr·dah*
I'm visually/hearing impaired.	**Tengo discapacidad visual/auditiva.** *tehn·goh dees·kah·pah·thee·dahd bee·swahl/ awoo·dee·tee·bah*
I'm unable to walk far/use the stairs.	**No puedo caminar muy lejos/subir las escaleras.** *noh pweh·doh kah·mee·nahr mooy leh·khohs/ soo·beer lahs ehs·kah·leh·rahs*
Can I bring my wheelchair?	**¿Puedo traer la silla de ruedas?** *pweh·doh trah·ehr lah see·yah deh rweh·dahs*
Are guide dogs permitted?	**¿Permiten a perros guía?** *pehr·mee·tehn ah peh·rrohs gee·ah*
Can you help me?	**¿Puede ayudarme?** *pweh·deh ah·yoo·dahr·meh*
Please open/hold the door.	**Por favor, abra/aguante la puerta.** *pohr fah·bohr ah·brah/ah·gwahn·teh lah pwehr·tah*

In an Emergency

Emergencies

ESSENTIAL

Help!	**¡Socorro!** soh·<u>koh</u>·rroh
Go away!	**¡Lárguese!** <u>lahr</u>·geh·seh
Stop, thief!	**¡Deténgase, ladrón!** deh·<u>tehn</u>·gah·seh lah·<u>drohn</u>
Get a doctor!	**¡Llame a un médico!** <u>yah</u>·meh ah oon <u>meh</u>·dee·koh
Fire!	**¡Fuego!** <u>fweh</u>·goh
I'm lost.	**Me he perdido.** meh eh pehr·<u>dee</u>·doh
Can you help me?	**¿Puede ayudarme?** <u>pweh</u>·deh ah·yoo·<u>dahr</u>·meh

In an emergency, dial: **112** for the police
080 for the fire brigade
061 for the ambulance.

YOU MAY HEAR...

Rellene este impreso. reh·<u>yeh</u>·neh ehs·teh eem·<u>preh</u>·soh — Fill out this form.

Su documento de identidad, por favor. soo doh·koo·<u>mehn</u>·toh deh ee·dehn·tee·<u>dahd</u> pohr fah·<u>bohr</u> — Your identification, please.

¿Cuándo/Dónde ocurrió? <u>kwahn</u>·doh/<u>dohn</u>·deh oh·koo·<u>rreeyoh</u> — When/Where did it happen?

¿Puede describirle?/describirla? <u>pweh</u>·deh dehs·kree·<u>beer</u>·leh?/dehs·kree·<u>beer</u>·lah? — What does he/she look like?

Police

ESSENTIAL

Call the police!	**¡Llame a la policía!**	*yah•meh ah lah poh•lee•thee•ah*
Where's the police station?	**¿Dónde está la comisaría?**	*dohn•deh ehs•tah lah koh•mee•sah•ree•ah*
There was an accident/attack.	**Ha habido un accidente/asalto.**	*ah ah•bee•doh oon ahk•thee•dehn•teh/ah•sahl•toh*
My son/daughter is missing.	**Mi hijo m/hija f ha desaparecido.**	*mee ee•khoh/ee•khah ah deh•sah•pah•reh•thee•doh*
I need…	**Necesito…**	*neh•theh•see•toh…*
an interpreter	**un intérprete**	*oon een•tehr•preh•teh*
to contact my lawyer	**ponerme en contacto con mi abogado**	*poh•nehr•meh ehn kohn•tahk•toh kohn mee ah•boh•gah•doh*
to make a phone call	**hacer una llamada**	*ah•thehr oo•nah yah•mah•dah*
I'm innocent.	**Soy inocente.**	*soy ee•noh•thehn•teh*

Crime & Lost Property

I'd like to report…	**Quiero denunciar…**	*keeyeh•roh deh•noon•theeyahr…*
a mugging	**un asalto**	*oon uh•sahl•toh*
a rape	**una violación**	*oo•nah beeyoh•lah•theeyohn*
a theft	**un robo**	*oon roh•boh*
I've been mugged/robbed.	**Me han asaltado/atracado.**	*meh ahn ah•sahl•tah•doh/ah•trah•kah•doh*
I've lost my…	**He perdido…**	*eh pehr•dee•doh…*
My…was stolen.	**Me han robado…**	*meh ahn•roh•bah•doh…*
backpack	**la mochila**	*lah moh•chee•lah*
bicycle	**la bicicleta**	*lah bee•thee•kleh•tah*

camera	**la cámara** *lah kah•mah•rah*
(hire) car	**el coche (de alquiler)** *ehl koh•cheh (deh ahl•kee•lehr)*
computer	**el ordenador** *ehl ohr•deh•nah•dohr*
credit card	**la tarjeta de crédito** *lah tahr•kheh•tah deh kreh•dee•toh*
jewelry	**las joyas** *lahs khoh•yahs*
money	**el dinero** *ehl dee•neh•roh*
passport	**el pasaporte** *ehl pah•sah•pohr•teh*
purse [handbag]	**el bolso** *ehl bohl•soh*
traveler's cheques	**los cheques de viaje** *lohs cheh•kehs deh beeyah•kheh*
wallet	**la cartera** *lah kahr•teh•rah*
I need a police report.	**Necesito un certificado de la policía.** *neh•theh•see•toh oon thehr•tee•fee•kah•doh deh lah poh•lee•thee•ah*
Where is the British/American/Irish embassy?	**¿Dónde está la embajada británica/americana/irlandesa?** *dohn•deh ehs•tah lah ehm•bah•khah•dah bree•tah•nee•kah/ah•meh•ree•kah•nah/eer•lahn•deh•sah*

ESSENTIAL

I'm sick [ill].	**Me encuentro mal.** meh ehn•kwehn•troh mahl
I need an English-speaking doctor.	**Necesito un médico que hable inglés.** neh•theh•see•toh oon meh•dee•koh keh ah•bleh een•glehs
It hurts here.	**Me duele aquí.** meh dweh•leh ah•kee
I have a stomachache.	**Tengo dolor de estómago.** tehn•goh doh•lohr deh ehs•toh•mah•goh

Finding a Doctor

Can you recommend a doctor/dentist?	**¿Puede recomendarme un médico/dentista?** pweh•deh reh•koh•mehn•dahr•meh oon meh•dee•koh/dehn•tees•tah
Can the doctor come here?	**¿Podría el médico venir aquí?** poh•dree•ah ehl meh•dee•koh beh•neer uh•kee
I need an English-speaking doctor.	**Necesito un médico que hable inglés.** neh•theh•see•toh oon meh•dee•koh keh ah•bleh cen•glehs
What are the office hours?	**¿Cuáles son las horas de consulta?** kwah•lehs sohn lahs oh•rahs deh kohn•sool•tah
I'd like an appointment...	**Quiero una cita...** keeyeh•roh oo•nah thee•tah...
for today	**para hoy** pah•rah ohy
for tomorrow	**para mañana** pah•rah mah•nyah•nah
as soon as possible	**lo antes posible** loh ahn•tehs poh•see•bleh
It's urgent.	**Es urgente.** ehs oor•khehn•teh

Symptoms

I'm…	**Estoy…** *ehs•toy…*
bleeding	**sangrando** *sahn•grahn•doh*
constipated	**estreñido** *m*/**estreñida** *f ehs•treh•nyee•doh/ ehs•treh•nyee•dah*
dizzy	**mareado** *m*/**mareada** *f mah•reh•ah•doh/ mah•reh•ah•dah*
I'm nauseous	**Tengo náuseas.** *tehn•goh naw•seh•ahs*
I'm vomiting.	**Tengo vómitos.** *tehn•goh boh•mee•tohs*
It hurts here.	**Me duele aquí.** *meh dweh•leh ah•kee*
I have…	**Tengo…** *tehn•goh…*
an allergic reaction	**una reacción alérgica** *oo•nah reh•ahk•theeyohn ah•lehr•khee•kah*
chest pain	**dolor de pecho** *doh•lohr deh peh•choh*
cramps	**calambres** *kah•lahm•brehs*
diarrhea	**diarrea** *deeyah•rreh•ah*
an earache	**dolor de oído** *doh•lohr deh oh•ee•doh*
a fever	**fiebre** *feeyeh•breh*
pain	**dolor** *doh•lohr*
a rash	**una erupción cutánea** *oo•nah eh•roop•theeyohn koo•tah•nee•ah*
a sprain	**un esguince** *oon ehs•geen•theh*
some swelling	**una hinchazón** *oo•nah een•chah•thohn*
a stomachache	**dolor de estómago** *doh•lohr deh ehs•toh•mah•goh*
sunstroke	**una insolación** *oo•nah een•soh•lah•theeyohn*
I've been sick [ill] for…days.	**Llevo…días que me encuentro mal.** *yeh•boh…dee•ahs keh meh ehn•kwehn•troh mahl*

For Numbers, see page 167.

Conditions

I'm...	**Soy...** *soy...*
anemic	**anémico** *m*/**anémica** *f ah·neh·mee·koh/ ah·neh·mee·kah*
asthmatic	**asmático** *m*/**asmática** *f ahs·mah·tee·koh/ ahs·mah·tee·kah*
diabetic	**diabético** *m*/**diabética** *f deeyah·beh·tee·koh/ deeyah·beh·tee·kah*
epileptic	**epiléptico** *m*/**epileptica** *f eh·pee·lehp·tee·koh/ eh·pee·lehp·tee·kah*
I'm allergic to antibiotics/penicillin.	**Soy alérgico** *m*/**alérgica** *f* **a los antibióticos/ la penicilina**. *soy ah·lehr·khee·koh/ah·lehr·khee·kah ah lohs ahn·tee·beeyoh·tee·kohs/ lah peh·nee·thee·lee·nah*

YOU MAY HEAR...

¿Qué le pasa? *keh leh pah·sah*	What's wrong?
¿Dónde le duele? *dohn·deh leh dweh·leh*	Where does it hurt?
¿Le duele aquí? *leh dweh·leh ah·kee*	Does it hurt here?
¿Esta tomando algún medicamento? *ehs·tah toh·mahn·doh ahl·goon meh·dee·kah·mehn·toh*	Are you on medication?
¿Es alérgico *m*/**alérgica** *f* **a algo?** *ehs ah·lehr·khee·koh/ah·lehr·khee·kah ah ahl·goh*	Are you allergic to anything?
Abra la boca. *ah·brah lah boh·kah*	Open your mouth.
Respire hondo. *rehs·pee·reh ohn·doh*	Breathe deeply.
Tiene que ir al hospital. *teeyeh·neh keh eer ahl ohs·pee·tahl*	You/he/she must go to the hospital.

I have...	**Tengo...** _tehn_·goh
arthritis	**artritis** ahr·_tree_·tees
(high/low) blood pressure.	**la tensión (alta/baja).** lah tehn·_seeyohn_ (_ahl_·tah/_bah_·khah)
I have a heart condition.	**Padezco del corazón.** pah·_dehth_·koh dehl koh·rah·_thon_
I'm on...	**Estoy tomando...** ehs·_toy_ toh·_mahn_·doh...

For Meals & Cooking, see page 66.

Treatment

Do I need a prescription/ medicine?	**¿Necesito una receta/un medicamento?** neh·theh·_see_·toh _oo_·nah reh·_theh_·tah/ oon meh·dee·kah·_mehn_·toh
Can you prescribe a generic drug? [unbranded medication]?	**¿Puede recetarme un medicamento genérico?** pweh·deh reh·theh·tahr·meh oon meh·dee·kah·mehn·toh kheh·neh·ree·koh
Where can I get it?	**¿Dónde puedo conseguirlo?** dohn·de pweh·doh kohn·seh·geer·loh

For What to Take, see page 159.

Hospital

Notify my family, please.	**Por favor, avise a mi familia.** pohr fah·_bohr_ ah·_bee_·seh ah mee fah·_mee_·leeyah
I'm in pain.	**Tengo dolor.** _tehn_·goh doh·_lohr_
I need a doctor/nurse.	**Necesito un médico/una enfermera.** neh·thee·_see_·toh oon _meh_·dee·koh/_oo_·nah ehn·fehr·_meh_·rah
When are visiting hours?	**¿Qué horas de visita tienen?** keh _oh_·rahs deh bee·_see_·tah _teeyeh_·nehn
I'm visiting...	**Vengo a hacer una visita a...** _behn_·goh ah ah·_thehr_ _oo_·nah bee·_see_·tah ah...

Dentist

I've broken a tooth/lost a filling.	**Se me ha roto un diente/caído un empaste.** *seh meh ah roh•toh oon deeyehn•teh/ kah•ee•doh oon ehm•pahs•teh*
I have a toothache.	**Tengo dolor de muelas.** *tehn•goh doh•lohr deh mweh•lahs*
Can you fix this denture?	**¿Puede arreglarme la dentadura postiza?** *pweh•deh ah•rreh•glahr•meh lah dehn•tah•doo•rah pohs•tee•thah*

Gynecologist

I have menstrual cramps/a vaginal infection.	**Tengo dolores menstruales/una infección vaginal.** *tehn•goh doh•loh•rehs mehns•trwah•lehs/ oo nah oon•fehk•theeyohn bah•khee•nahl*
I missed my period.	**No me ha venido la regla.** *noh meh ah beh•nee•doh lah reh•glah*
I'm on the Pill.	**Tomo la píldora.** *toh•moh lah peel•doh•rah*
I'm (... months) pregnant.	**Estoy embarazada (de... meses).** *esh•toy ehm•bah•rah•thah•dah (deh... meh•sehs)*
I'm not pregnant.	**No estoy embarazada.** *noh ehs•toy ehm•bah•rah•thah•dah*

My last period was... **La última vez que me vino la regla fue...**
*lah ool·tee·mah behth keh meh bee·noh lah
reh·glah fweh...*

For Numbers see page 167.

Optician

I've lost...	**He perdido...** *eh pehr·dee·doh...*
a contact lens	**una lentilla** *oo·nah lehn·tee·yah*
my glasses	**las gafas** *lahs gah·fahs*
a lens	**una lente** *oo·nah lehn·teh*

Payment & Insurance

How much?	**¿Cuánto es?** *kwahn·toh ehs*
Can I pay by credit card?	**¿Puedo pagar con tarjeta de crédito?** *pweh·doh pah·gahr kohn tahr·kheh·tah deh kreh·dee·toh*
I have insurance.	**Tengo seguro médico.** *tehn·goh seh·goo·roh meh·dee·koh*
I need a receipt for my insurance.	**Necesito una factura para el seguro médico.** *neh·theh·see·toh oo·nah fahk·too·rah pah·rah ehl seh·goo·roh meh·dee·koh*

Pharmacy

ESSENTIAL

Where's the pharmacy?	**¿Dónde está la farmacia?** *dohn·deh ehs·tah lah fahr·mah·theeyah*
What time does it open/close?	**¿A qué hora abre/cierra?** *ah keh oh·rah ah·breh/theeyeh·rrah*
What would you recommend for...?	**¿Qué me recomienda para...?** *keh meh reh·koh·meeyehn·dah pah·rah...*

How much do I take?	**¿Qué dosis me tomo?** *keh doh·sees meh toh·moh*
Can you fill [make up] this prescription?	**¿Puede darme este medicamento?** *pweh·deh dahr·meh ehs·the meh·dee·kah·mehn·toh*
I'm allergic to...	**Soy alérgico m/alérgica f a...** *soy ah·lehr·khee·koh/ah·lehr·khee·kah ah...*

Pharmacies are easily identified by their green neon signs in the shape of a cross. Opening hours are generally from 9:00 a.m. until 1:30 p.m., closed for **siesta** in teh afternoon and then open from 4:30 p.m. until 8:00 p.m. There are 24-hour pharmacies available in larger cities. A list of pharmacies that are open at night or on weekends can be found in the windows of all pharmacies, and the list is also published in the local newspapers.

What to Take

How much do I take?	**¿Qué dosis me tomo?** *keh doh·sees meh toh·moh*
How often?	**¿Con qué frecuencia?** *kohn keh freh·kwehn·theeyah*
Is it safe for children?	**¿Está indicado para niños?** *ehs·tah een·dee·kah·doh pah·rah nee·nyohs*
I'm taking...	**Estoy tomando...** *ehs·toy toh·mahn·doh...*
Are there side effects?	**¿Tiene algún efecto secundario?** *teeyeh·neh ahl·goon eh·tehk·toh seh·koon·duh·reeyoh*
I need something for...	**Necesito algo para...** *neh·theh·see·toh ahl·goh pah·rah...*
a cold	**el catarro** *ehl kah·tah·rroh*
a cough	**la tos** *lah tohs*
diarrhea	**la diarrea** *lah deeyah·rreh·ah*

a headache	**el dolor de cabeza**	ehl doh•lohr deh kah•beh•thah
insect bites	**las picaduras de insecto**	lahs pee•kah•<u>doo</u>•rahs deh een•<u>sehk</u>•toh
motion [travel] sickness	**la cinetosis**	lah thee•neh•<u>toh</u>•sees
a sore throat	**las anginas**	lahs ahn•<u>khee</u>•nahs
sunburn	**la quemadura solar**	lah keh•mah•<u>doo</u>•rah soh•<u>lahr</u>
a toothache	**el dolor de muelas**	ehl doh•lohr deh moo•eh•lahs
an upset stomach	**el malestar estomacal**	ehl mah•lehs•<u>tahr</u> ehs•toh•mah•<u>kahl</u>

YOU MAY SEE...

UNA VEZ/TRES VECES AL DÍA	once/three times a day
COMPRIMIDO	tablet
GOTA	drop
CUCHARADITA	teaspoon
DESPUÉS DE/ANTES DE/CON LAS COMIDAS	after/before/with meals
CON EL ESTÓMAGO VACÍO	on an empty stomach
TRAGUE EL COMPRIMIDO ENTERO	swallow whole
PUEDE CAUSAR SOMNOLENCIA	may cause drowsiness
DE USO TÓPICO SOLAMENTE	for external use only

Basic Supplies

I'd like...	**Quiero...**	<u>keeyeh</u>•roh...
acetaminophen [paracetamol]	**paracetamol**	pah•rah•thee•tah•<u>mohl</u>
antiseptic cream	**crema antiséptica**	<u>kreh</u>•mah ahn•tee•<u>sehp</u>•tee•kah
aspirin	**aspirinas**	ahs•pee•<u>ree</u>•nahs
bandages	**tiritas**	tee•<u>ree</u>•tahs

a comb	**un peine** *oon peyee-neh*
condoms	**preservativos** *preh-sehr-bah-tee-bohs*
contact lens solution	**líquido de lentillas** *lee-kee-doh deh lehn-tee-yahs*
deodorant	**desodorante** *deh-soh-doh-rahn-teh*
a hairbrush	**un cepillo de pelo** *oon theh-pee-yoh deh peh-loh*
hairspray	**laca** *lah-kah*
ibuprofen	**ibuprofeno** *ee-boo-proh-feh-noh*
insect repellent	**repelente de insectos** *reh-peh-lehn-the deh een-sehk-tohs*
lotion	**crema hidratante** *kreh-mah ee-drah-tahn-teh*
a nail file	**una lima de uñas** *oo-nah lee-mah deh oo-nyahs*
a (disposable) razor	**una cuchilla** *oo-nah koo-chee-yah*
razor blades	**hojas de afeitar** *oh-khahs deh ah-feyee-tahr*
sanitary napkins [towels]	**compresas** *kohm-preh-sahs*
shampoo/ conditioner	**champú/suavizante** *chahm-poo/ swah-bee-thahn-teh*
soap	**jabón** *khah-bohn*
sunscreen	**protector solar** *proh-tehk-tohr soh-lahr*
tampons	**tampones** *tahm-poh-nehs*
tissues	**pañuelos de papel** *pah-nyweh-lohs deh pah-pehl*
toilet paper	**papel higiénico** *pah-pehl ee-kheeyeh-nee-koh*
a toothbrush	**un cepillo de dientes** *oon theh-pee-yoh deh deeyehn-tehs*
toothpaste	**pasta de dientes** *pahs-tah deh deeyehn-tehs*

For Baby Essentials, see page 146.

The Basics

Grammar

In Spanish, there are a number of forms for 'you' (taking different verb forms): **tú** (singular) and **vosotros** *m* / **vosotras** *f* (plural) are used when talking to relatives, close friends and children; **usted** (singular) and **ustedes** (plural) are used in all other cases. If in doubt, use **usted/ustedes**. The following abbreviations are used in this section: Ud. = Usted; Uds. = Ustedes; sing. = singular; pl. = plural; inf. = informal; for. = formal.

Regular Verbs

There are three verb types that follow a regular conjugation pattern. These verbs end in **−ar**, **−er** and **−ir**. Following are the present, past and future forms of the verbs **hablar** (to speak), **comer** (to eat) and **vivir** (to live). The different conjugation endings are in bold.

HABLAR		Present	Past	Future
I	**yo**	habl**o**	habl**é**	habl**aré**
you (sing.)	**tú**	habl**as**	habl**aste**	habl**arás**
he/she/you	**él/ella/Ud.**	habl**a**	habl**ó**	habl**ará**
we	**nosotros**	habl**amos**	habl**amos**	habl**aremos**
you (pl.)	**vosotros** *m* **vosotras** *f*	habl**áis**	habl**asteis**	habl**aréis**
they/you	**ellos/ellas/ Uds.**	habl**an**	habl**aron**	habl**arán**

COMER		Present	Past	Future
I	**yo**	com**o**	com**í**	com**eré**
you (sing.)	**tú**	com**es**	com**iste**	com**erás**
he/she/you	**él/ella/Ud.**	com**e**	com**ió**	com**erá**
we	**nosotros**	com**emos**	com**imos**	com**eremos**

| you (pl.) | vosotros *m* vosotras *f* | coméis | comisteis | comeréis |
| they/you | ellos/ellas/ Uds. | comen | comieron | comerán |

VIVIR		Present	Past	Future
I	yo	vivo	viví	viviré
you (sing.)	tú	vives	viviste	vivirás
he/she/you	él/ella/Ud.	vive	vivió	vivirá
we	nosotros	vivimos	vivimos	viviremos
you (pl.)	vosotros *m* vosotras *f*	vivís	vivisteis	viviréis
they/you	ellos/ellas/ Uds.	viven	vivieron	vivirán

Irregular Verbs

In Spanish, there are many different irregular verbs; these aren't conjugated by following the normal rules. The two most commonly used, and confused, irregular verbs are **ser** and **estar**. Both verbs mean 'to be', but are used in different contexts (see page 164). Following is the past, present and future tenses of **ser** and **estar** for easy reference.

SER	Present	Past	Future
yo	soy	fui	seré
tú (sing.)	eres	fuiste	serás
él/ella/Ud.	es	fue	será
nosotros	somos	fuimos	seremos
vosotros *m* **vosotras** *f* (pl.)	sois	fuisteis	seréis
ellos/ellas/Uds.	son	fueron	serán

ESTAR	Present	Past	Future
yo	estoy	estuve	estaré
tú (sing.)	estás	estuviste	estarás
él/ella/Ud.	está	estuvo	estará
nosotros	estamos	estuvimos	estaremos
vosotros *m* **vosotras** *f* (pl.)	estáis	estuvisteis	estaréis
ellos/ellas/Uds.	están	estuvieron	estarán

Ser is used to describe a fixed quality or characteristic. It is also used to tell time and dates. Example: **Yo soy estadounidense.** I am American.
Here **ser** is used because it is a permanent characteristic.
Estar is used when describing a physical location or a temporary condition.
Example: **Estoy cansado.** I am tired.
Here **estar** is used because being tired is a temporary condition.

Word Order

In Spanish, the conjugated verb comes after the subject.
Example: **Yo trabajo en Madrid.** I work in Madrid.
To ask a question, reverse the order of the subject and verb, change your intonation or use key question words such as **cuándo** (when).
Examples: **¿Cuándo cierra el banco?** When does the bank close?
Literally translates to: 'When closes the bank?' Notice the order of the subject and verb is reversed; a question word also begins the sentence.
¿El hotel es viejo? Is the hotel old?
Literally, the hotel is old. This is a statement that becomes a question by raising the pitch of the last syllable of the sentence.

Negations

To form a negative sentence, add **no** (not) before the verb.
Example: **Fumamos.** We smoke.
No fumamos. We don't smoke.

Imperatives

Imperative sentences, or sentences that are a command, are formed by adding the appropriate ending to the stem of the verb (i.e. the verb in the infinitive without the **-ar**, **-er**, **-ir** ending). Example: Speak!

you (sing.) (inf.)	tú	**¡Habla!**
you (sing.) (for.)	Ud.	**¡Hable!**
we	nosotros	**¡Hablemos!**
you (inf.)	vosotros	**¡Hablad!**
you (pl.) (for.)	Uds.	**¡Hablen!**

Nouns & Articles

Nouns are either masculine or feminine. Masculine nouns usually end in **−o**, and feminine nouns usually end in **−a**. Nouns become plural by adding an **−s**, or **−es** to nouns not ending in **o** or **−a** (e.g. **tren** becomes **trenes**). Nouns in Spanish get an indefinite or definite article. An article must agree with the noun to which it refers in gender and number. Indefinite articles are the equivalent of 'a', 'an' or 'some' in English, while definite articles are the equivalent of 'the'.
Indefinite article examples: **un tren** *m* (a train); **unos trenes** *m* (some trains)**; una mesa** *f* (a table), **unas mesas** *f* (some tables)
Definite examples: **el libro** *m* (the book); **los libros** *m* (the books); **la casa** *f* (the house); **las casas** *f* (the houses)
A possessive adjective relates to the gender of the noun that follows and must agree in number and gender.

	Singular	Plural
my	**mi**	**mis**
your (sing.)	**tu**	**tus**
his/her/its/your	**su**	**sus**
our	**nuestro** *m*/**nuestra** *f*	**nuestros** *m*/**nuestras** *f*
your (pl.)	**vuestro** *m*/**vuestra** *f*	**vuestros** *m*/**vuestras** *f*
their/your	**su**	**sus**

Examples: **¿Dónde está <u>tu</u> chaqueta?** Where is your jacket?
<u>Vuestro</u> vuelo sale a las ocho. Your flight leaves at eight.

Adjectives

Adjectives describe nouns and must agree with the noun in gender and number. In Spanish, adjectives usually come after the noun. Masculine adjectives generally end in **–o**, feminine adjectives in **–a**. If the masculine form ends in **–e** or with a consonant, the feminine form is generally the same. Most adjectives form their plurals the same way as nouns.

Examples: **Su hijo *m*/hija *f* es simpatico *m*/simpatico *f*.** Your son/daughter is nice.

El mar *m*/La flor *f* es azul. The ocean/The flower is blue.

Comparatives & Superlatives

The comparative is usually formed by adding **más** (more) or **menos** (less) before the adjective or noun. The superlative is formed by adding the appropriate definite article (**la/las**, **el/los**) and **más** (the most) **menos** (the least) before the adjective or noun. Example:

grande	más grande	el *m*/la *f* más grande
big	bigger	biggest
caro *m*/cara *f*	menos caro *m*/cara *f*	el *m*/la *f* menos caro *m*/cara *f*
expensive	less expensive	least expensive

Possessive Pronouns

Pronouns serve as substitutes for specific nouns and must agree with the noun in gender and number.

	Singular	Plural
mine	**mío *m*/mía *f***	**míos *m*/mías *f***
yours (inf.)	**tuyo *m*/tuya *f***	**tuyos *m*/tuyas *f***
yours	**suyo *m*/suya *f***	**suyos *m*/suyas *f***

his/her/its	suyo *m*/suya *f*	suyos *m*/suyas *f*
ours	nuestro *m*/nuestra *f*	nuestros *m*/nuestras *f*
yours (inf.)	vuestro *m*/vuestra *f*	vuestros *m*/vuestras *f*
theirs	suyo *m*/suya *f*	suyos *m*/suyas *f*

Example: **Ese asiento es mío.** That seat is mine.

Adverbs & Adverbial Expressions

Adverbs are used to describe verbs. Some adverbs are formed by adding
-**mente** to the adjective.
Example: **Roberto conduce lentamente.** Robert drives slowly.
The following are some common adverbial time expressions:
actualmente presently
todavía no not yet
todavía still
ya no not anymore

Numbers

ESSENTIAL

0	**cero** *theh·roh*
1	**uno** *oo·noh*
2	**dos** *dohs*
3	**tres** *trehs*
4	**cuatro** *kwah·troh*
5	**cinco** *theen·koh*
6	**seis** *seyees*
7	**siete** *seeyeh·teh*
8	**ocho** *oh·choh*
9	**nueve** *nweh·beh*
10	**diez** *deeyehth*

11	**once** _ohn_·theh
12	**doce** _doh_·theh
13	**trece** _treh_·theh
14	**catorce** kah·_tohr_·theh
15	**quince** _keen_·theh
16	**dieciséis** deeyeh·thee·_seyees_
17	**diecisiete** deeyeh·thee·_seeyeh_·teh
18	**dieciocho** deeyeh·thee·_oh_·choh
19	**diecinueve** deeyeh·thee·_nweh_·beh
20	**veinte** _beyeen_·teh
21	**veintiuno** beyeen·tee·_oo_·noh
22	**veintidós** beyeen·tee·_dohs_
30	**treinta** _treyeen_·tah
31	**treinta y uno** _treyeen_·tah ee _oo_·noh
40	**cuarenta** kwah·_rehn_·tah
50	**cincuenta** theen·_kwehn_·tah
60	**sesenta** seh·_sehn_·tah
70	**setenta** seh·_tehn_·tah
80	**ochenta** oh·_chehn_·tah
90	**noventa** noh·_behn_·tah
100	**cien** _theeyehn_
101	**ciento uno** _theeyehn_·toh _oo_·noh
200	**doscientos** dohs·_theeyehn_·tohs
500	**quinientos** kee·_neeyehn_·tohs
1,000	**mil** meel
10,000	**diez mil** deeyehth meel
1,000,000	**un millón** oon mee·_yohn_

Large numbers are read as in English. Example: 1,234,567 would be **un millón, doscientos treinta y cuatro mil, quinientos sesenta y siete** (one million, two hundred thirty-four thousand, five hundred sixty-seven). Notice the use of **y** (and) between tens and units for numbers between 31 (**treinta y uno**; literally, thirty and one) and 99 (**noventa y nueve**; literally, ninety and nine).

Ordinal Numbers

first	**primero** m /**primera** f pree·_meh_·roh/pree·_meh_·rah
second	**segundo** m /**segunda** f seh·_goon_·doh/seh·_goon_·dah
third	**tercero** m /**tercera** f tehr·_theh_·roh/tehr·_theh_·rah
fourth	**cuarto** m /**cuarta** f _kwahr_·toh/_kwahr_·tah
fifth	**quinto** m /**quinta** f _keen_·toh/_keen_·tah
once	**una vez** _oo_·nah behth
twice	**dos veces** dohs _beh_·thes
three times	**tres veces** trehs _beh_·thes

Time

ESSENTIAL

What time is it?	**¿Qué hora es?** *keh oh•rah ehs*
It's noon [midday].	**Son las doce del mediodía.** *sohn lahs doh•theh dehl meh•deeyoh•dee•ah*
At midnight.	**A medianoche.** *ah meh•deeyah•noh•cheh*
From one o'clock to two o'clock.	**De una a dos en punto.** *deh oo•nah ah dohs ehn poon•toh*
Five after [past] three.	**Las tres y cinco.** *lahs trehs ee theen•koh*
A quarter to five.	**Las cinco menos cuarto.** *lahs theen•koh meh•nohs kwahr•toh*
5:30 a.m./p.m.	**Las cinco y media de la mañana/tarde.** *lahs theen•koh ee meh•deeyah deh lah mah•nyah•nah/tahr•deh*

Spaniards use the 24-hour clock when writing time, especially in schedules. The morning hours from 1:00 a.m. to noon are the same as in English. After that, just add 12 to the time: 1:00 p.m. would be 13:00, 5:00 p.m. would be 17:00 and so on.

Days

ESSENTIAL

Monday	**lunes** _loo_•nehs
Tuesday	**martes** _mahr_•tehs
Wednesday	**miércoles** _meeyehr_•koh•lehs
Thursday	**jueves** khweh•behs
Friday	**viernes** _beeyehr_•nehs
Saturday	**sábado** _sah_•bah•doh
Sunday	**domingo** doh•_meen_•goh

Dates

yesterday	**ayer** ah•_yehr_
today	**hoy** oy
tomorrow	**mañana** mah•_nyah_•nah
day	**día** _dee_•ah
week	**semana** seh•_mah_•nah
month	**mes** mehs
year	**año** _ah_•nyoh

Months

January	**enero** eh•_neh_•roh
February	**febrero** feh•_breh_•roh
March	**marzo** _mahr_•thoh
April	**abril** ah•_breel_
May	**mayo** _mah_•yoh
June	**junio** _khoo_•neeyoh
July	**julio** _khoo_•leeyoh
August	**agosto** ah•_gohs_•toh

> Spain follows a day-month-year format instead of the month-day-year format favored in the U.S.
> Examples: **el 25 de agosto de 2007** = August 25, 2007
> **25.8.07** = 8/25/2007

September	**septiembre** sehp·_teeyehm_·breh
October	**octubre** ohk·_too_·breh
November	**noviembre** noh·_beeyehm_·breh
December	**diciembre** dee·_theeyehm_·breh

Seasons

the spring	**la primavera** lah pree·mah·_beh_·rah
the summer	**el verano** ehl beh·_rah_·noh
the fall [autumn]	**el otoño** ehl oh·_toh_·nyoh
the winter	**el invierno** ehl een·_beeyehr_·noh

Holidays

January 1: New Year's Day, **Año Nuevo**
January 6: Epiphany, **Epifanía**
February 8: Carnaval, **Carnaval**
March 19: Feast of St. Joseph, **San José**
May 1: Labor Day, **Día del Trabajo**
July 25: Feast of St. James, **Santiago Apóstol**

> In Spain, the week begins with Monday and ends on Sunday. This distinction is especially apparent when looking at calendars — Monday will be the first column instead of Sunday.

August 15: Feast of the Assumption, **Asunción**
October 12: Spain's National Day, **Día de la Hispanidad**
November 1: All Saint's Day, **Todos los Santos**
December 6: Constitution Day, **Día de la Constitución**
December 8: Feast of the Immaculate Conception, **Inmaculada Concepción**
December 25: Christmas, **Navidad**

Easter festivities take place on different dates each year since this holiday is traditionally celebrated on the first Sunday after the first full moon, on or after the spring equinox.

Conversion Tables

When you know	Multiply by	To find
ounces	28.3	grams
pounds	0.45	kilograms
inches	2.54	centimeters
feet	0.3	meters
miles	1.61	kilometers
square inches	6.45	sq. centimeters
square feet	0.09	sq. meters
square miles	2.59	sq. kilometers
pints (U.S./Brit)	0.47/0.56	liters
gallons (U.S./Brit)	3.8/4.5	liters
Fahrenheit	5/9, after −32	Centigrade
Centigrade	9/5, then +32	Fahrenheit

Kilometers to Miles Conversions

1 km − 0.62 mi	**20 km** − 12.4 mi
5 km − 3.10 mi	**50 km** − 31.0 mi
10 km − 6.20 mi	**100 km** − 61.0 mi

Measurement

1 gram	**un gramo** *oon grah·moh*	= 0.035 oz.
1 kilogram (kg)	**un kilogramo** *oon kee·loh·grah·moh*	= 2.2 lb
1 liter (l)	**un litro** *oon lee·troh*	= 1.06 U.S/0.88 Brit. quarts
1 centimeter (cm)	**un centímetro** *oon thehn·tee·meh·troh*	= 0.4 inch
1 meter (m)	**un metro** *oon meh·troh*	= 3.28 ft.
1 kilometer (km)	**un kilómetro** *oon kee·loh·meh·troh*	= 0.62 mile

Temperature

-40° C – -40° F	**-1° C** – 30° F	**20° C** – 68° F
-30° C – -22° F	**0° C** – 32° F	**25° C** – 77° F
-20° C – -4° F	**5° C** – 41° F	**30° C** – 86° F
-10° C – 14° F	**10° C** – 50° F	**35° C** – 95° F
-5° C – 23° F	**15° C** – 59° F	

Oven Temperature

100° C – 212° F	**177° C** – 350° F
121° C – 250° F	**204° C** – 400° F
149° C – 300° F	**260° C** – 500° F

Dictionary

English–Spanish

A

abbey la abadía
accept v aceptar
access el acceso
accident el accidente
accommodation el alojamiento
account la cuenta
acupuncture la acupuntura
adapter el adaptador
address la dirección
admission la entrada
after después; **~noon** la tarde;
  ~shave el bálsamo para después
  del afeitado
age la edad
agency la agencia
AIDS el sida
air el aire; **~ conditioning**
  el aire acondicionado; **~
  pump** el aire; **~line** la compañía
  aérea; **~mail** el correo aéreo;
  ~plane el avión; **~port** el
  aeropuerto
aisle el pasillo; **~ seat** el asiento
  de pasillo

allergic alérgico; **~ reaction**
  la reacción alérgica
allow v permitir
alone solo
alter v (clothing) hacer un arreglo
alternate route el otro camino
aluminum foil el papel de aluminio
amazing increíble
ambulance la ambulancia
American estadounidense
amusement park el parque
  de atracciones
anemic anémico
anesthesia la anestesia
animal el animal
ankle el tobillo
antibiotic el antibiótico
antiques store la tienda de
  -antigüedades
antiseptic cream la crema
  antiséptica
anything algo
apartment el apartamento
appendix (body part) el apéndice
appetizer el aperitivo

adj adjective	**BE** British English	**v** verb
adv adverb	**n** noun	

appointment la cita
arcade el salón de juegos recreativos
area code el prefijo
arm el brazo
aromatherapy la aromaterapia
around (the corner) doblando (la esquina)
arrivals (airport) las llegadas
arrive v llegar
artery la arteria
arthritis la artritis
arts las letras
Asian asiático
aspirin la aspirina
asthmatic asmático
ATM el cajero automático
attack el asalto
attend v asistir
attraction (place) el sitio de interés
attractive guapo
Australia Australia
Australian australiano
automatic automático; ~ **car** coche automático
available disponible

B

baby el bebé; ~ **bottle** el biberón; ~ **wipe** la toallita; ~**sitter** el/la canguro

back la espalda; ~**ache** el dolor de espalda; ~**pack** la mochila
bag la maleta
baggage el equipaje; ~ **claim** la recogida de equipajes; ~ **ticket** el talón de equipaje
bakery la panadería
ballet el ballet
bandage la tirita
bank el banco
bar el bar
barbecue la barbacoa
barber la peluquería de caballeros
baseball el béisbol
basket (grocery store) la cesta
basketball el baloncesto
bathroom el baño
battery (car) la batería
battery la pila
battleground el campo de batalla
be v ser, estar
beach la playa
beautiful precioso
bed la cama; ~ **and breakfast** la pensión
begin v empezar
before antes de
beginner principiante
behind detrás de
beige beis
belt el cinturón

berth la litera
best el/la mejor
better mejor
bicycle la bicicleta
big grande
bigger más grande
bike route el sendero para
  bicicletas
bikini el biquini;
  ~ wax la depilación de las ingles
bill v (charge) cobrar;
  ~ n (money) el billete;
  ~ n (of sale) el recibo
bird el pájaro
birthday el cumpleaños
black negro
bladder la vejiga
bland soso
blanket la manta
bleed v sangrar
blood la sangre; **~ pressure**
  la tensión arterial
blouse la blusa
blue azul
board v embarcar
boarding pass la tarjeta
  de embarque
boat el barco
bone el hueso
book el libro; **~store** la librería
boots las botas

boring aburrido
botanical garden el jardín botánico
bother v molestar
bottle la botella; **~ opener**
  el abrebotellas
bowl el cuenco
box la caja
boxing match la pelea de boxeo
boy el niño; **~friend** el novio
bra el sujetador
bracelet la pulsera
brakes (car) los frenos
break v romper
break-in (burglary)
  el allanamiento de morada
breakdown la avería
breakfast el desayuno
breast el seno; **~feed** dar el pecho
breathe v respirar
bridge el puente
briefs (clothing) los calzoncillos
bring v traer
British británico
broken roto
brooch el broche
broom la escoba
brother el hermano
brown marrón
bug el insecto
building el edificio
burn v (CD) grabar

bus el autobús; **~ station**
la estación de autobuses;
~ stop la parada de autobús;
~ ticket el billete de autobús;
~ tour el recorrido en autobús
business los negocios;
~ card la tarjeta de negocios;
~ center el centro de negocios;
~ class la clase preferente;
~ hours el horario de atención
al público
butcher el carnicero
buttocks las nalgas
buy v comprar
bye adiós

C

cabaret el cabaré
cabin (house) la cabaña;
~ (ship) el camarote
cable car el teleférico
cafe la cafetería
call v llamar; ~ n la llamada
calories las calorías
camera la cámara;
digital ~ la cámara digital;
~ case la funda para la cámara;
~ store la tienda de fotografía
camp v acampar; **~ stove**
el hornillo; **~site** el cámping
can opener el abrelatas

Canada Canadá
Canadian canadiense
cancel v cancelar
candy el caramelo
canned goods las conservas
canyon el cañón
car el coche; **~ hire**
[BE] el alquiler de coches;
~ park [BE] el aparcamiento;
~ rental el alquiler de coches;
~ seat el asiento de niño
carafe la garrafa
card la tarjeta; **ATM ~** la
tarjeta de cajero automático;
credit ~ la tarjeta de crédito;
debit ~ la tarjeta de débito;
phone ~ la tarjeta telefónica
carry-on (piece of hand luggage)
el equipaje de mano
cart (grocery store) el carrito; **~**
(luggage) el carrito para el equipaje
carton el cartón; **~ of cigarettes**
el cartón de tabaco
case (amount) la caja
cash v cobrar; **~** n el efectivo;
~ advance sacar dinero de la
tarjeta
cashier el cajero
casino el casino
castle el castillo
cathedral la catedral

cave la cueva
CD el CD
cell phone el teléfono móvil
Celsius el grado centígrado
centimeter el centímetro
certificate el certificado
chair la silla; **~ lift** la telesilla
change *v* **(buses)** cambiar;
  ~ *n* **(money)** el cambio
charcoal el carbón
charge *v* **(credit card)** cobrar;
  ~ *n* **(cost)** el precio
cheap barato
cheaper más barato
check *v* **(on something)** revisar;
  ~ *v* **(luggage)** facturar;
  ~ *n* **(payment)** el cheque;
  ~-in (airport) la facturación;
  ~-in (hotel) el registro;
  ~ing account la cuenta corriente;
  ~-out (hotel) la salida
Cheers! ¡Salud!
chemical toilet el váter químico
chemist [BE] la farmacia
cheque [BE] el cheque
chest (body part) el pecho;
  ~ pain el dolor de pecho
chewing gum el chicle
child el niño; **~ seat** la silla
  para niños
children's menu el menú para niños

children's portion la ración
  para niños
Chinese chino
chopsticks los palillos chinos
church la iglesia
cigar el puro
cigarette el cigarrillo
class la clase; **business ~** la clase
  preferente; **economy ~** la clase
  económica; **first ~** la primera clase
classical music la música clásica
clean *v* limpiar; **~** *adj* limpio; **~ing
  product** el producto de limpieza;
  ~ing supplies los productos
  de limpieza
clear *v* **(on an ATM)** borrar
cliff el acantilado
cling film [BE] el film transparente
close *v* **(a shop)** cerrar
closed cerrado
clothing la ropa; **~ store** la tienda
  de ropa
club la discoteca
coat el abrigo
coffee shop la cafetería
coin la moneda
colander el escurridor
cold *n* **(sickness)** el catarro;
  ~ *adj* **(temperature)** frío
colleague el compañero de trabajo
cologne la colonia

color el color
comb el peine
come v venir
complaint la queja
computer el ordenador
concert el concierto; ~ **hall** la sala
de conciertos
condition (medical) el estado
de salud
conditioner el suavizante
condom el preservativo
conference la conferencia
confirm v confirmar
congestion la congestión
connect v (internet) conectarse
connection (internet) la conexión;
~ **(flight)** la conexión de vuelo
constipated estreñido
consulate el consulado
consultant el consultor
contact v ponerse en contacto con
contact lens la lentilla de contacto;
~ **solution** el líquido de lentillas
de contacto
contagious contagioso
convention hall el salón
de congresos
conveyor belt la cinta
transportadora
cook v cocinar
cooking gas el gas butano

cool (temperature) frío
copper el cobre
corkscrew el sacacorchos
cost v costar
cot el catre
cotton el algodón
cough v toser; ~ n la tos
country code el código de país
cover charge la entrada
crash v (car) estrellarse
cream (ointment) la pomada
credit card la tarjeta de crédito
crew neck el cuello redondo
crib la cuna
crystal el cristal
cup la taza
currency la moneda; ~ **exchange**
el cambio de divisas; ~ **exchange**
office la casa de cambio
current account [BE] la cuenta
corriente
customs las aduanas
cut v (hair) cortar; ~ n (injury)
el corte
cute mono
cycling el ciclismo

D

damage v causar daño
damaged ha sufrido daños
dance v bailar; ~ **club** la discoteca

dangerous peligroso
dark oscuro
date (calendar) la fecha
day el día
deaf sordo
debit card la tarjeta de débito
deck chair la tumbona
declare v declarar
decline v **(credit card)** rechazar
deeply hondo
degrees (temperature) los grados
delay v retrasarse
delete v **(computer)** borrar
delicatessen la charcutería
delicious delicioso
denim tela vaquero
dentist el dentista
denture la dentadura
deodorant el desodorante
department store los grandes almacenes
departures (airport) las salidas
deposit v depositar; ~ n **(bank)** el depósito bancario;
    ~ v **(reserve a room)** la fianza
desert el desierto
dessert el postre
detergent el detergente
develop v **(film)** revelar
diabetic diabético
dial v marcar

diamond el diamante
diaper el pañal
diarrhea la diarrea
diesel el diesel
difficult difícil
digital digital; ~ **camera** la cámara digital; ~ **photos** las fotos digitales; ~ **prints** las fotos digitales
dining room el comedor
dinner la cena
direction la dirección
dirty sucio
disabled discapacitado;
    ~ **accessible [BE]** el acceso para discapacitados
discharge (bodily fluid) la secreción
disconnect (computer) desconectar
discount el descuento
dish (kitchen) el plato; ~**washer** el lavavajillas; ~**washing liquid** el líquido lavavajillas
display v mostrar; ~ **case** la vitrina
disposable desechable;
    ~ **razor** la cuchilla desechable
dive v bucear
diving equipment el equipo de buceo
divorce v divorciar
dizzy mareado

doctor el médico

doll la muñeca

dollar (U.S.) el dólar

domestic nacional; ~ **flight**
el vuelo nacional

door la puerta

dormitory el dormitorio

double bed la cama de matrimonio

downtown el centro

dozen la docena

drag lift el telesquí

dress (piece of clothing) el vestido;
~ **code** las normas de vestuario

drink v beber; ~ n la bebida;
~ **menu** la carta de bebidas;
~**ing water** el agua potable

drive v conducir

driver's license number el número
de permiso de conducir

drop (medicine) la gota

drowsiness la somnolencia

dry cleaner la tintorería

dubbed doblada

during durante

duty (tax) el impuesto;
~**-free** libre de impuestos

DVD el DVD

E

ear la oreja; ~**ache** el dolor de oído

earlier más temprano

early temprano

earrings los pendientes

east el este

easy fácil

eat v comer

economy class la clase económica

elbow el codo

electric outlet el enchufe eléctrico

elevator el ascensor

e-mail v enviar un correo
electrónico; ~ n el correo
electrónico; ~ **address**
la dirección de correo electrónico

emergency la emergencia;
~ **exit** la salida de urgencia

empty v vaciar

enamel (jewelry) el esmalte

end v terminar

English el inglés

engrave v grabar

enjoy v disfrutar

enter v entrar

entertainment el entretenimiento

entrance la entrada

envelope el sobre

equipment el equipo

escalators las escaleras mecánicas

e-ticket el billete electrónico

EU resident el/la residente de la UE

euro el euro

evening la noche

excess el exceso
exchange *v* **(money)** cambiar;
~ *v* **(goods)** devolver;
~ *n* **(place)** la casa de cambio;
~ **rate** el tipo de cambio
excursion la excursión
excuse *v* **(to get past)** pedir perdón;
~ *v* **(to get attention)** disculparse
exhausted agotado
exit *v* salir; ~ *n* la salida
expensive caro
expert (skill level) experto
exposure (film) la foto
express rápido; ~ **bus** el autobús
rápido; ~ **train** el tren rápido
extension (phone) la extensión
extra adicional; ~ **large** equis
ele (XL)
extract *v* **(tooth)** extraer
eye el ojo
eyebrow wax la depilación de cejas

F

face la cara
facial la limpieza de cutis
family la familia
fan (appliance) el ventilador;
~ **(souvenir)** el abanico
far lejos; ~-**sighted** hipermétrope
farm la granja
fast rápido; ~ **food** la comida rápida

faster más rápido
fat free sin grasa
father el padre
fax *v* enviar un fax; ~ *n* el fax;
~ **number** el número de fax
fee la tasa
feed *v* alimentar
ferry el ferry
fever la fiebre
field (sports) el campo
fill *v* llenar ; ~ **out** *v*
(form) rellenar
filling (tooth) el empaste
film (camera) el carrete
fine (fee for breaking law)
la multa
finger el dedo; ~**nail** la uña
del dedo
fire fuego; ~ **department** los
bomberos; ~ **door** la puerta de
incendios
first primero; ~ **class** la primera
clase
fit (clothing) quedar bien
fitting room el probador
fix *v* **(repair)** reparar
flashlight la linterna
flight el vuelo
floor el suelo
flower la flor
folk music la música folk

food la comida
foot el pie
football [BE] el fútbol
for para/por
forecast el pronóstico
forest el bosque
fork el tenedor
form el formulario
formula (baby) la fórmula infantil
fort el fuerte
fountain la fuente
free gratuito
freezer el congelador
fresh fresco
friend el amigo
frying pan la sartén
full completo;
  ~-service el servicio completo;
  ~-time a tiempo completo

G

game el partido
garage (parking) el garaje;
  ~ (repair) el taller
garbage bag la bolsa de basura
gas la gasolina; **~ station**
  la gasolinera
gate (airport) la puerta
gay gay; **~ bar** el bar gay;
  ~ club la discoteca gay
gel (hair) la gomina

get to v ir a
get off v **(a train/bus/subway)**
  bajarse
gift el regalo; **~ shop** la tienda
  de regalos
girl la niña; **~friend** la novia
give v dar
glass (drinking) el vaso;
  ~ (material) el vidrio
glasses las gafas
go v **(somewhere)** ir a
gold el oro
golf golf; **~ course** el campo de
  golf; **~ tournament** el torneo
  de golf
good n el producto; ~ adj bueno;
  ~ afternoon buenas tardes;
  ~ evening buenas noches;
  ~ morning buenos días;
  ~bye adiós
gram el gramo
grandchild el nieto
grandparent el abuelo
gray gris
green verde
grocery store el supermercado
ground la tierra; **~ floor** la planta
  baja; **~cloth** la tela impermeable
group el grupo
guide el guía; **~ book** la guía;
  ~ dog el perro guía

gym el gimnasio
gynecologist el ginecólogo

H

hair el pelo; **~ dryer** el secador
de pelo; **~ salon** la peluquería;
~brush el cepillo de pelo;
~cut el corte de pelo; **~spray**
la laca; **~style** el peinado;
~stylist el estilista
half medio; **~ hour** la media hora;
~-kilo el medio kilo
hammer el martillo
hand la mano; **~ luggage [BE]**
el equipaje de mano; **~bag [BE]**
el bolso
handicapped discapacitado;
~-accessible el acceso para
discapacitados
hangover la resaca
happy feliz
hat el sombrero
have v tener
head (body part) la cabeza;
~ache el dolor de cabeza;
~phones los cascos
health la salud; **~ food store**
la tienda de alimentos naturales
heart el corazón; **~ condition**
padecer del corazón
heat v calentar; **~** n el calor

heater [heating BE] la calefacción
hello hola
helmet el casco
help v ayudar; **~** n la ayuda
here aquí
hi hola
high alto; **~chair** la trona;
~way la autopista
hiking boots las botas de montaña
hill la colina
hire v [BE] alquilar; **~ car [BE]**
el coche de alquiler
hitchhike v hacer autostop
hockey el hockey
holiday [BE] las vacaciones
horse track el hipódromo
hospital el hospital
hostel el albergue
hot (temperature) caliente;
~ (spicy) picante; **~ spring**
el agua termale; **~ water** el agua
caliente
hotel el hotel
hour la hora
house la casa; **~hold goods**
los artículos para el hogar;
~keeping services el servicio de
limpieza de habitaciones
how (question) cómo; **~ much
(question)** cuánto cuesta
hug v abrazar

hungry hambriento
hurt *v* **(have pain)** tener dolor
husband el marido

I

ibuprofen el ibuprofeno
ice el hielo; ~ **hockey** el hockey sobre hielo
icy *adj* helado
identification el documento de identidad
ill *v* **(to feel)** encontrarse mal
in dentro
include *v* incluir
indoor pool la piscina cubierta
inexpensive barato
infected infectado
information (phone) el número de teléfono de información; ~ **desk** el mostrador de información
insect el insecto; ~ **bite** la picadura de insecto; ~ **repellent** el repelente de insectos
insert *v* introducir
insomnia el insomnio
instant message el mensaje instantáneo
insulin la insulina
insurance el seguro; ~ **card** la tarjeta de seguro; ~ **company** la compañía de seguros

interesting interesante
intermediate el nivel intermedio
international (airport area) internacional; ~ **flight** el vuelo internacional; ~ **student card** la tarjeta internacional de estudiante
internet la internet; ~ **cafe** el cibercafé; ~ **service** el servicio de internet; **wireless** ~ el acceso inalámbrico
interpreter el/la intérprete
intersection el cruce
intestine el intestino
introduce *v* presentar
invoice [BE] la factura
Ireland Irlanda
Irish irlandés
iron *v* planchar; ~ *n* **(clothes)** la plancha
Italian italiano

J

jacket la chaqueta
jar el bote
jaw la mandíbula
jazz el jazz; ~ **club** el club de jazz
jeans los vaqueros
jet ski la moto acuática
jeweler la joyería
jewelry las joyas

join v acompañar a
joint (body part) la articulación

K

key la llave; **~ card** la llave
electrónica; **~ ring** el llavero
kiddie pool la piscina infantil
kidney (body part) el riñón
kilo el kilo; **~gram** el kilogramo;
~meter el kilómetro
kiss v besar
kitchen la cocina; **~ foil [BE]**
el papel de aluminio
knee la rodilla
knife el cuchillo

L

lace el encaje
lactose intolerant alérgico a la
lactosa
lake el lago
large grande; **~er** más grande
last último
late (time) tarde; **~er** más tarde
launderette [BE] la lavandería
laundromat la lavandería
laundry la colada; **~ facility**
la lavandería; **~ service** el servicio
de lavandería
lawyer el abogado
leather el cuero

to leave v salir
left (direction) la izquierda
leg la pierna
lens la lente
less menos
lesson la lección
letter la carta
library la biblioteca
life la vida; **~ jacket** el chaleco
salvavidas; **~guard** el socorrista
lift n [BE] el ascensor; **~** v **(to give
a ride)** llevar en coche; **~ pass**
el pase de acceso a los remontes
light n **(overhead)** la luz;
~ v **(cigarette)** dar fuego;
~bulb la bombilla
lighter el mechero
like v gustar; **I like** me gusta
line (train) la línea
linen el lino
lip el labio
liquor store la tienda de bebidas
alcohólicas
liter el litro
little pequeño
live v vivir
liver (body part) el hígado
loafers los mocasines
local de la zona
lock v cerrar; **~** n el cerrojo
locker la taquilla

log on *v* **(computer)** iniciar sesión

log off *v* **(computer)** cerrar sesión

long largo; **~ sleeves**
las mangas largas; **~-sighted** [BE]
hipermétrope

look *v* mirar

lose *v* **(something)** perder

lost perdido; **~ and found**
la oficina de objetos perdidos

lotion la crema hidratante

louder más alto

love *v* querer; **~** *n* el amor

low bajo; **~er** más bajo

luggage el equipaje; **~ cart**
el carrito de equipaje; **~ locker**
la consigna automática; **~ ticket**
el talón de equipaje; **hand ~** [BE]
el equipaje de mano

lunch la comida

lung el pulmón

M

magazine la revista

magnificent magnífico

mail *v* enviar por correo;
~ *n* el correo; **~box** el buzón
de correo

main principal; **~ attractions**
los principales sitios de interés;
~ course el plato principal

make up a prescription *v* [BE]
despachar medicamentos

mall el centro comercial

man el hombre

manager el gerente

manicure la manicura

manual car el coche con
transmisión manual

map el mapa

market el mercado

married casado

marry *v* casarse

mass (church service) la misa

massage el masaje

match la cerilla

meal la comida

measure *v* **(someone)** medir

measuring cup la taza medidora

measuring spoon la cuchara
medidora

mechanic el mecánico

medicine el medicamento

medium (size) mediano

meet *v* **(someone)** conocer

meeting la reunión; **~ room**
la sala de reuniones

membership card la tarjeta de socio

memorial (place) el monumento
conmemorativo

memory card la tarjeta de
memoria

mend *v* zurcir

menstrual cramps los dolores menstruales

menu la carta

message el mensaje

meter (parking) el parquímetro

microwave el microondas

midday [BE] el mediodía

midnight la medianoche

mileage el kilometraje

mini-bar el minibar

minute el minuto

missing desaparecido

mistake el error

mobile móvil; **~ home** la caravana; **~ phone [BE]** el teléfono móvil

mobility la movilidad

money el dinero

month el mes

mop la fregona

moped el ciclomotor

more más

morning la mañana

mosque la mezquita

mother la madre

motion sickness el mareo

motor el motor; **~ boat** la lancha motora; **~cycle** la motocicleta; **~way [BE]** la autopista

mountain la montaña; **~ bike** la bicicleta de montaña

mousse (hair) la espuma para el pelo

mouth *n* la boca

movie la película; **~ theater** el cine

mug *v* asaltar

muscle (body part) el músculo

museum el museo

music la música; **~ store** la tienda de música

N

nail la uña; **~ file** la lima de uñas; **~ salon** el salon de manicura

name el nombre

napkin la servilleta

nappy [BE] el pañale

nationality la nacionalidad

nature preserve la reserva natural

(be) nauseous *v* tener náuseas

near cerca; **~-sighted** miope; **~by** cerca de aquí

neck el cuello

necklace el collar

need *v* necesitar

newspaper el periódico

newsstand el quiosco

next próximo

nice *adj* amable

night la noche; **~club** la discoteca

no no

non sin; **~-alcoholic** sin alcohol; **~-smoking** para no fumadores

noon el mediodía

north el norte

nose la nariz

note [BE] el billete

nothing nada

notify v avisar

novice (skill level) principiante

now ahora

number el número

nurse el enfermero/la enfermera

O

office la oficina; **~ hours (doctor's)** las horas de consulta; **~ hours (other offices)** el horario de oficina

off-licence [BE] la tienda de bebidas alcohólicas

oil el aceite

OK de acuerdo

old adj viejo

on the corner en la esquina

once una vez

one uno; **~-way ticket** el billete de ida; **~-way street** la calle de sentido único

only solamente

open v abrir; **~** adj abierto

opera la ópera; **~ house** el teatro de la ópera

opposite frente a

optician el oculista

orange (color) naranja

orchestra la orquesta

order v pedir

outdoor pool la piscina exterior

outside fuera

over sobre; **~ the counter (medication)** sin receta; **~look (scenic place)** el mirador; **~night** por la noche

oxygen treatment la oxígenoterapia

P

p.m. de la tarde

pacifier el chupete

pack v hacer las maletas

package el paquete

paddling pool [BE] la piscina infantil

pad [BE] la compresa

pain el dolor

pajamas los pijamas

palace el palacio

pants los pantalones

pantyhose las medias

paper el papel; **~ towel** el papel de cocina

paracetamol [BE] el paracetamol
park v aparcar; ~ n el parque;
  ~**ing garage** el párking;
  ~**ing lot** el aparcamiento
parliament building el palacio de
  las cortes
part (for car) la pieza; ~**-time**
  a tiempo parcial
pass through v estar de paso
passenger el pasajero
passport el pasaporte; ~ **control**
  el control de pasaportes
password la contraseña
pastry shop la pastelería
path el camino
pay v pagar; ~ **phone** el teléfono
  público
peak (of a mountain) la cima
pearl la perla
pedestrian el peatón
pediatrician el pediatra
pedicure la pedicura
pen el bolígrafo
penicillin la penicilina
penis el pene
per por; ~ **day** por día;
  ~ **hour** por hora; ~ **night** por
  noche; ~ **week** por semana
perfume el perfume
period (menstrual) la regla;
  ~ **(of time)** la época

permit v permitir
petite las tallas pequeñas
petrol la gasolina; ~ **station**
  la gasolinera
pewter el peltre
pharmacy la farmacia
phone v hacer una llamada;
  ~ n el teléfono; ~ **call** la llamada
  de teléfono; ~ **card** la tarjeta
  telefónica; ~ **number** el número
  de teléfono
photo la foto; ~**copy** la fotocopia;
  ~**graphy** la fotografía
pick up v **(something)** recoger
picnic area la zona para picnic
piece el trozo
Pill (birth control) la píldora
pillow la almohada
**personal identification number
  (PIN)** la clave
pink rosa
piste [BE] la pista; ~ **map**
  [BE] el mapa de pistas
pizzeria la pizzería
place v **(a bet)** hacer una apuesta
plane el avión
plastic wrap el film transparente
plate el plato
platform [BE] (train) el andén
platinum el platino
play v jugar; ~ n **(theater)** la obra

de teatro; **~ground** el patio de
recreo; **~pen** el parque
please por favor
pleasure el placer
plunger el desatascador
plus size la talla grande
pocket el bolsillo
poison el veneno
poles (skiing) los bastones
police la policía; **~ report**
el certificado de la policía;
~ station la comisaría
pond el estanque
pool la piscina
pop music la música pop
portion la ración
post [BE] el correo;
~ office la oficina de correos;
~box [BE] el buzón de correos;
~card la tarjeta postal
pot la olla
pottery la cerámica
pounds (British sterling) las libras
esterlinas
pregnant embarazada
prescribe v recetar
prescription la receta
press v **(clothing)** planchar
price el precio
print v imprimir
problem el problema

produce las frutas y verduras;
~ store la frutería y verdulería
prohibit v prohibir
pronounce v pronunciar
public el público
pull v **(door sign)** tirar
purple morado
purse el bolso
push v **(door sign)** empujar;
~chair [BE] el cochecito de niño

Q

quality n la calidad
question la pregunta
quiet adj tranquilo

R

racetrack el circuito de carreras
racket (sports) la raqueta
railway station [BE] la estación
de trenes
rain la lluvia; **~coat** el
chubasquero; **~forest** el bosque
pluvial; **~y** adv lluvioso
rap (music) el rap
rape v violar; **~** n la violación
rash la erupción cutánea
razor blade la hoja de afeitar
reach v localizar
ready listo
real auténtico

receipt el recibo
receive v recibir
reception la recepción
recharge v recargar
recommend v recomendar
recommendation la recomendación
recycle v reciclar
red rojo
refrigerator n la nevera
region la región
registered mail el correo certificado
regular normal
relationship la relación
rent v alquilar
rental car el coche de alquiler
repair v arreglar
repeat v repetir
reservation la reserva;
  ~ **desk** la taquilla
reserve v reservar
restaurant el restaurante
restroom el servicio
retired jubilado
return v **(something)** devolver;
  ~ n **[BE]** la ida y vuelta
rib (body part) la costilla
right (direction) derecha;
  ~ **of way** prioridad de paso
ring el anillo
river n el río
road map el mapa de carreteras

rob v atracar
robbed atracado
romantic romántico
room la habitación; ~ **key** la
  llave de habitación; ~ **service** el
  servicio de habitaciones
round-trip ida y vuelta
route la ruta
rowboat la barca de remos
rubbish [BE] la basura; ~ **bag [BE]**
  la bolsa de basura
rugby el rubgy
ruins las ruinas
rush la prisa

S

sad triste
safe n la caja fuerte; ~ adj seguro
sales tax el IVA
same mismo
sandals las sandalias
sanitary napkin la compresa
saucepan el cazo
sauna la sauna
save v **(computer)** guardar
savings (account) la cuenta
  de ahorro
scanner el escáner
scarf la bufanda
schedule v programar;
  ~ n el horario

school el colegio
science la ciencia
scissors las tijeras
sea el mar
seat el asiento
security la seguridad
see v ver
self-service el autoservicio
sell v vender
seminar el seminario
send v enviar
senior citizen jubilado
separated (marriage) -separado
serious serio
service (in a restaurant) el servicio
sexually transmitted disease (STD)
  la enfermedad de transmisión sexual
shampoo el champú
sharp afilado
shaving cream la crema de afeitar
sheet la sábana
ship v enviar
shirt la camisa
shoe store la zapatería
shoes los zapatos
shop v comprar
shopping ir de compras;
  ~ **area** la zona de compras;
  ~ **centre [BE]** el centro comercial;
  ~ **mall** el centro comercial
short corto; ~ **sleeves** las mangas

cortas; ~**s** los pantalones cortos;
  ~**-sighted [BE]** miope
shoulder el hombro
show v enseñar
shower la ducha
shrine el santuario
sick enfermo
side el lado; ~ **dish** la guarnición;
  ~ **effect** el efecto secundario;
  ~ **order** la guarnición
sightsee v hacer turismo
sightseeing tour el recorrido
  turístico
sign v (name) firmar
silk la seda
silver la plata
single (unmarried) soltero; ~ **bed**
  la cama; ~ **prints** una copia;
  ~ **room** una habitación individual
sink el lavabo
sister la hermana
sit v sentarse
size la talla
skin la piel
skirt la falda
ski v esquiar; ~ n el esquí; ~ **lift**
  el telesquí
sleep v dormir; ~**er car** el coche
  cama; ~**ing bag** el saco de dormir
slice v cortar en rodajas
slippers las zapatillas

slower más despacio
slowly despacio
small pequeño
smaller más pequeño
smoke v fumar
smoking (area) la zona de fumadores
snack bar la cafetería
sneakers las zapatillas de deporte
snorkeling equipment el equipo de esnórquel
snow la nieve; **~board** la tabla de snowboard; **~shoe** la raqueta de nieve; **~y** nevado
soap el jabón
soccer el fútbol
sock el calcetín
some alguno
soother [BE] el chupete
sore throat las anginas
sorry lo siento
south el sur
souvenir el recuerdo; **~ store** la tienda de recuerdos
spa el centro de salud y belleza
Spain España
Spanish el español
spatula la espátula
speak v hablar
special (food) la especialidad de la casa

specialist (doctor) el especialista
specimen el ejemplar
speeding el exceso de velocidad
spell v deletrear
spicy picante
spine (body part) la columna vertebral
spoon la cuchara
sports los deportes; **~ massage** el masaje deportivo
sporting goods store la tienda de deportes
sprain el esguince
square cuadrado; **~ kilometer** el kilómetro cuadrado; **~ meter** el metro cuadrado
stadium el estadio
stairs las escaleras
stamp v (a ticket) picar; **~ n (postage)** el sello
start v empezar
starter [BE] el aperitivo
station la estación; **bus ~** la estación de autobuses; **gas ~** la gasolinera; **muster ~ [BE]** el punto de reunión; **petrol ~ [BE]** la gasolinera; **subway ~** el metro; **train ~** la estación de tren
statue la estatua
stay v quedarse
steal v robar

steep empinado
sterling silver la plata esterlina
sting el escozor
stolen robado
stomach el estómago; **~ache**
  el dolor de estómago
stop v pararse; **~** n la parada
storey [BE] la planta
stove el horno
straight recto
strange extraño
stream el arroyo
stroller el cochecito
student el estudiante
study v estudiar
stunning impresionante
subtitle el subtítulo
subway el metro; **~ station**
  la estación de metro
suit el traje
suitcase la maleta
sun el sol; **~block** el protector
  solar total; **~burn** la quemadura
  solar; **~glasses** las gafas
  de sol; **~ny** soleado; **~screen**
  el protector solar; **~stroke**
  la insolación
super (fuel) súper; **~market**
  el supermercado
surfboard la tabla de surf
surgical spirit [BE] el alcohol

etílico
swallow v tragar
sweater el jersey
sweatshirt la sudadera
sweet (taste) dulce; **~s [BE]**
  los caramelos
swelling la hinchazón
swim v nadar; **~suit** el bañador
symbol (keyboard) el símbolo
synagogue la sinagoga

T

table la mesa
tablet (medicine) el comprimido
take v llevar; **~ away [BE]**
  para llevar
tampon el tampón
tapas bar el bar de tapas
taste v probar
taxi el taxi
team el equipo
telephone el teléfono
temporary provisional
tennis el tenis
tent la tienda de campaña;
  ~ peg la estaca; **~ pole** el mástil
terminal (airport) la terminal
terracotta la terracotta
terrible terrible
text v **(send a message)** enviar
  un mensaje de texto;

~ n (message) el texto
thank v dar las gracias a;
~ **you** gracias
that eso
theater el teatro
there ahí
thief el ladrón
thigh el muslo
thirsty sediento
this esto
throat la garganta
ticket el billete; ~ **office**
el despacho de billetes; ~**ed**
passenger el pasajero con billete
tie (clothing) la corbata
time el tiempo; ~**table [BE]**
el horario
tire la rueda
tired cansado
tissue el pañuelo de paper
tobacconist el estanco
today hoy
toe el dedo del pie; ~**nail** la uña
del pie
toilet [BE] el servicio; ~ **paper**
el papel higiénico
tomorrow mañana
tongue la lengua
tonight esta noche
too demasiado
tooth el diente; ~**brush** el cepillo

de dientes; ~**paste** la pasta de
dientes
total (amount) el total
tough (food) duro
tourist el turista; ~ **information**
office la oficina de turismo
tour el recorrido turístico
tow truck la grúa
towel la toalla
tower la torre
town la ciudad; ~ **hall**
el ayuntamiento; ~ **map** el mapa
de ciudad; ~ **square** la plaza
toy el juguete; ~ **store** la tienda
de juguetes
track (train) el andén
traditional tradicional
traffic light el semáforo
trail la pista; ~ **map** el mapa de
la pista
trailer el remolque
train el tren; ~ **station** la estación
de tren
transfer v cambiar
translate v traducir
trash la basura
travel v viajar; ~ **agency**
la agencia de viajes; ~ **sickness**
el mareo; ~**er's check**
[cheque BE] el cheque de viaje
tree el árbol

trim (hair cut) cortarse las puntas
trip el viaje
trolley [BE] el carrito
trousers [BE] los pantalones
T-shirt la camiseta
turn off v apagar
turn on v encender
TV la televisión
type v escribir a máquina
tyre [BE] la rueda

U

United Kingdom (U.K.) el Reino Unido
United States (U.S.) los Estados Unidos
ugly feo
umbrella el paraguas
unattended desatendido
unconscious inconsciente
underground [BE] el metro; ~ **station [BE]** la estación de metro
underpants [BE] los calzoncillos
understand v entender
underwear la ropa interior
university la universidad
unleaded (gas) la gasolina sin plomo
upper superior
urgent urgente
use v usar

username el nombre de usuario
utensil el cubierto

V

vacancy la habitación libre
vacation las vacaciones
vaccination la vacuna
vacuum cleaner la aspiradora
vaginal infection la infección vaginal
valid validez
valley el valle
valuable valioso
VAT [BE] el IVA
vegetarian vegetariano
vehicle registration el registro del coche
viewpoint [BE] el mirador
village el pueblo
vineyard la viña
visa (passport document) el visado
visit v visitar; ~**ing hours** el horario de visita
visually impaired la persona con discapacidad visual
vitamin la vitamina
V-neck el cuello de pico
vomit v vomitar

W

wait *v* esperar; ~ *n* la espera;
~**ing room** la sala de espera
waiter el camarero
waitress la camarera
wake *v* despertarse; ~**-up call**
la llamada despertador
walk *v* caminar; ~ *n* la caminata;
~**ing route** la ruta de senderismo
wallet la cartera
warm *v* **(something)** calentar;
~ *adj* **(temperature)** calor
washing machine la lavadora
watch el reloj
waterfall la cascada
weather el tiempo
week la semana; ~**end** el fin de
semana; ~**ly** semanal
welcome *v* acoger
well bien; ~**-rested** descansado
west el oeste
what (question) qué
wheelchair la silla de ruedas;
~ **ramp** la rampa para silla
de ruedas
when (question) cuándo
where (question) dónde
white blanco; ~ **gold** el oro blanco
who (question) quién
widowed viudo
wife la mujer

window la ventana; ~ **case**
el escaparate
windsurfer el surfista
wine list la carta de vinos
wireless inalámbrico; ~ **internet**
el acceso inalámbrico a internet;
~ **internet service** el servicio
inalámbrico a internet; ~ **phone**
el teléfono móvil
with con
withdraw *v* retirar;
~**al (bank)** retirar fondos
without sin
woman la mujer
wool la lana
work *v* trabajar
wrap *v* envolver
wrist la muñeca
write *v* escribir

Y

year el año
yellow amarillo
yes sí
yesterday ayer
young joven
youth hostel el albergue
juvenil

Z

zoo el zoológico

A

a tiempo completo full-time
a tiempo parcial part-time
la abadía abbey
el abanico fan (souvenir)
abierto *adj* open
el abogado lawyer
abrazar *v* hug
el abrebotellas bottle opener
el abrelatas can opener
el abrigo coat
abrir *v* open
el abuelo grandparent
aburrido boring
acampar *v* camp
el acantilado cliff
el acceso access;
~ **inalámbrico a internet**
wireless internet; ~ **para
discapacitados** handicapped-
[disabled- BE] accessible
el accidente accident
el aceite oil
aceptar *v* accept
acoger *v* welcome
acompañar a *v* join
la acupuntura acupuncture
el adaptador adapter
adicional extra

adiós goodbye
las aduanas customs
el aeropuerto airport
afilado sharp
la agencia agency; ~ **de
viajes** travel agency
agotado exhausted
el agua water; ~ **caliente**
hot water; ~ **potable** drinking
water
las aguas termales hot spring
ahí there
ahora now
el aire air, air pump;
~ **acondicionado** air conditioning
el albergue hostel;
~ **juvenil** youth hostel
alérgico allergic;
~ **a la lactosa** lactose intolerant
algo anything
el algodón cotton
alguno some
alimentar *v* feed
el allanamiento de morada
break-in (burglary)
la almohada pillow
el alojamiento accommodation
alquilar *v* rent [hire BE];
el ~ de coches car rental [hire BE]

alto high
amable nice
amarillo yellow
la ambulancia ambulance
el amigo friend
el amor *n* love
el andén track [platform BE] (train)
anémico anemic
la anestesia anesthesia
las anginas sore throat
el anillo ring
el animal animal
antes de before
el antibiótico antibiotic
el año year
apagar *v* turn off
el aparcamiento parking lot
  [car park BE]
aparcar *v* park
el apartamento apartment
el apéndice appendix (body part)
el aperitivo appetizer [starter BE]
aquí here
el árbol tree
la aromaterapia aromatherapy
arreglar *v* repair
el arroyo stream
la arteria artery
la articulación joint (body part)
los artículos goods; **~ para el
  hogar** household good

la artritis arthritis
asaltar *v* mug
el asalto attack
el ascensor elevator [lift BE]
asiático Asian
el asiento seat; **~ de niño** car
  seat; **~ de pasillo** aisle seat
asistir *v* attend
asmático asthmatic
la aspiradora vacuum cleaner
la aspirina aspirin
atracado robbed
atracar *v* rob
Australia Australia
australiano Australian
auténtico real
el autobús bus; **~ rápido**
  express bus
automático automatic
la autopista highway
  [motorway BE]
el autoservicio self-service
la avería breakdown
el avión airplane, plane
avisar *v* notify
ayer yesterday
la ayuda *n* help
ayudar *v* help
el ayuntamiento town hall
azul blue

B

bailar v dance

bajarse v get off (a train, bus, subway)

bajo low

el ballet ballet

el baloncesto basketball

el bálsamo para después del afeitado aftershave

el banco bank

el bañador swimsuit

el baño bathroom

el bar bar; ~ **de tapas** tapas bar; ~ **gay** gay bar

barato cheap, inexpensive

la barbacoa barbecue

la barca de remos rowboat

el barco boat

los bastones poles (skiing)

la basura trash [rubbish BE]

la batería battery (car)

el bebé baby

beber v drink

la bebida n drink

beis beige

el béisbol baseball

besar v kiss

el biberón baby bottle

la biblioteca library

la bicicleta bicycle; ~ **de montaña** mountain bike

el billete n bill (money); ~ ticket; ~ **de autobús** bus ticket; ~ **de ida** one-way (ticket); ~ **de ida y vuelta** round trip [return BE]; ~ **electrónico** e-ticket

el biquini bikini

blanco white

la blusa blouse

la boca mouth

el bolígrafo pen

la bolsa de basura garbage [rubbish BE] bag

el bolsillo pocket

el bolso purse [handbag BE]

los bomberos fire department

la bombilla lightbulb

borrar v clear (on an ATM); ~ v delete (computer)

el bosque forest; ~ **pluvial** rainforest

las botas boots; ~ **de montaña** hiking boots

el bote jar

la botella bottle

el brazo arm

británico British

el broche brooch

bucear to dive

bueno adj good

buenas noches good evening

buenas tardes good afternoon

buenos días good morning
la bufanda scarf
el buzón de correo mailbox
[postbox BE]

C

la cabaña cabin (house)
el cabaré cabaret
la cabeza head (body part)
la cafetería cafe, coffee shop, snack
bar
la caja case (amount);
~ **fuerte** n safe
el cajero cashier;
~ **automático** ATM
el calcetín sock
la calefacción heater [heating BE]
calentar v heat, warm
la calidad quality
la calle de sentido único one-way
street
calor hot, warm (temperature)
las calorías calories
los calzoncillos briefs [underpants
BE] (clothing)
la cama single bed; ~ **de
matrimonio** double bed
la cámara camera;
~ **digital** digital camera
la camarera waitress
el camarero waiter

el camarote cabin (ship)
cambiar v change, exchange, transfer
el cambio n change (money);
~ **de divisas** currency exchange
caminar v walk
la caminata n walk
el camino path
la camisa shirt
la camiseta T-shirt
el cámping campsite
el campo field (sports);
~ **de batalla** battleground;
~ **de golf** golf course
Canadá Canada
canadiense Canadian
cancelar v cancel
el/la canguro babysitter
cansado tired
el cañón canyon
la cara face
los caramelos candy [sweets BE]
la caravana mobile home
el carbón charcoal
el carnicero butcher
caro expensive
el carrete film (camera)
el carrito cart [trolley BE] (grocery
store); ~ **de equipaje** luggage cart
la carta letter
la carta n menu; ~ **de
bebidas** drink menu; ~ **para**

niños children's menu; **~ de vinos** wine list
la cartera *n* wallet
el cartón carton; **~ de tabaco** carton of cigarettes
la casa house; **~ de cambio** currency exchange office
casado married
casarse *v* marry
la cascada waterfall
el casco helmet
los cascos headphones
el casino casino
el castillo castle
el catarro cold (sickness)
la catedral cathedral
el catre cot
causar daño *v* damage
el cazo saucepan
el CD CD
la cena dinner
el centímetro centimeter
el centro downtown area; **~ comercial** shopping mall [centre BE]; **~ de negocios** business center; **~ de salud y belleza** spa
el cepillo de pelo hair brush
la cerámica pottery
cerca near; **~ de aquí** nearby
la cerilla *n* match

cerrado closed
cerrar *v* close, lock; **~ sesión** *v* log off (computer)
el cerrojo *n* lock
el certificado certificate; **~ de la policía** police report
la cesta basket (grocery store)
el chaleco salvavidas life jacket
el champú shampoo
la chaqueta jacket
la charcutería delicatessen
el cheque *n* check [cheque BE] (payment); **~ de viaje** traveler's check [cheque BE]
el chicle chewing gum
chino Chinese
el chubasquero raincoat
el chupete pacifier [soother BE]
el cibercafé internet cafe
el ciclismo cycling
el ciclomotor moped
la ciencia science
el cigarrillo cigarette
la cima peak (of a mountain)
el cine movie theater
la cinta transportadora conveyor belt
el cinturón *n* belt
el circuito de carreras racetrack
la cita appointment
la ciudad town

la clase class; **~ económica** economy class; **~ preferente** business class

la clave personal identification number (PIN)

el club de jazz jazz club

cobrar *v* bill (charge); **~** *v* cash; **~** *v* charge (credit card)

el cobre copper

el coche *n* car; **~ de alquiler** rental [hire BE] car; **~ automático** automatic car; **~ cama** sleeper [sleeping BE] car; **~ con transmisión manual** manual car

el cochecito stroller [pushchair BE]

la cocina kitchen

cocinar *v* cook

el código de país country code

el codo elbow

la colada laundry

el colegio school

la colina hill

el collar necklace

la colonia cologne

el color color

la columna vertebral spine (body part)

el comedor dining room

comer *v* eat

la comida food, lunch, meal;

~ rápida fast food

la comisaría police station

cómo how

el compañero de trabajo colleague

la compañia company; **~ aérea** airline; **~ de seguros** insurance company

comprar *v* buy, shop

la compresa sanitary napkin [pad BE]

el comprimido tablet (medicine)

con with; **~ plomo** leaded (gas)

el concierto concert

conducir *v* drive

conectarse *v* connect (internet)

la conexión connection (internet); **~ de vuelo** connection (flight)

la conferencia conference

confirmar *v* confirm

el congelador freezer

la congestión congestion

conocer *v* meet (someone)

la consigna automática luggage locker

el consulado Consulate

el consultor consultant

contagioso contagious

la contraseña password

el control de pasaportes passport control

el corazón heart

la corbata tie (clothing)

el correo *n* mail [post BE]; **~ aéreo**
airmail; **~ certificado** registered
mail; **~ electrónico** *n* e-mail
cortar *v* cut (hair); **~ en
rodajas** to slice
cortarse las puntas *v* trim (hair cut)
el corte *n* cut (injury); **~ de pelo**
haircut
corto short
costar *v* cost
la costilla rib (body part)
la crema cream; **~ antiséptica**
antiseptic cream;
~ de afeitar shaving cream;
~ hidratante lotion
el cristal crystal
el cruce intersection
cuándo when (question)
cuánto cuesta how much
el cubierto utensil
la cuchara spoon;
~ medidora measuring spoon
la cucharadita teaspoon
la cuchilla desechable
disposable razor
el cuchillo knife
el cuello neck; **~ de pico** V-neck;
~ redondo crew neck
el cuenco bowl
la cuenta account; **~ de ahorro**
savings account; **~ corriente**

checking [current BE] account
cuero leather
la cueva cave
el cumpleaños birthday
la cuna crib

D

dar to give; **~ el pecho** breastfeed;
~ fuego light (cigarette);
~ las gracias a *v* thank
de from, of; **~ acuerdo** OK;
~ la mañana a.m.; **~ la tarde**
p.m.; **~ la zona** local
declarar *v* declare
el dedo finger; **~ del pie** toe
deletrear *v* spell
delicioso delicious
la dentadura denture
el dentista dentist
dentro in
la depilacion wax;
~ de cejas eyebrow wax;
~ de las ingles bikini wax
deportes sports
depositar *v* deposit
el depósito bancario
deposit (bank)
la derecha right (direction)
desaparecido missing
el desatascador plunger
desatendido unattended

el desayuno breakfast
descansado well-rested
desconectar v disconnect
(computer)
el descuento discount
desechable disposable
el desierto desert
el desodorante deodorant
despachar medicamentos v fill
[make up BE] a prescription
el despacho de billetes
ticket office
despacio slowly
despertarse v wake
después after
el detergente detergent
detrás de behind (direction)
devolver v exchange, return (goods)
el día day
diabético diabetic
el diamante diamond
la diarrea diarrhea
el diente tooth
el diesel diesel
difícil difficult
digital digital
el dinero money
la dirección direction
la dirección address;
~ **de correo electrónico**
e-mail address

discapacitado handicapped
[disabled BE]
la discoteca club (dance, night);
~ **gay** gay club
disculparse v excuse (to get
attention)
disfrutar v enjoy
disponible available
divorciar v divorce
doblada dubbed
doblando (la esquina) around
(the corner)
la docena dozen
el documento de identidad
identification
el dólar dollar (U.S.)
el dolor pain; ~ **de
cabeza** headache; ~ **de
espalda** backache; ~ **de
estómago** stomachache;
~ **de oído** earache; ~ **de pecho**
chest pain
**los dolores
menstruales** menstrual cramps
dónde where (question)
dormir v sleep
el dormitorio dormitory
la ducha shower
dulce sweet (taste)
durante during
el DVD DVD

E

la edad age
el edificio building
el efectivo cash
el efecto secundario side effect
el ejemplar specimen
embarazada pregnant
embarcar v board
la emergencia emergency
el empaste filling (tooth)
empezar v begin, start
empinado steep
empujar v push (door sign)
en la esquina on the corner
el encaje lace
encender v turn on
el enchufe eléctrico electric outlet
encontrarse mal v be ill
la enfermedad de transmisión sexual sexually transmitted disease (STD)
el enfermero/la enfermera nurse
enfermo sick
enseñar v show
entender v understand
la entrada admission/cover charge; ~ entrance
entrar v enter
el entretenimiento entertainment
enviar v send, ship; ~ **por correo** v mail; ~ **un correo electrónico** v e-mail; ~ **un fax** v fax ; ~ **un mensaje de texto** v text (send a message)
envolver v wrap
la época period (of time)
el equipaje luggage [baggage BE]; ~ **de mano** carry-on (piece of hand luggage)
el equipo team
el equipo equipment; ~ **de buceo** diving equipment; ~ **de esnórquel** snorkeling equipment
equis ele (XL) extra large
el error mistake
la erupción cutánea rash
las escaleras stairs; ~ **mecánicas** escalators
el escáner scanner
el escaparate window case
la escoba broom
el escozor sting
escribir v write; ~ **a máquina** v type
el escurridor colander
el esguince sprain
el esmalte enamel (jewelry)
eso that
la espalda back
España Spain
el español Spanish
la espátula spatula

la especialidad de la casa special (food)
el especialista specialist (doctor)
la espera *n* wait
esperar *v* wait
la espuma para el pelo mousse (hair)
el esquí *n* ski
esquiar *v* ski
los esquís acuáticos water skis
esta noche tonight
la estaca tent peg
la estación station;
  ~ de autobuses bus station;
  ~ de metro subway [underground BE] station; **~ de tren** train [railway BE] station
el estadio stadium
el estado de salud condition (medical)
los Estados Unidos United States (U.S.)
estadounidense American
el estanco tobacconist
el estanque pond
estar *v* be; **~ de paso** *v* pass through
la estatua statue
el este east
el estilista hairstylist
esto this

el estómago stomach
estrellarse *v* crash (car)
estreñido constipated
estudiando studying
el estudiante student
estudiar *v* study
el euro euro
el exceso excess; **~ de velocidad** speeding
la excursión excursion
experto expert (skill level)
la extensión extension (phone)
extraer *v* extract (tooth)
extraño strange

F

fácil *adj* easy
la factura bill [invoice BE]
la facturación check-in (airport)
facturar check (luggage)
la falda skirt
la familia family
la farmacia pharmacy [chemist BE]
el fax *n* fax
la fecha date (calendar)
feliz *adj* happy
feo *adj* ugly
el ferry ferry
la fianza deposit (to reserve a room)
la fiebre fever

el film transparente plastic wrap
[cling film BE]

el fin de semana weekend

firmar *v* sign (name)

la flor flower

la fórmula infantil formula (baby)

el formulario form

la foto exposure (film);
~ photo; ~**copia** photocopy;
~**grafía** photography;
~ **digital** digital photo

la fregona mop

los frenos brakes (car)

frente a opposite

fresco fresh

frío *adj* cold (temperature)

las frutas y verduras produce

la frutería y verdulería
produce store

el fuego fire

la fuente fountain

fuera outside

el fuerto fort

fumar *v* smoke

la funda para la cámara
camera case

el fútbol soccer [football BE]

G

las gafas glasses;
~ **de sol** sunglasses

el garaje garage (parking)

la garganta throat

la garrafa carafe

el gas butano cooking gas

la gasolina gas [petrol BE];
~ **sin plomo** unleaded gas

la gasolinera gas [petrol BE]
station

gay gay

el gerente manager

el gimnasio gym

el ginecólogo gynecologist

la gomina gel (hair)

la gota drop (medicine)

grabar *v* burn (CD); ~ *v* engrave

gracias thank you

los grados degrees (temperature);
~ **centígrado** Celsius

el gramo gram

grande large

los grandes almacenes
department store

la granja farm

gratuito free

gris gray

la grúa tow truck

el grupo group

guapo attractive

guardar *v* save (computer)

la guarnición side dish, order

el guía guide

la guía guide book; **~ de tiendas** store directory
gustar v like; **me gusta** I like

H

ha sufrido daños damaged
la habitación room;
  ~ individual single room;
  ~ libre vacancy
hablar v speak
hacer v have; **~ una apuesta** v place (a bet); **~ un arreglo** v alter; **~ una llamada** v phone;
  ~ las maletas v pack;
  ~ turismo sightseeing
hambriento hungry
helado icy
la hermana sister
el hermano brother
el hielo ice
el hígado liver (body part)
la hinchazón swelling
hipermétrope far-sighted [long-sighted BE]
el hipódromo horsetrack
el hockey hockey; **~ sobre hielo** ice hockey
la hoja de afeitar razor blade
hola hello
el hombre man
el hombro shoulder

hondo deeply
la hora hour
el horario n schedule [timetable BE]
los horarios hours; **~ de atención al público** business hours; **~ de oficina** office hours; **~ de visita** visiting hours
las horas de consulta office hours (doctor's)
el hornillo camp stove
el horno stove
el hospital hospital
el hotel hotel
hoy today
el hueso bone

I

el ibuprofeno ibuprofen
la ida y vuelta round-trip [return BE]
la iglesia church
impresionante stunning
imprimir v print
el impuesto duty (tax)
incluir v include
inconsciente unconscious
increíble amazing
la infección vaginal vaginal infection
infectado infected
el inglés English

iniciar sesión v log on (computer)
el insecto bug
la insolación sunstroke
el insomnio insomnia
la insulina insulin
interesante interesting
internacional international
(airport area)
la internet internet
el/la intérprete interpreter
el intestino intestine
introducir v insert
ir a v go (somewhere)
ir de compras v go shopping
Irlanda Ireland
irlandés Irish
el IVA sales tax [VAT BE]
la izquierda left (direction)

J

el jabón soap
el jardín botánico
botanical garden
el jazz jazz
el jersey sweater
joven young
las joyas jewelry
la joyería jeweler
jubilado retired
jugar v play
el juguete toy

K

el kilo kilo; **~gramo** kilogram;
~metraje mileage
el kilómetro kilometer;
~ cuadrado square kilometer

L

el labio lip
la laca hairspray
el ladrón thief
el lago lake
la lana wool
la lancha motora motor boat
largo long
el lavabo sink
la lavadora washing machine
la lavandería laundromat
[launderette BE]
lavar v wash
el lavavajillas dishwasher
la lección lesson
lejos far
la lengua tongue
la lente lens
las lentillas de contacto
contact lens
las letras arts
las libras esterlinas pounds
(British sterling)
libre de impuestos duty-free
la librería bookstore

el libro book
la lima de uñas nail file
limpiar *v* clean
la limpieza de cutis facial
limpio *adj* clean
la línea line (train)
el lino linen
la linterna flashlight
el líquido liquid; **~ de lentillas de contacto** contact lens solution; **~ lavavajillas** dishwashing liquid
listo ready
la litera berth
el litro liter
la llamada *n* call; **~ de teléfono** phone call; **~ despertador** wake-up call
llamar *v* call
la llave key; **~ de habitación** room key; **~ electrónica** key card
el llavero key ring
las llegadas arrivals (airport)
llegar *v* arrive
llenar *v* fill
llevar *v* take; **~ en coche** lift (to give a ride)
la lluvia rain
lluvioso rainy
lo siento sorry
localizar *v* reach
la luz light (overhead)

M

la madre mother
magnífico magnificent
el malestar estomacal upset stomach
la maleta bag, suitcase
la mandíbula jaw
las mangas cortas short sleeves
las mangas largas long sleeves
la manicura manicure
la mano hand
la manta blanket
mañana tomorrow; **la ~** morning
el mapa map; **~ de carreteras** road map; **~ de ciudad** town map; **~ de la pista** trail [piste BE] map
el mar sea
marcar *v* dial
mareado dizzy
el mareo motion [travel BE] sickness
el marido husband
marrón brown
el martillo hammer
más more; **~ alto** louder; **~ bajo** lower; **~ barato** cheaper; **~ despacio** slower; **~ grande** larger; **~ pequeño** smaller; **~ rápido** faster; **~ tarde** later; **~ temprano** earlier

el masaje massage;
~ **deportivo** sports massage

el mástil tent pole

el mecánico mechanic

el mechero lighter

la media hora half hour

mediano medium (size)

la medianoche midnight

el medicamento medicine

el médico doctor

medio half; ~ **kilo** half-kilo;
~**día** noon [midday BE]

medir v measure (someone)

mejor best

menos less

el mensaje message;
~ **instantáneo** instant message

el mercado market

el mes month

la mesa table

el metro subway [underground BE]

el metro cuadrado square meter

la mezquita mosque

el microondas microwave

el minibar mini-bar

el minuto minute

el mirador overlook [viewpoint BE]
(scenic place)

mirar v look

la misa mass (church service)

mismo same

los mocasines loafers

la mochila backpack

molestar v bother

la moneda coin, currency

mono cute

la montaña n mountain

el monumento conmemorativo
memorial (place)

morado purple

el mostrador de información
information desk

mostrar v display

la moto acuática jet ski

la motocicleta motorcycle

movilidad mobility

la mujer wife, woman

la multa fine (fee for breaking law)

la muñeca doll; ~ wrist

el músculo muscle

el museo museum

la música music; ~ **clásica**
classical music; ~ **folk** folk music;
~ **pop** pop music

el muslo thigh

N

nacional domestic

la nacionalidad nationality

nada nothing

nadar v swim

las nalgas buttocks

naranja orange (color)
la nariz nose
necesitar v need
los negocios business
negro black
nevado snowy
la nevera refrigerator
el nieto grandchild
la niña girl
el niño boy, child
el nivel intermedio intermediate
no no
la noche evening, night
el nombre name;
  ~ de usuario username
normal regular
las normas de vestuario
  dress code
el norte north
la novia girlfriend
el novio boyfriend
el número number; **~ de fax**
  fax number; **~ de permiso**
  de conducir driver's license
  number; **~ de teléfono** phone
  number; **~ de teléfono de**
  información information (phone)

O

la obra de teatro n play (theater)
el oculista optician

el oeste west
la oficina office; **~ de correos**
  post office; **~ de objetos**
  perdidos lost and found; **~ de**
  turismo tourist information office
el ojo eye
la olla pot
la ópera opera
el ordenador computer
la oreja ear
la orina urine
el oro gold; **~ amarillo** yellow
  gold; **~ blanco** white gold
la orquesta orchestra
oscuro dark
el otro camino alternate route
la oxígenoterapia oxygen
  treatment

P

padecer del corazón heart
  condition
el padre father
pagar v pay
el pájaro bird
el palacio palace; **~ de las cortes**
  parliament building
los palillos chinos chopsticks
la panadería bakery
los pantalones pants [trousers BE];
  ~ cortos shorts

el pañal diaper [nappy BE]
el pañuelo de paper tissue
el papel paper; **~ de aluminio** aluminum [kitchen BE] foil; **~ de cocina** paper towel; **~ higiénico** toilet paper
el paquete package
para for; **~ llevar** to go [take away BE]; **~ no fumadores** non-smoking
el paracetamol acetaminophen [paracetamol BE]
la parada n stop; **~ de autobús** bus stop
el paraguas umbrella
pararse v stop
el párking parking garage
el parque playpen; **~** park; **~ de atracciones** amusement park
el partido game; **~ de fútbol** soccer [football BE]; **~ de voleibol** volleyball game
el pasajero passenger; **~ con billete** ticketed passenger
el pasaporte passport
el pase de acceso a los remontes lift pass
el pasillo aisle
la pasta de dientes toothpaste
la pastelería pastry shop
el patio de recreo playground

el peatón pedestrian
el pecho chest (body part)
el pediatra pediatrician
la pedicura pedicure
pedir v order
el peinado hairstyle
el peine comb
la película movie
peligroso dangerous
el pelo hair
el peltre pewter
la peluquería de caballeros barber
la peluquería hair salon
los pendientes earrings
el pene penis
la penicilina penicillin
la pensión bed and breakfast
pequeño small
perder v lose (something)
perdido lost
el perfume perfume
el periódico newspaper
la perla pearl
permitir v allow, permit
el perro guía guide dog
la persona con discapacidad visual visually impaired person
la picadura de insecto insect bite
picante spicy
picar v stamp (a ticket)

el pie foot
la piel skin
la pierna leg
la pieza part (for car)
los pijamas pajamas
la pila battery
la píldora Pill (birth control)
la piscina pool; **~ cubierta** indoor
pool; **~ exterior** outdoor pool;
~ infantil kiddie [paddling BE]
pool
la pista trail [piste BE]
la pizzería pizzeria
el placer pleasure
la plancha *n* iron (clothes)
planchar *v* iron
la planta floor [storey BE];
~ baja ground floor
la plata silver;
~ esterlina sterling silver
el platino platinum
el plato dish (kitchen);
~ principal main course
la playa beach
la plaza town square
la policía police
la pomada cream (ointment)
ponerse en contacto con *v* contact
por for; **~** per; **~ día** per day;
~ favor please; **~ hora** per hour;
~ la noche overnight; **~ noche**

per night; **~ semana** per week
el postre dessert
el precio price
precioso beautiful
el prefijo area code
la pregunta question
presentar *v* introduce
el preservativo condom
la primera clase first class
primero first
los principales sitios de interés
main attraction
principiante beginner, novice
(skill level)
la prioridad de paso right of way
la prisa rush
el probador fitting room
probar *v* taste
el problema problem
el producto good;
~ de limpieza cleaning product
programar *v* schedule
prohibir *v* prohibit
el pronóstico forecast
pronunciar *v* pronounce
el protector solar sunscreen
provisional temporary
próximo next
el público public
el pueblo village
el puente bridge

la puerta gate (airport); ~ door;
  ~ **de incendios** fire door
el pulmón lung
la pulsera bracelet
el puro cigar

Q

qué what (question)
quedar bien v fit (clothing)
quedarse v stay
la queja complaint
la quemadura solar sunburn
querer v love (someone)
quién who (question)
el quiosco newsstand

R

la ración portion; ~ **para
  niños** children's portion
la rampa para silla de ruedas
  wheelchair ramp
el rap rap (music)
rápido express, fast
la raqueta racket (sports),
  ~ **de nieve** snowshoe
la reacción alérgica
  allergic reaction
recargar v recharge
la recepción reception
la receta prescription
recetar v prescribe

rechazar v decline (credit card)
recibir v receive
el recibo receipt
reciclar recycling
recoger v pick up (something)
la recogida de equipajes
  baggage claim
la recomendación
  recommendation
recomendar v recommend
el recorrido tour; ~ **en autobús**
  bus tour; ~ **turístico** sightseeing
  tour
recto straight
el recuerdo souvenir
el regalo gift
la región region
el registro check in (hotel);
  ~ **del coche** vehicle registration
la regla period (menstrual)
el Reino Unido United Kingdom
  (U.K.)
la relación relationship
rellenar v fill out (form)
el reloj watch; ~ **de pared** wall
  clock
el remolque trailer
reparar v fix (repair)
el repelente de insectos
  insect repellent
repetir v repeat

la resaca hangover
la reserva reservation;
~ **natural** nature preserve
reservar v reserve
el/la residente de la UE
EU resident
respirar v breathe
el restaurante restaurant
retirar v withdraw; ~ **fondos**
withdrawal (bank)
retrasarse v delay
la reunión meeting
revelar v develop (film)
revisar v check (on something)
la revista magazine
el riñón kidney (body part)
el río river
robado stolen
robar v steal
el robo theft
la rodilla knee
rojo red
romántico romantic
romper v break
la ropa clothing;
~ **interior** underwear
rosa pink
roto broken
el rugby rugby
la rueda tire [tyre BE];
~ **pinchada** flat tire [tyre BE]

las ruinas ruins
la ruta route; ~ **de**
senderismo walking route

S

la sábana sheet
el sacacorchos corkscrew
el saco de dormir sleeping bag
la sala room; ~ **de conciertos**
concert hall; ~ **de espera**
waiting room; ~ **de reuniones**
meeting room
la salida check-out (hotel)
la salida n exit; ~ **de urgencia**
emergency exit
las salidas departures (airport)
salir v exit, leave
el salón room; ~ **de**
congresos convention hall;
~ **de juegos recreativos** arcade;
~ **de manicura** nail salon
¡Salud! Cheers!
la salud health
las sandalias sandals
sangrar v bleed
la sangre blood
el santuario shrine
la sartén frying pan
la sauna sauna
el secador de pelo hair dryer
la secreción discharge (bodily fluid)

la seda silk
sediento thirsty
la seguridad security
el seguro insurance
seguro safe (protected)
el sello *n* stamp (postage)
el semáforo traffic light
la semana week
semanal weekly
el seminario seminar
el sendero trail; ~ **para bicicletas** bike route
el seno breast
sentarse *v* sit
separado separated (marriage)
ser *v* be
serio serious
el servicio restroom [toilet BE]; ~ service (in a restaurant); ~ **completo** full-service; ~ **de habitaciones** room service; ~ **inalámbrico a internet** wireless internet service; ~ **de internet** internet service; ~ **de lavandería** laundry service; ~ **de limpieza de habitaciones** housekeeping service
la servilleta napkin
sí yes
el sida AIDS

la silla chair; ~ **para niños** child seat; ~ **de ruedas** wheelchair
el símbolo symbol (keyboard)
sin without; ~ **alcohol** non-alcoholic; ~ **grasa** fat free; ~ **receta** over the counter (medication)
la sinagoga synagogue
el sitio de interés attraction (place)
el sobre envelope
el socorrista lifeguard
el sol sun
solamente only
soleado sunny
solo alone
soltero single (marriage)
el sombrero hat
la somnolencia drowsiness
sordo deaf
soso bland
el suavizante conditioner
el subtítulo subtitle
sucio dirty
la sudadera sweatshirt
el suelo floor
el sujetador bra
súper super (fuel)
superior upper
el supermercado grocery store, supermarket

la supervisión supervision
el sur south
el surfista windsurfer

T

la tabla board; **~ de snowboard** snowboard; **~ de surf** surfboard
la talla size; **~ grande** plus size; **~ pequeña** petite size
el taller garage (repair)
el talón de equipaje luggage [baggage BE] ticket
el tampón tampon
la taquilla locker; **~** reservation desk
tarde late (time)
la tarde afternoon
la tarjeta card; **~ de cajero automático** ATM card; **~ de crédito** credit card; **~ de débito** debit card; **~ de embarque** boarding pass; **~ internacional de estudiante** international student card; **~ de memoria** memory card; **~ de negocios** business card; **~ postal** postcard; **~ de seguro** insurance card; **~ de socio** membership card; **~ telefónica** phone card
la tasa fee

el taxi taxi
la taza cup; **~ medidora** measuring cup
el teatro theater; **~ de la ópera** opera house
la tela impermeable groundcloth [groundsheet BE]
el teleférico cable car
el teléfono telephone; **~ móvil** cell [mobile BE] phone; **~ público** pay phone
la telesilla chair lift
el telesquí ski/drag lift
la televisión TV
el templo temple (religious)
temprano early
el tenedor fork
tener v have; **~ dolor** v hurt (have pain); **~ náuseas** v be nauseous
el tenis tennis
la tensión arterial blood pressure
la terminal terminal (airport)
terminar v end
la terracotta terracotta
terrible terrible
el texto n text (message)
el tiempo time; **~** weather
la tienda store; **~ de alimentos naturales** health food store; **~ de antigüedades** antique store; **~ de bebidas alcohólicas**

liquor store [off-licence BE];
~ de campaña tent; **~ de deportes** sporting goods store;
~ de fotografía camera store;
~ de juguetes toy store;
~ de música music store;
~ de recuerdos souvenir store;
~ de regalos gift shop;
~ de ropa clothing store
las tijeras scissors
la tintorería dry cleaner
el tipo de cambio exchange rate
tirar v pull (door sign)
la tirita bandage
la toalla towel
la toallita baby wipe
el tobillo ankle
el torneo de golf golf tournament
la torre tower
la tos n cough
toser v cough
el total total (amount)
trabajar v work
tradicional traditional
traducir v translate
traer v bring
tragar v swallow
el traje suit
tranquilo quiet
el tren train; **~ rápido** express

train
triste sad
la trona highchair
el trozo piece
la tumbona deck chair
el turista tourist

U

último last
la universidad university
uno one
la uña nail; **~ del dedo** fingernail;
~ del ple toenail
urgente urgent
usar v use

V

las vacaciones vacation [holiday BE]
vaciar v empty
la vacuna vaccination
la vagina vagina
la validez valid
valioso valuable
el valle valley
el valor value
el vaquero denim
los vaqueros jeans
el vaso glass (drinking)
el váter químico chemical toilet

vegetariano vegetarian
la vejiga bladder
vender v sell
el veneno poison
venir v come
la ventana window
el ventilador fan (appliance)
ver v see
verde green
el vestido dress (piece of clothing)
el viaje trip
el vidrio glass (material)
viejo old
la viña vineyard
la violación n rape
violar v rape
el visado visa (passport document)
visitar v visit
la vitamina vitamin

la vitrina display case
viudo widowed
vivir v live
vomitar v vomit
el vuelo flight; ~ **internacional** international flight; ~ **nacional** domestic flight

Z

la zapatería shoe store
las zapatillas slippers;
  ~ **de deporte** sneaker
los zapatos shoes
la zona area; ~ **de compras** shopping area; ~ **de fumadores** smoking area; ~ **para picnic** picnic area
el zoológico zoo
zurcir v mend

Resounding Praise for Tom Deitz's

"A midnight train ride of a story, departing from a normal-seeming station, traversing increasingly wild country, plunging down a steep mountain track"

Roger Zelazny

"Tom Deitz is trying something more~~~~~~ tlous, darker, and he's writing bet~~~~ ever"

Mercedes Lackey, author of Magic~~~~

"A refreshingly different kind~~~~~ story and characters captu~~~~~ tion"

A.C. Crispin, author of The Staro~~~~

"Successfully combines such disparate elements as ancient Welsh mythology and Southern Gothic . . . Tom Deitz weaves a potent spell indeed"

Josepha Sherman, author of Child of Faerie, Child of Earth

"May well be the finest fantasy of the year, or even of the decade . . . A riveting read, brimming with grief, ecstasy, and the sweet pain of being Other . . . Tom Deitz is a master of modern fantasy"

Brad Strickland, author of Moondreams

DREAMBUILDER

TOM DEITZ

AVONOVA

AVON BOOKS • NEW YORK

AVON BOOKS
A division of
The Hearst Corporation
1350 Avenue of the Americas
New York, New York 10019

Copyright © 1992 by Thomas F. Deitz
Cover illustration by Tim White
Published by arrangement with the author
Library of Congress Catalog Card Number: 92-93075
ISBN: 0-380-76290-0

First AvoNova Printing: October 1992

AVONOVA TRADEMARK REG. U.S. PAT. OFF. AND IN OTHER COUNTRIES, MARCA REGISTRADA, HECHO EN U.S.A.

Printed in the U.S.A.

RA   10   9   8   7   6   5   4   3   2   1

For Bettie and Grace and Wilma
who showed me the secrets of books
and
for James Robert Nicholson
who did the same for cars

Acknowledgments

Sheri Bender
Russell Cutts
Joel Dukes
Gilbert Head
Greg Keyes
Adele Leone
Betty Marchinton
Buck Marchinton
Larry Marchinton
Chris Miller
Klon Newell
B. J. Steinhaus
Brad Strickland
and
An anonymous someone in Huntsville who wouldn't spill the beans about Stealth paint. Your government has spent its money well.

Prologue

Light My Fire

Oglethorpe County, Georgia
Beltane—midnight

Fire from a flaming wagon flicks his face with red, while wood chars and canvas flares and metal melts. Color becomes blackness as paint renders up its own bright spark and drinks in night, even as the delicate carvings that held those hues shrink to shapeless knots when heat takes hold and warps handwork to its artless will.

Wind carries pops and crackles, and hurls the thunder of oxidation at his ears. Goats cry in the forest, newly freed.

Smoke spreads thin among the stars but does not hide them; a shroud of midnight lace lurks close above the leaves.

Naked, he watches the pyre burn its course.

He is iron and carbon, calcium and zinc. He is Earth.

He pours creek water from a pewter cup upon his head. It is cold and it shimmers down his shoulders, sucking up the warmth, steaming on his skin. He scoops two handfuls of ash from the mound before him and smears them across his face—his chest—his back, legs, arms, hips, stomach—genitals: Earth and Water.

He breathes deep, inhales smoke that before was wood and bone and wonder: Earth and Air.

He reaches into the ghost of conflagration and does not shrink from the heat or pain, though it crisps the hair from his arms. His fingers find solidity and he draws it forth: a bar of steel, red, as from a forge. It hurts, oh how it hurts! Pain beyond pain, yet he holds it: grips it in both hands and waits.

Earth and Fire.

And still he waits, and the pain increases, spreads through his palms and fingers and into his wrist, up his arms, until all the world is pain. Until nothing of Earth remains except awareness. No light. No heat. No sound. No smell.

He simply *is*, as is the pain.

A voice: Soft . . . Female . . . Annoyed but not surprised.

"My . . . son?"

"Mother?"

"And who else could it be?"

"Mother . . . I have come to the Wall."

"I know."

"Is it time for the Crossing?"

"You tell me."

"I feared that would be your answer."

"Then why ask?"

"Because someday your reply will change."

"It will *never* change—until you change the question."

"And when will that be?"

"You will know."

"So I must return again? I must back up once more?"

"You know that answer, too."

"Can you not aid me at all? Not give me at least a hint of what I must accomplish?"

Her voice is impassive—though she *has* no voice. "Finish what you have begun. Become what you have not yet finished."

"So I feared."

Silence. Silence and pain, but fading. He can remain where he is but a little longer.

"You have not yet asked the other question: the one you *know* I will answer."

"Suppose I do not."

"You will be lost."

Silence, and pain fades further. He once more senses light and the smell of burning wood.

"Ask!"

"I . . . oh, very well."

"Ask!"

"Who is the Man? What is the Beast?"

A gentle chuckle, one with the snapping of embers: "Come, my son, I will show you."

Pain fades. Wind tickles his ribs, and he shivers. Dried mud flakes from his chest. His shadow is not the same. And there is more than ever to remember.

PART I

HURTING

Chapter 1

Rocky Top

Welch County, Georgia
Friday, June 18—dusk

When the bulb in the overhead light made a sputtering, buzzing sound like someone stir-frying a bumble bee, and then, with a soft, resigned *clink*, blinked out, plunging her makeshift mobile-home office into a spirit-depressing gloom, Brandy Wallace finally knew for certain that she had been cursed by the gods—though *which* gods and for *what* nefarious reason, she hadn't the foggiest notion. No, scratch that: the *perpetrators* she could pretty well narrow down to two—or at least two general genera.

Either her mounting tide of afflictions betokened the caprice of some clan of sky divinities—why *else* would it have rained for two months solid *just* when she needed clear days and firm ground in which to complete the northwest foundations of the enormous modular manor that already rose (in its more finished eastern portions) to second-story battlement level fifty yards beyond the trailer's front windows?—*or* her trials were born of a race of earth elementals she had inadvertently angered by delving trenches into their heretofore sacrosanct hillside homes.

The latter, at the moment, seemed more likely, especially as the latest calamity (ignoring the abdicated light bulb) did, in fact, involve undermined footings. The ones in the northwest corner, to be exact; the ones that had *seemed* like solid granite when she'd jackhammered out the eighteen-inch square groove that was to house the foundations of the office/studio.

The ones that, quite unbeknownst to her, had rested atop a layer of stone so near the surface of an underground spring that the rock had collapsed beneath the added weight—with the result that an L-shaped section totaling twelve feet long had sagged six inches overnight. *Last* night, to be precise.

The ones she didn't know what to do about, unless it was to dig up everything, excavate farther to either side, and reinforce the bejesus out of the whole mess with steel rebar. And, of course, look for something besides her own faulty engineering to blame.

Like maybe the *Nunnehi*, she decided—the Cherokee elves: invisible spirit people who sometimes aided strangers lost in the deep mountain woods, and whose drumming could occasionally—it was said—still be heard thrumming up through the earth from their underground townhouses. Shoot, according to James Mooney's *Myths of the Cherokee*, which had been a sort of second Bible to both her and her half-Cherokee mother when she was a child, there was supposed to be a tribe of the magical guys beneath Blood Mountain a few miles away to the east. And she'd heard similar stories about Bloody Bald two counties farther over. The fact that no such tales were told about her own hunk of terra firma only meant that no one had been listening at the right place at the right time.

Or—more likely, given the tendency of her countrymen to befoul every place they lingered for more than a minute—that none of the Immortals felt like playing.

—Not, she added to herself, that there weren't plenty of *other* supernaturals on which to fix the blame. The shelves to the left of her drawing board/desk were crammed with books with mythological leanings, historical and fictive alike—including both *The Mabinogion* and *The Leabhar*

Gabhala Erenn; the aforementioned copy of Mooney; and her treasured, much dog-eared, editions of *The Lord of the Rings, Gormenghast,* and *Titus Groan*—which, with their emphases on elves and architecture respectively, were bibles themselves, after a fashion.

Still, Brandy considered wryly, given the circumstances, the native species of sprite was probably the most likely culprit. At least *they* lived underground.

Which, of course, was *total* bullshit. She no more believed in elves than the Man in the Moon—which in no wise diminished her interest in them, or (she had admitted to only two people in the world) a secret desire that they were real.

She sighed and lifted an accusing eyebrow at the now defunct light fixture, muttered an irritable "Shit!" and leaned back from the drawing board where she'd been feverishly erasing, relocating, and reruling lines for the last few hours. Lines that, when she finally got them realized in three dimensions, would embody a lifelong dream, the various evolutionary images of which papered the flimsy paneling of what had been intended as a spare bedroom six layers thick in places.

On the wall before her, for instance—the one that contained the single window—were the photographs that had sold her on this wild corner of north Georgia in the first place. And if sheer splendor of scenery alone was any inducement, her hunk of real estate truly should be the haunt of elves (whether local, European, or Tolkienian did not matter), for Brandy could never have lucked onto more spectacular territory, at least not east of the Rockies.

Here in the southeast corner of remote Welch County, the land rose and fell more dramatically than it did any-where else in the state, and though Brasstown Bald over on the Towns/Union County line was officially taller, it held no other candle to the peaks that poked at the heavens whichever way Brandy looked whenever she stepped outside. They reminded her, in fact, of the Smokeys up on the border of North Carolina and Tennessee. They were *that* steep and ruggedly formed, the valleys between them *that* precipitous. Waterfalls slid and frolicked in half of the neighboring hollows, and most of the timber hereabouts

was old-growth forest, hoary with age. It was primar-
ily federal land, too (in fact, the Chattahoochee National
Forest enclosed Brandy's property on three sides); but it
had somehow escaped the bouts of clear-cutting that had
rendered much of Georgia's other woodlands pale shadows
of their pre-Columbian splendor. It was the influence of the
Welches, she'd heard: one of the more positive benefits
of having a powerful family nearby—though how any
patrician Southern clan could have been environmentally
enlightened the necessary years ago to preserve the local
woodlands, she had no idea. Better not to ask; better to
enjoy blessings than subject them to the cold-eyed scrutiny
of logical analysis.

Typical of when she was tired and poised between staring mindlessly and active thought, Brandy's gaze was
drawn to the particularly impressive view beyond the window. A shoulder of mountain showed there, one rendered
largely devoid of trees by the presence too close underground of the enormous boulders that began emerging
from the soil a few feet beyond her front patio before
thrusting out like the rampart of some medieval fortress a
hundred yards farther downhill. Trees rose on either side—
oaks and hickories to the left, hemlocks to the right—and
beyond and a quarter mile lower, she could just make out
a finger of Haroldson Lake, its silver waters tinged faintly
pink by the westering sun. She had never figured out why
whoever had drawn the borders of the public land had not
used that sparkling water as a natural boundary and gone
on to include her knoll as part of the permanent preserve,
but the proof of their negligence showed in half a dozen
topographical maps tacked to the wall beneath the photographs. Each one was in a different scale, but all depicted
the fifteen acres that served as backdrop to her dream.

If she could keep the damned thing going!

That was what occupied the rest of the room: plans
for the preposterous quasi-castle she had taken to calling
Brandy Hall, after one of the Hobbit estates in her beloved
Tolkien. She had every last incarnation, too: from the
first rough sketch she'd scrawled in the margin of her
seventh grade history notebook after seeing a photo of the
Alhambra, through the intervening stages she'd contrived

in the dozen-odd years since then, to the final meticulously drafted design that was now rearing skyward down on the rock—but which was not in fact even yet the *final* iteration, because even at this late date, she was constantly revising details.

Still, that *was* the version that had commandeered the right-hand wall: elevations and elaborations, floor plans and perspectives, and a perfectly executed 1/24 scale model—of what looked more than anything else like a medium-sized Roman villa with a combination Byzantine basilica and Norse mead hall plopped in the middle where the atrium ought to be. *Except* that the top of every wall, including the four stubby corner towers, was crenelated to within an inch of its life, and the whole thing was slathered with enough stained glass and strapwork, gargoyles and Gothic arches, bay windows and bas reliefs, to make even the most jaded Pre-Raphaelite jealous.

And she had designed it all: *everything*—right down to the switchplates. And even beyond that, she intended to do as much of the actual construction herself as possible; that way she could see it was executed correctly—as the team of skinny teenagers she'd experimented with earlier in the spring manifestly had *not* accomplished.

Her *plan* was to have the basic structure sufficiently finished to be habitable by the resumption of school in the fall, at which time she'd have to shift hats from architect-cum-contractor-cum-day-laborer to the less comfortable one of neophyte art teacher in the local high school. It would be less satisfying, but at least the pay was good: fifty percent better than anywhere else in the state, courtesy of heavy local subsidies.

But, she now knew, that was a wildly unrealistic goal. At this point she'd be happy if she merely had the rest of the superstructure roughed in and roofed, a bedroom finished, and a usable kitchen and bathroom. With those modules to build from, she could work outward by slow degrees, maybe completing one wall or floor or ceiling per week. At that rate, she'd still be done in no time.

If the blessed *Nunnehi*—or whoever—cooperated.

She scowled, but did not switch on the fluorescent desk lamp in spite of the gathering gloom, then paused to lean back in the maroon corduroy swivel chair that was the room's one concession to comfort. The black crescents of her bear-claw necklace clicked against one another; one of the long raven-feather earrings she wore to invoke inspiration brushed her neck, making her flinch reflexively. The soundtrack to *Local Hero* started over on the unseen CD player programmed for REPEAT. A yawn found her, and she stretched luxuriously, feeling the tension flow out of the firm, lean muscles a spring's intensive labor had given her. She squeezed a biceps appreciatively: hard as rock— as hard as any man she'd ever known, if not so massive. And the rest of her body was the same: long and trim and tanned, her hands dry and rough, her nails worn to nubs. Not an ounce of fat anywhere, beyond the minimum biology reserved to feminize her curves. She was like her knoll: hard parts poking out of a softer outer layer where nature had scoured weakness away.

Her face was like that, too: hard and soft at once, with a pointed nose and chin framed by rounded cheeks and arching brows, and the whole tanned beneath a shoulder-length mane that had borne the brunt of her one recent indulgence. A natural blonde, she had dyed her locks sooty black a week ago in hopes the tradesmen hereabouts might take her more seriously. Unfortunately, it hadn't helped, and the main attitudinal alteration she'd noticed was that fewer folks now thought she looked like Candice Bergen, and more of them like Cher. Not that it really mattered: she was planning to lop off the whole mess soon anyway, what with the resistance it was offering to the rubber bands and bandannas that most often confined it these days. At least her jeans were cooperating—by getting looser; and workman's muscles or no, she'd never had any trouble overfilling T-shirts—or the sleeveless, fringed buckskin singlets she had taken, as now, to wearing in their stead.

But if she didn't perk up and figure out what to do about the damaged foundations, tomorrow would find her without a course of action, and she did not dare waste even an hour if she could help it. Besides, tomorrow was supposed to be sunny, and if she was good, she'd be able to work outside all day.

Sighing, she snagged a fresh pencil from the blue ceramic mug to the right (legacy of her most recent underachiever boyfriend), and scowled once more. Maybe the *Nunnehi* didn't appreciate what she was trying to do here; though she imagined she'd be pretty pissed if somebody stuck a concrete plug in the roof of her house, too. Perhaps she should just go out there on the outcrop and explain things to whatever spirits might be lurking around, and hope they heard. Or maybe not. She'd once read a tale about a house in Ireland beset by strange occurrences until someone pointed out it was built on one of the paths the Fairies used in their ridings. The house was summarily moved (or else had the offending corner chopped off, she could never remember which), and the disturbances had ceased.

But she was damned if she was going to lop a corner off *her* dream!

The very thought of it made her bite down on her pencil hard enough to make her fillings twinge. Maybe if she just cut a set of satellite grooves at right angles to the main footing, reinforced them with rebar, and filled them in, *that* would spread the stress over a wider area without her having to reexcavate one ninth of the whole foundation.

Or maybe . . .

She stared out the window, thinking. Watching the evening shroud the hardwoods to her left even as the hemlocks to her right glowed with a hint of red from the last rays of sunlight.

Maybe . . .

She blinked, rubbed her eyes, blinked again, then squinted harder into the thickening dusk.

Something had *moved* out there: in the shadow of that stubby oak to the left. Something white. But where was it now? And what had it *been*? It had been big, that was for certain: too large to be merely a random light effect. But it was gone now.

Or *was* it? She squinted again and was rewarded with another flash of white weaving in and out among the fringe of trees. And then stopping.

Without taking her eyes off the hazy shape, Brandy reached to her right and snagged the binoculars she always kept handy for bird-watching (and to spy on her infrequent work crews when she couldn't actually join them). They were good ones: expensive Zeisses. And when she had adjusted the focus, she was rewarded with a sight that at once gave her chills and roused a wonder she had not felt since she'd first seen *Fantasia* as a child.

Perhaps her recent speculations about the *Nunnehi*, elves, and their kindred had not been so far off the mark. For what she saw lurking under the eaves of the forest less than fifty yards from her trailer truly was a creature born of some other world than her own.

Her breath caught; a lump formed in her throat as she gazed upon it. Her eyes misted in spite of herself.

It was a deer—an old buck, from the form and length of its head and the depth of its massive chest. And it was equally obviously the standard Georgia whitetail, to judge by the shape of the tangle of antlers arching around its head like a crown of thorns.

But what made it different, what made every hair stand up on her body, was that—saving only its eyes, its hooves, and the tip of its fine, narrow nose—it was as white as new-fallen snow. Even the antlers—all twelve-plus points of them—looked more like ivory than bone.

And it was simply standing there at right angles to her, frozen in the classic pose so often depicted in bad wildlife art. (And she should know; she'd won some prizes with wildlife art herself.)

For at least a minute, awe ruled Brandy's senses. But then, inevitably, more practical considerations invaded her mind. That was a *very* large deer, and a *very* white one. The hide alone would bring a fair bit from the right sort of collector, never mind what a trophy hunter would pay for the head.

And the meat . . . why, that big bruiser must weigh two hundred pounds easy, more than enough to refill the growing hollows in her freezer where the neatly packaged remains of two of his fellows had to last until the resumption of deer season in the fall—if she didn't want to fall back on the squirrels, rabbits, quail, and doves that occupied the other odd corners. Them she'd eat if she had to, but venison was her addiction of choice.

Except that she would no more shoot that fine-looking buck than she'd walk through downtown Cordova in the nude, for the simple reason that deer season was still four months away, and her father, from whom she had learned to hunt (as she had learned to plant and harvest and can by the signs from her mom) had taught her never, *ever* to poach, no matter whose land she was on. And that she would do forever, in tribute to the dead man who had given her so much. If she shot that buck now, she could just imagine Dear Old Dad's ghost (perhaps crowned with ensanguined antlers, like Herne in the old *Robin of Sherwood* TV series) haunting her for the rest of her life.

Besides, by the time she dug out her trusty .308, found the right ammo, and got out the door, old Whitey there would likely have hightailed it anyway.

Besides, it was simply too beautiful to kill.

And at that very minute, as if it had somehow been party to her silent speculations, the deer turned and walked very calmly into the welcoming woods. The invisible sun promptly dipped below the horizon, and the whole knoll lapsed into purple shadow.

Brandy did not move for a very long time, as the room darkened around her and the wilderness outside was lost in the night.

Finally, though, she switched on the desk lamp and turned once more to her drawing board. Seeing the deer had given her an idea. Maybe if she echoed the cantilever shape of its antlers with some rebar reinforcements, she could . . .

Antlers?

And then realization hit her. This was the middle of June—which meant that buck deer should at best be displaying only the first velvety spikes of their autumn racks. Yet *that* big white guy had sported at least twelve points, all of them fully formed, and none with even the slightest trace of velvet.

And *that*, she thought, was very strange indeed.

Either that, or she'd just seen the *Nunnehi*.

Interlude 1

Safety Dance

Welch County, Georgia
Friday, June 18—midnight

He runs because that is the only means he can muster to bring the pain. He runs through fields and forests. He runs uphill and down. He runs across highways and through backyards. He is seen but not recognized; more a shape than a substance with a name. Names limit; he is limitless. Names distill complexity down to nonsense words—and it is in fear of such reduction that he runs.

He is pursued by dogs, and though he has not seen them *this* time, he has heard them: the long, lean hunting hounds that seek his spoor through wood and town and meadow. They will not catch him, but they may come close. He does not know what would happen then, for they never have—so far. But he does know—and fear—their master, and so he flees them.

But he mainly runs to bring the pain.

It has found him now; for muscles, bones, and nerves can only bear so much before they protest. He is relieved

16

by that, for he wondered how long it would take before it came. And wondered where.

Feet? Blistered and run raw?

Arms? Legs? Scraped by twigs and thorns until they bleed?

Side?

It is side.

He should have known: the familiar catch that gathers under the ribs then grabs so hard everything stops—except him. He has run through that first grip and many others, and now the pain has grown so great that little remains *to* feel: Feet still fall on earth; eyes and ears still plot his path; lungs and heart fight to sound loudest inside where his *self* lives. But everything else is pain.

Pain: like fire in his side. Like the fire he needs to Transcend. And this time the fire comes from within. This time he needs no other flame.

Running . . . running . . . pain . . . pain . . . fire . . . pain . . . running—pain—fire—pain—

And he is there: running still, gasping desperately for every breath; but his mind is free and floating.

"You have run enough, my son."

"Mother, I hurt. Must there always be pain?"

"Everything worth having is born of pain. *You* were born of pain."

"And will die in it, I have no doubt."

"And be Changed, and that will be a thing worth having, trust me."

"Have you died?"

"I may have. I may yet. Who knows what may alter in time?"

"Everything—so you say."

"Everything. It Changes—or is Changed."

"I know. But at least *I* sometimes work the Changes."

"And are worked upon in turn."

"I also know that."

"You dream, by the way: you began some time ago."

"I know. I can hear the Hounds."

"Do you follow them or flee them?"

"I . . . both."

"When you do neither, you will pass the Wall."

"And until then?"

"You must make Changes."

"And how shall I make them?"

"Dance—for now. For now, this night, you must dance."

"Dance?"

"Like flames."

"Where?"

"Where you will. More to the point, where you were."

"I—"

"You must go. You have run to summon pain to summon me. Now dance to summon joy for them all."

She is gone.

He breathes, and the pain has vanished. He is in the forest, and he feels the need to dance.

He dances on leaves and moss and needles. He dances on asphalt and tile. He dances on wind and water.

And finally he dances on stone that is more and less than stone.

The stone dances with him, and is Changed.

Chapter 2

Fortune Teller

Jackson County, Georgia
Saturday, June 19—morning

Brandy Wallace was not the only person in Georgia to suspect Unseen Influences of meddling in her affairs. For in an artfully decrepit nineteenth-century farmhouse five miles north of Athens (but still a hundred miles southeast of Brandy's Knoll), a young man the citizens of Welch County would have remembered as Ronny Dillon had his own brand of beef with the Powers That Be . . .

. . . Either the steam from the shower had already poached Ron's brain without him noticing—which was a distinct possibility, given the near-boiling temperatures he preferred bathing in, and the level of muddleheadedness that generally afflicted him early in the morning—*or* he had neglected to pay proper obeisance to one of those nebulous Higher Intelligences normal people thought of as gods, and had been punished for his transgression by being cursed with stupidity. Or *else* those absent Agencies who ordered the omens he occasionally consulted in the innocent guise of radio station play lists (all unknown to their disc-jockey oracles) were once again conspiring to tell him what *they* wanted him to know—which was *not*, by any stretch of the imagination, what was bugging *him* at the moment.

And to add insult to injury, were doing so in the most oblique manner possible.

Ron flicked a nose-long mass of soggy, walnut-colored hair out of his eyes, slathered his smooth, clean-muscled torso with soap—and wished that, just once, the Secret Forces of the Universe would be straight with him. Or at least be a trifle less obscure when (as this morning) he had a particularly critical decision to make and very little time to make it in, courtesy of an alarm clock that had not gone off when it should.

Or that his girlfriend, Wendy, hadn't reset when she'd split to take her last final the previous morning, to fix the blame where it most likely lay.

Which meant that he'd had to start assembling omens far later than he liked (and yet, much sooner after arising than was optimum), and that he was having to rush through a shower instead of taking his usual leisurely bathtub soak.

And Lord knew he'd wrestled with the query in question enough on his own already. Surely the Gods (or Fate, or Wyrd, or the Norns, or Vanna White, or *somebody*) ought to be generous enough with one of their faithful minions to render him a clear pronouncement every once in a while. But if the music presently echoing around the bathroom's black tile walls was any indication, it was too late for that already.

The song under suspicion was The Animals' cover of "House of the Rising Sun" (the long version with the organ solo and the extra verses). But the fact that it was the tenth tune he'd heard since awaking—which meant that it occupied the position in the peculiar musical Tarot he'd adopted from his uncle Dion that in the traditional Celtic cross spread represented Hopes and Fears—had him utterly confounded.

Of course, it wasn't *his* system, anyway. The Tarot his flaky musician-scholar-jurist-jailbird kinsman had devised as a means of divination while in the slammer (where he had been denied an actual Tarot deck, but not a radio) was not one with which he felt perfect affinity—he wasn't nearly well enough versed in song titles, for one thing, never mind recording artists or lyrics. And more to the point, he disliked mucking about with what most folks would have called magic (and the family he had found himself shoved into a few years back more coyly referred to as Luck) with a true and abiding passion, and only stooped to reliance on even this bastard adjunct because Uncle Dion's form of fortune-telling was both simple and capable of wide (and therefore unreliable—he did not want to believe in magic) interpretation. Conversely, he had no urge whatever to follow clan tradition and devise a means of augury uniquely his own.

Which left him depending on the first eleven songs he heard that morning to resolve one simple quandary: should he, or should he not, succumb to his strong inclination and eschew his—and by extension, Wendy's—college graduation?

On the affirmative side, it *was* his first degree, and that really was something to be proud of: a Bachelor of Fine Arts from the University of Georgia, summa cum laude, with a concentration in metalwork. All completed in the requisite four years—and that didn't even count the summers spent at Georgia Tech studying metallurgy and automotive engineering on the side, which would have been more than enough to constitute a double major had the university allowed the classes to transfer, which they had not.

On the *other* hand, he had precious little family to show off for, and what he did have was both unimpressionable and largely unavailable—in a couple of cases due to federal intervention. And the university would cheerfully mail you your sheepskin if you chose not to collect it in person. Which effectively whittled his rationale for going through with the whole charade down to two: the prospect of seeing the sheriff of Clarke County leading a procession of grinning, black-clad loonies across the Sanford Stadium football field with his sword upright before him (which tradition allegedly dated from the days when there were still real live Indians in the rolling hills nearby)—but which, in practice, was hardly worth two hours of his life.

And the fact that his girlfriend wanted him to.

Trouble was, you couldn't have commencement without crowds, and crowds gave him headaches of a particularly virulent kind, the origin of which he could discuss with no one outside the clan. Including Wendy.

All of which left him back where he'd started.

And, regrettably, the omens did not seem inclined to offer an opinion either. As Significator, for instance—the tune that represented himself (which he'd heard above the buzz of his black German coffee grinder roughly an hour before)—they had served up Cream's version of "Crossroads." Which seemed fair enough: having just completed his degree, with the actual ceremony pending shortly past noon, his life was indeed at a crucial juncture.

But then things had gotten tricky. The next item on 96 Rock's oldies play list had been Jimi Hendrix's version of "All Along the Watchtower," with which he identified strongly because it was a Bob Dylan song, and Ron's last name was Dillon, which automatically made it worthy of more than typical attention. Unfortunately, it *also* meant that, however vigilant he was, something was about to sneak up on him from an unsuspected quarter and knock him off balance. And the *subsequent* three tunes—in the positions representing the nature of obstacles; either his aim or ideal, or the best that could be achieved; and the factors underlying whatever the situation was—had been real lulus: Heart's "Magic Man," Roy Orbison's "Oh, Pretty Woman," and Santana's "Black Magic Woman." (Someone in Atlanta obviously had a sense of humor.) All of which had left him completely confounded.

Or at least they did if it was graduation being addressed.

There was simply too much in there about both magic and women—and though his trepidation was inextricably bound up with both, the pieces in question almost always referred to *specific* people, not ceremonies or events. Unless, of course, there was a lot more to the university administration than anyone let on—which, given the paucity of staff pay raises and football victories lately, he doubted.

Then affairs *really* became confusing.

Song number six—Influences Passing Away—had been the Rolling Stones' "She's a Rainbow." Ron hadn't a clue what to make of *that* little bit of Sixties psychedelia, for the simple reason that he'd never *heard* it before, much less had to deal with it in a reading. He'd have to look it up in dear old Uncle Dion's concordance, he supposed—when he got the time.

The next two slots had been filled while he was loading the dishwasher after his hasty breakfast, and had made no more sense than their fellows: Looking Glass's inane "Brandy" in the place for Influences Coming into Being; and "Goin' Up the Country," by Canned Heat, representing his place in the whole affair. Again, the first had nothing to do with his dilemma, though it *was* about women, so that pattern, at least, still held. And the latter—well, that could mean nearly anything to do with travel. And though it usually implied a northern journey, he went that way a lot anyway, so any relevance to graduation was pretty moot.

That had left three positions vacant: those signifying Ron's House, in the sense of his environment; his Hopes and Fears; and, finally, What Will Be.

He almost couldn't stand the anticipation, and the first mystery had promptly been solved just as he stepped into the shower—with "It Ain't Me, Babe," as rendered by The Turtles. He'd scowled at that, not only because it was another Dylan song, and thus a double alarm, but because its primary meaning exactly fit the title: the denial or ending of a relationship, usually one with—yet again—a woman. He didn't like *that* at all. Oh, he had problems with Wendy, of course; but then again, what guy *didn't* sometimes find himself at odds with his lady? But he certainly had no desire whatever to dissolve his "association" with pretty Wendy Flowers.

And position number ten? Hopes and Fears? "House of the Rising Sun," which was now ending? What could *that* portend? Well, it generally meant a change of fortune, usually for the worse, possibly even destruction brought about by one's own shortsighted failure to deal with circumstances as they really were. Typically it carried undercultural overtones.

It was all *very* encouraging.

And pigs could fly!

"House" was on its final verse now, Eric Burden's dark-voiced wailings drawing to a despairing close. The next song would be the clincher, the one that would reveal how all the others interacted: the one that represented What Will Be. Ron sighed wearily and decided that he was probably sufficiently steam-cleaned to venture back into the real world for the verdict. He'd give himself one more rinse in hot, then blast himself with a couple of seconds of cold, and step out to meet his prerecorded fate, as naked and wet and confused as when he'd first entered Fortune's realm.

Any second now . . .

And then four things happened almost simultaneously.

The telephone rang.

The front doorbell chimed.

In the process of turning off the taps in order to address the first two, Ron missed the COLD and damn near scalded himself.

And in his haste to escape being boiled alive, his flailing left arm smacked against the radio he'd left atop the flush tank and swept it to the floor. It smashed into the black tile with a sickening crunch—and immediately fell silent, its oracle silenced on the verge of its most important pronouncement.

"What?" Ron shrieked. "No *way*! No *fucking* way!"

For a bare instant he stood as if paralyzed, torn with indecision, while the ringing went on in the living room and the chiming gave way to a pounding in the hall-way beyond. Then, as both persisted, he clutched a thick white towel around his hips and bolted for the bathroom door.

Bbrrrinnnnnggg—as he burst into the adjoining bed-room. That was number three, if he'd counted right, which meant he could still make the front hall on four. The answering machine wouldn't pick up until six rings had elapsed.

He snagged his crutch as he passed his dresser—it had been rainy lately, which always made his bum knee hurt, and occasionally go out on him—and sort of bounded-leapt-hopped into the hall, just as number four commenced. A dark shape was clearly visible beyond the frosted glass of the front door, and Ron did not have to resort to arcane measures to determine who it was. He flipped the dead bolt on ring five and, when it opened, stood dripping on the carpet—blinking into the clear blue eyes of a perplexed-looking Wendy Flowers.

It took his girlfriend no more than a second to assess the situation, whereupon her expression immediately ran a gauntlet from embarrassment through irritation to amusement, on which it finally settled. For Ron's part, he scarcely knew *what* to think, since his fricaseed shoulder was still smarting, he needed drying badly, and Wendy had caught him with more than his physical pants down. The omens were incomplete, dammit, their portents yet unpondered. Yet here she was, on the ragged edge of laughing at him (probably at the way he was gaping so stupidly, which expression he immediately altered), obviously dressed for commencement, and him with no decision made about *his* participation in the dratted affair at all.

In the adjoining living room, the answering machine whirred and clicked and began unreeling its lengthy speil.

"Well," Wendy giggled, when she regained a semblance of composure, "either I'm *extremely* early, you're *preposterously* late—or your entire house has sprung a leak." Her eyes twinkled mischievously.

Ron couldn't stand it. Pissed though he was at half a dozen things at once, there was no way in the world he could turn that anger on Wendy. Not with her flawless, heart-shaped face aglow with anticipation beneath curly blonde hair obviously freshly cut and styled, and accented with a white silk rose just oversize enough to be funky. Not with her body slim and impossibly beguiling in an antique green velvet dress (and with the inevitable trademark flowers—this time Art Deco daisies—appliquéd around the neck, armholes, and hem). Silver dogwood blossoms Ron had made himself glimmered on her earlobes. She was beautiful: beautiful, and—like her name—too, too fragile for pain.

"C-come in," he stammered, backing away to allow her entry, distantly aware that the shoulders of her dress bore dark splotches and that beyond the porch, it was sprinkling. "Sorry—but about a thousand things have gone wrong at *exactly* the same time."

An arched eyebrow lifted delicately, followed by a wrinkling of her perkily turned-up nose. "And are you saying that I'm something *wrong*, Ron Dillon?" she teased. She wasn't mad, though, which was fortunate. But Ron wished he knew what she *was* feeling. Anyone else he could have found out about, because anyone else he could have Listened to. But Wendy was Silent. Wendy Flowers, alone of all women he had ever met, had no Voice.

He could not even begin to read her thoughts.

Wendy ducked past him and made her way toward the living room, which opened off the hallway to his right. He followed her—dripping all the way—and arrived exactly as the recorded message ended and whoever had violated his vigil began to dicker with his machine.

Ron had already determined to ignore the caller until he got his morning reassembled, but he was not prepared for the voice that rasped and crackled from the tinny speaker. Even a bad connection could not disguise his half-brother's soft, gentle drawl.

"Uh, hi, Ronny," the voice began tentatively. "This is Lew. It's"—a pause—"ten-fifteen. Not that it matters, I guess, since you're not there to hear this, and all. But . . . I just wanted to wish you a happy graduation . . . and"—another pause while the speaker swallowed, as if he were nervous and unsure whether or not to proceed—"and to . . . to tell you that I need to talk to you *real* bad about—"

It had taken Ron a moment to find the portable phone, which was not on the floor by the TV, where he usually left it, but under the sofa where his black tomcat, Matty Groves, had evidently batted it in the night. And during the recovery, he had forsaken both his crutch and his towel, so that he was only marginally drier but quite a bit more bare when he finally managed to push the button that let him talk to his kinsman direct.

Not that he wanted to, not now. But he had to do *something* to curtail the conversation lest Lew inadvertently let something slip that he shouldn't. Oh, he'd try to be discreet, Ron knew, since Lew had no way of knowing who might be around when the recording was played back. But his idea of circumspection did not always jive with Ron's, especially where family affairs were concerned—

and the less Wendy heard about *them*, the better. They'd been a couple for nearly three years now, and so far he'd managed *never* to talk to Lew when she was around. But it looked like his luck had finally run out.

"Hey!" Ron gasped breathlessly. "How's it goin'?"

"It goes," Lew replied noncommittally. His voice had calmed now that he was "live," but even without the tentative nature of the aborted message, Ron could sense something was wrong. A hint of tension hid among his brother's words that hadn't been present the last time they'd conversed, back on Thursday. No, scratch that, it *had* been there, but subtle, controlled. Job pressure and that sort of thing. Nothing, so Ron had thought, to be concerned about.

Still, there was no point in rushing things if Lew seemed disinclined. "Sorry I took so long," Ron mumbled, searching the floor for his towel. "I was in the shower, and—"

"Uh-huh," Lew interrupted with what sounded like forced good humor. "More likely you were sacked out with that cute little—"

"Cool it! For God's sakes, *Cool* it!" Ron hissed frantically. "She's right *here*, man!" He slid his hand over the receiver and shot a furtive glance at Wendy—who was trying, with little success, to extract the cat from the towel. "Besides," he added archly, "how do you *know* she's cute? You've never seen her."

"And whose fault is that?"

Lew had said that in the same casual tone he'd used earlier, but Ron caught the edge of resentment in the words. "I think we *both* know the answer to that," he replied tersely. Phone still in hand, he gave up on covering himself and padded across the room to power up the big Sony stereo in hope of catching at least the final bars of the cumulative omen.

Lew did not answer immediately; then, very softly: "Ronny . . . I *really* need to talk to you."

"So talk," Ron mumbled distractedly, spinning knobs and pushing buttons with his free hand. "But make it quick and careful, 'cause now's not a good time—if you know what I mean."

"Why not?"

" 'Cause I've got company, for one thing, stooge! 'Cause I'm standing in my living room stark naked, for another; and 'cause I still haven't decided whether or not I'm going through with the frigging ceremony, for a third."

"You mean you might not?"

"I've got good reason, in case you forgot."

"I *never* forget, man! I live all the time with what you only live with once in a while, and . . . and . . . Dammit, Ronny, I just can't *wait* any longer!" Lew blurted out, sounding on the verge of tears. "There're a bunch of things been bugging me for weeks now," he went on desperately. "Things I haven't called you about 'cause of your finals, and all. But I've *got* to get at least a couple of 'em off my chest now, or I'll go bonkers! I've been pacing around the house all bloody *night* trying to decide what to do about . . . *something*. Trying to get up enough nerve to ask *you* about it. And now that I've finally called, I . . . I . . . dammit, I *can't* tell you—not yet. I mean, I *want* to, but you're obviously in a hurry and there's no way I can get into *this* in a hurry. Except . . . Ronny, I . . . *need* you to come home."

Ron left off fiddling with the radio. "You *know* how I feel about that," he said coldly.

"I *need* you, man."

"I've needed you, too!" Ron shot back, refusing to relax his guard, now that it had been triggered. "And where were you?"

"You know where—where I *always* am. Always and forever." Lew sounded absolutely miserable.

"*That* again, huh?"

"It's not an *again* with me, man; it's *ongoing*."

"But why call *now*?" Ron sighed in exasperation, once more spinning dials. (Where the hell was 96 Rock?)

"I told you . . . I just now got up enough nerve to ask the favor I *did*."

"Nothing else?"

"Well . . . Grandma's traveling again, if that makes any difference. She left last night."

"It *should* mean you can speak freely." Ron had found the station now, but only caught the last few bars of the song—not enough to pin it down, which griped him royally.

"It's ironic, isn't it?" Lew said bitterly, reclaiming Ron's attention.

"What?"

"That I can have every *thing* I want—except freedom. And—"

"Lew," Ron inserted flatly. "Whatever's bugging you can obviously wait, or you'd have gone ahead and spilled it whether you intended to or not. So I tell you what: I'll call you back after . . . after the ceremony. Then you can tell me all about it."

"No," Lew whispered sadly. "I can't. You'll have to come up here."

"Lew, I . . ."

"Come. Please."

"Maybe."

"Please?"

"Maybe."

A pause; then, very softly: "I'm sorry I can't be there, bro. But congratulations. And you know I mean that."

"Thanks. Take care . . . bro."

"Thanks."

" 'Bye."

"Catch you."

"Right." And with that, Ron punched the button that turned off the phone.

Wendy looked up at him inquiringly. "That your brother?"

"Yep," Ron replied, scowling. He recovered his towel and wrapped it around his hips with a flourish.

"What'd he want?"

"Nothing that can't wait. Uh, what was the name of that song? The one I just caught the tail end of."

" 'It's the End of the World as We Know It'—I think that's the title. It's by R.E.M.—*that* I know for sure."

Ron's heart skipped a beat. He flopped down in the overstuffed chair in the corner, the one he always thought of as his throne. "Oh *great*," he grunted sarcastically, digging his fingers into the thick red velvet arms. "That's just *wonderful*."

Wendy's expression shifted from confusion to concern. She rose and joined him, slipping onto his lap. "What's wrong, sweetums?" she murmured.

Ron shrugged listlessly. Wendy did not know about the Tarot. She did not know about magic or Luck or Listening. She did not know he was anything more than he appeared to be: a nice, bright, middle-sized white boy— good-looking in a Kevin Baconish way—who just happened to be richer than most, and a hell of a lot more driven and creative. No *way* she'd understand the portent of a song with a title like that. Not when it occupied the last position in a reading. Shoot, he didn't know what to make of it himself—except that something was definitely up. Some dreadful shift of circumstance, he feared, if the omens were to be believed. Something he would not be able to avoid. But at least he now knew who the magic man was. It was obvious, given the phone call: it was his brother, Lew.

Wendy bent over and licked his ear. "What's *wrong*?" she repeated.

"What's not?" he grumbled sourly.

"Well, we're graduating in a couple of hours. That's good, isn't it?"

"In the abstract, yes; in actuality, I doubt it."

"What do you mean?"

Ron took her hand, studied it: the petal-soft skin, the fine bones. "I'm . . . I'm not going."

Wendy stiffened. "But why? It's a big deal, Ron. A big deal for you and a big deal for me."

"Yeah, I know that, love; but—"

"But what?"

"It's gonna rain," he told her lamely. "I'm, uh, not keen on sitting in the middle of Sanford Stadium in a soggy cap and gown."

"They'll move it to the coliseum, then."

An eyebrow lifted wryly. "Not good enough, huh?"

Wendy shook her head. "No."

"Okay, so how 'bout if I told you I didn't want to drive? I mean, parking's gonna be a bitch; and the T-Bird's in the shop, so I'll have to take the Centauri, which means there'll be crowds slobbering all over it like there always are; and

I'm afraid it'll get dinged up; and—"

Once more Wendy shook her head. "I'll drive. So scratch objection number two."

"My knee hurts?"

"Better, but that's never stopped you from anything you *wanted* to do."

"How 'bout if I just said I didn't like crowds?"

Wendy regarded him coolly. "Better, because it's more honest. But you wouldn't be telling me anything I didn't know. You won't go to games, won't go to concerts—and apparently won't even go to our own graduation."

"Yeah, but you *know* why that is: the thing about crowds, and all."

"They give you headaches . . . so you say."

"Damned right. Killer ones."

"Which you won't get seen about."

"Because it would do no good."

"And because they give you a convenient excuse to avoid whatever you want, and—" She paused, then: "Ronny, isn't it worth a headache to make me happy once in a while?"

Ron took a deep breath. "Well, they're a lot worse than you can possibly imagine, to start with, so you're asking a lot more than you think you are; but no, it's not that, not at all. It's got nothing to do with you, in fact; it's just that . . . oh, jeeze, girl; why is it such a big deal? I mean, why don't we both just hang out here for the rest of the day? I'm sure we could find *something* to do."

For the first time since he had known her, Wendy's eyes flashed fire. "Because I'm sick of being a nonperson," she flared. "Because I'm sick of not having any past beyond three years ago. Hearing my name called would make me more a person . . ."

"Bullshit. You're a perfectly fine person."

"With no memory."

"With selective amnesia."

"Who thinks rites of passage are important," she countered, shifting to her scholarly persona. "Who thinks rituals give structure to our lives, and that it's the decline of those rituals that's made people so listless and unfocused these days."

For a long moment Ron remained silent, simply holding her hand. He didn't *want* to hurt her. But he couldn't go, dammit; *couldn't*. Not already predisposed against it, and now with something screwy going on with Lew that he needed to resolve.

"This has something to do with that phone call, doesn't it?" Wendy asked suddenly.

Ron nodded. "Somewhat. Lew told me some . . . troubling things. I need to do some hard thinking."

"Anything you can talk about?"

" 'Fraid not. You know how that is."

"I know how you *want* it to be, which isn't the same thing."

"I'm sorry."

"He wants you to go up there, doesn't he? I figured out that much from the part I heard."

Ron did not reply.

"He does, doesn't he?"

"Yeah."

"And are you going?"

A shrug. "I don't know. I don't want to, that's for sure . . . but I'm afraid . . . that I may have to."

"So? Why don't you just do it? We're both through with school for a while. We could—"

Ron shook his head. "Not *we*, Wendy, *I*. I'm not even sure *I'm* gonna do it yet . . . but I think . . . something tells me I'd better."

"But I *want* to go! You've never taken me home with you, not once!"

"That's because I haven't *been* home but once since we met."

"Which is all the more reason we should go now," Wendy countered quickly. "It's such a rare occurrence, I'm afraid I'll never get another chance!"

"You're not missing a thing." Ron assured her. "Welch County's just about the dullest place on earth."

"It produced *you*, didn't it?"

"Not in any real sense! I'm from Florida, remember? I only spent senior year there. And that wasn't by choice, I guarantee you."

"Well, I hear the scenery's great!"

Another shrug. "No better than the counties to either side, and we've *been* to both of them—lots of times."

"All of which makes me even more curious. I can't help but think that you're hiding something."

"You can think what you want," Ron replied wearily. "But the fact is . . . It's just that . . . I don't *like* going up there. It hurts too much, I guess."

Wendy bit her lip, then exhaled slowly. "I *know* about your mom," she said softly. "I know you saw her die. And I know that had to have been tough. But that was a long time ago. There *has* to have been some healing since then."

"Not enough. Not nearly enough."

"But you're going anyway . . . ?"

"Because my brother practically begged me to, and because he sounded so desperate that I don't think I have any choice *but* to go."

"You guys are close, aren't you?"

Ron nodded. "Close as . . . as brothers, I guess—with all that implies."

"Which means you'll do stuff for him you won't do for your girlfriend?"

"Which means I'll do stuff for him I won't do for anyone else on this planet!"

Wendy looked pensive for a moment. "So . . . if he wants to see you so bad," she began tentatively, "and since you don't like going where he is . . . then why doesn't he just come down here?"

Once again, Ron fell silent. Wendy wasn't usually this inquisitive—which was one of her many virtues. But even this sort of light-duty drilling about his brother had not occurred before, and he wasn't sure how to handle it. He didn't *want* to lie, but the truth defied simple explanation. And if he wasn't careful, he'd *really* open up a smelly kettle of fish.

Finally he simply said, "He can't."

"But *why*?"

"Because . . . because he's got a weird kinda phobia that makes it impossible for him to travel much. If he leaves home for more than a few hours at a time, he gets really wired. More than that, and he goes completely psycho."

"Must be contagious, then," Wendy muttered, much more sarcastically than was her wont.

"Huh?"

"Well, *none* of your family's coming, are they? Why's that? Are they psychos, too? Or gorillas, or vampires, or what?"

"Possibly, no, and not that I know of," Ron shot back. He was on the absolute verge of pointing out that none of her kin would be attending, either, when he remembered exactly why that was.

For Wendy Flowers was the recipient of one of Fate's crueler double whammies: she was both an orphan and an amnesiac. She had no memory at all before three summers ago when she'd attracted his attention at an Exxon station a few miles south of Macon, Georgia. It had been late August; and rising sophomore Ron had been returning to Athens from visiting Uncle Dion down at good old Homestead Federal Pen. And there she'd been: a pretty girl in a new white Toyota Celica—crying her eyes out and looking like she'd just seen about half a dozen ghosts. She remembered nothing. *Nothing*, she'd insisted, until she'd found herself driving up I-75 with the backseat and trunk stuffed full of four suitcases of new clothes, and one box each of books; cassette tapes; housewares; kitchen supplies—and potted plants. Oh, and there was also a key to a brand-new apartment in Athens, a set of registration forms that identified her as an entering freshman, completed and approved paperwork on two very lucrative multiyear scholarships, a thousand dollars in cash, two bank cards, and the address of a recently deceased Charleston psychologist who had evidently been utterly unsuccessful in plugging the holes in her memory either by helping her reawaken them herself, or through the efforts of the private detective he had subsequently hired. Ron had retained one, too, once they became a couple (as they quickly had)—to as little effect, and had even flirted with using Listener connections via brother Lew. He'd stopped pushing the matter, though, when Wendy proved more concerned with building a future than uncovering her past. Which was fortunate, because as far as anyone could tell, she *had* no past beyond a conveniently defunct South Carolina orphanage, S.A.T. scores (and good ones at that, though she had no high school transcripts, courtesy of botched computer files), and an assortment of addresses that had all led to post office boxes or more incomplete files. As far as the world was concerned, she hadn't existed before three years ago.

But it was also true that she was smart as a whip (she was, after all, finishing college in three years, courtesy of regular overloads), and beyond having no personal past to speak of, her mind was a veritable sponge of information. Her grades were fine; and there was nothing wrong with her ability to reason or recall post-trauma facts. It was only when she pushed beyond the three-year limit that she found an impenetrable wall. It didn't bother her, officially—or only once in a while, like now. Except that Ron knew it did. A lot.

And he had nearly exacerbated it again! He smiled what he hoped would be sufficient apology for his tone and squeezed her hand. "I'm sorry," he murmured. "I just can't. I know you want to go—want to prowl around in my roots since . . . since you don't have any of your own. But there's just nothing you can gain by going with me. I won't be happy, so I won't be good company. And the only thing that *is* good for me up there is my brother, and if he and I get to talking about things you don't know about, and folks you never heard of, and all, you'd get *really* bored."

"But that's what I *want*," Wendy wailed. "I *want* to hear those little things you guys talk about, 'cause they're the kinds of things you never talk about around me!"

"Because I don't *like* talking about 'em!" Ron countered. "And 'cause Lew's the only person I *can* talk about 'em to—and I won't feel free to do that with you there."

"More of those family secrets, huh?"

"Not like you're thinking."

"But what could be worse than what I already know?"

"Lots."

"Worse than being put up for adoption 'cause your mom was pregnant by two different men at once and didn't want you ever to find out about it?" Wendy snapped. "Worse than falling off a diving board and trashing your knee so that you could never dive competitively again? Worse than having your foster folks get killed on their way to the hospital to check up on you? Worse than having to leave all your old friends and move to a new school and then finding out your adopted mom's actually your real mom, and then losing her, too? Jesus Christ, Ron; what kind of stuff *can't* you talk about?"

"*Lots*, okay? So can we just drop it? I mean, is that okay with you?"

Wendy did not answer, and Ron was sure he'd gone too far. He was being a jerk. But he also knew that it would be a mistake of the worst order to take Wendy home with him. Amnesiac or not, she wasn't stupid. And no matter how discreet he and Lew were, there was no way she'd not come back loaded down with questions. Even if she didn't ask them, he'd know they were there, simmering in the back of her mind, ready to trip him up if he didn't watch every word and deed like a hawk.

But instead, Wendy bit her lip and tried to smile, and said, "Well, at least *think* about it, okay? I really do want to go. And I really don't think you've ever given me a good reason why I can't. I'll still be your girlfriend if you go without me. But I'll also be hurt as hell—and you can take *that* however you want to."

"I will, too," Ron sighed.

Wendy stood, and he noticed, to his surprise, that she was shaking. Tears glistened in her eyes. He felt like a cad. He'd never hurt her before—shoot, they'd barely even had a fight. And here, now, on what should be one of the biggest days of her life, he was letting her down.

"We'll . . . talk about it," he said finally.

"And what about graduation?"

Ron shook his head. "I can't . . . I just *can't*."

"And that's it?"

"I'm sorry, but . . . yeah. I've got a headache, I guess. One of *those* headaches." He rested his head on the back of the chair and closed his eyes. God, how he hated this, having to lie to his lady—though, in fact, he could feel a garden-variety throbber coming on. But it was a real pill trying to maintain the facade of normalcy when things were not, never mind having to contrive mundane excuses for acts that had their origin . . . somewhere else. It would help if he could, just once, *Hear* what Wendy was thinking. But unlike any other woman he had ever known, he could not. That was one of the things that had attracted him to her in the first place. That, and the fact that she was pretty and trusted him and did not, so far as he could tell, want anything out of him at all.

But he wished he knew, dammit; he wished he *knew*!

Without really intending it, he took the three deep breaths that triggered a very light trance. That accomplished, he entered that place only his kind could go: the Realm of the Winds, where thoughts—what folks like him called Voices—could be heard, and emotions read like novels. And once there, he focused his attention on Wendy, and Listened.

And found, as he always did, a vast echoing emptiness where her memories, her feelings, her very *soul*, ought to be. There was no ego at all, no *self* shouting its needs into the Winds. But there *was* something new this time that both surprised and troubled him.

For the first time in the three years he had known her, that emptiness was occupied! This time, very faintly, he caught one image—or feeling—or thought; one was never quite certain which. It was a ghost, really; the merest wavering hint of a Voice. But that Voice was proclaiming one thing in words that were beyond language: it was repeating over and over that Wendy loved him.

But when he eased his consciousness back into its more accustomed place an instant later, he was alone. The radio was playing "Take a Giant Step." He had not heard Wendy leave.

Chapter 3

The Letter

Brandy Hall
Saturday, June 19—early afternoon

It was probably fortunate that she was running wildly behind schedule and that Atlanta was a solid two-hour drive to the south, Brandy thought sourly, else there was a good chance she'd be wanted for murder by now.

Specifically, she would cheerfully have hanged every single TV weatherperson in Georgia's largest city from the ridgepole of Brandy Hall—assuming, of course, that she *had* a ridgepole, which (since the great hall, which was the only room that was even *supposed* to have one, still lacked most of one wall) she did not. It might even be worth it, too—certainly it would have given her considerable satisfaction to have succumbed to her more primal instincts when she had first drawn back her bedroom curtains and peered outside that morning.

It was raining: pouring in heavy pulses, like endless curtains of silver beads being bounced up and down across the landscape—doubtless by those selfsame vengeful deities that had so inflamed her fancy the day before.

Raining.

When all three major networks *plus* two of Ted Turner's *and* The Weather Channel had unanimously *promised* that daylight would bring a continuation of the clear skies that had finally given her a chance to make reasonable headway on her house during the last few days.

Raining.

Son-of-a-bitchin' rain.

Brandy sniffed loudly and straightened from where she'd been alternately pounding fractured slabs of collapsed concrete footings into manageable chunks and flinging those same fragments as far into the monsoon as her scarce-abated ire could manage. Something clammy and rough brushed her head as she came full erect, and she started so violently, she almost lost her grip on the sledgehammer she'd been wielding with such grim aplomb for more than three hours. "Shit *fire!*" she yipped, aiming a particularly baleful glare up at the dangerously sagging center of the tarpaulin she'd jury-rigged between a pair of makeshift poles and the nearest library wall to keep the *worst* of the rain off her head and out of the trenches while she attempted to reexcavate them. A sharp upward poke at the offending bulge with the handle of the hammer unleashed twin waterfalls from opposite sides of the canvas square, both of which immediately declared themselves rivers-in-training and made muddy beelines toward the growing lake around her sodden feet—which promptly sank another inch.

"Shit-*fucking*-fire! *Enough* of this shit!" she shouted to the storm. She dropped the hammer (which promptly splashed her jeans to midthigh), wiped her hands on the tail of her filthy T-shirt (no buckskin and feathers *today*), and stalked off in search of shelter. Her sneakers—cheap old Sears items she wore only in bad weather—squished smugly as she crossed the few yards to the west entrance to the library.

Once there, she snagged a black plastic thermos bottle from a gaping window niche, poured the last of the morning's Maxwell House into another of her seemingly endless horde of handmade mugs, and flopped up against the cinder-block wall to contemplate her day's endeavors.

Not much, she conceded, surveying the half-drowned landscape between herself and the woods. Most of what she could see was lonely islands of cinder blocks, sand, and plastic-shrouded lumber poking up from a sea of tan-brown mud, where they weren't actually inundated by equally murky water. And straight ahead was the gaping hole that, along with the twin ditches that intersected it at ninety degrees, two days ago had cruelly pretended to be finished foundations—and one day later had resembled the late, unlamented Berlin Wall, complete with fractures, fissures, and her own irate spray-can graffiti reading, "Fuck you, too!" Except that *the* Wall hadn't actually sagged into the ground, as *her* foot-high edifice had so inconveniently done.

Nor had it mysteriously fractured even further the previous night.

She scowled in disgust and took an absent sip, wincing at the bitterness of the beverage, which she took black. Maybe she really *should* consider offing the state's crop of meteorologists. Certainly the clerestory windows in the more complete side of the nearby great hall would make dandy scaffolds. She could dangle a weatherman from each Gothic arch and leave 'em there for the buzzards to snack on. It would be very Celtic—and, if she tortured them correctly, American Indian, too.

Though now she thought of it, maybe a sun dance would be more appropriate—or at least more positive. Not that she knew how to do any such thing; her mother hadn't had much truck with such foolishness, and it wasn't Cherokee, anyway—*or* Celtic. But at least that would be accentuating the positive, not wallowing in the negative. That's what her tobacco-baron grandpa—the one who had set up the trust fund that was paying for her house and keeping her afloat—would have said: "Now, Brandy-girl," he'd have drawled between puffs of the cigarettes that would eventually kill him, "It don't do no good to dwell on bad things. The thing to *dwell* on is how to make bad things better."

Brandy gnawed her lip. Maybe he was right. Maybe she *was* enjoying her misery a mite too much. Maybe—

She paused on the border of repondering a certain few perplexing somethings she had overpondered that morning already. A sound had fought its way through the white-noise thuddings of the raindrops to invade her ear: something mechanical and rapidly approaching. And by the time she had grabbed her jeans jacket and sloshed her way through the great hall and the foyer to the likelier (and drier) vantage point of the sheltered arcade that spanned the front between the two southern towers, she knew what it was.

A blue Toyota four-wheel-drive station wagon was alternately lurching and sliding along behind the last fringe of hickories between the clearing and the rutted pigtrail that was also her official driveway; and even through the rain she could make out the blue and white door decal that identified it as one of the rural carriers for the ever unreliable United States Postal Service—late as usual, but for once, she didn't care.

Today, she admitted resignedly, she didn't really have the heart to work, anyway—especially as it now looked as if she was not only going to receive mail, but have company as well.

The vehicle squirmed to a halt (nowhere near her actual mailbox, which was up by the main highway a quarter mile away). The near-side door squeaked open. Rain-obscured movement inside blossomed into a large red and black umbrella that tilted at a forty-five-degree angle toward her to more effectively fend off the latest squall. The galoshes and jeans that comprised the visible part of the body beneath paused by the wagon's front fender, as if their owner was uncertain whether to tend right toward the trailer or left toward the house.

Brandy solved *that* problem instantly.

"Weedge!" she hollered hoarsely. "Over here!"

The figure spun in place, revealing a flash of female features beneath a dark green raincoat and hood, then marched decisively in her direction—the purposeful precision of which maneuver was spoiled by the last two yards being executed in a series of staggers, slips, arm flails, and slides that would have ended with the unfortunate public servant on her fanny in the mud had Brandy not stuck out her non-coffee-wielding arm to steady her.

"Thanks," the mailwoman grunted, stomping onto the dry concrete of the arcade. "Jesus! Where the hell did *this* crap come from?" She turned to confront the downpour, inserted her umbrella at its very fringe, and spun it quickly, drying it faster than even the huge droplets could soak it again, then folded it and tucked it into the corner between the center wall and the southwest tower. Without a word, she reached out, deftly removed the mug from Brandy's hand, and drank from it gratefully.

Brandy waited patiently while her visitor drained the cup and shucked out of her mac, revealing the somewhat bedraggled form of a tall, dark-haired woman, even more wirily slim than she was. She looked girlish in spite of it, though, and had Brandy not known for a fact that Weedge was thirty-nine, she would have sworn she was no more than twenty-five. Typical of rural carriers, too, she was wearing no more uniform than new (though water-darkened and mud-spattered) jeans and a plain black sweatshirt. They'd been nodding acquaintances since Brady had moved to the county (reasonable enough, given Weedge's job), but their friendship was new, begun barely two weeks before when they'd met at an exhibit of Brandy's wildlife paintings in the gallery down in Cordova. Weedge had bought one. They'd talked, discovered they had a common interest in hunting and herb lore, and shared bad experiences when it came to men. The rest was history.

Brandy inclined her head toward the sodden gray world beyond the nearest of the three archways. "Don't blame this on *me*! I like working in this kinda stuff about as much as you like driving around in it! Now, let me guess, you've finished your rounds and your car's overheating, so you've stopped by here to let it cool off awhile."

Weedge grinned broadly, which made her narrow face look even younger. "That's what I'm gonna tell 'em back at the P.O., anyway."

"Figured as much," Brandy chuckled, attempting to refill the cup before remembering the thermos was empty and setting it down in disgust. "Wish *I* had that good an excuse for doing nothing."

"A friggin' *monsoon's* not enough?" Weedge snorted.

"Christ, gal, I figured even *you'd* stay inside on a day like this!"

Brandy shook her head and slumped against the wall, sliding down the rough surface until she was hunched up on the floor with her arms across her knees. A prickle of rain tickled her cheek even there, but she ignored it. "Can't afford to, not since the dratted foundation collapsed—I told you about that, right?"

Weedge nodded solemnly, then squatted in turn and began rifling through the mound of raincoat. "Five minutes after you discovered it—and a finer string of curses I've not heard since you and me watched that Eddie Murphy video."

Brandy sighed. "It really is a bitch."

Another nod. "I know, Bran, I know. But"—she broke off and attacked another portion of the raincoat—"maybe this'll make you feel better." Whereupon she twisted around on her heels and held out two bags—one a standard brown grocery item, the other a much larger plastic garbage type—both bunched together at the top.

Brandy eyed her warily. "Am I supposed to choose, or what?"

Weedge's eyes glinted girlishly. "Nope, they're both for you—one's your mail, the other's . . . maybe you'd better check; I'd hate to spoil the surprise."

An eyebrow lifted in delicate bemusement, but Brandy snatched the bags, setting the smaller, lighter one on the sandy concrete beside her. The other brow went up inquiringly as she began unrolling its fellow. "I'm not gonna get bit, am I?"

"That's for you to find out," Weedge countered quickly. "Though my guess is that you'd be more likely to do the biting."

Brandy shot her friend a quick, but well-tempered, glare, and reached inside without looking. Her fingers brushed the slick coolness of plastic wrapping, and she drew out the topmost of two smaller packages.

It contained a variety of yellowish shelf fungi Brandy wasn't familiar with. "Am I supposed to eat these or poison folks with 'em?" she asked pointedly, when a bout of unsealing and sniffing had told her nothing except that they smelled pungent and earthy—and very, very tempting.

"Whichever," Weedge shot back cryptically. " 'Course, what *I'd* do is sauté 'em in butter and serve 'em with a side of tenderloin, preferably of the venison variety."

"And invite a certain friend to dinner? Maybe I'll do that," Brandy laughed. She stowed the fungi beside the bag of mail and made a second assault on the parcel.

What she found was soft and heavy, and she had a little trouble dragging it out, finally ripping the outer bag in her eagerness. She suppressed a little cry when she saw the limp, dark-feathered shape the bundle contained.

"A hawk!" she crowed: "It's a goddamned red-tailed hawk." Then, more suspiciously, "You didn't *kill* this, did you?"

Weedge looked scandalized and shook her head vigorously. "No way! That was a road kill I found just past the foot of the mountain. I knew you were into feathers and stuff, so I figured maybe hawk plumes might be harder to come by than some, what with 'em being protected species, and all; so I—"

Brandy did not let her finish, but flung herself impulsively forward to give her friend a rough, awkward hug.

"I guess you like it," Weedge gasped shakily.

"I guess I do."

"So what're you gonna do with it?"

Brandy shrugged in the midst of examining her still flexible prize. "I dunno—yet. Maybe make some more earrings, or use the claws on a pair of rattles, or something." She unfolded a wing and pressed it against the sooty hair just above her left ear. "Shoot, I might even make a magic helmet; what d'you think? It won't go to waste, believe me."

"Does *anything?*" Then, when Brandy showed no sign of abandoning her new toy: "Aren't you gonna check your mail?"

"There's mail?" Brandy replied with an air of mock incredulity. "You give me a *hawk*, and you want to talk about mere *letters?*"

"There *is* an outside world," Weedge noted ruefully.

"There is?"

Weedge nodded solemnly. "So I'm told."

Brandy sighed expressively, laid the hawk aside, and reached for the other bag. "Am I the only person around here who gets her mail in plain brown wrappers?"

"The only one I can *talk* about—the only one I'm inclined to give presents to, anyway."

"Anything interesting?"

"Not that I know of. Then again, I'm not supposed to *know* anything except that the address is correct."

Brandy did not reply, but quickly sorted through the pile. She eliminated the circulars immediately, saved those local enough to include usable coupons. The county paper, the *Witness*, she also set aside. The remainder included copies of *Fine Homebuilding*, *Mother Earth News*, and *Foxfire*; some sort of memorandum from the Welch County Board of Education; a letter from one of her college friends; and the expected weekly gossip sheet from her mom. She tucked the last two into her jacket pocket and contemplated the single remaining item.

It was a heavy, legal-sized envelope made of thick, obviously expensive ivory paper. She studied it curiously, noting that the neatly calligraphed address simply gave her residence as Brandy Hall, Cordova, Georgia. There was no Zip Code and no return, but there was a local postmark, and a slight roughness on the backside indicating a seal there. She turned it over, but had to squint to read the embossing: Lewis Welch, Esq., Cardalba Hall, Cordova, Georgia. Once again, there was no Zip.

"Open it," Weedge urged eagerly, her eyes twinkling mischievously.

Brandy's eyebrows lifted again, but she slitted the top edge with her one sufficiently long nail.

It contained a folded sheet of paper, identical to the thick parchment of the envelope. Opened, it read, in the same calligraphed hand:

LEWIS WELCH
MASTER OF CARDALBA PLANTATION
INVITES YOU AND ALL YOUR KIN AND COMPANIONS
TO
THE ANNUAL MIDSUMMER CELEBRATION

OF
ANOTHER PROSPEROUS YEAR FOR WELCH COUNTY
TO BE HELD (AS USUAL) IN
FOUNDERS' PARK
ON
MONDAY, JUNE 21
REFRESHMENTS AND ENTERTAINMENT PROVIDED
EVERYONE WILL BE THERE
NO R.S.V.P.

Underneath, a different but obviously masculine hand had added,

> Sorry to be so late with this, but sometimes new folks get lost in the shuffle. We really do need to get better acquainted. Wear what you want, the funkier the better, and prepare to eat a *lot*. If you have any questions, just ask anybody local. Looking forward to it.
>
>   Lew

Brandy refolded the invitation and stuffed it back into the envelope. She looked at Weedge hopefully. "So . . . have you been here long enough to know what this is all about?"

Weedge responded with a listless shrug. "Almost a year. Will that do?"

"If it gives you knowledge to salve my ignorance."

"I don't know about that," Weedge chuckled. "But what I *do* know is that every year around this time the Welches throw a big catered bash for the whole county, and I do mean *bash:* food like you wouldn't believe—everything from Iranian caviar, lobster salad, and sushi, to venison stew, hominy grits, and chitlins; and drinks from Coke through moonshine to hundred-buck-a-bottle champagne. Dolly Parton played there once; so did the Black Crowes; so did R.E.M and Wet."

Brandy regarded her dubiously. "And it's *free*?"

"Absolutely. I think it's a tax write-off, or something. You *do* know who the Welches are, don't you?" she added suddenly.

Brandy glanced at her friend askance. "Is this the same Lewis Welch who's on the school board? Young guy—almost pretty?"

"The very same. Why?"

Brandy did not reply. That was about the millionth time since she'd moved to Welch County that she'd heard mention of the powerful clan that had first settled the area somewhere around the end of the eighteenth century. As far as she could tell, they practically controlled the place: owned vast tracts of prime bottom land, as well as the bank, insurance agency, two real estate companies, the newspaper, and various other businesses, including the sawmill that cut her lumber—most of which they managed through nonfamily surrogates, presumably to maintain as low a profile as possible. In fact, now she considered it, she'd never actually *seen* but two Welches, and wasn't sure there were any more. One was an old lady—Martha, she thought her name was. She was supposed to be quite a traveler, but Brandy had only encountered her once: the day she'd arrived. They'd met briefly in the Registrar's office at the courthouse, where Brandy was signing up to vote. From what she'd overheard, Martha had been planning another of her overseas jaunts and was making certain she wouldn't be up for jury duty any time soon.

As for Lewis Welch: she'd encountered him exactly twice, both times at school board meetings—which surprised her, since he barely looked out of high school himself. In fact, he was only a few years shy of her own twenty-five (she'd made discreet inquiries), but he looked far younger: seventeenish, with fair skin, no visible whiskers, and a riot of curly blond hair that made him resemble a Renaissance angel—or one of Tolkien's elves (Legolas, perhaps), though at maybe five foot seven, he was a bit short for that. His looks made him very hard to take seriously, too—until he spoke, at which point he became at once witty, commanding, and charming; with a secret sparkle in his eyes she'd found quite captivating—until she'd mentioned it to one of her more tenured future cronies and been informed that the Masters of Cardalba (that term again; she'd meant to ask Weedge for an explanation and hadn't had the chance) were almost always bachelors.

That had prompted more questions in the ladies' lounge, and the tersely worded replies had been that no, he wasn't gay so far as anyone knew, but that the family inheritance somehow went through the female line, with the Master's sister's sons taking over the lands and de facto title. That Lewis had no known sister was also noted in a very low, almost scandalized, tone; but Brandy had not been able to gauge why. It was all very mysterious.

Weedge was staring at her speculatively. "You okay?"

Brandy sniffled and wiped her nose, suddenly unaccountably uneasy. "Uh . . . well, you know I've only been here for a couple of months; and I *know* I'm an outsider and don't know everything that's going on and that I shouldn't make judgments without access of facts. But . . . well, seems like every time I turn around, somebody's talking about the friggin' *Welches*!"

"So? They're rich and powerful, they're charismatic, they own half the county. Lew's damned good-looking, as I'm sure you've noticed."

"Yeah, he is," Brandy nodded ruefully. "But what's all this Master of Cardalba crap? It sounds like something out of a bad romantic novel."

Brandy thought her friend tensed a little before answering. "It's nothing really," Weedge said at last, "just a convenient title. A holdover from the last century probably, when they had slaves, and all. I mean, they *do* own Cardalba Plantation, so it's a reasonable thing."

"Bullshit," Brandy retorted. "It smacks of feudalism, and that's been defunct for five hundred years."

"It wasn't necessarily bad, though," Weedge gave her back. "I mean, think about it: There was an awful lot of security tied in with it; and the lords—the good ones— gave as much as they got."

"And does Lewis Welch give as much as he gets?"

"You've seen the invitation. What do you think?"

"I think," Brandy sighed, rising to her feet, "that you're not gonna tell me as much as I want to know—and that I'm getting damned tired of evasions."

"Sorry," Weedge apologized. "But there're some things I'm just not comfortable talking about—not yet."

"Not even to me?"

"One should speak from a position of knowledge," Weedge informed her flatly, rising as well, and reaching for her raincoat. "And I'm almost as ignorant about the Welches as you are."

Brandy shrugged, aware that their friendship had just flirted with dangerous territory, and relieved that it seemed to have moved to safer ground. "Speaking of mysteries," she began, "—which we sort of were—I haven't told you about *my* latest two."

It was Weedge's turn to raise an eyebrow. "Oh yeah?"

Brandy grinned smugly and told her about the white stag she'd seen the night before.

Weedge listened intently and without comment until she had finished. "And you're *sure* it had antlers? *That's* very odd indeed."

"Yeah, *tell* me about it! But believe me, they were there. God knows I've killed enough of the suckers to know 'em when I see 'em. Never mind the ones I've drawn."

"I believe you."

"Glad somebody does—'cause I'm not sure I believe myself right now. I mean, there I was: sitting in the dark feeling sorry for myself, and then—bam—out strolls a critter straight out of *The Mabinogion*."

Weedge shook her head. "You just lost me."

"It's the Welsh national epic—but don't get me started on *that* or you'll never get back to work. Basically, though, white deer in Welsh myth are almost always supernatural beings—things out of the underworld, and all that. The most famous story has a Welsh king named Pwyll hunting one and getting in trouble with the King of Annwyn— that's the underworld in Welsh myth—for his pains. And that doesn't even count the fact that the Cherokees *also* had legends of a sort of archtypal deer called *Awi-Usdi*— except that probably wasn't him I saw, 'cause *that* means 'little deer,' and the guy I saw definitely wasn't *little!* And—"

She broke off when she saw the too patient expression her friend had assumed. "Uh, you haven't heard any reports of any critters like that, have you?" she asked sheepishly. "While on your route, or whatever?"

Weedge shook her head. "Sorry, no."

"Let me know if you do, okay? I mean, it's no big deal, but I *am* kinda curious."

"Sure." Weedge turned in place. "Uh, you *did* check out the place you saw it for tracks, and all, didn't you?"

Brandy looked embarrassed. " 'Fraid not," she replied ruefully. "I was going to, but I kinda detoured by here on the way to the woods, and that's when I discovered the *second* mystery."

Weedge folded her arms, and slumped back against the nearer of the two concrete block pillars that defined the arcade's archways. "Looks like I'm gonna be here awhile longer," she sighed. "So shoot."

"Well," Brandy began, "it's like this: You know about the foundations right?"

"Okay," Weedge affirmed carefully, "go on."

"Right. Well, obviously the entire thing had to be redone, so I figured I'd be spending the whole day out here breaking everything up and lugging the pieces out. But you know what?"

"What?"

Brandy paused for effect. "When I got down here, I found it *already* broken up—well, not broken exactly, but it was so cracked and fissured, it amounted to the same thing. It's only taken me half as long to clear out as I expected—and that in spite of this friggin' rain."

"And this is *mysterious*?" Weedge snorted. "Probably the stuff just set some more and contracted along stress fractures, or something."

"Maybe so," Brandy acknowledged doubtfully. "But I've worked with a lot of concrete in my time, and I've never seen anything like that before."

"You used the same mix as usual, and everything?"

"Absolutely. I've got *that* down to a fine art."

"Well," Weedge replied, "*I'm* certainly the wrong one to make any guesses; *you're* the expert."

"I wonder, sometimes."

"Yeah," Weedge grunted, reaching for her umbrella. "And right now I'm wondering what I'm gonna tell the folks back at the P.O. when I come dragging in half an hour late."

"What you always tell 'em, I suppose," Brandy laughed.

Weedge rolled her eyes. "Yeah, but one day they're gonna ask me why I don't fix my thermostat."

"Just tell 'em you're a woman and didn't know you were supposed to," Brandy growled sarcastically. "That's what they'll all blame it on, anyway."

"You're being unfair," Weedge shot back. "Most of 'em are real nice guys. I mean just 'cause *some* guys are jerks doesn't mean all of 'em are."

"Just the ones I get hooked up with, I guess."

"You *do* make a certain amount of trouble for yourself, you know," Weedge volunteered carefully.

Brandy did not reply, and Weedge, after a pause to open her umbrella, stepped back into the yard. Brandy followed, oblivious to the now rapidly slackening rain.

"Catch you later," Weedge said, when she had reached her car. She shut the door and started the engine, and an instant later was gone, though Brandy could hear tires spinning and gravel playing shrapnel in the undergrowth for a good half minute thereafter.

The rain had stopped by then, and Brandy stood where she was for a long moment, trying to choose between returning to work (which notion she did not relish), slipping into the house and curling up with something hot to drink and maybe justifying the waste of a Saturday with some more design work, or checking out the woods for signs of the deer she had seen the night before.

The latter won—because it was the most mysterious (and thus the most exciting) and would only take a minute. Besides, the rain would probably have washed away anything resembling spoor unless it was very well protected, anyway. God knew it had made short work of the numerous prints she'd left back at the house the day before. Still, she was curious, and while she didn't actually believe there was anything supernatural afoot—after all, a white deer could very well have other screwed-up genes as well, certainly enough to maybe make it keep its rack year-round—a part of her truly wanted to believe that she had seen something uncanny. Even if it *did* lead her off to Annwyn.

But she never made it far enough to check, because just as she reached the forest side of the muddy red ruts that passed for a driveway, she saw something that *truly* gave her pause.

She had mixed up a small batch of concrete the previous afternoon in a hasty, vain effort at a stopgap repair on the foundations before she had realized that they needed far more serious attention. And, uncharacteristically, she'd made up too much of the stuff and had dumped the surplus up here in the road in an attempt at filling one of the more treacherous ruts.

That had been in late afternoon, right before she'd gone inside to spend the next three hours worrying over her drawing board.

Which was also about three hours before she'd seen the deer.

Three hours.

Just enough time for the particular concrete mix she'd been using to harden but still be a little tacky.

And sometime during that period, an impression had been made: the print of a large, bare—and unmistakably human—right foot, facing directly toward her trailer.

She was still staring at it, still having cold chills and wondering why, *and* whether or not she should call the cops to report what had obviously been a prowler, when the sound of another vehicle approaching jerked her from her reverie—this one accompanied by a particularly virulent strain of heavy metal music. She glanced around, alarmed; then, when she saw the red Ford truck that was lumbering down the road, relaxed.

Well, at least *some* things were going right that day. At least the lumber she'd ordered two days ago was arriving on time—not that she could use it just yet, not with the foundations like they were.

The truck ground to a rough-idling halt beside her, and a teenage boy stuck a red-bandannaed head through the open window. He did not look reliable. The music blaring from the cab behind him (possibly the new Skid Row) bordered on pain.

"Where you want this stuff?" the boy shouted, peering down at her with the scarce-concealed contempt she was far too used to from young males of his type. She wondered suddenly what the odds were of him being one of her students come fall. Lord, she hoped not.

She bit back a retort that would probably have set the lad's head rag ablaze, and pointed toward the house instead. "Come on," she snapped, "I'll show you."

It was only when she was halfway there and heard the distinct brittle snaps of concrete shattering behind her that she realized that the truck had just driven over the evidence of her prowler and ground it to soggy gray powder.

And then the rain returned.

Interlude 2

Fire and Rain

Welch County, Georgia
Saturday, June 19—midnight

An inch-long candle gutters in a can lid, centering a bare wooden table that rests on a bare wood floor. A three-legged stool stands beside it. He sits there, staring, as he has stared at fire so many times before.

Fire: the Maker and Unmaker.

Fire that always brings Change.

He stares until his eyes go dry, until the empty room dissolves around the edges. He does not blink, and his eyes ache dustily.

It is time.

A deep breath and he raises his hand. He slides it beside the candle and examines them together. His eyes shift but do not refocus. The candle is white and pure, its flame clean and bright, blue and yellow. His flesh is firm and smooth, ruddy, with fewer calluses and more hair than he remembers. He has blisters: new ones, from the work he has just begun.

54

But there is other work he must be about, for which he must seek direction.

He turns his hand palm downward and closes his eyes. Darkness enfolds him as he shifts the hand sideways—into the flame.

Pain—but he does not remove it.

Pain—he gasps once, but the sound is slight.

Pain—and more pain, and then he is falling.

Into cool.

"It is twice in two days you have called, my son—surely you must be about your business."

"My business is yours in a way, for I am but a part of you—or so you have told me."

"A part may have *many* parts, and some are best not remembered."

"I know. I have *been* many parts—*had* many parts—*played* many parts."

"And will play others."

"How many?"

"At least one more."

"I . . . see."

"You do not."

"A figure of speech."

"Ah . . . so."

"Are you content, my son? Are you finished?"

"I am content. Things seem simpler than heretofore; there are not so many memories."

"Have you danced?"

"I have."

"Have you danced away your shadows?"

"So I imagine."

"Then you imagine a very great deal. It is your blessing—and your curse."

"One I seem compelled to pass on."

"It was ever the way."

"Mother?"

"Yes, son."

"There is a woman. There will be a man. There may be a . . ."

"What?"

"I don't know, but I . . . I think I fear it. It is not natural."

"Are you?"

"So you have told me."

"I must go, my son."

"So do you ever."

"You have what you need? You have once more become one man?"

"I do. I have."

"Will you remain so?"

"I doubt it."

"You have—"

"I have enough."

The candle winks out and he sits alone in darkness. There is no pain in his hand. On his roof he hears a gentle tinkle.

Chapter 4

She'll Be Comin' 'Round the Mountain

Just south of Welch County, Georgia
Monday, June 21—midmorning

The Centauri had developed a miss in the third rotor's number two spark plug, and there was something awry with a fuel injector as well—or that's what Ron *thought* was causing his car to be down on power as he found himself pressing the accelerator ever harder to maintain his current considerable clip up the first of the deceptively long grades that snaked their way through the forests of Keycutter Knob up to Clanton Gap. He sighed, clicked the transmission back a notch, and watched the tachometer needle swing right half a thousand revs as he prodded the power band back where it ought to be. The plugs—like the injectors, brakes, transmission, and about a million other high-tech components—were *always* plaguing him, either because they were made of plastic or ceramic and thereby beyond his areas of expertise, or because when he'd assembled the car from four years accumulation of carefully designed and chosen parts, he had lacked the equipment or materials, if not the actual engineering and machining skills, to construct alternatives of his own design.

But at least the long, metallic burgundy hood gleaming beyond the car's steeply raked windshield was as flawlessly executed as that of any Ferrari or Aston Martin. He should know: he'd sketched and modeled, then rolled, filed, filled, and shaped every curve and plane himself, all from raw aluminum alloy. And likewise for the entire chassis, most of the suspension, and every inch of the bodywork except the lights, windows, windshield—which had come from a late-model Thunderbird—and the deformable urethane bumpers he'd had custom-molded at preposterous expense in Atlanta. But with that much handwork, that many systems working together that had not been *intended* to cooperate, he supposed it was only natural that something would screw up once in a while.

And in any event, the only real-world effect of the glitch was a slight hesitation upon acceleration—which meant a second, max, added to the car's zero-to-sixty time, and possibly ten miles an hour lopped off a top speed that was useless in the mountains anyway. Which meant he might get to Lew's two minutes later than he would have otherwise.

Which, given that he really didn't want to be going there at all, was scarcely a problem when you got right down to it.

Still, he hadn't had a chance to give the car a workout in a while—what with the ever vigilant Georgia State Patrol all too eager to rev up their Taurus SHO's and take pursuit. Not that he couldn't dust them, either in a straight line or (especially) on crooked roads where their front wheel drive was no match for the complex all-wheel system that fed the Centauri's power to the ground. Never mind that all that gleaming paintwork contained certain substances that absorbed radar just like a Stealth aircraft, so that they rarely noticed him anyway. It was just that when they *did* . . . well, the Centauri was the only one of its kind in the world, and thus impossibly conspicuous; and even Listeners were not immune to radio-orchestrated roadblocks. As for tickets: every one he'd ever received had conveniently slipped through the cracks in the system, courtesy of a bit of well-applied Luck. He hated being reduced to that, though, especially when all he wanted was to have a little fun. Lew would not approve. But Uncle Dion would.

Ron grinned and clicked down another gear as the first curve worthy of the term loomed before him: a solid wall of rust-colored rocks on the right, the topmost twigs of a grove of cedars beyond the guardrail opposite. He tapped the brakes, barely moved the leather-padded wheel—and floored the accelerator halfway through the bend. His tires—big Pirelli P-Zeros on titanium wheels he had also designed and cast—uttered not a chirp as the G forces mounted, and then he was on a straightaway and gathering speed again. Wind whipped past his ears, whistling through the ear-pieces of his Ray Bans, even as it threatened to unseat the black baseball cap that confined his shoulder-long hair.

"Rrroowwwrrrr!" In the red leather bucket seat beside him, Matty Groves protested the sideways slide that had roused him from his nap with a plaintive yowl.

"Can't take the heat, huh?" Ron chuckled, reaching down to scratch between the feline's pointy ears as he continued to gather speed. "Or are you just pissed 'cause I didn't buy us a Jag?"

"Rrroowwwrrrr," Matty replied cryptically, and oozed to the floor, where he promptly curled up in the thick crimson carpet next to the heel of Ron's silver-encrusted crutch and once more affected sleep.

"You just *think* I'm gonna let you do that," Ron informed him slyly. "You ain't seen nothin' yet, kitty!"

"Rrrowwww?" Matty yawned politely, obviously non-plussed.

"Good idea, let's have some music. I haven't checked out the mojo today."

Ron took Matty's silence as agreement and powered up his latest Blaupunkt—which he did not commonly do when he took the car for a run. The sharp-edged whirr of the engine—four reprofiled Mazda rotary pistons geared together in a way the factory had never satisfactorily accomplished—was usually sufficient entertainment for his ears. Besides, with the top down, you couldn't hear without headphones anyway—though with the increasingly cloudy sky looking like it did, he wondered how much longer *that* objection would be valid.

What with the graduation hoo-ha, parties, and all, Ron had had no time to collect omens yesterday; no time, in fact, since Lew's troubling phone call Saturday A.M. Which meant he was overdue. Unfortunately, 96 Rock didn't pick up well this far north of Atlanta, so it took a moment to find a suitable alternative—and once he had, Ron wished fervently he hadn't. For the first complete song—the Significator—was "All Along the Watchtower." And when that was the second time in two readings that particular piece had appeared, Ron had a strong suspicion he was in very deep shit indeed.

Nor was the next tune more encouraging.

It was another Hendrix number—"Voodoo Chile," to be exact. And that really put the wind up him, because there weren't *that* many songs about magic, and when the few that did exist started showing up right and left in Tarot readings, as they'd been doing in recent days—witness "Magic Man" and "Black Magic Woman" the last time around—that could scarcely be accidental.

Thus it was with considerable trepidation that Ron found himself holding his breath through a short commercial while awaiting the third component of the oracle. This one should be *real* interesting, because this one would be in the Crossing slot: the one that would reveal the nature of the obstacles he was facing. Nor could he believe his ears when he finally heard it.

It was a song by The Association. Specifically, it was "Wendy."

And that, Uncle Dion would have told him, had he been sitting in the other seat instead of serving out the last months of an embezzling sentence down at Homestead Pen, was a *big*'un. For, like songs about magic, tunes with the names of one's close associates weren't that common in the grand scheme of things (he could think of none called "Ron" or "Dion" or "Lew," for instance—unless you counted "Louie, Louie," which was probably stretching things), so when one *did* finally turn up . . . well, then it was time to look out!

But he certainly didn't consider Wendy an obstacle— or hadn't until that annoying assertive streak had started manifesting back on Saturday. Up until then she'd seemed content to cut him as much slack as he needed—which he appreciated. She gave him all the personal time he asked for, never questioned the time or money he spent on his hobbies, generally kept herself out of crises or handled them alone (beyond the obvious one of being an orphan with no memory), had more than enough to live on from her various scholarships so that she never had to hit him up for cash—and rarely asked him for anything in return beyond pleasant companionship. It was, Ron conceded, basically a low-maintenance, if rather one-sided, affair.

Did he love her? He didn't know. He supposed he did—as much as it was possible for him to love anyone, given the number of people he cared about whom he'd lost during the last few years, which tended to make him cautious about forming close attachments.

But she certainly loved him! Of *that* he had no doubt; not with what he'd discovered back on Saturday, when he'd finally detected signs of an awakening Voice. That was great, in a way, because he thought it might mean her lost memories were finally returning. But what it revealed about her unshaking devotion to him made him feel doubly guilty about both this trip and graduation.

He should have attended the latter, he knew, but there was no way she'd understand the Voices in his head. Voices on the Wind, his Listener kinsmen would have called them—and Lord knew they *ought* to know; they'd been hearing them for about three thousand years. Or that's what the books up in Lew's vault intimated.

Ron called them a pain in the butt—or the head, to be precise. Sometimes they were thoughts; often, in fact, distinguishable sentences. But crowds were different. Crowds rarely assembled without a reason, and that reason was usually associated with some sort of strong emotion—like anticipation/impatience/joy/apprehension/regret, in the case of graduation. And when there were that many strong feelings concentrated in one place—well, the effect was a lot like several hundred marbles being swished around in a wok, with the whole thing amplified a thousandfold, only it was all inside his head.

Usually—most of the time, in fact—he could raise a mental shield to shut it out. That was an art Listeners mastered early on if they wanted to retain their sanity. But a sufficiently large crowd simply broadcast too much emotion to resist. The result would be one of Ron's famous headaches. Which didn't keep him from feeling like a cad.

But at least Wendy had forgiven him for his refusal to bring her along on this trip; or had said no more about it at any rate. True, she'd looked a little sad-eyed and droopy for the hour between the time they'd reconnected and the first of the postpartum parties that had occupied the rest of Saturday; but to be honest, he'd been so intent on shielding his own fragile psyche from the continual bombardment of the manageable but still strong emotions that inevitably slipped past his shields at such times that he hadn't been able to pay her much mind. Besides, by the time they'd joined friends for dinner at Pearl's Coastal Grill, she was her old perky self again; was sneaking him kisses and pokes in the ribs and sly assaults on his crotch as if nothing had ever happened.

And he'd get back to her real soon, he promised himself. As soon as he figured out what was up with brother Lew.

True to his word, Ron had tried to call again on Saturday afternoon. But Lew had either been out or wasn't answering his phone, which reduced Ron to leaving messages on his answering machine—guarded ones, initially, then more definite ones that had finally culminated in him making a unilateral vow to go up for a visit come Monday morning, which was today.

Ron was frankly worried.

Of course, he *could* have used the Luck, have girded up his loins and tried to Listen to the Voices up Welch County way. Except that he was not a Master, and therefore not as strong as Lew, and might not have been able to get through. Oh, he could *still* have made the attempt, but it would have taken a hell of a lot out of him. And frankly, he wasn't really sure he *wanted* to know what was up with Lew that bad.

But he was sure as bloody hell curious about all those songs about magic and women and warnings and change and dissolution! Lew was the Magic Man, he'd pretty well concluded. And the cryptic content of the rest of the call had all but convinced him that the reading had been in reference to whatever was bugging his brother, not to anything as prosaic as an empty ceremony.

But what, exactly, did it *mean*?

Perhaps he'd find out from the next batch of songs— *if* he ever got another, now that "Wendy" had ended and commercials had taken over again.

He sighed once more, and braked hard for the first of the several light switchbacks that constituted the final mile of the upgrade. The tires were stressed enough to howl this time, and then he was on the accelerator again and the engine was howling, too. Voices in the head notwithstanding, there *were* advantages to being a de facto Welch. Like money. Specifically, in his case, a pair of multi-hundred-thousand-dollar insurance policies he'd collected when his foster parents had bought it, not to mention their Tampa house, not to mention certain codicils in his late mother's will, not to mention the bit Lewis sent him now and then ostensibly as a tax write-off. The car, he thought, would have cost about five hundred K to duplicate.

And here he was, an overstressed twenty-two-year-old, driving it like a maniac.

Which really didn't matter anyway, as he already had plans for a much-improved replacement.

But in the meantime, he really *did* want to catch the next two songs; for if he was lucky, they would reveal first what slight good might come out of all this, and— more important—what underlay Lew's cryptic summons.

And there was the first one now, following an ad for Bill Elliot Ford over in Dahlonega: the Beatles' "She's Leaving Home." But who was *she*? Ron wondered. Wendy, or who? He was still puzzling over this when the Underlying Influences tune began. It was "Frankenstein," by Edgar Winter.

Which was *damned* disturbing. For according to Uncle Dion's iconography, that song more or less meant that someone had created a monster. The question was, who had done the creating, and who (or what), exactly, could the critter be?

It was then that he saw the other car.

"Crap," he muttered under his breath, for he had first thought that the sleek white vehicle a quarter mile ahead was dawdling along the highway at that infuriating crawl outlanders used when they were bent on absorbing scenery. But as he quickly caught up to it, he realized that it was not moving at all, but parked off the side of the road. And a closer inspection revealed three more things, none of which eased his mind.

The first was that the car was a late-model Toyota Celica coupe exactly like Wendy drove.

The second was that there was a good reason for that resemblance, which was that it *was* hers. He recognized the Greenpeace bumper sticker.

And the third was that it was most likely parked on the shoulder a hundred yards short of the gap because either a hose or the radiator itself had inconveniently given up the ghost. Or those were the *likeliest* sources for the steam rising wraithlike from beneath the unopened hood, at any rate.

Ron grimaced irritably and bit his lip. What his girlfriend was doing here, he did not want to contemplate—not when Lew clearly had problems he needed to talk out one on one. On the other hand, she *was* his girlfriend, and she *was* obviously in trouble. And—mechanical inept that she also was—he likewise knew he had no alternative but to play knight in shining armor and ride to her rescue.

But *Black* Knight maybe. Because the most aid he intended to render was to give her a ride into Cordova, find an obliging mechanic who did road service (and they'd *all* oblige, once they recalled that he was kin to Lewis Welch), and send the willful little wench packing for the southlands. No way he was gonna invite her home with him, uh-uh.

Or at least that was the plan when he eased the Centauri in behind the Toyo, set the transmission and brake, checked to see that Matty was still fast asleep in the floorboard, and turned off the ignition. But by the time he'd snagged the crutch, limped half a dozen steps up the roadside, and caught the sickly sweet scent of hot antifreeze wafting down the breeze, his resolve had begun to waver.

Fortunately, it was still sufficiently fortified for him to affect a scowl when he stumped up to the driver's window and tapped gently on the tinted glass.

The curved pane immediately whirred down—to reveal a bewildered-looking Wendy furiously paging through the owner's manual with one hand while she worked the window switch with the other. She had not looked up, which struck Ron as both odd and foolish. Either she was more distracted than he had ever seen her—or more trusting than any city-dwelling woman ought to be. He was on the ragged edge of announcing himself by pointing this out when he noticed a large, potted barrel cactus neatly belted into the passenger seat—and a brace of obviously fresh daisies peeping from the map pocket on that side. True to her usual affectation, too; Wendy was *wearing* flowers, this time a blue-green T-shirt batiqued with water lilies; and Ron found the overall tableau so amusingly typical that instead of launching into a tirade about the virtues of self-preservation, he had to mask a giggle by clearing his throat. Wendy promptly blinked up at him, her befuddlement changing quickly to joy when she recognized her rescuer.

"Ron!" she cried breathlessly, a dazzling smile spreading across her elfin features. "Jeeze, am I glad to see you! I wasn't sure when you were leaving, so I didn't know if I ought to wait, or hitch on into town and try to give you a call, or what. So I—"

"Well, you *couldn't* have called—not Lew," Ron broke in tersely, trying hard to regain his former ire, which was impossible before such guileless relief. "He's got an unlisted number."

"But . . . I thought he was an important person, and—"

"He is," Ron interrupted again. "That's *why* the number's unlisted. Otherwise he'd be so swamped with calls, he'd never get anything done."

He stepped away automatically as Wendy tossed the manual into the backseat, gave the cactus an encouraging pat, and opened the door. Once she was standing beside him, he returned her enthusiastic hug rather more mechanically, then reached inside to pop the hood release, though he already knew what he would find.

"What did you say he did?" Wendy asked innocently, apparently unconcerned for her wheels now that Ron was there to tend to whatever gremlins had waylaid her. "Your brother, I mean. I've never been clear on that."

"Because I've never told you," Ron retorted—far more sharply than he intended, even allowing that his anxiety level had just about reached overload sometime in the last two minutes. "Those who need to know, know; those who don't shouldn't care. Let's just say it's neither obvious nor illegal."

"But Ron . . . !"

"If you *have* to stick a label on it, you could say he's in the service industry, I guess. He works out of his house," he added unnecessarily, and cursed himself, since he'd long ago vowed never to volunteer information about either himself or the clan. He wouldn't lie if he could possibly avoid it—the Luck could trip you up if you did things like that. But he could hedge, or evade, or simply retreat into a brooding silence until the cows came home. It had served him well—so far. But he wondered how much longer he could keep it up. Wendy's presence here did not bode well at all.

Nor was she happy now—not that he blamed her. *"Sorry!"* she snapped, with a degree of sarcasm he had never heard from her before. "I didn't *realize* it was any big deal. *Thanks* for letting me know!" She frowned over his shoulder as he waved away the cloud of steam and fell to inspecting the plumber's nightmare under the hood.

It took less than ten seconds to locate the culprit: a radiator that had split for nearly an inch along its underside. So much for Japanese reliablity, he thought, noting the incomprehensible hieroglyphs that followed the English part number. Unfortunately, it also meant that the car would probably have to be towed and a new radiator special-ordered.

"I guess you're wondering what I'm doing up here," Wendy ventured a few minutes later, after Ron had explained the situation and had used his car phone to summon a wrecker from Cordova, twelve miles up the road. He was lounging against the right rear fender, fidgeting with one of the cast silver warriors that encrusted most of the crutch and wishing humidity didn't make his knee hurt like it was, while his lady rifled through the clutter in her trunk.

"I *was* a little curious, as a matter of fact," Ron answered, his tone as neutral as he could manage.

"Well," she began slyly, her earlier peevishness evidently dissipated now that salvation was in sight, "you *could* say I'm on vacation."

"Vacation!" Ron flared before he could stop himself. "Following me's more likely. Welch County's no place for a holiday, *that's* for sure!"

Wendy's face hardened immediately, her jaw taking on the firmer set he had noticed with increasing frequency in recent days. Ron hoped he wasn't in for a row. He hated contention, especially with women—not only because of the strong emotions that inevitably accompanied such occurrences, but simply because there was too much chance of someone getting hurt, which, his present mood notwithstanding, he also loathed. But he wasn't used to Wendy's new assertiveness, and therefore—

"You can *think* whatever you want to," she told him stiffly. "But the fact is that it suddenly occurred to me after you dropped me off last night that while I may *be* your girlfriend, I'm also a free and independent person, and I've got time and money enough to do what I please. And then I realized that just 'cause *you* didn't want me to go home with you didn't mean I couldn't come up on my own. It's a free country, after all. I don't have to have permission from you!"

Her voice had been rising steadily, and her eyes were flashing with the fire Ron had first seen back on Saturday. He was too stunned to speak. She apparently noted his amazement as well, and her face and voice softened immediately, as though she had surprised even herself—but both retained a hint of warning as she continued. "So what I've decided to do, I guess," she went on, "—assuming I get the dratted car fixed—is to spend a week in Cordova on my own. And if we just *happen* to run into each other once in a while, that'll be fine with me. And if we *don't*, well, I guess that'll just give me more time to find out about this mysterious family of yours."

Ron could only nod in resignation. Five minutes later the Toyota's emergency flashers were blinking merrily, Wendy's suitcase was snuggled beside his in the Centauri's shallow trunk. And the conniving little vixen herself was curled up in the seat beside him with a cat, a cactus, and a crutch contending for space in her lap. Due to circumstances beyond his control, Ron had abandoned any hope of collecting more omens. But that didn't stop him from trying to Listen to Wendy's thoughts—officially in what he already knew would be a futile effort to discover if she really was as pissed at him as she seemed. But also covertly curious to find out whether that trace of Voice he'd detected earlier still existed. It did—but once again, the only thing it Spoke of was love.

Chapter 5

Rescue Me

Cordova, Georgia
10:01 A.M.

"Do you think I'm *stupid*?" Brandy gritted in a hard-edged growl that was her only alternative to a shout. "Do you think that just 'cause I'm a woman, I don't know substandard material when I see it?" She glared past the bulk of a drooling redneck loon named Marcus Jones to the jumbled pile of damp two-by-eights who had just unceremoniously dumped into Mason Hardware's lumberyard, and raised an eyebrow meaningfully.

Jones (or so the script on his blue coverall proclaimed) was close to her own age, she guessed: no more than twenty-five. But already he looked old. A dropout, no doubt, which meant he probably *wasn't* a Welch County native. Which was no excuse whatever for the recalcitrance he'd been displaying since he'd discovered her pointedly ignoring a protesting teenage underling roughly a minute before. The boy had promptly lost himself amid the neat stacks of lumber that towered all about, but Jones, regretfully, had not. He wasn't saying a word, though, merely

69

staring at her with that indulgent, bemused smirk men like
him used when they were letting a woman have her say but
had no intention whatever of acquiescing to her obviously
absurd demands.

But this idiotically gaping moron bloody well wasn't
going to ignore Brandy Wallace! Hell no! Not when Brandy Hall was at stake!

"Now then, wait a minute, gal," Jones drawled at last.
"Ain't you kinda—"

Brandy's eyes flashed fire, silencing him in midprotest,
even as the eyebrow darted higher yet. "Don't gal *me*,
you asshole!" she raged, venting the anger that had been
building steadily ever since that morning when the skies
had finally cleared enough for her to examine the lumber
she was now so vehemently rejecting. "Don't you *ever* hit
me with that condescending shit!" she continued. "I may
be a woman, but I can do *anything* as well as you can,
and most things better. And I can *sure* as hell by God tell
warped boards from straight, and knotty ones from clear—
and *frigging* well tell top grade from bottom!"

"You're pretty top grade yourself, ain't you?" Jones
replied placidly, having already regained sufficient composure to slough off her tirade. His gaze shifted from her
face to her bosom, and Brandy found herself wishing the
target zone was armored with more than a sweat-stained
T-shirt and an old bra. Unfortunately, she'd been so angry
when she'd finally got a good look at the boards, she'd
come to town as she was, mud, sweat, and dirty face all.

Fortunately she still had her tongue.

"Would you like to keep your job?" she shot back icily.
"One more crack like that and I'll report you to your
boss. And if *that* doesn't work, I'll file sexual harassment
charges against you!"

"*What* about her ass?" Jones sniggered derisively, taking
a step forward—which effectively reduced the distance
between them to something on the order of three feet: easy
pouncing range for either of them.

Brandy instantly thought of so many replies simultaneously, she could not speak.

"Tell you what I'll do," Jones rumbled into the resulting
verbal vacuum, drawing himself up to a probable six foot

four in what she knew was an attempt at physical intimidation. "I'll take back them boards—even them you messed up by draggin' 'em through the mud. An' all *you've* gotta do is . . ."

Brandy folded her arms and glared at him distrustfully. "What?"

Jones's mouth twisted into a leering grin as he began casually unbuttoning his fly. "Why, all you've gotta do is play a little tune on my ol' flute here!"

In spite of herself, Brandy blushed furiously. God she hated this: trying to accomplish something as simple as buying lumber in a man's world. No way her brother, Tommy, would have had to put up with crap like this, no more than they'd have given him grief about car repairs, or moving her trailer, or selling her concrete in bulk. All because of what Tommy had between his legs; all because of what this overpumped asshole was all too aware he had between his. But she wouldn't be cowed, by God. No way. She'd call this bumpkin's bluff.

—In a manner of speaking.

She had already begun tensing herself to give the goon a kick in the gonads hard enough to ring his chimes up *past* his flute when she caught a flash of movement behind the head-high stack of lumber to her left. But before she could zero in on it, a large hand grasped Jones's shoulder from the rear, another cupped his crotch and lifted—whereupon he vented a strangled gasp and then was sailing through the air. He crashed heavily against a twin flat of boards that she'd been standing beside and crumpled to the ground, whereupon he promptly doubled up, clutching his groin with both hands, his face—now very white and sweaty— an almost comical mixture of pain, rage, and confusion.

The still unseen someone chuckled loudly, and Brandy shifted her attention from her fallen foe to her unsuspected benefactor—not, she hastened to add, that she hadn't been about to achieve much the same end herself.

The man who sauntered out to meet her looked to be a few years older than she—twenty-seven, say—but she only realized that after the fact. What caught her attention immediately was that he was about as handsome a piece of man-flesh as she had ever happened on: tall and red-haired, fair-skinned and muscular, with merry blue eyes, a square-cut chin, and a youthfully turned-up nose that would have been pug had it been any shorter. He was also grinning in a remarkably self-satisfied manner, the teeth between full red lips as white and shiny as fresh-glazed china. But it was an innocent expression, unlike that young Marcus Jones had so conveniently been deprived of.

The man's eyes shifted toward the fallen yardman, and the grin widened sufficiently to reveal a pair of dimples. "That piece of trash botherin' you, was he?"

Brandy nodded dumbly, only then realizing that this fellow knew perfectly well what had transpired. No way he *couldn't* have, with him standing as close as he was. Shoot, he'd *acted* on her behalf. Which meant he was basically being polite now: preserving her dignity by relieving her of the onus of explanation.

"You all right?"

Another nod. "I'm fine . . . uh, thanks," she added, glancing down and dusting herself off unnecessarily.

"Glad to hear it," the man replied, sparing her an appraising glance that did not give her the heebie-jeebies the way Jones's had done. "It'd be a shame to lose a customer that can tell top grade from bottom. There's few enough men can do that, never mind women."

Brandy's eyes narrowed reflexively. *Oh, this is just great*, she thought. *Out of the frying pan . . .*

"Just teasin',", the man amended quickly, taking a step back and looking wide-eyed and apologetic—and therefore at least five years younger. Something sparkled in his left earlobe, and Brandy noticed a golden stud set there—no, make that two: a plain gold stud, and a tiny Celtic cross. "Guess I oughta know better than to tease about stuff like that, shouldn't I?" the man continued. "At least when the wounds are fresh. Still, a woman that's gonna act like a man's gotta put up with men, sometimes."

"I'm glad you showed up," Brandy shot back acidly, "but I could have handled him. I've had martial arts training."

The man's eyebrows lifted inquiringly. "What kind?"

Brandy looked a little sheepish. "Uh, mostly T'ai Chi."

"Inoffensive stuff," he opined. "Exercise, really."

Brandy had just started to counter with something to the effect that a kick didn't need a name to be effective where she'd planned on delivering hers when the object of their discussion made his presence known by groaning, rising to his feet, and stumping over to glare at the man who had so recently humbled him.

"I don't know who the hell you are, mister," Jones gasped from between clenched teeth. "But you damned well better—"

"*Fire* you?" the red-haired man supplied helpfully. "Thanks, I will. Come by my office in ten minutes and we'll start the paperwork."

"Fired?" Jones looked as if he'd been hit where it hurt all over again. "*Fired*? Just who the hell do you think you are?"

The man smiled fiendishly. "I'm your new boss," he said softly. "I was hired this morning to get this yard in shape and to get rid of dead wood . . . like you. If you don't believe me, you can ask Mr. Mason. You can tell 'im Van Vannister sent you."

"But . . . you don't have on no coverall or nothin'."

Vannister glanced down at his black T-shirt, blue jeans, and Frye boots. "Didn't have one in stock to fit me 'cause of my shoulders. But that doesn't change a thing."

"The hell it don't!"

"The hell it *better*! Or next time I really will rupture your ball."

Jones colored to his hairline and commenced backing away.

Vannister shifted his gaze from Jones to Brandy and winked conspiratorially. "He hasn't got but one, you know," he confided. "Don't think he had much of a flute, either. Doubt you coulda played more 'n a couple of notes on it . . . not that you'd have wanted to, of course."

Brandy was completely floored. First this man rescues her, then acts chivalrous, then sounds sexist, then starts talking about the most scandalous matters imaginable as if they were ancient buddies.

Vannister winked again, breaking in on her reverie in the most disconcerting manner possible, and inclined his head toward the departing Jones. "Gets 'em every time," he went on. "You hurt a man worst by ridiculin' what makes him most intrinsically male. It was all true, by the way: what I said about him. I've had both medical and military trainin', and they teach you how to tell stuff like that in a hurry—so you can recognize hernias, and all. And—" He broke off abruptly.

Brandy was regarding him dubiously, wondering how much bullshit he expected her to swallow.

"You don't believe me?" Vannister ventured, with obviously feigned disappointment.

"Not a word."

"How 'bout if I said I heard his wife complainin' to one of her gossips about certain . . . deficiencies."

Brandy expected another wink, but this time Vannister produced a shrug—which made his T-shirt tighten alarmingly across his impressive pecs. And made her wish she hadn't been staring at them so intently for the last half minute or so. Not that they weren't worth looking at . . .

Her solution to the whole confounded problem was to change the subject. "Uh . . . well, since you say you're now yard foreman," she began briskly, "I was wondering if—"

"I'd help you with your order?" Vannister finished for her. "Sure. That's what I'm here for. 'Sides," he added, striding past Brandy to give the rejected load of ceiling joists a quick, scowling examination, "I hear young Mr. Welch's sawmill produces more'n enough good wood to go around. Isn't any need *a'tall* to sell stuff like this. It oughta be chipped up and used for pressboard—or paper."

"Or to keep stray employees in line?" Brandy suggested slyly. And immediately wished she hadn't, since it tended dangerously close to flirting—and the last thing in the world she needed when she was trying to be taken seriously as a customer for heavy building materials was to be caught doing something as frivolous as flirting.

Vannister turned to face her. "You got an order on file inside?"

She nodded. "Ought to."

"Fine. I tell you what, then: it's gonna take a little time to get what you want together—but if you're not in a *huge* hurry, I can have it to your place this afternoon. Might even stick in a board or two extra, just for your trouble—that is, if you need 'em."

"I can always use a good board," Brandy told him with a smile. "And yeah, this afternoon'll do fine. I've still got some concrete to fiddle with this morning—if I can ever get my shopping finished."

"Fine," Vannister concluded. "And in the meanwhile, *I've* got some paperwork to do. I don't want that piece of crap on the clock a second longer'n I can help. There's too many good men wantin' work for anybody to ever hire a bad 'un."

"And you're a good 'un?" Brandy teased.

"Finest kind," Vannister replied instantly, flashing his smile. "*Finest* kind."

Fifteen minutes later, Brandy dumped an assortment of tools and other staple building supplies atop the checkout counter. The plump, fortyish woman next to her eyed her speculatively, but the younger woman commanding the cash register (someone as new as Vannister, apparently, or at least Brandy hadn't seen her before) simply smiled and began ringing up her purchases, then told her the total.

Brandy already had her checkbook out and the date and signature filled in when the older woman first cleared her throat, then scratched her nose, and finally blurted out, "You're the new art teacher, aren't you?"

"Yeah," Brandy murmured absently as she finished the check. "Or I will be when school starts this fall."

"And until then . . . ?"

"I'm building a house."

"A *house*?" The young clerk sounded positively incredulous.

"A house," Brandy stated flatly.

"By *yourself*?"

Once more Brandy nodded, sick to death of this sort of interrogation, but too polite to admit as much. At least this time it was a woman staring at her as if she'd just announced that her mother was a pumpkin and her daddy a head of cabbage, and her expression showed more admiration than derision. "By myself . . . as much as I can, anyway."

"You've met the new foreman, then?" That was the older woman again. She looked familiar, but Brandy couldn't place where she'd seen her. That was the price of being a hermit, she supposed: not knowing anybody in the county except those on the board of education, the high school faculty, and the relative few she traded with.

"Well, have you?" the woman prompted.

"Yeah," Brandy replied—more snippily than she'd intended. Then again, she'd been caught off guard by a question which implied that this woman knew more about her business than she wanted her—or anyone—to.

"Good-lookin' boy, ain't he?"

"Boy?" Brandy repeated aloud before she could catch herself. She'd definitely thought Vannister a man, though perhaps that was because he was so much taller than she—or simply differing perspectives. "Uh, yeah," she finished lamely, "I guess he is." Feigning a cough in hopes of curtailing that line of conversation, she secreted her checkbook in her backpack, picked up the paper bag the clerk had provided, and prepared to depart.

"You goin' to the party tonight?"

She stopped in her tracks. *What party?* she almost snapped at the nosy woman, who was gazing at her inquiringly. And then she remembered. There was some kind of county-wide bash that evening, the one she'd gotten that fancy calligraphed invitation to: Lewis Welch's wingding. "Oh . . . right," she mumbled awkwardly, "I'd forgotten it was today . . . Time kinda slips up on me sometimes."

The woman nodded knowingly. "Up on that mountain, I can see how it would."

"Yeah."

"But you're comin', right?"

A shrug. "I guess." Then, for no clear reason: "Monday seems like an odd night for a celebration, though—seems like Saturday or . . . or even Sunday would make more sense. I mean if it's not a *specific* date or anything . . ."

The woman's response was instantaneous: "That's when Mr. Welch wanted it, and that's when it's gonna be."

Brandy shrugged again and continued on her way, then stopped once more, puzzled, completely at a loss as to why the population of an entire county would bow to the whims of someone who was barely more than a boy.

Except, she realized, that they'd soon be letting someone only slightly older teach their children art. She had her prejudices, too, she conceded. God help Jones, who judged her first by her appearance. And yet here she'd done the same for Lewis Welch!

"See you there, then?" the young clerk chimed in hopefully.

Brandy sighed and turned once more. "I guess . . . if I get finished with my chores."

"I'd try," the woman confided. "I'd try *real* hard."

"Lewis'd appreciate it, I'm sure," a tall, thin man in overalls added from where he was comparing brands of duct tape, his weathered face deadly serious. "Things always go much better if you have a Welch around, preferably *the* Welch."

"But why . . . ?"

"Luck."

"Luck?"

"You'll figure it out. You're a bright young woman; just keep your eyes and ears open . . . and your questions a little less obvious."

Brandy's brows lowered immediately, but the man's expression softened. "Don't worry about it, honey," he murmured. "But if I was you, I'd go to that party, and I'd sure as hell get to know Lewis Welch."

"But I've already met him."

"Right, but you need to get to *know* him. Things'll work out better for you, trust me."

"Sure will," a second male voice inserted from behind, which irritated her beyond words, because she liked her conversations to be private, and she was being given grief by three people already. "You really should come. You really should make it a point to get to know the Master."

"Right," a fifth party affirmed, another woman. "No way that house of yours'll be finished right unless the Master approves it."

Brandy's only reply was a stiff "Thanks for the advice." Whereupon she turned and walked briskly toward the door. Her face was like stone.

Superstitious mumbo-jumbo, she thought. Fantasy was fine when it was only that: a thing to be read or watched on a screen; an impossible dream to be wistfully desired. But what she'd just heard sounded more like the Middle Ages than modern America. Or like a bad horror movie, the way everybody's ·voices had gone hushed and strange when they spoke about the Master. That which seemed special and magical in private suddenly became cheap and tawdry when distilled through half a dozen Southern mountain twangs.

Master indeed! She was her *own* master, and nobody had better forget it!

By the time she reached the Mylared-glass door that let out onto the lumberyard where she had left her pickup, her keys were already jingling in her hand. She leaned into the push bar, but met sufficient resistance (courtesy of an unoiled hydraulic assist ram) that she had to draw back and try again. Just as she exerted herself, though, a dark shape filled the space beyond and she found herself staggering through onto the pavement outside.

And for the second time in fifteen minutes, facing a grinning Van Vannister.

"Thanks," she grunted as she edged past his outstretched arm.

"No problem," Vannister replied with another of those confidential winks she found so disconcerting. "You looked like you needed help. Oh, and by the way, it appears I'll be able to make that delivery this afternoon, if that's okay."

"That'll be fine," Brandy agreed shortly, in no mood for further conversation—since it suddenly seemed that every one she engaged in turned into a fencing match. She started toward her old F-150 at a brisk trot.

"I'll bring it personally," Vannister shouted to her back. "And if every board's not perfect, I'll trade you two for one to replace 'em—no charge!"

"You're gonna cost poor old Mr. Mason some money if you're not careful," Brandy called over her shoulder, still walking. "But thanks."

Footsteps sounded behind her, and Vannister jogged up to pace her at her left. He did not offer to carry her bag, though, which was some relief. "Something else bugging you?" he inquired seriously. "If it's something we did . . ."

Brandy paused in the act of inserting the key and glanced up at the man—it was hard not to look at him, with those eyes, that smile. He was at least superficially interested in her, too, she thought. But the last thing in the world she needed right now was a man complicating her life. Especially when that man did not know her at all beyond what she looked like, that she was building a house, and probably that she had a bad temper, none of which offered sufficient foundation on which to construct a relationship.

An eyebrow raised quizzically, boyishly.

Brandy shook her head. "Sorry, but no, it's not your fault. It's just . . . just . . ."

"Just what?"

She grimaced uncomfortably. "Oh, nothing, really. It's . . . Can I ask you something?" she managed finally.

"Sure."

"How long have you been up here? In Welch County, I mean?"

"You mean, when did I arrive?"

"Yeah."

"Saturday morning."

Brandy stared at him incredulously. "And old Mr. Mason's already giving you run of the lumberyard, with power to fire, and all? Jesus Christ!"

Vannister smiled wanly. "I guess I look good on paper."

"You *must*!"

"I've also got a certain . . . presence."

"And a very high opinion of yourself."

"But that's not what's botherin' you."

Brandy shook her head. "Well, then, you probably haven't noticed this yet, but . . . but it seems like nobody up here can take a blessed crap without an okay from the Welches. I mean I *know* the county's named after them and all, and I *know* they own about half the businesses— or control 'em, anyway. And I *know* they're major benefactors and that everybody up here seems to be prosperous. But honest to God, do they have to have their fingers in *everything*?"

"Anything in particular?"

Brandy told him about the party, and about the reference to her house not being likely to prosper without Welch intervention.

"And have you *seen* Lewis Welch?" Brandy finished. "The one they call the Master? He's nothing but a kid— well, not a kid, he's got to be close to our age; but . . ." She stopped, blushed, realizing she'd made an assumption about Vannister she had no right to make, and which might not be appreciated.

He apparently guessed what was on her mind, too. "How old *do* you think I am?"

Brandy shrugged and guessed low. "Twenty-five may-be?"

"Wrong. Wildly wrong."

She did not take the bait, merely shrugged again. "I need to be going."

"Oh, right. Sorry to have kept you." Vannister shifted his weight to his other leg, and she couldn't help but notice the way the muscles bunched and strained beneath his skin-tight jeans. "You're right, though," he added. "All this stuff about the Welches. I don't understand it either— but then again, I'm not from around here. But one thing I *do* know."

"What's that?"

"I think you'd be well advised to go to that party."

"Maybe I will," Brandy said, and climbed into her truck.

"Know something else?" Vannister asked through the open window.

"What?"

"I think I'd be well advised, too."

"Thanks again," Brandy mumbled awkwardly, and twisted the key.

"Catch you later," Vannister called.

Brandy wondered why she took that as a challenge.

Chapter 6

We Are Family

Cardalba Hall
Late morning

"Jesus *Christ*!" Ron gritted, stamping hard enough on the brakes to feel the pulse of the antilock kicking in, "I'd forgotten how sharp that turn is." He braced himself and swung the Centauri sharply right, to cross the humpbacked cobblestone bridge that marked the southern entrance to Cardalba Plantation in a series of noisy sideways jolts. As he resumed speed along the narrow paved road between the Talooga River and the piled stone wall that defined the limits of the inner grounds, Wendy seemed nonplussed by his automotive acrobatics—but *he* had to suppress a chill. Too much had happened among these haunted hillsides: too many things too strange to even hint at outside the clan.

But if he was trepidatious as he navigated that last quarter mile beside the river, Wendy was oblivious.

"Wow, those are fine-looking willows!" she exclaimed breathlessly, gazing to her right where the steadily flowing Talooga was curtained by trailing tendrils of green. "I don't know if I've ever seen weeping ones that tall. Oh, gee . . .

and the way they're barely hanging on to the banks there, yet don't seem to be undermined . . . I mean, wow! And look at those azaleas! I've *never* seen anything like them. You folks must have some kind of gardeners."

Ron merely shrugged and slowed minutely to permit his girlfriend a better look. From what he could catch out of the corner of his eye, someone had indeed done some serious azalea planting since he'd last been by, for the spaces between the willows were full of them, some miraculously still displaying crimson blossoms. "Must be Lew's doing," he remarked. "He's evidently gotten into plants lately."

"Yeah, but these look too old to have been put in recently."

"I dunno, then," Ron replied shortly. "This isn't my place, remember? I never lived here, and only came over so I could hang out with Lew."

Wendy looked puzzled for a moment, but then her eyes narrowed suspiciously. "Hey, but wait a minute," she began. "This was in high school, right?"

Ron nodded reluctantly, aware he'd just let a minor secret slip. "Yeah," he acknowledged, "it was."

"And you only went to school here a couple of years, correct? The rest of the time was in Florida, didn't you say?"

"Okay . . ."

"But you guys were just kids then!" Wendy blurted out. "Yet . . . you just showed me the place your mom used to live, and you've told me before that she died while you were a junior. Which means . . . you weren't living in her house by *yourself*, were you?"

Ron grimaced irritably. Here it went: the questions were starting to snowball. "Yeah, as a matter of fact, I was," he acknowledged finally. "Well, technically Aunt Martha— she was my mom's grandmother, actually, but me and Lew didn't know that for a long time, so we always called her Aunt—anyway, she was our guardian the last year we were in high school, so I used Cardalba as my address to keep the social workers happy. But I didn't live there. I hate the place."

"Why?"

"Because something happened there I'd like very much to forget."

Wendy sighed in exasperation. "Which means you want to drop the subject?"

"You've got it."

"Well, maybe I will for now," Wendy replied tartly. "But that doesn't mean I will forever. And—*Jesus Christ!* Is *that* it?"

"You got it!" Ron repeated, unable to resist a relieved smirk. "Yonder lies Cardalba Hall."

Wendy did not reply, but her eyes had grown wide in wonder.

It was not that the house Lew had inherited on the death of their great-uncle, Matthew, five years before was actually that imposing; it was not. In fact, though larger than any other house in the county, and boasting a seemingly endless supply of rooms, the post-Victorian pile that had just slipped into view from behind a screen of cedars to their left was actually quite plain—clapboard even, not brick or stone. Only its facade saved it from austerity, with an imposing two-story porch fronting three-fourths of its southern side, a projecting bay window on the remaining quarter, and a mass of gables piled two more levels above that. But what *did* make it worthy of note was, first of all, its location: atop a low hill with a dark frame of mixed oaks and cedars encircling it on three sides, while a long line of boxwoods led up from a circular drive on the fourth (which they were now bypassing in favor of the private one that branched off a bit farther on). And secondly, the fact that even at this distance, both building and grounds were obviously in absolutely perfect repair. Every window shone like a diamond; the paint was the same pristine white as new-fallen snow, and there did not appear to be so much as a lone stray leaf atop the jade green shingles. The gutters would be clear, too, Ron knew with an absolute certainty. And every rug inside would be spotless, every light bulb functional. Not a faucet would dare to drip, and not a doorframe would be scratched, nor a doily misaligned.

And Wendy was taking it all in.

By the time she had regained sufficient composure to punctuate her earlier exclamation with an awestruck "Wow," Ron was easing the car up the arc of the family drive. There was more new planting beside it: more azaleas, a few clumps of laurel, and a stand of dogwood so dense, it hid the carport until he was almost on it. He braked hard as the structure loomed ahead: another mass of clapboard, green doors, and gables elling off the mansion's northeast corner, newer construction, but definitely of a piece with the older design. Lew had obligingly raised one of the three matching entrances in order to accommodate Ron's car—which had forced him to leave a black Mercury Sable station wagon outside. Ron wondered if it had replaced the Miata Lew had been so proud of last Easter when his brother had briefly ventured out to meet him for lunch on the neutral ground of Dahlonega—the one he had subsequently totaled. Ron doubted it. Such restraint was not typical of a Master's style.

But an emerald green Jaguar convertible was, and so was a matching XJ-6 sedan. A glimpse into the backyard as Ron eased the Centauri between the pair showed two more automotive shapes under tarpaulins. One was the fading bulk of Uncle Matt's aging Ford pickup; the other was a longer, lower form that probably hid the old man's classic Thunderbird Sports Roadster.

Wendy saw him gawking. "The clan's really into 'things,'" he muttered apologetically. "'Specially cars. That's one thing I've got in common with 'em, I guess. I mean, I really haven't thought much about it before; but I reckon we've always kind of been into gadgets, and machines, and all."

And with that, he patted the Centauri's leather-clad dash, pushed the button that would raise both top and side windows as soon as the doors were shut, snagged Matty Groves by the scruff of the neck, and climbed out.

Wendy followed, cactus extended reverently before her like a catatonic porcupine about to be sacrificed; and Ron could hear various electric and hydraulic servos muttering to themselves in the car behind him as they went about their appointed tasks. He wondered briefly if he should retrieve the crutch, then rejected the notion on the grounds that he wasn't certain who the Sable belonged to, and didn't want to draw undue attention to himself (as such an ornate object was bound to do) before he'd assessed the lay of the land— or the Luck, as it were. After a further moment's waffling, he led the way: *not* toward the door inches in front of the car's nose, which let into Cardalba Hall's nether regions, but back outside and around to the front, so they could present themselves at the main entrance, as was proper for arriving company.

Which was not as simple as it sounded. Sometime since Ron's last visit, Lew had replaced the short cobblestone path from the carport to the side steps with a longer, more circuitous alternative that meandered around half the front yard, bypassing a lavish assortment of flower beds in the process, before doubling back almost to its point of origin. And unless one wanted to wade through knee-deep foliage, there was no alternative but to hoof the entire circuitous route—which they did.

Nor did it speed things that Wendy felt compelled to either exclaim over or actually inspect every single species along the way—which seemed to Ron like a couple of hundred. He should be used to it by now, he realized grimly; but a rose was still merely a rose to him, a daisy only a daisy. And in spite of Wendy's best efforts, and somewhat to his embarrassment, that was about as far as his knowledge of ornamental horticulture went.

Ron thought he had weathered the worst, though; and the Holy Grail of the steps was actually in sight when a skinny, hip-high hound chose that moment to lope into view from behind a nearby boxwood. It was white with alarmingly red ears—and frightened Matty Groves out of at least two lives by the simple expedient of padding up to Ron and poking him in the crotch with its narrow nose. Matty promptly hissed and spat and would have made for the nearest dogwood by way of Ron's head had Ron not collared him at the last minute and shooed his assailant away. But the scratches he received as souvenirs would be with him until the Luck got around to healing them—which might take a while, given the unreliability of that "talent" when it came to *minor* injuries.

Eventually, however, they reached the steps, and thus the porch, which now sported a veritable jungle of potted plants and hanging baskets, all of which had to be circumnavigated before they could win through to the massive oak front door. The library curtains were drawn, Ron noted as they passed—

which was no surprise; but the front door was cracked invitingly. Cut glass glittered beside it, and a stained-glass fanlight gleamed darkly overhead. Ron glanced in Wendy's direction, shrugged, and entered without knocking.

Wendy's only response was to mirror the shrug, deposit the cactus by the door, and follow. Matty Groves demanded to be set free and was accommodated. He promptly zipped through the nearest door and disappeared. And would find no mice; of that Ron was certain.

The wide hallway they entered was familiar—too much so, if Ron allowed certain memories to surface. He had seen that space too many times before, seen too many strange folk wander across the Persian carpet that led past two pairs of doors to the stairs at the opposite end. The only thing that had changed was that there were a lot more plants about: potted palms in brass urns at all four corners, a taller one lurking beside the stair, and sprays of near-black gladiolas atop the narrow tables to either side. There was music, too, now he was aware of it, wafting from unseen speakers: the low trumpet notes that heralded "Also Sprach Zarathustra." Lew, it seemed, still had a sense of humor.

A door stood open to the left, revealing a collection of overstuffed red velvet chairs, gleaming woodwork—and enough ferns to stock a dozen funeral homes. "Parlor," Ron told Wendy, ignoring it in favor of a twin door to the right, which was merely cracked. "Library," came his whispered follow-up.

He'd guessed his brother's whereabouts correctly, too, for when he gently pushed against the dark wood (it moved silently, of course; no hinges *ever* squeaked in Cardalba Hall—not that he could have heard them anyway, what with the escalating thunder of recorded kettle drums) and eased into the room beyond, the first thing he saw was Lew.

That his brother had known the instant of Ron's arrival was obvious from the way the music had kicked in precisely upon his entrance. But he was not prepared for the style in which Lew had chosen to receive his guests. True to the flare for theatrics that seemed to run in the clan, he had staged their reunion for maximum effect. The library was dimly lit, the curtains drawn, the surrounding bookcases wrapped in shadow. A single fixture in the exact center of the plaster ceiling medallion directed a tightly focused cone of blue-white light straight down. And in the center of that cone, framed by a vertible jungle of the ubiquitous palms, Lew sat enthroned in a black leather Art Deco armchair—naked save for a skimpy pair of white denim cutoffs. The light bleached all color from his skin and hair and washed out his features as well, but Ron could tell that the thick blond curls that would have been the envy of any rock star had grown longer and wilder in the three months since they'd last been together. Lew still had the same compact, muscular wrestler's body, though, that made his every movement soft and sure, his every gesture a graceful undertaking; but he'd slimmed down a bit, and Ron remembered that he'd said he'd taken up running. At the moment, however, his only exertions seemed to be maintaining a glass of what almost had to be sherry upright in his right hand, where its facets glittered like frozen fire.

—And nestling his slim bare feet in the lap of a pretty, brown-haired, teenage girl in a white Atlanta Olympics T-shirt and black Spandex biking shorts.

The music swelled to a defining crescendo—then faded past discernment.

"Welcome to my nightmare," Lewis whispered.

"Shit!" Ron stated flatly, and backed right out of the room, herding a very confused Wendy behind him. No way he was going to let her see his brother like that! But it was already too late, for even as he moved, the inquisitive little wench snaked her way around him and surveyed the Master of Cardalba for herself.

And then something very odd happened. Wendy's abrupt appearance inevitably drew Lew's gaze in her direction, and Ron, who was watching from the doorway, had the rare experience of seeing his brother look surprised. No, not surprised exactly, but something between confused and apprehensive. He was staring at Wendy as intently as Ron had ever seen him when not in a trance.

Wendy stared back, her mouth open, and her brow wrinkled in a particularly troubled-looking perplexity—almost as if Lew either scared or angered her.

But then whatever odd tension had passed between them dissolved, Lew did something with his left hand under the arm of the chair, and normal light flooded the room with vibrant color. Lew's skin went from deathly pale to healthy tan, his hair from faded gilt to brilliant gold, the palms from moldy gray to vivid green. For a moment he maintained his mask of dissolution, but then a muscle twitched in his jaw, and he first smiled, then smirked, then grinned, a mischievous sparkle in his eye. He swung his feet out of the girl's lap and rose gracefully, as she pirouetted sideways into the shrubbery. And then Ron could stand it no longer, and was hastening forward to enfold his brother in a hearty hug.

"Asshole!" Ron growled into Lew's shoulder.

"Ronny, my man!" Lew laughed back. "How the hell've you *been*? What d'ya think of my *homage* to MTV?"

"Is *that* what that was?" Ron chuckled nervously, still very much off guard and uneasy, but trying to cover.

"Well, it's more fun than just answering the door and saying, 'Hi,' " Lew giggled with a shrug. "But if you really want me to enslave myself to decorum, I *could* ask if you had a good trip up—so . . . did you?"

"All but the last thirty seconds," Ron grumbled, easing out of the embrace. "Jesus, guy; what're you tryin' to do, anyway?"

"Freak you out, of course."

"And what's the deal with all these blessed posies?" Ron gestured around the room. "I mean I *knew* you'd been talking about that kind of stuff on the phone a lot; but I . . . I wasn't expecting anything like this!" He paused, raised an eyebrow doubtfully. "You—uh, haven't gone *veggie* on me, have you?"

"Not a chance!" Lew shot back with a vehement shake of his head. "I'm a carny till I die. Plants're just my latest affectation. You like 'em?"

"*I* do!" Wendy inserted, prancing forward and fixing Lew with a guileless, expectant smile that belied her earlier trepidation. They were the same height, Ron noticed: his brother and girlfriend. And had the same color and texture of hair.

"Ooops!" Ron grimaced awkwardly. "Uh, sorry: Wendy, this is my brother, Lewis. Lew, my girlfriend, Wendy. She . . . uh, kinda decided to come up on her own and then had car trouble up on the mountain, so I figured you wouldn't mind if she . . ." He let the sentence trail off and raised an eyebrow helplessly.

"No problem," Lew responded carefully, puffing out his cheeks. And with that, he grinned again and extended a hand toward her. She took it immediately—whereupon Lew bent over and brushed her knuckles with a kiss.

Wendy beamed.

Ron scowled—and casually flopped a hand on Lew's bare shoulder and told him, by a means only the two of them could access, *Sorry, bro . . . I'll give you the whole scoop later.*

Lew merely shrugged and nodded. He turned back to Wendy. "I presume you have a last name," he prompted, eyeing Ron speculatively.

"Flowers," Wendy replied instantly, "Wendy Flowers."

"Flowers?" Lew exclaimed delightedly. "Oh, that's right, Ronny told me that, but I just forgot, I reckon. He just calls you Wendy on the phone. But it's kind of appropriate, isn't it? I mean, my hobby and your name, and—" He stopped in midsentence, blushing furiously. "It's nice to meet you, by the way," he finished abruptly. "I guess I'm getting ahead of myself, and all. I . . . uh, well, I've obviously heard a lot about you."

"Good, I hope."

"Dare I say otherwise?" Lew chuckled. "Old Ronny'd beat me with a stick if I got him in trouble with you. I thought he was *never* gonna find anybody who could put up with him."

Ron shot his brother a glare that could have lit the nearby candles.

"Actually," Wendy corrected mischievously, "I'm not sure I put up with him—but I like him anyway."

"So what's the problem with your c—" Lew began. But Wendy had already drifted away. For a moment both brothers watched amazed as she danced lightly around the library, gave the massed and weighty volumes a cursory examination, swept the heavy emerald velvet curtains aside—and promptly flopped down atop a matching sofa and stretched out luxuriously, as if she'd lived in Cardalba Hall all her life.

"Well, I was gonna say make yourself at home," Lew sighed with a smirk. "But looks like you already have."

Ron could only roll his eyes in resignation, as Lew steered him toward the sideboard.

"Aren't you gonna introduce us to your friend?" Wendy wondered, obviously completely at ease.

Lew, who had barely begun filling Ron a glass of sherry from the crystal decanter on the sideboard, shot his brother the quickest of wary glances, stopped in midpour, and smacked himself on the forehead with his free hand. "Christ!" he exclaimed "That's right! I'm being a worse host than I even thought: You guys haven't met *Karen* yet!"

Ron's gaze swept the cluttered room and quickly located the girl he'd last seen cradling his brother's feet, now standing quietly between a pair of the palms that had served as background for Lew's tableau. At the mention of her name, she smiled radiantly, but Ron noticed that her eyes were out of focus—and had a good idea why.

Wendy, who had been reclining on the sofa like an Egyptian queen, was likewise studying the younger woman with a curious intensity; and Ron wondered if she'd also observed that aberration. More to the point, he wondered what someone as relatively naive as she was would make of meeting her boyfriend's brother with his feet in a teenage girl's lap. Karen *looked* to be about thirteen, after all, which would have put her enough younger than Lew to raise eyebrows in most quarters. And though Ron knew such was not the case, Wendy probably thought Karen was Lew's live-in paramour—and was appropriately scandalized by the notion of such apparent youngsters cohabiting.

Which, he realized helplessly, raised yet another bugaboo: Wendy *also* knew he and Lew were twin sons by different fathers, but Lew clearly looked younger than he— though not by much. That was the sort of thing she *would* notice, too; and though it was more a peculiarity than a problem, it added to the already lengthy list of potentially awkward subjects any reasonably curious and perceptive person might be prompted to inquire about—and that in roughly two minutes time. He didn't want to *think* about what a day's worth of observation might uncover.

Still, Ron betrayed nothing as he crossed the room in a pair of easy strides to give the dark-haired girl the quick embrace which indicated that, by virtue of her association with his brother, he acknowledged her as de facto kin. Almost unconsciously he Listened to her—and found, as he'd expected, that she had no Voice, though not the same way Wendy lacked one. Which meant that she was exactly what he suspected: Lew's footholder—a virgin female whom a Master Listener could draw on to augment his power or increase his range should his personal resources not prove equal to the task. They were bound to their "patrons" by a ritual that rendered them tractable, but in so doing, damped their Voice. Or so Ron had heard. He'd never had cause to use one. On the other hand, *he* wasn't a Master.

"Uh—hi!" Ron said pleasantly, using a cough to cover his lapse into psychic exploration as he released her. "I guess you've figured out by now that I'm that uncouth asshole's brother, Ron—Ronny, he calls me." He did not offer his last name, since he had no idea what she knew about his and Lew's situation. "Oh, and as you probably heard, this attentive young couch potato here is my girl-friend, Wendy."

"Nice to meet you!" Karen said a little too brightly for the slightly awkward situation. Ron couldn't place her accent beyond urban Southern. "Uh . . . welcome to Cardalba Hall," she added tentatively, biting her lip and directing a doubtful glance at Lew, who was still occupied at the sideboard. She reached past Ron to take Wendy's hand. But when their fingers brushed, Karen's expression suddenly altered from shyly curious to distrustful bordering on afraid. The greeting that had begun warmly ended with a cool, almost abrupt, dropping of hands. Karen's eyes, Ron noted, were now clear.

"Still having trouble with your feet, are you?" Ron asked Lew pointedly, to cover.

Lew shot him a wry half smile. " 'Fraid so. Karen's obviously my friend—she's that first of all. But besides that, she's also my housekeeper, and my . . . physical therapist, I guess you could say. I generally need to have her energize my tootsies a couple of times a day." He had managed to fill two more glasses by then, and crossed the room to present one each to the two women. "I'm Lucky to have her, too," he added, with a slight emphasis on *Lucky* that Ron caught immediately.

"And yeah, I know it probably looks funny," Lew went on—mostly for Wendy's benefit, Ron suspected. "But it's not what you think. Mostly, Karen just keeps me company—keeps my mind from going stale, and all. You can only play so many video games single-handedly."

Perhaps surprised at his frankness, Wendy looked at him oddly, shook her head, and blinked, as if momentarily confused. "Actually, I was just *wondering* what the deal was. But I guess that would be a problem, wouldn't it—playing by yourself, I mean? I mean, if you really *can't* leave here."

"Where'd you hear *that*?" Lew asked innocently, shooting Ron an accusing look.

Wendy looked suddenly flustered. "I—uh . . . well, Ron told me, I guess. I didn't think it was a secret."

"It's not," Lew sighed after a pause. "But actually I *can* leave, for a few hours at a time; it's just not very comfortable. I'm told it improves with age—and if you don't strain yourself."

"So it's mostly psychological then?" Wendy asked with genuine interest. "Like some sort of dependency, maybe?"

"Wendy!" Ron hissed, and raised a finger to silence her.

"Y-eah," Lew said hesitantly, biting his lip. His expression showed a return of that startled puzzlement that had marked his first sight of Wendy. He closed the topic by returning to the sideboard.

Ron caught the exchange but didn't know what to make of it. For the briefest moment it had seemed as if Wendy really did know what Lew was about with Karen—and the Mastership as well. But he'd certainly never told her—nor would have. Still . . .

"Well," Lew announced suddenly, rejoining them with his own glass in hand, "now that we've all made it through the official part, why don't we all boogie off to the back parlor and really loosen up?" He eyed Ron critically. "Looks like you could use some loosening up, too, bro. You want something stronger than Uncle Matt's sherry?"

Ron shook his head and obligingly took a sip. "Not at the moment—I thought you'd be out of this stuff by now," he added, taking a long swallow and letting the wine—it was very good, though he hadn't a clue as to the origin or year—swish around in his mouth.

"I keep finding barrels of the stuff the old guy stashed in odd places," Lew explained. "Turns out there was a whole other wine cellar under the carport I didn't even know about. It was behind that door we never could find the key to."

"*Which* door we couldn't find the key to? There were about a dozen, as I recall."

Lew nodded gravely. "Good point. I've gotten into most of 'em now, though. I'll give you the grand tour later."

"And speaking of grand tours," Ron said, "do you think we could—ah, get the show on the road? This place kinda gives me the willies."

It did, too—and with good reason. For as many times as Ron had visited Lew in Cardalba Hall during their last year of high school, never mind the far fewer times he'd dropped by after beginning college, he could never forget the first time he had seen that room.

Murder had been done in the library of Cardalba Hall: murder and magic. Ron and Lew's uncle Matthew had been clubbed to death in that room by the same warrior-encrusted silver crutch Ron still used when the weather got cold and damp and the pain in his knee kicked up. Lew had nearly been killed there the same night—stabbed repeatedly by a half-insane cousin who coveted Matthew Welch's Luck badly enough to risk homocide to gain it.

That cousin was dead, too: slain by his own fear—if the miniature warriors encrusting the crutch had not. And that day had ended with the library awash with blood.

There was new carpeting now; new chairs, new woodwork. The paneling that showed between the plants and bookcases had been bleached to a lighter tone, and the masses of books now included many titles that would have either perplexed or scandalized the former Master of Cardalba. The various *Whole Earth* catalogs figured prominently, as did the works of Paolo Soleri. There was now an extensive section on American Indian society, folklore, and religion (and a genuine buffalo skull set between the windows that overlooked the porch). There were also a fair number of fantasy novels and some science fiction (mostly works by newcomers Keyes, Cutts, and Bramwell), and a huge number of books on gardening and horticulture.

But every time Ron closed his eyes for more than an instant, he saw blood.

"This way," Lew said brightly. "Like I said, I was mostly just doing this to try to weird you out." He clapped a hand on Ron's shoulder and steered him toward the door. Karen obligingly followed. Wendy caught Ron's helplessly raised eyebrow, shrugged in turn, and followed.

"So do you do that often?" Ron wondered. "Try to weird people out, I mean. That doesn't sound like the Lew I used to know."

Lew paused in the doorway and turned to face him. "That's 'cause I'm *not* the Lew you used to know. Too much has changed since you left for *that* poor innocent to ever surface again." He tried to keep his voice neutral, his expression calm. But Ron caught the hint of weariness there.

"Well, I guess I'll just have to do something about that, then," Ron said seriously, shaking his head theatrically. —And before Lew knew what was happening, Ron had grabbed him from behind and flung him down atop the Persian carpet in the hallway. He managed to get his legs astride Lew's hips before his brother could react. Which gave him about two seconds in which to find the tickle spot that lurked just below Lew's armpit.

Unfortunately, Lew also knew *his* ticklish place *and* had lettered in wrestling in high school, so that Ron soon found himself on the bottom, with his shirt rucked halfway up his chest and the sensitive areas on the sides of his now bare tummy being assailed unmercifully. In an instant he was giggling like a fool—not purely from reflex—and Lew was laughing as well. A moment later Lew had helped him to his feet and the two of them had their arms around each other's shoulders. Wendy and Karen, who had been exchanging bemused—if somewhat wary—glances, simply fell in behind.

Chapter 7

The Green, Green Grass of Home

It was only when Ron felt the comforting weight of Lew's arm across his shoulders, the warm solidity of his bare torso against his side as they maneuvered each other awkwardly down the hall, that he truly realized how much he had missed his twin. Missed the simple security of his presence, the unspoken communication that had nothing to do with Listening, missed the relief from the weighty responsibility of the secret knowledge they shared that was too much for anyone to bear alone for very long. Missed everything—except the fact that they were so very different, not only from each other, but from the world at large.

Three months had passed since they'd last seen each other, four years since they'd abandoned the constant companionship of youth, yet Lew looked scarcely older than when Ron had arrived in Welch County as a bitter seventeen-year-old junior. Or at least he still had the same hair, the same eyes, the same clear, guileless features that had always reminded Ron of a Botticelli angel. This close, though, Ron could see that he'd added an earring: a red cloisonné dragon in his left-hand lobe.

But what was really different—*disturbingly* so—was his expression. Ron could fix on no specific alteration, but he could sense that the air of ruthless frivolity Lew was affecting overlaid a deeper melancholy, a drifty resignation completely inappropriate for his twenty-two years. Maybe it was the way he no longer let his smile widen the extra few millimeters for its true glory to blaze forth. Or perhaps it was the trace of shadows under his eyes—or the tendency to focus those eyes a few inches lower than heretofore.

But did it really matter? He was back with his beloved brother, and even the fact that he resented the circumstances of that reunion could not dispel his joy at being with his best friend again. Sun and moon, they'd sometimes been styled in school, because Lew-the-fair was always energetic and enthusiastic and optimistic, while dark-haired Ron tended to be introspective and moody and morose—understandably in light of the staggering personal losses that had brought him to north Georgia in the first place, but not conducive to generating the sort of charisma Lew had possessed from birth. Too, the sun and moon were both lords of separate domains, and though they sometimes ventured into each other's turf, they never shared their sovereignty equally. Which was too bad, in a way.

"In here, m'lad!" Lew's half gasp, half giggle jolted Ron from his few seconds of introspection as they jostled each other through the last doorway to the left.

"Watch the frigging doorknob, asshole!" Ron grunted—and, upon seeing what lay beyond, fell silent.

Cardalba Hall had been built in the late nineteenth century, long before the advent of dens, so Ron had only seen the room he had entered in the guise of Matthew Welch's private parlor—but now Lew had transformed it into something very different. The paneled walls had been replaced with Sheetrock sprayed with noise-absorbing paint in an off-white tint that flirted with both mauve and gray; the inch-thick carpeting was a rich charcoal; and the leather sofa that took up most of the wall to the left and elled around the opposite wall to the window was black pigskin, as were a pair of matching loungers. A thick slab of smoky glass bowing the backs of a pair of crouching black marble panthers made a coffee table, and similar arrangements of felines and glass were scattered about the room. Oddly, however, the only flora was a single white rose in a slender vase on a table by the door.

The *big* change, however, was to the north. The window there had been filled in, and dominating the now blank wall was a darkly gleaming mass of buttons and monitors, switches and speakers and video screens. There were three twenty-five-inch Sony TVs, for instance, and four more smaller ones. The CD player was a triple-mag Pioneer, and the Polk Audio speakers to either side would have done any rock band proud. A floor-to-ceiling cabinet just inside the door held thousands of CDs; and a pair of guitars, one an acoustic Martin, the other an electric Rick, rested in chrome-plated stands next to a state-of-the-art Rhodes synthesizer. In spite of his new obsession with botany, Lew had clearly not abandoned electronic culture—nor given up on the talent for music Ron recalled so fondly.

"Well, gee," Ron said drolly, "you're just *full* of surprises, aren't you? I don't suppose it ever *occurred* to you to mention any of this in your calls, did it?"

"What? And spoil the surprise?" Lew chided, obviously delighted. "It's a lot more fun watching your chin bounce along the floor."

Silence—while Ron tried very hard to act unimpressed. "Good thing you own the power company," he said at last.

"Nobody *owns* the power company," Lew shot back with good-natured sarcasm. "I'm just on the board."

"Not chairman?"

"Not on a bet. I do it 'cause it's expected, not 'cause I like it. I wasn't brought up to that sort of crap, remember?"

"Well, thank God for that!" Ron sighed, wondering if that had actually been resentment in his brother's voice or if he'd merely heard what he expected. And did it really matter anyway? God knew Lew had a right to a certain amount of bad feeling, seeing as how there was no *real* reason Ron could not have been Master as easily as he, bum knee or no.

It was with that in mind that he flopped into the nearest lounger, took a sip of sherry, and folded his hands neatly on his tummy, glass in hand. And smiled up at his brother like an expectant Cheshire cat.

Lew thumped down on the sofa, Karen at his side. Wendy simply dragged a white leather beanbag chair from the corner, flung it down at Ron's feet, and curled into a comfortable ball in the center. Just like Matty Groves, Ron thought, reaching down to scratch behind her ears. Meanwhile, Lew had snagged a remote control from somewhere and was pushing an assortment of buttons, which caused certain lights to awaken on the wall of electronics. A moment later music began to waft through the room from more than just the obvious speakers. It was harp music, slow and gentle, with the slur and hiss of waves in the background: Alan Stivell's "Ys," which had always been one of Ron's favorites.

"Nice," Karen murmured.

"Yeah," Wendy echoed. "I've always been real partial to that one. Sentimental value, and all. That's what we were playing the first time Ron and I—"

"Hush, wench!" Ron interrupted cheerfully. "We don't want to give my poor repressed brother ideas."

Wendy glanced automatically at Karen and raised an eyebrow. "Doesn't look like he *needs* ideas," she muttered back softly, so the younger girl couldn't hear. Apparently she had not believed Lew's explanation for an instant— which was unfortunate, since Ron knew it to be true. Karen *was* special to his brother, but not in any way a non-Listener could understand.

"So how was graduation?" Lew asked suddenly, looking at Wendy. "I understand you couldn't get my rascally womb-mate to go."

Wendy shrugged. "It was a graduation. Long. Boring. Rained enough to make everybody miserable. Speaker was no great shakes."

"So why'd you bother?"

Another shrug. "Conditioning mostly. I guess I wouldn't have felt like I really had my degree otherwise—and I needed that so I could . . . I dunno . . . *validate* myself as a person, I guess."

Karen's brow wrinkled in perplexity. "What do you mean?" she asked almost fearfully. "That is, if you don't mind explaining?"

"She's got—" Ron began, mostly from reflex.

"*I* can talk!" Wendy interrupted, with an icy edge to her voice that disconcerted Ron no end, unaccustomed as he was to these sudden, unpredictable bouts of assertiveness. If such was to be her primary persona, fine, he could handle that; it was all this switch-hitting that was keeping him off balance and tangling up his nerves.

"I've got amnesia," Wendy went on coolly, directing her full attention to Karen, as if the brothers were not present at all—and in spite of the odd wariness the younger girl kept displaying, which seemed to make Wendy edgy in turn.

Karen colored to her hairline and looked down. "Oh, gee . . . I'm sorry, I—"

"Why? It's not *your* fault," Wendy assured her with a solemn smile. "It's nobody's *fault*, as far as anyone can tell. It's just that I don't know anything about my life before I started to college. It's—I dunno—a little like being born as an adult with a full complement of information and skills but no background to hang 'em on."

"Gosh! But you seem so . . . so *okay* about it, I guess," Karen managed, forgetting to be cowed in her excitement. "I mean, if that happened to me, they'd have to cart me off to the—oops! There I go again."

"Better quit while you're ahead," Lew cautioned between swallows.

"No . . . I *need* to talk about it," Wendy countered, shifting her attention to him. "The doctor said that would help. Said there was no telling when somebody might ask a question that would make all those locked doors start opening."

"Well, I guess I can't use the standard ice-breaker, can I?" Lew sighed.

"What's that?"

"Where you're from."

Wendy shook her head. " 'Fraid not. We're not even sure of my birthdate. Oh, my driver's license gives one, but there's reason to think it might be a fake."

Lew raised an eyebrow, suddenly attentive. "Oh *yeah*? How?"

"I don't know—exactly," Wendy replied slowly. "But the private detective that worked on my case said that everything was free and clear about it—except that there were no backup records: no paper copies, no temporaries, no computer files. Which would make it *sound* like a forgery—except that there're apparently enough glitches in state government that they can't *prove* it's a fake, so they had to give me the benefit of the doubt."

"Interesting," Lew mused, taking another sip. "So if we can't ask you where you're from, I guess the next obvious one is: What was your major?"

"Ornamental horticulture," Wendy replied instantly. "My shrink thinks it's 'cause of some long-ago identification with my name."

"Then you should really like it here," Karen laughed nervously, much more at ease now that the conversation had wandered back to her own turf. " 'Cause if there's anything we've got plenty of around here, it's flowers."

"Oh, I like it already!" Wendy assured her. "And I feel really comfortable here, like—I dunno—like I belong or something. And—Oh Jesus!" she exclaimed suddenly, springing to her feet. "That reminds me! I left poor Tony out on the porch!"

Karen looked utterly confused. "Tony? Who's Tony?"

"Tony Hillerman—my new pet cactus."

Ron and Lew could only exchange bemused shrugs as Wendy made a beeline for the door.

"We've, uh, got a sunroom out back," Karen called helpfully, rising to follow her—having apparently come to terms with whatever had been bugging her earlier. "He'll like it there. Come on, I'll show you."

"Well, gosh," Lew chuckled, when the two women had left, "I guess we know where *we* stand now, don't we?"

"I guess so," Ron agreed.

"Women."

"Can't live with 'em; can't live without 'em."

"I do okay—living with one, I mean."

"Speaking of which, whatever happened to—what's her name?"

"Which one?"

"The last one: the blonde. Mary, or whatever."

Lew shrugged. "She got tired of me staying at home all the time and split."

"I was afraid of that."

"They all do."

"I was afraid of that, too."

Another shrug. "It happens. Comes with the turf, I reckon."

"So what's up with those two, do you suppose?"

"What do you mean?"

"Uh—well, there was something kinda weird when they met each other. Like, Karen shook hands and then let go real quick, almost like—like Wendy burned her."

"I didn't notice."

"And they were kind of awkward to each other just now. Sort of feeling each other out, polite, but not; wanting to be friends but unable."

Lew's brows lowered slightly. "Ah, now, that I *did* catch. But I just figured it was territoriality or something. I mean Karen *is* used to being queen of the roost, sort of."

Ron shifted to a more comfortable position and took another sip of sherry. "Oh well, if we try to understand women, we'll be here all day. So—uh, how's the family business?"

"You mean Lucky Day Enterprises?" Lew's eyes twinkled smugly. "I'm thinking of putting an ad in the Yellow Pages."

"You'll attract crazies, too."

"And probably piss off the other Listeners."

"Speaking of which . . ." Ron inclined his head toward the closed door. "You really think we should be talking so freely about this kinda stuff with the girls likely to turn up again any minute?"

Lew eyed him curiously, and maybe with a trace of pity. "Hmmm. You really *don't* fool with this stuff much, do you? 'Cause if you did, you'd remember that I can pretty much determine what Karen remembers and what she forgets. And I could surely do the same for Wendy, even given her . . . peculiarity. As, no doubt, could you."

"Except that I don't like fucking with people's minds."

"With a body like Wendy's, I'd think that's the last thing you'd want to—"

Ron felt his cheeks starting to burn. "Hush."

"I do it all the time."

"Fuck?"

"Rearrange memories along more pleasant and convenient lines."

"Well, bully for *you!*" Ron snorted, and looked away.

Lew's brow wrinkled with genuine perplexity. "You have a *problem* with that? Jeeze, it comes with the blessed *job*, Ronny! I didn't *ask* to have to fool with footholders!"

"I know, man, I know!" Ron replied quickly. "It's just that . . . well, it kinda bums me out to see you treading so close to Uncle Matt's style."

"There's no way to avoid it, bro. But I'm careful, *real* careful."

Ron eyed him dubiously. "Sure."

"You haven't told her, have you?"

"Who? Wendy? Not a word. All she knows is that I don't like crowds."

"And you really didn't want to bring her up here?"

Ron sighed listlessly and rearranged himself again. "I *didn't* bring her! She honestly came on her own. She's always been very cooperative before, very accepting and accommodating—but then the last couple of days . . . well, all of sudden she's gotten, like, really contentious."

Lew's frown deepened. He steepled his fingers and peered through them. "Which is not what you want, right? You want someone who's beautiful, smart, and talented—and has no ego."

"No, you're wrong there. I really do want her to be independent; I just don't want her poking around in my private life any more than I can help. She'd only get hurt, and I don't want that. There're just too many things I'd have to fudge about up here, and—oh, crap, Lew, *you* know!"

"I know you were right about what you told me when you guys got hooked up. About her not having a Voice."

Ron grimaced resignedly. "Yeah, I kinda *figured* you'd have confirmed that by now. You got any idea why?" he added. "Now that you've actually met?"

Lew scratched his chin. "Hard to say. I presume it's got something to do with the amnesia."

"Except that she's *got* emotions!" Ron countered quickly. "Or a least she bloody well *acts* like she does! And it's emotion that gives force to Voice, isn't it?"

Lew looked troubled for just an instant, and Ron wondered what had prompted that reaction. "Supposedly," he replied. "But remember that there are other folks that can't be Heard either. Like the Road Man, for one. Or take footholders: them you can hear perfectly well until you do the binding charm on them so you can tap into their power, and after that, you might as well be Listening to a beach ball."

Ron nodded grimly. "*Tell* me about it."

"And you *really* can't Hear her? Not even when you're . . ."

Ron shook his head. "Especially not then—which is one of the reasons we're still together. I mean, I'm sure you know how that is: you start getting it on with a lady, and pretty soon her emotions start sloshing out all over, only they're always selfish—stuff about how they're enjoying doing it with you a lot, but only 'cause you're rich and good-looking, not 'cause they like the person inside the body and the bank account."

"Could be worse. You could be homely and poor."

"I could whip your ass, too—except that you'd probably enjoy it too much. But to answer your question precisely: No, I *can't* Hear her—no more than the merest whisper, and even that only recently. But . . . there's another odd thing," Ron added cautiously. "Something I've only noticed since we arrived."

Lew looked troubled. "Which is?"

Ron wriggled uneasily in his chair. "Well, she seems to be—I don't know . . . it's just odd how comfortable Wendy seems up here. I mean, you saw her: dragging the furniture around like she'd lived here all her life. She *never* does things like that; she *always* asks before she takes any unilateral action at someone else's house. I get onto her about it a lot."

"So maybe your advice has taken—finally. Or maybe she just looks at this place differently. After all, this *is* your house as much as mine—ethically, if not legally."

"Anything else?"

"Well, there's the small matter of the omens."

Lew leaned forward attentively. "Oh yeah? You're still using Uncle Dion's system, right?"

"Yeah. 'Fraid so."

"Hey, it's *fine* with me, man. Whatever works."

"Glad you approve. But seriously, they've been really freaky lately. Lots of stuff about magic, and all. You were even in there."

"Moi?"

Ron told him—full details about both Saturday's complete array and that day's partial. "So . . . any suggestions?" he asked when he had finished.

Lew did not reply, but the troubled look was back, as if he no longer had the energy to maintain the illusion of happiness. "I . . . I've never liked that system," he began. "It's both too literal and too vague. On the other hand, it's evidently worked before. And you say it showed Wendy as your main obstacle?"

"More or less."

"And is she?"

"Not that I know of. Oh, we've been sparring a bit more lately, courtesy of that new temper, but other than that . . . nothing major. She's certainly not kept me from doing anything I want to do."

"So maybe it hasn't come to pass yet—whatever it is that she's in the way of."

Ron pondered this for a moment, but was unable to reach any viable conclusions. "Well, that's all fine and dandy," he said at last. "But that's not what's bugging me the most."

"And what is?" Lew asked cautiously, as if he already knew.

Ron took a deep breath and looked his brother straight in the eye. "Why don't you just go ahead and tell me what this is about?"

"Because it'll probably make you mad, and I want to enjoy your company as long as I can."

"Thanks a *lot*!" Ron shot back bitterly, then took another deep breath and continued more calmly. "You know, of course, that if you make me wait, it's only going to make me even more hostile. And you *have* to know I didn't want to come up here."

Lew smiled, but it was a sad smile: the expression of one who has lost the will to defend himself. "I missed you, bro," he whispered. "Can't you accept that? Oh, granted there's more, and I'll tell you soon enough, but can't we at least go through the motions of being friends as well as brothers?"

"Friends level with each other when asked to," Ron snapped, unable to restrain himself. "Brothers do it as naturally as breathing. Brothers like *we* were, at least."

"You could *always* Listen to me," Lew observed pointedly. "I'll even lower my shields."

Ron shook his head. "I may *be* pissed at you, but I won't do that. What's in your head stays in your head until *you* tell me. I'll be glad to share the rest with you later. But I want to link with you to share, not to prove a point."

Lew eyed him steadily. "You've grown up, bro."

"I don't have any choice. Neither do you."

"I *will* tell you later, too. I promise."

"I'll hold you to that. I—"

A loud thumping interrupted Ron in midacceptance. His hackles rose suddenly—whether from fear or anticipation, he could not tell.

"It's not Grandma, if that's who you're afraid of," Lew said calmly. "*Or* the girls. Probably it's that cat of yours."

Ron relaxed visibly. He *thought* Lew had mentioned that their great-grandmother Martha was gone, and would surely have sensed her presence had she been anywhere near, whether he wanted to or not. Then again, one never could tell about the matriarch of the clan. "So where is she, then?"

Lew checked the calendar in his watch. "Ireland, I think."

"She due back anytime soon?"

"When she pleases, I reckon. She *says* it won't be until around Halloween."

"And of course, she didn't say what she was going to be up to."

Lew shook his head. "Of course not."

"Probably checking up on our apocryphal sister."

"Probably."

"Any more on that?"

"Not a word. All Granny'll ever say is that she rues the day she ever let slip there was such a being."

"Such a *being*?"

"Her exact words."

"Hmmmm. And she's always *very* exact with words."

"Very."

"We're going to have to look into that someday, you know."

Lew nodded sadly. "But not now. I don't even wanta *talk* about it now."

"At least she told us."

"Told *you*!"

"Pure accident."

"Wrong! She always liked you best."

"She was just sorrier for me than for you."

"Was not."

"Was, too!"

"Was not!"

"Was—" Ron broke off, grinning again. The brittleness between them had withdrawn for a while. For a while longer they could once again be comrades, could be young, without the responsibility three thousand years of tradition laid on both of them.

Lew grinned back, and Ron felt a brush of his brother's thought, probing gently through surface memories. Ron let him, reciprocated. Found real joy there, real relief—and a terrible undercurrent of pain Lew swiftly suppressed.

Lew smiled wanly. "Not yet."

Finally Ron took another sip of sherry and stood, wandered over to inspect the ranks of gleaming CDs. "So how's my old place?" he asked. "Aunt Erin's house? That race driver you rented it to hasn't put a drag strip in the flower garden, has he?"

"Not that I know of. Drop by if you want to; he doesn't mind visitors. In fact, he'd probably get a kick out of seeing that car of yours—you did drive it up, didn't you?"

Ron nodded. "Naturally. It's out in the garage."

"Reinforcing the myth, without a doubt," Lew chuckled.

"Damn, that's funny. As much as you try to be a regular guy, you just can't resist being flaky and flamboyant and weird."

"The car's not weird."

"No, but you've got to admit that a University of Georgia senior building one basically from scratch is. Most kids are happy if their daddy buys 'em a Beamer."

"The guys who designed the first Lamborghini were no older than we are, Lew."

"And were also engineers, not art majors. Never mind that they were also Italian, with all that implies."

"You're starting to sound as bigoted as Uncle Matt," Ron observed sourly.

"I am not!" Lew cried in mock indignation.

Ron started to reply, but just as he opened his mouth, footsteps sounded in the hall: small feet almost at a run. And there was laughter: the careless mirth of young women. Ron glanced at Lew, who looked mightily relieved at getting off the most recent of the several hooks Ron had set for him, and sighed. "We *will* discuss that later," Ron informed him, with a flourish of eyebrows.

And at that instant the door burst open and Wendy and Karen tumbled in, all flushed and breathless and young-looking, their earlier awkwardness with each other seemingly disappated. The brothers swapped glances at each other and rolled their eyes as one.

"I just felt like running," Wendy snickered simply, all signs of adult decorum fled.

"And I just felt like chasing her," Karen chimed in, straightening her sweatshirt, on which earth stains were plainly visible.

"But the question *is*," Lew began slyly, sparing a mischievous sideways glance at Ron, "do you guys feel up to a little *partying* tonight?"

Wendy's face brightened immediately, but Ron had a hard time controlling his frustration. He'd come all the way up here unwillingly, expecting to find Lew wrestling some dire problem he could not, even with his Luck, confront. And now, beyond a few cryptic references, he was acting as if nothing at all was wrong, was actually wanting to party!

"Oh, it's not one of *my* bashes," Lew amended quickly. "It's a traditional town occasion. Surely, my dear sibling, you recall what *day* this is?"

"It's Monday," Wendy volunteered instantly.

"Yes," Lew replied archly, rising to his feet with a theatrical flourish. "But it's *also* Midsummer's Eve."

"Midsummer's Eve?" Wendy wondered, exchanging glances with Ron. Her eyes looked troubled, too, like they did when one of her memories was right on the verge of returning but wouldn't resolve.

"Midsummer's Eve," Lew repeated flatly, shooting Wendy a strange, probing look like the one he had first given her. "The day when the sun lives longest."

"Which doesn't do me a helluva lot of good," Ron snorted.

"Why not?" Lew asked innocently.

"*Because*, oh my brother, if you think back to what they called us in school, the sun's yours; *I* was always the moon."

"Speaking of which," Lew said, "I think it's time for one."

And before Ron knew what was happening, his brother had bent over and dropped his shorts.

Ron chased him out of the room with the rose he'd snatched from the vase by the door.

And the women were simply left staring.

Chapter 8

·Special Delivery

Brandy Hall
Noon

"Lord, I'm tired," Brandy grumbled aloud to the pair of recklessly bold gray squirrels that were watching her from just inside the curtain of drips that defined the edge of the tarp. At the sound of her words, they lifted onto their hind feet and skedaddled in their characteristic arching leaps toward the nearby woods, leaving tiny, hand-shaped prints in the film of mud that skinned most of the rockier parts of her knoll. She watched them go and wished it was hunting season: game she didn't have to thaw in order to cook would taste mighty good right now. For, much as she hated to admit it, the impossible had happened: she was getting tired of venison.

As if reinforcing that point, her stomach growled—which sound unhappily segued into a much more annoying one, as the portable cassette player that had, until seconds before, been contentedly providing her company in the form of the soundtrack to *Local Hero* chose that instant to begin munching that most favorite of all her tapes.

"I didn't ask for your opinion, either," she growled at the recalcitrant appliance, snapping it off with her single unbegrimed finger before it spewed *too* much of its meal into the ooze. Probably the humidity had got to it, she concluded wearily. God knew it was certainly getting to *her*.

She allowed herself a purposeful sniff and flipped half a trowel-load of mortar back into the nearly empty wheelbarrow whence it had come, then flopped back on her butt, oblivious to whatever effect sitting in mud might have on her already filthy jeans. Her knees cracked, and her back felt as if one of the numerous lengths of rebar that lay scattered about like jackstraws had been rammed up her spine. She scanned the surrounding area speculatively, determined that nothing else could be done on the foundations for a while—and tried *not* to think about the footprint she'd discovered back on Saturday.

That was still bugging her; though there *was* the slimmest chance, that the bare human print had been hers. She *had* trotted around that area sans shoes on the day in question, after all. Any other possibility—including the obvious one: that a barefoot man had been watching her trailer—just seemed too preposterous, if for no other reason than that she couldn't imagine how, preoccupied or no, she could have missed seeing him. Still, it was something she *couldn't* blame on her imagination; and, unfortunately, the nearest reported sightings of Sasquatch-type critters came from Tennessee—and in the last century. Weedge had told her not to worry, that she was probably the most secure and best-defended woman in Welch County. But that hadn't helped her nerves, nor had it diminished that awful sense of having been violated, of having something going on around her she could not control.

But at least she had regained mastery of the foundations; Lord knew she'd been at 'em long enough that she'd better! What with half of last night consumed (with Weedge, to whom she had dutifully served dinner) laying rebar and pouring concrete during a lull in the monsoon. Never mind Friday's reengineering, and most of the earlier parts of the weekend spent clearing out the damaged originals, bending and laying more rebar, mixing additional mortar, and pouring the last of the new footings according to the revised plan. She hoped it was worth it. It had damned well *better* be.

Sighing, Brandy stood, wiped her hands on the one spot on her T-shirt tail that was both clean *and* dry, and executed a quick set of stretching exercises. Various joints obligingly popped, and she yawned hugely, wishing she could afford to indulge in a nap. Unfortunately, tomorrow's weather forecast called for more heavy rain, during which she'd have little option *but* to sleep. Which meant she had to make hay while the sun shone.

It was at that exact instant that she heard the sound of a vehicle grinding cautiously down the driveway from the main drag a quarter mile to the southwest.

An instant later she caught a glimpse of shiny red paint, and bare seconds after that, a gleaming new Ford F-350 bearing a white Mason Hardware logo on its near-side door hove into view, the tan-gold lengths of a bundle of two-by-eights plainly visible hanging out the back. The pickup bounced alarmingly on a pair of boulders Brandy had long since learned to avoid, but made steady progress until it ground to a halt at precisely the location she would have indicated had it not been tending that way already.

The driver's window was down, and Van Vannister himself was at the wheel, T-shirted and grinning, and with an emerald green bandanna-cum-sweatband perfectly complementing his thick auburn hair.

Vannister shifted gears and set the parking brake, then powered up the window and climbed gracefully from the cab. The grin widened: a flash of white between lips that Brandy once more noted were remarkably full and red.

And wished she hadn't, because when she started noticing details like that, it meant that she was getting interested— or at least indulging in aesthetic appreciation—and that was something she neither desired nor could afford right now. The *last* thing she needed when she was already behind schedule was the sort of distraction emotional entanglements inevitably resulted in. She had exactly two more months in which to make Brandy Hall habitable, and nothing, by God, was going to stand in her way.

And *certainly* not a presumptuous hunk with whom she'd exchanged something less than five minutes of conversation, infectious grin and great bod notwithstanding. Never mind that he had shown up barely two hours after their morning meeting.

Which meant one of two things: Either Van Vannister was one of those rare men who was as good as his word simply because that was the way he was.

Or that he wanted to make a favorable impression on her in particular.

Without really being aware of when she had started, Brandy found herself walking in Vannister's direction—which (unless she wanted to wade through mud even deeper than that she was already mired in) required that she navigate the entire rough cement floor of the unfinished great hall and stamp across the plywood decking of the foyer to reach the front arcade. She was standing within in the empty ten-foot-high archway that would one day contain her front door when Vannister came within hailing range.

"Mornin'," he called cheerily.

She checked her watch unconsciously, noted that it was in fact 12:01 P.M. and, before she could stop herself, countered with, "Better make that afternoon."

Vannister consulted his own timepiece. "I've got noon now, so why don't we call it a draw? Besides, it's *bound* to be mornin' *somewhere*."

Brandy laughed in spite of herself. "Well, you're earlier than I expected, anyway."

He shrugged. "I know a lady in distress when I see one."

Brandy ignored the remark, not wishing to provoke a confrontation by taking exception to it. She eased past him to the back of the truck and inspected the lumber. It looked good—*real* good—straight, smooth, and almost knot-free. The prickly sweet odor of conifer resin rose from the freshly sawn ends to mingle with the scent of damp metal, raw earth, and hemlocks that pervaded the knoll. She barely suppressed an urge to sneeze.

"I also knew you were in a hurry," Vannister continued, joining her at the back, "so I figured I'd work through lunch and come on up."

She glanced sideways at him. "You didn't have to do that. I could have waited."

Vannister sat down on the tailgate and surveyed the construction with a critical eye. "Not much longer, though, judging by what it looks like you've been up to today. Been pourin' some concrete, have you?"

Brandy nodded. "Had some trouble with a bit of foundation the other night. Had to tear out a bunch and replace it with more reinforcements."

Vannister frowned. "What was the problem?"

A tired shrug. "Rock wasn't as solid as I thought it was."

"Ummm-hmmm." Vannister murmured his approval. "Well, it looks like you're doing a first-class job. But I guess we're both burning daylight, aren't we?"

"I guess we are."

He prowled in a pocket for a pair of strap cutters, then reached for the nearest board. "Now then, where is it you want these puppies?"

Brandy indicated a cleared space a dozen feet from the southwest corner. "Over there's fine. If you'll wait a minute, I'll help you. I need to get a drink first."

"No need," Vannister shot back quickly. "It won't take but a minute. Oh . . . and I did throw in a few extras, by the way," he added, with another grin.

Brandy scowled slightly. "You didn't have to do that, either."

"No," he conceded, "but there's a fellow who *did* do what he shouldn't have, if you get my drift."

"Okay, then," Brandy sighed, folding her arms. "But only on one condition."

"What's that?"

"I don't like to be beholden, Mr. Vannister, and you've made me beholden to you. Therefore, the only way I'll accept the extra material is if you'll let *me* fix you some lunch."

An eyebrow lifted skyward. "Fine—but now *I've* got a condition."

Brandy eyed him dubiously, recalling the distasteful bargain young Marcus Jones had so lately attempted to negotiate.

Vannister didn't give her a chance to verbalize her misgivings. "I don't like for folks to watch me work," he said almost shyly. "So the only way I'll accept your offer is if *you* go inside."

"That's an odd request for a man like you."

"I'm an odd man."

"I'm beginning to get that idea," Brandy agreed, turning to go, then pausing and spinning back around. "It'll go a lot quicker if I help, you know."

"You'd be surprised" was Vannister's only reply.

She had barely found time to snag a couple of cans of Coke from the refrigerator, fill a pair of glasses with ice, and carve a half dozen pink-brown slices from last night's haunch of venison when Brandy heard a heavy tread on her doorstep. She frowned and stabbed the knife into the roast, wondering if Vannister had run into some a problem—or, more likely, had decided he needed her help after all. As she padded barefoot into the living room, a knock rattled the screen door: firm, but polite—if a knock could be said to *be* polite.

The dark shape cut out against the brilliant sky visible through the aluminum mesh proved to be Vannister, all right. He was panting slightly, but not—as she observed when she opened the door—sweating, which she thought odd. Perhaps he hadn't got started yet.

"Something wrong?" she asked before he could speak.

Vannister looked deliberately innocent. "No, ma'am," he replied. "I just wanted to let you know I'm done. I was wonderin' if you had a spigot"—he pronounced it mountain-style: *spicket*—"somewhere out here where I could wash my hands."

Brandy stared at him stupidly. "But that was a *big* load," she managed at last. "There's no way . . ."

Vannister shrugged. "It doesn't take long if you know what you're doin'. Nothing does, really . . . though there are *some* things you *want* to last as long as possible."

Brandy's eyes narrowed minutely as she tried to determine if that was an intentional come-on or not. In the end, she chose to ignore the remark, but could not resist peering beyond Vannister's impressive shoulders to where, sure enough, the truck stood empty while the boards lay neatly stacked exactly where she'd suggested—and in precisely the manner she'd have arrayed them herself.

"The spicket?" Vannister prompted.

Brandy blinked, then realized she'd been gaping like a fool—and had left her guest standing on the porch steps. "Uh, you can clean up in here if you want to."

Vannister shook his head. "No, ma'am. I've got mud all over my shoes."

"Oh," she mumbled finally, to Vannister's patient stare. "Yeah. There's a hose over by the cement mixer." She pointed past him to the right. "Hang on, and I'll get you a towel."

"Don't trouble yourself. I've got one in the truck."

"Suit yourself," Brandy told him shortly, annoyed at having her already sketchy hospitality so casually refused. "I'll meet you out on the patio with the sandwiches when you get back—I forgot to ask, by the way . . . but is venison okay?"

Vannister's grin returned. "That'd be *great*!" he laughed delightedly. "I haven't had any of *that* in ages."

"It's last year's," she admitted. "I've got a freezer full—or it used to be full, anyway," she amended.

"And let me guess: you shot it yourself, too, didn't you?"

Brandy couldn't resist a smug nod. "I like to carry my own weight as much as I can."

"I can tell," Vannister replied. "Are you a witchy-woman?" he added suddenly.

Brandy stiffened defensively, then realized that he had some basis for that question, given that the part of the trailer he could undoubtedly see behind her probably gave that impression, what with the strings of garlic, and the assorted oddly shaped and colored jars of herbs and spices in the kitchen to her left; never mind the various bones, skulls, and feather ornaments clearly visible in the living room directly behind her. Or simply the whole pack-ratty nature of the place in general.

She did not answer him immediately, though; not because she had anything to hide, but simply because she thought it too forward a question for a stranger to ask. On the other hand, it wouldn't do at all for word to get out that the odd new art teacher was brewing potions back in the woods . . .

"No," she muttered at last, fixing Vannister with a steely glare she hoped expressed more than her verbal denial. "I'm a wildlife artist, among other things."

"What other things?"

Brandy sighed, hoping this conversation wasn't going to turn into another sparring match. "I'm into the natural world," she said. "Self-sufficiency—hunting, canning, all that."

"And the unnatural world?" Vannister wondered, with a strange gleam in in eye.

"I'm interested in that, too," Brandy admitted before she could stop herself. "Or reading about it, anyway."

"And the reality-unreality interface?"

Brandy studied his face for a long moment. He raised an eyebrow quizically. "That's a subject for conversation, not chitchat," she informed him finally. "Maybe another time."

"I hope so," Vannister shot back with a knowing twinkle in his eye—whereupon, to Brandy's surprise, he sketched a hasty bow, hopped off the steps, and loped off in the direction of the hose.

She watched him go, enjoying the way he moved: fluid and sure like a big cat. When he had disappeared beyond his truck, she returned to the kitchen, loaded the sandwich fixings onto a tray, and backed through the screen door with them. The slab of concrete at the foot of the steps beyond served as both front porch and patio—and often enough as dining room as well, for which purpose an ancient redwood picnic table and benches stood in one corner. Brandy deposited the tray there and went in quest of drinks.

Vannister was back before she had quite finished arranging things, his bare arms and hands gleaming, water stains darkening most of his shirtfront—which scrvcd to display his impressive musculature to even better effect. He evidently saw her looking, too, and glanced down reflexively, obviously embarrassed. "Wasn't paying attention," he explained sheepishly. "Lots of distractions 'round here."

Brandy wondered what he meant by that, but chose not to pursue the matter. "Have a seat and a sandwich," she offered. "I didn't know what you liked on yours, so I just brought a little of everything."

"Thanks." Vannister seated himself on one of the benches and fell to, spreading mayonnaise, mustard, and a bit of horseradish across the thick slices of brown bread Brandy had provided. Two slabs of meat joined it, garnished with a good bit of salt.

"You bake this yourself?" he asked absently, indicating the bread.

"Of course!"

"Figured."

He took a bite of sandwich and a sip of Coke, and stared toward the uncompleted house.

"Mind if I take a look-see down there?"

"Don't you just want to *sit* for a spell?" Brandy replied with a start, honestly surprised. "All that work should have tired you out."

Vannister countered with a listless shrug. "Not really," he chuckled, rising to his feet, food in hand. "Besides, that way I can do two things at once."

"Suit yourself," she grunted, not moving from the bench. "I work when I work, and when I play, I play."

"And which is eating?" The grin reappeared—and the twinkling eyes. And the dimple.

"Play."

"Thought as much."

"Be careful around the edges," Brandy called, when it became obvious Vannister was not going to be dissuaded, and lacking the mental energy to try. "And *don't* step in any fresh concrete," she added—unnecessarily; no man as on the ball as he obviously was would make a mistake like that. Which meant, she decided, in that self-analytical way she had of examining her every action, that she'd evidently changed her opinion of the guy just since he'd arrived. She was even—cursed word—actually starting to *trust* him. Which meant she'd have to be careful. No way she wanted to start trusting men again. Not after what had happened with her and Jake.

But she was not going to think about a skinny, self-centered grad student named Jake Carlin right then. Not when she could watch Van Vannister steer his graceful way through the maze of supplies and equipment downslope. It looked like he had gone straight to the new construction, too: was standing right by her weekend's work, poised in exaggerated contraposto, with a Coke in one hand and the sandwich in the other. And even at that distance, even with his back to her, she could almost see the appraising look in his eyes, the jaw muscles bulging as he chewed his sandwich reflectively.

Critically?

Brandy suddenly had the uncanny feeling Vannister did not like what he was seeing. Or at least he certainly wanted to take a closer look, for at that exact moment he squatted down in the precise place she had vacated upon his arrival. She watched curiously as he first ran his hand along the ground, then shook his head and stood again, took a few paces to the left—toward the fault in the footing—and repeated the process.

Unable to help herself, she stuffed the last of her sandwich into her mouth, rose, and followed him, chewing frantically.

"This that section you were havin' trouble with?" Vannister asked when she had joined him. He had not turned to acknowledge her approach.

She nodded, a scowl wrinkling her brow. "Why? What's wrong?"

"This problem you had: what was it . . . exactly?"

"I don't know—*exactly*," Brandy retorted move irritably than she'd intended. "I thought it was solid stone there, but apparently it wasn't."

"Have you checked for caves and springs and things like that?"

She glared at him accusingly. "I'm headstrong, Mr. Vannister, not stupid."

"Which doesn't answer my question."

An exasperated sigh. "There aren't any caves, at least not that I can find—these are the wrong kinds of rocks to produce 'em, for one thing. As for springs . . . well, as it happens, there *is* one. But there wasn't any way *to* check until the rock collapsed over it."

Vannister stared at the fresh concrete for a moment longer, then shook his head. "Well, Miss Wallace," he said at last. "I'm afraid that's not gonna hold."

"What do you *mean* it's not gonna hold?" she cried furiously, letting her temper slip before she could stop herself. "Granted I may have screwed up to start with, but I've reengineered the whole thing since then! The stress is distributed over a much wider area now."

"Maybe so," Vannister replied calmly. "But it's not gonna hold."

"And how do you know so much?"

"Because I've been around a lot."

"So have I."

"Not as much as I have."

"That's debatable." Brandy really was pissed now, and the fact that Vannister was delivering his responses in an even, considered monotone didn't help things at all.

He did not reply to her last barb, either. Instead, he merely shrugged (he did that a lot, she noted) and said, "Do it your way, then; but a day from now you'll know I'm right. I guarantee it."

"But what's the matter with it?" Brandy demanded, irritation replaced with honest curiosity.

"Isn't slaked right," Vannister told her flatly. "And now I reckon I'd best be goin'."

"But how . . . ?"

He wasn't listening, though, and Brandy imagined she'd blown it with him by letting herself get worked up like that. Her first impulse was to follow him—he was halfway to his truck by then—but her pride wouldn't let her. No way she'd run after *anyone* crying out that she was wrong when she knew she wasn't.

Vannister had reached the pickup. He opened the door, then paused and skinned his shirt over his head, moving with the slow, deliberate languor of a man who had a good body, knew it, and didn't mind showing it off—especially when he knew someone was watching. Brandy eyed his bare back curiously and with more than a little appreciation as he folded the garment neatly and slid it into the seat— probably because he didn't feel like riding around in wet clothes with the air conditioner going. Damn, that man had a fine bod!

Vannister continued to fumble around inside for at least another minute, but only when the engine had roared to life did she remember that she hadn't thanked him for his efficient delivery or the extra lumber. Swallowing her pride, she trotted toward the truck.

He watched her approach impassively, but maybe with a trace of humor in his eyes that almost pissed her off all over again.

She halted a yard from the driver's door. Vannister rested his left arm on the sill and waited, an eyebrow lifted quizically.

Brandy found she could not look him in the face. "I'm not going to apologize," she said slowly. "I don't like to do that, especially when I think I'm right. But I *do* owe you thanks for being so prompt, and for the extra material."

"No problem," Vannister replied without inflection. "And if that foundation holds through tomorrow, I'll apologize to *you*."

"Fair enough," she conceded, managing a smile.

"Thanks for the sandwich."

"No problem," Brandy echoed, backing away as Vannister shifted into reverse.

It was only when he had dragged his arm back inside that she realized he'd had a tattoo on his shoulder.

The head and antlers of a deer.

A *white* deer.

Chapter 9

Party All the Time

Cordova, Georgia
Evening

Evening snuck up on Ron long before he had finished with the afternoon, leaving him musing in muddleheaded perplexity where eight hours of his life had wandered off to. A good part of it was into the sherry glass Lew had kept perpetually full, he suspected—and *that* was most likely because his brother knew perfectly well that if he got Ron buzzed and mellow, he'd be more inclined to kick back and enjoy himself, and therefore be *less* likely to raise the matter they both knew would have to be dealt with sooner or later. It worked, too: and though Ron never actually *felt* more than a vague disjointedness—a subtle distancing from himself, as if he watched his every action at one slightly bemused remove—each activity and conversation seemed to slip seamlessly into another utterly without volition. It was manipulation, but not malicious. And, he admitted, he probably *needed* to chill out some after the stress of the last few weeks. One didn't finish college every day; and finals were still finals, even for Listeners. *Especially* for Listeners, in fact, since it wasn't cool to use the Luck for direct personal gain.

Lew had given him and Wendy the nickel tour of Cardalba Hall, of course—mostly for her benefit, though there were scads of alterations Ron hadn't seen, either. The new media room was the most radical addition, but Lew had also redecorated his second-floor suite in a more contemporary style than the mix of Victorian and Art Deco Matthew had affected. It was much less intimidating now; far more conducive to laying back and hanging out now that the big, high-ceilinged rooms were slathered with posters for rock bands, and the thickly carpeted floors were strewn with discarded T-shirts, sneakers, and jeans. Even better, a monstrous new Jacuzzi had been installed in the master bath—and to Ron's great delight, a twin lurked in the loo adjoining his and Wendy's quarters. Also, as he'd already suspected, given the Richard Straus fanfare that had heralded their arrival, Lew had had the entire house wired for sound, so that every room contained both an intercom and at least four stereo speakers that connected by built-in computer terminals to the big system in the media room. Ron didn't even want to *think* about what the setup had cost. On the other hand, what *else* did Lew have to spend his fortune on?

"I—that is, *we*, the family, such as it is—make a lot of money off the county," Lew had told Wendy, in answer to the question she had asked over the fresh orange juice and fried crawfish that were allegedly a surrogate supper. "We own huge chunks of both woods and bottomland, and rent a lot of it, so it only seems right to plow some of the revenues back into the folks who help us earn it. Therefore, once a year I throw a bash and blow one day's worth of rent income on it. That's a tradition old as the hills—older, actually," he'd appended, sparing a knowing glance for Ron, who'd simply glowered at him and slipped Matty Groves a mouse-sized crawdad under the table.

The snack had ended with a bit more than two hours still to spare before sunset, which was the official kickoff time for the do. And while the women bathed and made themselves beautiful ("It's not formal," Lew had told them;

"it's too hot for that outside, even up here"), Ron had busied himself changing two spark plugs, cleaning a fuel injector that sure enough had gotten clogged, and wiping the bugs off the Centauri's windshield.

Lew had joined him in the carport, and since he'd never seen Ron's "hobby car" in its completed state, they'd spent an enjoyable thirty minutes comparing notes on matters automotive. Which they were still doing.

"And to think that you'd never set hammer to metal until you moved up here," Lew mused thoughtfully, sliding a hand along the crest of the hand-built car's gleaming fender. "Was it a fair trade, you reckon?"

Ron shrugged. "I dunno. If I look at it logically, I'd say yes. When I was a diver, I was good, granted. But there were beaucoup guys as good as I was in just my own town, and I had to work like hell to stay ahead of 'em. On the other hand, I doubt there were three people in all of Tampa who had the aptitude for metalwork I did—or for design, if only I'd known about it then."

"It's magic, you know," Lew observed, with a sly smile.

"Maybe," Ron replied tersely. "But don't let's get started on that, okay?"

It was Lew's turn to shrug. "I don't *need* to, since I know the truth. We've all got a talent; every one of us Listeners has, if you haven't figured that out yet: something we're really, *really* good at. They sneak up upon us unaware, and then we somehow become *uncannily* good at them. Mine's in gardening, oddly enough, though I never knew that until I was almost an adult. I always figured it'd be music, like Uncle Dion; or poetry, like Uncle Gil—"

"But we're *all* musical, more or less," Ron interrupted. "Or at least we can all carry a tune and pick up instruments fairly easily."

"Yeah, and we're all natural good shots with guns, and never have weight problems and are above average good-looking, too. It's something to do with the genes. But somehow I think the talents are tied up with the Luck in particular. That *it's* magic."

"*Is* it?"

Another shrug. "We've been over that, too, bro, and I doubt we'll agree on that, either. You'll keep on saying it's just psychic powers—undiscovered science. And I'll say it's something from Outside, but I can't tell you how I know that. We'll just have to agree to disagree, I reckon."

Ron chuckled. "Yeah, and there's even precedent for *that*, dammit. Seeing as how no two books in that vault of yours say the same thing."

Lew did not reply, but stretched across the now open cockpit to snag the crutch Ron had left there. One of the cast-silver warriors with which most of the upper half was encrusted in a never-ending struggle to win to the arm-cushion summit snagged the door panel with its tiny sword. Ron held his breath as Lew freed it. Fortunately the expensive leather was not damaged. "Still lugging this thing around, huh?" Lew wondered. "I'd have thought you'd have gotten tired of hassling with it by now, seeing as how you don't need it to motivate on anymore."

Ron looked up from his polishing. "Ah, but I *do* need it—sometimes. We've gone into this before, remember? First of all, it makes a first-class calling card when I need to show off examples of my work. And secondly, the Luck kicked in *just* as the knee was healing, so it could never quite decide if I was complete or not—which means that when it rains a lot, or gets real cold, I still have twinges. There's still no kneecap, in case you forgot. What looks like one is a plastic fake they shoved under there to salve my rampant vanity. But evidently the channels that carry the Luck got straightened out on their own, so there're no jammed-up places or blockages or anything. Nothing to make me crazy, in any case."

"*That's* debatable!"

"One has only to look at you, *mon frère*."

Lew ignored the jibe. "So you still heal okay?"

Ron nodded. "Fine, except for small stuff—I'm sure you know how that is. Like those scratches old Matty gave me when we first got here'll probably be around for ages. Which reminds me—you haven't seen him lately, have you?"

Instead of answering, Lew took three deep breaths. His eyes went out of focus for the merest instant, and Ron felt the stirring of energy that was the Luck in use—whereupon Lew took two more breaths, blinked, and exhaled slowly.

"He's back in the sun-room tantalizing one of the hounds through the glass."

"Sounds like him."

"He loves it. So does the hound."

Ron merely rolled his eyes and shifted his efforts to the hood.

Lew flopped an arm across Ron's shoulders and gave him a quick, brotherly hug. "And you're covered with grease, and smell like sweat and motor oil, and have a party to be at in less than an hour. Don't you think it's time you started primping? Surely your wheels can make ten more miles without giving up the ghost."

"Bad phrase to use around here," Ron muttered darkly.

"I want you to build me one sometime," Lew added as Ron straightened and started toward the door that opened into the back hallway. "The Jag's fine, but seems like everybody's got one, all of a sudden."

"In Welch County, I'd believe it," Ron chuckled. "Style setting just comes with the turf, I reckon."

"I guess," Lew grunted.

"And speaking of which, I'd best go make myself beautiful," Ron sighed, tossing the polishing chamois to his brother. "Here, make yourself useful, *boy*."

Lew snatched the rag and flipped Ron on the rump with it. "Boy? Who you callin' a boy, *son*?"

"You've drooled all over the hood of my car, stooge!" Ron laughed back, fending Lew off with his baseball cap. Ain't no *way* I'm drivin' my lady to a party in a car what's covered up with drool."

One bath, one shave, plus thirty minutes later, Ron swung the Centauri in behind Lew's XJ-6 in the space someone had thoughtfully reserved for them in the parking lot between the Gothic spires of the Welch County Courthouse and the ancient oaks of Founders' Park, which fronted it. Ron doused the lights and debated raising the top, then decided it was unnecessary. The sky was clear— *of course*; the weather *always* cooperated with important activities in Welch County; the car was burglar-alarmed to the nines anyway; and he had obviously been seen arriving with Lewis Welch, which, even if no one recognized him immediately, would be a certain tip-off that he was no one to be trifled with. So it was with a clear conscience that he helped Wendy from her side and joined his brother and Karen on the sidewalk that bordered the park—and immediately became aware of bright light stabbing out from between the trees, and of steadily pounding music too heavily biased toward bass.

An unseen someone whistled appreciatively, causing Ron to grimace sourly and wonder for the tenth time that hour why he had let Lew and Wendy talk him into attending. Not that the four of them hadn't deserved that spontaneous accolade, given that each of their outfits had been purposefully contrived for maximum effect *and* carefully coordinated in compliance with some obscure master plan of Lew's. Which meant that they were all decked out in white jeans and long-sleeved light silk shirts— his and Lew's burgundy and midnight blue respectively, Wendy's emerald green, and Karen's tawny gold. In addition, Wendy's pale hair was crowned by a wreath of wildflowers Lew had scrounged from the meadow behind Cardalba Hall, and Karen sported a preposterous orchid corsage that looked as if it might bite anyone venturing too close. So much for decorum and keeping up appearances, Ron thought, especially as Lew was too young to bow entirely to convention—which was why he had tied his hair into a ponytail with a blue velvet ribbon, wore his shirt tail-out over a black Cats Laughing T-shirt, had exchanged the dragon stud in his earlobe for a larger dangly one, and was wearing white Reeboks. Ron had settled for moussing his hair into a semblance of spikes and wearing his own Reeboks—and for tucking a large tiger lily into his shirt pocket buttonhole.

They paused together on the sidewalk, exchanged smirking glances with one another—and walked arm in arm toward the source of all that light and noise.

Founders' Park occupied roughly two acres smack in the center of Cordova. It was perfectly square and ringed by a double row of ancient white oaks that effectively screened its grassy center. Once that ring had been breached, however, the park opened out into a pleasant maze of terraces and planters, all rising to an open pavilion made of rough

stone slabs that were supposed to have been reared by the
Indians for some nameless rites but which in fact looked
a great deal more like a miniature Stonehenge. The whole
area was ablaze with torchlight, and the air was heavy
with the odors of food and the sound of voices. And, of
course, there was music: a live band playing something that
sounded like a mix of bluegrass and traditional Celtic.

" 'Wildwood Flower' on bagpipes?" Ron observed curiously.

Lew nodded. "Uillean pipes, actually. They've gotten to
be a big thing up here. I'm thinking of starting a record
company and hyping it as the next wave."

"Cordova replaces Athens?" Ron chuckled. "That'll be
the day!"

Wendy was looking troubled. They had reached the
outskirts of the crowd by then, and Ron was aware of
eyes drifting their way, of conversations falling off as they
drew near.

"I hate being late," Wendy murmured. "People always
look at you."

"Ah, but the Master *always* arrives late," Lew informed
her with a smile. "We *have* to make an entrance. After
that, there's no big deal."

"If you say so," Ron grumbled warily, remembering
what crowds did to him—and hoping Wendy hadn't caught
that use of his brother's de facto title.

Lew laid a hand casually on his arm. *Don't worry*, the
thought came into his head. *I can damp out most of it as
long as you stick close by. If you wander off, you'll be on
your own, though. And no, your lady didn't notice.*

They had jostled their way to the first food table now,
and Lew absently reached down and snagged a plate (real
china, Ron noted, not the expected paper or plastic)—
and, true to the never full adolescent he still mostly was,
proceeded to heap it with hors d'oeuvres ranging from two
colors of caviar and lobster salad to what Ron suspected
were mountain oysters and fried medallions of rattlesnake.
And brownies. *Lots* of brownies.

Ron followed his example only slightly more conserva-
tively. Both Karen and Wendy were much more prudent,
choosing mostly nuts and fresh vegetable crudités.

As they progressed down the heaping tables, Ron became aware that the whole place had fallen silent, as if in anticipation. Eventually, even the music trailed off. Not until Lew had topped off an earthen mug beneath the wooden beer keg on the nearest table did the mumbling buzz of conversation resume. But the air of hushed expectancy did not truly cease until Lew had turned to face the crowd, raised his mug, bellowed a simple *"To you all!"*—and emptied his vessel at one draught. Ron took the cue and followed suit, as did Wendy. Karen, by contrast, contented herself with sipping fresh-squeezed cider.

And then the music resumed, louder and fiercer than before, with fiddles vying with the pipes in a wailing jig that was almost pagan in its energy and wildness. People began to separate from the crowd and dance. The beat was flexible enough, to permit almost any sort of interpretative movement from slam-dancing (which a small group of black-leather-and-chrome-stud-clad teens were indulging in), through more appropriate makeshift jigs, to the buck-and-wing that was traditional in this part of the Appalachians. Karen was appropriated by a handsome lad her own age, and Wendy eyed Ron speculatively and gave his arm a gentle tug. He shook his head, knowing he'd last about two minutes until his knee starting acting up. "Go have fun," he told her. "I guess I'd better stick to the sidelines and let Lew tell me who I oughta know."

Lew cuffed Ron's shoulder with his empty mug. " 'Fraid so. You're a Welch, and there're a fair number of people here who remember you. No way we can escape."

While Lew revisted the keg, Ron found himself scanning the crowd in search of a certain familiar someone.

"Winnie's *not* here, if that's who you're looking for," Lew said softly, passing him a refill. He was referring to the first girlfriend Ron had had in Welch County, the one with whom he'd shared so much fear and pain one fateful night five years before. "She's not been back in ages."

"Any idea what became of her?"

"Well, you *know* she went to Miami of Ohio. But the last I heard, she'd gotten married and was going to grad school somewhere up north."

"With her memories intact?" Ron asked pointedly. "*All* of 'em?"

"With those she wants dead dying—with a little help from me."

"*Lewis!*"

"Well, she doesn't *want* to believe what she saw that night," Lew countered defensively. "So I'm just helping her forget details. She'll always remember you, though; and she'll always remember being Uncle Matt's footholder— sort of—and that he and Anson killed each other. She just won't remember the . . . weirder aspects."

"Oh well," Ron sighed. "It's just as well, I guess. If I saw her again, I'd just feel guilty."

"I *can* point out a few new interesting folks, though, if you like," Lew continued, leading the way to a rough stone bench at the edge of the stone circle.

Ron took a sip of beer and leaned back against the cool rock, feeling its reassuring roughness through the thin silk on his back. "Suit yourself," he yawned. "*I* just want to sit here and veg out."

"Long night partying?"

Ron took a longer, deeper draught, and nodded. "*Real* long."

"You could have waited a couple of days, you know. I'm not *that* desperate."

Another swallow. "Yeah, but I *am* that curious—'specially when the last tune in the reading turns out to be 'It's the End of the World as We Know It.' "

"That's not the whole thing, though. There's a phrase in parentheses tacked on the end."

"There is?"

" 'And I Feel Fine.' "

"Small comfort, that," Ron snorted. "I still have to survive the end-of-the-world part."

Lew patted his leg. "We'll talk about it when we get home, I promise."

Ron grimaced irritably and began scanning the crowd. Most of the people were ignoring them—they'd do that so as not to be thought too fawning. But a few were already beginning to gravitate their way. Lew nudged him with his knee and rose. Ron followed, just as what looked to be a delegation from Mason Hardware just "happened" to wander up. Ron recognized old man Mason from his own tenure in Welch County. And two of the older clerks were familiar as well, along with Mr. Mason's large, well-scrubbed, and tow-haired family. He couldn't identify a fairly attractive younger woman, though. And he *certainly* hadn't seen that strapping redheaded lad in the tight jeans and black T-shirt before, the one who moved with such easy, unconscious grace that half the women present were following him with their eyes. As the retinue drew nearer, Ron felt the buzz of Voices growing stronger, and reinforced his shields. Lew caught his strained frown and winked an apology. The Voices immediately faded to a scarce-Heard whisper.

"Mr. Mason!" Lew cried, when the old man got close enough to hail, whereupon he launched into a complex round of acknowledgments and introductions—including Ron, who responded as politely as he could.

"Now let *me* introduce y'all to some folks," Mason said in turn, including the unknown newcomers in a gestured embrace. "This here is Marsha Mullins, my new clerk"—at which the pretty girl came forward, took Lew's hand, and nervously blurted out something about being glad to meet both of them—"and *this* is my new yard foreman, and a helluva good 'un he's gonna be, too, looks like. Lewis Welch, meet Van Vannister."

—Whereupon the strapping lad sauntered up and engulfed Lew's hand with one about fifty percent larger. "Happy to meet you," the redhead drawled in a nonspecific Southern accent. "I've been hearin' about you ever since I got up here. I'm pleased to finally be makin' your acquaintance."

Lew was frowning slightly. "And how long *have* you been up here?" he asked pointedly. "I usually hear about new folks pretty quick."

"I just hired him Saturday evenin'," Mason put in. "He started work for me this mornin'."

"Already fired Marcus Jones, too," Marsha added.

"I'm not surprised," Lew chuckled carefully. "Old Marcus is kind of a mess, ain't he?"

"That's one way to put it," Mason muttered, then glanced around. "Van—*you* ain't met Ronny yet, have you?"

The tall man turned his way and closed the yard between them in an easy half step. That near, Ron was suddenly aware that though Vannister was, in fact, only a couple of inches taller than he, if more heavily built, he *seemed* far larger. Maybe it was the way he moved, Ron told himself, maybe it was simply raw presence. Some people had that. Lew did, for instance; Ron did not. But Vannister was smiling pleasantly, displaying impressive white teeth in a tanned, handsomely angled, if rather pugnosed face. He looked disconcertingly familiar, but Ron couldn't place him.

"Nice to meet you," Vannister said, taking his hand.

"You, too," Ron gave back automatically, "I—"

He froze. There was something odd about the touch of Vannister's flesh—something he could not quite place. Without really intending to, he terminated the contact as quickly as he could.

"Something wrong?" Vannister asked, raising an eyebrow.

Ron shook his head, but frowned. "No—I just got distracted, I guess."

Vannister spared a glance toward the dancing crowd. "I can see that, what with the music and all those pretty girls, and all."

"Yeah."

"In fact," Vannister announced, "I think I'll go join 'em."

"Have fun," Ron called.

Mason's entourage had withdrawn by then, and Ron found himself once more alone with his brother. Only when Vannister had merged back into the crowd did he realize he had been tense as a board.

"Now, *he* was a strange one," Ron observed. "Though I'm damned if I know why I think so."

"Well, his Voice was funny, for one thing," Lew told him promptly. "I can't be more specific, but—well—it just sounded sort of artificial, or something. Like he was more aware of his thoughts *as* thoughts than most people are in situations like this."

"He had a weird handshake, too," Ron added. "Like—I dunno—like he was holding back, or something—like he could have crushed my hand if he wanted to, and knew it, and was thinking about it, but decided not to."

"I'll have to check up on him," Lew sighed.

"He seems familiar, too."

"Yeah, he does, doesn't he?"

"I wonder if—Whoa! What have we here?" Ron clamped a hand on his brother's shoulder and directed his attention toward an opening in the trees beside the food tables. "Now, *that's* what I call a woman!"

If Lew responded, he didn't hear, because Ron's attention was fully focused on the figure who had just made her way fully into the torchlit glare. She was fairly tall—probably five eight or nine—which put her a bit taller than Wendy. Slim, but not skinny, with a startling mane of wild black hair hanging loose down her back, and with high cheekbones that hinted of Indian ancestry—now accented by the firelight. She was clad simply, in new-looking black jeans and an oversize white blouse—or would have been, had she not also been wearing a handsome fringed and beaded vest that almost had to be brain-tanned buckskin. There was something fixed in her hair, too, but he couldn't make out what it was. He couldn't tell why he was drawn to her either, for beyond her exotic veneer, her features were in no wise outstanding. Except—she didn't seem to be wearing any makeup. Maybe that was it: in a land of test-tube beauty, this lass made do with what she had—and still managed to look just fine. As Ron continued to stare, she snatched a plate from the stack at the end of the table, handed it to the slender, dark-haired woman who had come in with her, then commandeered one for herself and began to heap it with food. She was, he observed with considerable satisfaction, leaning heavily toward the gamier offerings.

It took Lew a moment to figure out who he was gaping at, but then his brother nodded. "Ah yes . . . now, *her* I do know—sort of."

"And . . . ?"

"Her name's Brandy Wallace. She's going to be teaching art at the high school in the fall. According to her resume—which I conveniently got a look at, courtesy of being on the school board—she's got a triple major in drawing and painting, scientific illustration, and architecture, if you can believe that."

"I had a *double* major, if you recall," Ron shot back. "It's not *that* dif—" He broke off in midword. "*What* did you say her name was?"

"Brandy Wallace. Why?" Then: "Oh, jeeze, that name turned up in the Tarot, didn't it?"

Ron suddenly felt very light-headed. "Yeah. In the slot for Influences Coming Into Being." He sat down abruptly.

"Well, now, *that's* interesting," Lew replied thoughtfully. "Come to think of it, you two probably have a lot in common."

An eyebrow lifted warily. "Like what?"

"Well, for starters, you've been building your dream car—and she's supposed to be building some sort of preposterous castle up on Keycutter Knob."

"And you haven't *seen* it? Not been by to give it your blessing? My, my—you're gettin' lax in your old age."

"Indeed!" Lew snorted. "But in the first place, I haven't been *asked* yet; and secondly, I try not to snoop on the Voices as much as Uncle Matt did. I weed out the bad stuff and let as much of the rest go as I can. And as far as I can tell, there's nothing bad about Brandy Wallace— nor has she been bothered by anything. Except money, I think. She worries about that a bit."

"Understandable, if she's building a house on a teacher's salary—even a Welch County teacher."

"I hear there's family money—some. Apparently she's the favorite granddaughter of some kind of minor tobacco tycoon. He set her up, but not her dad, which I gather is a considerable source of friction. Or was."

"Hmmm." Ron mused. "Interesting. Who's her buddy?"

Once more, Lew peered into the crowd. "Tall, skinny gal? That's Weedge—W. G. Montgomery, to be exact. She works down at the P.O. I didn't know she and Brandy were friends."

"Just curious."

"Want me to introduce you?" Lew asked suddenly. "I've met 'em both—know Weedge pretty well, in fact."

Ron shook his head. "No . . . thanks, but I probably ought to handle this one on my own. It's liable to scare her off if she finds out I'm kin to you." He drained his mug impulsively, rose, and started down the hill, on the theory that pursuit of a refill should put him on a collision course with the intriguing Ms. Wallace.

Lew was regarding him speculatively. "What about Wendy?" he whispered, raising an eyebrow.

Ron started—and immediately felt a pang of guilt. Lew was right, of course; he had a perfectly good girlfriend already, one who loved him wholeheartedly and who trusted him implicitly. And here he was casting covetous glances at the first slightly exotic lady to wander by.

He simply didn't *do* such things—not usually. He was essentially a one-woman-at-a-time man. And besides, it was only a matter of time before this Brandy Wallace found out who he was and wound up like all the rest: so blinded by superficialities of birth that she never looked beyond to find the real him.

On the other hand, hadn't the Tarot essentially indicated that this was a fated meeting? How else could she be an Influence Coming Into Being if he *didn't* meet her?

Besides, Wendy was obviously having a ball on the dance floor, *he* was just high enough to deaden his reserve, and there was certainly nothing wrong with at least making the lady's acquaintance. Besides, as some of his raunchier, more pragmatic friends were fond of saying: "Just 'cause you're datin' somebody don't close up no holes."

Ron smiled to himself. Now, *that* was certainly putting the cart before the horse! He glanced sideways at Lew. "Nothing ventured, nothing gained," he sighed. "It's into the breach, I guess."

It took longer to make his way to the object of his curiosity than Ron expected, for as soon as he started walking, he realized that the rich-tasting brew he'd been swilling had been far more potent than he'd suspected. In fact, he felt positively reckless, willing for once to override his considerable sense of ethics (which was screaming at him to remember Wendy) and follow his baser instincts instead—or perhaps, he admitted, his hormones. A few people tried to engage him in conversation as he strode past, but hc brushed them off with inconsequentialities and promises to catch them later.

Thus it was that he found himself fidgeting beside the beer keg at almost the precise moment Brandy Wallace sauntered up. This close, he discovered that the unknown adornment in her hair was a hawk's wing affixed to some sort of costume-jewelry clasp, and there were more feathers, too: black ones depending on short silver chains from her ears. He'd also been right about the makeup: she wore none. All of which Ron noted on the fly, as he watched her juggling plates plus mug while manipulating the spigot on the keg. And since her friend had been seduced by the dessert table, he had an ideal opportunity to ingratiate himself by the simple expedient of murmuring, "Here, let me help you," and proceeding to turn the tap while she inserted the mug below.

"Thanks," she replied mechanically, sparing him only a brief appraising glance that reflected no desire for further conversation. Her eyes were wary, too, as if she were uncomfortable not only with his presence but with the entire situation. And her gaze kept darting toward his brother, and without consciously intending to, Ron Heard a thread of Voice—which meant she must be more concerned about something than she let on, to be broadcasting with such intensity. As best he could tell, she was here mostly out of a sense of obligation to her friend, and intended to split as soon as propriety permitted. Also, there was more than a hint of impatience, as if she had better things to do.

"That's enough," the woman finished shortly, while the beer was still a good inch below the top of the mug.

"You're sure? It's mighty good."

"I'm sure," she replied flatly. "I don't need to get drunk tonight, and I absolutely *cannot* afford a hangover."

"I can't either," Ron began. "I—"

"Excuse me," Brandy broke in, staring past him at the crowd, into which the dark-haired woman was wandering. "But I seem to have lost my buddy."

"Ah, Ms. Wallace," a male voice drawled as the woman turned preemptorially, "I see you've encountered Ronny Dillon."

It took Ron a minute to recognized the speaker. It was that same skinny Victor Wiley, in whose eleventh grade shop class he had first discovered the extent of his knack for metalwork. He hadn't seen the guy in several years, but they'd somehow managed to maintain erratic contact through cards and their mutual association with Lew. Wiley had apparently been bent on the same errand at the keg as Ron and Brandy—and not for the first time, to judge by his breath.

Brandy froze in place and grimaced as sourly as Ron grinned from relief. This way he was spared having to either introduce himself or explain who he was.

Wiley was plying the spigot by then, but kept on talking. "Ronny, meet Brandy Wallace. She's gonna be teaching art for us next year."

"So I heard."

Brandy's scowl deepened, but Wiley blithered on obliviously. "Ronny was my star pupil for a while. You know his brother, don't you?"

Brandy blinked in confusion. "I don't think so. I don't remember any . . ."

Wiley struck himself on the forehead with an exaggerated flourish. "Of course you don't! I'm five kinds of fool and four kinds of idiot. Ronny's Lewis Welch's foster brother!"

Ron didn't know whether to be grateful that Wiley didn't know how closely he and Lew were actually related, or irritated at how much he'd blurted out already. All he needed was someone judging him soley by his connections.

"I see," Brandy remarked distantly, not looking at either of them.

"You two have a lot in common," Wiley added helpfully.

"I'm sure we do," Brandy said. "It's nice to meet you, Mr. Dillon. But now I have to be going."

"Nice to meet you, too," Ron managed lamely as Brandy swept away.

"Mr. Dillon?" Ron exploded when it was safe. *"Mr. Dillon!* Do I look like a *Mr. Dillon* to you, Vic? I'm twenty-two fucking years old! And she, by God, can't be much older!"

Wiley shrugged helplessly. "Gosh! I wonder what got *into* her? She's usually a lot more polite—distant, but polite. Tough but fair, all that stuff. Not somebody you'd want to cross, but definitely someone you'd want on your side in a fair fight."

Ron took a sip of beer and shrugged back. "It's okay, man. Best I can tell, she wasn't interested anyway. Not that it really matters."

Wiley raised an eyebrow. "I *thought* I saw you come in with someone."

Ron nodded. "My girlfriend from Athens."

Wiley smiled sympathetically. "Yeah, but I don't blame you for casting your eye toward Brandy; she's a true original. You're probably wasting your time, though; she doesn't seem to like men."

"Christ," Ron moaned. "You don't mean—"

"Oh no," Wiley corrected quickly as he waited for the foam on his drink to disperse. "Not so far as I know. From what she's told some of the other women teachers at planning sessions, she's just had a couple of real bad relationships and doesn't want another. Doesn't trust us, I reckon—not that I would either."

"That's always the way of it, isn't it?" Ron grumbled sourly, surprised at the vehemence of his reactions.

"Seems like," Wiley agreed, between swallows. "You still got that fancy crutch?" he added abruptly.

"Yep." Ron nodded, and allowed himself to be drawn into a fifteen-minute discussion of his latest metalworking ventures, during which interval he swilled a great deal of beer and spent most of his time alternately watching Wendy, who was still dancing happily (mostly with old men and teens, he was relieved to note—safe partners, so as not to make him jealous); Brandy (who had payed token obeisance to his brother and moved on to join a few of the faculty members of the local high school he remembered); and Lew himself, who, to Ron's surprise, appeared to be having a fine old time carrying on serial superficial conversations with a graciousness and style quite out of keeping with his tender years. Maybe it was another talent, he told himself. Or genetic. But if that was the case, why hadn't he inherited it?

He was not at all certain when he ceased to enjoy himself, either. But somehow the more he tried to watch Wendy, the more he found his eye drifting toward the recalcitrant Ms. Wallace—and the more that happened, the more his conscience pained him. Besides, he really was tired (he'd been up late the night before, and Lew hadn't spared him time for a nap since his arrival), and *besides* it had somehow got to be almost eleven anyway. Which meant it was high time he was away. Maybe he'd collect his lady and—

No he wouldn't! Wendy was having the time of her life—he'd never realized how much she loved dancing, because the two of them never did it—so he just couldn't rain on her parade. Besides, Lew was here, and Karen, and the two of them together could surely take the light-footed little wench in charge when they got ready to split.

A moment later, he had weaved out to the dance floor.

Wendy conveniently chose that moment to gyrate by, and he called her name. Her eyes darted about before fixing on him, whereupon she smiled wildly and pranced over to his side, leaving the skinny teen who had been her partner to freeze where he stood and glower at him sullenly from under an inky forelock. "Havin' fun?" Ron asked seriously.

"Great!" Wendy laughed in reply, all trace of her former hostility having vanished. "I hope you're not jealous," she added uncertainly.

Ron shook his head and tried very hard not to let his words slur. "Not me. I'm just glad to see you enjoyin' yourself—God knows I'd never have lasted as long as these munchkins."

"You can cut in if you want to," she ventured hopefully.

Ron shook his head. "I'm not feelin' real good, all of a sudden—crowd's got to me, I guess. I'm gonna boogie. I'll ask Lew to give you a ride home, if that's okay."

Wendy's face suddenly became deadly serious. "You all right?"

"A little buzzed, but I'll be careful."

"Promise? I'd hate to lose you."

Ron's conscience poked him hard at that, and only then did he realize how uncomfortable he actually felt at being attracted to Brandy Wallace. "Me, too," he mumbled. "Can I get a good-night smooch?"

Wendy obligingly closed her eyes and puckered up, and Ron did his best to lay a good one on her—more out of guilt than desire. "Don't strain anything," he whispered as they eased apart.

"Don't worry."

" 'Bye."

" 'Bye."

And with that, Ron turned and steered himself toward the parking lot, making a slight detour to inform Lew of his intentions. Lew merely nodded and told him to be careful, but Ron could already feel his head clearing— if it wasn't a false alarm. But that wasn't likely, given that if Listeners wanted anything—like sobriety—badly enough, they generally got it if they bent their will to it. The question was: did he *really* want it? And did he have enough will?

He paused by the first of the oaks and scanned the party one final time. Seeing no sign of Brandy, he shrugged once again, stuffed his hands in his pockets, and strolled toward the parking lot, eyes fixed firmly on the ground ahead of him.

He did not bother looking up until he was no more than a dozen yards from the Centuari, and when he did, he discovered to his dismay that someone was giving it a *very* thorough once-over. Which he didn't need at the moment. Oh, he was used to strangers looking at it, asking questions. No way you could drive a one-of-a-kind hand-built car like his and not have that happen. But he was in no mood whatever for that kind of encounter just now.

And then he saw who it was.

He froze in place and stared. Brandy had her back to him and was walking slowly from one end of the vehicle to the other, apparently eyeing it critically. Every now and then she'd stop to inspect a detail or run a hand lightly over some contour or crease, and once she squatted down to inspect the juncture of fender, hood, and bumper.

Ron watched in silence as long as he could stand it, then started forward. His sneakers made no sound on the concrete walkway, so that he was able to come within a yard of her without being noticed.

He hesitated a moment longer, then cleared his throat abruptly.

Brandy started and leapt to her feet like an uncoiling spring, spinning around in the process, instantly on guard.

"You!" she snapped.

"I see you've found my wheels," Ron said easily, though he'd noted that she had the hair-trigger reflexes of someone who was high-strung and nervous. He slipped beside her to rest a hand possessively on the windowsill.

Brandy's eyes widened incredulously. "*Your* car! But I thought—"

"That I was just another poor little rich boy? That just 'cause I happened to be connected to the bloody Welches, I wasn't good for anything but holdin' court at parties?"

Brandy's face reddened visibly, and Ron half expected her to light into him—he had, after all, reacted more aggressively to the implied taunt than he'd intended. But to his surprise, she smiled shyly. "Teach me to judge a book by its cover—or its title, rather," she said ruefully. "This little baby buggy's handmade, isn't it?"

Ron nodded, and could not resist a grin. "As much as I could manage. All the bodywork, most of the hardware. And of course, I did the styling and basic engineering."

"Well, it's certainly a good job, or so it looks now. I'd have to see it in the daylight to be certain."

"Are you into cars?"

"Not really—not as cars. But one of my roommates at college was the daughter of some big wheel in NASCAR, so I got enough of a grounding from her to know there's no such thing as a Centauri. And I've seen enough bodywork to recognize a custom job."

"Thanks." Ron smiled.

"How long did it take you?"

"About four years, total, from concept to finished product—if it even *is* finished. I mean, I keep thinking of more things I want to do to it, and all; more technology I want to add."

"Like what?"

"Like a ten-disc CD player instead of the five job I've got in there now. Like eight-channel antilock brakes 'stead of four. Like traction control, and—"

An eyebrow lifted. "But how do you—" She cut herself off and looked away.

"How do I what?" Ron finished for her. "How can I afford it? Because I've lost two sets of foster parents in five years, both of whom were well insured. Because I used a lot of my various schools' equipment. And because most of the expense of any undertaking is labor, and I provided that."

"Tell me about it," Brandy sighed, and Ron thought that was the first time she had actually seemed relaxed.

"Oh, right," he took up. "You're building some kind of castle, or something, aren't you? Up on Keycutter Knob?"

"Yeah."

"What's the deal? You've seen my dream-in-the-metal; tell me about yours."

She did—for nearly thirty minutes, while the two of them leaned against the flawless sheetmetal of the world's only Centauri convertible. Brandy might have no obvious passion where men were concerned, but get her started on her house—then the fire awoke. Fortunately, he'd had enough art history courses that when she used terms like rose window and bas relief, or compared certain features to stave churches and others to Pompeian villas, he knew what she was talking about. At some point her diatribe turned to the subject of doors.

" . . . and I want to have bronze front doors," she confided. "Double ones four feet wide and ten feet high apiece, each with forty panels. Like the ones Ghiberti did in Florence, only I want mine to illustrate scenes from *The Lord of the Rings*."

"That'd be *great*!" Ron cried, picking up the torch of her enthusiasm. "But they're gonna cost you the earth."

Brandy's face clouded immediately, but her eyes flashed dangerously. "*Everything* costs money! Dreams cost a *shitload* of money." And with that, she fell silent, her former fire reduced to embers.

"I could help," Ron said suddenly. "I'm pretty good at bronze casting. And if I had something decent to go by, I could probably do the sculpting as well."

Brandy eyed him dubiously. "It's one thing to pound out steel fenders, it's another thing to sculpt bronze figurines."

"But I *have* sculpted figures. I—wait a minute."

Her face was impassive as he unlocked the trunk and fumbled around for his crutch. A moment later he held it out for her. "I made this back in high school," he announced proudly.

Brandy's mouth popped open, but she recovered her composure quickly. She could not, however, disguise the delight that covered her face as she examined the crutch. "I don't suppose you want a job," she ventured.

Ron had to suppress his shock, not only at the forthrightness of the question, but that anyone would even consider him available. On the other hand, he wasn't exactly wearing a neon sign proclaiming, "I hate Welsh County," either. "Not up here," he replied quickly. "I'm only visiting for a few days. Assuming I did it, I'd work out of my studio in Athens."

"Just as well, I guess," she went on, as if to herself. "No way I could afford you anyway."

"Ah, but you might be surprised there," Ron countered smoothly. "Money doesn't mean as much to me as the act of creation itself."

Brandy eyed him narrowly. "I'd still have to fork out for the bronze, and I'm not sure I could even afford that. But maybe . . ."

"What?"

She sighed. "Well, like I told you earlier, my goal is to design the whole place and everything in it down to the switchplates. I'm not nearly that far along yet, but one of the things I'd been worrying about was how to do 'em. See, each room's supposed to have a certain motif—there's to be a Celtic bedroom, and a Viking bedroom, and a Southeastern Indian bedroom, and all—like I told you. But I wanted each one to have appropriate hardware—no ivory plastic crap or anything. So I'd thought I'd do switchplates and stuff out of ceramic, which I know how to do. But what I *really* wanted was cast metal—at least where it's appropriate. So . . . would you maybe be interested in doing a few of those? I *could* afford to pay for them."

"Except that I wouldn't let you," Ron told her—to his surprise. "Like I said, money doesn't matter to me. It's the making itself that's recompense—long as I don't have to stay up here. Shoot, I'll work free, as far as that's concerned."

Brandy shook her head, suddenly grown distant again. "If you work for me, I'll pay you: that's the bottom line, no arguing."

"But—"

"I have to leave, Mr. Dillon," she said icily. "It's late, and *I* have work to do tomorrow." She rose from the car and started back toward the park. "Good night."

Ron was staring at her incredulously, wondering how, exactly, he'd managed to turn an amiable conversation back into a confrontation. "We'll talk again," he called helplessly.

"Maybe," she tossed over her shoulder, and continued on.

For a moment Ron considered running after her then decided against it. What was he thinking, anyway? This woman obviously wasn't interested in him as anything but a means to an end. And he equally obviously had a truly excellent girlfriend. But still . . .

Women! he growled to himself, when he'd watched Brandy disappear back into the din. He unlocked the car and climbed in, but did not immediately start it.

"Women!" And this time he said it aloud. Sighing, he turned the key and let the Centauri idle while he tried to locate music to suit his mood. None of the CDs seemed likely, so he dialed in 96 Rock on the radio and listened. Maybe he could at least summon up an omen.

He got Van Morrison's "Brown-eyed Girl."

And wondered suddenly what color Brandy's eyes had been.

But Van Vannister, who'd witnessed the whole encounter from the shadows, already knew.

Chapter 10

In the Midnight Hour

"Nice moon," Weedge ventured at last, shattering the increasingly awkward silence that had persisted through half a cup of coffee for her and almost a whole one for Brandy. She shifted her gaze from the starlit sky to the woman sitting beside her and raised an eyebrow hopefully. From somewhere in the nearby forest came the cry of a whippoorwill: sad, but strident.

Slouched forward on the stacked cinder blocks that formed the front steps of her trailer, Brandy sensed her friend's stare and nodded but did not reply. An unseasonable chill floated among the night breezes, rendering the warmth of the mug between her palms too pleasant to relinquish. She wished her tongue felt as good—or her head and tummy. The former she had scalded on her first sip of the hazelnut Gevalia Weedge had brewed as soon as they'd returned to the knoll after the party. The other two were—sort of— the cause of the first: too much of Lewis Welch's alcohol consumed too freely over too brief a period of time, and

145

mixed with too much rich food. She'd get an acid stomach, she supposed; but she needed the coffee to clear her head. As it was, her thoughts were flitting frantically about, like swifts circling a particularly enticing chimney: she never knew which one would light, or how long it would stay when it did.

"*Real* nice moon," Weedge repeated.

And that was a hint, Brandy knew: a cue that she should say something to reassure her friend that she was okay, that a stone-sober Weedge Montgomery had not followed her home and plied her with caffeine in vain.

Weedge was right, too—about the moon, and probably about a bunch of unspoken things as well. And as a point of fact, Brandy *had* been looking at it: alternately gazing at the rapidly waxing orb itself, and through the ghostly webwork of half-completed walls at its reflection in the mirror of lake. It was a beautiful, romantic image, one that should have relaxed her and lulled her to sleep, ready to begin another day's labor. *Should* have—and did not.

"Really, *really* nice."

And Brandy knew she had used up her grace. "Yeah," she grunted, "it is." She tried to reintroduce silence by taking a sip of coffee, but the mug was empty.

"You're wired," Weedge stated flatly.

"I'm drunk."

"You're a wired drunk, then."

Brandy shrugged, deposited the mug between her bare feet, and resumed her contemplatory pose: leaning forward, elbows on knees, chin in hand. "I'm pissed," she mumbled finally.

Which, of course, prompted the inevitable "Why?"

Another shrug, her gaze never leaving the vista before her. "What the *fuck* am I trying to do, anyway?"

"About what?"

She freed a finger and waved it toward the construction. "About . . . about all this, for one thing! I mean shit, Weedge, here I am: queen of my realm, Mistress of Brandy Hall, ruler of all I survey. I've got one goal in sight, one singular obsession, and—"

"You mean your place?" Weedge interrupted. "If *I'm* gonna be your shrink, *you're* gonna have to be specific."

Brandy's brow wrinkled in perplexity, but fortunately, enough swifts had returned that she was starting to become lucid—maybe too much so. "Not the place," she began, "not really. I guess I'm talking about even more than that: I guess I'm talking about self-sufficiency. Independence, and all that."

"Looks to me like you're getting there pretty fast."

Brandy shook her head. "Looks can lie," she chuckled bitterly. "Right now it's all a nebulous ideal. Oh, sure, the land's paid for—that's the first part. And I'm finally making some progress on the frigging house. But until I get *it* finished and paid off, I'm doomed to be a slave to the system. Doomed to work for the Man."

"What about your art?"

"What about it? It pays—sometimes. Sometimes it pays very well. But you can't count on making a living painting critters. The market's just too fickle, and I'm not a big enough whore to paint what the market wants. I was doing wolves before they were fashionable; I was doing photo-realism long before its time, and right now I'm riding that wave. But it may not last. And until the house is mine beyond possibility of foreclosure—I need a reliable income."

"Teaching's not so bad, though," Weedge told her. "I've done it; I *know* you can."

"And probably fairly well, because I truly do love kids— creative kids, anyway. The ones with a spark you can fan into a flame. But I'd drop the whole thing in a second if Brandy Hall was finished."

"And then what would you do? Be a hermit? Be the crazy woman up on the mountain? I can see you now: bumming around in the woods in a coonskin cap and buckskin, scaring the crap out of little animals—and probably small children, too."

Brandy could not resist a giggle, having entertained exactly that same notion more than once. "Not a bad idea," she affirmed. "And I really do think I could pretty well get by on gardening and hunting—'course, I'd still do art, but only to satisfy myself, and maybe just when I had to as a supplement."

"And then you'd be free?"

A nod. "Then nobody could put liens on my place. And once that's secure, nobody'll be able to put liens on my soul either—unless *I* want 'em to."

Weedge finished her coffee. "That's what this is really about, isn't it? This edginess you're feeling tonight. It's not about your place or self-sufficiency; it's about men."

Brandy did not reply.

"Yep, that's it." Weedge nodded with conviction. " 'Cause nobody can put liens on anybody's soul except the opposite sex. Not the kind you're talkin' about, anyway: the kind that can really threaten."

Silence.

"I'm waiting."

Brandy sighed. "What the hell am I gonna do, Weedge?"

"About what? Or whom?"

"About . . . Van Vannister—and, maybe, that Ronny Dillon guy, too." She paused, waiting for Weedge to supply an answer, but none seemed forthcoming. And now she'd opened her mouth, so she might as well blunder on and get the whole sorry thing out of her system. Maybe it'd help to talk about it anyway; maybe it'd help her see her way clear. Of course, Weedge had heard it all before—most of it, anyway; but now that she was buzzed and free-associating, perhaps she'd come up with some new slant that hadn't occurred to her previously; some way of integrating her desire for independence with her deep-seated fear of being alone.

"Well," she began, as if she was giving an oral report in a class, "first of all, the absolute last thing I need in my life right now is a man. I mean I *like* men, and all—at least I like their physical selves, at least in the abstract; they've definitely got their uses, as I'm sure you know. Trouble is, the last umpteen I've been involved with have all turned out exactly the same. Things'll always start out fine: good company—at a bar, say, or a party; a certain amount of physical attraction. Intelligent conversation of the sort you usually get in a college town. At some point they'll tell me their dreams. And that's generally when things screw up, 'cause that'll make me want to tell 'em mine—and then they'll just smile and act interested and take me to bed, or to meet their friends, or even back home to Mom and Dad.

But as soon as—as *soon* as, Weedge—as soon as I start doing something to *fulfill* my dream, like telling some guy I can't go somewhere or do something 'cause I need to save my inheritance money for a down payment on some land; or maybe that I've just got a new book on being your own contractor; or that no, I *don't* want to go to the game 'cause I really *do* want to design the mosaics for the bathroom floor *right now* 'cause I've got so much creative energy built up for that purpose, I'm gonna *pop* if I don't use it—or, even worse, the muse'll boogie off. Let me do *any* of those things—those things that don't hurt them in any way and that actually help me 'cause I enjoy 'em— and suddenly it's like I don't matter at all. That's when I have trouble with men. That's why I try just to think of 'em now as tools. I mean, that's how they think of *us* most of the time. Why should I be any different? And then you meet somebody like Vannister, or Dillon, who really are charming and accomplished, and you start to wonder if maybe you've been wrong, if there might not actually *be* good ones somewhere in the woodpile. And yet . . . and yet . . ."

Before she was aware of it, she was up and pacing. The moonlight rendered the whole outcrop almost bright as day, and its twin in the lake was uncannily beckoning. And she was suddenly so awash with built-up tension, she could hardly stand it. It had been a bad couple of days, she admitted. And it had been a long time since she'd had any physical attention. And both Ronny Dillon and—especial- ly—Van Vannister certainly fell within her acceptable aes- thetic parameters. Perhaps she should have invited one of 'em home, stated her needs clearly and concisely, empha- sizing that this was only pleasure of the moment, that no long-term commitment was either expected or desired, and gone with the flow.

"You're not finished, are you?" Weedge said softly, from behind her. "If you're gonna indulge in catharsis, get it *all* out. Bare your soul, for chrissakes. I mean, who am *I* gonna tell?"

Brandy spun around abruptly, on the verge of telling her best—probably only—friend to go the hell away and leave her alone. But she did not. "It's just too big a risk," she sighed. "Just too big a goddamn risk. Once you start letting a man get involved in your life, even a good one—probably *especially* a good one—they'll feel compelled to start fooling around with your dreams, and I just can't risk that. You let 'em in, and pretty soon they'll be wanting to make changes—only they'll *say* they're just suggestions—and before you know it, it won't be *your* dream at all!"

"Mightn't it be a better dream then? Or at least a bigger one?"

"I . . . Oh, fuck, I don't know. I don't even want to think about it right now. I just want—"

"What?"

"I dunno! That's the trouble, Weedge, I just fucking well don't *know*! I mean I *want* to dream. But I want it to be *my* dream. But I'm afraid I can't do it just by myself. But I'm afraid not to, and . . . Oh bloody hell! Just fuck it!"

She had reached the house by then, was leaning against one of the walls in the southeastern corner, ignoring Weedge, who was hanging back, a look of stoic patience on her face. Giving her space, Brandy knew. Which she appreciated. Available, but not pushing, perfectly able to sense when to do and when to let be. The moon was invisible here, but its light was not, and it shone on a labyrinth of half-completed walls, shored-up ceilings, and unassembled woodwork.

She certainly *could* use some help; that was a fact. She could also do everything herself; that was equally true. But it would take far longer. Maybe she *should* bite the bullet and let Vannister—or even Dillon, if she could persuade him to hang around awhile—have a go. If she were up-front about things, laid down the law right away that she *was* the law, perhaps they could get along.

But was there any real purpose in worrying about it at all, right now?

Sighing, she shook her head and started toward the gaping archway of the entry hall.

—And had just set her foot across the threshold when what she first perceived as a low-pitched grumbling-grating sound quickly increased in volume and became a snapping, grinding crash. The doorjamb to her right quivered alarmingly, then stilled. And in the cool night breeze she caught, faint but clear, the odor of concrete dust.

The same dust that was still dispelling when she reached the source of the noise.

And though she already knew what had caused it, it took the evidence of her senses to actually bring a lump to her throat and tears to her eyes.

It was the damned foundation again, that damned corner that had already collapsed once—then with no hint of warning, and now again after careful calculations, reengineering, and rebuilding.

Which was *all* she needed. It meant another day's work blown to hell (which made two gone already, and probably two more now, since she'd not only have to rebuild a second time, but reengineer *again*)—which meant that what should have taken one day had suddenly stretched to a week.

But it also meant that Van Vannister had been right.

And damn him for it, too; damn him for being a man and being right!

The next thing Brandy knew, she was leaning against her cement mixer crying.

And she hated herself for that, too.

Interlude 3

Lay, Lady, Lay

Welch County, Georgia
Midnight

The Road Man would have called it cleaving, what he does with this woman who was a stranger the day before. He knows her now, but he has known the oft-cleaving tinker for ages, even traveled with him a time, always in secret; been very close to him indeed, so that he knows what the Road Man would say and do, how he would sound, the expressions he would make. He even knows how the Road Man makes love, for he has seen that, too: fiercely, but with little honest passion.

He makes love more slowly, *very* slowly, in fact; and though he does not love this woman, he loves what he does to her, loves her body as much as his own, loves how he feels to her as much as how she feels to him; and loves most of all making them both feel as one. And slowly, slowly they rise toward climax. They are one now: one in body, one in reflex, one—almost—in mind. It has begun, he can feel it deep at the root of his manhood, and it grows stronger: a tickle—a throb—an explosion. He cries out—

152

—And is somewhere beyond.

"Mother?"

"Are you surprised to find me here?"

"I—yes."

"There is more than one kind of pain—as well you know. And many are very close kin to pleasure."

"So I have observed."

"There is also more than one way to contrive a Calling."

"This, too, I have found."

"We cannot speak long this time. This kind of pain cannot be sustained. It is too sweet."

"Of this, also, I am aware."

A sigh in the empty spaces. "You have found metal? Ingots for your forge?"

"That is not my art—but yes, I have found them: the ones I told you of."

"I forget. You are not him."

"No."

"But they have the fire? Do they glimmer? Or do they flame?"

"They glow red-hot: hot as the hottest star. But still, I think, they need a bit more temper."

"Then that is what you must provide."

"I wish the Road Man were here. He does this sort of thing better."

"But I have given this task to you."

"And this task I likewise have taken."

"Do it well."

"I will do it."

"I have no doubt." A pause, then: "Is love an art or a craft?"

"Love, oh my mother, is living."

She does not answer. But the woman beneath him does. She moans and opens her eyes. He sees his own reflected in them, and in *them* he sees only flame.

And soon he is cleaving again—like a beast.

Very like a beast.

Chapter 11

Deadman's Curve

Cardalba Hall
Tuesday, June 22—12:33 A.M.

Ron was tired of waiting for the bed to stop spinning. He was home now—make that back at Cardalba Hall, which was definitely *not* home; lying flat on his back atop the quilted black covers of a king-sized bed in the room Lew had assigned him and Wendy. The James Dean Suite, he had always called it, because it was where he had played crash-and-burn on those rare occasions he'd found it necessary to spend the night in the ancestral mansion and did not share Lew's quarters. But the fact that it had a clever moniker didn't make him like it any better, not by a long shot. He was still dressed, sort of, having shed only his shoes, socks, and borrowed silk shirt upon returning from his brother's bash; and beyond his bare feet, he had a fine view of the carved oak footboard (it appeared to be undulating slightly), and beyond *that*, of the massive oak door that let onto the upstairs hall. A matching portal to the left opened into an enormous bathroom he had already visited several times. Trouble was, Lew had papered the

154

walls of both chambers in a subtle op art pattern in two shades of gray—which was *exactly* the wrong thing to inflict on an unsuspecting guest's eyes when he'd had too much lubrication.

Such overindulgence wasn't like him, either, but somehow, what with the stress of the trip, the tension of the reunion, and the necessary confusion of the party, Ron had allowed himself to consume quite a remarkable amount of alcohol during the last twelve hours, not the least of it being the home-brewed beer he'd swilled in copious quantities at the soiree. Usually he could hold his liquor fairly well, but the stuff he had sampled there had evidently been much more insidious than most, and had truly, as they say, knocked him on his heinie—a good thirty minutes after he'd stopped expecting it, and a solid hour after he'd laid off imbibing. And unfortunately, he no longer had enough willpower to summon the Luck to fight it. It was a miracle he had neither trashed his car nor gotten arrested on the way here. Not that either of those would have been a real problem, not with the family money and connections— and Luck—all to call on. *Plus* an ace in the hole he didn't like to contemplate because it was another one of those "Listener things" that marked him as different from rank-and-file humanity.

What he *wanted* to do was sleep. Except that every time he closed his eyes, the bed commenced a gentle gyration, and every time he opened them, the op art walls took over. But he was *not* going to toss his cookies (his lobster salad, rather); he had already told himself that. And so far his tummy was staying in line.

He wished his brain was as tractable, because in those rare intervals when he was not monitoring his mortal state, his thoughts kept darting back to the tantalizing Brandy Wallace. He was, he admitted, infatuated. Some of the attraction was purely physical, of course. With her lithe body, wild hair, and abstinence from makeup, she was a near-perfect example of the sort of woman he found most enticing. (Wendy, in spite of her perky beauty, was a little too insubstantial for his tastes.) But there was definitely more to his interest than mere appearance. Perhaps it was Brandy's ruthless self-sufficiency. Perhaps in her he had

finally found someone as consumed by her passions as he
was. Shoot, she was even an artist, and he recalled with
slightly bleary delight the way her face had brightened
and her conversation had become more animated when
they started discussing their respective crafts. Only truly
dedicated artists could do that; poseurs needed not apply.
True artists did art because there was no way they could
not do it; because they got weird and antsy if not allowed
to practice their particular madness. Or at least he was that
way when he was hammering on a sheet of metal, and he
doubted it was any different for Brandy with a saw or a
nail or a brush.

Maybe that was his problem with Wendy: she was too
dependent, too clingy, too cautious—until very recently, too fearful of conflict to even stand up for herself.
Which made sense in a way: a person who had lost all
record of past attachments along with her memory would
naturally avoid risking the favor of her present friends.
Except that where Wendy seemed to have no consuming
passions beyond loving him and studying flowers, Brandy
obviously had a shitload—and meant to see them realized.
Brandy, in effect, wanted to *become*; Wendy was content
merely to *be*.

On the other hand, the illustrious Ms. Wallace hadn't
seemed to have much use for men, so maybe he was
fretting in vain. Or maybe—

A raucous guffaw, coupled with a pair of giggles, a
startled yip, and the badly muffled pounding of several
pairs of footsteps on the staircase outside shook him
from his reverie. He jerked himself upright, momentarily disoriented before he realized it was most likely Lew
returning with the ladies—which meant he might as well
forget catching Zs anytime soon. Between decompression
chatter and Wendy's nightly ritual, there'd be a God's
plenty of racket, both mental and actual—and he was
just befuddled enough to be unable to shut any of it out.
Hopefully Wendy would be wasted from all that dancing,
so he'd at least be spared worrying about any physical
demands from her—not that he was up for it anyway.
Sighing, he slid his feet off the bed and fought his way
out of the skintight black T-shirt Lew had lent him as part

of the impress-the-peasants ensemble, thinking to exchange it for a looser, more comfortable alternative. He had just got it over his head when he noticed that the cacophony outside had ceased abruptly—whereupon the door opened, and Wendy wandered in.

"Hi!" Ron began. "You're—" He broke off, staring. Wendy's face was so placid as to be almost blank; her eyes *were* blank—distant and unfocused—and she moved with a calm, if mechanical grace he had witnessed far too often. Something was wrong, he knew right away—and felt the first pitchfork proddings of guilt, until he realized he had made a misassessment. Wendy was fine, she was simply . . . different. Lew had obviously been fooling with her mind, and he had a good idea why. He was on the verge of Listening to confirm what he suspected, when the Master of Cardalba himself appeared silently at the open door—barefoot, red-eyed, and with his hair in wild disarray. He inclined his head toward Wendy, who was in the process of divesting herself of her earrings at the dresser to the left of the bathroom door, and mouthed, "She'll be okay."

Ron scowled, but nodded in turn, then raised an eyebrow quizzically.

Lew merely shook his head and gestured for him to join him.

Ron did, feeling a momentary twinge of giddiness as he gained his feet. He started to snag a shirt and socks, but decided against it. Cardalba was plenty warm, and anything beyond the minimum attire necessary for comfort was a concession to a tradition of Southern gentility both he and Lew despised, even as they reveled in its perks.

His brother seemed to read his mind, too (or might have literally; Ron was too far gone to tell), and was already unbuttoning his own shirt when Ron joined him in the hall. "It's time," Lew whispered.

Ron blinked at him uncomprehendingly, wishing vainly he was more lucid. Even worse, to judge by the way Lew was scowling at him now, his brother was only that moment realizing how far down the road to intoxication he had progressed.

Lew had paused at the top of the stairs and was staring at him critically. "You *up* for this, man? I don't *wanta* wait, but I reckon I can if I have to."

Ron shrugged sloppily but managed to reply with reasonable coherence—and without too much slurring. "Probably. The worst that can happen is that I won't remember any of it in the mornin'."

Lew grimaced resignedly. "That's true, and anyway I'll have it off my chest. If I have to do it again—well, that's my problem, ain't it?"

Ron nodded, noting that Lew's accent had started to slip, along with his diction, which meant he'd had more than his share of the sauce, too—though obviously not so much he couldn't hoodoo Wendy.

"I could prob'ly help you with that hangover," Lew drawled as he started down the stairs. "Or I could if I could ever get the hell shut of mine."

Ron shook his head and followed, holding tightly to the rail as he sought to clear what felt like a year's worth of cobwebs from his reasoning facilities. Now that he was more or less fully awake, he could repair the damage himself if he really wanted to. Shoot, the Luck would take care of it on autopilot, given sufficient time. A quicker recovery merely required more effort than he wanted to expend, especially when he didn't like fooling with Luck to start with. Besides, something told him a buzz—real or feigned—might be an asset at the moment.

And at any rate, he had made it to the bottom of the stairs, and Lew was padding toward the media room. Ron hesitated before accompanying him; the place had struck him earlier as sterile, cold, and forbidding—precisely the wrong sort of ambience to encourage intimate conversation. Once he actually entered, though, he felt vastly relieved. For by some trick of lighting, some subtle rearrangement of shadow or shift in dominant chroma, the formerly chilly cubicle now seemed warm and inviting. Clannadd's "Legend" whispered softly in the background, making its own contribution to the aura of tranquility. Ron flopped down on the chair he had occupied earlier and wiggled his toes luxuriously in the thick carpet. Lew dragged its twin up opposite, whereupon, as if summoned by magic, a tired-looking Karen came in, bearing a silver tray on which sat a black plastic thermos bottle, twin black china coffee cups with matching cream-and-sugar service, and a plateful of walnut-laced brownies. She set the apparatus on the round glass table near the brothers, gave Lew's hair a final affectionate muss, spared Ron a weary grin, and withdrew.

"G'night," Lew and Ron called as one.

"G'night."

And they were alone.

Lew filled a cup, sugared it, and offered it to his brother.

"I wish you wouldn't do that," Ron grumbled, accepting the drink with a frown. "Every time I turn around, you're playin' dutiful host, just like I heard Matt used to do. Can't we just be buddies without all this damned ritual?"

Lew's gaze flicked upward from more pouring. "I thought we were."

Ron shifted his position nervously. "Maybe . . . sometimes. But just when I get used to one Lew, another appears—and it's gettin' on my nerves."

"I'm sorry, I . . ."

"Oh, it's not your fault, probably," Ron went on impulsively, vaguely aware that he was letting his fading besottedness serve as an excuse for a loose tongue and loss of discretion. "I know you've got a lot of different hats to wear, but I wish to God you'd at least cut the shit around me. You're *only* twenty-two, man. You've got a right to act like it once in a while."

Lew spared him a bemused smile. "Profound words from a drunk."

Ron shrugged. "Maybe so. Or . . ."

"Or maybe you've rehearsed 'em so many times, they just came out on automatic?"

A shrug. "Probably. I'm sorry, I shouldn't have said that, either."

"Except that it's all true. I *do* have to wear too many hats, and it's not fun, not by a long shot. And speakin' of which"—Lew stood and shucked out of his shirt and T-shirt, matching Ron's bare-chestedness—"is that better?

There can't be anything more relaxin' for a couple of good old Southern boys than sittin' around with your shirt off, drinkin' coffee with your brother in your den."

" 'Cept doing the same thing while drinkin' beer," Ron corrected, with a chuckle. "And we probably oughta be watchin' football, or something."

"Want to?" Lew asked suddenly. "I've got all the Dogs' last season on tape."

"Didn't know you was a fan."

"I'm not. But I kept hopin' I might see you in the crowd and get some feel for what your life's like—out there in the real world."

"Real world, shit!" Ron snorted derisively, helping himself to a brownie. "Athens ain't the real world any more than Welch County is. 'Sides, you'd get a *better* idea of what it's like by watchin' R.E.M videos on MTV."

"It's got Listeners then, Athens has?"

"None I'm aware of—but that's not what I mean, and you know it."

"So what *do* you mean?"

Another shrug. "That . . . I don't know. That . . . that there's too much goin' on there that folks couldn't get by with in other places. It's a pretty tolerant environment, I guess. You can pretty much be whatever you want to be, long as you don't break too many laws."

"So it's not the outside world, either?"

Ron took a sip of coffee before answering. "I'm not sure there really *is* an outside world, Lew. If you get to the center of any place, every place is both predictable and utterly strange."

"I wouldn't know."

"No, I guess you wouldn't."

Lew regarded him steadily across the top of his cup. "I'd *like* to, though," he whispered, his gaze never leaving Ron's.

Ron felt his heart flip-flop, though he shouldn't have been surprised. Any reasonable person would have expected it. That he had not was more a matter of his questionable sobriety (and perhaps a desire not to name the unnameable less it manifest) than of ignorance. "I thought you might," he sighed at last.

Lew's face was calm, but Ron knew he was holding back, trying not to blurt out everything at once. He was at once sorry for his brother, furious at him, and in dread of what he knew would follow.

"How long has it been?" Lew asked softly. "How long since we first met?"

"You should know," Ron snorted. "Aunt Erin—Mom, I should say—started bringin' you down to Florida when we were about three or so. 'Course, I don't remember that far back."

"And how long since you moved up here to stay?"

"I *haven't* moved up here to stay," Ron snapped before he could stop himself. "I have no intention of *ever* livin' in Welch County."

Lew's expression did not change. "Humor me, bro. How long?"

Ron grimaced irritably. "Five years, plus a couple of months—which, of course, you know, probably down to the exact number of days, hours, minutes, and seconds."

"One *tends* to keep track of time when one's in prison."

"You chose it. You're the one who said he'd take the Mastership."

"There wasn't any choice," Lew replied quietly. "I knew *something* about it simply from observation; you knew *nothing* about it at all."

"Would you *can* the suffering aristocrat act?"

"I can't—not anymore. I . . . I don't think it *is* an act anymore."

"I was afraid of that." Ron rolled his eyes and looked away.

"And if I was an asshole, I'd tell you it was your fault, too: that you should have argued me out of it, that you should have agreed to be Master yourself, or that we split the job, or whatever."

"And *are* you an asshole?"

"Maybe . . . sometimes."

"So am I . . . sometimes."

"When?"

An exasperated sigh. "You know *exactly* when: When I put off visitin' my own brother whom I love, just 'cause the place he happens to live gives me the willies. When I bitch 'cause he won't come to my graduation when I know perfectly well it could drive him crazy. When . . . when I get the hots for some woman I've barely met when I've already got a jim-dandy girlfriend who's—how'd you put it—beautiful and talented and smart, and has absolutely no ego. The perfect woman, in other words."

"As perfect as I could . . ." Lew began, then turned pale, as if he had already said too much.

"What?"

"Never mind," Lew mumbled quickly, not meeting Ron's eye. "Maybe I should just lay out my case straight and let you answer. And please, Ronny, *please* let me finish before you interrupt, okay? It's been hard enough for me to get up nerve to ask you—and now that I'm at it, I've gotta get the whole mess out."

Ron set aside his coffee and sank back in the chair, arms folded across his bare stomach. "So shoot."

Lew took a deep breath, and Ron saw his posture stiffen subtly as he resumed his more formal persona. "Okay, then; straight shot: I'm tired. I am sick to *death* of being Master of Cardalba. You've had four years of college during which you were absolutely free to do whatever you wanted, wherever you wanted to do it. Whereas—"

"Not free," Ron interrupted in spite of himself. "No way one of us is ever really free. I had crowds to deal with; you didn't—not as many or as often, anyway. Don't forget that."

"I haven't and I won't," Lew replied. "And I'm certainly aware that I've got enough money to bring most of the world's pleasures to me. But that's one of the points. Vicarious living isn't the same as *real* living. And I'm bloody well ready to do some serious living!"

"I'm not stoppin' you."

"No . . . you're not, or at least not as much as Grandma is. But you're still holdin' me back some . . . in a sense."

"So what do you want me to do?"

Lew took another deep breath. "Okay, cards on the table. What I want from you, exactly, is for you to remember that I've been Master for five unhappy years and probably will be for the rest of my life, and with that in mind, that I'm asking you—make that *pleading* with you—for you to take just three years out of your life and hold down the Mastership while I finish this bloody B.A. of mine some way besides by frigging correspondence courses, and"—he hesitated—"then get a master's degree. I *think* I can finish 'em all that fast," he added hastily.

"Where? Not that it really matters."

"Georgia, probably; same as you. They've got a good landscape architecture program, and decent botany and horticulture departments."

"So you want me to assume your headaches so you can grow better petunias?"

"They're not just *my* headaches," Lew snapped. "And I want to grow a bloody lot more than petunias!"

"What? Orchids? Tiger lilies?"

"It's my *talent*, Ronny!" Lew pleaded helplessly, rising and pacing around the room. "You're good at metalwork, I'm a gardener—a goddamned gardener! I thought it was music, or even wrestling. I was wrong. It's plants. You've heard of green thumbs? I've got a whole green body! And . . ."

"What?"

Lew paused by the chair and polished off his coffee. "And I'm desperate. I didn't *want* the friggin' Mastership, but *somebody* had to take it, and you couldn't. But I'd always *planned* to leave; everybody does. Shoot, Mom wanted me to, for that matter. Things are too perfect up here; you should know that. Oh, it's peaceful and beautiful and secure, but there're no sharp edges, nothing to make you feel like you're really alive."

"You're talking about the edge, aren't you?"

"If you wanta call it that. But I've heard more than one person say you only really feel alive when you're walkin' the edge." He paused, took another deep breath, and continued. "I truly am desperate, bro. If I don't get out of here at least for a while, I'll go batty. And if that happens, you really will get stuck with it, 'cause there's at least an even chance I'll trash myself, and you know yourself that for a Listener to truly *want* to be dead is the same thing, almost, as *being* dead."

"Except that you *don't* want death," Ron countered instantly. "You want an end to pain. That's what most people who want to kill themselves are really after."

"Maybe so," Lew said, shrugging. "But the fact is that I hurt, and I'm tired of hurting. I'm entitled to be happy, too, Ronny. I can't help my genes—*our* genes—any more than you can."

"Life's a bitch, ain't it?" Ron chuckled ironically. "And bein' as different as we are's a regular ring-tailed bitch-kitty."

Lew lifted an eyebrow. "And where did you discover *that* quaint little metaphor?"

"Prof down at UGA. Taught natural history until he retired. He was fond of colorful phrases—and of walkin' the edge, too, I guess."

"I thought art was your big thing."

"It was. But I'm also into information, 'specially if it ties a lot of stuff together; so I took a lot of electives in classes that codified information."

"Very interesting," Lew replied. "But I seem to be detecting an evasion. And I don't want evasions from you."

"But I don't want to be Master either, man! I'd be a disaster at it, 'cause I'd be resentin' it every minute—and 'cause I don't know how to do it, anyway."

"I could train you some," Lew countered. "Obviously I wouldn't have to leave immediately, given that I haven't actually applied for school yet. And of course, Grandma'd help when she gets back, seein' as how she likes you so much."

Ron ignored the jibe. "Have you mentioned this to her at all?"

Lew glared at him askance. "Of course not! The old biddy'd raise holy hell, you know that! The only way we can possibly pull this off is while she's gone."

"But . . ."

"Please, Ronny? *Please?* Oh, I don't need an answer tonight, or even tomorrow. But promise me you'll at least think about it. Promise you'll at least *try* to see where I'm comin' from, that you'll . . . that you'll . . ." But he could say no more, because he was crying.

"For heaven's sakes, Lew, get a grip on yourself!"

"Why?" Lew sobbed. "Dammit, man, hasn't it got through to you yet that that's what I'm *sick* of? I'm goin' out of my mind tryin' to keep a grip on myself! I soak in emotions all day, I can't get rid of 'em. And unlike you, I'm not allowed to keep my shields up all the time."

"I . . ."

"Just shut the fuck up and let me talk, okay? Do you have any *idea* what that's like? You've got a girlfriend: you know what it's like just having to be responsible for her happiness. Think what it's like for me—to have a whole town, shoot, a whole bloody *county* that you've gotta look out for—and all behind the scenes. Responsibility without authority can be a real—what was your term? Ring-tailed bitch-kitty."

Once more Ron shook his head. "I just don't know."

"What're you afraid of?"

"I already told you."

"And I told you that was stupid."

Ron bit his upper lip thoughtfully. Most of his muddle had faded, burned away by the tide of strong emotions that were threatening to swamp both of them. "Okay," he sighed after a pause. "Now it's time to lay out *my* hand. I'm torn, man. I truly do love you, and I truly do hate to see you unhappy, and I'd love to help you; you've got to believe that. But . . . but a part of me is scared absolutely shitless that once I was sittin' there in the library with my feet in some virgin footholder's lap soakin' up Luck like I can't even imagine, *you'd* take to the high timber and never be seen again. I wouldn't blame you, either."

"And you know perfectly well there's a foolproof way to know my intentions," Lew shot back. "All I have to do is lower my shields, and you can read my deepest thoughts."

Ron regarded him skeptically. "Unless you've found out how to screen off certain parts, like dear cousin Anson did. You can learn a lot in five years, old buddy."

"But not how to trust your closest kin, apparently."

"That's not fair."

"Neither is being Master of Cardalba for the rest of my life."

"What about the others, then?" Ron asked after another long pause. "What about our alleged sister's kid?"

"It's like I told you before," Lew managed between sniffles. "Grandma won't say a word except that she regrets the words she *has* said. And there is absolutely no way I can find out a thing. She *sleeps* with shields up. Even Uncle Dion hasn't got a clue what to do about her."

Ron's eyes narrowed suddenly. "Ah, but *you* do, don't you? Maybe nothing she's said, but just intuition that might be more than intuition. Is that it? Is that why you want to leave? Not to go to school—though I'm sure you'll do that—but to look for the other heir? *Somebody* has to pass on our version of the Luck, after all, and God knows *we* can't."

"Shouldn't. There's a big difference."

"I'm not bringing a child into the world to be part of *this* crap!" Ron spat vehemently. "That's for damned sure! Never mind that there's an even chance he'd go crazy even if I tried to protect him. Shoot, we might be crazy ourselves, if we only knew."

"We probably are."

"Yeah."

"So . . . where does this leave us?"

"I don't know."

"But I *need* to know, Ronny. I at least need to know you'll think about it."

"Of *course* I'll think about it," Ron snarled, unable to restrain himself any longer. He leapt to his feet and stalked toward the door. "I haven't got any choice *but* to think about it, now, do I? I've seen my beloved brother reduced to tears over a decision he made out of a sense of misplaced nobility. And now he's determined to guilt-trip me for the rest of my life!"

"Ronny!"

"Fuck off," Ron shouted, wrenching the door open. "I'm gonna go *think*, okay? I'm gonna *think* for a bloody long time. But I'm fucking well not going to do it under your roof!"

"Ronny, I—"

"Shut up!" Ron screamed. *"Just shut up!"* And with that, he strode into the hall, slammed the door, and flipped the latch behind him.

Before Lew could unlock it, Ron—still barefoot and shirtless—was already into the kitchen and heading for the short corridor that led to the carport. His brother would not follow him now, but he locked the outside door anyway, leapt into the Centauri, and turned on the ignition. An instant later he roared out into the starlit night. Lew wanted him to think about things, huh? Well, by God, he would— in the only way he *could* think about such things: while blasting down a highway.

Unfortunately, while time and anger had burned off most of his buzz, that same stress-born adrenaline that had soaked up the alcohol in his system sufficiently to allow him to carry on moderately coherent conversation was still pouring into his veins without letup. Which had the net effect of producing quite another sort of high—and one potentially far more lethal.

Ron had a self-destructive side   probably all Listeners did; possibly as a side effect of their enhanced mental and physical abilities, or perhaps simply a flirtation with that actual insanity that oft times afflicted them. But whatever it was, it sent him racing down the Welch County roads faster and more recklessly than he had ever dared. Oddly enough, his deep brain, the part that controlled reflexes, was calm—hyperfocused, even. He noticed every bump in the road and twitch of the steering wheel, and responded to them instantly; could feel the big tires and electronically controlled suspension rams feeding him information about traction through the seat of his pants, and was not concerned. He could see the road as if it were day, feel the cool hiss of breeze as it tumbled past the lowered roof and windows to dance around his bare shoulders, hear the thunder of the CD player thumping out Jethro Tull's "Broadsword," all with almost supernatural clarity. But he was utterly without fear, utterly without regard for the uncountable man-hours of hand-formed metal he was risking, or the lives of those whose lesser vehicles he screamed past at over a hundred miles an hour. He had never really let the car have its head, after all, and now seemed as good a time as any. Maybe if he was lucky, something sufficiently traumatic would happen to make his decision for him. And in any event, even if his action (or overreaction, a part of him reminded him) didn't make Lew think again about his preposterous request, maybe he could find out something about the car.

Like its top end.

He was entering the longest straight in Welch County now: the one that bisected Swanson's Meadow, where an enigmatic traveling tinker called the Road Man had once made camp and taught him the mysteries of metal—and other secrets besides. So what better place to put his foot down and let the culmination of all that training fly? Maybe that final adrenaline rush would restore his reason enough for him to think rationally about Lew's request. Or maybe he shouldn't do anything this stupid at all.

But it was only raw fury that was in control when he saw the straight line up before him and stomped the accelerator to the floor.

Frantically spinning turbochargers immediately spooled up another notch, electronic overrides disengaged. Already cruising at over a hundred, the car began to gather speed. One-twenty . . . one twenty-five . . . one-thirty: all these barriers he breached in the first quarter of the two-mile straight. One-forty . . . one-fifty . . . one fifty-five. The rate of acceleration was decreasing now, as the inferior aerodynamics of open cars began to become a limiting factor. One-sixty, and there he stayed for the last half mile before he had no choice but to slow for the intersection at the end.

But which way now? Left went to Cordova. Right . . . well, that way led, among other places, away. Back to Athens, where Lew could never follow him, where Wendy would eventually catch up with him.

Should he, or . . . ?

What the hell? There was more open road between here and there than between here and Cordova. Which meant more time in which to calm himself enough to make a decision. Barely touching the brakes in obedience to the stop sign at the north-south intersection, he swung the wheel hard right. Tires screeched, brakes shrieked, and both produced smells he did not like, as gravel spat and ground. The needle on the temperature gauge, which heretofore had remained rock-steady, began to angle upward.

But so was the road, and curves were becoming more frequent.

He carved through them like an expert, shifting the automatic down two or even three gears by hand to keep the torque curve where he wanted it, inching the speed ever upward, while half a dozen halogen headlights illuminated raw rocks, treetops, and guardrails in rapid succession.

He was nearing the gap now—almost to that barrier beyond which Lew would not go. And he still had not decided.

The car chose for him. Or the road did. Or Fate. With less than a half mile remaining, he swung around a particularly blind right turn . . .

. . . And saw, blasted free of color by his high beams and standing stock-still smack in the center of his lane, the largest buck deer he had ever seen. And the whitest.

Fortunately, his reactions were faster than his realization, and he managed to avoid the beast—but only by standing on the brakes with all his might and launching the car into a sideways skid around it—which in turn resulted in a full spin a hundred yards beyond. His main impressions were of bits of landscape flashing by, of the tortured squeal of expensive tires being shreaded, and of the steering wheel bucking in his hands.

He was completely across the road now (fortunately no one was coming), and arrowing straight for the guardrail on that side.

When—unbelievable luck—he glimpsed an opening there: a gap that gave onto what looked like the overgrown remnants of an earlier road that had been abandoned when the new highway he had so flamboyantly exited had straightened out a curve.

He had just enough control to aim for it, and just enough fortune to make it through—though he heard metal scrape as he passed the rail, and felt any number of solid objects thump against the bellypan as momentum carried him down among the trees. He fought the wheel with success enough to stay on the track, but the brakes were gone—apparently something had severed the lines. The upshot was that he found himself pointing downhill and rapidly gathering momentum. He geared down as low as he could and yanked up on the parking brake, but to no avail.

And then the trail dipped more sharply, and there was nothing ahead but leaves.

A jolt, a bounce, a sickening metallic crunch as something tore loose up front, and then he was back in clear air, and trees were everywhere—*big* ones.

The car fit neatly into the gap between the first two.

And—blessedly, for the sake of all that handmade bodywork—the front crossmember exactly matched the height of the stump beyond, which worked more effectively than any brake ever could.

Ron pitched forward against the belts, but took no real damage beyond bruising his chest and biting his tongue. But the impact jarred a dead branch from the thicker tree—which grazed the side of his head as it plummeted down—straight into the cellular phone, which it smashed to flinders.

Ron saw galaxies for a moment, and then he balanced for a long, sick moment between dark and light.

Light won, though its victory proved transitory. But all Ron could think of was the little bottle of Glenlivet in the glove box. With all the stars of summer twinkling down between the branches of the bracketing pines, he had just enough lucidity left to guzzle half its contents before dousing his headlights and passing out completely.

It was stupid, a part of him knew, but it had been a day full of stupid things.

When he dragged himself back to groggy consciousness sometime later, it was to blink dumbly through the bug-smeared windshield at the dark woods beyond. And then he shut his eyes abruptly, deciding he was still in the midst of a dream. For he could have sworn that not a yard beyond the end of his leaf-shrouded hood, an enormous deer had been standing.

A pure white buck with a twelve-point rack.

But when he looked again, it was gone.

Chapter 12

Morning Has Broken

Keycutter Knob
Morning

Ron didn't know if it was rain, pain, or the machinations of a six-inch tall silver warrior that prodded him back to consciousness. But whichever it was, he became aware of all three more or less simultaneously, as he blinked into the green-tinged light of a drizzly woodland dawn.

And wished he hadn't—because the little he could make out through wisps of drifting fog and whatever liquid was trickling into his eyes brought back the preposterous stupidity of his conduct the night before with numbing force. They had all been true!—the nightmare images that had haunted him through what a glance at the Centauri's chronometer told him was close to seven hours of stupor. He really *was* in the woods. The car really *was* listing at a precarious nose-down angle, its doors wedged soundly between the scaly trunks of two pines, with its expensive front fascia inches from another. But at least there were no obvious dents, no clearly crumpled metal. No hopelessly shattered windscreen.

Another itchy-eyed blink showed a splattering of rain-drops on the steeply raked glass ahead of him, and spar-kling beads of the same among the leaves on the well-waxed hood—which he now connected with a persistant cold prickling across his bare arms, head, and shoulders. And another (accompanied, as had been its brethren, by flashes of pain behind his retinas and an intensifying of the already potent pounding in the back of his skull) revealed that the top of his right hand was indeed under determined assault by the silver spear wielded by one of the miniature metal warriors that had somehow come adrift from the crutch—which itself had gotten free from the package shelf and now rested in the passenger's footwell beside him.

He scowled at that, and had to blink twice more before he determined that the manikin *was* still attached to its anchor, just not very well; and was not, in fact, func-tioning as a sovereign entity, as it and its crucible-mates had once or twice been known to do. Or at least that's the way he remembered it: how, five years ago, when his cousin Anson had been on the verge of clubbing him to death with that same crutch while he lay semi-conscious on the floor of Cardalba Hall, he had wished so fervent-ly for those figures to quicken and assail his tormen-tor that they had. Yeah, that was the *recollection*, but the only living person who could confirm it was both absent and blessed with blanks in her memory, courtesy of Lew. As for himself . . . well, conventional science said that such things could not be; therefore, they had not been. Except that *he* wasn't so sure, not with what he knew about Luck, the power of will (especially Listener will), and the properties of certain obscure alloys. The only thing that was definite now was that the warrior he was peering at wasn't where he had affixed it, but was still attached closely enough to where it ought to be that it *might* merely have loosened accidentally; that it *was* poking him in the hand every time the breeze brushed its voluminous cast-silver cloak—and that it did not seem to have quite the expression he remembered sculpting there.

On the other hand, he hadn't really examined it closely in quite a while.

Nor, apparently—as he confirmed when he finally dared a glance in the rearview mirror—had he attended to his own appearance in some time either.

There were leaves in his hair, to start with; and that same hair was sticking out in wild tufts like Harpo Marx's, where it wasn't being flattened by occasional deposits of halfhearted shower or already matted to the side of his head by what looked very much like dried blood—which latter might be connected to the tree limb he dimly remembered thwacking him when he first arrived, which now made a gray-barked bridge between the console and the passenger door. Nor was his face any great treat: puffy, with dark circles under bloodshot eyes, and telltale stains across his chin that he suspected were residual vomit. As for the rest—well, he stank of sour food, sweat, and breweries, and the white jeans that appeared to be his sole garment were crusted with more of the same foul-smelling yellow/green crud that had mere hours before been his brother's magnificent buffet. They were ripped and muddy, too; and his fly was open. All he could conclude from the available evidence was that he must somehow have climbed out of the car and chosen the worst briar patch in the woods as ground zero for a whizz. He didn't remember it, however, as he didn't remember a bloody *lot* of things.

He was, in short, as much a wreck as the car.

And that didn't even count the games his conscience was playing—games that told him how stupid he'd been to risk other people's lives and property simply because he'd gotten pissed at his brother for what was actually a perfectly reasonable request. Games that told him he'd treated Wendy really badly by running off like he had without notice. That said he was a fool to even consider the intriguing Brandy Wallace as any *more* than intriguing.

That told him he was now going to have to spend days repairing the physical and psychological damage less than an hour had wrought.

So what did he do now? Well, the *first* order of business, obviously, was to free the car sufficiently to give it a thorough going-over and then get the hell out of there. As best he remembered, the brakes had gone out; he'd careened through the bushes for a while, collecting bashes on the bottom along the way; and then he'd impacted something low-down hard enough to halt further progress. If he was lucky, whatever it was had caught the front crossmember, not the more delicate mechanisms behind it. And if he was *extremely* fortunate, the brake glitch would prove nothing worse than a line severed when whatever it was had struck the underbody. He crossed his fingers and prayed that a bit of finagling with duct tape and spare brake fluid would suffice to see him to town.

If he could get the blessed beast running. Holding his breath, he closed his eyes and twisted the ignition key—and was immediately rewarded by a familiar hum. But when he shifted into reverse, the rear tires merely spun on the loose pine straw, and the fronts didn't seem inclined to do anything at all beyond grinding noisily when he moved the steering wheel—which meant that the forward drive section was out. The brake pedal, of course, went straight to the floor.

So what now? Well, phoning for aid wouldn't work, for the simple reason that the cellular job on the console was now in about half a dozen pieces. "And it's all *your* fault!" Ron spat to the perpetrator of the destruction as he gave it the heave-ho out of the cockpit. He did not want to think what might have happened if that chunk of wood had smacked his skull directly. He'd have survived, of course; the Luck wouldn't let him off the hook so easily and would have lighted right in to fixing him. But the result would not have been pretty—or explicable—for quite a while, and pain was pain regardless.

Which put him back to his original query: What now? The best thing, he supposed, was to fumble his way back to the highway and see if he could flag down a ride into town.

And then . . . what? Probably he should simply call Wendy, agree to collect her and Matty Groves somewhere besides Cardalba Hall, and get the hell back to Athens in a rental car. They could always retrieve the Toyo later—or buy a new one. And enough cash in the right pockets would easily get the Centauri trailered down. All of which presumed Wendy was still speaking to him, which might not be the case. Had Ron not been so muddleheaded yet so excruciatingly cognizant of the pain Listening imparted to those who assayed it with less than perfect mental clarity, he might have tried to check up on her that way—or more properly, in light of her lack of Voice, tried to Hear someone who was interacting with her. And then . . . again, what?

Well, if he split without giving Lew a reply, that would in itself be a answer—one that would further damage already deteriorating relations with someone he truly did love. Besides, Lew could still guilt-trip him: through letters, through phone calls. Through certain *other* means he also had at his disposal—like dreams. The first two Ron could circumvent, the others he could not. And he knew Lew, if pushed, might be desperate enough to try that: to mutter imprecations at him in the night like some kind of disembodied Jewish mom. All of which would have sounded like preposterous paranoia had Ron not known from bitter experience what lengths desperate Listeners could be driven to.

Which had nothing whatever to do with the problem at hand. Sighing, he levered himself backward out of the seat and onto the top boot, then swung his legs past the trunk of that side's pine and over the side. In spite of its carpet of damp needles, the ground hurt his feet, and he guessed he had bruised them in the night. Why he had gone off as he had, shirtless and barefoot, when he had no replacements in the car, he had no idea. His knee hurt, too, but whether that was due to damage or the weather, he couldn't tell. Happily, it had stopped drizzling, but he raised the windows and top anyway, before beginning his inspection.

A cursory glance at the tightly stuck doors showed only scratches and minor gouges, which nevertheless would require a repaint. And a more involved scrutiny under the back (the inversion this entailed made his head ache even worse) revealed a huge dent on the bellypan just inside the left-hand frame rail—which coincided neatly with the brake lines, which ran close together there. Both had been severed, and fluid made a dark, oily stain on the leaves and grass underneath. Blessedly, it looked to be a fairly simple repair.

If there was no other debilitating damage.

Another sigh, and he rose—too quickly, so that his head pounded and his vision darkened abruptly, full of stars and comets. He wondered, dimly, if he might not have a concussion, but didn't worry: Luck would see to that soon enough. It always did. Dammit.

So what now? Well, a break in the mist showed him to be at the terminus of what appeared to be an abandoned bit of highway leading back to the newer one he had abdicated some indeterminate time—and distance—before. He supposed he could make his way up it and so win back to civilization. Assuming there was anyone in Georgia foolish enough to pick up a dirty, half-naked, wild-haired bum.

But maybe there was another alternative, for a shift in the wind brought him the staccato blat of something mechanical working at closer remove. And given his physical state, he was more inclined to walk downhill than up. So it was, then, that before he was consciously aware of the decision, he had grabbed his crutch and was limping from tree to tree downhill.

The woods became wilder almost immediately, the terrain much rockier and more rugged. Inclines became banks, valleys became stony defiles. The pines that before had been impressive but not remarkable in either height, configuration, or girth were abruptly hulking hardwood giants straight out of the Pleistocene. Moss was everywhere—or everywhere that ferns and laurel and azaleas were not. And the few leafy crowns he could make out through the hazy light, the drifting fog, and the steady drip of residual rain looked to be at least a hundred feet above his head. The others he did not dare estimate save that they were surely records—or would have been had their existence been known, which he suspected was not the case. The taint of Welchness was everywhere. Maybe there *was* something hereditary to Lew's green thumb.

For perhaps a mile he made his way through that odd backwater of landscape—and then, abruptly, found himself once more confronting civilization.

He emerged from the dripping woods directly behind a house trailer: a ten-foot-wide, two-bedroom job, if the stubbiness was any indication. Old, too, to judge by the rust stains marking the faded paint. He wondered who had installed such a monstrosity here, and frowned. Certainly no Welch County native would *ever* have lived in such straits for longer than it took to acquire proper housing—the county was *that* prosperous. Which meant that it almost had to be a flatlander, some refugee from Atlanta or Florida mucking up the scenery like they always did: sticking in temporary structures while their showplaces were a-building on the ridgelines; building *there* so they could get a view—and everyone in the valleys could gaze upon their prosperity rendered into wood and glass and stone, and be amazed.

But what mattered *now* was that whoever called this place home would almost certainly have a phone. Only . . . who would he call? Not Lew; he simply did not have the fizz to deal with his brother at the moment, nor Wendy either, in the odd event she should answer Lew's phone. But there had to be *someone* about, someone he knew from high school, perhaps . . . someone like Victor Wilcy. Yeah, he'd give old Vic a buzz and con him into a lift into town. Then he'd get a motel, get cleaned up, find someone to go collect Wendy and the cat, and then get on with his life.

He was just starting to formulate an explanation when he passed the trailer's western corner. And caught his breath.

Before him stretched a level area of easily two acres—skimmed with mud and enclosed by trees on three sides; and with the fourth, northern, exposure open because it was a precipitous rock that overlooked more woods and, maybe a quarter mile away, a finger of lake. More mountains rose opposite, and a well-used dirt road snaked off to the left.

But what had drawn Ron's eye lay straight ahead—in the form of the partially completed superstructure of what he knew instantly would someday be a quite remarkable building. In fact, it looked from here as if the cinderblock facade *was* finished, at least in its major elements. Roughly sixty feet across, with the middle third set back several feet and faced with square pillars capped with semi-circular arches that continued the line of the outer walls, and with a round-topped opening visible, beyond which would probably be the front door, the place reminded him very much of a Moorish palace. And the comparison was not lessened by the presence near the outer ends of the flanking wings-cum-towers of narrow, Gothic-style windows, or by evidence of crenelation along the crests of all visible walls. Eventually it would be cased in stone, or so he gathered; for he could see sections where rock had been set against the blocks—probably as studies in technique.

He wondered, blearily, who could possibly be building such a folly. And then he knew.

But even before the name could register, he got visual confirmation in the form of a slender figure who chose that exact moment to stride purposefully around the southwestern tower with a jackhammer in her hand—which she proceeded to rinse down with a convenient water hose.

It was Brandy Wallace: absolutely, and without a doubt, right down to her inky mane and buckskin shirt. And this close to her until-then-apocryphal fantasy, Ron couldn't help but be impressed by the scope of her ambition. Brandy Hall—if she ever got it done—would be absolutely huge: easily thirty-six hundred square feet, if not more. Which made it a lot easier to understand why she was so intent on saving money by doing the work herself. Shoot, the place was already darn near as big as Cardalba Hall, and Ron suddenly found himself wondering what one woman alone could possibly want with so much space. Maybe she had a lot of friends, or a big family—parents, say, who were old and wanted to retire to the mountains. Or perhaps she just dreamed big.

So what should he do now? Before, he'd had little compunction about presenting himself to whatever outlander was inhabiting the eyesore and begging to use the phone. *Before*, he'd simply assumed that whoever it was would not know him.

But he *did* know Brandy Wallace, *definitely* wanted to see her again, and more to the point, was interested in making a good impression on her when he did, if for no other reason than to get the lowdown on this preposterous dwelling. The latter did not seem likely while in his current state of disarray.

Which meant, he supposed, it was time he did what he should have done in the first place, and trudged back up the mountain in search of the main road.

He had actually turned to do exactly that when he felt, rather than saw, Brandy's eyes shift toward him. "Ho!" she hollered. "Who're you?" Then, when he had spun back around and squinted in her direction, "Oh, good God, you're him! . . . The guy with the crutch! . . . I mean, you're Ronny Dillon!" And then, with wider eyes and increasing alarm: "But . . . but what the hell's *happened* to you? Are you all right?"

These last words rang progressively louder because Brandy was running toward him as she bellowed them. They made his head hurt, too, and too late he realized that his shields were down and that the intensity of Brandy's concern (which was also mixed with a certain amount of anger at having her day's work interrupted so early on, and with several other emotions he couldn't make out, nor wanted to) was ringing through his head like a gong.

With sufficient force, in fact, that it made him quite light-headed.

Before he knew it, he was sitting on the ground with his bum leg straight out before him and a very pale-faced woman kneeling at his side.

"Hello," he managed, attempting a smile, though her face was deadly serious and her eyes like ink. "Sorry to drop by like this, but I sort of had a car wreck last night, and—"

"So *that's* what all that commotion up in the woods was!" she interrupted with a snort. "I nearly went up there with my shotgun."

"I think I'd have welcomed someone to put me out of my misery," Ron countered with a groan, bending forward to rest his head on his knees as he fought to banish his headache, regain control of his senses, and fight down a strong urge to puke.

Brandy's nose wrinkled—justifiably, Ron knew. "You've been drinking," she stated flatly. "Last night." But at least there was no accusation in her voice. "This morning, I should say," she amended, producing a bandanna from her jeans and using it to scour his chin. "You had beer at the party; this smells stronger."

"Thanks," Ron mumbled, in response to her attentions. "And yeah, I guess I was. I got mad at my brother and . . ." He stopped in midsentence, on the verge of blurting out what was, after all, a *very* personal matter to an utter stranger. "Forget it," he finished lamely. "I don't want to foist my problems off on you—'specially when you're obviously busy. If you can point me to a phone, I'll be out of your hair in thirty minutes."

Brandy regarded him seriously. "Well, you can certainly use the phone if you want to. But no way I'm sending you out of here in the shape you're in. I don't know what you did, but you obviously need to take it easy for a while. So how 'bout you get in that trailer and take a shower, and I'll cook you some breakfast? I usually wear men's shirts, so I've probably got one around that'll fit you. As for your britches . . . well, they look like hell, but I'm afraid you're stuck with 'em, unless you want to rinse 'em off, toss 'em out, and let me stick 'em in the dryer."

Ron smiled wanly up at her, feeling minutely better. "You don't have to. I have no right at all to disturb your work."

Brandy chewed her lip, as if she were resisting agreeing with him. "No, you don't. But as a fellow human being, you have a right to feel as good as you can as fast as you can, and I'm in the best position to ensure that." She spoke quickly, matter-of-factly. Ron was certain she'd react exactly the same to any wounded animal that chanced into her clearing—the same ones she'd shoot under other circumstances. She wasn't being nice to him because he was him, only because he was human and had strayed into her domain.

Which was—he realized—exactly what he'd been wanting.

"Uh, maybe I *will* take you up on that offer," he managed finally. "If you're sure it won't be any trouble."

"Not really," Brandy replied with a shrug. "I need to stir up a bite for myself anyway. I just went out to look at some damage that happened last night, and couldn't stop myself from working on it a bit; and the next thing I know, my tummy's growling, I'm having caffeine withdrawal, and you're standing there looking like something the cat dragged in."

"You have a cat?" Ron asked, to keep the conversation alive.

Brandy shook her head. "I like 'em, but I can't stand the smell of litter boxes. When I get that finished, I'll have a screened area I can keep the box in. Maybe then . . ."

Ron chuckled in spite of himself. "Yeah, I have the same problem." He rose carefully, swaying just a little, but with the crutch to support him. " 'Course, I probably smell *worse* than a litter box right now."

"No comment," Brandy muttered, turning away. "Come on, let's get you going. You need some aspirin, or anything?"

Ron shook his head. "Maybe after the shower—with coffee."

Brandy did not reply, but an instant later, Ron had followed her into the trailer.

It was incredibly cramped in there, he noted at once, though basically well kept. Trouble was, there was simply a huge amount of *stuff* everywhere. Mostly it was art supplies, architecture magazines, and objets d'art— including a number of really first-class wildlife paintings bearing the initials B.W. But there was also a vast quantity of what he could only call "natural" material lurking in the myriad nooks and crannies: things like animal skins, bones, and skulls; odd bits of crystal, rocks, and driftwood; and a wide assortment of Native American crafts; never mind the canned goods and jars of herbs. But there were concessions to modernity, too: a sizable collection of cassettes and CDs, and a moderately large component system, along with a small but obviously brand-new Sony TV. Brandy evidently went first-class whenever she could. Which was a thing he also did: another thing they had in common.

"Shower's in the back just before the bedroom," Brandy called as she turned right into the kitchen. "Towels are in the rack above the john. Use whatever you need. Same for soap and shampoo."

Ron nodded numbly and followed her instructions. A moment later, he had dealt with his jeans and skivvies as instructed and was standing naked in the middle of a turquoise fiberglass bathtub, with a gold and green shower curtain shimmering to his left and a torrent of blessedly hot water pounding down on him. He remained there for a long time, letting the water beat the pain from his head, massage his back and shoulders. He could easily have gone to sleep had a thumping on the door, which coincided with a marked cooling of the spray, not roused him. "Just a sec," he called sheepishly.

"Don't use all the hot water!" Brandy shouted through the flimsy wood. Then, after a moment of fumbling noises: "They're not quite dry yet, but I'll lay your clothes right outside."

"Thanks!" Ron hollered back, and spent the next minute giving himself one final lather and rinsing the leaves from his hair. The water was cold enough to raise goose bumps by the time he stepped out, but the first towel he found—a large red item—quickly put an end to them. He dried hastily, arranged his hair with Brandy's comb, and rummaged in the medicine cabinet for the promised aspirin. He took two, then cracked the door and snagged his clothes. The skivvies were still damp, so he decided to forgo them. The pants, though no better, were more necessary, and a thorough spritzing with Lysol made them marginally presentable olfactorily. After a moment's further consideration, he wadded his underwear into a ball and stuffed them in his pocket. A final assessment in the mirror showed him halfway presentable, if unshaven. *It'll have to do*, he told himself—and padded up the hall toward the kitchen.

Brandy's back was toward him, but he scarcely noticed, so intoxicated was he by the cooking odors. All his favorites: coffee (some kind of gourmet blend, by the smell of it), bacon, eggs, oatmeal with more than the usual amount of cinnamon. "There's a shirt on the sofa for you," she called. "I hope you like bacon and oatmeal. Or if bacon's too greasy, I could—"

"It'll be fine," Ron assured her, retrieving a neatly folded khaki work shirt from the well-worn beige vinyl couch. It was one size too small, but acceptable if he rolled up the sleeves and left the tail out. Fortunately, he still retained most of his adolescent slenderness. "I feel a thousand times better already."

Brandy had set out breakfast by then—had cleared exactly enough space from the overladen kitchen table for two plates, two mugs, and a pair of bowls.

"You'll have to serve yourself from the stove," she told him flatly. "Oh, and do you take sugar in your coffee—or cream?"

"Neither, usually; both right now," he replied, appropriating the nearer plate and helping himself to several slices of bacon and an industrial-size dollop of oatmeal.

Brandy followed his example, save that she heaped her plate even fuller and included scrambled eggs. Ron wondered how she kept her figure if she ate like that. Probably it was all that physical labor. Aerobics with a purpose, so to speak.

The food was excellent, but the first few moments of their meal passed in awkward silence, as each seemed disinclined to initiate conversation. Finally Ron spoke, if for no other reason than to ease the growing tension. "That's a mighty impressive piece of architecture you've got goin' there," he observed through a mouthful of oatmeal. "You're not a bit shy when it comes to thinking big, are you?"

Brandy paused with her fork halfway to her mouth. "A dream that's not big isn't worth having," she replied promptly. "That's what my dad always said. I'm pretty much his child, I guess," she added more softly.

Ron looked up at her and raised an eyebrow curiously. "Wanta tell me about him?"

She would not meet his gaze. "He . . . was full of ideas he didn't know how to realize, and it made him unhappy. Eventually it killed him."

"How?" But then Ron caught the bitterness on her face. "Sorry, it's none of my business."

Brandy bit her lip. "No, it's . . . not," she began forcefully. But then her voice faltered and Ron could have sworn her eyes were misting. "But . . . maybe it's good for me to talk about it," she continued slowly. "He—just walked into the woods one day during hunting season and never came back. It was a week before my brother found him."

"Brother?"

"Tommy. He's got one more year of college. Gonna be a forest ranger."

"Sisters?"

"None."

"Your mom?"

A shrug. "Making it. I hope to bring her out here when I get this place finished—if she lasts that long."

Ron tried to grimace away his embarrassment. "Oh Christ, don't tell me . . ."

"She's got cancer. Forty-five years old, and dying of cancer."

"Jeeze!"

Brandy did not reply.

Ron could think of nothing appropriate to say. More food was eaten. "You, uh, mentioned something about having a problem with the house?" he ventured at last.

"Trouble with the foundation, actually," Brandy replied with a grim eagerness that Ron took as relief at being on less personal ground—continuing for several minutes with more detail than he was really in the mood for, though he tried very hard to appear interested.

Ron concluded his meal by draining his coffee. "Need any help?" he asked, when Brandy had finished.

She shot him the coldest glare he'd ever received. *"No."*

"Sorry," Ron apologized quickly, wondering how he was supposed to know what was kosher to ask and what wasn't. "I was *only* curious."

Her expression softed the merest bit. "It's okay. I'm just . . . really wired about being behind. I don't like to fail, to start with; and I absolutely *hate* wasting time, which is what rebuilding is."

Ron nodded sagely. "True."

Brandy pointed her fork toward the remaining oatmeal. "Want any more?"

Ron shook his head. "I'm fine. That was good."

"Glad you liked it." She rose, picked up her plate, and headed toward the sink.

"Need any help with the dishes?"

"I've got a dishwasher."

Ron pushed back from the table and folded his arms across his chest, staring at her speculatively. "It's gonna be quite a change for you, isn't it? When you move, and all. I mean these are pretty tight quarters, you've got to admit."

"So they are."

"So why is that? I mean I know you want to take care of your mom, but—"

"I want to start an artist's colony."

Ron leaned forward, genuinely intrigued. "Oh *yeah*?"

Dishes rattled. "Yep. Like Rivendell in Tolkien. Kind of a sanctuary where my artist friends can come and hang out and do their own thing. I'd give 'em a roof, as much space as I can, and whatever food I can spare. And they'd do odd jobs for me and pursue their bliss until they could get on their feet."

"Artists only?"

Brandy grunted noncommittally and continued loading the dishwasher. "Artists, poets, playwrights—you name it."

Ron's forehead wrinkled thoughtfully. "What was that you said about bliss?"

She shut the appliance door, pushed a pair of buttons, then turned to face him, leaning against the sink. "Ever hear of Joseph Campbell?"

"Sure."

"So you know what he said, then? About following your bliss? About doing the one thing that means most in the world to you; the one thing that you're absolutely supposed to do, the one thing you'll never be happy unless you *are* doing."

Ron nodded. "Yeah. I've heard all that. *Exactly* that, in fact."

Brandy raised an eyebrow. "Oh *yeah*?"

"Heard it from a guy who was doing it, as a matter of fact."

"And . . . ?"

Ron sighed. "It's a long story—and you said you were short on time."

"So stretch yourself: give me a short answer."

Ron grinned ruefully. "Touché. Okay, then, I heard it from somebody I only knew as the Road Man."

Her eyes narrowed. "Strange old tinker, wanders around with a bunch of goats and crazy machines, preaching and stuff?"

"That's him. You ever meet him?"

"Nope. Just heard a little about him from a friend one time. She said he wasn't reliable. Said all he wanted to do was spout nonsense and have sex—not necessarily in that order."

"Sounds like him," Ron chuckled, recalling the brief time he'd spent as the enigmatic tinker's so-called apprentice. "Cleaving, he called it."

"Huh?"

"Sex. He called it cleaving. He—" Ron broke off when he saw the warning flash in Brandy's eyes. "So," he appended quickly, realizing he was on sensitive ground, and seeking a less controversial topic, "why a castle, in particular—beyond the thing for Tolkien, I mean?"

"Better you should ask why medieval."

Ron folded his arms and leaned back in his chair. "Okay, then: why medieval?"

"Because on the one hand, almost everything that exists in Western society comes from there," Brandy shot back immediately. "And while I've got Indian blood, too, it's . . . different. My main influences in my formative years were European. At the peak of the Middle Ages there was a vast amount of art being done—art I can identify with both through my roots and through fantasy. But there's another thing, too, I guess," she continued.

Ron lifted an eyebrow expectantly.

"You . . . had to *think* about things then," she said. "There was no mass production to separate customer and crafts-man. If you wanted a shirt, you didn't go down to Kmart and pick your favorite color and fabric and size; you merry well had to shear the sheep, then spin the yarn, weave the cloth, and dye it yourself; and then cut it so you didn't waste anything, and try to come up with some way to decorate it that didn't cost the earth. And it had to last a bloody long time 'cause of all that labor, so you had damned well better know what you wanted before you started. Same way with everything: houses, furniture, spoons—saddles, you name it."

"Ever hear of William Morris?"

"Of course."

"He a hero of yours?"

"Of course. So are Wright and Fuller."

"Gaudi?"

"Too free-form. Too organic."

"Soleri?"

"Big dreamer. Bigger than me, even."

Ron fell silent, his usually far more extensive (and reliable) mental file of radical socialists-artists-architects having suddenly deserted him.

Brandy regarded him solemnly for a moment, arms folded across her chest in exactly the same pose he had affected earlier. "You've got something special, you know," she whispered. "I can see it in that car of yours."

Ron couldn't resist a grin. "Oh *yeah*?"

"Passion," she stated flatly. "You've got the same passion for metalwork I have for my house. And to judge from the figures I saw on that crutch of yours, you've got the same feel for myth as well. That's a bloody rare combination." She stared at him for a moment longer, gnawing her lip. He lifted his brows expectantly. Trying to appear receptive, guileless . . .

"I have a . . . I guess you could call it a proposition to make," Brandy went on while Ron was trying to decide if he *ought* to say something or not. "I guess you can tell I'm a pretty independent person. I don't like owing favors, and I *hate* having to be dependent on other people—especially when it comes to something as important as my house. I don't like delegating authority, and I'm prone to sudden changes of mood. I've got a temper like a mama bear in the springtime, and I'm a perfectionist like you've never seen. But I also think you're as close to a kindred spirit as I'm likely to find anytime soon, so . . . if for some odd reason you'd be willing to completely subvert your ego, I really would like for you to work for me.

"I *know* we talked about this yesterday," she went on relentlessly, "and I *know* you don't want to stay up here, and I *know* I have no right to ask you to—but would you maybe consider at least establishing a *sub*studio here on the knoll? I can rig up a tent or rent another trailer, or something; and you could stay there when you needed to—and have a forge, of course. That way you could do your thing, and I'd be right here to supervise without losing too much of my own work time. How does that sound?"

Ron hardly knew how to reply. A great deal of it sounded exactly like what he wanted, especially given that he'd made no plans for postgraduation employment at all. On the other hand, the whole concept was rife with potential problems, not the least of which was the fact that he had no desire to turn a brief visit into a summer-long incarceration. But would it really *be* incarceration? he wondered. Not if he was doing art. Not if he was working with someone like Brandy.

The corners of her mouth twitched, as if to prompt him.

Ron grimaced helplessly, shrugged, and somehow managed to stammer out a reply. "Uh, well, *jeeze!* I mean— well, I guess it sounds just great! Except . . . that I'm still not sure I could stand to stay up here as much as that would require."

"Why not?"

"Because . . . I have a lot of bad memories from Welch County, for one thing," he replied slowly. "It may be the Promised Land for you, but it's not for me. And besides . . ."

"What?"

"Well, I've got a *girlfriend*, mainly. I don't have a *clue* what she'd say about me suddenly deciding to hang around here for a while—never *mind* if I was spending a lot of time back in the woods with another woman."

Brandy mirrored his scowl. "This would be strictly a *business* arrangement, Ronny. And in any event, it's all hypothetical at the moment anyway, since you haven't given me an answer. I really *could* use you, though; I'll be honest about that. But I also know that I may be asking you to change a lot of plans you've already made, so I can't expect a yes or no just like that."

Ron smiled wanly. "I appreciate your honesty."

"You're the first man who has, then," she shot back fiercely. "Now, didn't you say something about needing to get back to your car? I truly can't spare the time to help you fix it, but you can use the phone here to call a wrecker. Or I can lend you some tools and give you a lift back up there, if you think that'll suffice."

Ron could only roll his eyes and shrug. "I have no way of knowing until I do some prowling. But I'd *prefer* to get back under my own power. It's less ignominious that way."

"So you're a control freak, too?"

He cocked an eyebrow wryly. "I guess I am."

Brandy strode toward the door. "Tools are in the shed out back; we'd best get going. How'd you happen to run off the road, anyway?" she added conversationally.

Ron sighed. "The long version is that I had an argument with my brother. The short version is that I nearly hit a deer—a big white buck, as matter of fact—with antlers. Strangest thing."

Brandy froze in place and stared at him askance. "Perhaps," she whispered in a tone that did not encourage further inquiry, "it was an omen."

Yeah, Ron told himself. *Perhaps it was.* He wondered, though, whether for good or ill.

Chapter 13

Fixing a Hole

Keycutter Knob
Late morning

Poor guy, Brandy was reflecting with considerable consternation as she gave the steering wheel a sharp tug to the right and sent her pickup jolting off the glassy pavement and onto the rutted track that sneaked down to her spread. *Poor trashed-out Ronny Dillon.*

She was surprised at her concern, too, because the smug young metalworker hadn't impressed her at all when she'd first been introduced to him back at the keg; nor—in spite of their sprightly conversation—much more on their second encounter in the parking lot. But somehow, this morning, when he'd come limping out of the forest all pitiful and bedraggled, with his rich-boy arrogance as tattered as his jeans, she'd had a change of heart.

She'd have to watch it, too, or heart would take complete control—which could be disasterous. Business arrangement *only*, she'd stressed when she'd laid out her offer. (And that had also surprised her: making concrete proposals when scant seconds before, the very concepts them-

190

selves had been the most nebulous of speculations.) True, she needed someone around occasionally—someone stronger and more available than Weedge. And Dillon *did* seem to be a kindred spirit—or at least they could talk creativity well together, liked some of the same food, and held similar regard for cats. But did she truly want someone hanging around as much as she might require, much less some footloose proto-yuppie land baron who, because of his sex, education, and station, was doubtlessly used to having his own way all the time?

Jeeze! First Van Vannister and now this!

Still, she couldn't help but chuckle when she recalled how preposterous Dillon had looked staggering out of the woods like a genuine medieval wild man, with his pants ripped, his face begrimed and bloody, and leaves sticking out of his hair. Or come to it, how silly he'd looked twisting around under the tail of his car with his butt (and a nice tight one it was, she had to admit) poking up in the air. "I can fix it," he'd assured her. "It'll only take about ten minutes, but I'd appreciate it if you could at least hang around that long, in case I'm wrong and things *are* screwed up major league and I need to phone somebody. Or"—he'd paused and peered up at her hopefully—"like maybe you could give me a tow?"

She'd agreed, in spite of her better judgment—and quickly depleting reserves of disposable time—and had spent what proved to be the next hour and a half fidgeting while he squirmed around beneath the one clearly visible fender with an assortment of wrenches, various kinds of tape, and a veritable miscellany of fittings. The coup de grace had been when he'd emptied a can of brake fluid into the master cylinder, pumped the appropriate pedal, and pronounced the vehicle minimally fit to be towed up to the highway, whence he thought he could nurse it back to his brother's place for proper attention. The front end had made painful grinding sounds as they bounced up what was barely even a trail (a screwed-up forward differential, he'd explained: expensive, but not so much as to preclude driving it the ten or so miles back to Cardalba), but eventually the extraction had been accomplished.

He'd thanked her once where he stood, again when the

ropes had been loosened, and then had returned her tools
and would have dismissed her had she not insisted on
staying put until he was actually under way. Her last
glimpse of him was as a tiny face in the rearview mirror
of a very low-slung and expensive car puttering sedately
down the mountainside as a Buick Roadmaster roared past,
its driver obviously giving him the finger. She'd seen the
brake lights flash once from behind their neutral-density
lenses, but something told her he'd be okay. Or as okay as
his kind ever was. There was nothing wrong with the boy's
car that money couldn't fix. And probably nothing wrong
with him that being broke for a spell wouldn't cure.

And speaking of being broke, she had to get back to
work on the recollapsed foundations pronto or *another* day
would go by with no progress made.

She had not yet lurched around the last turn in her
drive, nor cleared the final screen of projecting laurel,
when her sharp eyes made out a flash of all-too-familiar
red gleaming in the clearing beyond.

"Fuck!" Brandy shouted to the dashboard. For it was the
sight of Vannister's truck ensconsed precisely where he
had parked it yesterday afternoon that had so aroused her
ire. "Jesus Christ!—Doesn't that guy *ever* work? Doesn't
he *ever* mind his fucking job?"

Well, of course he did, her more rational aspect informed
her. He'd been minding it pretty well yesterday morning.
And that afternoon as well.

On the other hand, as best she could determine, he'd
spent roughly a third of his supposed on-duty hours dealing
with her in one capacity or another. Which plainly *wasn't*
the norm. Next thing Mr. Van Vannister knew, he'd find
himself hoofing it to the unemployment line.

Which would serve him right.

Except that she didn't believe that for a moment.

She was still frowning—though whether at the troublesome lumberyard foreman or her own unresolved attitude
toward him was unclear—and still bouncing merrily (if
noisily) along, when she realized she was closer to daylight
than she'd thought, braked hard, and slewed her pickup in
beside his. Tires squealed, gravel crunched, the backend
did a tidy sideways two-step, as she came within a handful

of inches of sideswiping the innocent Mason Hardware Ford. Which was *all* she needed.

She cut the motor with a snap, leapt out, and slammed the door behind her. Where *was* the son of a bitch, anyway? When she found him, she'd give him a piece of her mind, by God! And probably have to spend the *rest* of the day inventorying everything she owned in quest of missing items. Damn him, too. Damn him! *Damn* him! She started toward the trailer, which looked exactly as it had when she'd departed, then paused. Had she heard something? A soft sound over to the left, there in Brandy Hall? Heavy breathing, maybe? Or the sound of denim grating against itself?

Before she knew it, she was running toward the looming pile, leaping stacks of lumber, sidestepping mounds of sand or the odd tool, hose, or concrete block as she went, her mouth set in a thin, grimly determined line. In an instant she had skirted the completed southwest corner—and had gained thereby a clear view of Vannister. He was standing just outside the cursed section of foundation, apparently having just risen from a crouch. Sweat made a sharp V down the back of his coverall, and he held a trowel in his hand on which a glob of gray glistened dully.

She stared at him for a long, confused moment. He looked different—altered, even, from when she'd glimpsed him in passing at the party the night before. His hair was shorter—that was the main thing—and he was now wearing a baseball cap emblazoned with the Mason Hardware logo, and had traded his too tight jeans and provocative T-shirt for a plain blue coverall that likewise bore the Mason Hardware brand. The effect was much more understated, much more modest.

Or would have been had the jumpsuit not been unzipped almost to the navel, displaying to excellent (and no doubt deliberate) advantage a muscular chest thicketed with dark red hair.

A toss of his head presaged Vannister's characteristic grin, and it was then that she realized he was not shorn at all, but had simply bound his existing mane into a ponytail that flowed a good five inches past his collar.

"Mornin', Miss Brandy," Vannister drawled, when she

showed no sign of acknowledging his presence with anything more than a scowl. "I was just on my way to work
and still feelin' kinda bad about yesterday, so I thought
I'd drop off a couple of little items I found lyin' 'round
that it seemed to me you might find useful. And then I
thought I'd take a look-see at these foundations of yours,
and—well, maybe *you'd* better look . . ."

"You ass—" she began. But words failed her as Vannister
casually eased aside so she could see what his body had
been blocking.

When she had first surveyed that stretch of footing
early that morning—which had been the first time she'd
inspected the previous night's damage in clear light—a
good ten-foot section had sagged at least nine inches in
the middle, and cracks had been everywhere. And when
she'd *last* seen it, before her surprise encounter with Ronny
Dillon, she'd barely managed to jackhammer out ten feet
of the waste.

But now that section was gone, along with the awkward augmentations her hasty reengineering had necessitated.

Now there was only one clean, seamless line of masonry,
gleaming gray-white in the late morning light. It was a
masterful job, too. Every mortar line was true, every course
of blocks perfectly square. And there was no trace of stray
concrete, scattered sand, or random trash. It looked, in
short, less like a piece of construction than a work of
minimalist art.

It had also been executed far too well and *far* too quickly
for *anyone* to have done.

What she was gaping at was an impossibility. Yet there
it was: her senses told her that more surely than memory
could protest it had been otherwise.

And Van Vannister was grinning at her like a fool.
"Ass-what?" he wondered innocently. "Ass-istant, maybe?
Ass-ociate? Ass-trologer? Ass-trogator?"

"Ass*hole*, I was *going* to say," Brandy gritted quickly.
"But I see that wouldn't be wise just now."

"And why not—if it's true?"

"It *is* true," Brandy flared, remembering herself; for
whatever Vannister had accomplished here, he had done

so without her bidding. And *that* was intolerable. "Or at least it's true that you messed with my goddamn house without permission!"

"*Messed* isn't exactly the word I'd have chosen," he informed her in his lazy generic drawl. "It's much less a mess now than when I found it."

"But—but how did you *do* all that?" Brandy stammered. "It would've taken me *hours* just to get rid of the old stuff before I could even think of pouring new, never mind reengineering the whole blessed thing *again*. I mean, *really*," she finished, lamely.

"Maybe I've had more practice," Vannister suggested, with yet another cryptic grin, to which he added one of those damnably irritating twinklings of the eye. "Or *maybe* I just understand stone better than you—and what is concrete, after all, but very small stones?"

Brandy could only stare at him dumbfounded. "That doesn't answer my question!"

"No, it doesn't," Vannister acknowledged with a self-satisfied smirk. "But it's as much as I'm gonna tell you! Suffice to say that things don't usually take long if you yank all the wasted time out of 'em, all the time you spend standin' 'round wonderin', 'stead of doin'."

"But it's *impossible!*"

A shrug—and a more serious expression. "Maybe. But you've got the evidence of your senses, so that oughta tell you something about throwing words like 'impossible' around."

Brandy ignored him and spent the next several minutes inspecting his work, pacing the length of the wall and the adjoining ones as well, running her hands along edges, thumping joints to see if they held, occasionally bending over to examine a bit of footing. Finally she stood again, eyes narrowed, hands on her hips. "Okay," she said slowly. "I'll concede you've somehow replaced every bit of damaged structure. And I'll concede that you've done it god-awful fast. But I also notice that all you've *really* done is duplicate the way I'd already built it."

"So I did," Vannister affirmed.

"But *why?*" Brandy cried in exasperation. "All that means is that it'll collapse again!"

Vannister cocked an eyebrow. *"Will* it?"

She glared at him. "Physics doesn't change from day to day, last I heard!"

"Doesn't it?"

She chose to ignore the direction their conversation was tending. "Okay," she said finally. "How do you *know* it won't fall in again?"

" 'Cause *I* made it!" he said simply. " 'Cause I made it exactly right—the way it should've been made all along."

"And how was that?"

A secret smile. "I'll tell you later. Maybe."

"Indeed!"

Vannister's smile became a scowl. "You need proof, don't you? You've just seen what you've seen, but you still need proof!" And without further conversation, he ambled back to his truck.

"You wait there," he hollered, when Brandy would have followed. "You'd best watch this close up."

Brandy sighed, folded her arms, and wished she had a cup of coffee.

A sour sideways glance caught Vannister already in the truck—and then her hackles rose once more. He was rolling toward her, neatly avoiding both natural landscape and the piles of construction litter that made an obstacle course of the knoll. An instant later, he was beside her, and before she could move to stop him, he had driven into the square of foundation and was easing the truck back and forth across the new masonry. At least ten times he did that, each time very slowly, so that the full weight of the big pickup came directly to bear on the fresh work.

And that really was impossible, because even if the work could have been accomplished as quickly as it obviously had, there was absolutely no way the concrete could have set sufficiently in that amount of time to withstand such stress. Shoot, she'd checked it herself just minutes ago and found most of the mortar still moist. Which meant that the whole thing should have gone crashing down.

But it hadn't.

Vannister braked the truck to a stop beside her and stuffed it into park, but left it idling. "Satisfied?" he called from the open window.

"Do I have a choice?" Brandy snorted. "Okay, you've made your point."

"I could set off explosives, if you're not sure. I've got a recipe for Plastique I haven't tried."

"That *won't* be necessary."

"I didn't think it would. But I like my customers to know their options."

"So I'm a *customer*, now?"

"Finest kind!" Vannister grinned, and gunned the engine. In an instant, he had cleared the site.

Brandy was flabbergasted. Christ, but she was losing control of things in a hurry! On the other hand, there was still one card she could play, one way to regain the upper hand.

"What do I owe you?" she called, dashing toward the departing pickup, which was now trundling slowly toward the road.

The truck slowed fractionally, allowing her to catch up, but continued to roll along at a snail-like crawl.

Vannister's head appeared at the window as he brought the truck to a halt again. "Nothing," he replied. "In fact, I almost forgot: I brought *you* something."

An eyebrow lifted skeptically.

Vannister cut the engine and climbed down from the cab, then sauntered to the rear and dropped the tailgate, where, with a grunt and a grimace, he proceeded to haul out two man-long slabs of polished blue-green stone, each as big around as his leg. Brandy first thought they were marble, but a closer inspection proved them to be malachite. She'd never seen so much in one place before. "Don't know what these were doin' at the store," Vannister confided, wiping his hands on his thighs. "But I couldn't find any place *for* 'em, no record *of* 'em, and couldn't think of any good they'd do most folks anyway—so I figured I'd just drop 'em by here, seein' as how you're so creative and all."

"And what am *I* supposed to do with 'em?" Brandy asked airily, trying to mask her awe with cool aloofness. No way she wanted to encourage this big lout—never mind how she'd explain the presence of a king's ransom in semiprecious stone, should anyone have the temerity to ask.

"Search me," Vannister shot back with a laugh. "They just looked more like part of a castle than part of a cabin, which is mostly what folks are building around here nowdays—so I hear."

Brandy was examining the fine, smooth stone. It was beautiful. She'd never seen malachite that brightly colored before and couldn't guess where such material could have come from, never mind what it had cost. "I can't take these," she said. "No way. Uh-uh."

"And why not?"

"Because they're not yours to give away, for one thing—and besides—I don't have any use for 'em."

"You will," Vannister stated flatly.

And then, for no clear reason, given the conversation they were in the middle of, Brandy blurted out the question that had been haunting her ever since she had seen the new construction: "But what was *wrong* with the way *I* did the foundations?"

Vannister shrugged again. "It's like I told you yesterday," he drawled. "You hadn't slaked 'em right."

"And how'd *you* slake 'em?"

"The way you're supposed to slake *any* masonry you want to last," Vannister informed her seriously. "With blood."

He climbed back into the truck, cranked it, and once more began easing forward, gathering speed as he went, so that Brandy had to jog alongside to keep up.

"One last question," she gasped. "Or maybe I oughta call it a proposition."

This time he cut the engine. "I'm listenin'."

"Okay, then," Brandy began breathlessly, "well, I'm probably crazy to do this, but I was just thinking that . . ."

She did not talk very long, but she spoke with great conviction.

Vannister listened intently, eyes ablaze with satisfaction.

Chapter 14

I Had Too Much to Dream

Cardalba Plantation
Noonish

The Centauri was handling like a pig, and something on the engine side of the firewall sounded like a bucket of bolts agitating in an antique washer—both typical symptoms of a forward differential that was self-destructing, as Ron had known it would before he started down the mountain. The steering was bucking like a jackhammer, too; but at least the car was stopping—after a fashion. It took a lot *longer*, of course, and every time he tapped the brake, he held his breath, as each application required a bit more pumping and ended with the pedal closer to the floor. Still, what could one *expect* of hydraulic lines spliced together with plastic tubing and duct tape? If he was lucky (and here he used the conventional definition of that term), he ought to be able to limp back to Lew's intact; and once there, could delve into the damage in earnest. A day's work, he estimated (and maybe a little help from Pep Boys and Western Auto), should put the binders good as new. The front-end glitch would take longer, but he thought he

199

could get the beast sufficiently roadworthy to make it back to Athens by doing some discreet disconnecting.

If only his *personal* problems could be cured by loosening bolts and tightening bearings. If only he could stop dwelling on Brandy and her tempting overture—*and* disconnect himself from worrying about screwing up with Wendy—*and* patch things up with brother Lew—why, then everything *else* would be dandy! Or at least no worse than it had been before his brother's modest proposal sent him hurtling drunkenly into the night.

Which was probably, now he thought on it, really not all that great, either; worrying about one's future never was. It was just that today's crises seemed so much more . . . catastrophic than those of the day before.

But at least he was feeling better. Breakfast plus bath plus Luck had pretty much banished his hangover. And his concerns about concussion were fading with the pain—not that Luck couldn't handle one anyway, given time. He wished he had a cat to scratch, though; wished Matty Groves was curled up in the passenger bucket so that he could chuck him under the chin and hear him purr. That would soothe his nerves, as no amount of Luck, no amount of conditioning, ever had been able.

And he'd have given his *soul* for a set of omens. Unfortunately, he'd stupidly wired the radio into the same circuits as the totaled telephone, so that the destruction of one had effectively disabled the other. Which left him back with the auguries he'd collected already—like "House of the Rising Sun": unexpected reversal of fortune.

Boy, *that* was an understatement! He wondered if these were the interesting times threatened in the ancient Chinese curse.

Oh, he would *try* to do the right thing; that was essentially a given. He would hook up with Wendy back at Cardalba, would apologize to her—to her *and* Lew, better still. And then he would take her aside—maybe for a long walk on the willow-shaded path that followed the Talooga—and then he would simply tell her the truth.

But what *was* the truth? That he loved her? Probably not. Yet having admitted that, it was also true that he *did* love her as much as he loved anyone outside the clan—more, in fact. Only . . . *that* would be getting off the subject and would only start her verbalizing what he already knew: that she loved *him* completely and utterly and—until lately—without one selfish thought. As no other woman ever had or seemed likely to.

No, the thing to do would be to sidestep emotions and lay out the facts one by one.

But suppose Wendy then asked—as was almost certain, because she'd said exactly those same words the few other times his eye had gone roving—"But, Ron, tell me one thing for sure and for real: are you getting interested in this Brandy Wallace person?" What would his response be then?

Well, what if he leveled with her? What if he simply said, "Yeah, I'm interested—but I don't *want* to be, and besides, we haven't *done* anything." What then?

Well, in that case, it would be just like Wendy—the *old* Wendy—to simply smile wanly, sigh wistfully, and tell him that if that's what it took to make him happy, why then, that's what he ought to do. That he shouldn't take *her* into consideration at all.

And she'd be absolutely honest, absolutely self-sacrificingly sincere. And—if she was human—also be lying to herself in her soul of souls, Voice or no.

And *none* of this was taking into account what the new, more assertive, Wendy might do. God, things were complicated!

All of which speculation was getting him nowhere except back to Cardalba far more quickly than he wanted, given that he was rapidly approaching the contemplation/actuation interface—and still hadn't a clue what he really wanted, or even who he wanted to have it out with first.

Lord, what a cad I am! he told himself as he downshifted in lieu of braking for the bridge that led onto the grounds of Lew's plantation. *Lord, what a goddamned selfish bastard!*

He sighed, argued with himself a minute longer, then turned left into the driveway proper, vaguely aware that the brakes were going to last exactly long enough to see him to the carport. The middle door was retracted precisely as he had left it, but though the Sable was gone, he did not park inside, on the assumption that since he needed to work on the car, more space was available out here than inside.

"Okay, Dillon, here we go," he told himself, and without further hesitation, climbed out, stretched, yawned, snagged his crutch, and strode directly toward the front porch, oblivious of the plants he had to push through and the flower beds he thereby betrod.

The front hallway was deserted, devoid of movement save the languidly drifting dust motes that seemed always to inhabit the shafts of light angling through the stained-glass fanlight that capped the dark oak door. He could hear music, though: the heavy bass line of what sounded like Def Leppard thumping out from the media room, and also—just barely—something soft and sultry (probably Alanna Miles) wending its way downstairs from the floor above. He did not need to be told who was where.

But as he stood there waffling, a sleek black shape stole from beneath the nearest brass planter and trotted silently down the hall—straight toward the source of the din. "Rrrowwww?" Matty Groves prompted from outside.

"Okay, cat," Ron murmured. "Have it *your* way."

Lew turned toward him as soon as Ron eased into the room, his face flushed, his brow a-drip with sweat. He was panting heavily, and a glance at the topmost TV told Ron why: His brother had been watching—and working out to—one of those morning aerobics shows. He even had the costume for it: skintight white spandex that showed the well-cut muscles of his wrestler's physique to excellent advantage. A quick double take told Ron that the music was from the stereo. Evidently Lew didn't need—or didn't like—the kind of coaching most aerobic instructors provided. Which in turn implied that he'd been at this sort of foolishness for some time.

Lew had seen him, of course, but merely raised a finger in a gesture of postponement in lieu of breaking off his calisthenics.

It was while he stood there alternately stroking Matty Groves and fidgeting that Ron realized how bad his brother looked. No, not *bad*, exactly—not in the sense most folks in Welch County used it, which was that someone who "looked bad" was likely in ill health. Rather, it was . . . tired, maybe? Distraught? *Troubled?* Or possibly simply burned-out?

Ron tucked the cat under his arm and helped himself to a glass of orange juice from a pitcher on the sideboard while he waited for the song to end, which it did roughly thirty seconds later. And wondered, idly, if the musical Tarot applied to recorded, as opposed to broadcast, tunes when encountered without premeditation. If so, he was doubtless in deep shit for having chosen "Pyromania" over "Black Velvet": self-induced conflagration to comfortable sensuality.

As the last bass bars faded, Lew crossed to the electronic wall, flipped two switches, and pressed three buttons—whereupon the room filled with the soft strains of "The Pachelbel Canon."

"Mornin', Ronny," Lew panted.

"Mornin'."

"You doin' okay?"

Ron wrinkled his nose in distaste. "That's a bit heavy-handed, isn't it?"

Lew looked genuinely confused. "What?"

"The music, stooge. Wimpy crap to try to calm me down, to soothe the savage breast, and all. It's not gonna work," he added.

"Looks like *something* already has," Lew noted pointedly. "Compared to last night, I mean."

"We can talk about *me* later!" Ron snapped. "I just checked in here to let you know I'm back and all right. But I've *gotta* go see Wendy." He reached for the door. "She upstairs?"

Lew shook his head but would not meet his gaze.

Ron froze, eyes narrowed. "So where *is* she?"

Lew shrugged uncomfortably. "Gone," he whispered so softly that had the room not had perfect acoustics, Ron could not have heard him.

"*Gone?* What do you *mean*, gone?" Ron was so shocked, he let go of Matty Groves, who hissed at him and vanished. Ron didn't notice. A score of conflicting emotions had awakened in him, principal among them a twisted sense of relief that he had, perhaps, been spared a confrontation because Wendy had preempted him.

"Gone where?" he repeated. "When?"

Lew snagged a glass of juice and flopped down on the nearest chair. "She didn't *say* where—not precisely. She . . . uh . . . Well, actually, it was before I got up, so I don't *know* . . . exactly. But it was this morning, and she took her stuff with her, so Karen said. So she must have been going for good. Back to Athens, I assume."

Ron's eyes narrowed further. "But she didn't say specifically?"

Once more Lew shook his head. "Just called a taxi and left when it arrived."

"Karen didn't take her?"

"To Athens? Not bloody likely!"

"To town—to the bus station, stooge! Hell, *I* don't know! To the place that's fixing her car!"

"They, uh, seemed to have sort of an uneasy relationship, if you remember. Besides, Karen had to go shopping."

"But she saw her?"

"So she said."

Ron ignored Lew's last remark. "Did she leave a note, then? Anything like that? Any messages for me? She didn't take off pissed, did she?"

"How should I know?"

" 'Cause it's your frigging *house*, for one thing!" Ron raged. " 'Cause you're the frigging goddamned Master!"

"Which doesn't make me omnipotent. And lest you forget, I can't Hear her—*or* Karen!"

Ron was speechless for a moment, then recovered. "But . . . but . . . for God's sakes, Lew, this isn't *like* her! I mean, as far as she knew, when she went to bed I was still here. She didn't even know I was gone, not necessarily; much less that you and I had a fight and I was out all night. I could've been out jogging, for all she knew. As spaced-out and hair-triggered as she's been lately, she could've been pissed at me for just doing that without telling her—or worried 'cause I ran off, or . . . or even *jealous*!"

For an instant Lew actually looked frightened.

It was all Ron could do to control himself. "You *did* lift that hoodoo you put on her last night, didn't you?"

Lew's brow wrinkled in perplexity, then realization brightened his face. "Oh . . . yeah, sure. I took care of that before she went to sleep; then our friends the alpha waves took over. She should have been her old self this morning."

Ron snatched up the nearest phone (there seemed to be at least one in every room—this was a slim white portable) and, without asking permission, punched in Wendy's Athens number. "When would you *guess* she left?" he growled, distantly aware of the phone ringing, but already certain no one would respond.

Once again Lew shrugged. "Couple of hours, maybe? No more than that. To tell the truth, I wasn't paying a lot of attention when Karen told me. It *was* the morning after the night before, in case you've forgotten."

"Which you could have cured if you wanted to," Ron countered. "I—" But Wendy's phone had finally stopped ringing. Someone had picked up, and Ron wondered abruptly what he would say. He had acted completely on reflex, utterly without forethought. And now he was going to have to (he supposed) throw himself on the mercy of the court when he didn't even know if there was trial by jury.

"Hello!" Wendy's voice chimed sweetly. "You have reached Wendy Flowers's residence. I can't come to the phone right now, but . . ." Ron tuned out the rest of the message. He'd gotten Wendy's machine, which probably meant that she was still in transit. He drummed his fingers while the message droned on, then, when the promised beep had sounded, took a deep breath and blurted, "Wendy, this is Ron. I'm sorry about last night, but I need to explain some things, so—uh, give me a call when you get in." A pause, then, "I know you've got a right to be mad at me, but if you'll give me a chance to explain, we'll both feel better. If you don't, neither of us will." And with that, he hung up.

Lew raised an eyebrow and offered him another OJ.

Ron took it without comment.

"What now?"

"Hell if I know. I can't do anything until Karen gets back."

"Except call the taxi company," Lew suggested patiently, "and the garage where you left her car."

"Good point," Ron conceded. And did.

And learned exactly nothing except that the driver of the single local cab acknowledged having gotten out of bed to pick her up at Cardalba at 7:30 that morning and had subsequently delivered her to the garage where her car was being repaired. A call there confirmed that the Celica had indeed been fixed, that an attractive young lady had retrieved it, and that she'd had a suitcase in her hand. She hadn't seemed upset, though she had appeared rather sleepy and somewhat distracted. She'd paid her bill with a check and driven off. After that, no one had seen her. Which meant that it was waiting time. Ron would give her the rest of the afternoon to cool down, then call again— probably that evening.

"So," Lew said when Ron had finally hung up in disgust, "now you wanta do some explaining to me?"

Ron grimaced sourly but nodded. "Might as well get it over with."

Lew mussed his hair affectionately. "Come on, then," he murmured, rising and heading for the door. "I need to grab a shower, but we can talk while I do."

Ron rolled his eyes but followed his brother into the hall and thence up the main stairs. Lew's suite was to the left at the top, occupying both rooms in the western side above the front parlor and media room, with a palatial, marble-walled bathroom between. "Sherry?" Lew asked, indicating a decanter to the right of the door.

Ron glared at him. "Not bloody likely. It was all that stuff you foisted off on me yesterday that got me in trouble in the first place!"

Lew did not reply, but skinned out of his sweat-stained workout togs. Naked, and bathed in the golden morning sunlight burning through the northern window, he looked like a young, if rather small, Greek god. He was *that* well proportioned, his features *that* finely made. Lew flung the sweaty clothes in the general direction of an open hamper.

"Why don't you start at the beginning?" he asked as he padded toward the bathroom.

Ron couldn't suppress a grim chuckle as he followed him through the door. "Which *one*? See, there's a lot more than just the Wendy problem, all of a sudden."

Lew was already adjusting faucets at the end of a deep cubicle that housed a carved marble bench and a curtainless two-person shower, so Ron helped himself to a seat on the side of the Jacuzzi ten feet away. The lulling patter of water striking stone abruptly filled the room. And of course, there had to be music. Lew apparently never did anything without a soundtrack anymore. This time it was Handel's "Water Music"—a natural choice, but blessedly tuned low. In spite of the open door and exhaust fan, the room quickly became humid. Ron could smell soap and herbal shampoo—and kept his eyes busy following the looping spirals of the mosaics on the floor.

"I'm waiting," Lew prompted, when a minute had passed without Ron speaking.

Another sigh. "Oh, Christ, Lew, I don't really want to get into all this but to start with, I think I told you that I didn't want Wendy to come up here, but . . ."

He went on from there, repeating his earlier spiel about his fears regarding returning home, about how he really had not wanted to bring Wendy, about his misgivings concerning her. That part didn't take long, but then he came to the altercation of the night before, the wreck, him finding his way to Brandy's place, breakfast—and then her offer.

Lew finished just as Ron did and shut off the water. "Wanta throw me a towel?" he asked, "I always forget 'em." Ron grumbled, but found him one—a big, fluffy white job—which Lew applied to himself with vigor.

"So is that all?" Lew asked, stepping closer.

Ron wished he were somewhere else, answering—or asking—other questions. "Who knows?" he grunted finally. "*I* don't, that's for sure—'course, I don't seem to know *anything* for sure these days."

"What d'you mean?"

Ron took a deep breath. "Well, for one thing, I've got a terrible feeling I'm in love with Brandy. Sort of," he appended hastily.

To his relief, Lew did not chastise him. "I'm not surprised."

"Well, *I* sure as hell am!" Ron retorted, as he followed his brother back to the bedroom, where Lew busied himself yanking odd bits of attire out of drawers. "I certainly wasn't in the market when I got here—or *on* the market, either. I had no complaints about Wendy beyond the bare minimum. But now all of a sudden—"

"The number one thing in your life is trying to figure out how fast you can get back to Brandy?"

"How'd you know? I mean, it *shouldn't* be, but I guess it is." Then, abruptly: "You haven't been prowling in my head, have you? Surely to God I didn't let anything slip!"

Lew merely grunted and tugged on a pair of black bikini briefs. "Not my style. Not with family."

"Then how?"

Lew spun around. "*Because*, man, you're not the only one in the clan with a heart and hormones. Do you think that just 'cause I'm stuck here, I've never been in love? It's just that the pickings are damned thin on the ground 'round here—in case you haven't noticed!"

Ron nodded heavily, feeling like a heel. "Yeah, I guess you're right. I wasn't thinking about you much there, was I?"

"I'm used to it," Lew muttered. "Oh, and let's not forget the Tarot. *It* said Wendy's a barrier; *it* said you were supposed to meet someone named Brandy."

"And said it would be the end of the world as I know it, which I sure as hell feel like it is!"

Lew regarded him solemnly. "I have another hard question."

"Christ!" Ron groaned, rolling his eyes. "What now?"

"Well, basically . . . *are* you going to consider Brandy's offer?"

"How could I help it?" Ron replied hesitantly, pacing across the room and finally coming to roost beside the northern window. "God knows when I'll get anything better."

Lew stuck his face through the neck hole of a crimson T-shirt and grinned like a Cheshire cat. "Good. Now, does that also mean you'll consider staying at Cardalba?"

Ron glared at his brother askance. "As a matter of fact, she *said* I could stay up at her place."

"Oh-ho-ho!" Lew chuckled. Then, much more seriously, "You know what I mean, man. I'm talking about the Mastership."

"I was afraid you were."

"And?"

"Let's just say it makes it more likely than heretofore. Beyond that, there's no way I can say—not until I find out what's up with Wendy."

"Jesus, Ronny!"

Ron's eyes narrowed suspiciously. "Lew . . ." he began slowly. "Uh . . . *you* didn't by any chance have anything to do with setting me up with Brandy, did you?"

Lew turned to face him full on, jeans in hand. "You know me better than that."

A shrug.

Lew folded his arms across his chest and shifted his weight to his other leg. "Look, man. It's easy enough to prove. You can Listen to me if you want to. But you won't find any duplicity. The most you'll find is me thinking that you and Brandy had some things in common and that it might be nice if you met, but that you'd probably kill each other if you were around each other very long. But it was *all* speculation. I swear."

Ron studied him for a long moment, then shrugged in turn and strode toward the door.

"Where're you going?"

"Out."

Lew caught up to him in an instant, restraining him with a gentle but firm grip on his shoulder.

"You don't believe me?"

"Why don't you just stick your nosy mind in *my* head and find out?"

"Because that's *not* my style, dammit—not with people I care about."

"But you just wanted *me* to!"

"It was the only way! I mean look . . . bro. If we can't trust each other, there really isn't anybody we *can* trust. We've got no choice but to do that."

Ron flinched out of his grip and whirled on him. "It'd help if you'd stop playing games!"

"I haven't *been* playing games," Lew shot back, genuinely indignant. "The *worst* I'm guilty of is trying to be subtle—delaying tactics, and all. I mean, I *knew* this was gonna be tough on you. All I've done was try to mix some pleasure in with the pain."

"Well, you've certainly done that," Ron growled. "Now excuse me, but it looks like I've gotta do some traveling."

"So you're casting your lot with Brandy?"

"I don't know *what* I'm gonna do. I won't know until I get out on the road!"

"Ronny, I—"

Ron pushed past him, reached for the knob. "Don't mind if I borrow a car, do you?"

"Be my guest," Lew replied helplessly. "Keys are in the kitchen."

Ron didn't thank him.

"If Wendy calls, where should I tell her you'll be?"

"Hell if I know!" Ron spat. "Tell her I'll call her till I get her. I dunno!"

"And then?"

"And then I wait. We . . . *both* wait, I guess," he added more gently, suddenly unwilling or unable to leave Lew in anger two days in a row. "And I guess we both do a lot of hard thinking. Maybe we should have done it a long time ago."

"Yeah," Lew said softly as Ron eased into the hall, "maybe we should."

Ron paused in the doorway. "Lew?"

"Yeah?"

"You ever see a white deer 'round here?"

Lew scowled in perplexity, obviously startled. "No—actually. Why do you ask?"

" 'Cause I saw one last night."

"Where?"

Ron told him.

Lew listened quietly. "Well that's certainly interesting."

"Tell me about it. Well, it's no big deal, it's just . . . well, you know, they *can* mean something in certain contexts."

"Those were a long time ago."

"Just covering all the bases," Ron murmured, and left. "Oh, and Lew?" he continued from the hall.

"What?"

"Sometimes you're an asshole. I just wanted you to know that."

"I know."

"Sometimes I am, too."

"I know that as well."

"Friends anyway?"

"Always and forever."

"Nobody said it would be easy."

"Nobody ever will."

Ron started down the stairs, but just as he stepped on the topmost tread, he noticed Matty Groves curled up in the window at the north end. "Hey, fuzz-butt," he sighed, retracing his steps and wandering over to where his pet was soaking up rays. "You've got the right idea: just lie in the sun and let the world pass you by." He picked him up, leaned on the sill, stroking the jet black fur. "Unfortunately, though, I've gotta travel. And you, my furry friend, have gotta come with me."

Matty didn't bother to meow, but Ron remained where he was for a moment, simply enjoying the sunlight, the comforting feel of its warmth on his back, the soft burr of Matty's purring.

And quite by accident, glanced out the window. The sun porch was below and to the right—the one Lew had made into a sort of greenhouse; which Ron had never bothered to look at. It was glassed in, and through the glazing he could see ranks and ranks of potted plants of all sizes and species.

And perched very primly next to the outside door was a stubby bright green shape that could only be Tony Hillerman, the barrel cactus.

"Jesus!" Ron exclaimed to Matty Groves. "I guess that means she really *was* pissed."

"Rrrrooowwww?"

"No," Ron sighed, once more heading for the stairs, "I doubt Lew would be that interested."

Chapter 15

Love the One You're With

Cordova, Georgia
Early afternoon

"Karen!"

Ron's hoarse yell echoed down a canyon of canned tuna and caromed off jars of jams and jellies. "Yo, Karen!" he repeated, oblivious to the fact that he was standing—panting, sweaty, and red-faced—dead center in aisle three of the Cordova Kroger. A fat woman glared at him. Her wide-eyed son sent solemn blinks of approbation from the security of his mother's Levied leg. A dapper old gent in a suit looked startled but pretended he didn't hear and went on fingering tubs of peanut butter as Ron gazed with vast relief toward the end of the aisle, past which the object of his exhortation had just wheeled her grocery buggy.

"Karen! For God's sakes, wait up!"

She didn't.

Ron rolled his eyes and sprinted, rounding the corner in question at warp speed—and practically collided with his quarry, who had evidently heard him after all. The girl froze, stiffened, and looked very white-faced and frightened as she whirled about to face him. And guilty? *That* he couldn't tell.

"Ronny? What . . . ?"

"Wendy—" he gasped, still breathless from the mad dash he had made through the parking lot upon spotting the black Sable wagon outside.

Karen's face clouded immediately. "W-what *about* her? I—"

"You saw her last, didn't you?" he interrupted, too wired for either patience or politeness. "Did . . . she say anything before she left? Anything at all?" He paused for breath, having delivered his opening sally at one blurt. "Anything about—about being pissed at me?"

Karen simply gaped dumbly, as if he were a space alien from the cover of a nearby tabloid—understandable, given the frantic wildness that was no doubt evident from his face and demeanor. Her eyes flickered apprehensively, and she took a step backward, automatically putting distance 'twixt herself and this obvious loon. "S-so . . . Lew t-told you, huh?" she stammered finally. Her voice was stiff and strained, as if she had to fight to free the words.

"How could he *help* but tell me?" Ron snapped. "I mean she *is* my girlfriend, for chrissakes!"

"*Is* she?" Karen shot back much more boldly, her face coloring even as she spoke, as if she'd surprised herself. She looked down abruptly.

Ron took her by the arms, shook her gently but firmly. "What d'you mean?"

She met his gaze. "I—I wasn't g-going to tell you this 'cause she told me not to. And—"

"I thought she didn't *say* anything to you before she left," Ron broke in again. "That's what *Lew* said."

"Lew doesn't know everything," Karen shot back, brushing his hands away as she regained composure and people started to stare at them. "And he *sure* doesn't know everything that's in *my* head, as I'm sure *you* know."

Ron bit his lip, obviously chastened. He backed up, too, tried to relax, to regain control. "O-kay," he gritted slowly, "so what *did* she say?"

Karen took a deep breath. "Not much. Truly not much. I—I was cooking breakfast. She came into the kitchen. I said hi, and she grunted. I asked her if she was hungry; she said no."

"And . . . ?"

"She . . . uh, then she asked where you were, and I said I didn't know, but that I'd heard you and Lew hollering last night, and then your car driving away."

Ron's eyes narrowed suspiciously. "How do you know it was *my* car?"

"It—ah, sounds pretty distinctive, with that loud muffler, and all. . . . Anyway, she asked if you'd come back. I told her I didn't know *where* you were, but that your car was still gone."

Ron exhaled slowly. "But . . . how *was* she? I mean, what was she *like*? Was she—did she act pissed, or anything?"

"Wouldn't *you* be? I mean, put yourself in her place: you won't have anything to do with her at the party, and then you spend all your time talking to some other girl."

"It was hardly *all* my time," Ron countered icily. "And this 'other girl' barely gave *me* the time of day—at least when Wendy could've seen us talking. And I *didn't* desert her. She knows I can't dance, and—"

"She was pissed, Ronny," Karen said flatly. "In fact, she used exactly that word. Evidently she saw more than I saw—to be quite honest."

"Well, *that's* comforting," Ron sighed. "So what happened then?"

"I asked her if there was anything I could do, and she just kinda went all weird and distant like I wasn't even there, and started flipping through the phone book. I was getting sorta scared by then—and maybe a little mad, I guess— so I just walked out. Last time I saw her, she was calling a taxi."

"And you didn't try to stop her?"

"Wasn't my place, I didn't think. I mean, I barely know her, and all; and I don't know if I even like her or not. She's so . . . *changeable*."

Ron folded his arms and nodded sage agreement. "Tell me about it. But that's what worries me. See, she's always been very predictable, very—I dunno—nonaggressive. And then all of a sudden—boom—she's goin' off on all these screwy tangents."

"Ronny?"

"Yeah."

"There's one more thing."

For no clear reason, Ron felt a chill. "Okay . . ."

Karen took another deep breath, and when she spoke again, it was in very low tones. "She said to tell you not to bug her. Said that since *she* obviously didn't make you happy anymore, there was nothing else she could do. She'd seek her happiness elsewhere."

Ron could only gape incredulously. "She *said* that?"

Karen nodded sadly. "She did."

"And you didn't tell Lew?"

"She asked me not to!" the girl protested helplessly. "And I was . . . careful how I answered his questions."

Ron could not avoid a grim smile. "Yeah, I know how *that* is."

Karen's lifted eyebrow mirrored his expression exactly. "Figured you did."

"Uh—well, thanks, I guess," Ron muttered, shoulders sagging. He turned to go, then thought better of it. "Oh . . . uh, Karen: one last thing."

The girl was already wheeling her buggy away—without telling him he was welcome, he noted. She whirled around once more. "Yeah?"

"I believe you."

A disinterested shrug. "Cool."

Ron caught up to her. "But I really do—at least about Wendy being pissed. See, she went off without Tony Hillerman—that's her pet cactus—and there's no way she'd have done that unless she was *really* upset."

"I see," Karen said distantly. "So what're you gonna do now?"

Ron grimaced helplessly. "Hell if *I* know."

"Hell," Karen repeated slowly, as if she had never heard the word. Then: "Hell indeed."

Jesus, not again! Ron grumbled when he had made his way back to the Kroger parking lot. *Christ, this is all I need!*

"All he needed" was not, in fact, a very big deal: merely a fine film of yellow-green pollen dusted across the Jag sedan's glossy hood. Nothing to fret over; it would all slide off the faultless wax as soon as the car commenced moving. It was just that this was the second time such a thing had happened that day. It hadn't really bugged him before; he'd simply noted that there was powder on the windshield when he'd backed the borrowed car out of the garage and thought it vaguely odd that such a thing was possible in an air-conditioned carport. On the other hand, Karen *had* left one of the doors open, so he supposed it could have drifted in from the nearby forest. The air was pretty stagnant, he'd noticed, in spite of the recent rain. And there'd been a thicker coating of the stuff on the Centauri, though it had only been parked outside a short time. Too, it was summer, and there were a lot of trees and flowers doing their thing. And though the sprinkle that morning *should* have cleared the air, one thing Ron never quite got the hang of was the weather. No, it was just odd. One more minor irritation on a day he didn't need any.

Matty Groves looked up at him and meowed plaintively as Ron slid into the car, ending his comment with a delicate sneeze. "Whazzamatter, cat?" Ron chuckled, giving him a quick scratch under the chin. "Allergies acting up again? Just hang on a second, and we'll turn on the old AC."

Matty sneezed once more.

Ron had already cranked the car and shifted into reverse when someone tapped on his window. He stomped the brake hard enough to jerk himself against the shoulder belt and glanced left—to see a vaguely familiar dark-haired woman peering in at him. He frowned, stuffed the lever back into park, and flicked the power window switch. Where had he seen this gal before? There was a mailman's patch on her jacket, he noted. And then he remembered: it was whatshername Brandy's friend from the party. Wedgie, or something. No—*Weedge*: W. G. Montgomery. He didn't like the way she was looking at him, either— as if she couldn't decide whether to eat him or ask him to dinner. "Hi," he ventured carefully.

"Greetings," Weedge replied with an easy nonchalance

that took him completely off guard.

"Hi."(*Again?* That was certainly inane, he thought; what was his *problem* today? Couldn't he even speak his native tongue?)

Weedge didn't seem inclined to further pleasantries. "Two things," she said abruptly, "and then I've gotta go."

"So shoot."

"I hope I won't have to," she laughed, lifting an eyebrow in what could have been amusement—*or* warning. "Okay, then: I'm probably out of line telling you this, seeing as how I'm more or less betraying the confidence of a friend. But there are two things you oughta know about Brandy."

"Which are . . . ?"

A deep breath. "The first is that though I'll grant you that she and I haven't been friends very long, still, I think I know her pretty well . . . and . . ." She hesitated, as if choosing how best to continue. "And as best *I* can tell," she finished, "Brandy likes you better than any man she's seen since she's been up here."

Ron gazed at her askance. "She *told* you this?"

Weedge shook her head. "Didn't have to."

"So what am *I* supposed to do?"

"Be nice to her," Weedge shot back promptly. "No matter how hard it is. She's a neat lady, but she needs friends—and I'm simply not as available as I'd like to be 'cause of my job. She needs someone around, or she's either gonna get hurt or go crazy. She doesn't know it yet, but she will."

"Was that both things?" Ron wondered.

Weedge's eyes flashed with sudden fire. "The *second* thing is that if *you* hurt her, I swear to God I'll kill you. That young lady has suffered enough!"

"So why are you telling me this?"

"So you'll know which way the land lays. Good luck—and be careful."

"Uh, thanks," Ron stammered. "Uh—we'll be seeing you."

Weedge shot him a warning wink. "You can bet on it!"

Ron believed her.

                              *   *   *

Either the omens were becoming *too* obvious, the Powers That Be were taking an atypically intense interest in human affairs—or he was becoming a tad too gullible for even a Listener, Ron concluded as he launched Lew's XJ-6 around the first curve beyond the Cordova city limits. Tires howled their protest—of course—and for a change, he heeded them, unable to avoid a touch of chagrin when he recalled the last time he had driven this route. Just like he couldn't help but be a tad suspicious about the song that had just commenced thumping out of the radio—or irritated at himself for being so self-absorbed he'd forgotten to check on the auguries earlier.

But now it had begun, and—*Jesus*—how heavy-handed could oracles be? For it was Crosby, Stills, and Nash's "Love the One You're With." And that was a bit too coincidental for even him to fully accept. So much so, in fact, that he strongly considered picking up the cellular phone in the console and dialing up Homestead Pen to see if they could somehow, just *possibly*, round up Uncle Dion and get him on the line.

Ron was actually fondling the receiver with that intent when it jangled. He uttered a startled yip and jerked the wheel enough to dart over the centerline before recovering. Matty Groves raised his head and growled.

With a certain amount of trepidation, Ron lifted the receiver. "Hello?"

"Ronny?" It was Lew. He sounded tense, as if he was the bearer of bad news.

"What's wrong?"

"Nothing—not with me. But I . . . uh, just found something on my machine you probably ought to hear."

"Oh yeah?"

Lew took a deep breath. "It was from Wendy. She called the house, but I was out and couldn't catch it. She left a message. If you'll hang on a sec, I'll give it a play."

Ron hesitated, gnawing his lip, then nodded. "Sure. Okay."

The phone clicked and buzzed and then Ron caught the low hiss of an answering machine being activated. And though the voice was filtered through imperfect electronics, knew instantly it was Wendy when she spoke. "Hello . . . Lew, I guess," she said flatly, but with a faint waver in her voice, as if she were trying to retain control but wasn't quite able. "I . . . uh—well, this is for Ron, so please see that he gets it, okay? Fine . . . here goes. Ron: I—I, uh, just got in and got your message. And . . . I hate to do this this way, but maybe it's the best. I'm sorry I had to do what I did like I did, but I think it's for the better. Things . . . haven't been going well for you and me for a while, though I doubt you've really noticed. But I have, and it seems like I'm becoming less and less of a person to you. And after last night, I *knew* you really weren't interested in me anymore. Not when you can hang out with someone like Brandy. See, I saw you guys together, and I asked around a little, so I know you guys are, like, a good match. And—and there was no way you could hide what was in your eyes when you told me you were going back to Cardalba. So . . . I'm gonna make it so you don't *have* to hide—which I guess means I'm saying that it's over. Please don't try to find me, 'cause I won't be here. But I'll be okay, I promise." And then, very softly, "I don't have any choice but to love you, and I wish with all my heart you could love me—but you can't. So . . . 'bye."

More clicks, then Lew again. "Sorry, man. But maybe it's just as well."

"Maybe."

"Oh, and Ronny?"

"Yeah?"

"You remember last night when we thought there was something odd about Vannister? Something weird about the way his Voice Sounded?"

"Yeah."

Lew paused for breath. "Well . . . I Listened for him again today and got the same thing. It's hard to explain, but it's like a veneer of normality overlying something deeper that I can't reach."

"Hmmm. Any idea what that means in the real world?"

"Not really. The closest I've been able to come is that the few schizophrenics I've Listened to have been like that. Like you were Hearing one personality, but not the only one."

"So you mean old Vannister might be psycho?"

"He might."

"Well," Ron sighed. "That's certainly interesting."

"Yeah, well, I just thought you might want to know. Just in case. You know, to be careful of him, and all."

"Thanks."

"Catch you later?"

"Maybe."

" 'Bye."

"Lew . . . ? Oh, never mind. 'Bye."

And Ron once more faced a decision.

"What d'you say, cat?" he inquired of Matty Groves.

"Rrrowwww?"

"Ah yes, back to the radio."

The song just beginning—the Crossing song—was an ancient tune by Johnny Rivers: something called "Mountain of Love."

"Okay," Ron sighed in resignation. "So I guess this means Mohammed goes to the mountain."

A short while later he was bouncing (and sometimes scraping) Lew's low-slung car down the rutted road that led—he supposed—to a new episode of his life.

Chapter 16

Dust in the Wind

Brandy's Knoll

Ron was grinning like a possum when he finally thrust the Jag into the spotty sunlight that now bathed Brandy's Knoll—but his cautious optimism faded to apprehensive uncertainty when he observed that the proprietress was nowhere in sight. Her pickup was present, however, and his sharp eyes noted a pile of concrete sacks over to the left that hadn't been there that morning, all of which he took as promising omens. And when he cautiously eased the car door open, he heaved a small sigh of relief, for he immediately caught a familiar grinding noise from beyond the nearer tower, coupled with vehement female cursing. Great, she *was* here. Except—

God, what did he do *now*? He'd arrived intent on merely talking: on laying out the latest developments as clearly as he could, with minimal reference to Wendy—whom, come to think of it, he wasn't sure Brandy knew about anyway. Nor was he certain he was going to accept her offer—and if he did, whether he would stay at her place (if that option was still available) or somewhere in town. (He had already ruled out Cardalba, and his mom's former place was not available.)

Well, he'd never find out by standing there wondering.

"Okay, cat, here we go," he told the dozing Matty as he paused with one foot on the ground to lower both front windows for ventilation. "You know where I'll be—you'd better be sure I can find you!" Not that he was worried. Unlike his namesake, Matty Groves had never gone roving. Not ever.

Ron considered retrieving his crutch but decided against it. Now that it wasn't so humid, his knee was giving him less grief than earlier, and he was determined to make a good impression. So with that in mind, he quietly shut the door and rolled up his sleeves, stopping only for a sneeze (the blessed pollen was suddenly everywhere) before limping off in quest of the foul mouthed wench— who was not difficult to locate, given the frequency and volume of her utterances. Nor, as best he could determine once he had cleared the southwest tower, had she heard him drive up—understandable, given the grinding din the cement mixer two yards to her left was generating—so that he was able to observe her for a moment undetected. And was mightily impressed all over.

Sometime since that morning, she'd actually gotten the damaged bit of foundation repaired and was now completely engrossed in filling the resulting twenty-foot square of graveled-over stone with concrete, so as to form a slab floor. *She* was in the farthest corner, kneeling with her back to him, attempting to use a two-by-four to level a door-sized section she'd obviously just finished pouring.

"Here," he called casually, slipping around so that she could see him by glancing right, "let me give you a hand." Without waiting for acknowledgment, he knelt, grabbed the nearer end of the plank, and began working it back and forth across the lumpy concrete.

Brandy merely glared at him, but scooted a couple of feet to the left, to better manage the board. "What're *you* doing back so soon?" she asked sharply.

Ron countered her sarcasm with a halfhearted smile. "Well, to tell the truth, I came up here to let you know

that . . . something's come up, and I'm a lot more interested in your offer than I thought I was—assuming it
still stands. But now that I've got here, looks like I've
got another job."

She studied him with a mixture of amusement and contempt. "You're not exactly dressed for it," she observed
pointedly. He wasn't either, not in newish Reeboks, a
long-sleeved blood-red shirt, and fresh-washed jeans, none
of which showed the merest spot, fray, or blemish. Which
contrasted markedly with the old cammos, white T-shirt,
and red bandanna Brandy was wearing, all of which were
already generously spotted with concrete splatters where
they didn't bear the imprint of dirty hands, splashed water,
or ill-aimed sand. Her hair, he noted with some amusement, was near-green with adhering pollen.

Ron shrugged, then grinned. "Ah, but I'm a workin' man
now; I can *afford* new duds!"

"If you're talking about my proposal, it wasn't for money," Brandy reminded him quickly. "Board and experience—and satisfaction. That's it."

"Ah, yes," he chuckled. "And as I recall, the best way to
experience this is for one person to keep the mixer going,
one to spread it, and two to level. But since there's only the
two of us, looks like we'll have to double up. Unless you
can do this as fast as you fixed that piece of foundation,"
he added. "How'd you *do* that, anyway?"

Brandy stood and strode toward the mixer, which had
just finished kneading another load. "I'm not sure myself,"
she muttered cryptically, using a sneeze to end her explanation.

Ron thought she looked uneasy, as if there was something she wasn't saying, and actually considered Listening
to her and ferreting out the facts that way, then rejected that
notion as unethical. He wanted their relationship—however
it evolved—to be absolutely honest. "No big deal," he said
at last.

She wiped her nose and glared at him, but more from
irritation than anger, he suspected. "Well, if you're gonna
hang around and look pretty," she grumbled finally, "you
might as well be useful, too, I reckon." She nodded toward
the nearest finished wall. "There's a rake over yonder. How

'bout you grab it and start spreadin' this stuff around? Then we can take turns leveling while the other mixes another load, and we can work together on the final smoothing."

"Sounds good to me," Ron said, rising.

—Whereupon she swung the mixer's spout around ninety degrees and proceeded to deposit a sizable dollop of lumpy, gray-white ooze onto the layer of granite gravel she had already spread across the naked rock. Ron hopped back instinctively as the goop grated his way—and found himself simultaneously mired to the ankles in the section they'd just completed, and splattered to the knees with the raw material of the next. *"Shit!"* he yipped, executing an oddly graceful dance to escape the line of fire.

He glanced sheepishly at his partner—and for the first time caught her smiling without being self-conscious. The smile became a smirk—which quickly became a giggle when she noticed his hangdog expression. At which point he feigned indignation, reached down, seized a handful of thickening goo, and flung it so that it splattered beside her left foot, soiling her already crud-blotched cammos even worse.

She looked indignant.

He raised an eyebrow.

And then they both were laughing.

An hour later, Ron had sneezed half a dozen times, the slab was within an ace of being finished, and he had learned a couple of things.

The first, and most obvious, was that pouring concrete floors was damned hard work—as sore muscles, blistered hands, and sweat-soaked garments testified. He'd done his part, too: shoveling gravel and sand into the mixer's insatiable maw, dumping in bags of cement, manhandling the recalcitrant machine around, raking thick semisolids, wielding the board that leveled the whole enterprise. Oh, he'd be sore tomorrow—but it'd be the good sort of pain that assured him he was that much more secure from what had threatened to become a dangerously sedentary life.

The second bit of wisdom he had picked up was sufficiently pleasant to make up for any physical discomfort he had undergone as a result of the first—which was that his reluctant infatuation with Brandy didn't seem to be as one-sided as he'd suspected, at least in terms of aesthetic appreciation. Indeed, they'd sneaked appraising glances at each other pretty frequently during the previous hour—though perhaps that was due in part to the midsummer heat, which necessitated frequent trips to the lemonade jug, and which had quickly resulted in Ron trading his jeans for the cutoffs he normally bummed around his apartment in, and discarding his shirt altogether. Brandy had seen his bare torso that morning, anyway, so at least *that* minor revelation—and he *did* have fairly clear notions of the proper level of exposure for various stages of a relationship—had already been exploited.

And he was beginning to get a pretty good notion what *her* hard little bod was like, too; given that she'd obviously not been expecting company, so had set to work with only a plain white T-shirt above the waist—which sweat and random water quickly rendered more than sufficiently transparent for him not only to note that she wasn't wearing a bra, but that she looked damned good without one, with breasts just the way he liked them: nice, firmly rounded handfuls.

"Now if you'll just fling one more shovelful in that corner, we'll be done in a couple of minutes," Brandy sighed at last, nodding unconsciously toward the mixer while she reached for the rake once more.

Ron nodded mutely and obeyed, depositing the requisite quantity into the appointed place, then squatting down outside the foundation to help her drag the faithful two-by-four across the uneven surface one last time.

"This part doesn't have to be absolutely perfect," she told him for at least the tenth time that afternoon. "I'm gonna lay down flagstones, so as long as it's at least six inches thick over the underlying strata, we'll be fine."

She rose then, sighing, and Ron heard her joints snap in counterpoint, even as he felt his knee twinge. She set the board against a convenient bit of wall while he busied himself shifting the now empty cement mixer to a more upright position prior to wheeling it away for a good rinsing.

"We're done, then?" he asked hopefully, shifting his gaze toward her in quest of confirmation.

And immediately guffawed, even as Brandy had no choice but to do so. For they had been so involved in their labor during the previous hour that, beyond the frequent surreptitious glances, neither of them had really looked at each other as a whole—and now that they could, Ron discovered that he had learned a third thing while ostensibly preparing a floor. And that was that working with concrete was not only tiring, if occasionally titillating, it was also incredibly untidy.

Not an inch of either of them was unblemished, whether by dirt, sand, or globs of concrete. And now that the stuff was beginning to set in vise-like clumps around his body hair, he understood why Brandy had rolled her eyes so expressively when he'd stripped down to cutoffs and sneakers, while neglecting to dress as lightly herself.

Unfortunately, laughing with a woman, Ron had long ago discovered, was a vital step toward love. And while he liked Brandy a lot, he had only *just* got the news about Wendy and was far from coming to terms with it yet—which meant even the minimal pleasure of laughter was not without its trauma.

On the other hand, that was no reason not to enjoy the moment. "I can only think of *one* way to describe you," he observed, with a mischievous smirk.

"And how's that?" Brandy countered, her voice a-drip with a mock haughtiness he would have never suspected *was* feigned even an hour before.

"Why, as a Concrete Blonde," Ron giggled. "Or at least I *think* that's what color your roots are under all that gray."

Brandy's eyes sparked dangerously. *"What* gray?"

"The gray of concrete, I meant," Ron amended quickly, when she began to advance toward him with a trowel. He was suddenly unsure if she was pissed at him or still teasing. But then again, women could be sensitive about certain words—like *fat*, and *wrinkled*, and *gray*, and *old*. Just as he'd known grown men to turn pale and go weak-kneed when a ladyfriend casually mentioned the word *bald*.

Besides, he'd seen her in action, and if her muscle tone was any indication, there was a good chance she was at least as strong as he—which would do him no good at all in a fair fight.

"Truce!" he cried, when Brandy showed no sign of retreating. He had actually turned to run when she caught him. But instead of giving him a pounding or a lashing with her tongue, she simply upended a handful of sand over his head. Which promptly rode the ongoing stream of sweat down his spine to pool grittily between his nether cheeks.

"*Now* who's gray?" she chortled.

"Gray, hell!" Ron shot back. "What're you doin', girl? Research on river sand as a cure for hemorrhoids?"

Brandy wiped her hand on her pants and grinned smugly. "You go on up to the trailer and shower, seein' as how you're even groadier than I am. I'll hose this down and be right with you."

"Thanks," Ron sighed, flopping weakly against the nearest wall. "I could definitely stand a good scrubbing."

"Don't use all the hot water this time, okay? My water heater's not that big, and it took two hours to recover from the *last* shower you had here—and this time I need one, too: got it?"

"Sure," Ron acknowledged. He started toward the car to retrieve a change of clothes from the duffel bag he had brought along just in case, when he noted a glitter through the trees to his right.

"How deep is the lake 'round here?" he asked, turning and lifting an eyebrow.

She shrugged. "Couple of feet close to shore there in the cove. Maybe up to ten further out, but the slope's fairly shallow."

"Deep enough to swim in?"

"If you don't mind scraping the bottom."

"What about to bathe? I mean . . . if conserving hot water's such a big deal, I was just thinking that lake water that's been in the sun would be warmer than water that has to come out of the cold, cold ground."

Brandy's expression brightened. "Are you volunteering?"

Ron's eyes twinkled mysteriously. "To let you use all the precious *really* hot water you want, while I use all the precious *sort-of* hot water I want? Sure. That way we'll both be happy."

Brandy studied him for a moment, then shrugged again. "Be my guest—just be discreet, okay?"

Ron was edging toward what he hoped was the start of a trail heading down a steep forested slope toward the water a quarter of a mile away. He could hear a creek closer by, but knew that water would be much colder—*too* cold for his Florida-born blood.

"*Okay?*" Brandy repeated more sternly.

A shrug. "Sure—who's gonna see anyway?"

"Probably nobody," she conceded. "But real estate folks do come by now and then trying to sell those lots across the lake. And stray hikers wander through once in a while."

"Who have doubtless seen naked men before if they're male," Ron countered with a smirk. "And probably if they're female and over fourteen or have brothers."

"That stuff sets fast," Brandy noted wryly. "If you want dinner, I'll start in about an hour."

And on that inconclusive note, she reached for the water hose.

The last view Ron had of her before the outcrop was obscured by pine boughs was of her standing on tiptoes hosing down the inside of her cement mixer—and getting splattered unmercifully. He felt it his right to chuckle.

It didn't take Ron long to find a suitable place in which to wash half an afternoon's labor from his tired and aching body. Indeed, he almost stumbled on an ideal spot by accident: a narrow, flat shoal that sloped into the lake near where a stream emptied in—cool by that, but not too cold, and the fast-moving water kept the underwater stone swept clear of moss and algae and other aqueous slime producers—though there was a thin film of pollen on the surface: reasonable, considering how pervasive it had lately become in the air. The cove was private, too: screened by laurel on three sides, and further shaded by an impressive stand of what *looked* like live oaks but shouldn't be, while the fourth side opened onto the lake proper. Thus, Ron felt relatively secure in dropping his drawers on the dry, sunlit rocks, and leaving them, along with his sneakers (which he wiped off with his sopping cutoffs) there to dry.

The water, when he stepped into it, was colder than the earlier sampling with his fingers had suggested, and he almost reconsidered, then recalled his condition and marched bravely in, feeling the coolness rise up his body until it was nearly waist-deep. Steeling himself, he ducked under, and rose: sleek, goose-bumped, and already cleaner.

And only then remembered that in the madness of his teasing match with Brandy, he had forgotten clean clothes, towel, and soap. Which did not, however, alter the fact that he was enjoying the present physical sensations immensely. Almost, even, he forgot the twinges of regret he usually felt when taking a dip.

He did not actually swim, however (and even this long after the accident that had robbed him of a possible Olympic medal, still didn't really like to), but spent the next several minutes alternately ducking himself and scrubbing away as much of the grime as he could. Fortunately, the majority of the concrete splatters had not set, so most were easily removed, and the few chunks that could not be simply rubbed away by hand yielded to more determined tugs. That brought pain, of course, because it tore out hair, but Ron found himself enjoying even that, perhaps because it made him feel more macho—and with a woman as strong and competent as Brandy around, he *needed* to feel as manly as possible.

If only he could lay off *sneezing*! He'd been doing it ever since he arrived on the knoll, and it had gotten worse down here by the lake—presumably because whatever flora was producing the pervasive pollen grew in closer hereabouts. As a point of fact, he could actually smell the stuff: something spicy yet vaguely familiar that made him a little dizzy, even as it made his eyes burn and tingle in spite of frequent rinsing.

He had just resurfaced from his latest such effort, and was standing there with water streaming into his face, trying to decide what to do about his hair, when the sound of loud whistling, coupled with someone moving noisily through undergrowth, reached him from the bushes to the south. Since someone was obviously telegraphing his or her progress, he hunkered down obligingly, and was not at all surprised to see Brandy push through the foliage a moment later. She was still unkempt, still besplattered—but had brought him a towel and the jeans and shirt he'd been wearing when he'd first driven up. Her gaze found him—and he saw her face flush beneath her tan.

"S-sorry," she stammered, with a foolishly lopsided grin that looked so wildly out of place, Ron wondered if she'd been drinking. "I was . . . uh, hoping you . . . uh, wouldn't be that far along."

"No problem," he called back lightly, feeling rather giddy himself. "I reckon I was in a bigger hurry than I thought."

Brandy wouldn't meet his eyes, but inclined her head toward the bundles in her hand. "You, uh . . . seem to have forgotten a couple of crucial items," she continued, setting the piles of fabric down beside his cutoffs. "And . . . I brought you some soap and a washcloth," she concluded with a drunk-sounding giggle, blinking and wiping her nose. "I'll . . . I'll just leave them here and get on with my shower."

Ron felt distinctly light-headed. He took a deep breath that reeked of pollen—and felt more so. "Thanks a bunch!"

"No problem." She was backing away now, and turning around as well. But hesitantly, as if torn by indecision.

And then, to Ron's absolute surprise—and delight—she muttered a curt "Why the hell not?" sat down on the rock, and began unlacing her boots.

Her cammos joined them, and, after she had illogically turned her back, her T-shirt and panties.

But she had regained her composure when she eased back around, so that she looked, Ron thought, like some sort of barbarian queen.

He never forgot the way she looked that day, either: her carriage erect, her skin sleek and tanned in places he wouldn't have expected: essentially all over, in fact, which told him a couple of things about how she spent her free time. She was muscular, too—firm and toned, rather—but certainly had curves in all the right places. And her breasts were exactly as he'd imagined: high and perfectly shaped. He saw the nipples harden as she stepped gingerly into the lake.

"Y-you look great!" he heard himself stammer from a muzzy-brained distance that was more like being buzzed by the second. "You're beautiful."

And when he waded forward to meet her, so that she could see all of him, too, he was overjoyed to hear her say the same.

They swam briefly, simply to cool off. And in that dreamlike way such things sometimes have, Ron was never afterwards sure when swimming became touching, became a rigorous, giggly soaping down and washing of hair. Or when *that* segued into long, slow lovemaking on a patch of moss in the most sheltered end of the cove.

"It's been a long time," Brandy breathed once, between stronger bouts of passion.

"But you don't have to wait any longer," Ron panted back, his nostrils full of the scent of her hair—and the subtler, more pervasive odor of pollen. "You'll never have to wait with me, not if it's always like this."

"This wasn't supposed to happen. Shouldn't *be* happening. I—I don't even feel like myself!"

"You feel fine to me," Ron laughed, though he, too, sensed that odd distancing, as if he were high, as if he *knew* he ought to withdraw, that there was a very good reason he should not continue, but that something was interfering with his judgment.

"But I *shouldn't!*"

"I shouldn't either." And then he buried his head between her breasts and let other parts do the talking.

It was good, he admitted, in that aspect of his mind that always sat back and observed and judged; that never slept because a Listener never *dared* let it sleep, even now when he had somehow become intoxicated. But simply *because* he was a Listener, he couldn't help but pick up some of the emotions that Brandy was broadcasting all unknown. He shielded instantly, having lowered them in the throes of desire, and instantly felt his erection start to weaken. Dammit, it *always* happened like that! Things just got good, and instinct operated fine for a while, and then the brains kicked in, and pretty soon he knew things he didn't want to know, but could not escape because sex alone had sufficient strength to pierce even the strongest shields.

But he could not help himself, could not stop himself, in one mad consumption of thought and memory and emotion, from letting go of every inhibition and falling straight into Brandy's mind.

And there he learned that she really was attracted to him *as* him: for what he was, and what he could do, not how he looked and what he could give her. But there, too, he discovered, lay a blazing fury of self-possession such as he had never experienced: an awareness of self *as* self that was determined to maintain dominion over its own life no matter what; that was thinking, even as the body that housed that consciousness responded ever more heatedly, that this *was* only the pleasure of the moment, not a long-term thing.

Which was fine with him—except that he wanted this particular bout of lovemaking to go on for a very long time indeed, especially now that his no-longer-so-little friend seemed to have gotten over its momentary bout of panic and had risen to the occasion again.

An instant later, he was climaxing—or she was—or they both were. And at that precise point, when all barriers between them dissolved into what was at once instinct and ecstasy, he found himself confronting one other thing in Brandy's mind as well. There was something she was not telling him.

But what she *was* telling him right about then was to roll over, that it was *her* turn to be on top.

At some point Brandy left him there, spent, sated, muddleheaded—and so sweaty that he had to rinse off all over again. He would have gone with her, but she told him in that dazed, embarrassed manner they were suddenly sharing that cooking demanded concentration, and it was impossible to get started in any meaningful way with someone around, especially in light of what had just transpired.

So Ron was forced to lie on the rocks and dry off.

And sneeze until he could sneeze no more.

And doze.

But just as his eyes drifted closed, something made him twitch and open them again. It wasn't really a sound, nor even the brush of a wayward breeze. It was more subtle than that, was, truth to tell, almost exactly like being watched. Almost, in fact, like when he'd started awake the night before and found that strange white deer staring at him across the hood of his car.

No, he corrected, it wasn't like that at all, for that had felt threatening; this did not—though he could not say how it *did* feel. Peaceful, maybe? As if something were watching over him, protecting him. Approving of what he and Brandy had done.

God! And Wendy not even gone twelve hours! What in the world had gotten into him? He was never *that* spontaneously randy. He thought he knew, too—but somehow couldn't quite focus. And as he tried to pursue that nebulous knowledge, his eyes drifted shut again, and the only sounds were the tinkling of the brook, the sussuration of the breeze through the leaves, the distant call of birds. And maybe—possibly—just at the point where sleep began—a voice calling his name that might, just barely, have been Wendy's.

But when he awoke and looked around, with his body covered with goose bumps under a shimmer of pollen, all he heard were the sounds of wind and water. And those other Winds, when he lowered his shields to admit them, brought him no Voices at all except Brandy's wondering what was keeping him. Sighing, he rose, dressed, scooped up his towel, the soap, and his still damp work clothes, and started, barefoot, up the hill.

Dinner was excellent: venison steaks, fresh mushrooms, and even fresher blueberries from the year's first picking, and there was cider to drink, from a barrel Brandy's mom had pressed the previous autumn. And the company was marvelous as well: they ate on what was obviously Brandy's good china, and finally got around to asking the usual sorts of questions about background, family, and interests most people ask *before* intimacy, at least when there's some reason to suppose there might be something serious to their relationship.

As for that event itself, neither mentioned it, as if they both knew they had somehow overstepped their normal bounds and dared not subject themselves to further temptation even through talk. Indeed, Ron's memories of the occasion were already blurring, becoming as distant as a dream. And that was perplexing, too—if only he could remember why. At least he had finally stopped sneezing.

Inevitably, of course, talk turned to Brandy Hall and its mistress's plans for it. But *now* they included a new element. Now there was talk of how Ron fit into the completion schedule—and this without an actual "yes" having ever been spoken.

"Tell you what," he said, pushing back from the table and rubbing his tummy appreciatively with one hand, while he slipped a surreptitious tidbit to Matty Groves. "I'm pretty hot to get going—so if you *want*, I can go into town tomorrow and pick up a tent, and use that for a forge and studio. If I get the right kind, I could even pretty much move into it."

"Sure," Brandy replied absently, chewing her lip unconsciously, as if something yet remained she hadn't quite mustered nerve enough to say. Once more, Ron suppressed an urge to snoop. "Yeah . . ." she went on, "go ahead and look for a tent. But . . . while you're at it, maybe . . ."

She hesitated again, gnawing her lip even more vigorously.

"What?"

She grimaced decisively. "Oh, I was just going to say that you might as well go ahead and pick up two."

"Two?" Ron wondered. "I'm not *that* big," he continued, in an effort at dispelling some of the tension he unaccountably felt rising. "And I *sure* don't have that much stuff."

"Oh, didn't I tell you?" Brandy replied in that awkward way people have who aren't used to lying.

"I don't know," Ron shot back with a touch of irritation, "since I don't know what it *is* yet."

She took a deep breath, but regarded him steadily. "Well," she said at last, "you're not going to be the *only* one staying up here." Her voice was calm and decisive, but her words seemed to take a great deal of effort.

And in turn, it took Ron considerable fortitude to steel himself and murmur, "I'm not?"

Brandy shook her head. "I hired another assistant today. Van Vannister. I think you've met."

"Yeah," Ron managed weakly, trying very hard not to groan, "we have." He rose abruptly and carried his plate, silverware, and glass toward the sink. "No problem," he added.

But he very much feared he had just told a monstrous lie.

PART II

HEALING

Interlude 4

The Waiting

Welch County, Georgia
Thursday, July 29—midnight

It should have been the candle again, but it has burned far past redemption, lost to last month's Callings. Now it is a lesser flame that brings the pain, one longer-lived than a match, easier to manage than a taper: a cigarette lighter held 'neath the palm of the hand. The striker flicked, a spark, and then . . .

Fire.

Fire and pain.

He closes his eyes and breathes darkness. He is fearful, for this time there is some chance of discovery. Not like last time.

The scent of pines fills his nostrils—and the spicy scent of a certain pollen that disturbs him, for he has smelt its like before and it is not entirely of this world.

He suspects he knows whence it comes, too, and would ask if only time were not so urgent.

Urgent.

He has forgotten urgent.

A deep breath, another, a focus, and then . . .

Pain and . . .

"Mother?"

"Son."

"I have a favor."

"I have the power to grant such things."

"As you have granted them before."

"Spare me your flattery."

"Very well: I need to have speech with my father."

"He is dead—or should be."

"It is because of that I would seek him. He exists only as bones. And bones are what I have need of—after a fashion."

"Can you not Call them yourself?"

"Not bones. Only their lifeless kin."

"You speak in riddles."

"So I do. So do you. I have heard it is one of your few delights."

"I would strike you, impertinent boy, if I had a body here."

"I would cry if you did—*should* you be successful."

"It will . . . take some time to find your father."

"Not too much, or the fire may fade."

"Or flame too high and destroy you."

"Not me, much though I might wish it."

"Tomorrow?"

"As I number days, or you?"

"As your father would have done."

"I—never mind. Farewell, Mother."

"Farewell."

A pause, and darkness rings with silent hesitation.

"Mother?"

"Yes, son."

"I think it may soon be over."

Chapter 17

Every Breath You Take

Jackson County, Georgia
Friday, July 30—dusk

"Well, thank God *that's* over," Ron sighed, reaching up to slam the Thunderbird's decklid—which he had to do twice: the luggage compartment was that full. So was the Sable station wagon Karen had driven down to Jackson County behind him. The Centauri, alas, hadn't enough trunk space for a move—even if it had been running.

"Whew," Karen echoed, wiping her hands on her dusty black sweatshirt before flopping against the nearest inky fender. "Remind *me* never to try this!"

Ron dragged a red bandanna across his sweaty forehead. "Teach you to volunteer," he teased.

"What *choice* did I have?" the girl—Ron still couldn't think of her as more than thirteen—shot back indignantly. "It was the only way Lew'd let either of us out of his sight! 'Sides, Athens is a happenin' place. Or it's supposed to be," she added with a sly sideways glance that carried a very adult weight of accusation.

241

"Sorry I didn't have time to show you around," Ron apologized with a wry half smile. He stuffed the bandanna back into the single intact pocket in his work-worn jeans, gave the decklid one final push just to be certain—and gazed wistfully across the yard at the neat nineteenth-century farmhouse that had been his home for the previous three years. And wondered if he'd ever inhabit those big, airy rooms again. Oh, he'd retain ownership, he supposed: rent it out or use it as a base of operations when he came to Athens. But something told him it had been his permanent address for the last time. Assuming things worked out like he thought they might with Brandy.

Might was the operative word, too; because right now she was all business. School would start in another couple of weeks, and she was desperate to have Brandy Hall habitable by then. And *might* just make it. It was completely shelled in—finally—and there'd been no more trouble from the plague-prone piece of foundation. It was almost all roofed over, too, except for the Great Hall, which they'd left open in order to help illuminate the inner rooms, which had not yet been fully wired. And they were well along on detailing, which was *his* main responsibility.

Not that he hadn't done his share otherwise, of course; especially during those wild, giddy weeks after she'd hired him and Vannister. Shoot, back then they'd virtually completed a room every six days—basically by setting high but realistic goals and sticking to them, so that they finished a floor one day, a wall the next, and so.

The pace had slackened lately, at least for Brandy and the big redhead; but *Ron's* work was picking up, as archways suddenly needed filling with doors, and switch plates and hinges and a thousand other bits of decorative hardware needed crafting—mostly by hand to Brandy's exacting designs. Only the fact that he'd now reached the stage where he needed to retrieve a few specialized tools from his Athens studio gave him sufficient cause for a return to his old stomping grounds.

That, and making one final check on Wendy.

No! He wouldn't think about her, not now, not here; it would accomplish nothing except getting him wired. Instead, he spent one last moment staring at the house:

at the broad front porch that had seen so many parties, so much crafting, so many lingering afternoon conversations. At the high center gable where he'd installed a jewelry studio. At the stand of ancient oaks that grew thick around.

Finally he sighed again and checked his watch. "Oh jeeze," he cried. "It's nearly nine! We're gonna have to boogie if we want to make it back at a reasonable hour."

"But you promised me dinner!" Karen wailed in feigned dismay, pushing her lip out in an exaggerated pout. "You promised me the best dinner in Athens!"

"I was afraid you'd remember that," Ron groaned. "So I guess I'll have to keep my word, won't I?—considering I made a promise, and all. You *sure* you don't mind driving home late?"

"Fine with me," Karen told him promptly. "I like cruising along in the wee hours with just my thoughts."

I wish I did, Ron thought, but what he actually said was, "Okay then, you can follow me."

Karen nodded tiredly and headed off toward where the Sable was parked farther down the sandy driveway.

But Ron was not ready to leave—not quite yet. Something was calling to him, wanting him to remain there. Nothing tangible, really, and certainly not a Voice, just . . . something. For the barest instant he felt as he had on that strange, terrible, wonderful, dreamlike day that had begun with him hungover in the woods and had ended with him and Brandy making love; the day of the odd drifting pollen, when he'd napped down by the lake and heard—or *thought* he heard—Wendy whisper his name.

He had been edging around the back of the Thunderbird, though, but as he cleared the left rear corner, something caught his eye in the landscape reflected on the deeply waxed decklid. The house was visible—or its pale inverted doppelganger and the enfolding trees, like a background of monochrome paisley. But more branches reflected there, too, from a nearby hickory: branches that made a dark lacework pattern across the gleaming paint. And there was something odd about one clump of mirrored leaves: something familiar. Abruptly he had a chill.

For there, where the metal curved over to meet the vertical wall of the taillights, a face stared back at him:

a woman's face made of highlights and memory. No, it was really only leaves, he assured himself: one for a nose, others for cheeks, forehead, chin; and with shadows for eyes and lips and hair.

But it looked an *awful* lot like Wendy. And he could have *sworn* it smiled.

He shivered again and glanced around, searched the looming hickory for the image's real-world analog. And could not find one. He was still having goose bumps when he reached the driver's door.

Karen was staring at him intently from beside the Sable. "Jeeze!" she called. "You look like you've just seen a ghost!"

"Maybe I have," Ron whispered. "Maybe I just have."

"But you've done everything you *can*!" Karen informed him nearly three hours later, as she munched a mouthful of barbecued shrimp at Harry Bissett's New Orleans Cafe and Oyster Bar. "Don't you think you oughta, y'know, like just let this thing with Wendy *rest*?" In spite of her adolescent speech patterns, she sounded suspiciously like a very perceptive adult—which Ron found damned unsettling—especially when she was right.

"I would, except—"

"What?"

He stirred his jambalaya with his fork but did not sample it. "I . . . I still worry about her, I guess," he said finally. "I mean I wasn't exactly in the market for another girlfriend when I met Brandy. And it really was odd the way Wendy just up and disappeared without any warning *at all*. I guess that's what *really* bugs me: her acting like she always did, and then—bam—she changes."

"But people *do* change," Karen mumbled through another mouthful—the food had been *very* late and she was hungry.

"Not overnight, they don't! Not like Wendy did!"

She swallowed, gave him another one of those serious, intense little stares. "Yeah, but—I don't know—maybe she regained her memory or something. You ever think about that?"

"Sure I have. But I don't think that's what happened."

"Why not?"

Ron scowled and glanced around uncomfortably, not at all certain that the junglelike atrium of an expensive restaurant in downtown Athens was the proper place to be discussing such topics, even close to midnight when they were mostly alone. "Because—it's one of those things."

A delicate black eyebrow lifted skyward. "Oh . . . one of *those* . . ."

"Yeah," Ron grunted, then hunched forward over the table. "I still can't Hear her, and neither can Lew, and we both think we could if she had her memory back."

"Oh . . ."

He leaned back again. "See why I'm concerned?"

"She *has* called," Karen pointed out.

"Called Cardalba, not me," Ron countered. "And she's *got* my number, and shouldn't have Lew's, since it's unlisted."

Karen put down her fork and folded her hands on the table. "So? She probably jotted it down when she was up, or something. 'Sides, you've *heard* the messages—we both have—and they're definitely her. She *said* she's moved, for heaven's sake! She's *said* to tell you she's okay."

"Yeah," Ron finished for her. "And she *says* she understands; and she *says* she thought it best to leave Athens and get on with her life somewhere else."

"So why don't you believe her?"

Ron shrugged helplessly. "I don't *know*! I just don't. And when you're like I am—like Lew and I are—you have to trust those kind of hunches."

"What about the, y'know, omens?"

"Bubble-gum, rap, and beach music, mostly. Lots of soft stuff like the crap they're playing in here."

"Which means . . . ?"

Ron grimaced in exasperation. "They can't deal with major mojo *every* day, Karen. There just aren't that many songs that carry any weight. Also, they tend to address a specific question—though it's not always what *you* want to know, let me tell you. Or else they predict a particular event, and either way, they do it when *they're* ready. Lately things have been pretty much status quo. Which means they're not giving me anything I can work with."

"So? That should give you comfort, man! Give you permission to, like, get on with the rest of your life."

"Yeah, it should. Except—except . . . I dunno. Something still isn't right about it. I guess I feel like I'm still responsible for her. And before you ask, yeah, I've been in touch with her friends—what few she's got. And none of them have heard from her either—which sounds to me like she's pretty well adrift. Adrift in a world that has no obligation to take care of her."

Karen reached out and patted his hand. "She'll do okay. I mean, I didn't know her real well, and we kinda had some problems 'cause she was so changeable and all; but she seemed really, *really* together, too—in a way."

Ron nodded, oddly comforted by Karen's simple gesture. "She is—in *some* ways. But I guess what I'm saying is that while she's a free and independent person, and I've got no legal obligation to protect her, I sort of assumed a moral one when we paired up. And the fact that we've split doesn't change the fact that I still care about her."

The grip on his hand tightened. "You've done all you could, Ronny. You really have!"

He would not meet her gaze. "Have I?"

"Haven't you?"

A stiff shrug. "Maybe."

Karen withdrew the hand and started counting on her fingers. "Okay, guy, here we go," she began brusquely. "First of all, you've *called* her, right?"

Ron nodded. "And her phone's been disconnected."

"Fine, so you've *written*, too, right?"

"And it's all come back stamped MOVED, LEFT NO ADDRESS."

"And you've checked by her apartment?"

"Yeah."

"And found *it* empty?"

"Right."

"But with a next-door neighbor who said he hadn't seen her but *had* heard somebody moving around over there about the time she should have returned from up home, and had looked in the window and seen that her stuff was gone. *And* with a landlady who said she'd given notice."

"The whole thing being conducted by phone, though," Ron added sourly. "Nobody's actually *seen* her after she left Welch County."

Karen's brow puckered in exasperation. "Well, gee! Sounds to *me* like you're determined to think the worst."

"No comment," he murmured cryptically.

"What's *that* supposed to mean?"

"Nothing."

"But *something's* still bugging you, isn't it?"

"Maybe."

"Wanta talk about it?"

He shook his head.

"Why not?"

" 'Cause . . . 'cause I just *can't!*"

Because, confound it, this nosy little girl-child-sybil-wench was right: he couldn't shake the suspicion that something had happened to Wendy!

The main thing was that Voice: his name riding the sussuration of the wind. He'd heard it a couple of times since the first time, always in the woods, and usually at sunset or sunrise when he went there to meditate and let his consciousness drift. But it was never *more* than his name—"Ronny," long and drawn out. And always so close to a whisper that it was easily possible to ascribe it to the breezes that tended to be fairly rambunctious around Brandy Hall. He had always chalked it up to his guilty conscience deviling him.

If only there hadn't been *other* manifestations, of which this evening's, when he'd seen the ghostly reflection, was only the latest. And unfortunately, that episode wasn't unique, either. Most commonly he'd glance into a body of water—usually the still edge of the lake down at the cove, the place where the water lilies and cat-tails grew—and think he glimpsed Wendy's face. But it always proved to be his own visage distorted by ripples. Or a reflection of trees. Or clouds. And a closer examination always confirmed that.

A chair squeaked nearby and he started, then looked up to see Karen eyeing him curiously. And only then did he realize that he'd been staring at the glassy high-lights on his wineglass for at least the last two minutes, more than half afraid he might actually see his lost girl-friend *there*.

"You really *do* think something's wrong, don't you?" Karen asked softly.

Ron tried to smile. "Lew been giving you lessons?"

"I don't *need* lessons."

A sigh. "Okay, so maybe you're right—and for some reason I don't think . . . whatever has happened is *normally* wrong, if you know what I mean."

"I do . . . I think."

Ron glanced around again, and once he had ascertained that no one was in easy listening range, continued in a very low voice. "I . . . gee, Karen, I don't know . . . I guess I'd be a lot happier if I just didn't *know* so much."

"What do you mean?"

"Did you ever just want to be normal?" he asked abruptly, ignoring her question.

"I *am* normal," she replied promptly. "I just have an abnormal job."

"*Sure* you do," Ron shot back with a mock sarcasm that was not, however, entirely feigned. "Oh, and speaking of which: How's Lew's packing coming?"

She shrugged in turn and managed to get down a whole mouthful before answering. "Okay, I guess."

Ron, too, ate in silence. Then, "I still can't believe I agreed to do that."

Karen's eyes twinkled mischievously. "You mean pack? We did that all day, if you remember."

"I *wish* that's what I meant," he snorted. "But no, I was talking about . . . about the Mastership."

She eyed him warily. "Maybe you should, actually—talk about it, I mean. I mean if you won't talk to him, and you can't talk to Brandy and Van, who else does that leave?"

"Good point," Ron conceded with a chuckle. "Well, actually, there's Uncle Dion and maybe Uncle Gil, but they're both still in the clink."

"So *you* talk, *I'll* eat."

"And then we take turns, and you tell me what it's like to be . . . what you are?"

"Sounds fair."

"Okay," Ron began. "Well, I guess the thing that freaks me out most is, like, just the way it happened. I mean there I was having dinner with Lew after I'd sort of decided to stay up there and help out Brandy, but we were both real nervous about talking about his request 'cause of what happened before, so we were sort of flirting with it—you know, talking about it in the abstract and all: as a thing I *might* consider now that it looked like I was gonna stay in Welch County anyway. Or at least until Brandy got her house done. Or maybe, maybe, *maybe* always—*if* things worked out exactly right with her. But somehow, by the time we'd finished the last course, we'd shifted form saying *might* and *maybe* to *will* and *can*—and the next thing I know, we're toasting the deal!"

Karen smirked prettily. "That sounds like Lew!"

"Yeah," Ron agreed, nodding. "And that's what bugs me, 'cause it's a very Listener thing to do. It smacks of manipulation, only I *know* he wasn't pulling anything fast with me, 'cause he can't; only it also bugs me that I even think that, 'cause I used to trust him more than anybody alive, and all of a sudden now I don't."

"But . . . uh, you *are* gonna go through with it, aren't you? The deal, I mean."

He shrugged. "I reckon so. I mean we've sort of made a contract, and he's gonna transfer the Binding Ritual to me, and all. But—" He paused, uncertain whether he should continue, especially here, now, to this person. On the other hand, this had been bugging him for a long time, and beyond one too hasty and circumspect phone call to Uncle Dion, he'd had no chance at all to talk about it—and was discovering, now that he was actually blurting the whole mess out, that he'd truly needed this kind of catharsis.

"Go for it," Karen prompted with the absolute sincerity of the very young. "You can tell me *anything*."

Ron exhaled deeply and nodded. "Oh, crap," he sighed, "well, I guess the big thing is that now that I'm committed—now that I've actually had time to *think* about what I've done—I'm having second thoughts. But on the other hand, maybe it wouldn't really be that bad. I mean the basic agreement's pretty . . . well, pretty *basic*."

"What *is* the agreement, anyway?" Karen asked slyly. "I've never actually heard."

Ron finished his wine in one gulp—thus seeking, perhaps, an excuse for a wagging tongue. Nor did he call up that sort of Luck that could have quickly cleared his head. "Oh . . . well, essentially it's just a trade. See, first of all, I assume the Mastership for a maximum of three years, but practically speaking, for somewhat less than that. During that time I live wherever I want to as long as it's in Welch County, but I maintain Cardalba Hall in reasonable condition, which shouldn't be a problem, considering that Aunt Martha'll be back by then—though God only knows *what* that little old lady'll do when she finds out what's happened. But anyway, I'm also supposed to try to keep up the Luck to at least a minimum level—which mostly means preventing major disasters. Beyond that, Lew'll train me some, and probably dear Auntie—once we peel her off the ceiling."

Karen's eyes sparkled merrily. "Think she'll be pissed, huh?"

Ron glanced at his watch absently—and noted to his dismay that it was only moments before midnight. "Who knows? There's no precedent for Masters taking leaves of absence."

"And what about Lew? You think he'll pull it off? College, I mean."

"Of course he will. He's brilliant. We all are."

"And conceited."

Ron started to counter with a zinger of his own but froze. And then whispered in a very small voice. "I think you should make that 'paranoid as hell.' "

"Why?" Karen asked innocently, but with real concern.

"Just listen," Ron murmured even more softly. "Listen to what just came on the radio."

Karen's brow furrowed, and she closed her eyes, obviously intent on hearing what the local oldies station that had been providing background music was playing.

"Oh jeeze," she mouthed, when she opened them again. "It's . . ."

" 'Wendy,' " he finished for her. "It's just past midnight, which makes that the first song of the day—the *Significator* song. And they're playing 'Wendy.' "

"Whooosh!" Karen gasped, amazed.

"Oh sweet Jesus," Ron echoed, and fell silent.

Interlude 5

Down by the River

Welch County, Georgia
Friday, July 30—midnight

He has come to the place where the water is, because he
has had his fill of fire. He stands in it, and then he swims,
and after a while, he lets go—though to him it is more like
lying down.

The water embraces his head. Cold water. Dark water.
Water black as night.

Or death . . .

He sinks.

Deeper, deeper . . .

His lungs tighten. He cannot breathe. But must.

He opens his mouth, draws in . . .

Water.

He is drowning . . . drowning . . .

He sucks in more . . .

Water. And with it comes his old friend pain.

"Son?" The voice is distant, obscure. He who speaks has
long abandoned speaking.

"Father? *Father!*"

"I . . . my son, I cannot stay long. I cannot even think how this is, I being nothing but bones."

"Ah, and it is of bones I would speak—after a fashion."

"What . . . sort of bones? Not mine, I hope, for they would be hard to come by."

"They are one with the earth now?"

"So it seems."

"And yet you are here."

"So I am. I am a part of time, but I seem to be apart from it as well."

"That is a thing I know very well indeed."

"What?"

"Time—and how to be apart from it, how to dance with it and its brother, space. How to fit them into certain . . . dreams . . ."

"But you said you needed to speak of bones."

"So I do."

"Well?"

"Have you friends among them?"

"What?"

"Bones. Bones older than you. Tiny bones. Bones so small they think they are stone."

"What do you need them for?"

"I need them so that I may master my fate. Maybe so that I can someday join them. But they will not hark to me. You it is who must Call."

"It is a thing I have never done."

"Nor I—until I Called my mother."

"She is well?"

"Let us simply say that she . . . *is*."

"But is she—"

He interrupts, for water is a crueler master than fire and will not long indulge him. "I have to leave. But if you bring them, I will take them home."

"Where?"

"Here. Nearby."

"Within Time—or without it?"

"Yes."

"Son?"

"Yes."

"I pray you to be happy."

"I will."

"And I ask that you forgive me."

"I did that long ago."

"That was not you."

"It was—but now I must leave."

He gulps—gags, opens his eyes into darkness and seeks the light. He rises. His head breaks water.

He coughs and spews, and then he breathes in night.

Very soon he is dreaming. Dreaming of bones awakening to his Call.

Chapter 18

Walk Like an Egyptian

Brandy's Knoll
Saturday, July 31—late morning

Brandy stepped back reflexively, then froze, too stunned to do more than close her eyes and gasp. The tape-bound bundle of cornice moldings she and Weedge had just man-handled down the skeletal basement stairs slipped from her shock-numbed fingers to smack loudly against the bare concrete floor. A softer slap behind her was Weedge on the bottommost tread, easing the other end down with greater care.

"I'm . . . not . . . *seeing* . . . this!" Brandy groaned when she finally found her voice. She steeled herself and for the second time surveyed the windowless cinder-block room visible through the archway beyond: the room into whose corners four cast-concrete faux-Egyptian columns were now neatly tucked, with an additional two half columns in each wall breaking the spaces between into thirds, for a total of twelve. "No *way* I could've missed somebody making *those*," she continued, "much less put-ting 'em in!"

"Say what?" Weedge grunted impatiently, flexing her fingers before wiping them on her jeans and sauntering up the short corridor.

Brandy could only point mutely and flatten against the wall as her friend scrunched past to examine the additions for herself. Weedge remained in the archway for maybe fifteen seconds, puffing her cheeks thoughtfully, then stepped back and mirrored Brandy's pose on the opposite wall. Her eyes were wide. Concerned, too—but likely more for Brandy's mental health than anything to do with Brandy Hall.

"So what's the problem?" Weedge asked, with an uncertain tilt of her head. "Looks just fine to me. Better than I expected, actually. And I *really* like those new—what d'you call 'em? Pilasters?"

Brandy exhaled slowly and nodded. "Yeah, well, actually, *they're* the problem."

Weedge folded her arms and stared at her askance. "Oh *yeah*?"

Another nod. "They're not supposed to be there!"

"They're *not*?" Weedge looked genuinely alarmed. "But—how could they not be?"

Brandy shook her head. "Well, let's just say they weren't there when I measured that room last night for this friggin' molding we just dumped!"

"So what're you complaining for? I mean they look really neat now—and expensive. Maybe somebody likes you. Or—"

"Yeah, tell me about it!" Brandy interrupted, a nervous edge in her voice. "But see, that's part of the problem. They *are* too expensive, too *damned* expensive for anyone to just happen to have 'em lying around. Shoot, I couldn't afford 'em for the next several centuries—which is why I decided not to include 'em in the first place. But . . ." She paused, realizing she'd already said too much.

"What?" Weedge's question sounded casual, but stubbornness hid in her tone. Brandy would not weasel out of this one quickly.

Nor would Brandy meet her gaze. "Uh, well, basically," she began awkwardly, "basically, they were part of the original design—that first one I did with all the bells and whistles, the actual fantasy house I designed to get it out of my system before I scaled back to something halfway reasonable."

"Reasonable!" Weedge snorted. "That's debatable, but go on."

Brandy shook her head. "No, I want to check something."

Weedge shrugged indulgently but glanced at her watch. "It's your call."

Brandy fumbled in her pocket for a moment, then produced a pencil, a small notebook, and an industrial-strength tape measure—and with them in hand, strode purposefully into the suspect room. Weedge raised an eyebrow and followed.

"Here, hold this," Brandy ordered with an air of unconscious authority, handing her friend the writing materials. "You remember how much of that stuff we bought?"

"Exactly sixty-five feet," Weedge quoted. "Sixteen per wall, with one left over for waste. I ought to know," she added with a pointed chuckle, "seein' as how you told the poor salesman about twenty times."

Brandy's only reply was to stretch the tape between the nearest two pilasters. She called out a number, them moved on to the next and the next, and so on around the room.

Her friend followed, intent on jotting down numbers. When they had finished, Brandy retrieved the notebook and quickly ran up the total. Her face was troubled when she looked up again.

"And . . . ?" Weedge prompted cautiously.

A helpless shrug. "Well, unless I've forgotten how to do math, something damned strange is going on."

"So clue me."

Brandy grimaced in resignation and commenced a slow slump down the wall, though Weedge remained standing. "Oh gee, I really don't want to get into this—but I reckon I oughta."

"I've got ears, still got a little bit of time 'fore I have to boogie."

"Got a job interview in Cordova, if memory serves," Brandy shot back. "Which means you oughta be going."

"Which means you don't want to tell me!" Weedge snorted. "Except that you know you're gonna."

Brandy knew defeat when she was confronted with it. "Okay," she began, "I said sixty-four feet, right?"

"Y-eah," Weedge acknowledged hesitantly. "Go on."

"Well, those pilasters are each nearly a foot wide, and there're twelve of 'em, correct?"

"Okay . . ."

"So if you measure the distance between 'em, it ought to total *less* than sixty-four feet, 'cause the pilasters take up roughly twelve feet of it, wouldn't you say?"

"Sounds good to me."

Brandy took a deep breath and looked her friend in the eye. "Well, Weedge, the problem is . . . there's not."

"Huh?"

"It still adds up to sixty-four feet."

Weedge's brow wrinkled in perplexity. "But that means . . . but that's impossible."

Brandy nodded vigorously. "Yes, it is—or else the room's gotten bigger in the night."

"And that's impossible, too."

"W.G., my friend," Brandy sighed. "I think it's time we had a little discussion."

"I'm all ears," Weedge assured her. *"Believe* me."

"Sit down." Brandy waited until her buddy had gotten herself arranged. "Well, gee, where do I start? At the beginning, I guess, only I don't exactly know when that was."

"You're stalling, gal."

A dry chuckle. "So I am. But this is hard to talk about— *damned* hard, 'cause folks already think I'm crazy. You will, too, once I get into this. But—well, uh . . . this isn't the first time something like this has happened. I mean I told you about the foundations and all, but since then, there've been a lot of strange things. Like . . . well, the main thing is that there was supposed to be a set of closets between two rooms upstairs. They were in the plans, but I hadn't built 'em yet; but then yesterday I came back and there they were, clear as day: Vannister had run 'em up— or at least I *think* it was him, since he wouldn't actually admit to anything. But the weird thing, Weedge, the *weird* thing . . . was that it was just like we just saw: I measured the room to either side, and they were the same size as before. And then I measured the wall outside just in case, and got the very same thing—which means there somehow got to be forty-five feet of room inside a wall that's only forty feet long outside. Which I'm sure you'll agree can't happen."

Weedge eyed her skeptically. "And you're sure? I mean you couldn't have made a mistake or anything?"

"Not bloody likely!" Brandy snapped. "I've lived with the specs for this place for ten years. No way I'd forget a major dimension."

"And you checked this?"

"Me and Van did 'cause Ronny wasn't here. He took me aside and made me watch as he measured everything again and then compared his specs to the blueprints—and found everything kosher. Well—I was pretty freaked, let me tell you."

"Hmmm. But did you, uh, ever think he might be right? I mean you have been under a lot of strain, and—"

"And having two men around is causing lapses of lucidity? Sure!"

Weedge regarded her seriously. "Stress *can* affect the memory, you know. God knows *I* can attest to that from experience. And it can sure as hell make you vague and drifty, like you've been complaining about so much lately—even high under some circumstances."

"But not hallucinogenic, I don't think," Brandy countered. "But see, the problem is that Van's *always* doing things like that: making unauthorized alterations or additions or modifications. It *has* to be him, simply by process of elimination, 'cause I can always *account* for Ron's time. Trouble is, he always does 'em while I'm gone; and always while Ron's occupied—*pre*occupied, rather, 'cause God knows when he gets cookin' on a casting project, the elves could carry off the whole place and he wouldn't notice."

"And have you said anything to him? Vannister, I mean? It's hard for me to imagine that you haven't."

"Oh yes!" Brandy cried vehemently. "You can bet on that! But he just grins and tells me that if I don't like the

alterations, he'll be glad to change 'em back—but it'll cost
me more time than leaving 'em alone, and he can't hang
around indefinitely. And—dammit, Weedge, I always *do*
wind up liking 'em. In fact, a bloody lot of 'em are like
these pilasters: things I wanted to incorporate but discarded
as impractical—or too expensive."

"And yet you're complaining."

An apologetic smile. "And you don't have time to listen
to this kinda crap now."

Weedge checked her watch again and shook her head.
"Not really. Sorry, but I don't have a chance at a job
upgrade every day."

"I understand," Brandy replied. Lord only knew Weedge
had stood by her most of the times she'd needed her. She
couldn't begrudge her a few minutes now.

"Well," Weedge sighed, as if in summary. "*I* think you
should count your blessings."

"Yeah, but this is *my* friggin' house!" Brandy retorted
sharply. "*My* dream! And by God, I have a right to see it
finished according to *my* plan!"

She rose then, but as she came full upright, she dropped the tape measure she'd been fidgeting with, oblivious to the possible damage such an action might cause
the innocent tool. Several feet of tape had been hanging
out when she had done so and now began to rewind
like a thin metallic snake. She glared at it and stomped
to the stairs, completely ignoring her startled companion.

"Brandy, what . . . ?"

But Brandy had just slipped past her tenuous temper
limit.

Where was Vannister? Where *was* he? And why was he
never around when she discovered the kind of crap she just
had? Shoot, if she let him have his way, he'd have her so
far over budget, she'd never get out. (Though as a point
of fact, her materials cost had been almost nothing since
she'd hired him: the guy was a genius when it came to
scrounging, recycling, and reusing, and he often returned
from nameless nocturnal ramblings with a truckload of useful supplies he swore he'd acquired legitimately—mostly
by haunting other building sites and the town dump.) She'd

been wary of that at first, but had eventually come to accept it.

But she merry well wasn't going to accept any more unauthorized tinkering with her design! Not when she found what was supposed to be one of the few elegantly modern rooms in her house suddenly Egyptized.

"Brandy!"

"Come or go," Brandy gritted. "Just don't try to stop me!"

She had reached the four-foot-square landing at the top of the stairs by then, and turned left along a short hallway bridged by intersecting groined arches. A matching opening at the end (still without the door Ron was supposed to be completing the strapwork and hardware for at that very moment) led into the large, open space of the entry hall, which in any other house would have been considered finished—except that *she* planned to spend the next several years rendering the First Battle of Magh Tuireadh in Byzantine-style mosaics over every inch of the white-plastered surface. Assuming, of course, that money permitted.

The empty round-topped opening that would one day hold the front doors gaped to the left, a bright shape against the darker inside walls. And beyond she could hear music: something Celtic—possibly the Chieftains or Clannadd, counterpointed by Ron tap-tap-tapping at the forge.

"Brandy, wait up!"

She ignored the huffing and puffing a room behind her and stepped into the sunlit south arcade. Heat slapped against her face as she emerged into the full light of day, and only then did she realize how cool it had been within the thick basement walls, even in high summer—not that it had cooled her down! Not hardly. Her gaze darted back and forth automatically, seeking the suspect workman. But where *was* he? Maybe Ron knew. Slow he might be, but at least he did what he was told, was reliable, and predictable. And usually had at least *some* idea of what was going on.

Grimacing sourly, she stuffed her hands into her jeans pockets and strode toward the twenty-foot-square tent that sheltered both Ron's forge and the stacks of boxes and cheap furniture that did him for an apartment. Weedge jogged up to join her, saying nothing, but staring at her reproachfully.

Ron was there, as he always was: naked as legality and the fear of rambunctious sparks allowed, which basically meant he was wearing scandalously short cutoffs, a leather smith's apron, and a red bandanna-cum-sweatband—the latter a necessity, since he'd let his hair grow out in the month he'd been here. Which she approved of—but the sparse beard he was also sporting . . . well, she wasn't sure if that was good or not.

In spite of her anger, she couldn't help watching him for a moment, enjoying the way his muscles tensed and stretched beneath his sweat-sheened skin as he swung his hammer. He'd bulked up a bit in the last few weeks, mostly in his chest and shoulders. She liked that, too—when she had time for liking. And at least he was doing what he was supposed to: pounding away on the promised strapwork— very intensely, so it appeared. In fact, he looked to be working on two projects at once, if the vat of bronze bubbling in the back was any indication. For, unless she missed her guess, *that* would soon be transformed into yet another panel for the doors whose steel-channel framework rested on a brace of sawhorses beyond. Matty Groves was napping on them now—as he always seemed to be: a blot of blotchy shadow in the sunshine.

Eventually Ron saw them—or sensed their presence at any rate; he had an uncanny way of doing that. He raised a dark brow into his head rag. The hammering ceased as he looked up tiredly. "Trouble?"

"Irritation," she countered with a scowl, not liking to be preempted, even when he was right. "Have you seen Van?"

Ron squinted to left and right. "He's not downstairs? That's where he said he'd be."

Brandy shook her head vehemently. "Nope."

"His tent, then?"

Brandy glanced over her shoulder at the twin pavilion to this one. It housed most of the more perishable supplies, as well as Vannister's now permanently unrolled sleeping bag and the matching military knapsacks that, with his truck, seemed to be his only property. The flap was open wide, and unless the guy had added invisibility to his other skills, he wasn't there.

Ron was looking with her—as was the silent Weedge. "I guess not," he muttered wearily. "I don't know where he is, then. You know how quiet he can be."

"Make that sneaky," Brandy grumbled. "He's been at it again."

"At what?" Ron asked guilelessly, but Brandy suspected he knew perfectly well what she was referring to—or at least the general area. "Just come with me, okay?" she sighed finally. "I need to show you something."

Ron sighed in turn, shoved the length of glowing iron he'd been assailing into a vat of water to his right, and, when the resulting cloud of acrid-smelling steam had dispersed, smacked it twice with the hammer, and followed obediently.

A moment later, the three of them were inspecting the out-of-spec wall.

"Looks fine to me," Ron told her. "What's the trouble?"

"Those!" Brandy shot back fiercely. "Those goddamned pilasters that I can't afford and that nobody's had time to build, and that shouldn't jive with the amount of molding I just bought but still do. *You* didn't have anything to do with 'em, did you?" she added suspiciously.

Ron responded with the barely perceptible shrug that was his usual reaction when being falsely accused. "When would I have had time? Besides, metal's my thing—and clay. I don't get on well with limestone."

"They're concrete," Brandy corrected automatically.

"Well, they're limestone *now*," Ron countered, stepping forward to peruse the nearest more closely, then running a hand along the smooth, tapered length. "See? There's a fossil ammonite right here."

"Oh *shit*!" Brandy cried incredulously, exchanging troubled glances with an antsy-looking Weedge. "No way! I mean I was just down here a *second* ago, and . . ."

"Yeah, but you weren't expecting to see these, so you said. So maybe once you *did* see 'em, you just saw what you expected to see, not what was."

"Gimme a break!"

"I was."

"Asshole!"

"I don't feel like arguing now," Ron grumbled resignedly, "not when I've done nothing wrong."

"Except be inattentive while Vannister fools around with my goddamned house again!"

"I can't watch him every minute!" Ron snapped back. "That's not what I'm up here for. Never mind that I wasn't even in the county until after three this morning!"

"Hmmmph," Brandy grunted. "I oughta put a frigging bell on him, or a beeper, or something, just so I can tell where he is and what he's up to."

She fell to examining the remaining pilasters, amazed to discover that they were all limestone. But where had Vannister managed to lay hands on such stuff? The same place he'd gotten that malachite, maybe? That had come from Mason's, so he'd said, but now she wasn't so sure. On the other hand, these had been lately finished, and she hadn't seen any unworked slabs around. And to give him his due, Vannister *had* been sticking to home pretty much constantly for the last couple of days.

Which *still* didn't get him off the hook. Sighing, she turned back to Ron, who was still standing before the opposite wall. He looked wired, too; and she wondered suddenly what he was so intent on. Shoot, she could practically feel the tension massing around him, as if a swarm of invisible mosquitoes was gathering in the air—until, quite suddenly, it fell dead and flat, like it sometimes did in a plane right before your ears popped.

Even Weedge had noticed it, or had keyed into *something*, to judge by the way she was fidgeting and shifting her eyes—which was most unlike her.

But why was Ron staring at the wall like that? He did that sort of thing a lot, though she doubted he knew she'd noticed. But every now and then, especially when something odd was going on, he would just sort of go blank for a few seconds, then shake his head and—like as not—come out with some off-the-wall comment or prediction that almost inevitably came true. He was uncannily accurate at identifying approaching vehicles before they appeared, for instance; and batted near a thousand on guessing who the phone was for and what they wanted. But that still didn't explain his present action, and before she quite knew what she was about, her tongue had got ahead of her discretion.

"What're you *doing*?" she asked sharply, fixing him with a glare.

Ron blinked, then turned and regarded her sheepishly. "I dunno. What *was* I doing?"

"Staring into space!" Brandy snapped with a degree of exasperation she instantly regretted. Weedge shot her a warning glare.

"I *was*?"

"You got it."

"I . . . guess I was just thinking," Ron mumbled lamely, not looking at her.

"You think a bloody lot, then!"

"I *do*?"

"Don't lie to me, Ron," she raged. "I've got *enough* to worry about with Vannister being so damned mysterious all the time. I fucking well don't need that kind of shit from you!"

"I *know* you don't!"

"But you still do it!"

Ron regarded her steadily. "Look, I'm human, okay? I've got a functioning brain that can get pretty active sometimes, and since we both know that a lot of smithing more or less happens automatically, I occasionally indulge in a bit of daydream, *okay*?"

"You weren't smithing just now!" Brandy gritted.

"No, but I need to be," Ron countered irritably. "Or do you want something else?"

Brandy shook her head. "I'm sorry," she said with a resigned frown. "You know how I am: I get stressed, I get a shock, I overreact."

Ron nodded and gave her a quick if rather sweaty hug. "No problem." A moment later he was gone.

Weedge lingered a short while longer, looking impatient and worried, and about as indecisive as Brandy had ever seen her. Even as Brandy looked at her, she checked her watch. "I . . . uh, hate to do this to you, Bran, 'cause I really do think something's going on . . . but I have *got* to split. Some things I just can't get out of. But . . ." She hesitated. "But if you need me, call."

" 'Bye. Thanks a lot." And Brandy was left contemplating the wall.

For at least two minutes she stood there, simply staring at it, and—inevitably—arguing with herself. Part of her wanted to be happy: thrilled beyond words that the room was going to be exactly like she had wanted, not as she had conditioned herself to accept. But a different part was totally freaked out, because physics was physics and math was math, and she was more or less sane (she thought), and so were Weedge and Ronny, yet they had essentially corroborated what she had told them—which was that, apparently, physics was *not* always physics nor math consistently math when it came to Brandy Hall. And if she couldn't rely on *them* . . . well, it just didn't do to ponder.

And finally another part pointed out that, wish fulfillment or no, neither Vannister nor anyone else had any right at all to make such major unilateral decisions as the pilasters represented.

And while she couldn't do anything about some things, she could certainly attend to that! And the *only* way to put an end to it once and for all was to go have it out with the perpetrator—*if* she could ever catch up with him.

So where was he?

The woods? Not likely. For in spite of being a basically outdoorsy type, Vannister seemed to prefer sunlight to the dark, cool tree-trunk mazes that enclosed Brandy Hall.

And she was confident he wasn't in the trailer, because she and Weedge had stopped by there right before this latest troubling find.

Which left where?

The lake, she supposed, and come to think of it, that made a fair bit of sense, given that it was by far the hottest day they'd had so far, and that for the first time in memory, she hadn't given the guy an assignment before heading into town.

Sighing, she shot the offending room one final, warning glare and trudged back up the stairs. But this time she did not go straight out her incipient front door, but turned sharp right, and then right again, and pretty soon was snaking her way down the now well-worn path to the lake.

The trees were thick along the trail, and the underlayer of laurel and rhododendron seemed none the worse for having witnessed countless passings of one or the other of the three of them on their way to swim or bathe. Thus, she was unable to determine for certain whether or not Vannister was actually *in* the water until she was no more than twenty yards away. Oh, she could *see* the lake with no trouble: glimmering sun-bright beyond the darker oaks. But the nearer shore was obscured by a particularly dense laurel thicket until she was practically atop the granite shoals that comprised what passed for a beach. And since she wanted to be certain her prey was there before she pounced, she eased off the main trail and picked her way quietly through the screen of waxy-dark leaves. And was trying to disentangle her sleeve from an annoyingly persistent dead twig when she finally caught sight of her quarry.

It was Vannister, all right, flopping along on his back a few yards offshore. But she could not see him clearly, for the wind had picked up and was whipping the lake into ripples that glittered especially brightly where he was. As best she could tell, he was trying to float, but having considerable trouble. Probably the result of his muscle density; there was scarcely an ounce of fat on his body, after all. But in spite of his flailings, he looked happy: utterly, blissfully at peace.

Brandy could feel her resolve falter: Lord knew she was pissed, but she also knew peace—at least of the kind evident on the workman's features—was too fleeting a thing to ever be willfully shattered. And she was still trying to choose between allowing the big lug his indulgence and *then* lighting into him when he got back to the knoll, and the more satisfying alternative of confronting him now, when she at least had the advantage of physical, if not moral, high ground, when he solved the problem for her by the simple expedient of splashing toward shore, and— once he had found bottom—sauntering straight toward her hidey-hole. Fortunately, he was looking at the beach, not toward the surrounding foliage.

Brandy could not help but gape, first from shock, then from embarrassment, and finally from something closely approximating awe.

Vannister was naked—of course—which fact should not have surprised her. But moving as he was, striding unself-consciously through the shallows, with water cascading off him, and the sun turning every drop and rivulet to silver-white fire, while the spray kicking up behind him sparkled like diamonds and gold, he looked less like a man than some river deity, rising newborn from lakewater foam.

She had never seen him bare before, either, though he went shirtless constantly and sometimes seemed locked in an unspoken war with Ron over who could wear the most ragged jeans. But now she *was* seeing him, and could not help enjoying the view.

The river god analogy was not inapt, she decided. For like most of the swimmers she had known (of whom Ron was a sleeker exception), Vannister was tall, broad-shouldered, and flat-bellied, with the full chest and limbs of a man who gave all parts of his body equal—and rigorous—use. And wet as he was, with his body hair sleeked down, thereby enhancing rather than obscuring his contours, he did indeed look almost as if he were sculpted from stone.

Except for his stag's head tattoo (which seemed to have faded a lot recently) and his tan (and there *was* an obvious tan line).

And except for the fact that no Greek statue she had ever seen (or Roman—or Renaissance either, now she thought of it) was . . . *equipped* anything like that well. Nor, come to it, was any *man* she had ever seen, Ron included. And the fact that he was simply standing there, completely unaware of her presence (as far as she knew)—and *still* seemed to be flaunting his endowment—only made it more difficult for her to look away. Quite against her will, she found herself wanting to draw closer, to touch him, to feel the firmness of those shapes and planes, seeking, perhaps, to prove to herself that they bore the warmth of flesh, not the coldness of the carved stone they resembled.

Stone indeed! she told herself. *It was bloody stone that brought me down here.* But she couldn't accost Vannister now. He might be naked, but she doubted that'd bother him as much as it was bugging her. There was, she supposed, nothing more vulnerable than a naked man—or more threatening.

Vannister had come onshore by then. He yawned, stretched magnificiently, and turned his back to her (revealing a handsome set of buns that made her gawk all over again). And was strolling toward his clothes when she noticed something distinctly odd.

It wasn't his body—not hardly, for his marble-white backside looked every bit as impressive as his front. No, it was something more subtle, something she would not have noticed had she not had an artist's practiced eye for observing details.

Van Vannister was limping. Not badly, but the flaw was nonetheless clear. And it wasn't a function of the uneven terrain he bestrode. She wondered at that, tending to ascribe the condition to some recent injury she didn't know about, while another part noted the nonchalant, resigned quality of it and concluded that it was a condition the man had endured for a very long time indeed.

But why hadn't she noticed before? Surely she wasn't so preoccupied with the countless details of home-building that she had failed to note something so obvious. And yet . . . there was a certain amount of evidence to indicate that she *wasn't* as observant as she thought she was. Witness room dimensions that were not what she recalled them to be. Witness pilasters that got put up when she wasn't looking. Lord, it was enough to drive anyone batty.

She wondered, suddenly, if she *was* starting to crack—and distracted herself by turning her gaze (she could scarcely resist) back toward the bare-assed workman.

Vannister had dried himself off now, and was tugging on the same jeans he'd worn earlier that day—a particularly scuzzy pair with essentially no knees and only patches of white thread across his buttocks, through which (fortunately for her tattered modesty) bits of blue calico-patch were visible.

But *had* he hurt himself? she wondered. She hoped not, because she couldn't spare him. And, she admitted, asshole or no, she also liked him enough to be concerned for his well-being.

But if she didn't get herself out of here pretty soon, she was going to have some *real* awkward explaining to do.

Allowing herself one final, wistful appraisal, she turned, and as soundlessly as she could (which was pretty quiet, courtesy of her Cherokee kin), made her way back up the path to the knoll.

Ron was still forging away when she returned, but he looked up quizzically when she panted up. "You're blushing."

Brandy felt her cheeks growing even warmer. "Thanks a lot."

His face broke into a grin. "Ah-ha!" he cried. "Let me guess: you caught old Van in his birthday suit!"

Brandy did not reply.

"Am I right?" He was grinning now: grinning like a fool.

Still no answer.

"I am, aren't I? I *know* I am!"

"No comment," Brandy grunted at last, sparing him a scathing glare. "But if you say *one* word about it, I'll *kill* you."

And she could tell by the way Ron blanched that he more than half believed her.

And then the telephone rang.

"Crap," Brandy spat. And dived for the trailer.

As circumstances devolved, nearly two hours slipped by before Brandy had an opportunity to either confront Vannister about the unauthorized augmentations or quiz him about what she more and more suspected was a recent injury.

The call proved to be her mother, lonely beyond words, and phoning out of the clear blue, regardless of Brandy's countless earlier pleas not to do so until after dark because every second counted when she was working on the house. And since her mother was both a notorious gossip *and* notoriously long-winded, Brandy had no choice but to listen to almost an hour's worth of the happenings in Greensboro, North Carolina.

And then the hardware store rang her up to announce that they'd just gotten in the first pieces of that blue tile she'd been wanting, but they weren't sure it was the *right* blue and could she please come check, 'cause otherwise they were gonna have to send it back.

And by the time she got *that* settled, Vannister was securely ensconced sorting out the wiring in the fuse box, looking so self-absorbed and peaceful that she hadn't the heart to disturb him.

All of which meant that they were having a much-delayed lunch before she could broach the subject of Vannister's injury.

"How'd you hurt yourself?" she asked seriously, gazing straight across the picnic table on the patio to impale him with a meaningful stare.

Ron, who was sitting to her left, froze with a handful of potato chips halfway to his mouth and regarded her curiously.

And Vannister simply finished chewing his bit of rabbit sandwich and blinked at her. "What do you *mean*?" he asked absently.

Brandy found herself coloring in spite of her best efforts to be forthright. "You were limping. I saw you."

A barely visible shrug. "When?"

"Earlier today."

An eyebrow lifted slightly, and an amused twinkle awoke in the workman's eye. *"Where?"*

Brandy didn't want to answer, but found herself doing so in spite of herself. "D-down at the lake."

Vannister's lips curled fiendishly. "You saw more than *that* if you saw me then," he whispered with a wicked grin. "But one thing you *didn't* see was me limping." And with that, he rose from the table and walked straight toward his tent—with no trace at all of faltering.

Chapter 19

I've Just Seen a Face

Brandy Hall
Midafternoon

A swipe of file, a brush with crocus cloth, and one final quick pass with an engraving tool, and Galadriel *finally* began to look like she was supposed to: regal and distant and all-knowing—a woman to whom those few mysteries of the universe she had not already explored were choice tidbits to be set aside for savoring in the long boredom of her immortality.

But Ron, who was busily engaged in applying the final finesse to the foot-square bronze rendition of Tolkien's Elf-queen that would eventually grace the left front door of Brandy Hall, was beginning to suspect that there was no way *he* was ever going to untangle even the rather small enigmas that were vying for attention in his left brain while his right continued on its blissfully automatic way smoothing and refining as if nothing at all was awry.

"Mmmrrrrowwww?" Matty Groves grumbled, rising from where he'd been cutting Zs on the skeletal doorframe, to yawn, stretch, and pad smartly away, mystery incarnate.

Ron blinked and looked up, his vision blurring as sleep-deprived eyes shifted focus—first to the cat, who was already well beyond retrieval, then to the view beyond the worktable he had moved to the edge of the tent so as to escape the heat of the forge he'd been slaving over during the cooler morning hours. Brandy Hall was to the right, Van's empty pavilion to the left, and straight ahead a splinter of unobstructed landscape showed mountains, lake, and forest. *Not bad,* he told himself. *Not bad for a city-bred white boy.*

It was a beautiful day, too: the warm sunshine felt great on his bare back and shoulders, which still retained a trace of stiffness from the move of the day before. And the breezes were sultry and heavy with the scent of conifers—and, very subtly, a return of that strange spicy-smelling pollen. He wished he could ignore that, too, wished he could banish the memories it conjured. And yet he was almost—content: able to enjoy the beauty of the day, the delicate wonder of making.

Or would have been, had those things not been bugging him.

And there was one now!—as voices to his left drew his gaze to where Brandy and Van were bickering over who was going to carry a second batch of molding downstairs. The big redhead was asserting his masculinity as usual, and Brandy, equally typical, was refusing to be cowed, and now Van (who evidently had some sort of death wish) had started teasing her about how her boobs would just get in the way, and how she had the wrong center of gravity for that kind of toting, and of course, that just made her madder—especially as she was already pissed at him to start with, never mind that she and Weedge had already managed the same operation nicely just that morning.

Quite against his will, Ron felt a twinge of jealousy. Oh, he *liked* Van fine—most of the time. The guy could be damnably charming and witty when he wanted. And he was obviously an *incredibly* talented builder, equally at home with lumber or concrete, wiring or plumbing, each of which he attacked with a standard of workmanship Ron thought had vanished somewhere around the turn of the last century. And since Van's skills complemented rather than conflicted with Ron's own, he had little cause for envy there.

Trouble was, building wasn't the *only* thing Van was good at. He could recite the names of all the units of more than one hundred men who had fought for the Confederacy, for instance; and knew the founding dates of all the Georgia units, plus their commanders, their movements, their losses, their ultimate fates, and the date their last survivor died. But he could also do the same for both sides in the battles of Crécy, Poitiers, Agincourt, Culloden, and half a score others Ron had never heard of, some with African or Oriental names.

What's more, he could quote long passages from Vasari, Dante, Shakespeare, Poe, and—surprisingly—Lovecraft and Tolkien (including three of the master fantasist's obscure longer poems in their entirely), and could draw a passable copy of either a Holbein or Dürer.

Not to mention driving a nail with one blow, producing an uncanny (and hilarious) imitation of Bob Dylan singing, and being able to render any arms from a heraldry book simply by looking at the blazon.

But unfortunately, the arts Van seemed bent on practicing most appeared to be woman-wooing.

And even worse was the smug way he went about it: flaunting his sexuality with his constantly bare torso and the holey, skintight jeans he almost certainly wore without underwear. Never mind the way he moved: languid and easy-like, with slow flexes of his muscles whenever he thought Brandy was watching, and with knowing grins and devilish twinklings in his eye when she was in closer proximity. And absolutely *never* mind the fact that about every other thing he said was capable of at least one sexual interpretation.

As for Lew's warning, that the guy was some sort of schizo-psycho, the jury was still out. Beyond the somewhat aberrant Voice, Ron couldn't tell if there was anything odd about Van's psyche or not, and hadn't investigated to any degree—mostly because he didn't like to Listen in the first place, and disliked doing it to friends in particular. It was bad for the peace of mind. Otherwise you'd get into situations like what had occurred when Brandy had lugged him downstairs to look at those peculiar columns.

His *intentions* there had been completely honorable. Brandy was obviously growing ever more concerned about what she considered to be peculiar aberrations afflicting her house: oddities that to be perfectly honest, he hadn't paid particular attention to because he had his own store of conundrums to consider. Still, he *did* have resources at his disposal that normal folks did not, and Brandy *had* been upset, so he'd ventured a low-level scrying of the limestone columns, hoping thereby to discover who had set them there. But when he'd slipped surreptitiously into trance and projected his consciousness back along the few hours between current time, when the pilasters clearly *were* present, and the evening before, when they equally obviously were not, he had found something damned disturbing. Oh, he could *sense* the house easily enough, focus on that room, even—but only from the outside. It was as if the *interior* was in some other place—or time. And he could detect no sentient presence there at all. He didn't know *what* to make of it either, for he had never found a place like that. Not that places had Voices, exactly, but there was a sort of equivalent. Except that Brandy's downstairs den *didn't* have one, not for a couple of hours last night.

Of course, the logical culprit was Van, partly because of Lew's warning, but mostly because Ron hadn't been there to keep an eye on him for most of the night—never mind that Ron knew less about him than anyone else who had regular access to the knoll. But a cursory inspection of the Winds blown by last night's Voices had shown the big guy snoring away the entire time the pilasters could have been installed.

And unfortunately, Ron had learned something *else* when he'd tried his little bit of psychic eavesdropping. For with Brandy so near and keyed up, and with his shields necessarily at low ebb so as to permit the probe, he had inadvertently found himself brushing her consciousness along the way. And underlying all that overt concern about her house was a deeper thread of admiration for Van that Ron only *wished* she would ever feel for him. Unfortunately, too, once he'd accessed that aspect of Brandy's Voice, he'd been unable to resist following it a way, with the result that he had discovered that a part of her not only *appreciated* Van, but was also almost (if guiltily) *preoccupied* with him. And it didn't help that Ron had also learned that she was attracted to Van on a purely physical level as well. Trouble was, he also knew that she had her own ideas about personal independence and ultimate responsibility in relationships, and that if she took a mind to make a play for the big redhead, she would—and would have the backings of her entire ethical system to go with it.

God knew she'd wrapped *him* around her finger easily enough. They couldn't do it again, she'd told him; she didn't want to play favorites—but she still wanted him up there, still at her beck and call.

Fine!

He could deal with it—he supposed, as he (with the occasional aid of his right hand) was dealing with celibacy. But he wished he didn't have to. And he absolutely wished Brandy and Van wouldn't look at each other like they sometimes did: eager and hungry as a pair of horny wildcats.

The net result of all this speculation, of course, was that he was getting tense. Yeah, Ron told himself, it really would help if Van and Brandy'd just stay away from each other, so he wouldn't have to constantly keep an eye on them like the chaperon at a Southern Baptist sock hop.

But *that*, he suspected, was pure pie in the sky.

Just like it was a total pipe dream to hope that Lew would change his mind about the deal.

He was, he admitted, practically scared shitless about the Binding Ritual he and Lew would perform the day before Lew's departure. Up until then he had a choice; after that he'd have none. He'd be bound to the earth of Welch County without recourse, would be unable to leave its borders for more than a matter of hours (though apparently that time span increased as one got older). After that, the land itself would start to draw on him, making him feel more and more on edge until he finally went psycho—or returned. *That* was what frightened him more than anything else he had ever done—even more than the loss of his freedom of movement—for he had already seen what psycho Listeners could do.

And of course, there was still the small affair of Wendy.

"Gaaa!" he grumbled aloud. It was just too friggin' much to try to keep up with!

Scowling, he returned to his work, and had just completed the fine detail of Galadriel's bracelet when he found his mind wandering again.

No! he told himself ruthlessly. *Not now, not here. Today I am only a metalworker. Today I am lord of my craft.* He *needed* to work, dammit, *wanted* to work, was happiest *when* he was working. That was what he was here for; that was the one thing he was good at beyond taint or compromise. But it looked like the only way he was going to be able to deaden his own troubling notions was to distract them with the energy of others. So with that in mind, he rose and retrieved his portable CD player from inside, set it on the worktable beside him, and prowled through his disk collection for something raucous enough to completely obliterate intellect with emotion. It turned out to be the Bullitt Boys. He slipped in the disk, cranked up the volume two-thirds full, and returned to his labor.

An instant later, Brandy's Knoll exploded with the twang of electric guitars and heavy percussion. And Ron lost himself in artistry. The music energized him as nothing else he could easily access could, and he threw himself into his project, refining lines, smoothing surfaces, polishing, engraving tiny leaves on the trees in Lothlorien behind the Elf queen. Before he knew it, he had lost all track of time, and—finally—of his troubles.

Nor did he have any idea how long he'd been grinding and filing away when he became aware of a presence behind him. Had he been less self-involved, the Luck would probably have alerted him, but he had been so focused on his work that he'd suppressed even that.

But when a shadow fell onto the very area he was defining, and a slim hand reached from behind him to reduce the heavy metal to a light whisper, he had no choice but to stop and look up. It was Brandy, peering curiously over his shoulder, but even as he watched, her delighted smile slowly shifted to a frown. "It's a good likeness," she growled acidly.

Ron blinked in puzzlement. "What is?" But then he followed her gaze down to the nearly completed plaque.

And shuddered. For quite without being aware of it, in the process of his finishing work, he had somehow altered Galadriel's face into an uncanny likeness of Wendy's. And since Brandy had an eagle eye for such details, and had already approved the wax master mold before he'd cast it, it was unlikely she'd have missed the modification.

"It was—uh—an accident," he stammered awkwardly. "Or unintentional, anyway."

"You need to speak to your right brain," Brandy replied, with heavy sarcasm.

He bridled at that, almost too tired to resist the urge to zing her. "Maybe I do," he managed finally. "But it's a willful bastard, y'know." He tried to smile, to indicate that this last was an attempt at humor, but before he could even start the appropriate muscles twitching, Brandy had preempted him.

"Boy, do I!" she snapped. "Boy, do I goddamned ever!" She meant it, too—for the moment. But Ron could see that she was fighting with herself, trying not to let such a small thing upset her. She *knew* he had a tendency to put his friends into his works; the crutch was full of 'em, and there were several subtle portraits of him and Brandy and Van in the doors already, usually in subsidiary roles. "Still no word?" she added in a strained voice.

He shook his head. " 'Fraid not. I basically struck out in Athens, and there's been nothing up here since that last message on Lew's machine."

"Think you ought to call the cops? File a missing persons report?"

"I'd *like* to, believe me," Ron replied, though he went on engraving leaves. It was a mechanical process, one he could easily manage while talking. And it helped him relax—and God knew he needed to relax just then. "But I don't really think I can," he continued, "since as far as *I* can tell, *she* doesn't think she's missing."

"Still, maybe for your peace of mind . . ."

"Maybe so," he muttered, squinting at his work as a cloud drifted across the sun, and the wind brought the scent of the curious pollen. A drop of sweat fell on the softly gleaming bronze, but evaporated quickly. He looked up, wiped his eyes. Brandy had said nothing. "Maybe I—" he began, then: "What the hell is *he* doing?"

For, masked by the thunder of rock-and-roll, Van had returned to his tent, and though the interior was fairly dark, he could still be plainly seen calmly stripping off his jeans and padding around in search of another pair. And, as Ron already suspected, he wasn't wearing any skivvies. Ron prayed that Brandy hadn't noticed, and he thought it unlikely that the impromptu exhibitionist was aware of her presence in any event, given that she was lurking in the shadows behind him. But the mere fact that the big lug would be so indiscreet when there was even a possibility Brandy *might* happen by—well, that was just typical of the aspect of the guy he despised, especially as it had evidently happened once that day already. He'd joked about it then, but somehow it did not seem so humorous now.

"What?" Brandy had just begun, which he supposed meant she *hadn't* seen anything. But by then it was too late.

Because Ron's sudden flare of anger had caused him to clench his engraving tool so tightly, he flinched reflexively—with the result that he had dug the point deeply into the smooth surface of one of Galadriel's bare arms, then across it, through her bosom, and into her chin: possibly ruining it, certainly instigating a repair.

He gasped. A sick feeling flooded his gut.

And Brandy had seen the whole thing.

He looked at her. She looked at him, her face full of hurt accusation.

"That does it!" she said icily, hands on her hips. "You need to talk to your brother."

"Maybe I do!" Ron snapped, too tired and burned-out to hold back any longer. "Maybe I goddamned do!"

Brandy's only reply was to stalk away in the direction of the trailer.

Ron shot a scathing glare at Van, who had finally covered his nakedness and was gazing about in perplexity, having evidently heard the altercation but not divined its cause. He shrugged. Ron did not reply, and Van shrugged again, as if to say, "Have it your way."

Ron discovered that he was sweating. Muttering a disgusted "Shit!" he retired to the shadows of his tent, unearthed a towel and wiped the worst of the gunk off his torso, then put on a shirt and sneakers, and combed his hair. He was already fishing in his pocket for the keys to the Thunderbird when he decided to take one final peek at his ruined masterpiece.

The bronze really was in sad shape. But the face— the troublesome face—was still mostly intact. And as he stared at it, a second cloud shielded the sun, and in the resulting moment of squinty refocusing, Ron could have absolutely sworn that Galadriel winked at him. But when he blinked and checked again, the Elf-queen's eyes were open: wide and guileless. But she had somehow acquired a secret smile.

Chapter 20

Triad

Though she was *overtly* sorting through a two-day-old pile of Ron's sketches in search of the perfect design for the iron strapwork that would curl across the door of the Viking bedroom, and *covertly* taking the hard edge off the high heat of the day with a late afternoon mug of cider in the front arcade, Brandy had in actual fact spent most of the last half hour trying to determine when, exactly, she had lost control of her life.

Like those flare-ups of temper she'd been plagued with all day, for instance, as precipitated most recently by Ron's little slipup with the door panel. *That* shouldn't have fazed her. Shoot, the guy could probably patch up the damage in no time, and there was no *good* reason for him not to make Galadriel look however he wanted. He had a right to his feelings, and he'd been involved with Wendy for years before he'd even heard of Brandy Wallace. Never mind that as far as she could tell, he was not and never had been in love with the strange girl she had seen only once and never met. But the fact that so simple a thing as depicting his ex in a bronze panel still irked her galled her even more because it meant that she wasn't as much in control as she had either grown accustomed to being— *or* wanted to be.

Once again, she realized dully, she had allowed her life to become circumscribed by men.

The crux of the problem was that she both *liked* Ron and Vannister and *needed* them. Shoot, they'd been like mobile gifts from God, when you got right down to it. Both brilliant, charming, and talented as hell; both apparently willing to subvert their egos to hers—which was damned hard for a man to do.

She'd tried to be evenhanded in her treatment of the two. Except that she had somehow allowed herself to skew her favor toward Ron—had come to rely on the security of having him around to bounce ideas off of, which he was better suited for than Vannister. And since Ron was also the most secure person she had ever met, by virtue of his family contacts, he had patience aplenty to spare for her. As long as his *own* work wasn't threatened, which basically meant as long as he was allowed to work at all, he was fine. And since she had informed both her helpers more than once that theirs was first and foremost a business arrangement, and that friendship—or *anything* else—was strictly secondary, she thought she had the situation under control.

If not for that afternoon by the lake when she and Ron had made love. *That* she bitterly regretted. Not the act itself, she hastened to add—*it* had been quite marvelous— but the commitment that act implied. She *still* didn't know what she'd been thinking then. But it had just seemed so . . . right: two overwrought people who cautiously liked each other making each other feel good, with no further expectations.

But it was so unlike her, she couldn't help being puzzled. As best she'd been able to figure, she almost had to have been intoxicated—possibly some aftereffect of Lewis Welch's banquet plus the beer she'd had at lunch because that was all she had to drink on the knoll except water and coffee, neither of which she'd been in the mood for. But *whatever* it was, she couldn't let it happen again!

Not until she was living in Brandy Hall.

If only Ron wasn't so damned good-looking—as beautiful in his own way as the much larger Vannister, with a hard, sleek body that had only been improved by a month's work at his forge. Trouble was, she hated liking him for any such base and earthy reason, because it meant that her instincts, not her intellect, were calling the shots.

And that didn't even count Vannister himself. For if Ron was tame, his opposite number was wild. Ron was like Matty Groves (who had just wandered up to be stroked): a pet she had seen and coveted and called to her; Van was a wild thing that had come out of the woods and blessed her with his attention for a space of days. And *that* was damned flattering, even as another part of her insisted that she shouldn't be flattered at all because Vannister was exactly the kind of man who, because of his raw animal magnetism, could seduce any woman he wanted if he tried hard enough.

And, she very much feared, the way she felt right now, he wouldn't have to put forth much effort with her at all. She had seen him casually and completely naked, seen him gleaming and glorious in the morning sun, and to her everlasting chagrin, could not keep the image from her mind. In particular, she couldn't shake the memory of his manhood hanging heavy and primal, as if it contained in its astonishing length and girth every secret *man*kind (as opposed to *woman*kind) had accumulated in ten thousand years of sexual ascendency. Secrets she found she wanted to possess.

But Vannister was also brilliant and charming. And something Ron was not: he was mysterious. A month of his company had gained her no more knowledge of him than that he had lived many places and knew many things.

If only he would stick to the plans. And if only Ron would quit fretting about his brother and mooning over Wendy.

But neither seemed a likely possibility anytime soon, and her lack of control over both made her furious.

Scowling, she dispatched Matty with a swat of her hand and told him to go look for his daddy, then sorted through the sketches one final time and chose two that together embodied most of what she'd envisioned for the strapwork. That accomplished, she flipped through the copy of *The Art of Scandinavia* beside her and noted among its plates a couple of additional features that intrigued her. And rose.

She'd intended to dump the whole mess by Ron's tent and then get busy installing the molding she'd bought that morning when she noticed that the young metalworker was nowhere to be seen, nor was his black Thunderbird in its accustomed place beside the half-disassembled Centauri. Only then did she remember seeing it rumble off a good half hour before.

Her temper flared immediately, and only with difficulty did she resist venting a stream of profanity. *She* had suggested he talk to his brother, after all. And though she'd said that in the heat of anger, she'd meant it as well. But she'd also intended him to do it on his own time, not hers. On the other hand, she hadn't actually specified as much, so she supposed she had no right to complain.

But it still griped the bejesus out of her!

Before she knew it, she was pacing, too wired to make serious decisions, and too distracted to apply herself to even such mindless chores as tacking up trim. What she *wanted* to do—what she usually *did* in moods like this—was to throw herself into heavy manual labor, like jackhammering out recalcitrant foundations. But Brandy Hall was mostly beyond that stage now—which meant that she had little choice but to simply continue pacing: back and forth in the arcade at first, and later round and round the entire house.

She was just completing her eighth circuit when Vannister—whom she'd also misplaced—suddenly emerged from the gloom of the shallow arcade that shaded the double arched windows of the library on the northern side.

He had made no noise at all, and appeared so abruptly that she uttered a strangled yip of surprise—which first embarrassed her, then made her angrier still because it had made her look weak, stupid, or both, with which concepts she had already wrestled enough that day.

"Sorry," the big redhead drawled easily, ignoring the

thunderous scowl she fixed on him once she had turned around—which, of course, only made it worsen. "But I figured I oughta warn you."

"About what?" she snapped. "I'm in no mood for foolishness."

His brows lowered slightly. "Well, I was *gonna* say that you'd best stop pacin', or at least change your course, 'cause if you complete one more lap, you'll have walked nine times widdershins around your house, and God only knows what'll happen then."

She raised an eyebrow in warning.

"But I'm *not* gonna say that," he added with a grin. "Seein' as how you look like one pissed-off lady."

Brandy regarded him icily. "I *am* one pissed-off lady."

He flopped back into the shadow of the overhang and folded his arms across his bare chest.

"Wanta tell me why?"

She fixed him with a scathing glare. "You mean beyond the small matter of how a dozen limestone pilasters came to be in my downstairs den, and of how you generally assume that I'm supposed to doubt the evidence of my own senses whenever it pleases you?"

"Such as?"

"Such as when I distinctly see you limping and you swear you weren't."

"Oh, *that* again."

"It was never concluded."

"But that's not what's gettin' at you now, is it?"

She stiffened, then shook her head and crossed the few feet between them, to mirror his pose exactly: arms folded, shoulders propped against the wall. "No," she replied so softly she doubted he even heard her.

But evidently he did. "So what is it, then?"

"I don't wanta talk about it."

"Yes you do."

"Not to you!"

"Who better?" he asked gently. "I'm the only friend you've got who's actually here right now—and *now's* when you need to talk, not later. I'm discreet—you know that. And I'd never hurt you deliberately. And besides—"

"What?"

"You look like you're in the kind of pain that can only be cured by talkin'."

She looked at him askance. "Van the philosopher surfaces, huh? That's an aspect I haven't met yet."

He nodded solemnly. "Or you can think of me as Van the shrink, if you'd rather."

Brandy slid down the wall until she was squatting on the grass beside him.

"Or Van the Confessor," he prompted, joining her.

She stared into space, vaguely aware of her sneakered feet and beyond them of the rock and the ledge and then treetops and lake, with more mountains beyond.

"It's Ron, I guess," she whispered, hating herself for displaying even that much weakness.

"What about him?"

"What's *your* opinion of him?"

"We're not talkin' 'bout me."

"Humor me."

Vannister shrugged. "I like him well enough, I reckon. He's sort of a snob, but doesn't mean to be—noblesse oblige, and all that malarkey. But he's had a rough life, too, a whole lot worse than you think, or than he'll ever let on to you. He's got baggage very few folks could understand."

"And how do *you* know so much?"

"I've got my sources," he replied cryptically. "Now—what's *really* buggin' you? Not latent hostility, but imminently? What sent you off in a walkin' fit, in other words?"

"I—I guess I don't know how I *feel* about him," she murmured hesitantly, wondering how she dared discuss such personal matters with the man who could very well be Ron's rival. Shoot, it was hard enough hashing 'em out with Weedge.

Vannister did not seem to be concerned. "*Don't* you?" he shot back quickly. "If *you* don't, who does?"

This time Brandy shrugged. "I don't know. I . . . I don't want to *love* him, that's for sure. I don't want to love anybody right now. I don't need the distraction, not when the dream's so close to being realized."

"But *do* you? Love him, I mean?"

"I don't know that either. I mean, in a lot of ways he's everything a woman's supposed to want in a man: patient but energetic, brilliant but thoughtful, handsome but not flashy. Considerate, open-minded. You name it."

"Actually," Van inserted, "those're more properly good qualities for a *person*, not for a *man*, per se."

She eyed him warily, noting the subtle change in his syntax and vocabulary. "You, of all people, are accusing *me* of being sexist?"

He laughed loudly. "I'm not that stupid! But I *could* be dumb enough to tell you that you might wanta think about the possibility. It *is* kind of a two-edged sword, after all. Sauce for the goose, and all."

"Fortunately, I don't like paté," Brandy shot back, and wished she hadn't. It was far too inane a remark for the tone of the conversation. If Vannister was going to be intellectual, she felt honor-bound to return as good as he gave.

"Which has nothing to do with your feelings for our buddy, Mr. Dillon."

Brandy took a deep breath. "Yeah, well *jeeze*," she began awkwardly. "I—uh, I suppose the main thing is that I'm having a lot of trouble with not being sure I love him, yet hoping he does love me. I guess I think that'd feel good. And he really is somebody I could share my life with, if it came to that. That's part of my dream, too: having Brandy Hall, but having people come and hang out and do art and write, and compose. Art needs art to stay sane, Van; though I don't know if you know that or not. And once I get this place done, and can get the energy flow going . . ."

"But you don't wanta do it by yourself?"

"Right."

"So does that mean you love Ron for what he is, or simply 'cause he's the most perfect realization of a particular role in your life you're ever gonna encounter?"

She eyed him curiously, wondering where *that* bit of psychoanalytical BS had come from. "I'll have to think about it" was all the reply she would grant him.

"I'll make it simple then: Do you go to sleep thinkin' 'bout him, and wake up thinkin' 'bout him? When you see something that relates to one of those things he's into, does he automatically pop into your head? *Is* his *happiness more important to you than your own?"*

Once again she was slow to answer. "I . . . I don't know," she whispered finally. "I don't think that last part's possible; at least it hasn't been for me. And I usually go to sleep thinking about the house—when I'm not so tired I can't think at all."

"So what do *you* really want?" Van asked softly, his face deadly serious.

She shrugged and contemplated the lake until the sparkling of the sun on the water reminded her too much of what she had seen that morning and made her shift her gaze to the nearer boulders.

"I think it'd do you a heap of good if you answered that," Van urged even more softly than before.

Something brushed her wrist then, and she looked down—and was startled to see his hand resting lightly there: ruddy-tanned flesh against her gold. She did not flinch nor draw away, but the contact coursed through her like an electric shock. She swallowed and felt her cheeks start to burn. Against her will, she found herself recalling the naked Vannister and how she had wanted to touch him, to feel every part of him and thereby make him her own.

"Think about it, okay?"

She stiffened and removed her hand on the pretext of wiping a strand of hair out of her eyes. A breeze crept out of the woods to caress her, bringing with it the spicy odor of pine—and that more subtle scent that was the curious, intoxicating pollen. The lake sparkled. A distant Dead Can Dance tape began "Salterello."

"Just think about it," Vannister repeated, his voice barely more than a murmur. "What do you *really* want out of Mr. Ronny Dillon?"

Brandy started to rise, to abandon this conversation that was rapidly riling her up all over again. But then, clear as rainwater, the answer popped into her mind. "I want to be able to trust him completely," she stated flatly. "I want to *know* I can rely on him, that he'll *always* be there for me; that he'll *never* let me down."

Vannister replied with a low chuckle. *"That's* a pretty tall order."

"You asked."

He nodded. "I did. But I'm not sure that was the truth—not all of it."

"So what *is* the truth?" she flared.

A thoughtful pause. Then: "I think you want to control him."

"I do not!"

"Don't you?" Vannister countered instantly. "You try to control everything else! Why not Ron?"

She felt the pulse of her anger increasing rapidly. Who the hell did this lumbering fool think he was, to put her to the question like this? To trick her into betraying her innermost secrets, and then turn them around on her.

But he was also right. Or at least a cursory inspection of her emotions disclosed the possibility that control might, in fact, be the one thing she desired.

Vannister was simply looking at her, grinning like a fiend. "I hit it, didn't I?"

"No—maybe. Will you please just lay *off*?"

"You know what the main difference 'twixt old Ron and me is, don't you?" Vannister asked abruptly—which was not the sort of follow-up she'd expected. Trust him to change the topic and keep her off balance.

"Okay," she muttered. "I'm game. Tell me."

The grin widened, as if Vannister had just won a hand of strip poker she wasn't even aware she'd been dealt into. "The main difference between me and Dillon," he confided, "is that you *might* be able to control him, but you'll *never* be able to control me."

Brandy glared at him, not so much because he was probably right, but because his observation was an uncanny echo of what she herself had been thinking only a few minutes before: that Ron was a domestic pet she had chosen, while Vannister was a wild thing from the woods that had chosen her.

But there had been something more in his assertion, she realized; there had been an implicit challenge.

"Sure I can," she began. "If I want to, I can—"

But her sentence was cut off—because, completely without warning, Vannister reached over and kissed her fully and firmly on the mouth. An instant later, his arms enfolded her.

Her first response was indignation, her second righteous fury, which was followed by an even sharper anger at herself. For, quite against her will, she had found herself returning his kiss with a passion that at least equalled his. And then it didn't matter.

Vannister, not surprisingly, proved to be a master of the sensual arts. But he was also unexpectedly gentle. His kiss had been firm, yes, and craftily contrived. But as she began to respond, his touch softened, and she was aware only of the pleasure of his lips against hers, his tongue at play with her own.

And then those lips were roving, tracing her eyes and nose and ears, even as his hands began to quest across her body. A part of her resisted, protested that she didn't want this, that to even allow such familiarity as had already passed was being untrue to Ron. But at the same time, another part said to relax, that Ron had no exclusive lease on her soul, and that her body, at least, knew exactly what it needed, which was to explore completely and utterly and at extreme firsthand that glorious, full-blown form she had seen in all its naked glory earlier that day.

At some point she discovered that her breasts were bare and that Vannister's face was between them. A moment later, she was lying on her back in the scanty grass, while he slowly eased her jeans and panties off. She let him, content to feel his touch merging with the breath of the wind—and, in turn, to touch him. He had a wonderful body: hard as iron when she gripped him hard, but softer and unexpectedly smooth when she stroked his flesh more lightly. Her nipples hardened beneath his fingers, but his did likewise, and he let himself enjoy her caress.

Eventually he rose, but only long enough to slip off his Levi's, and she reveled anew at his brilliant nudity. For a while he lay beside her, simply teasing her with his fingertips, while she stroked his thigh and manhood in turn.

"What happened to your tattoo?" Brandy murmured dreamily as her gaze drifted toward Vannister's shoulder, where the white stag's head that had practically blazed at her from across the yard the first time she'd seen it was now faded almost past decoding.

"I wore it out," Vannister whispered cryptically. "I do that with a lot of things."

And then neither of them could hold back, and they drew together.

It was like being forged, she thought. Or like being sculpted out of stone. The daughters of men must have felt like this when the gods lay with them in the myths she was so fond of. Vannister moved surely and quickly, but with astonishing finesse, too, as if he knew exactly what she wanted, and precisely what his body could do to achieve it.

And it lasted, thank God, a very long time indeed.

They had only just slipped apart from a second round when Vannister tensed abruptly. He leaned up on his elbow, eyes darting back and forth, suddenly alert, head raised like a stag questing for the footfalls of approaching hunters.

"What is it?" she wondered nervously, suddenly recalling that if Lew wasn't home, just about enough time had elapsed for Ron to make a round-trip to Cardalba.

Vannister shrugged. "Maybe nothing. But I'd best go check." He rose and sauntered, still naked, toward the corner of Brandy Hall that faced the driveway. She watched him go and felt a glowing satisfaction that she, Brandy Wallace, had just made love with one of the ten best-looking men on the planet. She now knew everything about his physical person it was possible to know.

Or maybe not, for as he edged along the side of the house, she noted for the second time that day that he was limping. Once again it was not obvious, but this time she had no doubt about what she was seeing. Which meant that he *had* lied to her earlier. Which, given the intimacy they had just shared, made her feel utterly betrayed. Never mind that he had completely charmed her out of ethics as easily as he had her pants.

Vannister had halted by then; was peering around the corner. He remained there, alert, for a few seconds, then shrugged and relaxed. A moment later, he returned and flopped down beside her.

"What was it?" she asked nervously.

"Not what you were afraid of," Vannister replied with a wry smirk. "Not Dillon comin' back."

She glared at him, wishing she could be angry enough at him to consider what had just happened to be rape, and thereby regain the moral high ground she feared she had pretty well abandoned, at least as far as Vannister was concerned. But he merely smiled—sincerely, she thought—and whispered, very softly, "Thank you. I enjoyed that a lot."

Brandy blushed furiously, but had presence of mind enough—or honesty enough—to murmur, "So did I. But we can't do it again—not ever."

Vannister's only reply was to let his smile expand into a grin. And then he reached down, picked up his pants, and slowly began pulling them on. His socks and boots came next. Brandy followed his example rather more hastily, with the result that by the time she was buckling her belt, he was knotting his second boot lace.

And then, faint but clear, she heard the distant jingle of the telephone.

"Probably the hardware again," she grumbled. "Probably wanting to know when I'm coming in to see those blessed tiles."

"Better talk to 'em, then," Vannister chuckled. "Seeing as how you cheated 'em out of a first-class lumberyard foreman, you don't have as much karma there as you did."

"Good point," she conceded with a sigh. "But I think I'll let the machine do my talking first—just in case. Forewarned is forearmed, and all that."

"I'll talk to 'em if you want me to," Vannister volunteered.

She shrugged. "Whatever."

Vannister was strolling nonchalantly toward the trailer now, but Brandy had not moved. She was still gazing out at the landscape. "You coming?"

She glanced at him, shook her head. "Not yet."

"Whatever."

And with that, he turned and walked away. And once again there was something disquieting about the way he moved. But only when he was already out of sight did Brandy realize that the limp, once more, was absent.

Chapter 21

Brothers in Arms

Cardalba Hall
Midafternoon

It's a damned good thing I've got a key, Ron reflected sourly as he twisted the heavy brass knob for admittance into Cardalba's main hall, *or I'd probably have broken down the frigging door by now!*

It was comforting to imagine that the front porch boards were still thrumming from where he'd stomped across them, and the granite steps at the eastern end *did* show the marks of his muddy sneakers and the heel of the crutch he had not bothered to scrape clean after striding through his brother's precious petunias. But for once, he didn't care. For once he had no time for genteel formality. Yesterday's long labor—*and* too little sleep last night—*and* today's escalating tensions—had finally caught up with him and were making a determined assault on his usual tight control. His bum knee was acting up, too, growing numb and unreliable as it did when he overstressed it. All of which meant that, Listener or no, he was as tired and burned-out and irritable as he could remember—and for once, was allowing his emotions free reign.

The fact that the key Lew had given him almost five years before was proving to be recalcitrant wasn't helping matters, either. He withdrew the intricate length of scrolled brass, scowled at it, and inserted it again while wrenching the knob hard enough to rattle the faceted glass in the narrow windows beside the door. A fine mist of dust drifted down from the fanlight overhead to merge with the thin skim of that damned greenish-yellow pollen on the wide pine boards. The air smelled of unknown spices: elusive, yet familiar. One of the ghostly white hounds padded up to stare distrustfully at him. And the lock gave.

Fine!

He slammed the door behind him to announce his presence, though if Lew was anything like the Master of Luck Ron assumed he was, he would already be alert to his coming—and probably to the reason for the visit as well.

So where *was* Lew? Ron paused in the front hall, abruptly unsure of his convictions, where a mere fifteen minutes before—when he'd left the Knoll with Brandy's words still ringing in his ears, telling him he ought to go see his brother and try, once and for all, to exorcise the ghost of Wendy Flowers from his conscience—he had been completely convinced of his mission.

He would talk to Lew about Wendy, about everything he'd ever known or felt or suspected about her. He'd rehash yet again every action he'd taken to locate her; and, finally, he would pose those pointed questions he'd been postponing because they weren't the sort of things one asked a beloved, trusted brother.

For in the process of that short, frantic drive from Keycutter Knob to Cardalba Hall, Ron had somehow transferred his ire from Van for provoking him enough to damage a major casting project, through the lady herself for refusing to help him deal with matters in his own way and time, to Lew, who had summoned him up here in the first place—and who really was in a position to find out nearly anything he wanted, should he so desire, but didn't seem inclined to. He'd been here when Wendy left, for chrissakes! And while he hadn't actually seen how she

looked or heard a single word she said, he *did* have access
to Karen, who had. And though Karen, as a footholder,
could not be Heard by either of them (access to her
memories of the occasion would have helped a lot), they'd
both recapitulated everything they *could* recall to Ron in
excruciating detail several times. (Lew had even let him
browse through his memories of the morning in question,
including Karen's recounting of Wendy's departure.) But
in spite of all that, Ron still had a sense that his brother
knew even more, that Lew was somehow holding out on
him, that though he had no doubt words and descriptions
and acts were being reported accurately, a subtle spin was
being placed on them in order to dispose Ron toward a
certain set of beliefs.

Yet he hadn't a clue why he thought that, beyond a few
too cryptic omens, the fact that Wendy was weighing on his
mind more than she ought, and that there were reasons to
suspect that his former girlfriend's influence, if not actual
body, was still active in his affairs.

The business with the plaque was the last straw. No
way he'd have consciously made it look like his ex. And
he was more certain than ever that it *had* winked at him,
that the smile had twisted in the split second after he had
blinked in disbelief.

Maybe Lew could at least explain that.

But where *was* he?

Ron was calmer now—on the surface. Already he regretted stomping on the porch, doing violence to the flower
bed, slamming the door. But his psyche was still seething,
so full of a nervous energy that was neither anger nor fear
nor hurt nor mistrust nor confusion but a complicated
synthesis of all five, tempered with love and betrayal in
the bargain, that he could scarcely think straight. *God*, he
wished he'd had more than three hours of shut-eye.

If wishes were horses . . .

He bypassed the parlor to his left, knowing by that
instinct only Listeners possessed that his brother was not
inside, and ignored the closed door to the media room for
an identical reason. The library did warrant an inspection,
however, because it was sufficiently infused with latent
Luck that Lew might lurk there undetected. But the knob

resisted when he tried it, and a check with his own key proved that the place was empty.

Which meant Lew was probably in his room, else he'd have shown himself by now.

Sighing, Ron started up the stairs, his anger fading as quickly as it had appeared, replaced with that grim, sick dread he always felt when approaching confrontation. He made no effort to damp the step and hitch of his tread, either, though the thick, wine-colored carpeting had that effect anyway. Nor did he attempt to mask his steps as he limped down the hall from the upper landing to the half-open door of Lew's bedroom, from which, faint but clear, the soundtrack to *Twin Peaks* was softly wafting, obscuring but not overriding the thumps of someone padding around barefoot in the room beyond.

Steeling himself, Ron took a deep breath, eased the door the rest of the way back, and stood in the empty opening, taking in his brother's latest artfully incongruous tableau.

Lew was packing. Or there were piles of large cardboard boxes placed at strategic intervals around the room, at any rate, most crammed to overflowing with comic books, paperback novels, movie posters, and thematically unrelated sheets of paper. As for the man himself, clad only in red sweatpants, he was stooping over a large chest at the foot of his bed, his back to the door, stirring yet another brew of documents to a rattling boil.

Ron watched him for a long moment, certain that his brother sensed his presence, yet equally determined not to speak first. Let Lew acknowledge *him*, dammit! No way he'd give him the satisfaction of begging attention.

"You'll have to get a footholder, you know," Lew murmured finally, nonchalantly. But instead of meeting Ron's gaze, he squatted in place and continued poking through the rustling sheets. The portable CD player he was using in preference to the big system downstairs whirred and clicked and produced Hendrix's "All Along the Watchtower." "Are you the joker, I wonder; or the thief?"

Ron chuckled grimly, forcing himself to check the irritation bubbling up inside him before it developed into something more psychologically lethal. "Whatever I am," he sighed, "I'm *definitely* confused, and I *sho'* can't get any relief."

Lew twisted around to look at him, eyes wide and a little too innocent. "What's the problem, bro?"

"Don't bro *me*!" Ron snapped—abandoning his already shaky control in the face of such obvious theatrics. "And you can dump the coy act, too, since you know perfectly well you're playing games with me."

"What kind of games?" Lew asked mildly, returning to his delving.

Ron dropped the crutch and crossed the distance between them in three awkward strides, then grabbed his brother by the shoulder and spun him around, even as he joined him on the floor. "You know *exactly* what kind of games," he spat. "And I'm not talking about luring me up here, or the way you're putting on innocence when you couldn't help but know I was coming over, much less in your friggin' house! Shoot, the goddamned noise alone should've told you that much!"

"And should've dissipated your anger some, never mind burning off most of that adrenaline high you're on."

Ron gaped helplessly. Then, "Screw you, Lew! Just *screw* you!"

A flicker of anger awoke in Lew's eyes; his jawline tensed. His brow furrowed very slightly.

"You have," Lew shot back matter-of-factly. "And I'm not talking about that night we spent curing our curiosity about each other, either. I'm talking about the fact that it could be you up here packing to leave as easily as me, that it could've been you stuck up here while your brother traipses around free in the flatlands."

Ron relaxed his grip on Lew's shoulder but did not remove his hand. "*You* chose that course, as I recall," he snapped icily.

"Because there was no choice!" Lew snorted. "Because, like it or not, I was better conditioned for the job than you were; and because I *knew* I was a Welch, while you, even at the end, still wanted to deny it."

"Don't guilt-trip me!"

"I don't intend to. You do *that* well enough yourself."

"That's beside the point, and anyway, it's got nothing to do with why I came here."

"Then why *did* you? Obviously *something's* wrong, or you wouldn't even *be* here. I *know* how much you hate this place."

"Not the place," Ron corrected, "the symbol."

"Whatever."

Ron bit his lip, scowling furiously. "Wendy," he gritted finally, his jaw shaking. "What do you know about Wendy?"

Lew's eyebrows shot up in surprise, then lowered again, though not so much in anger as irritation. "Do we *have* to go over that again? I've already told you everything. I've even let you snoop in my memories—not that it did any good, given that I wasn't actually present when she left."

"Yeah," Ron grunted, "I know. Just like the only person who saw her leave conveniently happens to be one of the few folks you can't Listen to."

"It'd *help* if I could Listen to Wendy!" Lew snapped back. "It'd *help* if we were dealing with the here and now, not the then and somewhere else. The Luck wears thin over distance, you know that: time and space, too—and that's if you're looking for someone with a Voice! If it's *that* big a deal, you should have Listened for her yourself, when you were in Athens—maybe you'd at least have found somebody who *had* seen her or was interacting with her! But no!" he went on. "That'd mean you had to taint yourself with the Luck you were born with! It'd mean you had to use a god-awful wonderful gift for something besides low-level scrying. You'd have had to stretch yourself, and that wouldn't do, would it? 'Cause you're afraid you'd like it too much!"

Ron rolled his eyes in exasperation, refusing to be baited. "You're being evasive," he growled. "And I am bloody sick of evasions." Then, more softly, as he regained some semblance of control, "Look, guy, I know neither of us wants this. We've always been straight with each other before— why does this one little thing have to be different?"

But Lew did not reply. Instead, he reached into the chest, inundated his arms to the elbows, and finally pulled out a small stack of letters bound together with a fresh-looking rubber band. He tossed them in Ron's direction. "Here, maybe these'll quiet your nerves."

Ron caught the bundle handily and examined the address, return, and postmark on the topmost.

It had been canceled in Athens—two weeks ago, in fact. But what caught Ron's attention immediately was that the letter was addressed to *him*: Mr. Ronald Dillon, Esq., in care of Mr. Lewis Welch, Esq., Cardalba Hall, Cordova, Georgia. There was no return and no Zip Code, probably because the flaky little wench—for it was obviously Wendy's handwriting on the envelope and her initials in the otherwise empty upper left corner—hadn't felt inclined to look it up. He was holding, he realized, a pack of letters from his onetime lady.

And Lew was looking at him with an expression of guilty resignation—mixed with fear, probably that he had finally gone too far and alienated Ron once and for all.

"Well?" Lew prompted accusingly. "Aren't you gonna read 'em?"

Ron simply flipped through the stack of envelopes. None had been opened. And then he shifted his gaze to his brother, his expression blending shock, hurt, and confused perplexity, with no room left for anger. "*Why*, Lew?" he managed finally. "Why didn't you give these to me when you knew I was going out of my mind with worry?"

Lew shrugged and looked away. " 'Cause I figured that the sooner you put Wendy behind you, the sooner you could get on with the rest of your life and finally settle down and be happy. I knew that if you *couldn't* get back in touch with her, those wounds you're worrying with so much'd heal a lot faster than if I let what's probably in those letters reopen 'em."

"You did it for my own good, in other words," Ron snorted.

Another shrug. "More or less."

"And not for yourself at all?" Ron went on hotly. "It never *occurred* to you that Wendy was the major thing binding me to Athens, and if she was out of the way, I'd have one less reason not to take over the Mastership?"

"Well—I can't lie to you about that, can I?" Lew conceded with a resigned smile. "But it wasn't my first intention, believe me; nor my first choice. I did it 'cause I know what it takes to make you happy—what it *really* takes, not what you *think* it takes, or have fooled yourself into believing it takes."

"God," Ron spat, retrieving his crutch and rising abruptly. "You sound like the fucking Road Man. And I am so goddamned sick of half-baked, self-seeking obscure psychology, I could scream!"

"Why don't you?"

"Because I might not *stop*! Because if I let it go and got down and dirty and primal, my body might follow my mind and clamp my fingers around your throat!"

"Which would do precisely no good," Lew replied easily, "given what I am—and what you are, I might add. I'd be out a couple of minutes, then good as new."

"If I didn't hack you into pieces and toss 'em in the fire!"

"Except that the instant you saw me unconscious, you'd be scared so shitless with remorse, you'd do *anything* to have me back—including assume the Mastership."

Ron caught himself before he went too far—threats of death, even talk of death, among Listeners was a near taboo.

Lew rose smoothly and joined him. He flopped an arm across Ron's shoulders. Ron didn't resist, though he shuddered, disgusted with the failure of his convictions.

"It *was* for your own good," Lew said finally, his voice no more than a whisper in Ron's ear. "I knew as soon as I saw you looking at Brandy that, arch-bitch or no, she was the one woman in the whole world for you."

"You set me up, in other words."

"Not a chance. The party was a fait accompli before you ever showed. And you didn't tell me exactly when you were coming, if you recall—nor that you were bringing Wendy."

Ron bit his lip, trying to think, trying to regain an upper hand he was not certain he had even lost.

"Yeah," Lew continued. "I saw you look at old Brandy, and it was like something out of L'il Abner—something with whats-her-name? Stupefyin' Jones, or whatever. One glance, and there you went. I saw you talking to her, and I saw her looking at you, and I did just the tiniest little bit of Listening and I knew it'd work. So—"

"Asshole," Ron interrupted, shrugging out of Lew's grip and flinging himself down on the bed, where he lay on his back, feet on the floor, while he stared fixedly at the plaster roundel in the ceiling, from which hung Lew's collection of quartz crystals.

"Maybe so," Lew conceded. "But like I said, I know it'd work—so the first chance I got after you left, I simply woke Wendy up . . . and told her what I thought."

Ron sat bolt upright. *"Told her!"* he cried incredulously. "You *told* her I had the hots for a woman I'd barely spoken to? That had treated me like a fucking *turd* when I tried to talk to her?"

"That's what I said," Lew acknowledged softly. "The rest you know."

"The *hell* I do!" Ron snarled. He rose and began to pace, oblivious to the pain in his knee; it was all he could do not to simply deck his brother right there. "You *hid* those memories from me, Lew!—and that's the same thing as lying! You said things went one way about Wendy's leaving, which I have no doubt they did. But you neglected to mention you knew the how and why! And yet you stand there and say I *know*! Well, fuck you, man! 'Cause I bloody well *don't* know *what* you said *exactly*—which could be important. And I *certainly* don't know what *Wendy* said when you told her her boyfriend was a randy-cocked shit! But I—"

"Stop it, Ronny," Lew snapped, his voice grown suddenly cold as ice, and stiff with unconscious authority. "Just stop it, okay? Before somebody says something he'll never be able to take back."

"Christ," Ron groaned, slapping the wall in frustration. "Are you even *listening* to yourself, man? I don't suppose you even *considered* the fact that it might already be too late for that? That by denying me those letters, you've already done something you can't ever fix."

"It was a risk I had to take," Lew replied calmly. "And look at me with a straight face and tell me you're happier now than before you knew about 'em."

Ron glared at him, then stomped to the window and stared through the limbs of the surrounding oaks toward the tennis court, and beyond, the western lawns. "I don't *need* to look at you to tell you that."

"Then you believe me?"

Ron spun around. "Not bloody likely! Not when you've already lied to me about the most important thing in the world."

"I thought *Making* was the most important thing in the world."

Ron froze. "It is . . . was . . . Oh hell, you know what I mean. The most important thing in the world that I have any *choice* about."

Lew regarded him for a long moment, his usually cherubic mouth now a thin, hard line. His brow wrinkled with indecision, and then, suddenly, he squatted by the chest again, rummaged within, and produced another mass of envelopes. "Okay, then. Maybe *this'll* convince you." He passed the pile to Ron.

Ron took them, only then realizing he hadn't yet read the first ones, the ones that purported to be from Wendy. Those he deposited on the windowsill while he perused the latest set.

"Christ," he gasped, when he saw what he held. "These are bloody police reports!"

"Report," Lew corrected. "There's only one of any consequence. In there you'll find a copy of a missing person report I filed with both the local police *and* the GBI the day your sweetie split. And," he continued before Ron could respond, "you'll find the notes they sent me rejecting it: first because it was too soon, *then* because I'd had phone calls and letters which seemed to indicate that Wendy, at least, didn't consider herself missing at all."

"Okay, okay," Ron growled. "I get the picture." He glanced over the final pages, which proved to be transcripts of questions asked Lew by one Detective Jonathan Myllo on the afternoon of Wendy's disappearance, and dropped the bundle beside the unopened others. "Looks like your ass is covered after all," he went on. "But one thing still bugs me about all that."

Lew, who was helping himself to a drink—a screw-driver, by the look of it—raised an inquiring eyebrow. "Which is?"

"That no one bothered to interview Karen—or me! Which strikes me as being a pretty big oversight, don't you think? I mean if *I* was investigating a missing coed, the first people I'd check'd be the folks who saw her last, which, as best I can tell, was you, Karen, and me."

"We couldn't catch up with either of you at first. And by then we'd had the first call. The interview was mostly a technicality."

"I don't suppose you bothered to trace the call?"

"It came from a pay phone in Athens. They all have."

Ron was staring at him suspiciously. "You know, it occurs to me, oh my brother," he said slowly, "that if you hoodooed her that night, you could have stuck anything in her head you wanted to—any posthypnotic suggestion you thought might be useful."

Lew could only gape. Then, "Jesus, Ronny! I thought we were friends, never mind brothers! I thought we trusted each other! I thought if I laid out my dirty laundry, you'd—"

"What?" Ron snarled, rounding on him. "Pick it up and wash it with mine until it was all lily-white again? It don't work that way, man. Not when you start playing the kinda games you've been playing! It smacks too much of how Matt used to act. Or are you becoming like him, too?"

Lew glared at him furiously. "I resent that. It was only for your own good. You had the perfect girl—you thought. And then you met the *really* perfect girl."

"And you made damned sure to burn the bridges behind me. That's supposed to be *my* job, guy—not yours!"

Lew chugged his drink. "Well, it's done now, isn't it?"

Ron simply continued to glare; then, when his brother showed no sign of offering either protest or further explanation, snatched up the letters, collected his crutch, and stumped past him out the door. He did not close it behind him.

Karen peered out of the dining room door as he limped by, her tentative smile quickly fading as she saw his thunderous scowl. Ron caught a whiff of something scrumptious sneaking out the door around her, but ignored it stonily and pressed on down the hall.

He slammed the front door behind him hard enough that he heard the desperate crack of antique glass breaking, followed by a sorrowful tinkle.

He didn't care. Cardalba Hall could collapse into a heap for all the difference it made, and Lew with it. Bad blood had triumphed at last. His brother, his *beloved* brother Lew, was as much a manipulative shit as the previous Master had been—and a traitor in the bargain. Well, screw him! He could leave or go as he pleased, but Ron, by God, would never be Master of Cardalba, not while he was in his right mind!

Not while Lew hid things from him he needed to know; not while Lew let him stew in his own guilty juices when absolution might have been at hand!

He had reached the car by then (unattended by the ghost-hounds, which was a pleasant change), and immediately felt another pulse of anger. For, in addition to the road grime that was a necessary adjunct to living at Brandy Hall, the Thunderbird had acquired a film of the pervasive yellow-green pollen in just the few moments Ron had been inside. But as he reached for the door handle, his attention was drawn to a line of symbols someone had smeared into the powder on the hood with a finger. *Those* absolutely hadn't been present before. And there was certainly nobody around Cardalba Hall to put 'em there except Karen, who'd seen enough of him yesterday to know better. But it made him furious anyway, because such antics could damage paint by abrading it.

Grimacing irritably, he edged left to read the incised graffiti, expecting the usual WASH ME or DUST DURABIL-ITY TEST or some such juvenilia—probably of Van's contrivance.

Yet when he actually got a good look at the script, it was not in the big guy's hand at all. Indeed, the neatly slanting letters closely resembled *Wendy's* writing.

But what sent a chill up Ron's back and over his shoulders to knot in the pit of his stomach was not the *fact* of the inscription, but what it said. Just two small words: HE LIES.

Chapter 22

Refugee

"*Shit!*" Ron grunted as he caught himself on the ragged edge of punching the small, square button in the middle of the dash that would switch the radio station to something *besides* commercial chatter. He drummed his fingers nervously on the steering wheel and watched the landscape flashing by quickly become more rugged as the highway whipped onto the lower flanks of Keycutter Knob. And waited—which, as the Tom Petty song he'd heard in a nonoracular context earlier that day suggested, was the hardest part. It was true, too, especially when you desperately needed some sign to point the way to security and happiness ever after—and all you got was someone trying to sell you Toyotas.

Ron hated it: being reduced to external influences for charting the course of his life. And especially loathed having to deal with something as unreliable as radio station play lists that only chose to pass on useful information when it suited *their* nefarious needs.

God only knew they'd been of little help lately! Had given him nothing at all for weeks until just past midnight at the restaurant in Athens. But *since* then—Jesus! "Wendy" had only been the start. It had been followed immediately by "Magic Man"—*again*—this time in the Covering position; which had then been capped in turn by Aretha Franklin's stirring rendition of "Think," which in the Crossing role meant that he was supposed to do exactly that: *think*, as opposed to *react*. Which was precisely what stress and lack of sleep were rendering him incapable *of* doing.

Unfortunately, he'd caught no more omens last night, for the simple reason that the restaurant had closed. (As it was, he and Karen had been its last customers.) And after *that*, it hadn't mattered, because he had no idea what the station had been anyway, never mind that the necessary continuity had been shattered.

Which, however, did not mean he was totally without recourse. True, it was generally the *first* song of the day that counted. But Uncle Dion had also told him that *any* critical emotional disjunction—such as his latest spat with Lew—could be construed as a new beginning, so with that in mind, he'd switched on the radio as soon as he'd roared away from Cardalba.

And got two more songs very quickly, both of which seemed to indicate that he was still being fed portents left and right—if only he knew how to read them. It was damned frustrating, though: trying to catch eleven songs in sequence. And nerve-racking, given what those first two had been.

The Significator, for instance, had been Genesis's "Ball of Confusion"—which certainly mirrored his mental state admirably.

But the second—the song that represented Immediate Influences—jeeze! *It* had been Fleetwood Mac's "Rhiannon."

Which gave him the worst case of the apprehensive shivers he'd had in a while, because that was about as powerful an indicator of Female Magic at work as he could imagine. More to the point, Rhiannon was a character from *Celtic* myth, which was not only one of Brandy's major interests, but of particular significance to Listeners in general—especially when their last name happened to be Welch.

Welch: Welsh. According to what he'd read years ago in one of the ancient tomes back at Cardalba, one name had begat the other somewhere around the beginning of the last century, preserving most of the sound while cleverly obscuring the sense. Just like Cordova was a corruption of Cardalba, which was in turn a much-corrupted form of Caer Dathal, which had been the seat of a powerful Welsh magician named Math, itself not far from Matthew, which was by far the most common name among Masters.

Trouble was: he didn't *know* any Welsh sorceresses, famous, mythological, or otherwise.

Scowling, he tried to do what last night's Crossing tune had advised: to think, to lay out *all* the alternatives—and found it damned hard, as upset as he was, and as sleepy.

Perhaps the logical thing to do first was simply to consider the song in light of the women influencing his life at the moment. Like who? Well, Brandy was obviously interested in Welsh myth, but her gene pool was almost pure English, with a spicing of Cherokee sneaking in around early in the century. *Karen* had no power of her own beyond that she passed on to Lew by virtue of her virginity. And Wendy—well, she'd never evinced any interest in arcane matters. Though now he thought of it, she *was* into plants, which he supposed *could* relate to Earth Magic. Or unless that really *had* been her Voice, her half-glimpsed face—and still faintly visible through the windshield, her handwriting on his car—in which case, she was far gone into the Great Unknown indeed!

And speaking of Earth Magic, he had finally reached the turn-off for the dirt road that led down to Brandy Hall. *Just* as the everlasting commercial ended and the next tune began, the one that revealed the nature of obstacles.

Del Shannon's "Runaway."

Now, *that* was interesting. But did it refer to Wendy, as was surely the most logical conclusion? Or was there a subtler, more obscure interpretation?

Maybe when the whole array was complete, he'd know. *Maybe.*

He was still puzzling over the implications when he finally caught sight of the low battlements atop Brandy Hall.

"Oh, gee, Weedge, that's great!" Brandy enthused loudly, if automatically, into the portable black plastic phone Ron had "officially" only lent her.

"Why're you yelling?" came the distant crackle of her friend's voice.

"Because frigging Vannister's running two-by-fours through that blessed table saw of his!" Brandy shot back irritably, though her anger was not directed at her chum.

"Yeah, I can kind of hear it," Weedge replied carefully. "I thought it was static."

"Yeah, well, I don't have a clue about what he's actually gonna *do* with 'em—the boards, I mean. I—"

Weedge didn't let her finish but launched into a summary of how she'd won the job upgrade she'd left so precipitously to interview for. And Brandy really was glad for her. Trouble was, she had more pressing matters to consider at the moment, so she mostly went through the motions of conversation, without much minding the content. She let her best friend blither on for a while, then, at a suitable pause, inserted, "Weedge, can I ask you something personal? Something that has nothing whatever to do with your good news?"

The briefest of hesitations, then, "Sure."

Brandy paused as well. "I'm sorry I'm preoccupied now, but . . . something's happened."

"Not more measuring glitches, please God."

"They weren't glitches," Brandy corrected instantly, "but no, it's nothing to do with the house, at least not directly."

"Good Lord!" Weedge chuckled with gentle sarcasm. "You mean you've got problems *besides* finishing Brandy Hall?"

"Lots."

"So shoot."

Brandy took a deep breath. "Have you ever done anything you didn't want to, but did anyway, even though you actually knew *while* you were doing it that it was wrong?"

"Occasionally. Why?"

"Because I just did."

"Like what?"

Brandy took a second, even longer breath to steel herself—and hesitated once more. Did she *really* want to get into all this on the phone? Especially to Weedge, who did not need her parade rained on so soon after being made queen?

"Hang on a sec," Brandy shouted into the receiver, that being necessitated by a particularly prolonged and obnoxious shriek from Vannister's saw—during which interval she caught a flash of movement up on the driveway.

"Sure."

She looked up from *The Art of Scandinavia* she'd been absently paging through with her free hand while she held the phone with her other, just in time to catch the expected glint of shiny black paint hurtling along behind the trees two curves above the knoll. It was clearly Ron, he was definitely in a hurry, and God, but she hoped he wasn't pissed!

Not that he didn't have some small right to be, she conceded, especially in the unlikely event he found out about her dalliance with Vannister, which he *certainly* wouldn't from her! But she had a right to be upset at him, too, and not the least because his little fit had cost him—and therefore her—half a day's smithing. That Ron was probably as distraught, frustrated, and confused as she was didn't matter at all when viewed from that perspective. In fact, she'd probably been too easy on him. He'd get his work done properly and on time, and if he had any fizz left for talk—or *anything* else—later, that was okay, too.

But not—anymore—a necessity.

The saw's anguished howl was even louder now—loud enough to rattle the glass in what few windowpanes had actually been installed here up front. Yet through that cacophony, she could still hear the crunch of gravel, the slap of foliage—which meant Ron was driving *much* faster than he should along that road. Which in turn meant that he probably *was* upset.

"Brandy?"

"Uh, sorry, Weedge, I gotta go. Something's just come up."

"Sure. Catch you later."

" 'Bye." Brandy turned off the phone, set the book down, and rose, wiping her hands on her jeans as she did.

Vannister evidently noticed her shift to friskiness, looked around, and—to judge by the stream of profanity that followed a particularly sudden and nerve-jangling screech from his table saw—for the first time since Brandy had known him, savaged a board beyond redemption. Matty Groves, who had been pacing about looking furtive and lost, immediately fluffed to twice his normal size and dived for the shadows beneath the Centauri.

Brandy scowled, but just then the Thunderbird barreled from between the trees like a low black bullet and crunched to a rumbling halt in Ron's usual parking spot between his other car and the tiny flower garden in front of the patio.

Even across the twenty-plus yards that separated them, she could see that his expression matched his car's mechanical voice. For Ron looked seriously unhappy—and not, she thought, at her.

"Well, if you gotta, you gotta," she muttered to herself, whereupon she stuffed her fists into her pockets and strode toward him.

But Ron—who was not only disinclined to get out of the car but quite content to remain where he was inside it—was not, in fact, actually so much angry or upset as perplexed. Forgetting the omens for the moment (the next was being delayed by yet more commercials), all he had to do was to squint through the windshield at those cryptic words scrawled across the hood in pollen to be reminded that even for a Listener like him, there was still far more mystery in the universe than could ever be comprehended.

It *was* Wendy's handwriting, of that he had little doubt. And the accusation of lying—though by whom and to whom was not clear except by implication—was certainly more than troubling. But every time he tried to figure out how the message had actually come there, he reached the same conclusion. Either it was an impossibly well-timed and topical practical joke on the part of some nameless venturesome neighbors, or Karen had somehow gotten wind of their altercation and, knowing more about

Wendy's departure than she'd dared admit even in the relative security of Athens, had forged Wendy's writing there as a sign to Ron that he should keep his investigation alive. Or Wendy herself had somehow contrived them. Christ, but he wished he'd thought to try a scrying when he'd first found them—not that it would help much if it really *had* been Wendy. Still, if she only had a Voice! If he'd only delved deeply enough into her mind to find some equivalent psychic signature—at least enough to allow him to keep track of her presence and be assured she was okay.

Or at least *was*.

But beyond the Tarot, a conclave of Listeners working in concert, or an all-out investigation by the FBI, there was no way to find out now, and certainly not here.

Especially not when Brandy was stalking toward him with something less than eager welcome in her eyes.

And *especially* not when, in spite of his efforts to shield against such things, Brandy's Knoll was practically awash with some kind of odd psychic residue.

Still, if he stayed in the car, he'd be giving her a psychological advantage she didn't need. And that was a lot more important right now than figuring out what was upsetting the Winds. Especially when he suspected he was about to be subjected to a wind of quite another sort—given that Brandy was now close enough for him to see that she was definitely sporting her "We need to talk" expression (as opposed to the "You have now royally pissed me off" look she'd worn when he departed).

Which meant he'd have to commune with the Voices of nameless scribblers another time—pursue them into the past, if need be. *If* it was even worth the trouble.

Sighing, he unlatched the door and unfolded himself from the leather-lined security of the T-bird's cockpit. He made no move to greet Brandy, though; but simply leaned against the front fender and waited for her to come to him: yet another ploy in the game of one-upmanship. Matty Groves quickly joined him, appearing from nowhere to rub against Ron's legs as if he'd been gone for ages. "Well, I'm glad *somebody* still likes me," Ron murmured.

Brandy took the bait, and though she was already within hailing range, did not actually speak (probably because of the proximity of the howling table saw) until she was no more than two yards away. She stopped there, staring past him with a strange expression on her face. Ron tried to meet her gaze, conscious that at least one of them ought to apologize, and that both probably wanted to. But she wouldn't meet his eyes; instead, her gaze would catch on his, then flick away, as if something was bothering her that—great surprise—she *didn't* want to discuss.

She swallowed, as did he. He attempted a smile, which she weakly echoed. "Feeling better?" she asked finally, still not looking at him. She eased against the fender beside him, folded her arms across her breast in that pose she affected when she wanted to say something important and didn't want to be distracted by anything as hazardous as eye contact. A breeze ruffled her hair, smelling of honeysuckle and that damned pollen. A drift of pale blossoms floated down onto the hood behind them. Ron snagged one without thinking, sucked out the tiny drop of sweetness at its heart, and began absently dismembering it. Brandy watched him.

"Yeah," he said at last. "I feel okay—at least about some things. Trouble is, sometimes when you solve one problem, you get another."

Brandy nodded sagely. "Tell me about it."

Ron glanced sideways at her. "Was that a request, or were you just being rhetorical?"

"I—"

Ron started, wondering what had made her break off in midsentence like that.

"*Now* what?" she grumbled, pushing away from the car and starting toward where Vannister was frantically gesturing at them.

But she was hesitating, Ron saw instantly, with that mastery of the subtleties of body language that usually came as second nature to Listeners. He wondered what was wrong, and nearly risked a psychic probe in her direction, vacillating between desire for the peace of mind any revelations thus acquired might grant and fear of violating the vow he had made never to intentionally spy on her thoughts without permission.

Discretion won. But as he followed her toward Van's loudly whining saw, he had to make a conscious effort not to pry. The vibes were *that* strong, the resonances *that* pervasive.

And he *truly* had to fight to maintain control as he drew closer to his fellow workman.

"What is it?" Brandy asked the big redhead brusquely as she and Ron came into speaking range.

Van shut off the machine. "Nothin' really," he replied in what they all three knew was a mostly put-on good-ol'-boy drawl. "I just messed up the first piece of two-by I ever did while I've been up here's all, and I figured I'd show it to y'all."

Even without seeing Brandy's face, Ron could sense her irritation. She was not in a mood for frivolity. Surely even Van realized that.

Or maybe not, for he reached to a sawhorse-braced table beside him and dragged out a foot-long length of wood which he flourished before their faces as if it were the world's ultimate fertility fetish.

Which in a way it was, for the saw had evidently impacted a monstrous knot which even good-quality steel had proven unequal to assailing. And the resulting kicking of the blade and splintering of the surrounding matrix had freed the obstruction almost in its entirety. And, as Vannister brandished it triumphantly in the afternoon light, it looked exactly like an immense golden phallus.

Ron blushed in spite of himself, and he saw Brandy redden as well.

But he sensed something else, too: a heightening of that strange, latent tension that had pervaded the entire knoll since his return. And now he recognized it: sexual energy—an entity he was certainly familiar with, but not precisely this way—and never of this intensity.

And then he saw the self-satisfied grin that was lighting up Van's far-too-handsome features, and had a terrible sick feeling that he *knew*.

"Pretty cool, ain't it?" Van sniggered, flourishing the wooden member with an almost childish glee Ron had never seen him indulge in before. "Hey, *you* want it, Brandy?"

Brandy shook her head and turned far enough around that Ron could now see that she was absolutely furious—both at Van in general, and at being deviled when she was already in a prickly mood.

On the other hand, there *was* that grin . . .

But maybe it was time to defuse the situation. Ron fixed his fellow workman with a casual but forceful gaze. "That's pretty amazing," he observed with deliberate nonchalance. "But I *hope* you got more done this afternoon than that—'cause *I* sure as hell didn't."

Ron was watching Van's face when he made his comment—and caught the quick darting of his eyes in Brandy's direction, the sudden reddening of his cheeks, the tremble of his lips.

But then a challenging light awoke those eyes, and Van grinned at him so disarmingly that Ron had no choice but to look away. "I did," Van laughed knowingly. "Or *we* did, rather: Brandy and me." He winked at Ron. The grin widened.

It was all Ron could do to keep from decking him right there, never mind getting to the truth of the matter they all seemed to be dancing around. "What?" he asked, completely without forethought.

But then, suddenly, he needed no reply.

For, perhaps in response to Ron's implicit and probably imminent challenge, Van had stepped toward him. But that movement also took him slightly sideways, revealing one of the numerous patches of flowers Brandy suffered to flourish here and there amid the piles of construction materials. Pansies these were: tiny and delicate. And, in this case, of a uniform height.

But now Ron could see quite clearly that something had pressed a large section of them flat. Indeed, the ground beneath them was soft enough that he could make out with remarkable clarity the shape of a naked woman lying on her back, arms represented by elbow-length stubs, as if they had been raised to grasp something sprawled atop her.

Which they probably *had* been, because the legs were spread wide and showed between them, but a suspicious space lower down, the unmistakable imprint of obviously male knees, shins, and feet, with a trace of thigh as well. And just about level with the female's breast were the impressions of two large, widespread hands.

"I see," Ron whispered savagely. "*Boy*, do I see!"

Van simply gaped at him, but Brandy had already followed his gaze to the traitorous flower bed, where (she obviously had no more doubt than Ron) were impressed the forms of a pair of lovers happily engaged in the traditional male-superior position.

"But we never . . . !" she blurted before she could stop herself. "Not there!"

"*Hush!*" Van snapped harshly. But Brandy had already clamped her hands across her mouth and was gazing at Ron with eyes so huge with apprehension, he feared she was about to faint.

Unfortunately, he already had other things on his mind than assuaging the guilt of errant females, or laying their likely seducers low. For if he could believe the evidence of his senses—and he had no reason not to—and if he computed correctly, every single person he cared about had, in the last half hour, betrayed him. And when that basically amounted to only two names anyway—with Van a companionable but distant third that was *damned* depressing.

He was evidently not worth a turd to anyone. Or not enough to inspire either trust or fidelity, at any rate.

Clamping his jaw tight shut to keep it from quaking, he turned and, without a word, strode stiffly, not south toward his tent, nor north toward the beckoning glitter of the lake, but southeast toward the deepest part of the woods. Matty Groves stared after, but did not follow.

For the better part of a minute Brandy imitated the cat and watched Ron slowly diminish as he walked away through the calf-high grass, her mind so numbed by conflicting emotions, she was for all practical purposes paralyzed. How could this have *happened*? No way that damned tattletale impression should have been there—they'd done the deed at least thirty yards away, for Christ's sake! But even given that it *did* exist (and it was still blatantly present for anyone to see, right behind the equally shocked-looking carpenter), why in the world had she blurted out what she had? It was almost as if another will had seized her tongue for a crucial instant and demanded she speak what her heart forbade!

And now Ron was leaving—beautiful Ron, beautiful, dutiful, gentle genius-with-metal Ron.

And Vannister was looking at her very hungrily indeed.

Beautiful, wild, unpredictable master-of-all-trades Vannister.

Which did she really want?

And how on earth had an unassuming Saturday afternoon suddenly become an emotional D day?

Vannister smiled at her, eagerly, then winsomely, as if uncertain for once how far he should go, and perhaps aware at last that she truly did have limits beyond which even he was a fool to transgress—and that he very likely just had.

And then Ron tripped on an unseen something and stumbled forward onto his hands and knees before rising again and continuing on.

And she was running toward him, her decision made.

Yet when she finally caught up with him, there on the fringe of the forest where the familiar path commenced its long wind down to the lake, and a nearly invisible trail she'd never explored angled off into the deeper woods, she felt her old steel returning.

"I never *said* I was yours," she called helplessly, while he continued to hitch along, clearly in need of the crutch he had abandoned back in his car. "You wouldn't let that other love die: why should I?"

But Ron did not stop, did not turn, though she thought he slowed slightly. Or maybe that was merely a trick of light, a shift in footing where the roots of oak and hickory tugged at the deep, rich soil.

"I'm not gonna apologize for being human," she insisted. "I'm not!"

But Ron still didn't reply, though she saw his shoulders stiffen and caught a tightening of his jawline that probably meant he wanted to say something but didn't dare.

He was entering the underbrush now, pushing through it to take the straight path along the overgrown trail. Still ignoring her.

"Oh, what's the use?" she groaned, and followed him no further. Which did not keep her from watching until he was masked from sight by the protective waxy leaves of a stand of late-flowering rhododendron, leaving her alone beneath a canopy of hickory, wondering if she had just cut her own throat.

For a long time she stood there, wondering, fearing, vaguely aware of the scent of unseen flowers riding the wind, mocking her with their spicy sweetness. The sun slid behind a cloud, and a splatter of rain pricked at her shoulders, even as she heard the steel-drum rumble of thunder—yet still she stayed unmoving. If it rained, Ron would get soaked—but maybe that would wash some sense into his head.

Or hers.

The storm held off, but she still did not move, though her palms now bore red crescents where her stubby nails gnawed into them. Eventually she became aware of a presence behind her: a warm, sweaty muskiness that overwhelmed the flower scent, a sound of breathing, a swish of broom sedge against denim that could only be Van Vannister.

She did not turn to face him, but found herself tensing at the mere notion of such proximity, where little more than an hour before, she had welcomed it. But the decision was made now: the one she had fretted about all unknowing for most of the summer. Vannister was the snake in the Garden of Eden, not Saint Michael casting out the fallen Adam. Which, she supposed, made her Eve the Temptress—and by rights, Adam's companion in adversity. Except . . . that was wrong. It was time to rewrite the myth; she had to remain steadfast, had to endure. She would not allow Vannister, nor Ron—nor *any* man—to cast her from her bliss.

"What's up with Dillon?" Vannister asked with that practiced innocence she had no more patience for now that she knew it hid nothing but insincerity. He was close behind her—*too* close. She could feel his breath stirring her hair, warm on the sides of her throat.

"Is he pissed, or—"

"*Yes indeed* he's pissed," she shouted abruptly, spinning around like a cornered doe to confront the suddenly incredulous workman. There was a trace of satisfaction

in his expression, though, one that she could no longer
tolerate. The tension that had been brewing all day, that
had found temporary relief in sex, but which had rebuilt
again thereafter, suddenly rose to a boil, even as the sky
belled with closer thunder.

"Of *course* he's pissed," she continued at a knife-edged
yell. "Wouldn't *you* be if some asshole just seduced your
girlfriend and then rubbed pictures in your face?"

Vannister merely shrugged and grinned, but the spark
awake deep in his eyes hinted more of danger than amusement. "Don't give me that crap!" he snarled back. "You
needed fucking as much as I did."

"*Bullshit!* You took advantage of me."

"Bullshit, hell! I knew you wanted me. And I knew
you'd made it with him. I just gave you a choice; that
way you can make a more informed decision!"

"Some choice! Love or rape! Respect or domination—"

"*Wild or tame?*"

Brandy backed away reflexively, as a vast uneasiness
suddenly clamped around her heart. "Don't give me that!"
she spat. "Ron's here by my grace; so are you. And *I* call
the shots on my own place, and don't *you* forget it!"

Vannister's expression clouded. "How *can* I?" he
sneered. "You remind me of it every time I try to do
anything!"

"It's my right! It's my place! My dream!"

"And a damned lonely one."

Brandy's face was crimson with rage. "I *had* someone
to share it with—until *you* fucked it up!"

"*Down,*" Vannister corrected smugly, with a wicked
leer. "It was *down* that I was fucking. Don't forget that.
It happened. I enjoyed it; so did you."

"I can't imagine why," she gritted icily.

An eyebrow shot up in wry amusement. "*Can't* you? I
gave you a walk on the wild side. You can't go back now.
It'll haunt you forever."

Brandy drew herself up very straight. "*I* can go where
I please."

"Sure you can," Vannister chuckled agreeably. "And
wherever that is, *I'll* be right there with you, locked in
your memory, stark naked with a hard-on."

Brandy could do nothing but gape. "And I thought you were different," she growled finally. "I thought 'cause you were good at something worthwhile you weren't like all the rest."

"Oh, but I *am* different," Vannister countered instantly, with a fiendishly feral glint in his eyes. "You'd better hope you never know how much!"

"I don't *want* to."

"Don't you?"

Something about Vannister's complacency, his refusal to back off, to admit she had the upper hand, galled her. And wired as she already was, she found herself screaming, with all the force she could muster, "I hate you! You've destroyed every good thing I ever had!"

"Have I?" Vannister teased, before she could continue her tirade, a dangerous flash brightening his eyes. "Funny, *I* thought I was *givin'* you good things: good lumber, good workmanship, good company . . . good sex. All those things still exist . . . or can."

"Bullshit!" Brandy shot back, wishing she could think of something even more scathing. "But they're all tainted now."

"Only if you let 'em be."

"Shut up!"

"They can *not* be, too," Vannister warned silkily. "Somebody could drop a match—or leave a car outta gear. Maybe some kind of electronic glitch eats up your bank account. *How* much insurance did you say you had on this place?"

Brandy's mouth dropped open, but she quickly mustered herself again. "If you even *think* you're brave enough to risk that, do it and be done!" she snapped. "You've screwed with it so much already, it might as well be your fucking house anyway, 'cause it sure as bloody hell isn't *mine!*"

"It's *not*? I thought it was your dream house. Well, I've been giving you what's in your dreams. Screw blueprints! I've been building from the soul."

"Whose soul? Mine, or yours?"

"Yours, if you'd only look beyond deadlines and control and bein' a bitch!"

"Ah, so it's the 'B' word now," Brandy snorted grimly. "Well, as best I recall, there're two of 'em."

"You mean *brilliant*? *Builder*? Or—"

"You know what I mean."

"Tell me anyway."

But she could not. Something Vannister had said, something he'd inserted in passing, which he'd then glossed over, roared back to haunt her. What was that line about giving her her dreams? Dammit, that was true! Much as she hated to admit it, every single change he'd made to Brandy Hall had brought it closer to that impossible image she had in her head: the one she'd never quite been able to get down on paper no matter how she tried.

But there was no way he could access that information. *No way!*

"Cat got your tongue?" Vannister taunted, flopping against a nearby oak and folding his arms across his chest.

"You scare me sometimes," Brandy hissed, aware even as the words left her lips that she was opening a chink in her armor. Yet the thought would not leave her, remained there, seething, demanding to be released no matter what the cost. "You know that, don't you? These things you do when nobody's looking—they're not . . ."

She let the sentence trail off, dreading that final, awful word.

Vannister would not let her off the hook. "Not what?" he asked, his voice scarcely even a whisper.

"Not . . . not *human*."

"Ah!" he cried, with a sly smile that completely unnerved her. "But I never *said* I was human, did I? Then again, what else *could* I be?"

Brandy believed him. Yet her only response was to run. Only *instinct*, rather; her mind was too numb with shock and fear to give rational orders at the moment, so that before she knew it, she was darting across the shreds of grass, leaping the flower beds, sidestepping the mounds of sand and cement bags and lumber. Seeking whatever shelter she could in the heart of her dream.

Somehow she made it to the front arcade, then inside. But only when she had stumbled into the dubious sanctuary of the nearly finished master bedroom and slammed its thick oak door behind her did she realize that if Vannister had followed he was taking his own sweet time.

Which didn't necessarily mean anything, not if what he said was true: that he wasn't human.

Except that was preposterous!

Or was it?

—Whereupon she turned the key in the lock and leaned panting against the heavy wood, already aware of how insecure that room was, of how she was going to have to seek shelter elsewhere. But it also sent that same troublesome question gibbering through her consciousness. If he wasn't human, what was he?

One of the *Nunnehi*? Not hardly—not with his coloring! Which only left about a million others, none of which she believed in for an instant. Vannister was flesh and blood: flesh she had felt, blood she could almost smell. Strength of limb that could hurt her if he willed.

Only one thing she *did* know: she was going to fight him. But in order to accomplish that, she needed time to think, to defend—or attack, if need be—from a position of strength, which she couldn't do here, stout oak boards notwithstanding. Not when there was a pair of plate-glass doors opening onto a side patio not ten feet away. A rock in the hand of an angry man could do some damage there.

So she moved on, down the length of the room and into a smaller corridor, then right into what she intended someday to be a studio, nestled in the much-plagued northwest corner. She'd built a secret room there, tucked beneath the stairs. One she'd hoped to make a strongroom. She slipped inside and waited, aware at once of how hot and dry the air was—and how very, very stale.

She had not been there long at all when she heard booted feet approaching. Someone fumbled at the latch she thought she'd hidden. The bolt clicked home.

Her primary realizations as she heard those footsteps leave were how stupid she was not to have installed a failsafe to the lock on the *inside*. And better ventilation.

And then she began to have trouble breathing.

Chapter 23

Run Through the Jungle

Welch County, Georgia
Early evening

It was only when he tripped over the third root in as many minutes that Ron began to suspect that perhaps—just possibly—it was time to sit down.

He had paced and plodded, trudged and jogged (as best his bum knee permitted), and finally staggered for what were probably hours along what had first appeared to be a well-traveled deer trail but which had long since petered out entirely, leaving him alone in a very old forest indeed, without food, shelter beyond leaves, and with very little hope of salvation.

And that didn't even count the fact that it was getting dark and had been drizzling for quite some time. The first he could handle—he thought—*if* he made his way carefully or merely remained where he was. But the second was turning out to be a real ring-tailed bitch-kitty, not so much because he actually minded being wet (the canopy of leaves overhead was dense enough to screen out the worst of what had mostly been a light though steady shower anyway), but because it made the ground treacherous and the visibility even worse. And both of those, given the prevalence of hidden roots and stones among the thigh-tall ferns he'd been slogging through, strongly increased the odds that sooner or later he would fall and injure himself.

Not that he wouldn't heal—but it could still hurt like hell, which wasn't exactly a notion he relished. And he might lie there a long time without food or drink while the Luck worked its dubious spell. He wondered about that: whether it was possible for Listeners—whose bodies repaired themselves when damaged if the will that ruled their flesh desired to go on living—to die of starvation? Probably not. Probably you'd just waste away until you became unconscious, then revive at the taste of food or drink. But that really wasn't a thing he ought to be thinking about, as he finally halted beside a flat, car-sized boulder that rose waist-high from the bracken. Not when he was both literally lost in the woods and figuratively lost in the rest of the world besides.

The rain had stopped, for a miracle, and Ron climbed atop the mossy stone and simply lay there, panting, staring up through damp lashes at the blurred patterns of leaves and branches above: black lace against an indigo sky, with the barest trace of pink still visible through the thick trunks to the west. This was the oldest part of the woods, the section that had never been logged off, that had been exactly as it was (probably with a good many of these same trees) when his own white ancestors had arrived—possibly when the Cherokee had appeared, and *maybe* even when the tribes who'd built the Chiefdom of Coosa before *them* flourished. Now those trees—oaks and mountain ashes and hickories—were hoary with age: overgrown with shelf fungi lower down, and with their higher branches festooned with what he would have assumed to be Spanish moss had the ghostly parasite been able to prosper this far north.

It was a beautiful place, a peaceful place, a place slightly apart from time, even—he supposed—as the Listener folk like him were.

But just now, apartness was the last thing he needed.

He had screwed up royally. Two months ago he'd had it all: a wonderful girlfriend who loved him completely; a brother who, though consumed with bitterness over his own self-inflicted angst, nevertheless thought the world of him; interesting, creative friends in Athens; a house of his very own; two cars, one of them a hand-built special; and all the hi-tech toys money could provide.

And now he'd lost everything—and an even better woman and a potential friend in the bargain. Even worse, he didn't have a clue where to begin reweaving things— mostly because he wasn't certain where they had begun to unravel.

He *thought* the threads all ran back to Lew. Lew had summoned him up here, after all; Lew had made it possible for him to meet both Brandy and Van. And Lew had been a barely offstage presence when Wendy hit the road.

Trouble was, that smacked of conspiracy and cunning, and though his brother was as naturally brilliant as the rest of the clan, up until the last few weeks, he had never given any indication of being aught but scrupulously honorable and ethical. Of course, he was up to his neck in what had to be a nearly intolerable situation, especially for a well-off young man living among the myriad temptations of the last half of the twentieth century—which could, Ron supposed, send even the best-intentioned close to the edge, if not over it. That Lew was even willing to consider such deprivation as Mastership required spoke volumes about his character.

God only knew Ron wished him well.

But he *still* couldn't figure out what was up with him and Wendy; because, whether or not Lew had set him up with Brandy, there was no way to disguise the fact that he *had* concealed information about Ron's former fling. Like those letters she'd sent (and, dammit, he never had gotten around to reading them, and now they were back in the car). Like the fact that she seemed to have so thoroughly fallen off the face of the earth that it smacked to high heaven of the sort of machinations Listeners used to conceal their existence. Things like destroyed computer files, missing records.

Missing pasts!

Ron sat bolt upright, cursing himself a thousand times for being so stupid. Jeeze! He couldn't believe it had never occurred to him until that very moment that Wendy's supposed amnesia might actually be a function of Listener interference. It was certainly within the scope of their subterfuge, after all, though the few he knew all possessed far too many scruples to actually delete someone's entire memory. And Lew *certainly* wouldn't. Desperate he might be, but not that unethical, not that—dare he say it—insane.

Yet Lew wasn't being straight with him, either. But why? Was something going on between his brother and his former sweetie that it had never occurred to him to actually ask about?

He tried to think back to that first meeting between Lew and Wendy. It *had* seemed odd: Lew had looked shocked that Ron had brought someone with him unannounced (and now he considered it, none of Lew's invitations had ever included anyone else). He'd assumed that was for the obvious reason: the trouble it took to hide things, coupled with the fear of discovery.

But suppose that wasn't the situation at all? Wendy had seemed remarkably at ease at Cardalba almost from the beginning. And in light of these new possibilities, that was even more disturbing than he'd first thought, for the simple reason that the very structure of the mansion had been subjected to so much Luck for so long that the whole place practically hummed with psychic energy. Most ordinary people experienced that sensation simply as a vague disquiet that made them antsy to leave, but Wendy hadn't seemed to notice it at all. Indeed, it was almost as if . . . she'd come home.

Maybe she had! She hadn't been a virgin when he'd met her, so perhaps she was one of Lew's footholders who'd seduced him, gone recalcitrant, and had her memory wiped for her pains. Or maybe she was merely a former lover. Their meeting had had that sort of feel to it, and come to think of it, he never had actually asked her about Lew: either what she thought of him or why she seemed so relaxed in his presence. Maybe their meeting had jogged free a hidden memory Lew didn't *want* jogged.

Except that she usually talked about those right away.

Except, on the other hand, she'd never had that happen in the house of a sorcerer.

Too, there were more than a few odd things about Wendy's conduct just before her disappearance: one, though not the most obvious, being that peculiar assertiveness she'd begun to display around the time they'd left Athens. And coupled with that had come those first faint hints at a Voice, though it had only manifested as total and complete love for him. But together, what did they portend? That Wendy was somehow awakening, coming *alive* in a manner of speaking?

So was Lew the catalyst for that, then? Or was *he* in some way he didn't understand responsible? Or was it Welch County itself?

And what about Wendy's easy acquiescence to his new girlfriend, as if she'd sensed that relationship a-borning and bowed herself out instead of staying to fight for him? She'd never been the jealous type, but apparently one brief conversation with Lew had been enough for her to drop Ron like a hot potato—which didn't jive at all with that same assertiveness. Or jived with it too much, neither of which possibility was in character.

Which—again—meant what?

That Lew had somehow sensed that she might make trouble and put an end to her in some more subtle way? Surely not! Surely Lew would not sink so low or be so desperate as to actually resort to violence, not with the resources he had at his command. Or maybe not, since the alternative really was too much to accept: the one that implied that Lew was not merely a sneak and a manipulator, but—he forced himself to mouth the word— a murderer as well.

He frowned as a drop of rain obscured his vision, wishing the whole messy situation could be explained away as easily as blinking cleared his eyes.

And speaking of vision, what about the signs? They'd definitely been increasing in frequency and variety lately. Why, there'd been two just that day: the winking bronze plaque, and the cryptic inscription in the pollen on the car hood. But that did they have in common? He tried to think, to channel his mind past conventional thinking and into that part of the subconscious that connected things the conscious brain dissociated. And then he had it—maybe:

He'd been engraving leaves on the plaque, and the plaque depicted Galadriel, who was queen of Tolkien's Lothlorien, which was sort of a center for the natural world in Middle Earth. And the words inscribed on the trunk of his car had been written in a thick layer of that wretched hallucinogenic-aphrodisiac pollen that had been a nuisance all summer, that had—oh Jesus!—first appeared the day Wendy disappeared. And both those things had one thing in common: plants.

And both Lew and Wendy were into plants.

And there was also the matter of the imprint of Brandy and Van he'd seen in a *flower* bed. Was that coincidental, too? At the very least, it displayed remarkable negligence on their part.

Or *did* it? He tried to recall that encounter exactly, squinted his eyes shut and used a ghost of Luck and succeeded. Brandy had said something then, something that had gone completely by him in his anger. But what were the lines? He followed the Winds, heard them again, faint but clear: "But we never did . . . not there!"

Not a denial of the fact; merely a denial that it happened *where it had*!

And—Ron's gasp shattered the silence of the woods— Wendy's last *name* was Flowers!

But where had all these signs and portents come from? Well, obviously either Wendy had instigated them, or someone else had. If it was Wendy, either she was doing it herself, which meant that she had somehow managed to contrive some sort of hidden existence, which in turn implied that there was a lot more to her than he'd ever suspected, possibly even that she was a Listener herself.

Or else someone had manipulated her into doing those things.

And in either case, to consider all possibilities, either Wendy was alive . . . or she was dead.

Unfortunately, he was presently inclined to believe the latter. Not that he actually believed in ghosts, but he did know from firsthand experience that consciousness was a far more active principle than most people suspected, and that it was perfectly possible to separate it from the body, as long as it wasn't for too long and certain precautions were taken. And somehow, he thought, if she were physical, he'd have been able to detect more sign. But he'd had not a hint beyond vague feelings that were even more subtle than the half-heard voices, the ghostly faces, and the scarce-sensed Voice he'd a time or two felt pouring its love out on the Wind.

The Wind!

If only he could ride the Wind back into the past and actually watch the morning Wendy had departed. Or better yet, back to before Wendy had become aware of herself driving her white Toyota up the interstate.

If only . . . if only . . . if only . . .

But he wasn't strong enough; was no Master. And even if he were, those days were so long gone in time and space now that to even begin to seek them was to risk losing one's soul forever in the Realm of the Winds.

But he could at least try.

Sighing, he shifted to a more comfortable position upon the stone (better that than lying on damp leaves beneath soggy ferns) and closed his eyes. It had stopped raining some time ago, though the leaves were still dripping; and it was warm and humid enough for him to have worked up an unpleasant sweat that attracted both mosquitoes and gnats—until the quirkiness of Listener blood drove them to seek other prey. The forest was still. Waiting. Silent save for the slow *plip-plop* of water, the rustle of shifting leaves, the distant chatter of an irate squirrel.

Ron concentrated on his breathing, trying to shift into a deeper trance than he usually assayed. But it was no use: he couldn't take that final step, couldn't bring himself to let go and fall that last distance that was so much like death, he wondered how Lew put up with doing it as a matter of course.

Still, it felt good there, in that no-place on the threshold of that even stranger realm that was the domain of Winds and Voices. And so he remained there, suspended: on the border of two worlds and part of neither.

And that deeper aspect of him that looked after his own good even when his conscious mind would not, found him there and eased him into yet another alien country: slumber.

It was light that awoke him—a gilt-edged brightness lancing into his eyes—and as he slowly squinted to full, gritty awareness, he first thought it was someone with a very large, yellow flashlight standing directly over him. But a sequence of blinks and a return of higher brain functions showed it to be only the waning, but still enormous, moon gleaming through a break in the leafy canopy overhead.

He blinked one final time and sat up, achingly aware of how stiff he had become lying on the boulder. A yawn followed, then a languid, catlike stretch, as he felt his joints slide back into their familiar alignments, his muscles resume their accustomed seats. And in spite of the pain that still persisted, he felt better, at least physically. He was drier and no hungrier. And his problems were at marginally further remove.

But since he had no desire to spend the rest of his life as a hermit in the woods (however impressive and primal those woods might be), he supposed he'd best be making his reluctant way back to civilization.

Only, he realized suddenly, he hadn't a clue which way that was. When he'd left Brandy's Knoll, the trail had led downhill. But he could easily have come miles since then, both uphill and down, sometimes traversing ridgelines, sometimes haunting valleys. And at no time had he seen a trace of civilization. Most of the land hereabouts was national forest, and since little of it had been clear-cut (and since the previous Masters of Cardalba had evidently practiced certain subtle arts to discourage such activities), there were no logging roads. Of course, it *was* odd that he'd not encountered either the lake or highway, but he supposed even that was possible, given the meanderings of both, coupled with his own. For all he knew, he could have been twenty yards from either and not have known.

All of which meant that one way was as good as another.

Yawning one final time, he swung his arms down to push off the boulder.

And noticed another thing he had not been aware of before.

The rock had been covered with soft, prickly moss—so he thought: moss and lichens. But now that he rested his fingers on it, they encountered a softer, silkier surface. And he caught a whiff of a familiar spicy-sweet odor as well. He blinked, looked down in the silver-blue gloom, and saw that he had inadvertently lain down in a patch of some species of night-blooming flower that scratched out a thin existence of a surface of solid stone. He could see them clearly, now that his eyes had grown accustomed to the half-light: trumpet-shaped blossoms, something like tiger lilies—except that they were no more than an inch across and pure white. *White-tiger-cub lilies?* a part of him suggested in jest. But there was something odd about those flowers beyond their abrupt appearance and their odor: they seemed to be glowing softly, with a subtle phosphorescence that held no hint of decay.

Sighing one final time, and probing his knee to see what kind of shape it was in, he slid stiffly down from his perch.

And landed in more of the same blossoms—a veritable pavement of them, in fact, peeking in and out of the ferns. And now he looked, it seemed they made a softly glowing trail among the nighted trunks.

But did he really want to follow spooky posies through the woods? God knew he'd been manipulated enough lately. Was this more of the same? Was it—Heaven forbid—another of Lew's tricks? Shoot, was it a *dream*—a phantasm born of that damned pervasive pollen? Or even worse, like those he'd had back in Florida that had utterly wrecked his life?

But did he have anything to lose? Not bloody likely. Shoot, the *worst* that could happen now that he'd lost the two women he loved most, and probably his brother in the bargain, was that he'd get killed. And at the moment, that didn't sound like such an unpleasant notion.

He might even—he realized with a shudder that shook his very soul—want it!

Which meant it could actually happen.

Still, he'd get no answers standing here. And things did seem to be coming to some kind of head—or at least something beyond the norm was interested in him. So with that in mind, he squared his shoulders and stepped onto the path. The smell of flowers that drifted up to greet him was well nigh overpowering.

For a long time Ron rambled—once more curiously unstuck from time. He was grateful he was not wearing a watch (keeping track of time while being creative was not a good idea), for he feared what it would have shown him now. He was magic—sort of. But here, he sensed, was magic of a stronger, deeper kind than he had ever suspected existed. The trees became larger and taller, the moss that shrouded them thicker, the smell of leaves and plants and herbs more luxurious, eventually overpowering even the heady scent of the strange white flowers that limned a twisting road among the trunks before him. He was distantly aware of the sound of an airplane, once of the roar of a car on some unseen highway, but those things seemed remote, as his whole life up to that point now seemed a thing removed. It was like experiencing a waking dream, and that part of him that sat back and watched and analyzed wondered what it was about nighttime that conjured that effect. One spent as much time in darkness— theoretically—as in light, yet one did not regard daylight as a dream. Why, then, should the night be any different? Why should—

He halted abruptly, aware that the flowers were becoming less common, that their dim luminescence was fading. There was light of a different kind, though: moonlight, but of a purer form than had heretofore been fighting to filter through the leaves. He headed toward where it was brightest, first at a fast walk, then at a jog that pained his forever-injured knee.

The trail, which had already tended downhill, suddenly shifted to a slope so steep Ron found that he had to work to remain upright. The light was definitely stronger ahead, though: a break in the trees, which meant he was coming to some sort of clearing—if he was lucky, a road or farmstead; or at least a bit of lake shore he could follow to a boat dock or cabin.

But then, with very little warning, the terrain shifted again, became steeper yet, and Ron could no longer restrain his momentum. He ran—fast. Far faster than he wanted. And inevitably tripped and fell, landed on his knees, tumbled forward, fell again, and then was rolling along a slope that was now mostly low, tangled briars.

Eventually he stopped, sore, scratched, and winded. And for a moment he simply lay where he was, catching his breath, feeling the brush of cool wind, the dryness of which was welcome relief to the humidity of the day. And with that breeze came another odor, one that spoke to him as clearly as the perfume of flowers probably did to Lew: the scent of metal.

Tons and tons of metal.

He blinked, looked up, rose from the thicket of brambles that had sheltered him. Mountains loomed around him, tall and dark on three sides, only slightly lower on the fourth. But closer in, the ground was level; closer in, tall piles of dark shapes cut the sky like fantastic sculptures. Moonlight found much to play on there, sparking and glittering on chrome and filigree, on plastic and broken glass, on paint and rust and leather.

He had somehow stumbled upon an automobile graveyard: promised land—once—to one such as he. In a sort of haze he began to wander there, observing wrecks with an eye most people never had, seeing in each destroyed vehicle a story. The cars were of all vintages, he noted, from ancient Model Ts to the newest high-tech Japanese—which meant the yard was still in use: a comforting thought come tomorrow when he had to rejoin the world at large. And each car had once been new—chosen by caprice, or after much consideration; brought home to a delighted family, or shown to envious friends. All once the pride of some happy owner. And then circumstances had changed: parts had broken down, systems had ceased to function. Some had lost their luster, some had been run to death, neglected; others held together as long as their owners could support them, dispensed with only reluctantly. And some had died deaths as violent as their drivers—for the ghost of blood rested there, too: an acrid bitterness that hid in rust and cracked paint and torn upholstery.

But the place gave Ron peace. Metal was his friend as no person ever could be: that thing with which he held rapport as only other artists and craftsmen could ever understand. There was metal here that had been shaped and could be shaped again: new metal and old, raw metal and painted, bent metal and straight—copper and steel, zinc and chromium, magnesium and titanium and manganese. Gold on the crest of that shattered Cadillac, and silver on the badge of that otherwise rusty Continental.

Ron wandered there for a long time, coming at last to a place where the wrecks were newer, the paint brighter, though there was far less chrome. He recognized a Porsche—a Taurus—an S-class Mercedes Benz: signs of the prosperity of Welch Countians who had, nevertheless, managed to evade the Luck (for Lew only forestalled accidents when he foresaw them; and that was not the sort of thing the Winds commonly foretold).

And directly in front of him was a particularly impressive pile, twice his height and stacked, ready for the crusher. These were *bad* wrecks: new cars in all colors, but so horribly mangled, he could scarcely tell what brands they once had been. But then something struck him as familiar about one, and he trotted closer, until he was scarcely five feet away from the ruin in question.

The wreck was stacked atop another, its back bumper exactly eye level, and with most of a bronze Chevy Celebrity depressing its roof. But what Ron saw on that bumper made him start, made his heart leap into his mouth, and that mouth taste at once sick and dry.

It was a white Toyota Celica the same year as Wendy's. And on what remained of its plastic rear bumper was, plainly visible in the bright moonlight, a Greenpeace bumper sticker, exactly like hers.

He sat down with a thud on the upended engine block from a Dodge, narrowly missing impaling himself on a tatter of Pontiac fender.

It was Wendy's car; there was no doubt about it.

But how had it come here? The man at the garage who had repaired it had said she'd picked up her car. And she'd been down to Athens since then, to retrieve her stuff and move.

Or *had* she? He'd not been able to locate a single person who had actually seen her after she'd claimed her wheels. Only her voice on Lew's answering machine and her handwriting on those stupidly abandoned letters gave proof she had existed since then.

Which were both, he reflected, with another twinge of heartsickness, relatively easy things for a Listener to manipulate.

Which could easily mean—he forced himself to admit— that Wendy really was dead and that Lew had probably killed her and somehow faked the rest. He rose then, determined to search the mangled Toyo for signs of blood—or any other clue to his former girlfriend's fate.

But just as he rose, just as he took a deep breath to steel himself for that ordeal, something clanked nearby.

He looked that way, blinking into the gloom. Saw nothing that could have moved, only the shattered nose, twisted grille, and empty headlights of a ten-year-old Jaguar sedan.

Crrraaaakkk!

There was that sound again: metal popping and tearing. Ron stepped closer, bent over—and saw nothing save the cast metal badge that still adorned the car's hood: the one that depicted a snarling cat's mask affronté.

But as Ron stood gawking at it, the emblem began to move. And while he was never certain what he actually saw that night, he knew, without a doubt, that the Jaguar mascot looked at him, vented a whiskery hiss, and then growled in a very low voice, "She's not here."

Chapter 24

Liar, Liar

Welch County, Georgia
Night

"She's not here."

That a jaguar's mask of silver pot metal should speak; that molecules of lead and zinc should draw on who-knew-what arcane energies and move of their own volition in a manner recognizable to human perception as something 'twixt a snarl and a sneer; that sound should yet issue forth when there was no mechanism to drive it, no lungs to power speech: none of these seemed as remarkable to Ron at that moment as the implications of those simple words:

She. Is. Not. Here.

"She" obviously meant Wendy—the preeminent *she* of his present reality, the shell of whose flattened Toyota gleamed unnaturally white in the light of an equally suspect moon. And implicit in the use of the pronoun was the assumption that Ron would know who *"she"* was.

Is. Well, that was rife with possibilities. *Is* equated with existence, and while Wendy obviously had existed and apparently still maintained the ability to affect material reality, he was uncertain what else that indicated. But the mascot had said *is*, not *was*—which implied that Wendy, as a self-aware entity, was still active in some form.

Not here was obvious. Or should the negator be attached to *is*? *Is not*: a state of nonbeing.

Ron shook his head, exasperated, and glanced around once more. Stacks of twisted metal rose as far as he could see on either side: a maze of walls and towers worthy of any labyrinth, all sharp angles and jagged edges awaiting the smoothing only decades of rust could render. Or the smelter.

And Wendy was not there.

Which meant what?

Why, that she was somewhere else!

Why else would lifeless metal quicken to tell him so? Why else would all the laws of conventional science contravene for one brief burst of prophecy?

But why now?

Because whatever was contriving omens was only strong enough now? Or only now saw the need? Or only now had an opportunity? Or only now found Ron receptive?

In all this complex of doubt, one fact alone shone clear: metal only awoke for him in times of great crisis, when lives hung in the balance.

Ergo, this was a critical juncture.

In a moment, Ron was running.

He ripped his pants on the bumper of a '59 Mercury. The spiderweb spokes of a smashed MGB's wire wheel shredded his shirttail. The grille of a gutted Cadillac slashed his leg exactly across his injured knee, sending pain and numbness to fight for mastery there. Yet still he stumbled on.

And found, at last, the border of that vast junkyard he had never heard of. A barrier rose there: a multihued wall of severed van roofs bolted to decommissioned utility poles to bridge the whole north end of this mausoleum of dead automotive dreams. Mountains rose on either side: high, steep slopes older than the metal that made the machines— yet its source. And pines grew thick beyond the barricade, so that a man might pass the very gates all his life and not suspect this automotive charnal house was here. Certainly

Ron had not known. But *Lew* had.

Lew!

He had to get back to Lew. And this time there would be no storming out with the tale half told. This time there would be no forgiveness. He would learn it all, every shred of the truth, if he had to rip the knowledge from his brother's naked brain!

Trouble was, Ron neither knew where this junkyard was, nor had a way to reach Lew if he found out.

But both of those problems were solvable easily enough to one such as he. A limping jog along the palisade quickly led to a long cinder-block building with a wooden back door Ron prized open with a lug wrench from the trunk of a smashed Camry. A few paces through the structure— a warehouse stacked to the rafters with shelves of sub-assemblies—brought him to a poorly alarmed plate-glass door that let onto the world he knew.

And in the parking lot beyond, a black late-model Mustang GT gleamed darkly, both sheetmetal and drivetrain apparently intact.

A few seconds work with a pair of pliers purloined from a bin by the door disabled the alarm. After that, it was a matter of applying a screwdriver *just so* to jimmy the driver's door. And only a little more finagling with his pocket knife, the screwdriver, and the pliers to hot-wire the engine and set the motor rumbling.

"Sorry, old girl," Ron whispered to the dash as he thumped down inside and stabbed the screwdriver into the ignition slot. An instant later, he had disarmed the steering wheel lock. He hoped the owner would forgive him. But he hoped even more that Wendy would.

"Okay, here we go," he muttered, and stomped the gas.

It took exactly five minutes of blasting down narrow gravel roads surrounded by dense forests to locate an inter-section he recognized. After that, he was home free.

A half hour later, he was shutting off the engine beside Cardalba Hall.

And two minutes after that, was staring down at his brother.

Lewis Welch lay sprawled on his back in the exact center of his king-sized bed, his arms extended Christ-like to either side, the fingers of his left hand draped gracefully beyond the edge. He was naked save for a sheet drawn across his hips. Both northern and western windows were open in preference to air-conditioning, and the night breeze floated in, stirring his golden hair. The remaining moonlight washed all color from the room, reducing floor and furnishings alike to cutout ciphers of dark and pale. The only sound was the whisper of wind and the regular burr of Lew's breathing.

He was asleep; of that, Ron had no doubt.

In spite of his anger, Ron found himself moving softly, his footsteps muffled by the thick carpet. For a long time he simply watched his brother dream, while argument after argument fought themselves out in his head. Finally, impulsively, he crept atop Lew's trunk of secrets and from there climbed silently onto the wide, waist-high shelf of solid oak that comprised the bed's toe board. There, he folded himself into a shaky crouch, balanced on his haunches, and hunched forward with his forearms resting on his knees like some monstrous sculpture stolen from a Gothic spire.

Lew still slept.

And Ron had an idea—not one he liked, or one he relished, or one that was in any wise ethical at all. But one that was easily executed and should win him the answers he craved.

Closing his eyes, he slipped lightly into a trance and entered that not-place he despised so much. But in the Realm of the Winds it was no problem at all to locate Lew's Voice.

Lew *was* dreaming, his surface mind occupied with visions of himself in an Arab bazaar, dickering with a dirty urchin for the use of a red plastic telephone.

But Lew's dreams did not concern him. He went deeper, wading into territory that was at once achingly familiar and utterly unknown. For unlike the other times he and Lew had shared consciousnesses—which had been by choice, with both of them opening doors and showing ways—this was like having once been guided through a vast forest on a cold, clear winter day by someone who knew every hill and hollow intimately, and then attempting to locate the same landmarks alone on a summer night. It was all exactly the same, yet utterly transfigured into the alien and strange.

And, unfortunately, Ron was unpracticed and clumsy.

"Who's there?"

Ron never knew whether that challenge sounded in his ears or his mind alone. But it clearly signaled an end to his snooping.

"R-Ronny?"

Silence, as Ron withdrew from Lew's mind and snapped his shields into place.

"Ronny? What are *you* doing here?" And *that* had been Lew's actual voice.

Abruptly Ron was back in his own head, was gazing down at his brother, who was blinking up at him from his pillow, with much the same trepidation a road kill might display when regarding a circling vulture.

Ron steeled himself, suppressed the sick fury that made him want to shout and scream and throw himself atop his kinsman and wrap his fingers around his throat. "I think you know," Ron said quietly, a note of deep and sorrowful resignation tempering his words.

Lew was still blinking up at him uncomprehendingly, still half-asleep, still muddleheaded. "You look like a gargoyle," he mumbled.

"I'm supposed to," Ron replied grimly. "Or like Death—or maybe the Last Judgment. In fact," he added, "I kinda *like* that one—since I've come to open up some seals."

Lew yawned hugely. "What kinda seals?"

"You know that, too."

Another yawn. "Humor me."

"Why?" Ron raged, suddenly rising, to balance precariously on the foot-wide shelf, as a fire of emotion roused flamelike within him. "Why, Lew? So you'll have time to think of more lies? More deceptions? More half-truths? Well, there'll be no more of that! I'm on to you—and something *else* is, too: something beyond either of us. You've trespassed, man; you've crossed some line you shouldn't have, 'cause something beyond is out to set the record straight!"

Lew was still confused, still half-asleep, but moving toward full awareness quickly. He slid up in bed, drawing the sheet with him to shroud his waist, then folded his arms across his chest in what was probably an unconscious defensive gesture. Nor would he meet Ron's eyes, but sat gnawing his upper lip, his brow furrowed in thought.

Ron dared not wait for his brother to compose himself. "What've you done with her?" he demanded.

Lew did look up at him then, eyes wide and fearful, if not completely innocent. "I haven't done *anything* to her," he replied shakily. "Nothing worse than you'd have done under the same circumstances."

Ron's eyes flashed fire. "What the fuck do you mean by that? The worst *I've* done is admit that I'm human, that I might want something—or someone—one time, and then find out I wanted someone else another. *You've* lied to me, and that's a thousand times worse 'cause it means I won't ever be able to trust you again, and it hurts double 'cause I thought you were the one person on earth I *could* trust."

"But you *can* trust me," Lew protested miserably, and even in the half-light Ron could see that his eyes were glistening. "There're secrets between us we don't dare share beyond this room, things we can't tell anyone else, not even other Listeners. Do you honestly think I'd ever do anything to hurt you? I mean that would *really* hurt you in your soul, down there where you actually live? It's *hard* being a Listener, Ronny; surely you know that. And doubly hard being a Master when you never wanted to be one. That makes us special. But it also builds a bond between us that can't ever be broken."

"Bullshit. You've broken it now! Absolutely."

Lew shook his head. "I'm sorry you feel that way," he said wretchedly. "But you're wrong. I've never lied to you, not technically. I've been very careful how I put things— I'm sure you know how it is, seeing as how I've seen you do the same thing yourself."

"But you've still not told me all the truth—and that amounts to the same thing."

Lew did not reply.

"*Have* you?" Ron added. "Now I've made it a question, and you have to answer truthfully."

"No," Lew murmured, very quietly.

Ron could stand it no longer. In one long leap, he flung himself forward from the toe board to imprison his startled brother in an iron grip, his thighs clamped close around Lew's lower body, his brother's shoulders forced hard against the headboard by forearms made steely strong by months of smithing.

"What have you *done* with her?"

"Nothing!"

"What?"

"Nothing, goddamn it! Nothing!"

"You're lying."

Lew did not reply, but began to writhe and twist within Ron's grasp. Ron held him firm, exerting every bit of will he possessed, knowing that though Lew was cunning and a trained wrestler, *he* was heavier and stronger in the absolute sense, and that even if Lew *did* somehow manage to pin him, neither of them could retain their grip indefinitely, but that *he* could probably last longer—and was prepared to withstand any pain to gain the truth.

And pain could be of more than the body, as could strength. Ron closed his eyes and for the second time that night violated one of his longest held personal prohibitions. For some reason—probably instinctive conditioning—Lew had not assailed his shields; which meant he was free to lower them, and could thus, in turn, launch an attack of his own. He did, and though he met resistance, it was weak and wavering—almost as if Lew *wanted* him to win through to his subconscious. But the deeper he went among Lew's memories, the harder it was to find his way. And try though he would, he could not discover what he sought.

Which was not to say he could not locate *any* memories of Wendy; but the ones he found were all things he knew already, things he had seen before. It was even possible to replay yet again the whole morning Wendy had left, complete with Ron's arrival and all the hard words they had exchanged. They made him shudder. But Ron could get no further, except to note one thing: that there was a very tenuous connection to *another* set of memories much more deeply imbedded—too deep for him to venture without cooperation. And even the linkage was so fragile and insubstantial that Ron could easily see how Lew had concealed it from him before. It was, indeed, almost as if he had secreted that information even from himself; as Listeners knew, yet did *not* know, the single means by which they could be killed.

Help me! Ron pleaded, in that unheard speech of mind-linked Listeners.

You got yourself where you are! Go or stay, at your own risk!

You could make this easy.

I tried.

Then I have to try as well.

—Whereupon Ron took a mental gasp and followed the thread down to deeper knowledge.

—And met, hiding there, the one thing he had hoped never to confront again. And the one thing he had thought never to encounter in his brother's memory.

Lew had laid an ambush, all unknowing, but when Ron triggered those memories, they attacked. And before he could retreat, he was reliving that awful night five years ago when his and Lew's mother had died—the same night Uncle Matt had died, and Cousin Anson. The night Ron finally knew without doubt or denial that he was fundamentally different from other human beings.

The worst, most fearful, most emotional draining night of his life. And the one whose reverberations he was this very instant still suffering.

He couldn't stand it. He withdrew, felt Lew's shields rise as he passed them, and raised his own in turn.

But still had command of his tongue. And whether Lew could not move, or was simply choosing not to, was still pinning him below.

"What *is* it between you two?" Ron cried in exasperation. "I *know* there's something, but I'm damned if I know what! Were you . . . lovers? Was that it? Were you afraid I'd find out and hate you 'cause you saw her first?"

"No." Lew sobbed, shaking his head. "That wasn't it."

"What then?" Ron shouted, putting all the force of his will into his next question. "Was it jealousy, then? You were jealous of me and her?"

"No!" Lew countered desperately, and stopped resisting entirely, though Ron still dared not take the chance of easing his grip.

"Well, what was it, then? Goddamn it, Lew, I *know* there's something, 'cause I saw it in your mind, and you've all but admitted it already. For chrissakes, man, make it easy on yourself!"

"We . . . we weren't lovers," Lew gasped so softly, Ron could barely hear him.

"Then what were you?"

"We were much closer than that."

Ron's eyes narrowed, even as his heart described a sick flip-flop. "You don't mean . . . Oh my God, she's not our sis—"

"No!" Lew interrupted before he could complete the one word that would have truly made him no better than Uncle Matt had been.

"What then? How *could* you be closer than lovers without being kin?"

Silence, for almost ten seconds, during which Ron suddenly became aware of the soft whisper of wind, of the harsh rasp of his own breathing. He could almost smell Lew's fear.

And then Lew spoke. Three words, soft but clear, that forever changed everything Ron thought about his brother.

"I made her."

"What?"

Lew looked up at him, no longer trying to restrain his tears. "I made her, Ronny! Don't you see? I *made* her!"

"What do you *mean* you made her?" Ron shouted. "You can't make a person! *Nobody* can make a goddamned human being!"

Lew tried to shrug but was prevented by Ron's grip on his arms. Ron sensed the movement and relaxed his hold, sat back against the footboard, breathing heavily, trying without success to grasp the implications of what his brother had just told him. "You can't make a person," he repeated, his tone almost as low as Lew's had been.

Lew regarded him sadly, with an odd mix of honest fear and genuine concern in his eyes. "*I* can," he said in a voice so calm, it sent chills up Ron's spine. "We *all* can, actually, once we learn how—assuming we aren't too demanding. It's all in the books in Uncle Matt's library . . .

and a couple in a vault I conveniently forgot to tell you about."

Ron could only gape incredulously, barely half hearing his brother's words. "But . . . but . . . *how*?"

Lew rose carefully and crossed to the window where a single white rose glistened in the moonlight. "I made her out of flowers. Flowers and feathers. That's how it's always done."

Ron tried to fight simultaneous urges to scream and lash out and cry. "But *why*?"

Lew plucked the blossom from its vase and returned to the bed. Ron stayed where he was. They stared dully at each other across a distance now suddenly greater in mind than it ever would be in feet and inches. Lew puffed his cheeks thoughtfully. Ron waited. Eventually Lew stabbed a thorn against his finger and watched the blood ooze out: a single drop of black on ivory flesh. "It's all here," Lew said. "Everything it takes to make me *me*, at least in a physical sense. Every cell in here knows how to reproduce me."

"But doesn't tell *me* why you made *her*!" Ron prompted gently. "Lew, I really do want to know. I . . . I think I have to know, or . . ."

"Or what?"

"I don't know. But neither of us will like it."

Lew sighed and nodded. "I did it for you, bro. I've never lied about that; you absolutely have to believe me."

"For *me*? You screwed up my life, and you say you did it for *me*?"

Lew nodded. "I knew you were unhappy. As soon as you left for college, you started calling a lot, remember? You'd talk about classes and how much fun you were having being young and rich and free. And you'd talk about working on that car of yours, and how great that was going. But then . . . then you'd talk about your love life, and how shitty *that* was 'cause you didn't believe in having sex with women you didn't care about—only every time you liked a woman enough to have sex with her, you'd find out that she didn't care about *you* as much as she cared about your looks and your cleverness and your money. And . . . and I *knew* that was wrong 'cause you deserve better than that for all you've suffered losing your swimming, and all, and for all you went through for me that . . . night. So I knew you needed somebody to love you *as* you, somebody to love you above all else. And then one day I was prowling through some books and learned some . . . stuff. And then I just *made* her." He paused, as if expecting Ron to reply, but Ron could only stare at him, in sadness and in awe. "It was the *only* thing I could think to do for you, Ronny," Lew sobbed. "It was the only thing I could do for somebody *I* love! And whatever differences you and I may be having now, Ronny, *whatever* differences, I really do love you."

Ron did not reply, but simply remained where he was, staring mutely at the rose Lew held in one hand and the glistening drop of blood on the other.

"But why did you have to kill her?" he gritted at last, his voice shaking.

"I *didn't* kill her."

"But she's gone! No one's seen her in two months. And I've seen her car. She never made it back to Athens."

"But I didn't kill her," Lew insisted dully.

"You're lying," Ron shot back, his anger once again awake.

"No I'm not."

"Oh, for heaven's sake, Lew, just cut the shit, okay? I *know* you're lying because Wendy *said* you were."

"How?"

Ron told him.

"But I didn't kill her," Lew repeated when he had finished.

"So where is she then? Tell me that!"

Lew took a deep breath. "I didn't *kill* her, Ronny— 'cause she wasn't really alive *to* kill. I . . . I guess I just *unmade* her."

"*Lew!*"

"No, listen, man; you've gotta listen! She was the perfect woman for you 'cause I made her that way. I took flowers and feathers and a few other things, plus a drop of my blood, and I made her. But you have to understand why, you *have* to."

"I'm listening."

"I hope you are, 'cause I've been dreading this moment for years."

Ron did not reply.

Lew took another deep breath. "It's like I said, man. She was the perfect woman for you, because . . . because part of her was me, and I heard on TV somewhere that the perfect partner for someone is their own identical twin, only you and I aren't identical, and neither of us are . . . *that* way. But that didn't change the basic fact, so in most ways Wendy was me as a girl, except that she was supposed to love you."

"But—"

Lew shook his head. "No, let me finish. She was the perfect woman for you . . . until you found a *more* perfect woman in Brandy. Only Brandy's a *real* woman, and she's got levels Wendy could never have, no matter how well made she was. And as soon as I saw things start happening between you and Brandy, I knew what I had to do. I wanted out of here, and I knew there was no way you'd stay without more reason than I could give you. And when that reason just fell in my lap—without any intervention from me at all, I might add—I knew I had my chance. I knew that if you two got together, you'd want to stay up here; and then I'd have the perfect opportunity to leave. The only thing that was a threat was Wendy. So I removed her."

Ron was still flirting dangerously close with shock, and though he was hearing Lew's words, not all of them were getting through. "Did . . . did she know?" he asked at last. "Did she have any idea?"

Once more Lew shook his head. "Not that I can tell; at least I hope not. Though I was pretty surprised when you showed up with her, let me tell you."

"And she found herself so at home," Ron mused slowly, nodding.

"Yeah."

"But . . . oh, gee—this explains so much."

"I hope so."

"But the transcripts . . . the background . . ."

"Connections."

"Did Aunt Martha know?"

"With her connections? Of course—but not until it was too late. I, uh, used a drop of her blood for the female component in the Making—for the second X chromosome. And I had a *hell* of a time getting hold of it, let me tell you. But after that . . . I guess she sort of regarded Wendy as a kind of surrogate daughter."

"And the letters and phone calls?"

Lew shrugged. "Once I made her, it wasn't that hard to duplicate her again, or at least enough of her to write what I told her and to call when I needed her to—I guess I *did* sort of lie about the calls coming from Athens. It wasn't . . . pretty," he added carefully. "As for the rest: I just made sure folks saw what I wanted them to. That's a lot of everything, after all, isn't it?"

Ron nodded slowly. "I guess so, 'cause *I* was sure as hell seeing what I wanted to see."

"Heard enough now?"

Ron was silent for a long time. Then, "No."

"But what else *is* there?" Lew demanded helplessly.

A deep breath. "You said you made her, right? And then you removed her?"

Lew regarded him warily. "Yeah . . ."

"Well," Ron said heavily. "You obviously didn't remove her well enough."

Lew looked troubled for a long moment, then nodded in turn. "I'm afraid, oh my brother, that you're right." He paused, then went on. "Evidently I made her better than I thought I did, 'cause she's obviously a lot stronger-willed than I expected. And—Jesus! I should have noticed that when I brought her back!"

"Well then," Ron said wearily, smacking his hands against his thighs in a gesture of finality, "I guess it's time we got to work."

"Doing what?"

Ron's reply was to slide off the bed and gather Lew's piled clothing from the floor. When he had finished, he dumped the whole mess in his brother's lap. "You made her once, didn't you?" he snorted. "Well, then, *we're* gonna do it again!"

Chapter 25

Slip Slidin' Away

Brandy Hall
Night

Brandy was getting tired of the dark, and very, *very* tired of the slow, raspy hiss of her own laborous breathing.

She had no idea how long she had crouched there since some sourceless hint of fresh air had brought headachy consciousness creeping back; with her shoulders pressed hard against the unyielding cinder-block wall opposite the concealed strongroom door, and her eyes fixed vainly on where that invisible point of maximum vulnerablity lay. But strain as she would, she could *see* nothing, though she knew there was a long wall five feet beyond the toes of her sneakers, and shorter ones a like distance to either side. Indeed, she doubted she had ever *seen*—if that word could realistically be used—darkness so complete. It was like being in a sense-deprivation tank: a space at once (and logically) rigorously confined and (emotionally) so infinite, her mind rejected it.

She had, in effect, lost her anchor in space. And, since her perception of time depended mostly on visual clues (and being conscious), she had pretty well lost track of *it* in the bargain. Oh, it was night; she could tell *that* much because there had once been the merest sliver of light along one edge of her hidey-hole, and was no longer—which meant she'd been out several hours. Beyond that, she had precious little to center on save that her body ached in a whole variety of places from holding still; and that she had a tension headache from scowling. She tried to will *that* away, to unlock the frown that had furrowed her forehead since she had returned to her senses. She *wished* she could loosen the tightness from her chest, too—which came from having to breathe shallowly so long—but didn't dare on account of the added noise normal respiration would cause.

She wondered why she bothered.

Vannister wasn't outside—she didn't think—though how much time had elapsed since he had locked her in here, given that dread and anticipation tended to play tricks on how one determined such things, she had no way of telling.

But the truly irritating thing was that she didn't *really* know what she was afraid of! Or why she had run, when her usual tack was to dig in and fight. Shoot, even at the height of their argument, even in the midst of his most preposterous assertions, Vannister had never evinced any sign of actually wanting to *hurt* her, nor displayed any serious tendency toward violence, though he was obviously strong enough to inflict any sort of mayhem he desired. Yet the worst he'd done was play head games with her: teasing her with the power of his physical presence and the provocative way he moved and dressed; the subtle innuendo of his speech.

If only he had stopped there, she could have handled it—and in fact, she acknowledged a certain pleasure from the verbal fencing matches they'd oftimes engaged in. But now . . . what in the world was going *on*? Was she supposed to sit here and *dread* for the rest of her life? Not bloody likely! A day from now this would all be over. Either Vannister would release her himself; she'd somehow find a way out of this sanctuary on her own—in which case she'd either encounter Vannister again or she wouldn't; or else Ron or Weedge would show up and, not finding her, seek her out.

Knock on wood.

Once more she considered her options. Ron had left in a probably justifiable huff, but he'd been on foot and presumably would return sooner or later, if for no other reason than to retrieve his property. And she thought she understood him well enough to believe that eventually he'd cool down and look at things rationally, and at least give her an opportunity to state her case before casting her into the outer dark.

As for Weedge . . . actually, her friend was probably her best bet. Weedge had gotten her promotion and, if she knew her buddy, was *bound* to come bopping by with a bottle of bubbly to celebrate. Shoot, she'd probably phoned already—and if she got no answer often enough, would be doubly likely to check in.

Assuming Vannister didn't intercept her calls and lead her astray with some tale or other.

Vannister!

Damn him! This was all *his* fault: the way he had taunted her—seduced her, trumped her—terrorized her at last. And all because of six stupid words: "I never *said* I was human." Which didn't mean he wasn't, just that he was perfectly willing to blurt out absurd assertions purely to psyche her out.

Only . . . why did she believe him?

Because he could predict things before they happened?

Because he could do things faster than anyone should be able to, and never made mistakes or miscalculations?

Because he knew things about her innermost soul he had no way of knowing? Or any right to know, either.

But, supposing he was telling the truth, then what was he? Her only frames of reference were the myths and fantasies she loved so much. But beyond a superficial resemblance to the crippled smith archetype (which, how-ever, suited Ron far more aptly) and a possible peripheral association with the white stags so common in Welsh mythology, he fit none of the standard profiles for para-normal races. He looked *human*, dammit; felt and acted human, often earthily so. He sweated and bled, excreted and fornicated—which, with the exception of the last, were not qualities she typically assigned to the supernatural. Gods just didn't do such things—or shouldn't. On the other hand, saying one wasn't human didn't necessarily mean one was supernatural. It merely meant he was . . . something else. Or thought he was. Or maybe—

"I am what I am," Van's voice broke through the darkness, only lightly muffled by the intervening wall. Brandy started, almost cried out, and *did* jerk her arms to her mouth reflexively. "I am what I am," he repeated. "I won't go away, either—at least not far—but the door's unlocked now, so you might as well save yourself some trouble and a hell of a lot of fear, and come on out.

" 'Course, you don't know what you'll be comin' out *to*," he added, with a wicked chuckle. "I *could* be what you saw last, or I *could* be that god-awful something you're afraid I might be. I could be perfectly okay, perfectly civilized—or I could be that murdering psycho you fear. But just think, Brandy; even if I kill you the second you sneak out that door, wouldn't that be better than being terrified of death for hours and *then* walking into it? Isn't a fast death better than a slow one? Or are you one of those people who think any life is better than none? Myself, I'm not saying. I've tried to make decisions for you before, and look where we've wound up. You're gonna have to make the call now: go or stay. It's your choice. Myself, I'm gonna hang around. So no matter what you do, I'll be here.

"But," he continued even more gleefully, "forgetting me for the moment, there's no tellin' what *else* you'll find when you crawl out, no tellin' *what* I might do to your house, now that I've got the run of it."

Brandy did not reply. Why bother, when anything she said or did would only be turned against her?

"No go, huh?" Vannister laughed eventually. And once more Brandy heard the lock click closed.

Which gave her no choice but to settle against the wall, try to relax as much as she could, and resign herself to sleep as the only salve to bad air and terminal waiting.

Chapter 26

Where Have All
the Flowers Gone?

Cardalba Hall
Near midnight

"Yeah, front door'll be fine." A pause, then: "Yeah. Thanks. 'Bye." And with that, Lew hung up the media room phone. "They *swore* they'd be here in thirty minutes," he told Ron tiredly, steering a careful course around the boxes of dried leaves, driftwood, pressed-flower arrangements— and, incongruously, feather pillows—that littered the usually spotless carpet, before flopping down in the first chair he came to.

Ron could not suppress a grim chuckle.

"What's funny?" Lew asked sharply.

Ron raised an eyebrow wearily and gestured around the cluttered room. "You are. All this . . . stuff, all those flower beds, and that greenhouse—and you *still* didn't have everything you needed."

"Not for a complete job," Lew told him, sliding lower in his chair. "Not to do it right and have it last a reasonable lifetime—which I have to allow for."

"Thank God for FTD."

Lew snorted derisively. "Thank God for being a *Master*! No way I could get hold of two dozen Welsh primroses and fifty-five daffodils in thirty minutes otherwise."

Ron laughed again. "I'm still surprised you didn't have 'em back in your greenhouse."

Lew shrugged edgily and drummed his fingernails on the glass tabletop where the coffee thermos sat. "I wasn't into plants the first time I made her," he admitted at last. "I had to special-order 'em, and never figured I'd need 'em again, seeing as how I *thought* I'd made Wendy for keeps. Fortunately, the greenhouse in town thought they were neat and decided to maintain a stash. And I've ... uh, had to deal with 'em a couple of times lately, so they've maintained an on-hand supply."

Ron, who could think of nothing nonincendiary to say by way of reply, could only stare at his brother and wonder how someone as neat as Lew had once been, had been reduced to this dispassionate, neurotic creature who talked casually of making and unmaking living beings. And shuddered. *He* was going to take over the mantle of Mastership? Well, a promise was a promise, but only now was he coming to realize what he had committed himself to, not only in responsibility—*that* he thought he could handle—but in temptation as well.

He yawned hugely, stretched. God, he was tired! Not enough sleep the night before, plus a fair morning's smithing, plus enough angst to keep a dozen psychologists working overtime had seen to that. Never mind the unknown miles he'd tromped through those strange woods some few hours before. If not for the industrial-strength coffee Lew was plying him with, he'd be *totally* wasted. Luck might help—if he so willed it. But he feared he'd need all he had—and all Lew had, too—to see them through the next few hours.

And he hadn't a *clue* when he'd get to sleep. It all depended on how quickly Lew could reconstruct—if that was the word—Wendy. But he dared not acquiesce to his brother's pleas and postpone that undertaking. Otherwise, Lew might have a chance to pull another fast one. He intended to see Wendy resurrected, and then have her out of there that night. After that—who knew?

More time passed. Lew had closed his eyes. Not sleeping, though; conserving energy, centering his will.

"So . . . how did you do the deed?" Ron asked at last, to relieve the monotony of waiting.

An eyelid slitted open. "Do what?" Lew yawned.

"Kill Wendy—unmake her, whatever you did."

"That's a long story, and"—he checked his watch impatiently—"we *should* only have about five minutes."

"I got time."

"I thought you didn't *like* to talk about magic!"

"I *said* I've got *time*. Don't push me, man, okay?"

"Have it your way," Lew grunted, levering himself up from his slump and helping himself to a fresh cup of coffee. Then, "Well, to make what should be a much longer and more complex story short, once I'd figured out that Wendy, alive and running around—even if she really *was* willing to give you up—constituted far too serious a threat to my . . . uh . . . schemes, I knew I had to act fast and sort of work things out as I went. So . . . well, first I just waited until I knew she'd left the grounds—though let me stress that I did *not* see her go, or influence that going beyond what I've already told you. Anyway, after she'd split, I kind of did a little solo Listening—which was one of the reasons I looked so ragged-out that morning, *not* a hangover—and though she didn't have a Voice, I could track her through the folks she interacted with: mostly the cab driver and the guy at the import garage. After that, it was simple. Once she had her car, I zipped the old psyche into a buzzard and followed her *that* way. And—"

"Wait a minute," Ron interrupted with a troubled frown. "I didn't know you could *do* that with animals. God knows it's hard enough with people."

Lew shrugged and took another swallow. "Yeah, well, it's simpler in some ways and harder in others. Critters are easier to take control of 'cause they have no real will of their own beyond survival. But on the other hand, what they've got hiding out in their little braincases can be pretty weird. There's a lot of instinct that'll try to force you out, and a lot of reflex, a *bloody* lot of that—like flying. So you have to be careful to maintain enough control so that the critter does what *you* want it to, but not so much that it forgets how to be what it already is—and falls out of the sky, or something."

"Which is interesting, but beside the point."

"Yeah," Lew sighed, pausing to drain his cup. "But anyway, I followed her in the buzzard until she was on a piece of deserted mountain highway—and then I did . . . I guess it was a very bad thing, especially for a Listener."

"I already *know* that," Ron grumbled sourly. "Tell me something I *don't* know."

"Okay, then. Well, basically, I . . . uh, waited until she was on the steepest part of the mountain—and then I just . . . took total control of the buzzard and dive-bombed her. I flew straight into the windshield, and poor animal-loving Wendy tried to miss me and drove right off a cliff. Killed the buzzard."

Ron glared at him, disgusted with his cold-bloodedness. "But what about the car? How'd you get it out of there without anybody knowing? And . . . what about the *body*?"

"*What* body? There *was* no body! How many times do I have to *tell* you, Ronny, Wendy wasn't *really* alive, not like we are—or not in the same way, anyhow. Oh, she had enough physical presence to fool any number of folks, including assorted shrinks, doctors, and you. But she was mostly held together by her own will. And since even *she* didn't know she wasn't real, she believed in death; so when she trashed her car, she thought she ought to be dead—and just died! And once her will was gone, there was nothing holding her together. She went back to what I made her out of: flowers and feathers."

"But the car . . . ?"

"Wrecker service in the next county owed Matt a favor. I collected. He had a file of them, you know."

"What?"

"Favors. A Rolodex as big as a truck tire full of pluses and minuses, debits and credits. I computerized it," Lew added smugly. "That's how I found out about that guy in the first place. And"—he checked his watch again—"the florist we're waiting on—who should be here just about—"

The doorbell obligingly rang.

"—Now." Lew grinned. Before Ron could do more than glance around, his brother was on his feet and striding into the hall. Ron followed more slowly, courtesy of his still uncooperative knee, and watched from the door.

"FTD for Lewis Welch," a sleepy-sounding skinny blond teen-boy mumbled, thrusting a bundle of yellow, red, and white blossoms into Lew's hands. "Sorry it took so long."

"No problem," Lew told him with that phony affability that irritated Ron so much. "What do I owe you?"

The deliveryman muttered a number Ron couldn't hear, whereupon Lew fished in his jeans pockets and yanked out a thick wad of bills. He chose two and handed them to the startled lad. "Thanks." Then, when the boy reached for his wallet, presumably in quest of change, added, "No, take it *all*. I had to drag you out in the middle of the night, and you were *still* quick—and I'm in an ungodly hurry."

"Thank *you!*" the boy enthused, turning away.

Lew backed the door closed behind him, locked it with a flick of his elbow, and proceeded back down the hall, his upper body completely engulfed by an enormous mass of nodding daffodils—and something Ron couldn't immediately identify, which must be the Welsh primroses. In spite of the fatigue and apprehension that shadowed his face, Lew managed a grin as he slipped past Ron into the room. "Well, now that we've got the rest of the raw material, I guess we better get cookin'."

"I guess we had," Ron echoed sourly, joining his brother inside. Lew was already stacking boxes of dried flora atop one another. The new arrivals had been hastily dumped into a carton of their own. Lew indicated a pile with a finger, then looked across to Ron. "Make yourself useful."

Ron spared time for a final quaff of coffee and did as instructed, loading his arms with three of the seven boxes, plus two pillows. Lew took the other four boxes—heavier ones, but not so tall—plus a pillow. He did not pause to extinguish the lights or switch off the stereo, which had been playing Wagner's "The Death of Siegfried," as performed by the New Kazakhstan Orchestra. He also left the door open as he turned left down the hall, then pushed through the larger door that let onto the backyard.

The Sable was already parked there, partly on the sidewalk, partly in the grass. Its tailgate was open, and most of the space behind the front seats had earlier been crammed with more (and fresher) flowers, plus an odd assortment of tools and apparatus Lew had assembled from all over the house—including a zillion feet of water hose and two large aquariums. Ron stuffed his load in first and glanced around apprehensively while Lew fitted his into odd corners.

"That does it—I think," Lew sighed. "Like I said, I didn't expect to be doing this again, so I'd kinda put things away." He straightened and slammed the tailgate, then surveyed the surroundings a final time. Evidently satisfied, he motioned Ron into the car.

Ron obediently climbed in—and found himself waiting longer than he liked as his brother made one last foray into the house. When he returned, Lew held something small and dark. A book, as Ron discovered, when Lew vaulted into the driver's seat and passed the object to him. He caught the musty scent of dust, ancient leather, antique rag paper. It was the oldest one he'd ever seen, including those in the Rare Book Library at the University of Georgia; bound in some kind of dark leather that was still supple and lustrous, and with bits of tarnished metal studding covers Ron could tell from their stiffness were wood. He started to open it, but Lew stopped him with a hand on his. "Not now. Not this close."

"But what *is* it?" Ron wondered aloud.

"Instruction manual, you could say," Lew replied seriously. "Like I told you, I found it in one of Uncle Matt's secret vaults."

"Which you *didn't* tell me about," Ron growled.

" 'Cause I didn't think you were interested," Lew countered. "And anyway, I *did* tell you; you just forgot. I simply didn't tell you *everything* I found in there."

Ron only snorted contemptuously.

"I always feel like bloody Frankenstein," Lew confided as he turned the ignition key.

"Yeah," Ron shot back. "And that song was in the reading, too; only I didn't know what to make of it, except that it meant somebody had created a monster. Only I didn't know I was supposed to take it so damned literally."

"Teach *you* to neglect the arcane," Lew chuckled nervously as he twitched the station wagon across the back lawn and around the flower beds and topiary sculptures that, under his stewardship, were slowly taking over. For some reason, Lew was eschewing pavement in favor of that softer surface. And once he'd passed the hulks of Matthew Welch's defunct vehicles and come even with the front of the garage, he tugged the wheel sharply left and set off across the quarter-mile-long expanse of the east lawn—where five years before, Ron had had his first encounter with the strange white hounds that were loping along behind them even now, fortunately at nonthreatening range.

Ron, not unexpectedly, found himself getting fidgety. "So you're not gonna tell me anything about this tomfoolery?" he grumbled.

"No more than I have to. You wouldn't understand half of it, another part would only make you ask more questions, and the rest would nerve you half to death with anticipation."

They were almost across the lawn now; Ron could see the low stone wall that marked its western terminus as a pale line in the glare of headlights. Trees grew beyond: dark and troubling pines in a fifty-acre grove that had always given Ron the willies. There was something new, though: a rustic-looking gate in the exact center.

"What's—"

Lew silenced him with a glance. "Not now. I need to concentrate. I mean this isn't exactly the optimum time for this. Are you *sure* I can't convince you to wait?"

Ron shook his head. "No way, man. I . . . I just can't trust you anymore, not when I know what you're willing to do to get your way. And besides, the omens seem to think this is the time."

"And of course, you *firmly* believe them when it suits you!" Lew shot back sarcastically as he opened his door.

Ron followed his example, and joined him at the back of the wagon.

"This scares the shit out of me, you know," Lew confided as he swung up the hatch and commenced loading his arms. "Not the *fact*," he added without prompting.

"It's having to do it outside where you can be caught or observed—which, of course, I can handle, but would rather not."

"But what about—?"

"Karen? As you so quaintly put it, I hoodooed her. *Had* to, in order to get some female blood. She'll sleep the sleep of the blessed until morning."

"By which time we'll be done?"

"We *oughta* be done in about thirty minutes," Lew sighed. "Assuming we ever get started."

Ron stared at him. "It's that easy?"

A curt nod. "Once you've done it; once you've got the right stuff to work with. It's like a lot of things: only hard 'cause you *think* it will be."

"But—"

"How do you suppose I was able to call her back all those times?"

Ron shook his head. "I *don't* wanta know."

"No," Lew agreed heavily, "you don't. Fortunately, I only had to bring back part for that, just enough to talk, to write. It took a lot out of me emotionally, but it was worth it—I thought—in peace of mind for you."

"Hmmmph."

"Yeah, well, I was *trying* to do the right thing."

"I'm *sure*."

"Look, Ronny," Lew snapped in exasperation. "We can stand here exchanging pleasantries, or we can reanimate your old girlfriend. Which would you prefer?"

Ron nodded slowly. "Yeah, okay. So, what do you want me to do?"

"Tote," Lew replied promptly. "I want you to tote."

"Fine," Ron yawned. "Let's get at it." And for the next half hour they were busy.

Noise awoke Brandy: a vibration in the bare block wall at her back, followed by a crash, then a long, drawn-out rumble that sounded like the world's largest millstone being rolled across the great hall floor.

What was Vannister doing?

Wrecking her house, probably. He'd certainly threatened as much, saying anything that was made could be *unmade*. Maybe that was his plan: to level Brandy Hall floor by floor and wall by wall until all that remained was the cinder-block shell that shrouded her, and then as the ultimate spite, to drag her out at last to a vision of wrack and ruin. Yeah, that'd be just like him; the ultimate demoralization: for her to see her handiwork—her dream—laid waste. And even worse was the fact that he had to know that hearing all those noises would be even more torture for her because they'd play on her far-too-active imagination. Vannister had her pegged, all right: he knew exactly how to pluck her strings to make her squirm.

If only Ronny would return. Or Weedge. Or *somebody!* If only the sun would rise, or it would rain. *Anything* to shift the wildly uneven balance even slightly in her favor.

And even as she thought that, the noise redoubled: more rumblings, more snaps, more sounds of heavy objects being moved. But never the sound of breaking, never a crash. And eventually she could not have heard them anyway, for all she *could* hear was a muffled grinding roar that filled the whole world and made the walls shiver and thrum. It was exactly like being in the middle of a vast cement mixer—except that she was warm and dry. But at least it masked the sound of her breathing.

It was making her headache worse, though; reducing her whole world to dark and noise and pain. An hour ago—if it had *been* an hour—she had felt as if she were floating in space; now she felt as if she were being ground into dust at the center of the earth.

And the stony cacophony never abated, went on and on all around her, sometimes before her, sometimes behind or above: rumblings and thuddings, and gravelly hisses and gratings, and occasionally a muffled crunch. She had no choice but to try to tune it out, to find refuge as far inside her consciousness as she could.

Maybe she slept again.

When she awoke—if she did—it was to find herself lying on the floor with her back and hips stiff from resting on the unyielding surface, and her arms, legs, and neck knotted with yet more tension. Her lungs hurt, too, but that was probably due to the hot, stale air. The headache was also still present, but distant and dull.

But the noise was fading.

And there was light!

Something was glimmering ever so slightly around the edge of the hidden door.

Daylight?

Salvation?

Or . . .

The door was in the wrong place! She'd konked out facing it, and now it was at her feet!

And even as that registered, she felt the faintest touch of fresh air against her cheek—and the line of light along one side grew fractionally wider.

"This really should be done by daylight," Lew murmured, in answer to a question Ron had not asked. "Flowers like the sun, see; and *I* identify with it, and together we provide more total energy to draw on."

Ron rose stiffly from where he'd been using a whisk broom to clear pine needles, leaves—every movable object—from a ten-foot circle in the forest floor, leaving the earth bare save for the few stray weeds that had rooted there. He fixed his brother—who was busy with a troubling *something* in the middle of the wheel—with a weary scowl. "You've got *me* to draw on, though. That *should* make up the difference—so you say."

Lew aimed a steely glare in his direction. "What's *that* supposed to mean?"

"It means," Ron sighed, "that I still don't really trust you."

"Well, I don't reckon I can change that *now*," Lew told him flatly. Without further comment, he rose and began pacing the perimeter of Ron's handiwork. Evidently satisfied with the cleanliness of the circle, he glanced at the sky once more. The moon gliding overhead painted the woods blue and silver. "At least it's Lugnasadh," he grunted. "That'll help."

"Lugnasadh?" Ron echoed in confusion, then, when he recalled what the date was, continued, "Oh yeah, right. I— uh—kinda tend to forget things like that, seeing as how they're not part of my mainstream reality."

"You'd do better to remember 'em, too," Lew shot back. " 'Cause certain things really do work out better if undertaken at particular times."

"Gimme a break!"

"No, it's true!" Lew continued earnestly. "See, as best I can figure, the universe is mostly electromagnetic—shoot, it might *all* be that way with no real matter in it at all. And since every object in that universe produces gravity, it only makes sense that there would be times and places where gravity waves overlap differently than at others. And—"

"Fine," Ron interrupted. "Let's get going, before I boil alive in my own skin."

Lew sighed sagely. "You're right there."

He was, too. The trees grew too close here to admit breezes, and what little air *did* manage to stir carried with it the spicy scent of that weird pollen. Shoot, Ron's eyes were running already, and he'd twice had to lay off whisking to sneeze.

He fought down another attack, and finally ventured a close examination of the center of the circle—where his brother was putting the finishing touches on one of the strangest sights he'd ever seen.

Lew had set up an open-topped rectangular glass box there: roughly a foot high, two wide, and six long; its sides—which were embedded a few inches into the ground—made of panels pirated from the defunct aquariums. And within it lay what looked amazingly like a naked woman—but was not.

Rather, every single bone in the human skeleton had been approximated with lengths of rough wood—except the skull, pelvis, and shoulder blades, which were pieces of sun-dried gourd. And within and around that frame, vegetables from Lew's refrigerator made organs: a small squash (that was the gall bladder), grapes (for lungs), a wrinkled chili pepper as a pancreas, lengths of vines for nerves and major arteries, and half a score others Ron couldn't identify. The phial of Karen's blood poured upon an orange made a heart. After that had come muscles, features, and skin—that was where the flowers and feathers came in. It had been like making lasagne, Ron thought: first Lew laid down a layer of feathers from one of the pillows, then one of flowers—either the entire blossoms, or the petals alone—and then another of feathers, then of petals, and so on. There was definitely some logic to it, but Ron couldn't make out what it was except that certain species evidently went certain places, and that Lew had to consult that book of his to be sure what went where. But the upshot of it all was that in a phenomenally short period of time, there was a passable likeness of a woman lying there. Ron couldn't help but be reminded of Snow White in the crystal coffin the seven dwarfs had made her. All it needed was a bunch of cute Disney critters to sit around looking sad. Shoot, he could almost feel his own eyes misting— and that in spite of the fact that the features, which were merely suggested, in no way resembled Wendy's. At the moment, Ron couldn't tell whether Lew was finished or not, for though he hadn't added anything lately, one bundle of flowers remained unused.

And as if in answer to his question, Lew padded around to those blossoms and, with great reverence and solemnity, picked them up. He did not bestow them upon the effigy, though, but joined Ron at the foot of the glass box. There he separated a single bloom and handed it to Ron. Ron took it hesitantly, and noted to his great surprise that it was glowing, exactly as those odd flowers that had shown him the way out of the woods had glowed. It was larger than them, but of exactly the same configuration, and its petals were waxy, its stem silky smooth. Impulsively Ron took a deep whiff from its bell—and would have sneezed had he not been so stunned. For as soon as the pollen reached his nostrils, he felt giddy and lightheaded—almost drunk. His senses seemed heightened, too; and he recognized that heady, spicy scent: that damned pollen again! At last he was sure of its source.

"What . . . ?" he began, but Lew shushed him. "Not from . . . here," he muttered cryptically, then continued around the ring and gently laid the rest of the odd flowers on the bosom of the effigy.

"Okay," he announced finally, "what I'm about to do relies on something called the Law of Similarity, which basically means that things that look the same *are* the same—like something that's roughly the same size and shape as a bone, and porous like a bone, can substitute for a bone or be transformed into one. A lot of different mythologies use it, but I doubt you're up for a lecture now."

Ron shook his head and yawned, wondering idly whether he was on his second or third wind.

Lew stepped close beside him, laid an arm across his shoulders. "Okay, guy," he murmured, "you ready?"

Ron puffed his cheeks and nodded. "Let's get the show on the road."

"Good," Lew replied. "Well, I guess the main thing for you to do is . . . *nothing.* Just follow my lead. In the past I've done this alone, but I may need to draw on you if I get too weak, which I might, seeing as how it's dark and I'm tired and all. But you don't need to do anything active—just, if you feel me start to pull energy from you, don't fight it. This isn't like a thing with spells, or stuff like that; it's basically a focusing of will—*my* will. Oh, and I guess I'd better warn you: I may need a couple of drops of your blood, but I won't know until I get going. Is that cool?"

"Sure."

"Uh—to start with, just stay where you are, I guess," Lew concluded. And with that, he left Ron at the foot of the box and strode around to the other side of the circle. He stood there for a moment, eyes closed, lost in concentration, then opened them again and walked quickly out of the clearing, leaving Ron to gape.

Fortunately, he didn't have to wait long before Lew returned with the unlikely accompaniment of the length of water hose, which he was slowly uncoiling from around his arm. Presumably the other end led to one of the numerous sprinklers that studded the lawn. Ron raised an eyebrow, but Lew only shook his head, squatted by the upper end of the glass box, and inserted the nozzle into the enclosure close to the ground. A twist of the fixture and water began to trickle into the chamber. The earth would drink it, but not as fast as the box would fill. Ron wondered what its purpose was, but then remembered the Law of Similarity *and* the fact that the human body was mostly composed of water. Lew might be going to practice magic, but there was nothing so esoteric going on as actual transmutation of elements—or so he assumed. As best he could tell, *that* came later.

The water was rising quickly now, had pretty much engulfed half the effigy, so that it now looked more than ever like a woman floating in . . . a bathtub, he supposed, and had to suppress a chuckle.

As for Lew . . . he had knelt down at the head and closed his eyes. Ron did likewise, but kept his eyes open. Lew stayed like that for at least two minutes, as the water gradually engulfed the figure. When it was no longer visible (and why weren't any of the petals or feathers floating atop it? Ron wondered), he shut off the flow and withdrew the hose. Only then did he lift his lids again.

His eyes were blank, and Ron could tell his brother was in a trance; and, with his pollen-heightened awareness, could sense a pervasive presence that surely must be Lew's disembodied consciousness. It wasn't drawing on him, though, which he assumed meant things were progressing okay. He tried to relax, to will the stiffness from his joints—but tensed all over again when Lew reached behind him and produced an oddly shaped dagger with a glassily glittering blade that it took Ron an instant to recognize as obsidian. Where it had come from, he had no idea: he'd never seen it before. But then he had no more time for speculation, for Lew had grasped the haft (was it bone?) in his right hand and was drawing it across his left palm. Ron saw his jawline tighten. That done, Lew extended the hand before him and slowly reversed it. Three drops of blood plopped into the water—whereupon the surface immediately skimmed with red. More followed, and then Lew carefully eased the hand wrist-deep into the liquid. His breath caught at that, as if the effort pained him, and Ron felt a sharp intensifying of that unknown force that pervaded the circle. The breeze shifted, brought the scent of pine—and, more subtly, earth, water, pollen . . . and blood.

But there was a *strain* in the air, too, and Ron realized suddenly that he still had his shields up. He lowered them at once, and immediately sensed a vast surge of relief. Lew's expression softened, and Ron closed his eyes and let his brother draw on him: a peculiar sensation, but not unpleasant, as a sort of flow seemed to have been established that fed him energy as quickly as it drained away. Impulsively he raised his hand to his mouth and bit down hard enough to bring blood, then slid it into the water.

The pulse of energy increased at once, but with it came an even stronger feeling of comfort and contentment. He was almost in Lew's mind now, he noted distantly, and Lew was probably on the edge of his—but now it didn't matter. He wondered what was happening, though, and started to open his eyes (When had he closed them? When had he gone into a trance?) when Lew stopped him.

No, came the thoughts, soft but certain. *Some things one should* not *see.*

But . . .

No! But share with me, Ronny: share with me, and know.

Ron hesitated, then steeled himself and jumped—and *was* in Lew's mind. And there he saw—not what was happening—but what Lew knew to *be* happening: flowers and feathers were changing, giving up their chemical bonds, making others. Producing heat, too: lots of it, as electrons danced and dallied and drank in water to fuel and fix those changes. And driving it all was the awesome strength of Lew's will that was somehow coordinating everything at once, and the power of Listener blood that was providing more strength and, in Lew's case, a blueprint of what to do. Ron was frankly amazed. *Lew* was doing this! His brother! Lew, who was only twenty-two and looked younger! Lew who liked rock-and-roll and good food. Lew was not only a Listener and a Master, but a Sorcerer!

No, I'm not, came Lew's Voice. *This is all beyond me—the complex stuff is. I simply desire the end—and it* happens!

But . . . but with this, you could do anything! Make *any-thing—or anybody.*

'Fraid not! I can only do this one *time—make* one *person, I should say. And I can only do it if I* really *want to, and—*

So you really *wanted to do this?*

I really do. I told you I loved you. I wasn't lying. And I could only do this if I was motivated by love.

But—

Not now, Ronny! It's almost finished.

How could he tell? Yet Ron, too, could sense a change: a lessening of the thrum in the air, a cooling of the breeze, a diminution of that spicy smell. And . . . what? Yeah, it was true: a sudden, overpowering odor of flowers.

"You can open your eyes now," Lew whispered—or was that his Voice? *"We're through."*

Ron did—precisely as soft female tones murmured, "I'm cold."

"Wendy!" Ron cried, flinging himself forward, only to check himself halfway so that he could gaze into the face of the girl he once—perhaps—had loved.

She looked exactly as he remembered—though she was presently sitting soaking wet and naked on a patch of muddy earth in the middle of the woods. But then Ron noticed two things. The first was something he couldn't believe he had never noted before, which was that she really did look like Lew: their faces and bone structure were almost the same. And the second was the expression on that face.

Wendy was staring straight at him, her eyes wide, but no longer guileless. Love was in her gaze, too, but much more as well, of which chiefmost was a mixture of reproach and regret.

"W-welcome back," Ron stammered, then offered her his hand.

She took it—briefly, tentatively—and let him draw her up. And Ron suddenly felt so confused, he had no idea *what* to think.

Lew had said nothing since Wendy's reawakening, and Ron found himself looking past the girl toward him. "You okay?" he mouthed. Lew nodded, yawned, and raised an eyebrow—whereupon it dawned on Ron that this was probably not an optimum time for nudity. He hastily retrieved the red jogging suit Lew had thoughtfully brought along and presented it to the girl. A modicum of modesty thus contrived, he reclaimed her hand and gave it a gentle tug.

"W-where're we going?" she asked hesitantly, still obviously shaken.

"Back to Athens just as fast as we can," Ron replied instantly, sparing a warning glance over her shoulder to

Lew. "No way I'm gonna let you hang around up here!"

Her grip tightened, and it took him a moment to figure out that she was trying to pull away. "No," she said firmly. "We're *staying*."

"We'll talk about that later."

"No," Wendy repeated, her voice even harder—though not, Ron thought, in anger. "*I* may go back, but *you're* staying."

"But—"

"Hear me *out!* Ronny!" she insisted. "I know more than you *think* I know, and more than *I* did, too. And one of the things I know is that you love Brandy more than you love me."

"But I love you, too!" Ron replied helplessly.

"I know you do," Wendy shot back promptly, but without malice. "But it's not the same kind of love. It's . . . I don't know . . . love born of pity, or something: responsibility more than joy of company. If I hung around, or if you came back to Athens, I'd only hold you back. *She'll* make you better."

Ron hesitated, amazed at hearing truths he had not fully reconciled himself to stated so effortlessly. "There's a song," Wendy went on, "remember? 'If You Love Somebody, Set Them Free?' or something like that. But that's true. 'Cause I *do* love you, Ronny, more than anything in the world, but I care for you even more—that's what kept me . . . *alive*, I guess the word is . . . even when I really wasn't. And that's what brought me back again, more than any magic of Lew's."

"Yeah, but—"

"Let me *finish!*" she interrupted. "You've *got* to stay up here. In fact, you've *got* to go back to Brandy's as quick as you can. You gave up too soon. Since you quit diving, you've had things too easy, you've gotten scared of contention and challenge, when in actual fact those are the things that make you stronger. But you want Brandy more than Van wants her, and you sure as hell *deserve* her more, but you'll have to fight for her to get her."

"But what about you?"

"I'll be fine. *Brandy* should be your concern now. Why do you think I called up so much pollen that day? So you guys would get high and do what you both really wanted, and then you'd *know* Brandy was the one for you 'cause you'd lower your shields and *see*! I—"

She stiffened abruptly, eyes wide and blank, like Lew's when he was Listening.

"Wendy?"

The lids fluttered again; life returned to her gaze.

"Don't scare me like that!"

"Hush," she broke in urgently, grabbing his hand and tugging him toward the stone wall. "You've gotta get back to Brandy *now*—'cause if you don't . . . I'm afraid Van'll do something awful to her!"

"Van?" Ron echoed dumbly, refusing to allow himself to be dragged along. "But how do *you* know?"

" 'Cause I've *seen* it!" Wendy snapped. "When you're unreal you're also *completely* real; you know *everything*— I guess it just took a minute to register."

Still Ron held back, shaking his head. "But what about you?"

"I *like being alive*," she told him frankly. "But I know enough now that I can live without you. I think . . . *I* needed to be stronger, too."

Yet still Ron hesitated. He was tired, so tired. *God*, how he wanted to sleep. He cast his gaze wearily to where his brother was apparently just coming out of a trance of his own.

"She's right about Brandy," Lew sighed, his voice thick with apprehension. "There's a Silence up at her place like you wouldn't believe. Come on, folks, we've gotta hurry!"

Chapter 27

Trapped

Brandy Hall
Near midnight

Fresh air! Blessed fresh air! Balm to her laboring lungs, relief to her pounding head! Hope and clarity to her muddled mind.

Brandy could hold her breath no longer—and yet was almost too caught up in wonder and dread to breathe. The sun-bright sliver of golden light she'd been staring at, which admitted the clean thread of breeze that brought salvation, was an inch wide now and widening. It was lengthening, too: stretching halfway to the floor, as though someone were burning through the south wall of her hidey-hole with an acetylene torch. Yet still she sat, cowering in her corner, fearing to make any sound as a full-fledged opening slowly showed itself in what had—moments?—before been solid concrete. She *knew* it was solid: she had conceived it that way, designed and blueprinted it that way, *built* it that way! There was no other way it *could* be!

Yet there it was: a new door limning itself where none had been, while the old one yet remained—to her right, since she had shifted to face the more immediate threat.

And now that the crack was providing enough light to show more than the red inside her eyelids, she had no doubt that it *was* a door. More precisely, a round-topped archway plugged by a massive panel of shiny red-brown boards laid chevron-style, with ornate iron strapwork grappling across its face from the hinges like a phalanx of jet-black dragons scrambling sideways 'round a wall. The *same* strapwork—or its twin—that Ron had been forging just that morning.

And now the line of light had reached the floor, and the portal was slowly easing open, moving with absolute silence, absolute precision . . .

Brandy shivered uncontrollably. This was it! A few seconds more and it would all be over. Less than a minute from now she'd know what was up with Vannister, what he had done to Brandy Hall.

The door stopped abruptly, stilled no more than six inches into its arc.

Brandy waited.

Waited.

Straining her ears, her eyes—all her senses—in a desperate drive to determine the time and tack of the encounter that now seemed so imminent.

Only then did she truly become aware that the roaring, grinding, grating sounds that had assailed her ears for so long had ceased, replaced by a silence so thick, it was almost palpable. She imagined it out there, like a carpet of invisible dust: motionless until the force of her breath sent it clouding into the air when she exhaled at last.

Steeling herself—though against *what*, she had no idea—she groped her way dizzily to her feet, grinding her teeth in dismay as joints popped and snapped, and acutely aware of how stiff and sore she was. Her hair flopped into her face and she slapped it aside, then wiped her grimy hands on her jean-clad thighs before knuckling the grit from her eyes.

—And blinked incredulously, for the light had actually altered in just the few seconds she'd neglected it. What *was* it, anyway? It was too soft to be ordinary incandescents, and too yellow. But it wasn't one of the big floodlights she'd installed outside to aid nighttime construction either. And she *knew* it was neither moonlight nor sunlight, because . . . well, just because it didn't *look* like either of 'em: too bright for one, too wimpy for the other.

Which left what?

There was only one way to find out. And since the door *was* present, and *had* opened out, not in, she knew that the time for indecision had passed. Vannister was out there, sure; had done something inexplicable to what had definitely been a solid wall. But surely it was better to meet him there, where she at least had room to maneuver than in this cramped hole. What was she afraid of, anyway? He hadn't really hurt her—*or*, to be perfectly honest, done anything to either her house or her body she hadn't, in her heart of hearts, desired. So why *did* she fear him? Because he had said he was something else? Well, so what? That didn't mean he wasn't everything *else* he'd ever been, too—and the Vannister she saw day to day, she was pretty sure she could handle. The only problem was that she didn't trust him, and specifically didn't trust him not to play head games. But maybe he'd listen to reason (if she could think of anything reasonable to say), and even if he didn't, even if the psycho returned, she could always resort to violence if need be.

But with what? She patted her pockets, found them atypically empty; scanned the floor around her, and to her everlasting regret, saw not so much as a stray nail, lost tool, or sliver of wood. But maybe there'd be something outside, and if not—well, there was always her martial arts training. Shoot, if she was lucky, she might even make it to an outside door.

Sighing softly, she took a deep breath, straightened her shoulders, and strode the few feet to the new portal.

It swung effortlessly outward at her most tentative touch, and froze exactly in place as soon as she withdrew her fingers. But it had felt *odd:* not like oak or walnut or pine, but heavier, slicker, like . . .

Like *petrified wood*! Wood turned to stone by the action of ages. And so a closer inspection showed it to be. But she had no time to wonder at that, not when freedom beckoned.

Another deep breath, and she cautiously poked her head through, blinking into the warm, flickering glare of a bank of stubby candles ranged before the semicircular niche she'd intended to house the bronze statue of Odin one of her friends at Chapel Hill had promised her. The air, though still fresh, smelled of wax, smoke, and spices.

"No *way!*" she gasped softly. For where scant hours before the niche had only been roughed in, now it was complete—and the short, and very blessedly empty, corridor that included it as well. And all exactly as she had planned—except for the handsome petrified wood door behind her.

And except that, now her eyes had grown accustomed to the uneven light, what had been cinder-block walls the last time she'd been by were now undeniably stone—grainy, golden sandstone. The arches had changed, too, were fine limestone; and the floor, which she'd intended to cover with bricks, hard, slick marble.

Her heart flip-flopped: a sick double thump. *Jesus, oh Jesus, oh Jesus!* No way this could be real, no way this could have happened. It was all . . .

What? Her mind searched for an excuse, any rationale beyond the irrational. It was . . . it was that damned pollen, she finally decided. The stuff was almost certainly hallucinogenic, at least in large doses; and God only knew she'd snorted enough the last few days. Maybe there'd been a concentration in the secret room—though try as she would, she couldn't recollect having smelt the distinctive odor. Which meant that *possibly* she was still back there, still asleep. Dreaming. Or . . .

Without waiting to ponder the wisdom of such an act, she clenched her right fist and slammed it mercilessly into the nearest pillaster—hard enough to jar her shoulder and stipple her knuckles with red. And did not awaken.

Fine!

Grimacing sourly, she snatched the healthiest of the candles and made her way left down the short passageway. A right through the big doors there would put her in the great hall, whence lay the straightest route out.

Only . . . where was Vannister? She hadn't seen any sign of him, nor heard a sound beyond the soft, blurred scratching of her denimed legs rubbing against each other, and the faint hiss of her breathing. Well . . . either he was lurking about or he wasn't; and if he *was* around, he was either waiting for her or he wasn't. And in either case, she wouldn't find out here.

The arched corridor *should* have been only ten yards long, but somehow it looked longer than she recalled—wider, too. And different in yet another way when, a bare instant later, she crept between what *had* been the thigh-high south wall of the library and the tall, empty archway that graced the north end of the great hall. Only now, the incomplete section had been finished, down to the blind arcades she'd long ago rejected as too space-inefficient. And as for the archway . . . well, it certainly wasn't empty now! A pair of double doors hung there, wrought of the same woodlike stone she had encountered earlier; wide as her outstretched arms and half again as tall—a bit larger than she'd specified, but almost exactly the size she'd first envisioned.

Holding her breath, she pushed against the strapwork where the right half joined the left. It moved, slowly, ponderously, but as silently as the other. And opened into an echoing gloom lit only by shafts of silver-blue moonlight lancing through clerestory windows that were too narrow and high, to strike a procession of tall, slender columns that shouldn't have been present at all, much less in the number she saw. It had somehow acquired a roof, too; for stone spanned the space with Gothic arches.

"No way!" she repeated, as if mere words could banish what all her other senses affirmed. Without consciously willing it, she stepped forward, her feet falling on an unfamiliar surface as she came full into the room. Another tentative step, and she felt the coolness that only arises from night-drenched stone. A breeze found her and snuffed her candle, even as it slammed the door behind her with a deep-toned boom. She gasped, blinked, swore silently as fear rushed up her spine. Backing up reflexively, she paused with her shoulders to the wall until her eyes readjusted and her heart slowed its frantic race. She was nerving herself out, she realized dully; being her own worst enemy. On the other hand, she was also wandering around inside something quite irrational, something over which she no longer had any control. Which was just about the worst situation she could imagine.

But freedom was not far away: across this space, through the matching doors she could see glimmering opposite, and thence into the entry that let onto the front arcade, where—she prayed—sanity ruled once more. Taking a deep breath, she started across the chamber.

And had only gone a pair of paces before she noticed that the narrow aisles behind the columns that supported the clerestory gallery were not empty. Statues lurked there: stone, they looked like, and life-sized. And more to the point, the exact representations of the Lords of the Tuatha de Danaan—the old gods of Ireland—she would have installed had she possessed truly unlimited resources. Yet there they were. Which meant . . .

She shuddered. Vannister had not lied. And now she thought about it, she'd been totally blind. He had *told* her, for God's sake; had said every time he'd changed something that he was giving her what she really wanted. And he had!

But that didn't tell her how—or why—or what he was. She was halfway across the strangely attenuated space now, nearing the door, and though a part of her wished desperately to turn aside to inspect every figure, she ruthlessly passed them by. But there was one by the door she could not overlook: a slender, bare-chested boy-man with a hammer upraised above an anvil on which lay a human heart. She knew instinctively it represented Goibhniu the Faerie Smith. But it looked exactly like Ron Dillon, down to the beatific expression, which exactly mirrored Ron's when he was fully immersed in his craft.

"Good likeness, don't you think?" a low male voice drawled behind her, sounding a long way off, though uncannily clear for all there was an echo.

Brandy spun around, automatically assuming the best defensive position she remembered from T'ai Chi class. And saw nothing, though her eyes sought frantically from side to side.

No, wait! Something was moving in the shadows of the aisle to the left. And as she watched, tense as an overwound spring, a figure calmly sauntered from beneath the farthest arch. It was Vannister, of course, but not precisely the one she had last seen. Oh, he was still wearing his characteristic jeans, T-shirt, and work boots; still had his hair tied back and that damnable too white grin. But he was dusted from head to foot with some kind of fine gray powder that made his very flesh look like stone. And as Brandy gaped at him, he continued to walk toward her, moving in the slow, easy, almost feral amble she found so damned entrancing.

She should have bolted; should have thrust through that door behind her and sought the exit—but did not. Flight would admit defeat, and somehow during the last few minutes, she'd discovered she'd had enough of being defeated. Especially when there was no way to tell when Vannister might attack again. And so she waited.

"Evenin'!" Vannister cried cheerily, when he had come to within two yards.

In spite of her resolve, she stepped backwards. "What *are* you?" she whispered. "What've you done to my house?"

"What do you *want* me to be?" he replied with that winsome cocking of eyebrow he'd used on her the first time they met. He sounded sincere, too—damn him!

"I'm in no mood for riddles," Brandy shot back.

"And I'm in no mood for interrogation—'specially when you wouldn't know any more than you do if I actually told you. 'Sides, that presupposes *I* know—which might not be the case. You ever think about *that?* How maybe I know what I can do, and what I can't, but not *why* or *how?*"

"I am *so* sorry," Brandy snapped acidly. "But I repeat: what've you done to my house?"

A shrug. "Finished it—more or less. Given you what you wanted—what you *really* wanted. I—" He paused thoughtfully, then grinned. "Hey! Maybe *that's* what I am: maybe I'm a Dreambuilder. Yeah, that's a good term. Maybe I'll stick to that."

Brandy bit her lip to calm her quaking teeth, then gestured around her. "But . . . *why?* Why me? Why all this?"

Once more Vannister shrugged. " 'Cause this is what I do—and you needed to have it done. Just like you needed to have a *lot* of things done," he added with a wicked leer she did not like at all. She tensed instantly, cursing herself for having so easily fallen under the spell of his words.

Vannister raised an eyebrow and casually eased past her to block her access to the door she'd been seeking.

"I wouldn't go out there just yet," he purred. "I'm not sure things are . . . *finished.* 'Sides, we've got more important things to discuss."

"Like what?" Brandy countered warily.

"Like all this, of course," Vannister chuckled. "The question is: Is this a gift . . . or a game?"

Brandy glared at him in a helpless mix of rage, fear, and confusion.

"And if it's a game," he went on, "what happens to the loser?"

"I would *suppose*," Brandy gritted, trying to sound braver than she felt, "that would depend on who it is."

"Good point," Vannister shot back instantly, all amiability again. "I might not *want* the same thing as you."

"What *do* you want?"

"Officially? To do what I'm supposed to do."

She regarded him skeptically. "Which is?"

"To make the rational—which is you—confront the *irrational* which is me."

"And actually?"

"*Actually?* I want to fuck you again. In fact, I want to do it several times . . . in a variety of positions." He clutched his crotch lasciviously.

Brandy could take no more. Yelling inarticulately, mostly to startle him, she aimed a kick straight at his groin.

And missed—for Vannister leapt back so quickly, she half expected to hear thunder bell into the vacuum where he'd stood.

For her part, she overbalanced and staggered a pair of yards to the left, where she halted, panting, glaring at him for all she was worth.

"I can give you whatever you want," Vannister whispered, as if she had not attacked. "I can make whatever you want; you won't have to work for it at all. And all you've gotta do is keep my pecker happy."

"Bullshit!"

He took a step forward. "I'll even let you keep Dillon around."

"*Bullshit!*"

Another step, fingers clutching mindlessly. "I don't *care* if you fuck him. Long as I get to when I want to, and for as *long* as I want to."

"Go to hell!"

An eyebrow lifted. "Hmmm. Now, *that's* a thought. But honestly, to quote loosely from Mr. Marlowe, 'I *am* in hell, and where I am, there is hell also.' "

Brandy was still grasping the blown-out candle—and as soon as Vannister paused for breath, hurled it straight at him. It smacked him solidly in the forehead and thumped to the floor. But before he could blink away his surprise, she was moving. A flatfooted kick to midchest connected, sending him stumbling backwards into a slanting shaft of light, and that bought her time enough to shove through the door to the foyer. Across it, through one more door, and she'd be free.

Only she wasn't *in* the foyer. This was another hall-way—and definitely not one that had ever been present before, except in the first, all-out blueprint of Brandy Hall. For an instant she thought she'd simply gotten confused and returned to the candlelit corridor outside the library by which she had first entered the heart of all this strangeness. But now she looked at it, she saw that though similar in design and dimensions, the proportions were subtly skewed, and the stone had a different texture. There were still candles, however, though not so many as in the other one; and a door rose opposite: a twin to that she had just flung herself through. She tried it—both sides, since it was another double—and found it locked.

Locked! She whirled around, but saw to her relief that the door to the great hall had snicked shut behind her. She flicked the latch and held her breath, but heard nothing.

And ran: left toward an archway that *might* lead to the Viking bedroom.

Instead, it marked the terminus of another impossible corridor that must continue around the great hall on that side. Candles guttered along it as well: all shapes and sizes, some on the floor, some in wall niches, a few affixed to the ceiling by silver chains. More important, though, a door loomed straight ahead. She pressed at it—to no avail—but a matching one stood at right angles to it in the adjoining corner. She glanced at it furtively, flipped the latch—felt it give.

And heard a noise behind her.

Once more she spun about, all nerves and tension—and saw, picking its way calmly around the flames that studded that unlikely passage, a pure white stag, its rack so wide, it brushed the walls to either side, the tines on its magnificient ivory antlers scraping sparks from the vaulting as it passed beneath.

It would be upon her in seconds.

She abandoned the door and ran back the way she had come, past the entrance to the great hall, and on to the western side.

—And gazed upon *another* corridor that had no right to exist, this one leading north: again paralleling the great hall. Sparing a glance over her shoulder and seeing neither man nor beast, she turned down it, and—blessedly—saw that the second of the three doors in the left-hand wall was cracked open. She ducked through—into what would have been the master bedroom, had it not been about fifty percent larger than she'd remembered and rendered in stone, not cinder block.

But it had doors! Sliding plate-glass doors leading out! She reached the closest in seconds—yanked at the slide. It wouldn't budge. She unlocked it, unable to see beyond for her own reflection painted gold and tawny by the light of yet more candles. A push, a tug, but still it would not move. She tried harder, swore, broke a nail. Looked around for something to smash it with. Nothing at all. Save for the candles, all of which were small, and none of which were in any kind of holder, the place was utterly bare.

She rested there a moment, panting out her frustration. And peered beyond the glass. It was hard to see through, but she thought she could make out the familiar landmarks of the knoll.

Only . . . only . . . there shouldn't be a terrace beyond the windows, at least not one with crenelations along its edges. And the angle was all wrong, as if she looked down upon the knoll from a height.

"Shit!" she groaned, and turned her back on all that irrationality.

Where to now? Back to the passage? She didn't think so; the deer could easily have made it there by now. So where?

Well, there was a door in the adjoining wall that ought to open into the master bath. But it had windows, too; maybe she could escape that way!

She tried the latch—it was functional—and pressed through. And heaved a small sigh of relief as she found herself exactly where she'd expected.

—Where she expected to be in about six months, more properly, for except for the mosaics she intended to slather across every surface, the bathroom, too, was complete. And it really was a *bath* room. Sixteen feet square, with cubicles for auxiliary functions opening off either side, the center held a huge square tub—which was now, apparently, paneled in tigereye, where it had been only a concrete shell the day before.

Why, there was even water in it! And—

"Evenin'!" Van Vannister cried cheerily, strolling casually out of the shower stall that opened off one side. He was wet and naked and no longer covered with stone dust. Indeed, he looked *very* human. "Take off your clothes an' stay awhile," he continued, gesturing toward the tub.

Brandy glared at him and backed through the door whence she had come, slamming it behind her.

So where now?

The office, she supposed. That was the only accessible door she hadn't tried. Pausing only to catch her breath, she sprinted across the oddly attenuated chamber. The door was cracked. Good. She stumbled through.

—Right at the foot of a flight of stairs that absolutely did not belong there at all. But where else *could* she go? Wearily she started up them, grateful that whoever—or whatever—had built them had at least used a reasonable width and rise. A landing interrupted her trek halfway, kinking the whole flight back toward the center of the house. Again, she had no choice but to follow—and emerged, seconds later, into the western aisle of the gallery above the great hall, from which the clerestory windows looked out upon the mostly flat roof.

But she was not alone. The deer was back, staring at her from the east aisle: directly opposite, across the open space. Not advancing, but making no move to flee.

Brandy started to ease away from it, back the way she had come.

But the door had locked behind her! And it was twenty feet to the floor below—and she was afraid of heights!

And then she glanced out the nearest window and saw the tower.

But . . . Brandy Hall *had* no tower! Not like that! Not four stories high!

But it had no corridors around its great hall either, nor was it made of stone, nor were any of the rooms finished to the degree she'd just observed, as if they only lacked that veneer of fresco, stained glass, or mosaic she'd hoped to spend the next many years executing.

And it *certainly* had no tower.

She wondered, suddenly, if it was already haunted—whether the white deer that was also probably Van Vannister was likewise a spirit or a ghost. A chill raced up her spine at that, but she had no more time for such speculation, for she had caught a movement in the window glass: a flash of white, moving quickly.

She jerked around—and saw that it was only the deer, still where it had been, merely tossing its head. Lord, but that was a beautiful beast. What a brilliant coat, what magnificent antlers.

What fantastic eyes! Even at this distance, even in the uncertain light, they were gorgeous. It was staring at her, too: enticing her with those dark, glistening orbs. But when she tried to look away, she could not.

Chapter 28

Fortress Around Your Heart

Welch County, Georgia
Sunday, August 1—near 1:00 A.M.

"Oh, Lord, *no*, not that!" Ron grumbled from the front passenger seat of Lew's XJ-6 as his brother braked smoothly for the first serious curve on Keycutter Knob. Without waiting permission, he reached over and switched off the radio, which had just served up the Significator tune of the day: "The End," by the Doors. "*That* I absolutely do *not* need!"

He closed his eyes and tried to relax, to conserve energy for the ordeal ahead. And failed. "Jesus *Christ*, won't this thing go any faster?"

Lew merely clenched his teeth tighter and shot him a weary sideways glare as the headlights planed across the raw rock face two bends beyond. Wendy, wide-eyed in the backseat, picked at the jogging suit her and said nothing—but then, she'd been quiet most of the ten minutes since their rescue mission had hit the road. Ron, who, until the radio had proclaimed its dire warning, had been watching her speculatively and wondering what could be going on in the head of someone who'd just been called back to physical reality, gnawed his lip nervously and fidgeted with the armrest. He *hated* this: not being in control, especially in a situation this urgent. Brandy was in danger, Wendy had told them: some kind of threat from Vannister that appeared to involve magic—or Luck—or *something*— and they were rushing to her aid. But not fast enough, not *nearly* fast enough. Shoot, the tires weren't even squealing, and the low growl of the Jag's big six was nowhere close to the irate metallic scream that would mean they were really hustling. "Lew, for chrissakes, we're not out for a Sunday drive here!" Ron gritted, when he could contain his impatience no longer.

"No," Lew snapped back. "But you'd prefer to *get* there, wouldn't you?"

Ron scowled fiercely. "Which we'll *do* if you don't roll this thing into a ball and set it on fire. And with our Luck, we'd survive even that!"

"But *not* help Brandy," Lew countered calmly, though he was already picking up the pace: cutting apexes and braking later, accelerating harder. Ron could feel G forces pressing him against the tan leather door panel—finally.

"Nor me, either," Wendy added pointedly. "I'm not real keen on going back to being leaves and feathers."

Ron lapsed into a sullen, fretful silence. She was right, of course; three lives saved was better than one lost—if Brandy was even in *that* degree of danger.

Lew broke the peace. "Is there *anything* else you can remember?" he asked the girl.

Wendy shook her head. "No more than I've told you: that Vannister told Brandy he wasn't human—which he isn't, though I don't know what he *is*—and it freaked her. And that he's awakened some kind of power—I think in the earth. Or at least there's a shitload of energy at work there. I couldn't tell much after that 'cause I was focusing on Ron, except for just a minute before I incarnated— that's when I kinda went cosmic and picked up most of the magic."

"Which is exactly what we already knew," Ron grumbled, too tired to resist the temptation to gripe.

"And you *know* how much I know," Lew volunteered, as if he'd read the rest of Ron's thought—which maybe he had. "That when I tried to Listen for Brandy and Van, all I Heard was Silence."

"No sign of them at all?"

"Not a whisper. It was a weird kind of Silence, though: not so much around a person as around the whole place— which probably means they're inside . . . whatever it is."

"Which means we don't have a *clue* what we're getting into," Ron finished for him. "Great!" he appended bitterly.

Lew glared at him again. "Look, man, I'm at *least* as fried as you are, but this isn't a thing we can put off! You've got a responsibility to Brandy, and *I've* got a responsibility to you, her, and the rest of the people in this county. And if something involving rogue magic's going on, I've gotta deal with it!"

"Sorry," Ron murmured. "You know how it is."

Lew spared an instant to muss his hair. "Boy, do I! I wonder if—"

Ron's yell interrupted him. "There's the turn, man; there's the frigging *turn!*"

"Huh? Oh . . . *shit!*"

Lew stabbed the brake for all it was worth and jerked the wheel hard left. Ron felt the discs locking and unlocking, their alloy voices merged in a four-part shriek as the Jag skewed half around before angling onto the mass of ruts and boulders that led down to Brandy Hall. They caught the first rock at a horrendous pace, bouncing the car hard against its suspension stops before Lew straightened it out and thundered on. In spite of his seat belt, Ron's head smacked the sunroof. Wendy uttered a startled yip.

"*Jesus*, man!" Ron gasped, "I thought you knew how to get here!"

" 'Fraid not," Lew gulped back. "I only go where I'm invited, remember? And Brandy never asked me up here— nor did you."

"Sorry 'bout that," Ron mumbled sheepishly. And tried to hold his peace as Lew hustled the low-slung vehicle along as best he could, swearing colorfully—and very atypically—whenever a limb brushed the side, or the bottom smashed and grated against the rough surface. Ron and Wendy contented themselves with grunts when they caromed off solid surfaces. Ron caught a whiff of hot lubricant.

"You'll have to watch it up ahead," Ron cautioned when they had nearly reached their destination. "There's a bad curve that'll fool you if you're not careful."

Lew grimaced irritably. "I wish you'd make up your mind fast or slow," he hissed. "I'm not—" He broke off in midsentence. *"Jesus Christ!* What's *that?"*

Ron's view was still blocked by an outthrust clump of laurel, but an instant later, he, too, saw. "Jesus H. Christ! Shit and *double* shit!"

For he had finally caught sight of Brandy Hall. A handful of turns and a hundred yards separated them yet, but already he could tell that the place he was returning to was in no wise the one he had left less than nine hours before. And as Lew jounced them closer, a sick dread clotted in Ron's stomach as it dawned on him that they were approaching something far more powerful than he had ever imagined. But not until the car slid to a lurching halt at the edge of the clearing did Ron fully grasp the extent of the alteration.

Ron hoped—nay, *prayed*—that the shift was a trick of light, a phantasm wrought by moonlight on the familiar crenelations, walls, and windows. And maybe that *was* part of the effect—that, and the fog that had woven its way up from the lake and now lapped and frothed around the base of the building like an uneasy, stealthy army of drifting wraiths which the blazing silver-gilt moon blasted to stark blue-white.

But that was clearly not the limit of the change, not by a long shot. The whole building had transfigured, though the basic format—four stubby corner towers embracing recessed arcades, with a clerestory level capping the middle third—remained the same. It was, Ron thought grimly, exactly as though the concrete walls and arches had been infected by their rock foundations, so that the bones of the mountain had grown up through the artificial constructs and warped them to a less structured plan, like some kind of tumorous growth. Why, the facade wasn't even all on the same level anymore! Never mind that it had also been raised higher, as though the earth had swelled and fractured beneath it, rearing terraces and slopes and precipices where none had existed.

And Brandy was almost certainly inside.

"Jesus, oh Jesus, oh Jesus," Ron repeated as he wrenched at the door handle and tumbled out.

The wind was cold when it hit him, and whipped his hair into his face. But what unnerved Ron more was the way the rocky ground beneath his feet thrummed ominously, while the very air vibrated, tense with pent-up power.

"Brandy!" he yelled hoarsely, before the others could join him. "Brandy—where *are* you?"

Not even an echo replied.

"What—?" Lew began, arriving at his side.

Ron merely grunted, snagged his crutch from the Thunderbird, and waded into the fog, not bothering to check either tents or trailer as he limped past. No *way* Brandy could've slept through whatever had happened here. And even more to the point, no way she'd have stayed away once things started happening to her house.

Before he knew what he was about, he was running— *trying* to. His bum knee hurt abominably, and the sporadic numbness that afflicted that limb lower down became more pervasive with every step.

"Ronny, goddamn it, *wait*!" Lew bellowed.

He didn't.

The fog engulfed him to the waist as he forged ahead, and the nearer he staggered to the building, the more he was struck by how it had changed. Not that it mattered. *Nothing* mattered but finding Brandy and putting an end to this whole sorry mess so he could rest. He had reached what ought to have been a muddy forecourt by now, and this close, the air felt so taut with energy he feared it might rip asunder if he moved too abruptly. Not that it slowed him.

What *did* was when he tripped on an unseen obstacle and stumbled forward onto his hands and knees. He swore, fumbled for the crutch, and realized dully that he'd fallen onto the lower terminus of a brand-new flight of wide, shallow steps that angled up to a south arcade that was now at least five feet higher than heretofore, and looked out across what could either be rough-cut battlements or piles of fractured stone.

Forcing himself to ignore the pain in his knee and the now almost constant numbness below it, Ron drove himself upward. Lew and Wendy panted up beside him, already pale faces wide-eyed with concern as they helped him along, uttering vain pleas for caution. An instant later they rose out of the fog like scruffy gods newborn from the foam of a contentious sea. Ron spared scarcely a second for the view—Brandy Hall a craggy island in an ocean of fluorescent white—before he was moving on, straight toward the front door.

Where he got another shock.

It should have been empty: *should* have been only a gaping archway eight feet across and ten tall. Instead, the whole space—and it was much larger than before: wider and higher, even as the arcade itself seemed to have expanded—was now sealed by a massive door of some thick, woodlike stone, with neither lock, hinge, nor knocker; all set in a wall no longer cinder block but stone.

Which didn't prevent him pounding on it with his fist. *"Brandy!"* he screamed: *"Brandy!* Jesus, girl, *answer* me!"

No reply save the subtlest shiver in the stone.

"Brandy!" he yelled one final time as he backed up three paces and flung himself shoulder-first hard against the door. It hurt like the devil: jarred his teeth and sent pains shooting down his arm and into his chest. Which cleared his head, but did no good otherwise.

But he had no choice but to try again, and this time Lew joined him—to as little avail. He was on the verge of a third attempt when Lew restrained him with a decisive grip on his forearm. "It's no use," his brother murmured soberly. "We'll never get in that way."

Ron twisted free of Lew's grasp. "Fine!" he spat over his shoulder as he limped back onto that troubling new terrace. "So I'll try the fucking *windows*!"

Lew and Wendy exchanged wary glances, but followed him to the western end of the southwest tower, where stained-glass panes in narrow Gothic arches lit the master bath. But where the last time Ron had seen them, they were on ground level, the wall that held them now perched atop a sheer, man-high escarpment: clearly out of reach. Never mind that some sort of dense stone tracery filled them anyway.

"*Shit!*" Ron growled. "Well, maybe the *other* side's better." Whereupon he turned and stumped toward the south*east* tower.

The windows there proved more accessible—except that they were likewise blocked by a knotted piercework so tightly twined no amount of pounding with either fists or what few loose rocks littered the ground could affect it.

"This just can't *be!*" Ron groaned when Lew tried to ease him away. "No *way* this place could have changed *this* much so fast. No *fucking* way! Not even with magic."

"Not the kind *we* use, anyway," Lew conceded.

"Tell me about it!"

Lew said nothing, but his face was taut with fear and concern. "What about *other* entrances?"

Ron shrugged gloomily. "I reckon we'd better try. But something tells me it won't help. The place doesn't *want* to let us in."

"Not the place," Lew corrected. "Whoever's maintaining that Silence."

"Or *whatever*," Wendy blurted out. Then, "Oh jeeze, I shouldn't have said that!"

"It's okay," Ron told her, patting her hand. "We're all tired, all burned-out."

"So, what about those other entrances?" Lew prompted.

Once more Ron shrugged, but led the way around the corner to the eastern wall—where yet again the windows were too high, or the walls below them too sheer, or the openings themselves too densely blocked with stone filigree. And the north side, which overlooked the lake, was now rendered totally inaccessible by a precipitous drop of at least twenty feet, where before there had been level ground.

West was the same: more slopes and terraces, more unyielding doors and inaccessible battlements. Nothing that would serve to admit them to Brandy Hall.

It was hopeless, Ron conceded, staring down at hands ripped bloody by contending with too much stone. Lew laid an arm on his shoulder sympathetically, tried to draw him away from the source of all that despair. "Come on, man—there's nothing you can do."

"But there *has* to be!" Ron protested, half in tears. "Shoot, we've got more power than anybody in the state—and can't get inside a fucking *house*?"

"But—"

"No, Lew; I won't accept it. You've gotta try one more time: use the Luck—use whatever you've got to . . . to at least see what's going on in there!"

"Ronny, I—"

"*Use* it, Lew!" Ron demanded, grabbing his brother's shirtfront. "Use it, or I'll never forgive you!"

"But I already *did*, man! I—never mind." Without another word, Lew flopped against the nearest wall, closed his eyes, and took the three breaths that triggered a trance. Ron immediately sensed the tightening in the air that was the physical side effect of Luck—though here it was almost lost within that heavier tension that thrummed up from the earth. For maybe a minute Lew remained as he was: not moving, breathing shallowly, with a single muscle twitching in his throat. Then he drew a long, ragged breath and opened his eyes, blinking in confusion. His pupils were huge with awe and apprehension.

"I can't do it!" he managed weakly. "I'm just not strong enough."

Ron slumped to the ground, utterly devastated.

Wendy joined him. Lew laid a hand on Ron's head, ruffling his hair. "*You* could try," he said softly.

"*Ha!*" Ron snorted, staring at his feet. "Not bloody likely! I'm a wimp, remember? Besides, *you're* the Master. This is your land; you're supposed to be the strong one."

Lew grimaced wearily. "Yes and no," he sighed. "Actually, I think we're both about even as far as raw Luck goes. I've had more practice, but that doesn't necessarily mean anything. And I'm used to working with a footholder, and without one, I'm nothing special—not that I'd risk Karen even for this. *You*, on the other hand, haven't ever developed that dependency. Also, the further from Cardalba I get, the weaker I become, while *you're* at the absolute center of your power, 'cause you've invested this place with your creative and emotional energy—the power of Making, if you will.

You're stronger here than I am!"

Ron regarded him warily, then nodded. "You're right, of course. It's just that—Lew, I don't know how much I've got left in me!"

"Enough to see you through tonight," Lew assured him. "This *can't* go on indefinitely. Sooner or later something'll give. You just can't fiddle with the kind of force that did all this for very long—you'd attract too much attention."

"Fine," Ron gritted. "Okay, then, I reckon I'll give it a go." And without further comment, he closed his eyes, triggered the trance . . . and Jumped.

The Winds engulfed him immediately: howling around him with their burden of Voices, which were also thoughts and dreams, emotions and ideas. With Lew so close in that unheard chorale, he was like a perfect tenor belting out a joyful overture: brilliant, but so strong and clear, he rose above all other singers. Which made it hard to key into any other Voice. Ron tried to blank Lew out—but could not. *Brandy?* he called desperately, freeing his own Voice in the unlikely hope she might hear.

But if she responded, he missed it amid so vast a cacophony. Yet he *had* to keep trying. If he couldn't locate Brandy herself, he'd do as Lew suggested and focus on her house. Places had—not precisely Voices, but Presences, anyway. And Brandy Hall, with its vast accumulation of invested emotion, should have a very strong Presence indeed: like a bass booming amid the higher whistles and shrieks that were human lives. Which meant it should produce a profound disturbance. But when he finally fought his way there, he found not the familiar comforting resonance, but a Silence so vast and smooth and impenetrable, it was terrifying.

It was hopeless. No way he'd ever find a chink in that armor!

He drew back immediately. *Nothing* Lew could have said would have prepared him for this. It was as if a dome of Silence had taken form in the Realm of the Winds, rather like (to use a more physical metaphor) a boulder in a stream forcing the water that rushed past it aside. But as for Brandy—or Van—they might as well not exist. Which undoubtedly meant that Lew was right: they were inside that Silence. And since Silences were born of conscious desire, and since Brandy certainly could not manage more than the most rudimentary of shields behind which to hide her psyche, that only left one possible source: the supposedly inhuman Van Vannister, who *certainly* had something screwy about his Voice. Lord, but Ron wished he'd paid more attention to that aberration—or that Lew had. It was obvious now that Vannister had power—and had been deliberately constructing inconsequential surface memories to mask a deeper deceit.

Ron was right on the verge of bringing himself back to what passed for the real world when he became aware of a new Voice among the Winds: a small change that took a moment to key into. Something was approaching, was thinking about him. In a favorable way, so it seemed. He reached toward it automatically—and brushed an alien mind. Nonhuman. *Animal?* Yes. He withdrew from that, frightened by the unlikely thoughts. Yet it had seemed familiar—*very* familiar. Steeling himself, he returned, explored that awareness more thoroughly—and all at once found himself looking up at his own inert form through the slitted green eyes of Matty Groves.

And had an idea.

The barriers that kept him out of Brandy Hall were purely physical: actual walls around which the Silence he'd been battling was merely an intangible shield against thoughts. But Matty was small and might be able to enter bodily where no human could. And if Ron stashed his consciousness inside the cat's, perhaps he could breach the boundary of the Silence that way. If nothing else, it was certainly worth a try.

Once more bracing himself against the alien instincts he now knew he would find, Ron insinuated himself into Matty's mind and eased into control. The cat resisted, but not as much as Ron expected, and before he was aware of it, Matty was scrambling up the bank toward the nearest window. It was gridded over, of course, but apparently not glassed in. And contained openings large enough for a cat to slink through—which Matty did.

Ron felt the Silence lap at him as he breached its physical analog, felt it drag at him, try to press him back. But he'd been right! Matty's instincts shielded him from the worst of it, and before he knew it, he was inside and Listening.

He found a Voice instantly: Brandy's—alone, and desperate with fear, yet filled with a grim determination. She seemed to be intact physically, which was a vast relief; but something was threatening her—something that had no Voice in exactly the same way the Egyptian room had been Silent that morning. He quested, tried to merge with Brandy's consciousness and look out from her eyes; but her mind was too awash with jumbled emotions for anything as subtle as an outside thought to register. He could not project reassurance to her either, but at least he had located her. At least he knew she was okay.

But then Matty saw something that alarmed him quite independent of Ron, and bolted. And with that outswelling of reflex, Ron felt his awareness flung not only out of the cat's mind, but into his own as well.

He blinked, squinting into the bright moonlight, felt for his breath and finally found it. "She's there," he gasped. "And she's in trouble. Beyond that . . ."

"So we *have* to get in, then."

"Or at least give it our best shot," he sighed. "Come on, maybe we can find a sledgehammer or something."

It was then that he heard the grating crunch of a vehicle grinding its way down the drive.

Ron looked up, searching the rugged, moonlit landscape—and quickly saw the flicker of headlights winking in and out among the trees to the south. "My God," he gasped. "Who the hell . . . ?"

Lew blinked for an instant, then closed his eyes—and blinked again. "That wasn't hard," he said, "not this close. It's Weedge Montgomery."

Ron could only gape. "Weedge!" he cried. "What's *she* doing here?"

"She's been trying to call Brandy all night and hasn't been able to get her—so she got worried and decided to get out of bed and come on up. Evidently some kind of hunch, or something."

Ron rolled his eyes. "Well, that's just great! All we need is to have to explain all this."

Lew's eyes narrowed thoughtfully. "No," he said slowly. "I don't think that's gonna be a problem. I think . . . we might actually be able to use her. She's Brandy's best friend, after all, has a huge emotional investment in her. And any time you can draw on something like that, it's an asset."

"But—"

Lew shook his head. "No time to talk now. She's liable to drive up, see all this weirdness, and bolt. We have to be there to meet her."

Before Ron knew what he was about, he was slogging through the fog behind his brother, with the high new walls of Brandy Hall looming ominous beside him.

When they reached the top of the steps, Weedge's car had cleared the woods. And by the time they had limped and tripped and stumbled down them, she was out of the vehicle and striding forward. Confusion contorted her face, then anger, as she recognized them.

"What's going on?" she demanded without preamble. "And what the hell's happened here? Where's Brandy?"

"In there," Ron sighed heavily, pointing back the way they had come.

"What . . . ? How . . . ?"

Ron had just taken a deep breath in anticipation of far more explanation than he had energy for, when Lew preempted him. Without being obvious about it, he eased beside Weedge and laid a hand at the juncture of her neck and shoulder. She started, her face blanked for an instant, then relaxed. Lew's face was slack, too, but the air was alive with Luck. Ron guessed what his brother was about: mind-to-mind communication—far faster than words and much clearer. Lew was pouring all his memories of the last few hours into Weedge's mind. Ron hoped she was up to accepting it. He found out quickly, for an instant later Weedge's lids flicked open.

"Jesus!" she gasped. "Well, *that* was certainly interesting." Her face was haunted: tense and strained—though not as much as might be expected of someone who'd just had her whole concept of reality realigned. Ron knew how she felt: he'd experienced much the same thing that awful night five years ago when his dying mother had funneled all her long-suppressed knowledge of his conception, of who and what he was and could become, into the mind of a guileless teenage boy who heretofore had assumed the *real* world was the one most people saw.

He was poised on the verge of suggesting that the quest for the sledgehammer continue, when Weedge folded her arms, nodded once with conviction, and strode straight toward her Toyota. "Come on," she told them tersely. "You guys need to get inside fast? Well, I know *one* good way!"

Wendy's brow wrinkled with uncertainty as they found themselves with no alternative but to follow or abandon the conversation. "But what about—" she began.

"Oh, *I* see," Lew interrupted absently, trotting faster to keep up. "Yeah, it might just work—if you're willing to risk it."

"Get in, or don't," Weedge snapped, reaching for her keys. "Go, or stay. But I'm taking the fastest way." She thumped into the driver's seat and slammed the door.

Ron hesitated only seconds, then piled into the back, utterly confused. Wendy joined him there, with Lew in the vacant front shotgun seat. It was not until Weedge commenced backing up that Ron understood what she was about. "Can't get through that door, huh?" the woman snorted. "Well, I bet a ton and a half of Toyota can! 'Sides, *I've* got four-wheel-drive!" And with that, she shifted into first, revved the engine to a banshee scream, and popped the clutch. The little car bucked, squeaked, then surged forward, bounding across the scarred ground and into the fog, which engulfed it to dashboard level.

"There're steps!" Ron yelled—but the car had already struck the first one. It lurched, bounced, listed—rattled a lot—but somehow continued to gather speed up the corrugated slope. The instant they reached the terrace at the top, Weedge floored it, arrowing straight toward the arcade's center arch. "You're gonna owe me a car," she laughed grimly. And then Brandy Hall was looming up *very* fast indeed. Ron barely had time for a strangled gasp, a muttered half prayer, before they had bumped onto the arcade pavement and the near-side pillar was flashing by. Metal scraped. Sparks flew. Something underneath broke with a sickening *twang*. Ron saw nothing but the huge door dead ahead, rushing to fill the whole world—until masked by the windshield webbing to opacity as they struck the woody stone head-on. Ron felt himself lifted and thrown against the driver's seat. He bit his tongue, tasted blood, heard Wendy scream and Weedge and Lewis swear, as rock splintered and metal collapsed.

More metal shrieked and tore, and then they were through, careening across a candlelit corridor Ron did not recall, into another enormous door, and through *it* into a vast vaulted space full of columns braced by slanting shafts of moonlight.

Yet *more* metal crumpled. Brakes squealed. Weedge swore colorfully. The car skidded sideways—

—And stopped.

There was no noise, no movement save drifting dust motes—until four people gasped out their wonder at being alive.

"Yep," Weedge chuckled shakily as she yanked at an obviously jammed door handle. "You guys definitely owe me some wheels." Then: "Oh, shit! Oh, fucking bloody *shit!*"

"What?" Lew asked, concerned.

The woman's face was suddenly very pale. "Nothing," she grunted from between clenched teeth. "It's just that I . . . think my right leg's broken. I—Oh *Jesus!*" She tried to move the limb again, went white—and was unconscious.

Ron swapped uneasy glances with his companions. "You guys check her out," he sighed finally. "I've *gotta* look for Brandy."

"I'll go with you," Wendy offered.

Ron shook his head. "No," he said softly. "This is *my* battle. I . . . think it's *always* been my battle."

Lew regarded him seriously, oblivious to the cut over his eye. "Yeah, maybe you're right. But if you're not back before we finish tending to things here, we're comin' after you, got it?"

Ron mumbled an affirmative and wrenched his door open.

Chapter 29

Up on the Roof

The little Toyota was totaled, Ron knew in an instant, its front sheetmetal crushed back to the middle of the wheels; even the roof was buckled. It was a miracle none of them had been killed. Or maybe not, since Weedge had been wearing her belt, and the rest of them were . . . different.

And in any event, it didn't matter. What mattered now was finding Brandy.

But where did one begin in this monstrous labyrinth that was no longer in any wise the building he remembered. He swallowed, took in the new hugeness of the great hall, the slender stone columns, the clerestory windows, the gallery, the arching Gothic ceiling. Even those fantastic sculptures—even the one that looked like . . . oh, Jesus!—*him!* It was all new, all different, utterly and completely changed: a place where cement had incarnated as stone, where concrete caterpillar had become rocky butterfly.

But where was Brandy?

And then he saw her: on the western side of the clerestory gallery—which put her about twenty feet up. Not far away at all, but inaccessible for all that. Yet in spite of the commotion all their automotive cacophony must surely have engendered, she didn't seem to have noticed them. In fact, to judge by her wide, unblinking eyes, she didn't appear to be noticing anything; was simply standing as if frozen, with her back pressed hard against the outside wall as though she were trying to merge with the stonework there. Ron followed her line of sight. And finally saw what so completely absorbed her attention.

A pure white buck deer shared the gallery, facing her head-on from across the great hall. It was moving no more than she, but its gaze never left her. The instant Ron saw its eyes, he had to look away. They were too bright, too steady, too *unafraid*! Impulsively he shut his own lids, breathed deep, Listened . . .

Silence! That awful greedy Silence lurked there. But there was something odd about it now; something dark, almost bestial, as if it was born of instinct, not intellect. Yet in spite of that, he could feel a ghost of will grating against the shield he had automatically raised upon entering Brandy Hall. *But what was a deer doing with a will?*

Or a Silence?

And how could it exert its will and yet maintain a Silence?

But he already knew that this was not, in any sense, a creature from the everyday world. And given Vannister's absence and what Wendy had implied . . .

"Brandy!" he shouted so loudly, the effort nearly tore his throat. "Brandy! Snap out of it! For God's sake, there's a door right beside you! *Run!*"

She didn't move. And Lew and Wendy were too preoccupied with their injured comrade to be of any assistance. Very well, if Brandy couldn't rouse herself and come down, he'd just have to go up! Bracing himself against a whole assortment of pains he didn't recall acquiring, he rummaged inside the ruined Toyota until he found his crutch, then limped as fast as he could toward the nearest door—which, if memory served, led to a short hallway whence he could access the stairs.

But he couldn't resist one final assessement of the stand-off playing out on the gallery. And even as he stood gnawing his lip, the deer snorted, tossed its head, turned—and advanced a step.

Which apparently roused Brandy from whatever odd stupor she'd been thrall to. She blinked, looked down, stared at him—*recognized* him! "*No*, Ronny!" she yelled, when she saw him advancing. "Not this way! The stairs are all screwed up. You've gotta come up direct!"

Ron gaped helplessly. What did she mean? Did she actually want him to climb up to the gallery? He couldn't do that! The columns were too smooth and tall; he had no ladder or rope, and there was no way he could jump twenty feet.

The deer took another step.

"Where's Vannister?"

Brandy pointed across the gulf between herself and the animal. "There—I think. I don't *know*!"

"The door . . . ?"

"Locked."

"Then you've gotta jump down!" Ron called frantically. "I—I'll try to catch you."

"I . . . I *can't*," Brandy yelled back. "It's too far, and . . . I'm afraid of heights! More than anything in the world!"

"Brandy!"

Another step. Hoofs clicked loud against hard stone.

Ron had no alternative but to act.

The statue of himself as Goibhniu was half again life-sized and, alone of all the half-seen sculptures, projected far enough into the room that its upper parts were within marginal leaping distance of the gallery floor. Without waiting to consider the wisdom of what he was about, Ron hitched toward it. An instant later, he had scaled the anvil, and seconds after that, had made his way onto the marble shoulders. He clung there, panting, disgusted at the effort even that small exertion had required; though to be fair, he could have accomplished it easily had he had full use of his leg—and *not* had to lug that dratted crutch. As it was, he'd had to rely almost exclusively on the smithing muscles in his arms. He was close though, could almost stand on his own stony shoulders and brush the lower edge of the gallery. *If* he jumped. And *if* he had two good legs . . .

"Brandy," he shouted frantically. "Lew . . . anybody! Gimme a hand!"

Shoe leather slapped against stone: hasty, yet hesitant. He looked up to see a furtive-eyed Brandy leaning over the railing, stretching her hand toward him. He steeled himself, then rose shakily on his one good leg, balanced precariously on the statue's shoulder, with its upraised arm as brace. But strain though they might, their reach still failed by almost a yard. He tried harder, ventured an awkward hop. But the stone was too well polished, and he slipped . . . started to fall. He flailed out, caught the statue's head, and hung there for a dreadful eternity before he could right himself.

And once more heard the nervous clicking of hoofs, this time accelerating rapidly—their way.

"Shit!" Brandy growled in helpless frustration as she was forced to withdraw.

"Run!" Ron shouted desperately. "Keep what distance you can until I get there!"

Brandy hesitated only an instant before dashing around two sides of the gallery, so that she once more stood opposite the buck—and fifty feet away from Ron.

He had to help her, *had* to! Straining himself to the utmost, he managed a more secure perch, but as he tottered upright, the crutch that had been such a nuisance to manhandle slipped. He snatched at it, felt it snag on something below, freed it—and had an idea.

Before he could talk himself out of it, he swung the figure-encrusted staff up and over his head in a long, smooth arc. It smacked into the new stone grillwork that fronted the gallery rail—and stuck, lodged firmly within that lattice. If only it would hold. And if only he was strong enough. Gritting his teeth, Ron let go with his feet and climbed, using every ounce of that wiry strength a summer's labor had given him. Inch by inch he worked his way upward, knotting his fingers among the cast-silver warriors he had wrought so long ago, feeling them bend and crumple as he brought his weight to bear. They cut him, too, for they wore armor, carried swords, and glittered with spikes and sharp edges. But he dared not falter, even when blood trickled down his arm.

Less than a minute that effort took, but for Ron it was an eternity during which he was helpless—a lifetime during which Brandy might lose her insane waiting game with that buck. The crutch was loosening, too; he could feel it shifting, hear the grate of metal against stone. But just as it finally jerked free, his fingers clamped the bottom edge of the rail.

The crutch fell noisily to the flagstone floor, but he no longer needed it to make his way. One awful moment of superhuman strain, and he released his other hand and started to pull himself over.

Just in time to hear a frantic clatter of hoofs—and stare straight into the buck's liquid eyes from less than a yard away.

He understood now how Brandy had been beguiled; for the creature was beautiful beyond belief, wild beyond dreams. And those eyes! Dark brown ringed with green ringed with white; lashes jet-black against that snowy hide. Eyes one could get lost in.

But why wasn't it attacking—or doing whatever it had done to hoodoo Brandy? That's what he'd been expecting, for chrissakes: that it would try to match wills with him and—surely—lower that Silence long enough for him to Jump into whatever consciousness lurked there and battle it out that way.

Instead, it was simply staring at him, almost sadly, pleading to him with those eyes—those damnable, lovely eyes. He tried to look away—and not only couldn't shift his gaze, couldn't move a muscle! He was snared as surely as Brandy had been.

Perhaps. For while he could not break eye contact, neither was there any sign of additional aggression. He was merely trapped: locked in another of those dratted standoffs. If only he could close his eyes, he could go into a trance, and then he'd be fine. Then he could focus his will and maybe win free. If nothing else, the effort would beat this feeling of helplessness.

Or *was* he helpless? Eyes were the windows of the soul, it was said. But what did shutting them before Listening actually accomplish? Closing off the outside world, of course; eliminating distractions. But with those cervine eyes dark as they were, and filling much of his field of vision, most of that was already done. And he had nothing to lose by trying. So he stared—hard; took the three breaths—and Jumped.

And met that same troubling Silence that so completely blocked access to whatever intelligence lurked behind it.

Well, what did he expect? That was what Silences were supposed to do!

On the other hand, as he'd noted before, this Silence was different from those he was accustomed to. Usually they were wrought by intention or desire, and were functions of conscious volition: intentional constructions. But this one seemed to have a different feel to it. It was more like what he'd experienced when he'd hitched his way in here under cover of Matty Groves's sneaky little brain: instinct, not intellect. Inadvertent as opposed to intentional. And instinct could be stronger than conscious desire, which maybe explained the ease with which his own desires had been overpowered.

But what if he *also* relied on instinct? Might his not be stronger than this . . . creature's? Strong enough to shatter these peculiar bonds?

But if so, how did he access it?

He tried to recall how it had been with Matty, what the cat's instincts had been like, and then locate that part of himself. The memory, though recent, had not been particularly pleasant, and was already buried deep—but he found it, and once that was done, quickly found their connections to his own analog and followed them down to his deep brain, where nothing existed but the desire to eat and procreate and survive.

Survive!

To survive, he had to be free; and to be free, he had to break the bonds that held him.

But what was holding him?

Some kind of power. A power fueled by instinct. An instinct that hid its driving force behind Silence.

Though he had no idea how he did it, Ron shunted his conscious desire for freedom into his instinct for survival, drove them both through his deep brain, and then Jumped again. Past Silence and into—

Nothing!

There was nothing behind the Silence! No Voice, not even that odd superficial one Vannister displayed. Instead there was—he could not help thinking visually—only a vast hollow sphere with emptiness at its heart.

But how could Nothing power so much strength?

Ron had no idea. But as he floated there in that no-place, pondering how to retrieve himself from this perplexing dead end, he Heard something.

It was soft—as soft as Wendy's ghost of Voice had been when she'd first begun to awaken into selfhood. But it *was* present. Ron Listened that way, focused all the odd strength of his peculiar kind, and Listened harder.

And heard—not softly, but *weakly*—a Voice calling out, *"Help me!"*

Ron never fully understood what happened next, but as best he could tell, he was so surprised by that request that his reflexes took over. And since his most basic reflex was fight-or-flight, and there was nothing tangible *to* fight, his only alternative was to flee.

He did: out of that no-place, past that impossible Silence—and back into his own skull.

He blinked—base reflex—and saw the deer's eyes once more.

Only . . . they weren't exactly *deer* eyes anymore; they were shifting: shrinking, changing color, all faster than he could rightly register.

Before he could blink again, they were human: the bright blue eyes of Van Vannister—now wild with fear. Or were they mad?

"Thanks for the ride!" Vannister cackled loudly. And ran—naked as a jaybird—not toward the gawking Brandy, but toward the single door in the gallery that appeared to lead outside.

"You asshole!" Ron grunted. "Come the hell back here!"

"Come and get me!" the crazy man taunted back—and ducked through the beckoning portal.

"Ronny!" Brandy called, rushing toward him as he tried frantically to flounder across the rail. "God, what just happened?" she added, thrusting an arm under his to help him down.

He had to lean against her for support. "Nothing—I don't know," he replied shakily. "It's . . . I don't think it's over yet!"

"But what . . . ?"

Ron took a deep breath, waiting for the room to stop spinning and his various mental processes to reseat. "Please," he panted. "I beg you: not now. I've still gotta . . . find out what's going on, and I've . . . gotta do it alone!"

Brandy's expression showed hurt, fear, and resignation all—along with vast fatigue that was bordering on shock. "Okay," she managed, "do it. But for God's sake, be careful!"

"Oh, believe me, I will!" he replied, attempting a smile. "Now, scoot. See if you can get back downstairs. Get Lew and Wendy to help you if you have to, and get the hell *outta* here!"

She stared at him a moment longer, then nodded and jogged toward what Ron presumed was the entrance to the stairs.

He spared an instant to glance over the rail, to where his brother and former girlfriend were finally easing Weedge out of the car; shouted a hasty, resigned "End of round one"; and hurried, as best his leg allowed, toward the archway through which Vannister had plunged.

It took far too long to limp-jog the distance, which was halfway around the gallery, and Ron wondered why he bothered. The guy—whatever he was—would be long gone by now. But he *had* to know—had to at least make the effort. There were too many mysteries loose in the night for him to call off the chase. Never mind minor things like justice, like restitution. Like revenge! And he'd at least like to have something to tell his companions.

Damn him! he thought—and stumbled through the arch (which he could have sworn had held a door seconds before) into a darkened vestibule between the gallery and the roof.

Vannister was waiting for him there, a half dozen yards away, leaning casually against the battlements beside a shocking four-story tower Ron had never seen before. Though still barefoot and bare-chested, he had on jeans; and his long red hair was whipping wildly in the night breeze. He looked both pale and determined. A smirking tip of his head acknowledged Ron's scowling presence.

"I'm not gonna hurt you," Ron called from the vestibule. "Come on, guy—we need to talk."

"Ah, but maybe I *need* to be hurt," Vannister chuckled, folding his arms across his magnificent chest. There was no trace of his characteristic drawl. "Maybe I need to *feel* what I have done."

"Van, I—"

"It didn't work this time," Vannister interrupted thoughtfully, as though he were not addressing Ron except peripherally. "There was too much beast, I reckon."

Ron blinked at him uncertainly, but did not approach. Something told him not to—not yet. "What—what do you mean?"

"That you've found me out, maybe?" Vannister replied softly. "But then, what exactly have you found? That there's more to me than there is to most folks? That I can do things other folks can't? Well, the same can be said of you! So what right do you have to judge me?"

"But I'm not *trying* to judge you!" Ron stammered uncertainly.

"*Aren't* you? You want to hurt me; I can feel it in your soul. And no civilized . . . being . . . wants to hurt another unless it's threatened. And it doesn't usually feel threatened unless it thinks it's right—it's easier that way: to feel instead of think. And what is that, in essence, but judgment?"

"Come here, Van," Ron repeated mildly, his anger having lapsed into a reluctant compassion. "There're better places to do this than out here."

Van shook his head. "You'll have to come get me."

But still Ron hesitated.

"Cat got your tongue?" Van teased. "Little Matty Groves, maybe? Or maybe a deer? Well, I guess I have to talk instead, then, won't I? And I'll just tell you one thing: I haven't hurt you in any meaningful way. I haven't hurt Brandy either, nor have I hurt anyone else since I came here. I'm actually kinda like you, in a way: I'm a smith—a builder, rather. But the thing *I* build is dreams. It was all deliberate, every bit of it was."

"But you just said you *had* hurt . . ."

"Ah, but that was a different me; that was the me of a minute ago, which is not the same me as now."

Ron heard him, but he heard something else, too: he heard smooth words and subtle manipulation. And he knew he was looking at the man who had played games with him and Brandy that no man had a right to play. If nothing else, Brandy had been irrevocably exposed to the strange. Her world would never be the same again—and that was not a thing one person should do to another.

"I fucked your girlfriend!" Vannister crowed suddenly, unzipping his pants. "I made your girlfriend scream!"

Ron simply gaped, dumbfounded; and then, unable to cope with reason any longer, flung himself forward.

Pain caught him exactly as he passed under the arch. He could feel his bones exploding with fire as they stretched into new shapes, his muscles straining into agony as they sought to accommodate those alterations. Odd instincts awoke, and he became aware of hard things confining his waist, his chest—legs—feet. Muscles strained harder, fabric ripped, tore free. He shook it away—all of it. And somehow, when he finally made it onto the roof, he was a deer.

Facing a huge white buck.

And while Ron stumbled foolishly, still trying to figure out what was going on, that other deer lowered its head and charged.

He had no choice but to respond. Before he could stop himself, the animal reflexes took over and hurled him out to meet his adversary. Halfway there, he dipped his own head—on which, presumably, grew a rack—to match.

They hit. Antlers harder than bone sent the clatter of their impact echoing into the night. Ron felt the jolt like a hammer smashed between his eyes. Light flashed, he staggered, backed up—and lunged again.

Twice more they came together. Twice neither gave ground.

But the fourth time—

Ron closed his eyes at the moment of impact—he always did. But this time he did not feel the expected jolt, did not hear the characteristic crack and clatter. Rather, his antlers struck something soft, and a very noncervine "Unh" whispered into the night. *No!* He would have cried out in dismay at what he knew he had done in that final second of lost control.

And in that instant, Ron was standing human and naked on the flagstones of the roof.

Vannister lay before him, likewise nude. His eyes were bright and alert, but his face was contorted with pain. Seven bloody holes patterned his stomach.

"It won't kill me," the carpenter grunted. "But I reckon it'll mess me up awhile."

Ron was at his side instantly, trying to staunch the wounds, but Vannister motioned him away. "I *told* you I needed to get hurt. That's what I did—that's what I'm *doin'*!"

"But that's crazy!"

Vannister flashed his famous grin. "Yeah, it is, isn't it? I reckon I get crazier every time."

"What do you mean?" Ron demanded.

The bleeding man ignored him. "I guess it just didn't work very well this time through. I reckon I didn't pay proper respects to the beast. And it got me, it did: caught me there when I wasn't lookin'. That's what I get for showin' off, I guess—for tryin' to do too much too quick." He paused, coughed up blood, and continued. " 'Course, it's all that other girl's fault—the flowery one. I hadn't counted on her. She made me have to hurry—and that wasn't a good idea."

"Who *are* you?" Ron gasped, appalled.

The grin again. "Who do you *think* I am?"

Ron's eyes narrowed suspicously. "Well, you kinda remind me of the Road Man. But I don't suppose you know who he is."

"Oh yes I do," Vannister told him through gritted teeth. "I know *all* about him."

Ron stared at him warily. "But you're *not* him. No, of course you're not—you're too young."

"So you've answered your own question."

"Maybe. Or maybe I'd better ask it anyway: *Are* you the Road Man?"

"No."

"Were you telling the truth just then?"

"You have no way of knowing."

"Okay then, are you *like* him?"

"Maybe."

"Are you . . . like *me*?"

"Somewhat."

Ron gestured around the battlemented roof. "But what were you trying to *do*?"

A shrug, another grin. "The Road Man taught you a craft; I was supposed to find you someone to share your life. I was goin' to give you what you wanted, and her what she wanted, and then make you both forget there was anything odd about how it all came to be. Trouble was, I didn't count on fallin' in love with her—which I did, in a way. That kinda fucked things up."

"But back there on the gallery . . . what was that all about?"

"I was just tryin' to hold her there so you'd fight for her and never take her for granted. Trouble was, I was weak, and I woke the beast—and it just took over. Trapped me in my own head, it did—till you came along. That's the trouble when you wake the beast. On the other hand, it made for a better fight, didn't it?"

"But . . ."

Vannister's face blanched with pain. "Look, boy, I've told you exactly as much as I'm goin' to! I've done what I came to do, and you've got friends inside who need you a lot more than I do. So why don't you just tend to them, and let me take care of myself?"

Ron was still staring incredulously, trying to think of some reply that would regain him the moral high ground, when he heard Brandy call his name. He whirled around, then shot Vannister a warning glare. "You be here when I get back! I've still got a shitload of questions!"

"And where would I go?" the man wondered calmly " 'Cept, maybe, to meet my Maker—and we both know that's unlikely."

Ron merely snorted and trudged back across the roof to where Brandy was waiting for him in the vestibule door. He retrieved what remained of his pants on the way and struggled into them. The shirt was a total loss, and he didn't feel like fooling with shoes. "You okay?" he sighed wearily.

"You should ask!" Brandy shot back. And Ron could see that she was trying very hard to remain calm in what was obviously an impossible situation. He knew how she felt. He'd felt the same way the night his mother died, and he'd had the whole weight of his uniqueness thrust upon him.

"Sorry," he managed, taking her in his arms. She resisted for a moment, then relaxed. "What happened?"

"How much did you see?"

"Two naked guys butting heads . . . and then two naked guys talking to each other."

Ron breathed a silent prayer of relief.

"So what do we do with him?" Brandy asked practically.

"*I* dunno," Ron replied honestly. "Somehow I don't think it's our call."

"The hell it's not!" she snapped, then more softly: "Sorry, I'm just real wired—*real* wired. And I'm in no mood for riddles."

Ron steered her toward the archway that led to the gallery. "I'm sorry, too," he murmured. "But it's gonna take us years to solve all *these* riddles."

"But he's . . . not human!" she protested, resisting a little. "We should . . . we should call the cops, or something . . . Turn him over to science—study him."

"No," Ron whispered, "we shouldn't."

"But—"

"I'm not human *either*!" he blurted, before his head could overrule his heart. "At least not by ordinary standards—though I try very hard to be."

"But—"

"You don't want to put *me* in a lab and study me, do you? Much as I hate to say it, old Van's got the same rights I do. I guess you really oughta say we're both human—but we're both *more* than human, too."

Brandy tensed abruptly, and Ron feared she would bolt. Instead, she took a deep, shaky breath, and asked, "What about Lew?"

"Same deal. He's like me."

"And Wendy?"

"She's . . . strange, too, but in a different way."

Brandy didn't reply for a long moment, then looked him straight in the eye. "I *knew* you were too good to be true," she said feistily. "But you wanta know something? It doesn't bother me—not really. Now that the mystery's been solved, I don't think there'll be any more barriers between us."

"I hope not," Ron replied wearily. "But there's still a bloody lot to know. I'm not sure if you really *want* to know all of it."

She started to reply, then apparently thought better of it and shook her head. "Not now. But someday, I guaran-damn-tee you!"

"We'll see."

When they reached the inner archway, poised between within and without, Ron couldn't resist a final glance over his shoulder toward where Vannister lay. He was gone. All that remained were his jeans. But up the slope, at the fringe of the clearing that framed the knoll, the fog had drawn back, and he thought he could see a huge white buck silhouetted against the dark forest. When he blinked, it, too, had vanished.

"What?" Brandy wondered, gazing at him expectantly, apparently not having seen what he had.

"Nothing—not that we can do anything about." He drew her inside then, and with her help, began making his way slowly along the gallery, where he paused to peer over the rail. Lew and Wendy appeared to have Weedge in good order, had laid her, still unconscious, on the floor. Wendy was doing something at her head, while Lew ministered to her leg. The air hummed with the tension of Luck empowered.

"Good God!" Brandy gulped. "That's Weedge!"

"You didn't *notice*?" Ron cried incredulously. "What were you *doing* while I was out there?"

"Trying to open a locked door! Until I gave up and went to watch you. What the hell happened, anyway?"

"Come on," Ron sighed. "It's a long story."

The house gave them no surpises as they made their way to the lower floor, and Ron explained as much as he could on the way. When they reached the great hall, Lew was just finishing whatever he'd been about with Weedge's leg. He yawned, stretched, and rose to greet them, his face very haggard indeed.

Brandy's brow furrowed with massive concern. "How is she?" she asked instantly.

Wendy glanced up, looking at least as tired as Lew. "Broken leg, which Lew set. She's sleeping—*very* deeply."

Ron raised a warning eyebrow at Lew. "You *didn't* . . ."

"It was one of *my* things," Wendy inserted before Lew could reply. She shook her hair—whereupon the air immediately smelled of spices, and a familiar yellow-green pollen mingled with the dust motes in the slanting shafts of moonlight.

Ron nodded numbly. "It's over."

"I know," Lew said, reaching forward to enfold his brother with as much hug as Brandy's support permitted. "I was in a trance there at the last, trying to get rid of some of Miss Weedgie's pain, and kind of slopped over into what you were doing. But did you ever find out what he was?"

Ron shook his head and freed himself gently. "Not really. And the notions I *do* have would be better discussed late at night over good food and beer."

"He *said* he was a Dreambuilder," Brandy put in. Her brow furrowed again, then: "I thought he meant that he just gave me my dream—my *material* dream. But now . . . I'm pretty sure it was more than just the actual building."

Before anyone could ask for an explanation, she continued. "See, folks, it seems to me he figured out that it's one thing to plan every last detail down to the nuts, bolts, nails, and boards; but much as I hate to admit it, it's a heck of a lot more fun to always be finding something new that you hadn't expected. Not just fun in the making, in other words; but fun in the having, too."

"Oh, *I* see what you mean," Ron acknowledged slowly. "Becoming is more interesting than being. And you can only have the joy of discovery once."

She bit her lip awkwardly. "Yeah, but there was one more thing, too."

Ron frowned. "Like what?"

"I mean," she replied almost shly, blushing a little, "that I, uh, had more dreams than just finishing Brandy Hall. Oh, I *wanted* this place, sure; but the plan was always to find someone I could share it with, someone who loved the things I did, who lived and breathed creativity as much as me."

Ron raised an eyebrow hopefully. "And . . . ?"

She took a deep breath, colored more. "And I think I've accomplished that. But I also think that if Vannister hadn't set up that tension between the three of us, I'd never have known *who* I loved."

"Oh *yeah*?"

"Yeah," Lew yawned, "but where do the rest of us fit in?"

"I dunno," Ron mumbled through a yawn of his own, then: "Maybe it was, you know, vicarious. Like, what was *your* big dream, man? To get the hell out of here, right? But you already knew that I had to have a reason to hang around besides the Mastership. Except that even after you pulled that little trick with Wendy, I was *still* bouncing back and forth between Brandy and her. But right up until the last, when I had to break down and actually fight, I didn't know which way I'd go. I guess old Van made me look hard and deep and see what I really wanted—just like he did with Brandy. Otherwise, I'd have wound up taking her for granted—like I did Wendy. Sorry about that," he added to his former flame, by way of apology.

She shrugged. "No problem."

"I mean, *think* about it, Brandy," he went on earnestly, feeling a sudden need for complete catharsis. "If I'd come up here to the knoll like I was king of the mountain, like I always *have* done, I'd have alienated you right off, wouldn't I? 'Cause I really *have* had it too easy. I mean, I've always been the best at anything I wanted to do; always been able to do things most folks can't. And that's great. But"—he paused for a thoughtful moment—"it's also scary as hell . . . and damned hard to live with, 'cause you're always scared you'll fail."

"And it's frustrating, too," Lew broke in. " 'Cause if you're *too* good, folks'll either hate you, or be jealous, or both. Yet you've got a responsibility to use your talents absolutely as much as you can—or so the Road Man said. So you can't win."

"Yeah," Ron countered. "Only, I guess what Van did was set me up so that I *had* to be me, *had* to use my Luck, even though I don't like to, 'cause to deny it would be to deny a gift, just like it would be to deny metalwork."

"In other words, you had to face your fear," Brandy told him.

"Yeah," Ron acknowledged, "I guess I did."

"But what does it mean in the real world?" Lew wondered.

"It means," Wendy informed him, "that Van made Ron choose between Brandy and me, and when he did, he decided to stay up here—so you get your time of freedom."

Lew regarded her curiously, and Ron, too, raised an eyebrow. "And what *else* do you know, Little Miss Insightful One?"

Wendy squared her shoulders. "I know exactly what he did for me—though I don't think he *intended* to do anything at all—but he did anyway."

"Which was?"

She took a deep breath. "He gave me hope that in spite of everything, Ron might give up Brandy and throw in with me again—maybe even figure out what had happened and see me remade. That's what kept me . . . *aware* long enough to figure some other things out; even though I *knew* that Brandy really was the perfect woman for Ron. But as long as there was still a possibility she'd go for Van . . . I still had a chance, I guess. And by then I knew enough to plan otherwise."

"But you don't know who he was?" Lew asked pointedly. "Or what?"

She shook her head. "Only that if he hadn't pushed Ron to the absolute limit, I'd still be just a voice crying on the wind; a face in a field of daisies. But instead, I'm alive again—and this time"—she fixed Lew with a level glare—"I'm gonna stay that way."

"Yeah," Lew sighed, "you are."

"What about Vannister?" Brandy asked suddenly. "I mean—jeeze, he's still up there."

"No he's not," the other three chorused as one.

"Who's not where?" Weedge groaned, behind them. "Jesus, folks, what the hell just *happened*?"

"Hell *is* what happened," Ron told her. "Uh, tell me, Weedge, do you . . . which do *you* believe in? Dreams, or magic?"

Epilogue

Take a Walk on the Wild Side

Brandy Hall
A few days later—morning

There was a lot to be said for sleeping in a real bed, Ron reckoned. He stretched luxuriously, feeling clean new sheets slide and swish against his bare skin, even as he reveled in the comfortable firmness of an actual mattress beneath him—far better than the cot in the tent he'd grown accustomed to. He slitted an eyelid just open enough to tell if it was day. It was—barely. The light seeping into the master bedroom from the west was pearly gray: bright enough to see by, yet sufficiently dim to soften every contour of the vast stony space around him. It was a warm, soothing sort of light, too, which suited his mood perfectly—especially when a lazy shift of position brought him in contact with Brandy.

She was warm as well, her silky skin smoother than the sheets on which they lay. For a long time he simply sprawled there, enjoying. Eventually, however, she moved. He scooted to accommodate her, eased an arm across her waist as she made to get up. "Not yet," he murmured, opening his eyes to meet hers.

A twitch of the familiar contentiousness awoke in her face as she blinked across the short space between them, but faded when he smiled. "I need to get going," she whispered. "I need to start on those bathroom mosaics."

"They'll wait," he told her firmly. "You don't have to finish it all today."

"But—"

"No!" he insisted, his voice firm but gentle. "The house is *done*—given that you'll always be fooling with it. It's finished in its . . . unfinishedness, in other words." He paused, confounded by his own inarticulateness. "*You* however, don't have to get up every day and work on it. You can relax now, do what you want when you want. And I can, too."

Brandy regarded him with a wry smirk. "Philosophy before coffee's a bad idea, lad."

"So make some, then."

"*You* make some!"

Ron stretched lavishly and hid his head under the covers, with only his eyes peeking out. "Gosh, Miss Brandy, do I *hafta*?"

She grinned wickedly and nodded. He yawned back, then sighed, rolled off the edge, and padded toward the sliding glass doors that opened onto the west terrace. Limped, rather; his knee still pained him, and the leg below was plagued with spells of numbness that were apparently beyond the Luck to heal. He didn't care. A limp was a small thing to worry about in the midst of so much bliss.

They hadn't gotten around to hanging curtains across those huge plates of glass yet (Brandy planned to etch carpet pages from the Book of Kells into the panes eventually), but they had tacked up bed sheets—not that anyone was likely to come prowling, much less actually peer in. Ron brushed the thin fabric aside to admit more light— and tensed. He still hadn't gotten used to the changes: stone where concrete had been, crags where once was level ground, the terrace out there with battlements born of solid stone. But it was fine: was Brandy's dream incarnate—and now very much a dream of his own. Far more lavish than

Cardalba Hall, more chaotic, infinitely more . . . alive.

He stood there a long moment, drinking in the vista of mountains, the edge of the lake, then turned his gaze hard left, where his latest project was taking form at the rim of the terrace. It wasn't finished yet, but the clay statue he was sculpting in the very place where the completed work would eventually stand would be ready for casting in another day or two. He hoped Brandy understood why he'd felt compelled to erect a life-sized effigy of Van Vannister.

"It still there?" she called. "Didn't wake up in the night and wander off?"

"Yep."

"Well, thank God for that!"

He returned to the bed, thumped down on the edge, and sat scratching Brandy's back until she purred like Matty Groves. "You doin' okay? Dealin' with all this mojo, I mean?"

She nodded sleepily. "I guess so, now that you've explained most of it. It's gonna take some time to rearrange my worldview, though."

"Shoot, I'm still working on *mine*!" Ron chuckled. "Probably always will be."

"Most people are," Brandy told him, easing her hand over to stroke his thigh. "But at least I've got somebody who'll understand if I go crazy."

"You won't go crazy."

"I hope not."

"You *better* not! Not after I lose Lew, anyway."

"He know when he's leaving yet?"

Ron shrugged. "Sometime this month. Beyond that, he hasn't said."

"You guys okay now?"

"More or less."

Brandy yawned once more and pulled herself up against the headboard, then craned her neck to gaze beyond him at the work in progress. "You still have no idea who he was?"

Another shrug. "Not really. For a while I thought he might be the Road Man, or one of his by-blows. He looks a lot like him, but Van was younger, more urbane, more—"

"Nonhuman?"

"In an odd way, yes. The Road Man was crazy all the time—or acted that way. But in his heart he was sane. I think there was something else with Vannister. He was saner on the outside, but crazy as a peckerwood down deep."

"But he knew exactly what he wanted to achieve—and did it."

"Yeah," Ron conceded, "he did."

"But you don't know what he was?"

"Mostly I know what he wasn't," Ron sighed, rising. "But whatever he was, it ain't gonna get that coffee goin'."

"I'll have mine in bed!"

Ron shot her an easygoing glare. "You *wish!*"

She aimed a slap at his butt which he narrowly avoided before crossing to the antique carved chest that held his clothes. He knelt beside it, found skivvies and jeans. The former he slipped on, but he paused with the Levi's halfway to his hips. "Jesus, these things are baggy!" Then, suspiciously, "Whose *are* these, anyway?"

Brandy squinted into the half-light, and Ron thought she looked embarrassed. "Uh, well, actually, they're probably Vannister's. He abandoned all his clothes, so I just dumped 'em in with the rest of the laundry and forgot 'em. Sorry," she added wryly.

"No problem." Ron yanked them the rest of the way up. They were too long and sagged on his hipbones, but they'd do fine to make coffee in. And with that, he wandered off in quest of the kitchen.

—And was back a moment later, his eyes huge, and smugly strange with secrets. Brandy saw him, and he could tell she was curious about the look on his face. "There's something weird about these britches," he said, grinning.

"What?"

"Just look!"—whereupon he turned, and proceeded to pace the length of the room.

Brandy was staring at him in amazement when he returned. "You're not limping!"

"And I was a minute ago."

"But—"

"It's these jeans, apparently."

Apparently, hell! he added to himself. It *was* them, as sure as the world, and he had no idea how the change had been accomplished. On the other hand, a lot of things had simply *happened* lately—enough to constantly remind him that he still had a tendency to bind himself to certain assumptions about reality, when he knew the *real* world wasn't necessarily what it appeared to be. Maybe he should look at the facts.

He had once known an enigmatic tinker called the Road Man. The Road Man had limped when bare-legged, but not when he wore pants. And he'd always worn ragged jeans like Vannister's. Which meant that in spite of the obvious differences between the two, these were either those *same* jeans, or somewhere in the world somebody was making magic Levi's. The latter seemed extremely unlikely. Which only left one alternative.

But Vannister had *said* he wasn't the Road Man.

But, Ron wondered, did that mean he never *had* been?

"Ron?" Brandy called, shaking him from his reverie.

"Huh?"

"I think you'd better take 'em off. I don't feel like weirdness today."

"Right," Ron agreed with an even wider grin. "Besides, who needs pants to make coffee?"

TOM DEITZ grew up in Young Harris, Georgia, and earned bachelor of arts and master of arts degrees from the University of Georgia. His major in medieval English (it was as close as he could get to Tolkien) and his fondness for castles, Celtic art, and costumes led Mr. Deitz to the Society for Creative Anachronism, of which he is still a member. A "fair-to-middlin' " artist, Mr. Deitz is also a car nut, has recently taken up horseback riding and hunting (neither with remarkable success), and *still* thinks every now and then about building a castle.

In his *Soulsmith* trilogy—of which *Dreambuilder* is the second volume—Mr. Deitz has begun an ambitious new work dealing with the powers, and the dangers, of one family's Luck. He is also the author of a very popular contemporary fantasy series comprising *Windmaster's Bane*, *Fireshaper's Doom*, *Darkthunder's Way*, *Sunshaker's War*, *Stoneskin's Revenge*, and the related novel, *The Gryphon King*, all available from Avon Books.

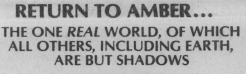

"You may be right. About going public, I mean."

"Whether I am or not, that was my recommendation this afternoon. . . . I'd like another bottle of wine." Tyrell signaled the waitress, pointing at the ice bucket; she nodded, and walked to the outside bar.

"Did you . . ." Cathy began gently, "did you tell them who Bajaratt was?"

"No," replied Hawthorne quickly, raising his clouded, tired eyes, locking them with Catherine's. "There was no reason to, and every reason not to. She's *gone*, whatever demons that drove her gone with her. Her traces were strictly to the Baaka Valley; everything else was a cover that could damage people who were used—just as I was used."

"I'm not arguing with you," said Cathy, placing her hand on his arm. "I think you made the right decision. Please, don't be angry."

"I apologize, I'm not angry—God knows, not with you. I just want to get back to the charter business and watch a boat cut through the water again."

"It's a good life, isn't it?"

"The ultimate 'balm of Gilead,' as my erudite father and brother would say." Hawthorne smiled, no appeal for sympathy in his expression.

"Yes, I guess it is," said Cathy, seeing beneath Tyrell's facade. "Still, I'm sorry, so *very* sorry for everything that's happened to you."

"So am I, but there's no point in belaboring it, is there? Apparently I have a talent for attracting, or being attracted to, women who get killed—for the wrong reasons or the right ones. If I could bottle it, a lot of divorces might be prevented."

"That's not a very nice thing to say, and I don't believe for an instant that you mean it."

"I don't. I'm just not feeling very nice, okay? The déjà vu has come around once too often. . . . But I don't want to talk about me—I'm *sick* of me, *very* sick of me. I want to talk about you."

"Why?"

"We've been over that. Because I'm interested, because I care."

"Again, why, Commander Hawthorne? Because you've been hurt—*desperately* hurt, I'll give you that—and I'm here, a person who cares for you, someone you can turn to as you did with your Dominique?"

"If you think that, Major," said Tyrell stiffly, moving back his chair and starting to rise, "this conversation is over."

"Sit *down,* you ass!"

"*What?*"

"You just said the words I wanted to hear, you damn *fool.*"

"What the hell did I say?"

"That I'm *not* Dominique, or Bajaratt, or whatever her name was. And I'm not the ghost of your Ingrid. . . . I'm *me!*"

"I never thought otherwise—"

"I had to hear it."

"Oh, Christ!" said Hawthorne, sitting down and leaning back in the chair. "What do you want me to say?"

"Offer a suggestion or two, maybe. The President himself ordered the air force to give me an unlimited furlough, for my recuperation, which the doctors say will take three or four months."

"I understand Poole turned his leave down," Tyrell said.

"He didn't have anywhere to go, Tye. The air force, computers and all, are his life. That's Jackson, not necessarily me."

Hawthorne slowly moved forward in his chair and leaned over the table, his eyes again leveled with Cathy's. "My God," he said softly. "Do I see someone else crawling out of that uniform? Maybe a young kid who wanted to be an anthropologist?"

"I don't know. The services are crying for early retire-

ments, the country can't afford the military status quo.
I just don't know."

"But did you know that the Caribbean is loaded with
undiscovered anthropological mysteries? For example,
the lost colonies of the Ciboney and Couri Indians,
traced from the islands back through the Guianas and
down to the Amazon. And the primitive Arawaks, whose
laws to keep a civilized peace were a couple of hundred
years ahead of their time. Or the warrior Carib nation,
at one time covering most of the Lesser Antilles, who
perfected guerrilla tactics so well, the Spanish conquista-
dores ran like hell to stay out of their way . . . and also
to stay away from their evening barbecues, where the
king's men would naturally be the main entrees. Von
Clausewitz would have approved, both strategically and
psychologically. . . . It all happened long before the slave
trade; whole spread-out civilizations held together by
huge drums and war canoes and leaders who meted out
justice from island to island, like the traveling judges in
the Old West when they weren't drunk or dishonest.
Those few centuries are so fascinating and so little is
really known."

"Good Lord, you're the one who should study them.
You get really wound up."

"Oh, no, I'm the sort who sits around a fire and listens
to the stories, I don't study. But you could."

"I'd have to go back to school, to a university."

"There are some great ones, from Martinique to
Puerto Rico; and I'm told some of the finest anthropolo-
gists are teaching in them. It's a place to start, Cathy."

"You're probably making that up . . . but are you
saying—"

"Yes, Major, I'm saying come back with me. We're
not children, either of us, we'll know if it's right given
some time. Let's face it, our personal agendas aren't
overcrowded, so what's a few months? Where would
you go, back to the farm?"

"Maybe for a couple of days. After that Dad would

point me to the barn to clean up the cows. And God knows my agenda's a clean slate."

"Why not give it a try, Cath? You're a free agent; you can always walk away."

"I like it when you call me Cath—"

"Lieutenant Poole has his insights."

"Yes, he does. Give me your telephone number."

"Is that all I get?"

"No, it isn't, Commander. I'll be there, my darling."

"Thank you, Major."

They both smiled, the smiles growing into quiet laughter as each reached for the other's hand.

About the Author

ROBERT LUDLUM is the author of eighteen novels published in thirty-two languages and forty countries, with worldwide sales in excess of 200 million copies. His works include *The Scarlatti Inheritance, The Osterman Weekend, The Matlock Paper, The Rhinemann Exchange, The Gemini Contenders, The Chancellor Manuscript, The Road to Gandolfo, The Holcroft Covenant, The Matarese Circle, The Bourne Identity, The Parsifal Mosaic, The Aquitaine Progression, The Bourne Supremacy, The Icarus Agenda, Trevayne, The Bourne Ultimatum,* and *The Road to Omaha*. He lives with his wife, Mary, in Florida.